LIBRARY
COLLEGE OF THE REDWOODS
EUREKA, CALIFORNIA 95501

P9-DUI-122

E
185.93
C2
B4

Beasley
The Negro trail blazers of California

21443

LIBRARY
COLLEGE OF THE REDWOODS
EUREKA, CALIFORNIA 95501

Ever grateful

Delilah L. Beasley

LIBRARY
COLLEGE OF THE REDWOODS
EUREKA, CALIFORNIA 95501

THE
NEGRO TRAIL BLAZERS
OF CALIFORNIA

A Compilation of Records from the California Archives in the Bancroft
Library at the University of California, in Berkeley; and from the
Diaries, Old Papers and Conversations of Old Pioneers in
the State of California. It is a True Record of
Facts, as They Pertain to the History of
the Pioneer and Present Day
Negroes of California

BY
DELILAH L. BEASLEY

NEGRO UNIVERSITIES PRESS
NEW YORK

21443

Originally published in 1919, Los Angeles, California

Reprinted 1969 by
Negro Universities Press
A DIVISION OF GREENWOOD PUBLISHING CORP.
NEW YORK

SBN 8371-1768-2

PRINTED IN UNITED STATES OF AMERICA

FOREWORD

The author's reason for presenting a book of this kind to the public at this time is not due to the fact that she is not cognizant of the fact that, within the past fifty-four years, much has been written regarding the Negro, but to our knowledge, practically no attempt has been made to put into permanent form a record of the remarkable progress made by Negroes in the State of California.

For eight years the author of the "Negro Trail Blazers" has worked incessantly. At her own expense she has covered the great State of California, visiting small towns and villages, with like zeal with which she visited the larger cities, gathering facts concerning the early pioneers of the race in the State. In gathering the data for this most unique volume, she has sacrificed money, and health. She, however, shall feel well repaid for her labor, if, through the perusal of these pages, there shall be an incentive to even greater efforts by the Negro Race in this State in the future.

Miss Delilah L. Beasley, author of this volume, has contributed many articles of interest to the race, published in some of the leading journals and magazines of this country. This volume is her greatest effort, and it is without a doubt her greatest contribution to the literary world. It is hoped that the appreciation of her people for these earnest efforts for their uplift and general enlightenment, will place this book in a conspicuous place in the home of every Negro, and that as a work of literary and historical value, it will occupy its place upon the shelf in every Public Library. In writing this little foreword I consider it a very special privilege and favor to be permitted to recommend Miss Beasley and this work.

CHARLOTTE A. BASS,
Managing Editor of the *California Eagle*, Los Angeles, October 30, 1918.

(**The author** is especially proud of this foreword, for it was dictated from the heart of a great and noble woman.)

DEDICATION

The author is aware of the fact it is the custom to dedicate a work of this kind to one person, and yet, few writers have been as heavily indebted to a group of persons as is the author of this work, owing to her long and almost fatal illness during the past year. Hence she feels that the highest appreciation she can render these sincere friends is to dedicate this work to them; for, had it not been for their devotion and many acts of kindness, it would have been impossible for the author to have had the courage to finish the book.

These friends are:

Dr. Wilbur Clarence Gordon, of Los Angeles, for careful medical attention and words of cheer.

Miss Mary O. Phillips, of Berkeley, who, besides her financial aid, contributed much in her constant letters of cheer and hope to the author's final recovery and publication of this book.

Mrs. Undine Bradley, of Pasadena, who, aside from her financial aid, by visits and letters of hope and cheer never allowed many weeks to pass without sending assistance in some form or other.

Mr. and Mrs. Ernest A. Coons, of Los Angeles, who, especially after her relapse, did all they could to aid the author to regain her strength by long auto rides, afterward furnishing her with a home, typewriter and paper that the book might be completed.

Last but not least, the sacred memory of her mother, who would have been her greatest reader, and kindest critic.

To these, ''The Negro Trail Blazers of California'' is most sincerely dedicated.

PREFACE

In presenting to the public this history, the author will state that she had spent eight years and, six months to the very day it was ready for the publishers; notwithstanding fully ten years was previously given over to the reading and study of the subject, before actual work was begun. This reading was done while a resident of Springfield, Ohio, and through the courtesy and use of the private libraries of Mr. and Mrs. J. E. Heffelfinger, Dr. and Mrs. Henry Dimond, Mrs. Asa Bushnell, Mrs. J. S. Crowell, Capt. and the late Mrs. E. L. Bushwalter, and many others, who, together with Mr. and the late Mrs. E. C. Dyer, of Berkeley, encouraged the author to go to California and write a book on the "Negro."

The research work, covering years, has included the careful examination of many records of interest to the Negro contained in the California Archives and the Bancroft Library at the University of California in Berkeley; interviewing old pioneers of the Negro Race in every section of the State wherever a railroad or horse and buggy could go; carefully examining all old newspapers contained in the Bancroft Library from the first one published in 1848 to the late nineties and every Negro weekly paper published in the State from the first one in 1855 to the present date; examining the files and records of county hospitals and poor farms, and many old papers in the hands of pioneer families, and sending letters of inquiry to every board of supervisors in every county in the great State of California seeking data concerning old pioneer Negroes, the property holdings, business and other questions of vital interest to the history of the Negro Race in California. The author will state that the boards in Los Angeles and Marysville were the only ones who knew or took the trouble to send any reply of value; the others usually dismissed the subject by stating "They knew nothing concerning the condition or history of the Negroes in that county." The author has spent much time in Boalt Hall of Law at the University of California in research work in the California Reports, statutes, Assembly and Senate journals.

After securing sufficient data, the author by chance read to Father David R. Wallace, of Oakland, a short description of "My City of Inspiration—San Francisco." It was the original intention of the author to write a series of lectures, and not a history. Father Wallace immediately suggested that she include the Pioneer Negro, and gave her a letter of introduction to a pioneer lady by the name of Mrs. Annie Peters in Oakland. After spending a day in talking over the pioneer history of the State with Mrs. Peters, the author decided to write a history, and has spent five additional years in producing this work.

The author is not only grateful to Father David R. Wallace, who afterward gave her several additional names for the pioneer list, but to Captain Floyd Crumbly, who has loaned her books, and furnished the names of Negro United States army officers, and offered many helpful suggestions including the criticism of the chapter on "The Negro Soldier." The author is grateful to Mr. and Mrs. Arthur Wilson (deceased), who permitted her to quote from many old records in their possession, and to Mrs. Mary Grasses, and brother, Mr. Sanderson, for permission to quote from the diaries of their father, the late Rev. J. B. Sanderson. The author is also grateful to the late Col. Allensworth and wife for many helpful suggestions, and to Mr. and Mrs. Levi Booth, Mrs. Lois Voswinkle-Stevens, Mrs. C. M. Kinnie, Mr. and Mrs. Bert W. Perks, Mrs. Emma Voswinkle, of Berkeley, Mr. B. A. Johnson, of Sacramento, California, for data, and to Miss Ruth Masengale, of Oakland, for translating Spanish documents for use in this work. The author is grateful to Prof. Charles Edward Chapman, of the History Department of the University of California, for calling her attention to data concerning the California Negroes in the Spanish Archives, and to Professor Herbert Priestly, Assistant Curator of the Bancroft Library for criticism of the creative work, and to the memory and relatives of the late Hon. Theo. Hittell, who assisted the writer in verifying the creative work. The author's last visit to this grand historian was just one month before his passing, when, owing to his advanced age, she read to him from her manuscript. He paced the floor of his library and exclaimed: "Oh, that I could live to see your book published. Every Negro in the United States ought to buy a copy and more than one white person will buy one."

The author also wishes to sincerely thank the Hon. Frances B. Loomis, who, while managing the *Oakland Tribune*, accepted articles from her pen that she might have confidence in herself and complete the book. She is sincerely grateful to Mr. Owen C. Coy, Archivest of California, for furnishing her copies of the "Freedom Papers" contained in the California Archives, and in a very great measure she is thankful to the Hon. John Steven McGroarty, author of the "Mission Play," who so very kindly criticized the historical part of the book, and gave the author very many helpful suggestions which have made it possible for her to give the public a better history. The author cannot say too much for the tremendous value of a letter Mr. McGroarty gave her after his review of the creative work. This letter was the direct means of creating confidence in the members of the Negro Race that the work promised to be worth while.

During the past year the author has been in very serious ill health and all during the long months of illness there were a few good, staunch friends who voluntarily sent money whenever they wrote and never allowed her for one moment to entertain a thought that she would not get well nor complete the book. These ladies have the author's sincere thanks: Mrs. Frances B. Loomis, Mrs. D. Gordon, the late Mrs. Alice Kinnie-Burnham, Mrs. Yeazell, Mrs. Undine Bradley, Miss Mary O. Phillips, Mrs. C. C. Bliss, and Mrs. Maude Warmington Coons. They stood by in many dark hours, and threw around the author a mantle of love that would not let her sink. There was another group of ladies who did many comforting things during these long months of illness, to whom sincere thanks are given. They are especially: Mrs. Alice Harvey-Patton, whose true devotion and constant attention did much to aid the author's recovery, and Mesdames Scott and Slayton and Miss Ellen Prowd. So, dear reader, this book has been made possible by friends ever helping on up the hill with the load, and ''May God never let me be unmindful or ungrateful of my friends.''

DELILAH L. BEASLEY.

AUTHORITIES CONSULTED

Afro-American Press (I. Garland Pen).
History of California (Howe Hubert Bancroft); Bancroft Co., San Francisco.
History of California (Theo. Hittell); published in San Francisco, 1888.
History of California (Friar Z. Engelhardt).
History of California (Franklin Tuthill); published in San Francisco, 1878.
History and Romance of California (John Steven McGroarty).
National and Civil History of California, from the original Spanish of Miguel Venegas, a Mexican Jesuit; published at Madrid, 1758.
History of California (Venegas); published in London, 1759.
History of California (Norton).
Palou's Notices de la Neva (Alexander Forbs).
The Approach to California (Frederick J. Taggart); published in the Reports of the Southwest Historical Quarterly, July, 1912, vol. I.
Spanish California (Prof. Charles Edward Chapman).
California Historical Papers, in Bancroft Library.
California, an Intimate History of (Gertrude Atherton).
California of the Padres (Helen Hunt Jackson).
California, What I saw in; being the journal of a tour by the immigrant route and South Pass of the Rocky Mountains across the continent of North America, the Great Desert Basin and through California, in the year 1846-7 (Edward Bryant); Appleton & Co., New York-Philadelphia, 1848.
California, The Transition Period of, from 1846 to a State of the American Union, 1850 (Samuel Willey).
California, Three Years in (Rev. Walter Colton, U. S. N.); A. S. Barnes & Co., New York, 1850; H. W. Derby & Co., Cincinnati, Ohio, 1850.
California from the Conquest 1846 to the Second Vigilante Committee (Josiah Royce).
California, Douglas' voyages from the Columbia river to, in 1840.
California (Bennett Papers); published by the General Association in Sacramento Union, 1869.
California, Who Conquered (Ide's Biographical Sketch).
California in Pioneer Times (Gray).
California, Sixty Years in (W. H. David).
California State Register and Year Book of Facts for the Year 1857.
California Records of Men in the War of the Rebellion (Richard Arton)
California, Overland Stage to (Frank Root, M. E. Connely, Sam Clemmens).
California, First Steamship Pioneers; edited by a committee of the Association of Pioneers (George Gorman).
California, Early Days in; an attempt to assassinate Justice Fields (Stephen Fields).
California Supreme Court Records on the Public School question of 1872.
California Statutes for 1863 to 1869; Assembly Journals 1863.
California Reports, Number 56 (Forbs) "People vs. McGuire."
California, Romantic (Ernest Pexiotte).
The following books have been consulted concerning Slavery in California:
Catholic Kings (Prescott).
Christianity and Humanity (Thomas Starr King); edited with Memories (Edward P. Whipple).
Congressional Globe, 446, of the First Session and Thirty-First Congress, April 8, 1850, and Congressional Globe, March 11, 1850; Thirty-First Session, "California, Union and Freedom."
Conquerors of the New World, and their Bondsman (Sir Arthur Helps); published in London, 1848-52, volume 2.
Contact of Races (John Archibald).
Colton's Independence on the Pacific Coast before 1850.
Conquerors of the New World and their Bondsman, being a narrative of the principal events which led to Negro Slavery in the West Indies and America (Sir Arthur Helps); published in London, 1848.
California under Spain and Mexico (Irvin B. Richmond); Houghton and Mifflin.
California from 1846 to 1888 (Jacob Wright Harlan).
California Society of Pioneers and their celebration of the Tenth Anniversary of Admission to the Union, September 10, 1860 (Edward Randolph); published in San Francisco.

California Pioneers of New England; Nicollas and Brown, San Francisco.

California by Oxteam, a narrative of crossing the plains in 1860 (Mrs. Lavina Honeyman Porter); published in *Oakland Enquirer,* Oakland, California, 1910.

California Reports, Number 51, ''Slavery in California.''

California Reports, Number 9, ''Ex-Partra Archy.''

California Reports, Number 2, ''Carter and Robert Perkins.''

California State Assembly and Senate Journals for 1850 to 1906.

California Debates in Convention on the founding of the State Constitution, September to October, 1849 (J. Ross Brown).

Conquest for California (Eligar Kennedy); Houghton & Mifflin, New York, 1912.

History of Santa Clara County, California (J. P. Monroe).

History of Slavery and the Slave Trade, Ancient and Modern, the African Slave Trade and the Political Slavery in the United States (W. O. Blake); J. & H. Miller, Columbus, Ohio, 1858.

History of the Negro Race from 1619 to 1880 (George W. Williams).

History of the Pacific Northwest (Joseph Schafer); McMillan Co., New York.

Historical Papers in Bancroft Library, Berkeley.

John Brown (Herman von Host).

Journey of Alva Nuez Cabeza de Vaca, and his companions, from the Floridas to the Pacific, 1526-36. Translated from his own narrative (Fanny Bandilier) together with the Report of Friar Marco of Nizza (Edited with an introduction by Adlf. Bandilier).

Junipero Serra (A. H. Fitch).

Mining Camps, a Study in American Frontier Government (Charles Edward Shinn); Charles Scribner's Sons, New York, 1885.

Memories (Cornelius Cole).

Negro in the New World (Sir Harry Johnston); The McMillan Co., New York, 1910.

Negro Problems (Seig).

Palaces and Courts of the P. P. I. E. (Julett James), San Francisco, 1915.

The Negro and His Needs (Raymond Patterson, with a Foreword by Hon. William Howard Taft); Fleming H. Revells, New York and Chicago.

Spain in America (Edward Gaylor Bourne); 1450-1580, published in New York and London, Harper & Brothers, 1904.

Spanish Conquest in America and its relation to the history of Slavery and the Government of Colonies (Sir Arthur Helps); Harper & Co., New York, 1856-1868.

Story of the Pony Express (Glenn D. Bradley); McClurg & Co., Chicago, 1913.

Slavery in California after 1848 (C. A. Dunaway); before the American Historical Society, 1910, in Bancroft Library, Berkeley.

Slavery in California (Marion Reynolds); *Boston Transcript.*

Establishment of Government in California (Cardinal Goodman).

The following books have been consulted concerning San Francisco, California:

The Beginning of San Francisco, from the expedition of Anza, 1774, to the City Charter of April 15, 1850, with biographical and other notes (Eldridge-Zoe Skinner); published by Z. S. Eldridge, San Francisco, 1912.

San Francisco Great Register of the City and County up to 1872 (in Bancroft Library); A. S. Bancroft, San Francisco, 1872.

San Francisco Directories, regarding San Francisco, Sacramento and Marysville, July, 1850 (Bancroft Library); W. B. Cook & Co., Portsmouth Square, San Francisco.

San Francisco, As it Was, As it Is, and How to see it (Helen Throop Purdy); Eldridge & Co., San Francisco, 1912.

San Francisco, a History of (John Hittell); San Francisco, 1878.

San Francisco, a History of the Vigilante Committee of.

San Francisco, Discovery of San Francisco Bay (George Davidson).

San Francisco, The Fogs and Sky of, (A. George McAdie); A. M. Robertson, San Francisco, 1912.

San Francisco, Pioneer Times in.

San Francisco, Martin Monahan's Recollections narrated (Edward S. Meeny); published in Seattle Newspaper for January 28, 1906.

San Francisco, Annals of, 1852.

San Francisco (Helen Lockman Coff).

San Francisco, Colonial History of.

A Senator of the Fifties (Lynch).

A Tribute of Thomas Starr King (Richard Frothington).

A New Light on Sir Frances Drake (Mrs. Zelia Nuttall) Hackluyt Society, London.

American Digest, 1906.

History of Hayti and Life of Toussaint l'Ouverture (Charles Mossell).

CONTENTS

LIST OF ILLUSTRATIONS

THE NEGRO TRAIL BLAZERS
OF CALIFORNIA

CHAPTER I

DISCOVERY OF THE NAME OF CALIFORNIA

We are told by historians that for centuries before California was discovered every explorer started out to find the Northwest Passage to the Indies, and the seven cities of Cibolia. These cities were reputed to be rich in turquoise and gold. I think even in this day if explorers were told that somewhere, undiscovered, there were cities with houses of gold and pillars of turquoise, they would sacrifice every thing, even life if necessary, that they might behold such beautiful cities on earth.

Consequently, when Columbus sailed on his fourth voyage of discovery he wrote a letter to King Ferdinand and Queen Isabella (original note in ''His Level Best'' by Hale). This letter contained the following in regard to the South Seas, then undiscovered, and known to us as the Pacific Ocean: ''I believe if I should pass under the Equator in arriving at this high region of which I speak, I should find a milder temperature and a diversity in the stars and in the waters. Not that I believe that the highest point is navigable, whence these currents flow, nor that we can mount them, because I am convinced that there is the Terrestrial Paradise, which none can enter but by the will of God.''

Immediately following Columbus's letter, Mr. Hale quotes from Dante's ''Divina Comedia,'' and Longfellow's Notes to the ''Purgatories'' to prove that Columbus had these writings in mind when he made use of the passage referring to the ''Terrestrial Paradise, which none can enter but by the will of God.'' The writer would not attempt to say these writings influenced his words or his great, though unsuccessful, attempt to discover the Northwest Passage or were the cause of his speaking thus, but if we follow the trend of discovery and occupation on this coast we will find Columbus's words like the notes of a beautiful symphony ringing through it all—''None can enter but by the will of God.'' This letter was written by Columbus in the year 1503, and in the year of 1510, there was published in Spain a romance called ''La Sergas de Espladian'' by Garcia Ordonez de Montalvo, translator of Amadis of Gaul. In this novel the author speaks of the ''Island of California.'' The name is spelled the same as it is today. It has been said that Cortez had the romance in mind when he discovered and named the peninsula in 1535. For this statement we have the authority of the historian Herrera.

California! What a charm the name carries with it! There seems to be a romantic inspiration in the very pronunciation, but whence did it originate? We are told that for years scholars debated its origin; one tracing it to the Latin, another to the Greek, others claiming that it was given by the natives.

The reading public refused to accept as satisfactory any of the statements offered until after Mr. Edward Everett Hale read a paper before the American Antiquarian Society at a meeting held in Boston, April, 1862. In this paper Mr. Hale told of having read a Spanish romance called ''La Sergas de Espladian'' by Garcia de Montalvo. In this book the author speaks of the ''Island of California,'' with the same spelling for the name ''California.'' Mr. Hale explained that the failure of the great authors to find the origin of the name ''California'' was because that ''after 1542, no edition of the 'Sergas of Espladian' was printed in Spain so far as we know until 1575, and after that in 1587, and none for two hundred and seventy years more. The reaction had come when the Curate burned the books of Don Quixote. He burned this among the rest. He saved Amadis of Gaul, but he burned Espladian. We will not spare the son for the virtues of the father.'' These words show Cervante's estimate of it as early as 1605.

Mr. Hale further stated that when he read this romance pertaining to the Island of California, and noted the similarity of spelling, there were only two copies in the world, one copy in Mr. Ticknor's collection in the Public Library of Boston, Mass., and another copy in the Congressional Library in Washington, D. C. Mr. Hale, in ''His Level Best,'' gives a chapter from this romance, an extract of which is now quoted:

CHAPTER CLVII. LA SERGAS DE ESPLADIAN

"Know ye that on the right hand of the Indies there is an island called California, very near the Terrestrial Paradise which is peopled with black women without any men among them, because they were accustomed to live after the fashion of the Amazons. They were of strong and hardy bodies, of ardent courage and of great force. The island was the strongest in the world from its steep rocks and great cliffs***Their arms were all of gold and so were the caparisons of the wild beasts which they rode after having tamed them, for in all the island there is no other metal but gold.

"They lived in caves very well worked out of the rocks with much labor. They had many ships in which they sailed to other climes to carry on their forage to obtain booty***The various Christian knights assembled to defend the Emperor of the Greeks and the city of Constantinople against the attacks of the Turks and the Infidels and on this occasion the Queen of California and her court entered this war."

The discovery of the name is equally as interesting as the land of California. The story of the ox-team and prairie schooner to California after the discovery of gold readily recalls to mind the words of Columbus, "None can enter but by the will of God." It has been said that in the trail of the ox-team to California or "The Eldorado," meaning "the home of the Gilded One," were strewn with the bleaching bones of persons who lost their lives trying to reach the land of California.

Columbus longed to discover what he thought must be a land very near the Terrestrial Paradise. Let the reader compare his wish to the oft repeated expression that "California is next door to heaven;" an expression frequently made by eastern tourists after their first winter in California. The modern writers speak of the land of California as the "Land of Heart's Desire." It is so generous to mankind. It can supply almost the entire United States with its deciduous and citrus fruits, its cotton, rice, gold, silver and quicksilver. Any time of the year, somewhere in California there are fresh vegetables growing. Nature seems to be inexhaustible in its desire to please mankind and supply his every wish.

If one is of an artistic temperament he can have that instinct developed without the aid of any other teacher save a constant view of the beautiful valleys, lofty mountains, and glorious and bewitching sunsets. The great variety of wild flowers which in the spring time cover like a carpet the foothills and valleys of the high Sierras, scattered with the gold of the poppies, the blue of the Lupin, wild violets and buttercups make a picture of perfect harmony. Few artists can paint a picture of spring in California and tell with the brush half of its inspiring beauty. It has been said that following the rainy season, the wild flowers on Mount Tamalpais near San Francisco are of so many varieties that it is given for a fact that three hundred and twenty-five different kinds and colors adorn its dells and canyons.

Aside from wild flowers, California abounds in majestic palms, and magnolias, crepe myrtle and pepper trees. The shrubbery and small flowering trees of every species known to civilized man from all parts of the United States, Japan and Australia grow in California in all their beauty as they would in their native land.

The part of Columbus's wish in the letter to King Ferdinand and Queen Isabella: "I believe that if I should pass under the Equator in arriving at this high point of which I speak, I should find a milder temperature and a diversity in the stars and in the waters; Not that I believe that the highest point is navigable whence these currents flow, nor that we can mount them, because I am convinced that there is the Terrestrial Paradise, which none can enter but by the will of God." The people of the entire world are realizing this wish now that the Panama Canal has been completed and vessels are thereby enabled to pass through the Equator and not under in passing through the locks and waters of the canal.

The repeated and unsuccessful attempt of the French Government to cut the canal, and the difficulty the American Government encountered in the terrible battles between the forces of nature and the engineering skill of the American civil engineers, however, led as if by the will of God to a final completion of a navigable canal. Note Columbus's words, "None can enter but by the will of God."

Let the reader compare the fictitious California as given in the Spanish romance, and the present-day American State of California. The fictitious California was supposed to be rich in gold and so is the real California. The fictitious supposed to have been the home of beautiful black women with strong and hearty bodies. The writer challenges the world to produce more beautiful women than the State of California. They are strong and hearty, because they engage in almost every kind of outdoor exercise often acquiring a heavy coat of tan. This does not worry them in the least, for they immediately proceed to sleep out of doors by night, confident in the fact that if too much golf and tennis has produced this tan, the glorious fog comes in through the Golden Gate and down the valley and kisses roses into their cheeks making them the most beautiful and healthy appearing women in all the world.

If Columbus had ever reached California he would not only have thought it was very near the ''Terrestrial Paradise,'' but he would have said with Joaquin Miller:

> ''Be this my home till some fair star
>   Stoop earth-ward and shall beckon me,
> For surely God-land lies not far
>   From these Greek heights and this great sea.
> My friend, my lover trend this way
>   Not far along lies Arcady.''

CHAPTER II

BEGINNING OF THE DISCOVERY OF CALIFORNIA WITH FRIAR MARCO, AND THE NEGRO GUIDE ESTEVANCIO, TOGETHER WITH CORONADO AND THE NEGRO PRIEST AND THE FINAL DISCOVERY BY CORTEZ, THE EX-VICEROY OF MEXICO, IN 1535

The reader in the preceding chapter has been given the tracing of the discovery of the name ''California'' to a Spanish novel published in 1510, while California was not discovered by Cortez until 1535. Nine years previous to its discovery there started from Spain an exploring expedition ''under the direction of Governor Panfilo de Narvaez, who departed from the port of San Lucar de Barameda with authorities and orders from your majesties to conquer and govern the provinces that extend from the river of the Palms to the cape of the Floridas, these provinces being on the mainland. The fleet he took with him consisted of five vessels in which went six hundred souls.'' (From the translation by Fanny Bandelier of the Journey of Alva Nuez Cabeza de Vaca, and his companions). This translation further states that ''The expedition met with many hardships. Several ships were destroyed by a West Indian hurricane and hostile Indians killed a large number of the remaining members of the party; and at one time the party was so reduced that it seemed they were all doomed. It was then a thought occurred to Cabeza de Vaca, who in the beginning of the expedition acted as treasurer of the company; he decided to act as leader in an effort to save the lives of the remaining members of the party, turned 'Medicine Man,' saying the 'Rosary' and making the 'Sign of the Cross' on the sick Indians.'' This pleased the Indians, who afterward passed the party in safety from one tribe to another.

''Nevertheless the party grew smaller every year until at the end of nine years, when they reached Culiacan, out of six hundred souls there were only a party of three Spaniards and one Negro remaining.'' This translation also gives a graphic account of the nine years of exploring by Cabeza de Vaca and his companions before they reached Culiacan, and how they would pass tents which showed that civilized men had spent the previous night. Cabeza de Vaca said that, ''Having positive traces of Christians and becoming satisfied they were very near, we gave thanks to God our Lord for redeeming us from our sad and gloomy condition***That night I entreated one of my companions to go after the Christians who were moving through that part of the country.***Seeing their reluctance in the morning, I took with me the Negro and eleven Indians, and, following the trail, went in search of the Christians.''

He then tells how he and the Negro were the first to meet Diego de Alcaraza, who was an officer of Nueno de Guzman, and that he asked for a ''certified statement of the year, month, and day when he met them, also the condition in which he came.'' To which request this officer complied. Cabeza de Vaca then tells how that, afterward, he sent the Negro as guide with a party of horsemen and fifty Indians after Dorantes and Castillo, who were the remaining members of the party. He stated that ''Five days afterward they joined him, returning in company with the Negro and those sent after them.''

Cabeza de Vaca then decides that it will be well to give the names of those who after nine years of exploring should be fortunate in reaching the Pacific Coast and said, ''And now that I have given an account of the ship, it may be well to record also who those are and where from, whom it pleased God to rescue from all those dangers and hardships. The first is: Alonzo de Castillo Maldonado, a native of Salamanca, a son of Dr. Castillo Maldonado, and Dona Alonza Maldonado. The second is Andrew Dorantes, son of Pablo Dorantes, born at Benjar, but a resident of Gilraleon. The third is Alvar Nuez Cabeza de Vaca, son of Frances de Vera and grandson of Pedro de Vera, who conquered the Canary Islands. His mother was called Dona Teresa Cabeza de Vaca and she was a native of Xerez de la Frontera. The fourth is Estevanico, an Arab Negro from Azamore on the Atlantic Coast of Morocco.'' The writer has quoted the four names to show that the Negro was in the original party when they started from Spain, and that he came from Azamore on the Atlantic Coast of Morocco.

Through this translation the reader is given the knowledge that the first two persons to reach the west coast of Mexico in an exploring overland expedition from Florida to the Pacific Coast were one Spaniard and a Negro, and that in five days afterward they were joined by two other Spaniards and a number of Indians.

In another translation by the same author of the ''Report of Father Marco of Nissa and his expedition to Cibolia in which Estevanico, the Negro, acted as guide and perished,''

LIEUTENANT-COLONEL ALLEN ALLENSWORTH (deceased)

DR. LEONARD STOVALL
First Lieutenant Medical Reserve Corps.
Served in National Army in France.

LIEUT. JESSE KIMBROUGH
365th Infantry (The Buffaloes).

ATTORNEY WILLIS O. TYLER
Corp. 8th Indiana U. S. Volunteers,
Spanish-American War.

HON. WM. EASTON
War Historian.

CAPT. WILLIAM T. REYNOLDS
Spanish-American War Veteran.

SERGT. RAOUL T. REYNOLDS
Promoted for efficiency to Platoon
Sergeant, Co. I, 365th Infantry,
U. S. A., in France.

is given an interesting account of the part Estevanico, the Negro, took in the discovery of the Southwestern part of this continent, which eventually led to the discovery of California, as the following will show:

"Soon after these three Spaniards and the Negro reached Mexico City and told of their strange experiences and the many cities they had passed through during the nine years of travel across the continent, Cortez, who had been deposed as Viceroy of Nueva Espana, but at the same time was given permission by the King of Spain to explore and discover at his own expense, whereupon after hearing of the arrival in Mexico City of these three Spaniards and the Negro and their experiences in exploring, decided to use the power given to him by the King to explore. He then proceeded to build some ships to be used by him in an expedition of discovery, and started out. He sailed into the Gulf of Lower California and hence into the Pacific Ocean, where he discovered the Santa Cruz Islands, which he named "California."

In the meantime Cabeza de Vaca and his party decided to return to Spain. They embarked in separate boats; Cabeza de Vaca and Castillo in one boat, and Dorantes and the Negro in another. A terrible storm drove them back to port. Soon afterward they again set sail, when a more severe storm again overtook them, and Dorantes and the Negro returned to shore. They did not attempt again to leave. Since there was no "Wireless" in those days, Cabeza de Vaca did not know that the boat with Dorantes and the Negro was not following him until he reached Habana, Cuba. After waiting for the boat a reasonable time he sailed for Spain. "Upon his arrival, he was made Governor of a province as a reward for his nine years of hardship while exploring in the interest of the Crown of Castile."

Viceroy Mendoza, the then ruler of Nueva Espana, being anxious to explore in the interest of the King of Spain, hearing that the Negro and Dorantes were still in Mexico City, sent for Dorantes and told him he would fit out the necessary outfit for an expedition of exploring. Dorantes consented, but afterward decided not to undertake the task. He had not forgotten the nine years of exploration with Cabeza de Vaca.

Viceroy Mendoza was not discouraged and determined to send out a party and to that end employed the Negro. His success at this is told in a letter to the King of Spain. It has been translated by Fanny Bandelier and says: "A letter written by the most Honorable Lord Don Antonio de Mendoza, Viceroy of Nueva Espana, to discover the end of the Firmeland of Nuena Espana toward the north. The arrival of Vasquez de Coronado with Friar Marco at Saint Michael of Culiacan with commissions to the governors of those parts to pacify the Indians, and not make slaves of them any more." Mendoza then tells at great length of fitting up an expedition for Dorantes which was given up "and he still had in hand the Negro who returned from the aforesaid voyage who, together with certain Indians born in these parts, whom I sent with Friar Marco de Mica and his companions, a Franciscan Friar because they had long traveled and exercised in these parts and had great experience with the Indians and were men of good affairs and consciences—for whom I obtained leave of their Superiors. So they went with Friar Vasquez de Coronado, Governor of Nueva Galicia, unto the city of Saint Michael of Culiacan."

Mendoza, then speaking of Governor Coronado, says: "Because I had likewise advertisement of a certain province called Topria situated in the mountains, I had appointed the Governor Vasquez de Coronado that he should use means to learn the state thereof. He, supposing this to be a matter of great moment, determined himself to go and search it, having agreed with the said Friar that he should return by that part of the mountain to meet with him in a certain valley called Valle de Coracones, being 120 leagues distant from Culiacan." Mendoza closes the letter by saying: "The Governor, traveling in those provinces, found great scarcity of victuals there and the mountains so scraggy that he was forced to return home to Saint Michael. So that as well as in the choosing of the entrance as in not being able to find the way it seemed unto all means that God would shut up the gate to all those which, by strength of human force, have gone about to attempt this enterprise and hath revealed it to a poor and barefoot Friar and so the Friar began to enter into the land."

Hittell's History of California (p. 69), in speaking of Coronado, says: "Coronado, believing that the approaching winter would seriously embarrass his movements, determined to hasten back. He therefore hurriedly set up a cross with an inscription commemorating his progress thus far and then as rapidly as possible retraced his steps. A few of the people, however, including Father Juan de Padilla, Father Luis de Escabona and a Negro Priest, were so fascinated with the beautiful diversity of river, hill and plains at Quivera that they determined to remain there." Mr. Hittell gives Herrera as his authority. The writer called on this author and asked if his reference referred to the Negro Priest or other members of the party. He frankly said that it referred to the Negro Priest, and because of his interest in the Negro Race he made note of it in his history.

However, in a desire to remove any possible doubt as to the Negro Priest being with Coronado's expedition of exploration in an effort to discover California, the writer has been fortunate in having a friend, Miss Ruth Masengale, voluntarily to offer to translate some Spanish documents, among which was the one given by the historian, Hon. Theodore Hittell. This translation, as found by Miss Masengale, read that "Francis Vasquez de Coronado returned to New Galicia pleased with this land. Many would have populated it but they could not. The Friar Luis de Escalone of Saint Vida wished to stay in this land to watch over the service of God and to see if preaching could possibly save them, and moreover, if necessary, he would suffer martyrdom and not wish another thing but a perfect slave of a captain for his consolation, and to learn the language and change the love of religion. They would stay with him in this land of the Recorteas some Christian Indians of Melchoacan, and two Negroes, one with his wife and children; beside, the Friar Juan disputed the return to Quivera and after the declaration there went with him, Andres de Campo, a Portuguese, and another Negro that took the habit of a friar. He carried sheep, chickens, a horse with embellishments, mules and other things. Some that were with him killed him when they came to the cape. If it were to take what he had brought from him or for other reasons is not known. A Mexican Indian called Sebastian and a Portuguese brought the news." It seems passing strange that after hundreds of years, a colored girl and a native daughter of California should be the one to translate this document for its use in the history of the Pioneer and Present Day Negro of California, thereby giving the reading public the knowledge that Governor Coronado on his trip of exploration in an effort to discover in the interest of the Crown of Castile, should have in his expedition several Negroes and even a "Negro Priest."

Let us continue the tracing of the journey of Friar Marco and the Negro, Estevancio. The translation by Fanny Bandillier which said "Friar Marco rested on Palm Sunday, sending the Negro and certain Indians who, if he thought it worth while, would send back messengers. The Negro always marked his own journey by large wooden crosses. After Easter, Friar Marco proceeded to follow the 'journey' of the Negro in an effort to reach the Seven Cities of Cibolia." In another passage this translation says, "Friar Marco traveled thus nearly two weeks and traversed several deserts, guiding his course by the wooden crosses which Estevancio had erected to direct the road. But before he reached Cibolia, he met an Indian messenger who told him that the Negro had reached Cibolia and when he entered the city he found hostile Indians, who killed him." Friar Marco of Nissa in his report says, "Having seen the disposition and situation of the place, I thought it good to name that country, 'El Nueva Reyno de San Francisco.'"

In an effort to give the reader all the knowledge possible concerning the Negro, Estevancio, and the cause for which the Indian killed him upon his entering the city of Cibolia, the writer had Ruth Masengale translate Friar Marco's report as given by Antonio Herrera "dec. 6, libro 7, cap. 7", which she found as follows: "First upon arriving at the villa of Saint Michael in Culiacan, as advised by the Castillano, that they should assure the Indians that the King had been concerned about the bad treatment they had had and that there will be none henceforth and those who do contrary will be punished and they will not become slaves any more; nor will they be drawn out of their country and they will lose fear and serve God that is in the heavens, and the King in whose hand the country has been placed to rule and govern it temporarily, that notice as decreed by Francis Vasquez de Coronado, the conversion and good treatment of the natives. Upon finding a command to enter into the country, we carried with us Estevancio, who was called Dorantes, he that went out with Cabeza de Vaca, Castillano and Orantes of the Floridas, he that was the good companion of the Indians which went with the above mentioned and the rest of Petaland and in this made the best of that which presented itself."

In the portion of the letter pertaining to the death of Estevancio, Ruth Masengale's translation says: "Your fathers, sons, and brothers are dead, more than three hundred men, and cannot come from Cibolia; and Estevancio sent his gourd and told the governor that he was to head (or save) and gave peace and the governor flung the gourd to the ground and said they were not his own***The other day Estevancio went out of the house and some principals with him and many from the city fell upon them and they, fleeing, tumbled over one another, being more than three hundred, beside women, and when they themselves were shot with arrows and wounded as it seemed they fell down among the dead until night***that they had not seen Estevancio any more; but believed that he had been shot with the others. Friar Marco prayed for some to go and see what was become of Estevancio, which none would." This translation has given to the reader the words of praise the Friar Marco wrote to the King of Spain in regard to the "Negro guide, Estevancio."

The following is quoted from another account of the death of Estevancio as given by

Hackluyt's collection of voyages of early English Nations, (1600 edition), which says: "The cause, therefore, Stephen Dorantes was slain I demand upon what occasion he was killed, and he answered me that the Lord of Cibolia, inquiring of him whether he had other brethren, he had answered that he had an infinite number and that they had a great store of weapons with them and that they were not very far from thence. When they heard this, many of the chief men consulted together and resolved to kill him that he might not give news unto these brethren where they dwelt and that for this cause they slew him and cut him into many pieces, which were divided among all the chief Lords that they might know assuredly that he was dead, and also that he had a dog, like mine, which they likewise killed a great while afterward.''

The following is quoted from another edition of Hackluyt's discoveries, which says: "And going on our way in a day's journey of Ceuola we met two other Indians of those which went with Stephen, which were bloody and wounded in many places, and soon as they came to us, they which were with me began to make great lamentation. These wounded Indians I asked for Stephen and they all agreed in all points with the first Indians, saying that after they had put him into the aforesyd great house without giving him meat or drink all that day and all night, they took from Stephen all the things which he carried with him. The next day when the sun was a lance high, Stephen went out of the house and some of the chief men with him and suddenly came a score of people from the citie. Whom, as soon as he saw, he began to run away and we likewise, and forthwith they shot at us and wounded us, and so we lay till night and durst not stirre and we heard great rumors in the citie and saw many men and women keep watch and ward upon the walls thereof and after this we could not see Stephen any more and we think they have shot him to death as they have done all the rest which went with him, so that none escaped but we only.''

It gives the writer great pleasure to quote the following from the Negro Year Book by the Hon. Monroe N. Work, in which he says in regard to Estevancio: "A number of Negro slaves were in the expedition of Panfilo de Narvaez to conquer the Floridas. Among them was Estevancio***This expedition was unsuccessful. Estevancio (Little Steve), a Negro, was a member of this expedition***In 1538 he led an expedition from Mexico in search of the fabled 'Seven Cities of Cibolia' and discovered Arizona and New Mexico. He was killed at Cibolia in what is now New Mexico. He was the first member of an alien race to visit the North Mexican pueblos. After a lapse of three and a half centuries the tradition of the killing of Estevancio still lingers in a Zuni Indian Legend which, among other things, says: 'It is to be believed that a long time ago when the roofs lay over the walls of Kya-Ki-Me, when smoke hung over the housetops, Mexicans came from their abodes in Everlasting Summerland. These Indians So-No-Li, set up a great howl and thus they and our ancients did much ill to one another. Then and thus was killed by our ancients right where the stone stands down by the arroyo of Kya-Ki-Me, one of the Black Mexicans, a large man with chili lips, (lips swelled from eating Chili pepper).' ''

The Honorable Monroe Works is the director of research work at the Tuskegee Institute, which was founded by the late Hon. Booker T. Washington, and is not only an author of note, but is thoroughly reliable.

CHAPTER III

END OF THE SPANISH RULE IN CALIFORNIA

To give the reader a clear understanding of conditions prior to the coming of the Franciscan Missionaries and afterward the occupation by the American Government of California, would require considerable time. Hence in an effort to give the facts in a short chapter the writer is quoting from a paper by Mr. John T. Doyle in which he gives an accurate history of the "Pious Fund of the California Missions," which really is a short history of the "Spanish rule" up to the time of the occupation of the territory by the Americans.

In this paper the writer says: "From the time of the discovery of California, in 1534, by the expedition fitted out by Cortez, the colonization of that country and the conversion of its inhabitants to the Catholic Faith was a cherished object with the Spanish Monarchs. Many expeditions for the purpose were set on foot at the expense of the Crown during the century and a half succeeding the discovery, but, though attended with enormous expense, none of them were productive of the slightest good results. Down to the year 1697 the Spanish Monarch had failed to acquire any permanent foothold in the vast territory which they claimed under the name of California.

"The success of the Jesuit Fathers in the Mission on the northwest frontier of Mexico and elsewhere induced the Spanish Government, as early as 1645, (on the occasion of fitting out an expedition for California under Admiral Pedro Portal de Casanti), to invite that religious order to take charge of the spiritual ministration of it and the country for which it was destined, and they accepted the charge. But that expedition failed like all its predecessors.

"The last expedition undertaken by the Crown was equipped in pursuance of a Royal Cedula of December 29th, 1679. It was confided to the command of Admiral Isidro Otondo, and the spiritual administration of the country was again entrusted to the Jesuits, the celebrated Father Kino being appointed Cosmograph Mayor of the expedition which sailed on the 18th of March, 1683.***Many precautions had been taken to ensure its success, but, after three years of ineffectual effort and expenditure of over $225,000, it was also abandoned as a failure, and at a junta general assembled in the City of Mexico, under the auspices of the Viceroy, when the whole subject was carefully reviewed, it was determined that the reduction of California by the means heretofore relied upon was a simple impossibility, and that the only mode of occupying it was to invite the Jesuits to undertake its whole charge at the expense of the Crown.***It was declined by the society.***Individual members of the society, however, animated by a zeal for the spread of the Christian Faith in California, proposed to undertake the whole charge of the conversion of the country and its reduction to Christianity and civilization and without expense to the Crown, on condition that they might themselves select the civil and military officers to be employed.*** This plan was finally agreed to and on the fifth of February, 1697, the necessary authority was conferred on Father Juan Maria Salvatierra and Father Francisco Eusebro Kino to undertake the reduction of California on the express conditions: First, that possession of the country was to be taken in the name of the Spanish Crown, and second, that the Royal Treasury was not to be called on for any of the expense of the enterprise."

This paper then at length tells how that Father Kino and Salvatierra, realizing that they would need money to carry on the enterprise, raised through private subscription and religious societies a fund to conduct the work of advancing Christianity according to the faith of the Catholic Church by establishing Missions, preaching, teaching and administering the sacraments of the Church. The funds collected were placed in a trust fund, and then invested at a safe rate of interest, the income to be used for the purpose for which it was collected. This fund was given the name of "The Pious Fund of the Missions of California." The paper then gives the names of the first and subsequent donors to the fund, and the Missions established in Lower California through the income derived from the Pious Fund.

The paper further states: "The Pious Fund continued to be managed by the Jesuits and its income applied according to the will of its founders, and the Missions of California remained under their charge down to 1768, in which year they were expelled from Mexico in pursuance of the order of the Crown or pragmatic sanction of February 27, 1767. The Missions of California were directed by the Viceroy to be placed in charge of the Franciscan Order. Subsequently a Royal Cedula April 8, 1770, was issued directing that one-half of their Missions should be confided to the Dominican Friars; in pursuance of which and a Concordate of April 7, 1772, between the authorities of the two orders sanctioned by the Viceroy, the Missions of Lower California were confided to the Dominicans and those of Upper California to the Franciscans.

"The income and product of the Pious Fund were hereafter applied to the Missions of both orders. The Church, when first established in Upper California, was purely missionary in its character. It first dates from 1769, in July of which year Fr. Junipero Serra, a Franciscan Friar, and his companions reached the port of San Diego overland from the frontier Missions of Lower California and then founded the first Christian Mission and the first settlement of civilized men within the territory comprising what is now the State of California. The Missions were designed so that, when the population should be sufficiently instructed, to be converted into parish churches and maintained as such, as had already been done in other parts of the Viceroyalty of New Spain.

"But in the meantime and while the necessary missionary character continued, they were under the ecclesiastical government of a President of the Mission. Fr. Junipero Serra was the first who occupied that office and the Missions were governed and directed by him and his successors as such down to the year 1836, when the authority of this office was superseded by the appointment of a bishopric or diocese. Francis Garcia Diego, the last President of the Missions, was the first bishop of the new diocese of Upper California.

"The text of the decree of pragmatic sanction expelling the Jesuits from the Spanish domain is very brief. Under this provision the Crown took all the estate of the order into its possession, including those of the Pious Fund, but later constituting a trust estate,*** charged with this trust. This was fully recognized by the Crown, and the property of the Pious Fund, so held in trust, was afterwards managed in its name by officers appointed for the purpose, called a Junta Directive.

"This income and product continued to be devoted through the instrumentality of the ecclesiastical authorities to the religious uses for which they were dedicated by the donors.***On the declaration of Mexican Independence, Mexico succeeded to the Crown of Spain as trustee of the Pious Fund, and it continued to be managed and its income applied as before down to September 19, 1836, when the condition of the Church and the Missions established in California seemed to render desirable the erection of the country into a diocese or bishopric for its government.***

"The two Californias, Upper and Lower, were erected by His Holiness, Pope Gregory XVI into a diocese and Francis Garcia Diego, who until that time had been President of the Missions of Upper California, was made bishop of the newly constituted See. As such he became entitled to the administration, management and investment of the Pious Fund as a trust.

****"On February 8, 1840, so much of the law of September 19, 1836, as confided the management and investment of the fund to the bishop was abrogated by a decree of Santa Ana, the President of the Republic, and the trust was again devolved on the State, but that decree did not purport in any way to impair or alter the rights of the trust. On the contrary, it merely devolved on the Government the investment and money of the Pious Fund.***On October 24, 1842, another decree was made by the same President,*** directing that the property belonging to the Pious Fund should be sold for the sum represented by its income capitalized on the basis of 6% per annum,*** and that the proceeds of the sale as well as the cash investment of the funds should be paid into the public treasury and recognized as an obligation on the part of the Government to pay annually thereof thenceforth."

The reader has learned from the quotation of extracts from the paper by Mr. Doyle that the missionary fathers financed their own establishment of the California Missions, through the income derived from the Pious Fund. This paper fully stated the banishment from Mexico of the Jesuit Order of missionaries. The reason for allowing the Franciscan Order to do such wonderful work in laying the foundation for civilizing the Californians is explained by Father Engelhardt, who says: "When the royal decree expelling the Jesuits from New Spain had been executed, Viceroy de Croix and Inspector General Jose de Galvez resolved to place the California Missions in charge of the Franciscan Mission College of San Fernando, in the City of Mexico.***There were still some Jesuit Friars in the Missions of Lower California. The Crown sent Captain Gaspar de Portolo, a Castilian, to execute the Royal decree in California. He was at the same time made Governor of the Peninsula of California. Don Gaspar de Portolo sailed from Spain with fifty soldiers and fourteen Franciscans."

Seven years previous there also had sailed from "Spain August 28, 1749, Fr. Junipero Serra, a Franciscan, and Francisco Palou, who came to the College of San Fernando, in Mexico City, arriving in January, 1750." These two Friars were anxious to Christianize the heathen in California.

Fr. Serra immediately engaged in missionary work in Mexico. After Portolo had seen to the return to Spain of all the Jesuit Friars in Lower California, by virtue of his office or appointment as Governor of the Peninsula of California, he and his soldiers formed the military part of the expedition of the conquest to civilize and Christianize Upper California. It was necessary to have the Holy Fathers accompanied by a military escort for their protection, and because, in an effort to secure the country for the Crown of Castile, the government requested that every expedition should be accompanied by a military escort.

The college at San Fernando, Mexico City, selected to head the religious part of the expedition Friar Junipero Serra, who at the time of the selection was in the interior of Mexico engaged in his missionary labors among the Indians, and hence was not consulted as to his wishes in the selection. When he arrived in Mexico City and was told about the selection, he was very happy, saying that all his life he had wanted to go to California— to save souls for the glory of Christ, our Lord. There could not have been a better selection made for the office of President of the missionary part of the expedition. He was a strong character and had unshakeable faith in God and his blessing on his work of saving souls in California.

During his nine years of missionary work in Mexico, at the very beginning of his duties, he was shot in one leg and it never healed. While making the trip overland to San Diego he suffered great pain and Portolo desired a litter made that they might carry him. Whereupon he replied: "Do not speak of this dear sir: for I trust in God. He must give me strength to reach San Diego, as he has granted me so far, and, in case that it is impossible, I conform myself to his Holy Will, but though I die on the road, I will not go back. They may bury me and I shall gladly rest among the pagans if it be the will of God."

Inspector Jose de Galvez gave the Friars orders to establish Missions in honor of certain saints. They were to first find the ports named in honor of these saints. When Junipero Serra asked if they were not to establish a Mission in honor of Saint Francis, Galvez replied: "If Saint Francis wants a Mission, let him cause his port to be discovered."

After the establishing of a Mission at San Diego, Don Gaspar de Portolo and his soldiers decided to go on up the coast by land and locate the Bay of Monterey. It had been recorded that Ascension had said Mass in Monterey under a tree in 1602. The expedition decided to divide; part remaining with the President, Father Junipero Serra, at San Diego, until the arrival of the ship that was to follow with supplies from Mexico City. The ships named in the expedition were the San Antonio and the San Carlos.

Portolo and his party were gone a long time. A number of the party died from scurvy, and they were unable to locate the Bay of Monterey. In an effort to do so they proceeded to walk on up and through the valley of Santa Clara and over to where "they viewed from the Berkeley Hills the most beautiful, large, land-locked bay they had ever seen." Even so they were discouraged because this bay did not correspond to the description given them of the Bay of Monterey. Sick at heart, discouraged and disappointed they decided to return to San Diego, which meant another long walk, but they finally reached there and were welcomed by President Father Junipero Serra and the remaining members of the expedition.

Junipero Serra and his band also were discouraged, because the ship that was to bring the supplies was months over-due, and there had not been any conversions among the Indians. Rations were getting short and they had told Serra that they would like to return to Mexico and abandon California as a hopeless place. Portolo and his party were hurrying as best they could to reach San Diego. Not wishing to hastily decide the best course to pursue, the President, Father Junipero Serra, ordered a Novena said to determine the problem. He had much faith in God and believed that he would save California, and bless the efforts of the missionary fathers to save California to the glory of God, our Lord, and the Holy Catholic Church.

A Novena is devoted prayers said for nine consecutive days asking God's blessing on any thing desired by you or any number of people who may be making the Novena. The Catholic and Episcopalian churches often have a Novena when they wish a special blessing from God. The missionaries and other members of the expedition said their prayers in the Mission, but Junipero Serra was so sincere that he climbed the hill near the Mission, and alone he poured out his soul in prayer to God to send him guidance. Before the end of the Novena, Portolo and his part of the expedition returned to San Diego and told of their trip, and the beautiful large, land-locked bay they had discovered from the Berkeley Hills. They also added that it could not be the Bay of Monterey because it was too large. The President Father immediately recognized from their description that they had discovered the Bay of San Francisco. Its discovery made him more than happy because

Galvaz had said to Junipero Serra: "If Saint Francis wants a Mission let him cause his port to be discovered."

Portolo was told of the unsuccessful efforts to convert the heathen and that the ship with the supplies was months overdue. He, too, wanted to return to Mexico City before they were out of supplies, and could see no reason for longer remaining in California. He tells Serra that he is an old man and that they will take him back by force, whereupon Junipero Serra ran up on to the hill back of the Mission and said: "Though you all return, I will remain alone with God to save California."

Let the reader for a moment think of Christ in the Garden of Gethsemane and this saint of the order of Saint Francis climbing the hills of San Diego that he might be alone to talk and plead with God and finish his Novena. He prayed all day, wrestling as it were with God to send him help that the expedition would not abandon California, and that the Missionary Fathers would yet win many souls to the glory of God, our Lord. He had been sending his petitions to the court of heaven for nine days. The entire party were packing and making ready to sail back to Mexico with the setting of the sun. Even so, Serra continued to pray, unheeding their working. The sun was fast setting, no relief ship in sight, no baptism, no conversion. The party said that they would sail at the setting of the sun. Portolo ordered the sails unfurled and they began to embark (so historians tell us), but behold, there is nothing impossible with God, and just as the sun was almost setting over the beautiful Bay of San Diego, just around what is now known as Point Loma appeared a white sail. In a few moments the full view of the San Antonio loomed in sight. On the shore there were Monks and the rest of the party unfurling the sails of the San Carlos and embarking ready to sail at the setting of the sun, abandoning California, while only one member of the party was willing to trust God to answer his prayers in his own way and time.

The land party was convinced that they had sighted the San Antonio and ran to tell Junipero Serra that California was saved. The day before the ship reached port, the first Christian baptism according to the Holy Catholic Church was performed. Serra did not care if they did return to either Spain or Mexico. He did not care if they reported their efforts to the King of Spain or the Ruler of Mexico, he had come to California to wage war against sin under the leadership of a captain who had never lost a battle, the Captain and King of Glory, Christ our Lord, who heard his prayers. The ship San Antonio was so much overdue, they supposed the party had all gone to Monterey and did not stop at San Diego. But, just before she reached Santa Barbara, we are told, she broke a rudder and went into port to repair it, and while there the natives told them of the land expedition going south, resulting in the San Antonio reversing her course and returning to San Diego. Junipero Serra's prayers were answered. Portolo and the expedition did not abandon California.

Mr. John Steven McGroarty, in the "Mission Play," and also in his "History of California," pays a beautiful tribute to the Bay of San Diego, calling it the "Harbor of the sun and the bright shores of glory." The writer read his description before fully studying the history of California, but she is convinced, since reading the life of Junipero Serra by his lifelong friend Palou, and taking into consideration the beauty of the Bay of San Diego, the answer to the earnest prayers of Serra, resulting in the Missionary Fathers remaining and not abandoning California, that many tributes have been paid to this State which at first may seem overdrawn, but afterwards prove fitting.

The San Antonio was sighted off Point Loma in San Diego Bay, returning from Santa Barbara, while, in sight of the shore, that saint of God, Junipero Serra, was on the hill talking alone to his Maker. Through the anxious prayers and labor of the President Father Junipero Serra, Crespi, Palou and the other Franciscan Friars composing the company of missionaries, we find in a few years the shores of California which, during the previous hundreds of years had lain a barren waste, dotted with successfully managed Missions. George Wharton James says of their work in "The old Franciscan Missions" (p. 65): "Personally, I regard the education given by the Padres as exemplary, even though I materially differ from them as to some of the things they regarded as religious essentials, yet, in honor it must be said that if I, or the church to which I belong, or you, and the church to which you belong, reader, had been in California in those days, your religious teachings or mine would have been entitled justly to as much criticism and censure as have been visited upon the Padres. They did the best they knew how and, as I shall show, they did most wonderfully well, far better than the enlightened government to which we belong has ever done."

It was the aim of the Holy Fathers to establish Missions about a day's journey apart on California's coast, and they established twenty-four Missions to the glory of God, our Lord, and the Catholic Church. The Padres also taught the Indians how to farm, and do all kinds of labor intelligently. In a measure they mastered the manual arts. They were also taught music and painting. Specimens of their handiwork can still be seen in the Santa Barbara Mission, which has never been abandoned or allowed to go to ruin. The writer once visited it and was surprised to hear the monk who was acting as guide say that in an effort to teach the Indians music, not being able to make them understand in any other way, the Padres resorted to painting the notes on the scale different colors. In explaining the effort to teach them art, he pointed to the ceiling of the Mission, saying that, even in this day, its decoration after a hundred years would compare favorably with the art in mural decoration of today, unquestionably showing that the California Indians were capable of being civilized even if they had been enslaved by the Mexican people for untold generations.

The greatest thing the Padres taught the Indians was the value of virtue and the sacred duty of the male to protect the virtue of the female. Judging from the different reports submitted at the annual meetings of the Friars, the Missions were in a prosperous condition up to the death of Friar Junipero Serra, and had they been unmolested in the work they no doubt would, in a few more years, have taught the Indian the value of becoming self-sustaining and other necessary steps to a true civilization. Friar Engelhardt says: ''The secularization was like taking children from their parents and turning them over to selfish strangers.''

The last Mission was established in 1823, and shortly afterward President Father Junipero Serra passed to his reward, which was a great loss to the Missions and also to California.

The Crown appointed Jose Maria de Echeandia as Governor of both the Californias, February 1, 1825. He was very indifferent to the Missions and immediately began planning to secularize them. The plan was adopted by the Mexican Congress on August 17, 1835. Mexico declared her independence and assumed trusteeship over the Pious Fund, and it was still managed in the interest of the Missions. Governor Micheltorena, the first Governor appointed by Mexico for Upper California, ordered the restoration of all the property taken from the Mission Fathers, but the order came too late to benefit the neophytes.

The Missions of the Jesuits passed from their control to the Franciscan Order in 1767, which was about a hundred years from the discovery of San Diego and California. During this period there were many ships sailing the Pacific Ocean and touching California's coast. Some were explorers; others were pirate ships, but the greater number were ships sent out by Russia to procure fur.

In early days this coast was rich in fur-bearing animals, such as seal and otter. The news reached Spain in regard to the Russian adventure on the Pacific Coast. The Spanish Crown was anxious to discover the Northwest Passage to the Indies, which they supposed led through the Straits of Anin, and which, if discovered, would open another avenue of trade whereby their ships could extend the possessions of the Crown of Castile. In view of this fact, the Crown of Castile fitted out expedition after expedition, in an effort to establish a claim to the country. The historian H. H. Bancroft says: ''For sixty years or since Sebastian Viscano, in 1602, as much had been known of the country as now, the general trend and appearance of the coast, the fertility of the country was known, also the general description of the ports of San Diego, Monterey and under Point Reys called San Francisco, with a tolerable accurate knowledge of Santa Barbara Channel and Islands. Thus it was no new information about the country that prompted the California Conquest.'' Note Columbus' words: ''None can enter but by the will of God.''

California was not civilized until the Church was given comparatively unlimited and practically unmolested authority to civilize and Christianize by establishing Missions. Then the military part of the expedition completed the plans for the execution of the civilization and for holding the country for the Spanish Crown. Presidios established then are still in use, namely, San Diego, Monterey and San Francisco.

CHAPTER IV

BEAR FLAG PARTY

During this unsettled period in California's early government by Mexico, the United States government sent out an expedition under Captain John C. Fremont, topographical engineer, to survey the interior of the continent and the Pacific Coast. This expedition left Washington City under orders of Col. J. J. Albert, Chief of the Topographical Bureau. In Captain Fremont's narrative he speaks of his party, which was composed of about thirty-nine persons, consisting of Creole, Canadian, French and American, leaving for the West in the early spring of 1843. Captain Fremont spent several years in surveying the interior of the continent and California, also Oregon. He afterward returned to Washington City and both wrote and talked in glowing terms of California. He had several talks with his father-in-law, Senator Benton, and they arranged a set of secret codes with which Senator Benton promised to send secret messages to Captain Fremont when he returned to California.

Senator Benton saw a possibility for his son-in-law to distinguish himself as a United States army officer in California, if he could in some way seize the Territory of California, in the interest of the United States Government. The United States Government was supposed to be then preparing to go to war with Mexico in regard to the boundary which involved the territory of Texas, Arizona and New Mexico. Senator Benton decided that in the event of war, he would let Captain Fremont know when the time was right to act by sending a secret message which would be perfectly plain to him through the pre-arranged set of codes.

The year previous to Captain Fremont's first visit to the Pacific Coast, a United States navy officer, Thomas Catesby Jones, seized the port of Monterey, California, and raised the Stars and Stripes. But on the following day, finding that war had not been declared by the United States Government, immediately lowered "Old Glory" and hastily paid a visit to Governor Micheltorena, who was located in Los Angeles. This United States officer offered the Mexican Governor an apology.

The country on the other side of the Rocky Mountains was full of rumors of the approaching war with Mexico, and the possibilities of the United States Government owning California. Royce says: "As the reader will know from the foregoing, our hearts were set upon California as the one prize that made the Mexican war worth fighting. The Bay of San Francisco, the future commerce of the Pacific, the fair and sunny land beyond the Sierras, the full and even boundary westward, the possible new field for the extension of slavery; such matters were powerful with some or all of our leaders. The hasty seizure of Monterey in 1842, although disavowed by our government, was a betrayal of our national feelings to say the least, if not of our national plans, which no apology could withdraw from plain history. Meanwhile with more or less good foundation we had strong fears of both England and France as dangerous rivals in the acquisition of the western land."

Royce then cites the disorganized condition of the Mexican rule in California and to prove his statements of the United States' intentions in regard to California he has drawn his evidence from the correspondence of the Department of State with Council Thomas O. Larkin, who at the time was located in Monterey, California. Professor Royce then tells of plans that the government of the United States would try to use in acquiring peacefully the Territory of California. He says: "To wait until war had been forced upon Mexico and actually begun and thereupon to seize the Department of California as an act of war, to undertake with semi-official support of some sort the colonization of the country by an unnatural rapid immigration of Americans into it, and to take advantage of the strained relations already existing between Californians and the mother country, and by means of intrigue, to get the land through the acts of its own native inhabitants."

It was under such exciting rumors that Captain Fremont returned to California with another surveying expedition and after completing his surveying he continued to linger in California. "He marched his little band of thirty-nine souls as far north as Sutter's Fort, when he left them and personally returned to Monterey to ask permission from General Castro to spend the winter in the valley of the San Joaquin." The news soon reached General Castro that Captain Fremont and his men were in the valley of the Salinas. They had already stayed on California's soil longer than they could give a satisfactory excuse for doing, and as the Mexican rule was still in force in California, acting upon his authority, "General Castro ordered all Americans to leave California." He was then having trouble enough with his own countrymen. General Pio Pico wanted to be ruler and so did General Castro. A former ruler, General Mariana Vallejo, withdrew from the quarrel, believing that sooner or later the Americans would take possession of the country and that it would be the best for everyone if they did.

Captain Fremont insisted upon wintering in the Salinas Valley with his men, and when told to move, raised the Stars and Stripes and invited anyone to dare lower them. Finding that the Mexican General did not attempt to molest the Stars and Stripes, he then proceeded to march his expedition, slowly northward, passing Sutter's Fort and reached the Oregon boundary on the banks of Klamath Lake, when a messenger overtook him telling him that Lieutenant Archibald Gillespy was riding post haste to overtake Captain Fremont, and that he carried important messages from the United States Government for Captain Fremont. It seems that Senator Benton, learning that both the English and the French were planning to seize California, decided to send a secret message to Captain Fremont telling him to seize the territory in the name of the United States Government. There being neither a rapid mail service nor telegraphic communication between Washington City and California, the opportunity presented itself to Senator Benton when the United States Government selected Lieutenant Gillespy to go to California with important messages to Consul Thomas O. Larkin, who was then stationed at Monterey, California.

Professor Royce, who had personal talks with Captain Fremont in after years, says that ''Gillespy had left Washington City with a secret dispatch early in November, 1845, and met Fremont May, 1846. But the really important official part of his mission, namely, his secret dispatch, had been committed to memory by the Lieutenant and destroyed before he landed in Mexico. In California he repeated its contents to Captain Fremont, who was a United States army officer engaged in official duty in California.''

Upon the receipt of this secret code letter, Captain Fremont and his expedition returned to California and to Sutter's Fort. In the meantime the news reached General Castro of Lieutenant Gillespy's ride in quest of Captain Fremont with important dispatches from the United States Government. General Castro could not understand the motives of either Captain Fremont and his soldiers again coming on California's soil and this visit of Lieutenant Gillespy. He ordered all Americans to leave California immediately. Unfortunately about this time General Pio Pico had declared himself ruler of California, and General Castro was gathering his forces to go to the southern part of the territory to battle with Pico. All was excitement among the Spaniards and also the American settlers. Neither understood the motives of the other.

Upon the return of Captain Fremont and his men to Sutter's Fort the American settlers went to him to talk over the numerous proclamations issued by the Mexican ruler, General Castro. Whereupon Captain Fremont told them that he could not start a revolt without receiving permission from his home government in Washington, D. C., but that if they got into trouble with the natives of California, he could come to their assistance. The Californians were rounding up horses for General Castro to use in his campaign in Los Angeles against Pio Pico. These horses were seized by ''Lieutenant Arce and a Mr. Merritt, and sent to Captain Fremont. The men with the horses were told to carry the news to General Castro. The Americans then proceeded to Sonoma, California, where they made prisoners of General Vallejo and his brother Salvador and a Mr. Leese, also Mr. Pruden''—(Royce). They were not organized, but after some parley they selected Dr. Semple and William Ide and then formed or drafted a constitution of the Republic of California. Afterward they decided that they needed a flag. Space will not permit giving the constitution of this Independent California Republic. It was one that they need not be ashamed of and neither should any loyal Californian of today; in fact, it has the ring of independence and justice so characteristic of the Native Sons and Daughters of the Golden West.

But this chapter would not be complete were the writer to fail to give a description of the Bear Flag. The following is quoted from Hon. John Steven McGroarty's ''California, Its History and Romance'' (page 195), which says that ''As there has been considerable controversy and dispute concerning this flag, it is obviously proper to give the statement of the man who made the flag. It is he, if any one, who ought to know all about it. Mr. Todd published in June, 1872, the following: 'At a company meeting it was determined that we should raise a flag; and it should be a bear enpassant with one star. One of the ladies at the garrison gave us a piece of brown domestic and Mrs. Captain Sears gave us some strips of red flannel about four inches wide. The domestic was new, but the flannel was said to have been part of a petticoat worn by Mrs. Sears across the mountains. For corroboration of these facts, I refer to G. P. Swift and Pat McChristian. I took a pen and with ink drew the outlines of a bear, and a star upon the white cotton cloth. Linseed oil and venetian red were found in the garrison and I painted the bear and the star. To the best of my recollection, Peter Storm was asked to paint it but declined, and as no other person would undertake to do it, I did it. But Mr. Storm and several others assisted in getting the material and I believe mixed the paint. Underneath the bear and star were printed with a pen the words ''California Republic'' in Roman letters. In painting the words I first outlined the letters with a pen, leaving out the letter i and putting c where i should have been and afterward the i over the c. It was made with ink and as we had nothing to remove the marks of the letters it is now on the flag.' '' It is the writer's delight to state that a colored man secured the paint with which the bear was painted.

In speaking of the Bear Flag in the history of the Negro in California, the question will occur to the reader, were there any colored people in the party? Yes, there were several, and the following is a record of them: First, the writer has found in the account of the expedition of Brevet Captain Fremont, topographical engineer, who, in writing the narrative of his expedition in the early spring of 1843 (page 123-4) speaks of the personnel of the party, which was composed of Creole, Canadian, French and American. He then gives the names of the different men in the party, and at the end of the list the following appears: ''Jacob Dodson, a free colored man of Washington, D. C., volunteered to accompany the expedition and performed his duties manfully through the voyage.'' Bancroft, in his history of California, speaks of Jacob Dodson among the twenty-five persons selected by Captain Fremont to accompany him in the discovery of Klamath Lake, and he was also with Fremont on his famous ride from Los Angeles to Monterey.

Through the courtesy of Miss Ward, of San Jose, the writer has learned of another colored man who was with Captain Fremont on his trip to California, by name James Duff, of Mariposa county, California, the lady's former home. Judging from the picture shown the writer, he was one with only a dash of Negro blood. He recently died at the advanced age of ninety-three years. Lieutenant Gillespy had a bodyguard or servant with him, a colored man known as ''Ben.'' The writer's authority for stating that these colored men were in the Bear Flag Party is established by the following quotation from the *Western Outlook* of San Francisco, October 7, 1914: ''Recalling memories of 'Forty-nine' John Grider, the only survivor of the Bear Flag Party, rode in solitary state in an automobile, a vehicle his wildest imagination never pictured in the strenuous days of California's fight for membership into the Union. Those who read this item in the daily papers about the Admission Day parade in Vallejo did not know that the pioneer was a colored man. From a letter from Mr. George Van Blake, of Vallejo, we learn that Mr. Grider was treated royally and accorded every honor pertaining to the hospitality of the city.'' After reading the above the writer hastened to visit Vallejo and have a talk with the gentleman. He was highly interesting and, although he came to California in 1841, the facts in regard to the Bear Flag Party were as fresh in his mind as if of recent date. When questioned concerning the forming of the Bear Flag Party he replied: ''Yes, it was formed in Sonoma City, but it did not amount to much,'' also adding that he found the paint in the loft of an old barn nearby. This paint was used to paint the bear and star on the flag. He was then asked if there were any other colored men in the Bear Flag Party. The writer gave the names of the colored men with Captain Fremont already mentioned, whereupon Mr. Grider replied that they were all present in the forming of the Bear Flag and that I might add the names of Joe McAfee, Charles G. Gains and Billy Gaston.

While in Vallejo the writer interviewed Dr. Vallejo, the son of the late General Marianna Vallejo. After stating her mission, the writer asked the doctor if he could tell her anything concerning the Bear Flag Party. He replied that he was a mere lad, but that he remembered when the men came to his father's house in the early morning hours demanding a surrender. His father was so friendly with the Americans that he had withdrawn from the quarrel between Generals Pico and Castro, and had retired to his home at Sonoma as a private citizen, believing that sooner or later the Americans would take possession of California, and feeling that it would be a good thing for all concerned. His friendliness was so well known that when this band of Americans came to his house demanding a surrender, he invited them in and, according to Spanish hospitality, ordered breakfast for them, and while drinking a friendly glass of wine, they talked over the terms of peace. As well as he could remember his father's object in talking over terms of surrender was, that he wished to protect his own interest with the Americans, and also keep friends with the Spaniards, since he was a wealthy man. Dr. Vallejo stated that after the Bear Flag Party had partaken of his father's hospitality they ordered his arrest. Some of the party insisted that he was a friend to the Americans, the leader then said: ''Take him to Sutter's Fort that he may not change his mind.'' The party then ransacked the home of General Vallejo, and when they were leaving with a gun of his father's, an heirloom brought from Spain, his brother, who was older than the Doctor and yet only a mere lad, interfered saying: ''The one who proves the best shot can have the gun.'' The challenge was accepted and the lad took turns shooting at a target. The boy proved the best shot, and the gun remained in the Vallejo family. Doctor Vallejo then called a servant and had the gun brought to him and the writer had the pleasure of closely examining it. The gun was inlaid with a beautiful scroll of silver.

Doctor Vallejo then spoke of his father's rule in California, showing the writer a report sent to the home government by General Figueroa, in which he spoke in the highest terms of General Marianna Vallejo's rule in California. The home government was so delighted over the report sent concerning this ruler in California they had the report printed in a pamphlet form and forwarded a copy to General Marianna Vallejo. After his death the report fell to Doctor Vallejo, together with other valuable books and papers. A number of these books were shown the writer. The Vallejo family had one priest who was a great historian. One of whose books had been published in Spain.

Bancroft in his Pioneer Index has the following to say of Marianna Vallejo: ''From 1835 he was the most independent and in some respects the most powerful man in California***The year '36 brought new advancement, for though Lieutenant Vallejo took no active part in the Revolution, yet after the first success had been achieved such was the weight of his name that under Alvarado's new government he was made Commander General of California, taking office on November 29, and was advanced to the rank of Colonel by the California authorities. In the sectional strife of 37-9, although not personally taking part in military operations, he had more influence than any other man in sustaining Alvarado***I have found none among the Californians whose public record in respect of honorable and patriotic conduct, executive ability, and freedom from petty prejudices of race, religion or sectional politics is more favorable than his. As a citizen, he was always generous, and kindhearted, maintaining his self-respect as a gentleman and commanding respect of others; never a gambler or addicted to strong drink. He is a man of some literary cultivation and has always taken a deep interest in his country's history. Many of his writings are named in my list of authorities. His service to me in this connection has been often and most gladly acknowledged. His collection of Documentary History of California is a contribution of original data that has never been equaled in this or any other State.''

Historian Bancroft personally knew General Vallejo. The Spanish people in that period of California's history were constantly being misunderstood, which can be explained because the life of any nation or race is not an easy one when another nation invades their shores, whether for conquest or peaceful pursuits; if they come in large numbers, they cannot learn the customs and language of the resident in a short time, neither can the natives learn or grasp the meaning of their presence or understand the language readily, hence both sides suffer. The reader can perhaps more fully understand the position in which the California Spaniards were placed if they will read the ''Rose of the Rancho,'' which has also been dramatized. This book shows the difficulty and disadvantage in which the Spanish people were placed by not being able to understand the American language and laws. It also shows how unscrupulous men, bent on taking advantage of their ignorance in such matters, robbed the California Spaniards of vast tracts of land in pioneer days in California.

General Vallejo should be highly commended because of his attitude toward the Negro in the constitutional convention of 1849. As a member of that body he voted against every amendment put before that body that was intended to bar from the State the admission of Free Negroes. He always voted for the best interest of the Negro while a member of the First California Legislature. He was personally acquainted with the immortal Lincoln, and often visited him in Washington City and discussed the advisability of freeing the Negroes, and paying them to build a railroad from Mexico City to Washington City. His last visit to President Lincoln was after entering his son, who is now Doctor Vallejo, in Columbia College. Before his return to California he stopped to visit and entreat the President to set the Negroes free. The President replied to him, so the son told the writer: ''Well, suppose, Mr. Vallejo, I did set the Negroes free and send them to Mexico to build a railroad to Washington City, I have been told that Mexico is not a very healthy place for white people, and the Negroes would have to be accompanied by white people to teach them how to build a railroad.'' After listening to the President's remarks General Vallejo replied: ''Well, Mr. President, suppose a few Yankees did die and go below; they always change things so wherever they go, that by the time you and I arrive they will be serving ice cream on marble top tables.''

Dr. Vallejo told the writer that the freedom of the Negroes had been a familiar subject at their fireside; when the War of the Rebellion started he enlisted in the hospital corps. After the close of the war he returned to college and graduated as valedictorian of his class, and is proud of having served in the Union Army. In Rose McKedzie Wood's book, ''Tourist California,'' is given an account of the large tract of land Vallejo gave to the United States Government in California.

Returning to the Bear Flag Party and Captain Fremont, it has been proven that he was not present at the launching into history of that memorable party, but that he came afterward and claimed the Territory of California in the interest of the United States Government for fear the English would seize the territory. His fears were well sustained by future events. A few months afterward Commodore Sloate raised the Stars and Stripes at Monterey, claiming the Territory in the name of the United States Government. He afterward told how an English vessel raced him up the coast from Mexico, but Commodore Sloate's boat being the faster, he reached Monterey first and the Stars and Stripes were waving over the land when the Englishmen landed. Mrs. Nuttall has just published a book covering years of research work in which she tells that Sir Francis Drake had sailed up the Pacific Coast and had drawn a map of all the harbors of the western coast in the interest of the English Crown.

Senator Benton had inspired Captain Fremont, but the task was too great to be successful in any other way than the right way, the way that Commodore Sloate used by raising the Stars and Stripes, the emblem of a government able to sustain its position on any coast in any land. If the revolters at Sonoma had raised the American Flag instead of the Bear Flag, they would have registered their names among the immortals of America, but what they did, while noble and perhaps inspiring to those then in California, still the United States Government never recognized the Bear Flag Party.

Father Zephelian Engelhardt, of Santa Barbara Franciscan Mission, in delivering an address before the American Historian Society at their annual meeting in Berkeley, 1915, among other things said: ''Bishop Nichols remarked after the fire of 1906, that there should be erected a statue of Saint Francis at the Golden Gate, the same as the entrance to New York Harbor, and to act as a beacon light representing 'Union with God.' The Franciscan missionaries came to California to possess nothing, but to convert the Indians, and had the American Flag been raised in California fifteen years before it was it would have been the best for all concerned.''

CHAPTER V

Landing of Commodore John D. Sloate—Constitutional Convention, 1849

The Bear Flag Party was formed in May, 1846, and in July, 1846, Commodore John D. Sloate entered the harbor of Monterey on the United States frigate Savanna, and by his orders on July 7th, 1846, the Stars and the Stripes were raised over the custom-house at Monterey, California, in the name of the United States Government.

The Congress of the United States in 1847 appropriated three million dollars for the purchase of California, and the Treaty of Peace was signed in 1848, when California was annexed to the United States. Commodore John D. Sloate, after raising the flag at Monterey, immediately ordered Captain Montgomery to raise it in San Francisco. He never recognized the Bear Flag Party, and neither did the United States Government.

The United States Government having purchased California from Mexico, the Mexican rule in California was at an end, and it was expected that the United States Government would soon send the citizens of California a territorial form of government. In 1848 gold was discovered and the news soon spread to the East. Brevet Mason, then Commander of the Department of the Pacific, finding men deserting the army to go to the mines, decided to investigate conditions. He visited the mines in company with Lieutenant W. T. Sherman and others, and sent a report to his government. His report as to conditions was so clear, giving the amount of gold procured by the miners, that after the report was read before the Congress of the United States it was published through the entire civilized world. As a result men were coming by the thousands to California during the early part and after 1849. The trip was difficult, long and full of dangers, but it did not matter, for at the end of the trail was the Eldorado, or the land of gold and plenty. As a result of this great influx of people the Alcaldes found it difficult to control the situation. The people were anxious and needed a stable form of government.

In regard to California at the period following the report of Brevet Governor Mason, Rev. Willey, who at the time was a resident and active in the affairs of California, has said in his book, "Transition Period in California," (p. 77): "Governor Mason made known to the people of California that the Mexican rule having come to an end, he believed that the civil government was now on the way to this country to replace that which had been organized under the right of conquest, but the looked-for government was waited for in vain."

The question of the admission of slavery in this newly acquired territory divided Congress; they could not agree upon legislation replacing the Mexican rule. The President of the United States in his message to Congress in July of that year had said that "since the cession of California to the United States the Mexican rule has no longer any power, and since the law resulting from our military occupation has come to an end by ratification of the treaty of peace, the country is without any organized government and will be until Congress acts."

The Territory of California was added to the United States in 1848 and session after session of Congress adjourned without giving to California any form of government. The large number of people of all descriptions then coming to California to hunt gold were not all peaceful, and it has been stated that their actions were lawless because they knew that there was no law to suppress them. Under the distressing state of affairs Brevet Governor Mason asked to be relieved from his post of duty. The United States Government then sent as Commander of the Pacific, Brevet Riley, Brigadier-General of the United States Army, to act as Governor of the Territory of California. The newly appointed Governor retained as his secretary the former secretary to Governor Mason, a well educated gentleman, who fully understood the situation in California.

Mr. Hallack, as secretary to the Governor, and at his command as the representative head of affairs for the United States Government in California, issued a proclamation recommending the formation of a State constitution or plan of a Territorial form of government. The proclamation was issued in June, but the convention did not convene until September 1, 1849.

FIRST CONSTITUTIONAL CONVENTION

"In pursuance of Governor Riley's proclamation of June 1st last, the convention for the formation of a State constitution for California met in Colton Hall, in the town of Monterey, at 12:00 M. on Saturday, September 1, 1849. The minutes; prayer by Rev. Willey; a quorum was not present; on motion of Mr. Hallack the convention met in pursuance to adjournment; prayer by Rev. Willey; the minutes of Saturday's meeting were read and approved; the chairman announced the receipt of a communication from the Governor through the Secretary of State, transmitting the election returns from the various districts of California, together with the names of the delegates elected.''

The convention being duly organized, let us see how it dealt with the Negro question in the formation of its constitution. In the debates in the convention of California, in the formation of the State constitution, September to October, 1849, by J. Ross Brown, the following appears: ''The 15th Section of the report of the committee being under consideration, 'Foreigners who are, or may hereafter become residents of this State, shall enjoy the same rights in respect to the possession and enjoyment of property as native-born citizens.' Mr. Shannon moved to insert as an additional section the following: 'Neither slavery nor involuntary servitude, unless for the punishment of crime, shall ever be tolerated in this State.' Mr. Garver moved to amend the amendment by adding thereto the following: 'Nor shall the introduction of Free Negroes under indenture, or otherwise, be allowed.' Mr. Hallack moved that a declaration against the introduction of slavery into California should be inserted in the 'Bill of Rights.' The motion was unanimously adopted. Mr. Garver had an amendment which he desired to offer as an additional section.

'' 'Section 19. The Legislature shall at its first session pass such laws as will effectually prohibit Free persons of color from immigrating to and settling in this State, and to eventually prevent the owners of slaves from bringing them into the State for the purpose of setting them free.' He deemed this necessary because the house had already made provision prohibiting the introduction of slavery, the object of which he thought would be defeated by a system already in practice. He had heard of some gentlemen, having sent to the States for their Negroes to bring them here on condition that they should serve for a specific length of time. He was informed that many had been liberated with the understanding after serving a few years they were to be set loose in the community. He protested against this. 'If the people of this Territory are to be free from the herds of slaves who are to be set at liberty within its borders.***The slave owners possessed of a hundred Negroes can well afford to liberate them if afterward they engage to serve them for three years. What is to support them after that? Are they to be thrown upon the community?' ''

This address was followed by a lengthy appeal by another member of the Constitutional Convention, a Mr. Wozencraft, who said among other things: ''Mr. President, the capitalist will fill the land with these living labor machines with all their attending evils. Their labor will go to enrich the few, and impoverish the many.***The Legislature may, and doubtless will, pass laws effectual in preventing blacks from coming to or being brought here, but it will be an extended evil even at that date when this constitution goes forth without a prohibitory clause relating to the blacks.''

This address was followed at length by Mr. Jones, who spoke as follows: ''I stand upon the floor as a representative of a community of California which has a right to be heard upon the question; a part of California that is determined to carry this provision into effect. It is a question of immense importance to the mining district of California; it is to these districts that are threatened; it is not to the South, but it is to these mining districts where the money is to be made that these persons will go.***The danger is this: the citizen of the southern States whose slaves are gaining nothing will emancipate them under certain contracts of servitude. Slaves are worth from $300 to $400 in Mississippi; it would be a very good speculation to bring them here to serve either in the mines or for a certain time as servants. We know that such is the intentions and it has been manifested to members of this house by private letters received from the States.''

This gentleman was immediately followed by Mr. Snyder: ''Let us make a calculation about the matter for the Yankees are a calculating nation and they are making calculations every day on the other side of the sunny ridge. What is a Negro worth in Missouri? That is, take the average value, say $600; well, what is the clear profit that a slave holder in Missouri or Kentucky calculates to derive from the labor of each able-bodied man per year? $160 to $200. Then the slave will yield $200 a year from the time he is 16 years of age until he is 50 years of age, which will net the owner $6800 up to the time that he may be considered useless, to say nothing of sickness or death. Then we can see that if the owner makes $6800 from the labor of each slave he is doing as much as can be expected in a general way. Now suppose that the slave holder will say: 'Mose, if you will go with me to California, I will give you your freedom, after working there four years, or I will give you your freedom now, and have indentures made for the fulfillment of this agreement.' Do you suppose, Mr. President, Mose would object? No, never.

Now what would the slaveholder make by the operation in three years? A working man by one year's labor will procure $4000 at least in gold dust, which, at the same rate for four years, will be $16,000, leaving the handsome sum of $9,200 more by one-half thousand than what the Negro would have paid by working his whole life in Missouri, and this is accomplished in the short space of four years. Do you suppose that this will not be tried?''

There were a number of gentlemen who delivered lengthy addresses upon the admission of slavery into the State of California, and while some were intended to excite the passions against the introduction of slavery, the fear of placing the slave on equal footing with the miners was just like men of today when, wishing to close the door in the face of the Negro laborer, they cry ''social equality,'' when in truth all the Negro has asked for or wants is an equal chance to make a living and will seek his social life among his kind. Hence, men in the Constitutional Convention, in the battle against the admission of slavery into California, resorted to first inflaming the minds of the members of the convention by speaking of ''equality of the races.''***The Negro slave laborer would be the equal of the white miners. They usually ended their addresses in nine cases out of ten as Mr. Wolzencraft, Jones and Snyder, showing very clearly that the supreme reason they wished to keep the Negro slave or Free Negroes out of the State of California was because one of the gentlemen said they would all go to the mines and that ''their labor would go to enrich the few and impoverish the many.'' Whom did the speaker refer to when he said ''enrich the few;'' No other than the slaveholder; and in a few years there would be an aristocracy of capital upon this coast in which the slaveholder would hold the full hand or balance of power.

Mr. Snyder's address was very clear on the subject, for he made a calculation, showing how the slaveholder would be willing to take the chance in bringing his slaves here, because his gain derived from the labor of his slaves in the mines would yield him more in California in a few years than a whole life of labor of the average slave in the Southland. He was perfectly right, as the reader will learn in another chapter on ''Slavery in California,'' in which is recorded the lives of slaves who paid for their freedom by working in the mines in California, paying often thrice the price asked on the other side of the Rocky Mountains. Nobody paid any especial attention to the Negro until after the Constitutional Convention. The year previous there was appointed by the government agent a Negro to prevent illegal otter hunting in the Pacific Ocean, especially along the California coast. The writer refers to Allen B. Light, mentioned in Bancroft's History of California. This case is recalled to prove the statement that the color of the skin was no bar to recognition before the ''Constitutional Convention of 1849.''

Some of the gentlemen wished to know what was to become of the slaves after they had been brought to California and had been set free. Who was to take care of them, They said that the slaves would corrupt society. The pioneer Negro was neither shiftless nor immoral at the period of California's history when this convention was debating his admission either as a Slave or Free Negro. In the chapter treating on the industrial and moral status of the Negro at that period the reader will learn that the only shoe store, either retail or wholesale, in the city of San Francisco was owned by a Negro by the name of Mifflin Gibbs. The Negroes there had a private school and also a church. The best miner, either as a mining engineer or metallurgist on this coast, at that period, was Moses Rodgers, a colored man who was located at Horneitus, and he also owned a group of mines at Quartzburg. In after years he had a daughter graduate at the University of California in Berkeley.

Mr. Edwin Booth came to California in the early forties and mined enough gold before the rush to return to Baltimore and pay for the passage to California of his sisters and two brothers, and also to pay for the education of the widow sister's son, sending him to Oberlin College, located in Ohio. If the reader will consider the difficulties of travel at that period and the expense of a trip to California, Mr. Booth's case is a befitting answer to the question as to whether the Negro pioneer was either shiftless or capable of taking care of himself.

The writer had the pleasure of meeting in Sacramento the surviving brother, Mr. Elige Booth, a dignified and stately gentleman with a delightful personality. His mind was fresh in regard to the history of mining conditions in early California and in regard to the treatment accorded to colored miners. He said that while the miners had laws of their own, a Negro miner was a man even for all that. He recited an instance in which some miners were attempting to jump his claim and how the white miners immediately came to his rescue. The writer has talked with other Negro miners who were in the California mines during pioneer days who spoke of fair treatment by the white miners, especially those mining upon Mokelumn Hill.

CAPT. QUARTER-MASTER
T. NIMROD McKINNEY
Served with U. S. Army in Philippine
Insurrection.

WILLIAM NAUNS RICKS
Spanish-American War Veteran
and Poet.

CAPTAIN FLOYD H. CRUMBLY
Past Department Commander United Spanish War Veterans.

HON. FREDERICK MADISON ROBERTS
First Negro elected to the California State Legislature.

The true reason they did not wish either slave or free Negroes in California was because the question of slavery was then prominent before the public against the extension of the slave territory, and it was necessary to have a definite clause in their constitution deciding the issue before going before Congress to ask for Statehood for the Territory of California. If the question was not decided in California the probability of Congress debating the issue or else ignoring their request, would have delayed the admission of the Territory into the Union. The settlers were anxious to secure a speedy admission and prevent the slaveholders from becoming rich in California's gold through the importation of, as one speaker said, these "living labor machines." They were just like the citizen of today living in California, when they see some of the best vineyards in the State cultivated by a foreign race of people, they legislate to prevent the immigration of any more of their kind into the State. The question was the same and created the same kind of an issue.

To prove the writer's statement that no one paid any attention to the Negro miner in California until after the Constitutional Convention, the following is quoted from Charles Shinn who, in his book on "Mining Camps," presents in an impartial way a study in American frontier government. He is considered an authority on the subject as there were a number of Negro miners at the time working at Placerville, Grass Valley, Negro Bar and Mokelumn Hill, his statements can be safely considered as including the Negro, as well as others of whom he speaks. Mr. Shinn says that "The vast body of gold seekers known afterwards as the Argonauts, did not reach the Pacific Coast until early in Forty-nine (1849). The organization of the smaller mining communities of 1848 must be considered before we can discuss the more complex element of later camps. When, early in 1849, mining began at Coloma, near Sutter's Mill, Captain Sutter himself had alcalde powers over the region. That autumn Mr. Belt was elected Alcalde at Stockton. The nearly two thousand Americans who were in the mines before the end of June, and most of them knew what an alcalde was, knew that he had no legal right to elect an officer and knew, also, that Col. Mason, the de facto Governor, was the only other authority. But there was no general acceptance of Sutter as Alcalde. Some of the very first miners attempted to own, hold, control and rent to others a large and valuable mineral bearing tract. After paying rent for a short time the newcomers, who were in the majority, began to equalize matters and adopt laws respecting the size of claims.

Nothing in the early history of these camps is more evident than the unpremeditated and unsystematic nature of their first proceedings; officers were never elected until they were needed to give an immediate decision and, as we have said, local customs in rgeard to the amount of ground a man could mine took form before officers were formally chosen. Everyone knew that most of the land on which they worked was government land, and the use of it belonged to all alike until such time as the government made other regulations. Equality of ownership was the only logical conclusion. Here the laws of the camps had their beginning. Long before the first California gold had reached New York, claims of a definite size were being measured out in the mining camps for each gold seeker. The ownership of land was the beginning of organization. Its ownership in equal parts is significant of the form of society that prevailed, for an unconscious socialism it certainly was. The miners put all men for once on a level. Clothes, money, manners, family connections, letters of introduction, never before counted for so little. The whole community was substantially given an even start in the race. Gold was for a time so inexhaustible that the power of wealth was momentarily annihilated. Social and financial inequality between man and man were swept out of sight. Each stranger was welcome, told to take a pan and pick and go to work for himself. The richest miner in the camp was seldom able to hire a servant; those who had formerly been glad to serve others were digging on their own claims. The veriest greenhorn was likely to uncover the richest mine on the gulch as was the wisest ex-professor of geology, and on the other hand the best claim on the river might suddenly "give out" and never again yield a dollar, the poorest man in camp could have a handful of gold dust for the asking from a more successful neighbor. The early camps of California did more than to merely destroy all fictitious standards; they began at once to create new bonds of human fellowships." Mr. Shinn's estimate can be relied upon because he was on the ground and studied conditions at first hand.

There were not a great number of Negroes at that period in the State, and yet there were enough to have caused a difference had there been any desire on the part of the mining camps to have a difference, if we are to believe that the census was correctly reported. Goodwin, in his "Establishment of Government in California," gives the following in regard to the Negro population of California at that period, in which he says: "The seventh Census, 1850; total population in the State, 92,597; white inhabitants,

91,635; colored, 962. Men, colored, 872; women, colored, 90. Six counties, containing the largest colored population: Sacramento, 212; Mariposa, 195; El Dorado, 149; Calaveras, 182; Yuba, 66; Tuolumne, 66. Sixty-nine of the colored population were born in the State, 709 other sections of the United States and 175 foreign countries.'' These figures prove that the majority of the Negro population then living in California were in the counties in which were located the mining camps. Elsewhere in this book will be found copies of Freedom Papers recorded in these counties, some of which give the price the Negroes paid by working in the mines after night for themselves in an effort to earn the price of their freedom. In the chapter on ''Slavery'' will be found other slave records and the price they paid and the sections of the State where they earned the money working in the mines; these places can be located in some one of these counties.

If one will study in an impartial manner the debates on the boundary and also slavery, as it was debated in the Constitutional Convention, they can readily see that they were intensified through the great desire for admission as a State into the Union. Mr. Norton, in his address before the Constitutional Convention, in speaking on Mr. McDougall's substitute amendment, said: ''I am opposed to this reconsideration for the simple reason that I want this whole matter submitted to the Legislature. If the people desire such a clause they can instruct their representatives and then an enactment of the Legislature can be made that will prevent any discussion of this question in Congress and the possibility of our being thrown out of the Union.''

The California constitution was finally formed with a clause preventing slavery in the State, and in due time a Governor and Legislature were elected. In the first message the Governor sent to the Legislature he recommended the exclusion of Free Negroes from coming to or residing in the State. He could not have done differently after the numerous amendments offered on the subject of slavery in the Constitutional Convention.

The Senate and Legislature of California at that period formed joint resolutions on the subject and intended to send them to the Congress of the United States, but were prevented from so doing by the parliamentary tactics of Senator Broderick, a splendid friend to the Negro. An amendment being offered against the Negro, Mr. Broderick would amend the amendment and then his amendment would be amended. At this point Senator Broderick would invariably move to indefinitely postpone the same. In this way be cleverly killed a set of resolutions which would have no doubt delayed the admission of California into the Union.

CHAPTER VI

ADMISSION OF CALIFORNIA INTO THE UNION

In Bancroft's political history the following appears: ''Early in 1848 the editor of the *Californian* in May of that year declared that he echoed the sentiment of the people of California in saying that slavery is not desired here and if their voices could be heard in the halls of our National Legislature, ''it would be as one man, rather than place this blighting curse upon us. Let us remain as we are, unacknowledged and unaided.''

The slavery question was so prominent that California never passed through a Territorial form of government. The citizens held a convention, formed their constitution and elected a Legislature without the permission of the Congress of the United States Their object was to be admitted to the Union of the United States Government as a Free State, before the slaveholders could locate their slaves in California.

There was no transcontinental railroads in pioneer days coming into California. The trip was dangerous, long and at the best it was not an easy matter to communicate with the government in Washington or locate in California. The majority of the citizens of the State at that date were people from the South and yet they were bitterly opposed to the slave traffic in California. Their position is better explained with a quotation from ''General U. S. Grant's Memories'' (p. 39): ''The labor of the country was not skilled, nor allowed to become so. The whites could not toil without becoming degraded and those who did were denominated 'poor white trash.' The system of labor would have soon exhausted the soil, and the non-slaveholder would have left the country and the small slaveholder must have sold out to his more fortunate neighbor.''

This quotation fully explains to the reader that the majority of the white settlers at that period in California belonged to either the northern element who were opposed to slavery from principle, or they were opposed to it because they were too poor to own slaves, while the other half of the white settlers in the Territory of California were for bringing their slaves because they saw a possibility of working the mines and reaping a fortune through slave labor.

The opposition to slave labor in California by those who did not own slaves in the Southland previous to coming west, was because of the terrible caste of being called ''poor white trash'' if they attempted to make their own living. There was among the settlers in California during pioneer days good material for the making of good humanitarians. They were sincere and believed, like Columbus, that California, with its balmy atmosphere and beauty, was too near the ''Terrestrial Paradise'' to blight it with human slavery. And to add an insult to their efforts to make their living by the sweat of their own brow, or be called for so doing ''poor white trash.'' The caste in a place as beautiful and rich with gold as California would have been thrice as hard as in the other parts of the United States.

If the Negro slaveholders could bring their slaves to work the mines they would soon have all the gold and the poor white people would be poorer than ever. They realized that no country can continue long beautiful that has for its object the oppression of mankind, whether black, red, yellow or white. The course these early Californians took at that early date in California's history is the same today. They may some time make mistakes, but they are not afraid to do the right thing as it appears to them, whether anyone else approves or not.

Long before the United States Congress met again California had formed its constitution, held one session of the Legislature and sent a representative to the United States Congress to ask admission into the Union, which was the beginning of the greatest chapter in American History. Congress, owing to the slave question, had been unable to agree on a Territorial form of government for California. There were some very eloquent addresses delivered for and against its admission. Both sides presenting arguments in defense of their views and rights. A few years previous the House passed the Missouri Compromise which was intended to limit the extension of slavery. It was afterward amended so that two States, Nebraska and Kansas, were admitted into the Union and without restricting slavery. Afterward the ''Wilmot Proviso'' was passed by Congress, which said that ''No part of the territory acquired from Mexico shall be open to the introduction of slavery.''

The southern members of Congress deemed it just that the newly acquired Territory of California should either admit slavery in all or part. There were at the time fifteen Free States and fifteen Slave States in the United States. Some of the members of the California Constitutional Convention who were friendly to the South had tried to have the convention adopt for California the entire territory recently purchased from Mexico. The eastern boundary of California would have reached to the Rocky Mountains, making a State so unwieldy and out of proportion that the Congress of the United States would either have thrown it out or divided it into two States, Northern and Southern California. The South would then have had another Slave State in the southern part of California and the North another Free State in Northern California. The statesmen debated the question of the admission of California for months, and for a while it seemed that it would not be admitted. Public opinion and conscience for years previous had been aroused through the work of such men and humanitarians as William Lloyd-Garrison, Charles Sumner, and a long list of advocates of human freedom and justice, that a few of the Congressmen raised their voices in speech and won others to think as they did, which resulted in the final voting in of California as a Free State, or without permitting slavery in her domain.

Space does not permit quoting from many of these masterful addresses. The following quotation is from the address delivered by Senator Benton, who was the father-in-law of General Fremont. His address will give the reader some idea of the justice of California's claim to admission into the Union. Among other things he said: ''It is proposed to make the admission of California a part of a system of measures for the settlement of the whole slavery question in the United States. I am opposed to this mixing of subjects which have no affinities and am in favor of giving to the application of California for admission into the Union a separate consideration and an independent decision upon its own merits. She is a State and should not be mixed up with anything below the dignity of a State. She has washed her hands of slavery at home and should not be mixed up with it abroad. She presents a single application and should not be coupled with other subjects. Yet it is proposed to mix up the question of admitting California with all the questions which the slave agitation has produced in the United States, and to make one general settlement of the whole somewhat in the nature of a compact or compromise. Now I am opposed to all this. I ask for California a separate consideration and object to mixing her up any more with the whole of the angry and distracting subject of difference which has grown out of slavery in the United States***What are these subjects? They are: the creation of territorial government for New Mexico and in the remaining part of California; the creating of a new State in Texas, reducing of her boundaries, settlement of her dispute with Mexico—and cession of her surplus territory to the United States; recapture of fugitive slaves; suppression of the slave trade in the District of Columbia; abolition of slavery in the District of Columbia***forts, arsenals, navy yards and dock yards of the United States; abolition of the slavery within the State and a catalogue of oppression, aggression and encroachment upon the South. This is the list of subjects to be mixed up with the question of admitting the State of California into the Union; and I am opposed to the mixture and that for the reasons which apply to the whole in a lump and to each separate ingredient in the detail. I am against it in a lump. California is a State and has a right to be treated as other States have been treated asking for admission into the Union, and none of which have been subject to the indignity of having their application coupled with the decision of other inferior and to them foreign questions. I object to it upon principle***that principle of fair legislation which requires every measure, unimpeded by weaker ones***on account of the subjects to be coupled with California all angry, distracting and threatening the Union with dissolution, while her application is calm, conciliatory, national and promises to strengthen the Union. I object because California herself has objected to it. Her constitution contains this provision: 'Every law enacted by the Legislature shall contain but one object and that shall be expressed in the title.' This is the opinion of California about mixing different subjects together in the process of legislation and a wise provision it is to be put into all constitutions. The Senator from Kentucky is in favor of the proposition to couple the admission of California with some other subjects. I think he limited himself to the territorial government and recommended that conjunction as the most speedy way of accomplishing the admission of the young State. Sir, I say honor first, speed afterward. I say honorable admission no matter upon what time, in preference to dishonorable one no matter how speedy.

''The subjects proposed to be coupled with California under the motion from which we move to except are all subjects impending in the Senate and which grew out of the institution of slavery in the United States. If she goes to the intended grand committee of thirteen under the proposition, she goes there to be coupled in the consideration and weighed in the balance and mixed up in the concoction and brought out in the product of all these subjects moulded and amalgamated in a compromise. I qualify this as dishonorable to California, and say that the latest admission is doubtless desirable to California, her position is anomalous and disadvantageous, a young government without the means of living, without character to borrow, soliciting loans and that in vain at three per cent a month. If she were a State of the Union, Wall Street would relieve her of her bonds. But being as she is without acknowledged legal existence, the capitalist eschews her and this young State, rich in inherent resources, and sitting upon gold, is driven to the resource of State bonds and a paper medium, which nobody will touch. All her operations are carried on at disadvantage, for want of a fixed legal character***Want of a branch mint and before that could be gotten ready an assayer to fix the value of gold in a lump is another want of California, neglected because she is not a State: The laborer loses largely on all his diggings for the want of this test of value. All the gold that is used in the country is used at a great loss of two dollars in the ounce, as I have been told, equal to twelve per cent on the amount dug. That is an enormous tax upon labor, such as no country ever beheld. Yet it has to be endured until the State is admitted, and even after that until Congress legislates for her. Those are some of the reasons for the speedy admission of California. They are great and many remain untold. But great as they are, dishonorable admission is worse than these.***Let us vote upon the measure before us beginning with the admission of California. Let us vote her in. Let us vote after four months' talk. The people who have gone there have done honor to the American name.''

The extract from the speech just quoted clearly explains the different objections offered by the Southern Senators in an effort to keep California out of the Union.

Mr. Benton in his address spoke of California's insecure banking or credit system due to lack of recognition as a State. I would that I could give the reader a few instances of the wild financial deals in pioneer times in California. But my history is concerning the Negro in California, hence will have to confine the subject to the effect upon the Negro and his interest. Speaking of banking in pioneer days in California recalls a remark made by the daughter of a colored pioneer who said that when the rumor that the banking firm of Page & Bacon, of San Francisco, had failed or was about to fail, her father, who was a depositor, immediately withdrew his deposit. He filled a champagne basket with the gold he drew from the bank, loaded the basket on a wheelbarrow and carted it home. She said that some time afterward the bank did fail. The name of this colored pioneer was Samuel Shelton, a fair representative of the class of colored people living at the time in California. Such could not be either a menace or a burden to society.

We will proceed with the address in favor of the admission of California into the Union, delivered by Senator Seward, in which he said:

''Let, then, those who distrust the Union make compromises to save it. I shall not impeach their wisdom as I certainly cannot their patriotism. But indulging in no such apprehension myself, I shall vote for the admission of California directly without conditions, without qualifications, and without compromise. For the vindication of that vote, I look not at the verdict of the passing hour, disturbed as the public mind now is by conflicting interest and passion, but to that period happily not far distant when the vast region over which we are now legislating shall have received their destined inhabitants. While looking forward to that day its countless generations seem to me to be rising up and passing in dim and shadowy review before me and a voice comes forth from their serried ranks saying: 'Waste your treasures and your armies, if you will; raze your fortifications to the ground; sink your navy into the sea; transmit to us even a dishonored name if you must, but the soil you hold in trust for us give it to us free. You found it free and conquered it to extend a better and surer freedom over it. Whatever choice you have made for yourselves, let us have no partial freedom. Let us all be free; let the reversion of your broad domain descend to us unincumbered and free from the calamities and sorrows of human bondage.'

''It is the part of the eternal conflict between mind and physical forces, the conflict of man against the obstacles which oppose his way to an ultimate and glorious destiny. It will go on until you shall terminate it by yielding in your own way and in your own manner indeed, but nevertheless yielding, to the progress of 'Emancipation.' You will do this sooner or later, whatever may be your opinion now, because nations which were prudent, and human, and wise, as you are, have done so already.''

This address was the most effectual one delivered in Congress in behalf of the admission of California into the Union. The reader will agree that it is grand, human and so much like a prophecy. A vote was taken in the Senate, and California was admitted to the Union.

Almost immediately after its admission a protest was framed and signed by ten southern Senators, members of the United States Congress. They protested against the admission of California as a Free State. There was considerable debate as to whether the secretary should read the protest, and then a lot more talk as to the advisability of it being entered on the Senate Journal. Finally, Jefferson Davis, from Mississippi, who at the time was a member of the Senate, addressed that body, and said that so much talk was creating outside criticism, and the newspapers were spreading alarming reports, which were doing more to create a sentiment to dissolve the Union than it would to enter the protest on the Senate Journal. The names of the Senators signed to the protest were as follows: J. M. Mason, R. M. T. Hunter, of Virginia; A. P. Butler, R. B. Barnwell, of South Carolina; H. L. Tunney, of Tennessee; Pierce Soule, Louisiana; Jefferson Davis, of Mississippi; David R. Atchison, Missouri; Jackson Morton, D. L. Yulee, Florida. Senate Chamber, August 13, 1850.

Senator Seward's address, appealing to a higher consciousness, caused the Senators to vote California as a Free State. Their actions proved that justice was about to rule, even if the Negro slaves had been held in darkness, ignorance, and cruelly treated in a land where people had come to escape oppression and had declared their independence. They allowed another class of people to come to America and for hundreds of years carry on human slavery, forgetting that the first human blood shed in the Revolutionary War was that of a Negro man by the name of Crispus Attucks. Still even this sacrifice was not sufficient to arouse the conscience of the masses against the enslaving of the Africans brought to America. The statesmen in those days could not see nor believe that it was right to allow California to become a Free State.

If the reader will review in an impartial manner the facts in the case and consider that for hundreds of years these southern Senators' ancestors had been dealing in human slaves, that some of their fortunes had been handed down to them in the form of human slaves, it would be more than human for them to give up the institution of slavery without a struggle. They were true to what they believed to be right.

There were others who did not believe in human slavery, and still others who, while believing in it, were too poor to own slaves, and wished California admitted as a Free State for fear that if the southern whites were permitted to bring their slaves and work the mines there would soon be an aristocracy of southerners in beautiful California. The latter legislated to keep the Negro out of California, whether either slave or free. They were afraid to be even kind to the Free Negroes, lest they would lose by that kindness. "Kindness is a perfume you cannot pour upon others without getting a few drops yourself." The admission of California as a Free State, a land very near the "Terrestrial Paradise" was as an opening wedge, an awakening of the public conscience and a call from the God of Justice. The poor slaves had no way of being heard or changing the laws against them, for their human bondage was so complete it was held a crime to teach them their letters. But somehow the Negroes learned to pray and they poured out their souls in prayer and songs, in their plantation melodies, and God was not deaf. The great Negro, Fred Douglass, at one time was addressing an audience and his heart was so oppressed at the cruelties of slavery that in the anguish of his soul, in a heart-rending, plaintive tone, he said: "Oh, God surely must be dead; he does not answer our prayers." In the audience sat a colored woman by the name of Sojourner Truth, who arose and said: "Fred Douglass, God is not dead! To your knees, oh ye benighted sons of Africa; to your knees; and remain there. There, if nowhere else, the colored man can meet the white man as an equal and be heard."

The effect of the protest of these southern Senators against the admission of California as a Free State was as an answer to the prayers of the Negro slaves sent to the Court of Heaven, for hundreds of years asking to be given their liberty. The abolitionists and humanitarians had been constantly campaigning against the system of human slavery. Like drops of water they had finally worn an impression upon human conscience. People were beginning to think. The battle was not won by the admission of California into the Union as a Free State, but the protest of the southern Senators was effective and the South began to realize that the time was coming when the country would no longer remain "one-half free and one-half slave." It really was the beginning of the end of human slavery in the United States.

There were many white persons living in the South who were too poor to own slaves, and yet too proud to work for a living; too much like a slave, the performance of common labor. All over the country there was fast developing a class of white people who were "shabby genteel." Their children, however, grew tired of the custom, especially when coming into contact with the northern whites who worked and earned their living by the sweat of their own brows and were happy and healthy.

This was demonstrated in a speech in the California Constitutional Convention when one gentleman, a member of the convention, said: "We left the South because we did not care to bring up a family in a half dependent sort of a fashion." In other words, they came to California because they wished to earn their own living without the aid of Negro slaves, and not be considered "common, or poor white trash" for so doing. He opposed the admission of the Negro either as a slave or freeman. Coming as he did from the South, he knew the tricks the southern slaveholders would resort to in an effort to retain their slaves in California and would soon become wealthy in California gold through the labor of the Negro slaves.

In an address given by Abraham Lincoln at Peoria, Ill., October 16, 1856, among other things the speaker said: "Slavery is founded in the selfishness of man's nature; opposition to it in his love of justice. These principles are in eternal antagonism, and when brought into collision so fiercely as slavery extension brings them, shocks and throes and convulsions must ceaselessly follow. Repeal the Declaration of Independence; repeal all history; you cannot repeal human nature. It still will be the conviction of man's heart that the extension of slavery is wrong and out of the abundance of his heart his mouth will continue to speak."

While this speech was delivered after the admission of California into the Union, still it is typical of the spirit that was dominating the minds of a large number of people at that period through the United States. The human heart of mankind that loved justice was crying out either in spirit or otherwise, to be delivered from the cause of slavery. The prayers of the Negro slave, his groanings and anguish for hundreds of years had to be heard and answered. In the language of the Honorable John Steven McGroarty:—

"So through the centuries he has borne,
With shoulders bowed to the wheel,
The whole world's burden and its scorn;—
Its bloodhounds at his heels.
Bound, he stood in the palace hall,
He was chained in the galleyed ships,
Yet with deathless courage he braved it all
With a challenge upon his lips."

Thus the Negro coming to California in pioneer days, with all the disadvantages and obstacles, ever kept the challenge on his lips which in time opened to him the door of hope. The records will show the wonderful strength of character and energy possessed by the pioneer Negroes of California. The writer is allowing them to tell their own story. So come visit with me to the aged pioneer Negroes all over the State. Listen to the tales from their memory of the days when California was young; gather from them the connecting links and trace the threads of the story of their struggles to obtain a right to live in California.

The Honorable John Hay has said: "Real history is not to be found in books, but in the personal anecdotes and private letters of those who make history. These reveal the men themselves and the motives that actuated them and also their estimate of those who are associated with them."

CHAPTER VII

PONY EXPRESS

It may be a great surprise to some people to learn that in January, 1855, Senator Gwin introduced in the United States Senate a bill which proposed to establish a weekly letter express service between St. Louis, Missouri, and San Francisco, California. The express was to operate on a ten days' schedule following the Central route and was to receive a compensation not exceeding $500 for each round trip.

This information has been obtained from Glen D. Bradley's "Story of the Pony Express." In this highly interesting book the author tells how Senator Gwin, while en route to Washington City from San Francisco to take his seat in the United States Senate, made the trip on horseback, and was accompanied part of the way by a Mr. Flicklin, general superintendent of the big freight and stage firm of Russel, Majors & Waddell, of Leavenworth, Kansas, who was an agreeable traveling companion and told Mr. Gwin of his desire to establish a closer service of transportation to the Pacific Coast.

Under the influence of this conversation Mr. Gwin introduced a bill and had hoped to work out a plan by which the United States Government would assist. This conversation and the introduction of the bill were the incentive to the firm and in a very short time they started the operation of the "Pony Express." The object was to shorten the time between St. Louis, Washington City, and the Pacific Coast.

There were three recognized routes at that date—the Butterfield or Southern, the Central and the Panama Route—all of which required a great deal of time. By a system of relay riders the Pacific Coast was brought within eight days of the Atlantic Coast. The "Pony Express" was a perfect success. Its value to California during the War of the Rebellion was inestimable. Senator Gwin, who introduced the bill in the interest of the State, made a speech in the United States Senate December 12, 1859, about six months before the express made its first trip, that ruined his career and left a cloud on his memory as a statesman.

The "Pony Express" was one of the greatest and most convincing adventures of that date, causing men to realize that nothing is impossible. The Pacific Coast and its newly discovered gold was a long way from the seat of the United States Government, the trip long and dangerous, over mountains and plains, facing hostile Indians and wild animals, yet after sixteen months of successful operation the telegraph line supplanted its usefulness, as messages could be sent quicker by wire.

The transcontinental railroad soon followed in the trail of the telegraph line. The "Pony Express" had proven beyond a possibility of doubt that if men could cross the continent riding horseback with valuable messages and packages in so short a time, why not a coach of steel? The stage for passengers was a success, and yet it was attended by great expense and danger of highway robbers, not counting other troubles.

The "Pony Express" was a system of relay riders and stations. Each rider was supposed to travel seventy-five miles. During that distance he was allowed three different horses, and just enough time to dismount and mount. The proprietors of the "Pony Express" were noted for the care with which they employed their men. They were bound by an oath of honor, the observance of which made the "Pony Express" a success. On entering the service of the Central Overland, California and Pike's Peak Express Company, employees of the "Pony Express" were compelled to take an oath of fidelity which was as follows: "I......do hereby swear before the great and living God, that during my engagement and while I am an employee of Russel, Majors & Waddell, I will under no circumstances use profane language, that I will drink no intoxicating liquors, that I will not quarrel or fight with any other employee of the firm, and in every respect I will conduct myself honestly, be faithful to my duties and so direct all my acts as to win the confidence of my employers. So help me God."

The firm adhered to a rigid observance of the Sabbath. They insisted on their men doing as little work as possible on the Sabbath day. The firm likewise clung to its policies. Probably no firm ever won a higher and more deserved reputation for integrity in the fulfillment of its contracts and for business reliability than Russel, Majors & Waddell.

It affords the writer much pleasure to record the names of three colored men who were connected with the "Pony Express:" Mr. James Frances, of San Francisco, who had charge of the horses at the end of the trail at Summit, and again at Sacramento, California; George Monroe, from Merced to Mariposa, who was a "Pony Express" rider between the above named points, and William Robinson, of Stockton, who carried the mail from Stockton to the Mines, after the Wells Fargo Express bought the "Pony Express" business. He served as such with this company for forty years. These men had to take the oath the same as other riders.

In Kennedy's Contest for California the author quotes Justice Field as saying in his Reminiscences: "I could have recounted the effort made in 1860 and '61 to keep the State in the Union against the movements of the Secessionists and the communications had with President Lincoln by relay riders over the plains." Hittell's History of California, which said: "But the Presidential election of 1860 when the line became drawn with great distinction between Union and Secession, California broke its Democratic record and wheeled into line as a Republican State, strong on the side of the Union." Mr. Hittell gives as his authority "Davis Political Conventions, (p. 110-116)." He further said: "Nominations by the Republican National Convention were Abraham Lincoln and Hannibal Hamlin as President and Vice-President, and, in a short time after the canvass opened, it was very clearly understood that the struggle, call it by whatever name they might, and without reference to individuals, was to be between Union and threatened Secession.***The Presidential campaign of 1860 in California was a memorable one. The people were thoroughly aroused and many able speakers took part in the conflict."

Kennedy's Contest for California said: "There were twenty-two newspapers pouring forth or repeating the arguments and confident boasts of the Breckenridge party, twenty-four supporting Douglass and only seven for Lincoln.***Col. E. D. Baker avowed his candidacy for the United States Senate from Oregon. But, after the nomination of Lincoln and Hamlin became known, he put that forward as being of the greatest importance, and I have been told that Baker's speeches did more than any other instrumentality to secure the electoral vote of Oregon for the Republican candidate."

Col. Baker delivered an address in Salem, Oregon, on the occasion of a Fourth of July celebration. The following is an extract from it: "Whatever service I have rendered on the field of battle in other days, I leave impartial history to record. But if it be reserved for me to lay my unworthy life upon the altar of my country in defending it from internal assailants, I declare here today that I aspire to no higher glory than that the sun of my life may go down beneath the shadow of Freedom's temple and baptize the emblem of the Nation's greatness, the Stars and the Stripes, that float so proudly before us today in my heart's warmest blood."

After the delivery of this speech the Republican committee of California persuaded Col. Baker to speak in the Commercial Metropolis of the Coast. The place chosen was the old American Theater, San Francisco. The writer has deemed it appropriate to quote from this address since Col. Baker was one, if not the greatest, friend the Negro had at that date in California:

"We live in a day of light. We live in an advanced generation. We live in the presence of the whole world. We are like a city set upon a hill, that cannot be hid. The prayers and tears and hopes and sighs of all good men are with us. As for me, I dare not, I will not, be false to freedom. Here many years ago I took my stand, and where in youth my feet were planted, there my young manhood, and my old age shall march. I am not ashamed of Freedom. I know her power. I glory in her strength, I rejoice in her majesty. I will walk beneath her banner. I have seen them give her ashes to the winds, regather them that they might scatter them yet more widely. But when they turn to exult, I have seen her again meet them face to face clad in complete steel and brandishing in her right hand a flaming sword, red with insufferable light."

In commenting on the speech Kennedy says: "During the utterance of these sentences the listeners were finding it difficult to repress their feelings. When Col. Baker, always as graceful in gesture as in speech, came to the mention of the sword, he, a veteran officer of two wars, appeared to draw his own weapon, so that the last words were spoken with his arm uplifted. The excited thousands sprang to their feet; the pent-up enthusiasm broke loose and the wild tumult that greeted the hero on his introduction was repeated with wilder power. Cheer after cheer rolled from side to side, from pit to dome. Even the reporters were swept away in the frenzy and left their desks and tables to fall in with the shouting multitude.

A young fellow, just come of age, afterwards famous as Bret Hart, leaped upon the stage and frantically waved the American Flag. In this era of prearranged demonstrations that would excite little attention, but no such scene had occurred in California. None, I think, ever occurred since, and it may well be doubted whether, except in National Conventions, the equal of it was ever witnessed in the United States. It was nearly a quarter of an hour before the uproad ceased. Meantime Col. Baker stood motionless, intent, transfixed. When at last there was perfect silence, he spoke as if he had not been interrupted and in a golden, throbbing tone that thrilled like an electric current said: ''And I take courage; the genius of America will at last lead her sons to freedom.''

After the conclusion of his address, Col. Baker made a personal statement to a few friends, since it would be the last time he probably would see them before sailing for the East. He reviewed his defeat in California for United States Congress and added, ''With my heart bruised, my ambition somewhat wounded, my hopes crushed and destroyed, it was my fortune one week later to stand by the bedside of my slaughtered friend, Broderick, who fell in your cause and on your behalf***and I cried, 'How long, oh how long shall the hopes of freedom and her champion be thus crushed?' The tide has turned. I regret my little faith. I renew my hopes. I see better omens. The warrior rests. It is true he is in the embrace of that sleep that knows no earthly waking. Nor word, nor wish or prayer, nor triumph can call him from that lonely abode***but his example lives among us. In San Francisco, I know I speak to hundreds of men tonight, perhaps thousands, who loved him in his life and who will be true to his memory always. And if I were not before a vast assemblage of the people, I would say that in a higher arena it may be my privilege to speak to him and for him.''

One writer in describing Col. Baker on this occasion, said: ''His countenance and bearing and his gray locks recalled the picture of Thorwaldsen, of whom it was said that when he moved in the midst of a crowd it would separate as if it felt the presence of a superior being. His disposition was the perfection of amiability. In his most heated forensic and political contests he was never betrayed into saying an unmanly thing of an adversary.''

Hittell, in his history of San Francisco, says of this speech by Col. Baker: ''It was in this campaign that E. D. Baker pronounced in favor of Freedom and the Republican party, what was supposed to be the greatest speech ever delivered in California. It will survive the English language if that can ever die. It will be repeated, cherished and appealed to until freedom, in every form the most precious of all the triumphs of humanity and the struggle for it the most sacred of all duties, shall have lost its interest. It surpasses any paragraph in Demosthenes, Cicero, Burk, Webster, Sumner, or Gladstone.*** It is the soundest reason on a subject appealing to the sympathies of our common Nation, expressed in the highest polish of rhetoric.''

The speeches just quoted were more than admirable because of the remoteness of California, and its mixed citizenship of Indian, Mexican, Chinese and Spaniard, and also the southern ex-slaveholder. It was so easy to be misunderstood, and men in California at that period settled their differences by dueling. Their code of honor did not admit of ignoring a challenge. The duel between Judge Terry and Senator Broderick was then fresh in the minds of the public. It was this duel Col. Baker referred to when he spoke of his slaughtered friend Broderick. Judge Terry was resentful to Broderick because of his known friendship toward the Negro. Consequently when the slightest provocation presented itself, Judge Terry challenged Senator Broderick to a duel of pistols. Mr. Broderick died from the wounds received in the duel. It has been said that his last words were: ''They killed me because I am opposed to the extension of slavery and a corrupt administration.''

Mr. Broderick had as a body servant a colored man by the name of John Jones, who was in the immediate vicinity of the duelling grounds when Senator Broderick, who had fired his gun into the air, was shot by Judge Terry. This colored man was more than a mere body servant. ''Senator Broderick had taken a great fancy to Jones and when he left for the National Capital to represent California in the Halls of Congress, he took Jones along with him as his valet and confidential servant. During the active period of the Vigilance Committee he was put in charge of the warehouse which served as an armory and as the council room of the committee. He was present when a barge load of rifles was seized by the committee. These rifles were coming from Sacramento and had been sent by the Governor to the Terry faction, who were opposing the Vigilance Committee.'' The quotation is from a pioneer whose life is given in full in another section of the book.

Col. E. D. Baker was not only a true friend of freedom, but he was a sincere friend to the immortal Lincoln. He showed his love and friendship for Lincoln by neglecting his own candidacy after the nomination of Lincoln for the Presidency of the United States. Abraham Lincoln was equally as true to him and, realizing the terrible odds E. D. Baker would have against him in this western country in the race for United States Senator, sent a letter to a friend asking this friend to give his regards to Baker. The letter is here quoted in full:

"Springfield, Ill., Aug., 1860.

Dear Friend:—If you see Col. Baker, give him my respects. I do hope he may not be tricked out of what he has fairly earned.

"Yours forever, As ever

"A. LINCOLN."

This letter was not intended for the public, but the friend made it public and saved the day for E. D. Baker in his race for the United States Senate. Afterward Lincoln was elected as President of the United States with a plurality in California of 614. As the President of the United States he relied upon the recommendation of Col. Baker more than once in appointments on the Pacific Coast as the following will show:

"Headquarters of the Army at the National Capital, Adjutant General Thomas, ignoring the Governor of Oregon, wrote to three loyal citizens of the State, Col. Thomas B. Cornelius, Hon. B. F. Harding and R. F. Maury, authorizing them to raise for the service of the United States, one regiment of mounted troops" and, after instructions as to officers and equipment, added, "unless otherwise ordered you will be governed by directions sent by Col. E. D. Baker, Senator from Oregon. The department relies confidently upon the prudence, patriotism, and economy with which you will execute this trust."

Col. Baker used his influence to defeat the Secession conspiracy to dislodge California. George W. Ficks, representing the Grand Army of the Republic, in an address at the Lincoln exercises in the Sacramento high school several years ago said: "James McClatchy, in a conversation with Edmond Randolph during those strenuous times, came into possession of the aim to dislodge California from the Union. Immediately after the conversation James McClatchy wrote to E. D. Baker, then Senator in the United States Senate, and as a 'Pony Express' was then starting it carried this important letter with all the plans to E. D. Baker." Kennedy in his Contest for California says: "For Baker there was one supreme demand that Albert Sidney Johnson should be removed and the army forces on the Pacific Coast be subject to the orders of a loyal man." Two weeks after the Inauguration, General Scott wrote to Brigadier General E. V. Sumner to prepare to sail for California. The following day formal orders were confidentially issued to General Sumner, directing him to without delay repair to San Francisco, and relieve Brevet Brigadier General Albert Sidney Johnson, in command of the Department of the Pacific; he was instructed to leave his orders sealed until he should have crossed the Isthmus of Panama and fairly out into the Pacific.

According to this address by Mr. George W. Ficks, when Gen. Sumner presented his credentials to Albert S. Johnson, the latter replied: "Give me one hour and I will turn the country over to you." Gen Sumner replied, "No, not one minute. I am now in command of the Department of the Pacific." Kennedy's Contest for California says that, "then, the crisis was passed."

Brevet Albert Johnson was relieved of the command of the Department of the Pacific. It was soon discovered that there was a strong Secession movement on this coast to that extent that when an order came for the soldiers under the command of General Sumner on this coast to leave for the East, the best citizens signed a petition entreating the Government not to remove the troops from the State. They gave for their reason that a majority of our present State officials are avowed Secessionists and the balance, being bitterly hostile to the administration, are advocates of peaceful policy at any sacrifice upon terms that would not be rejected even in South Carolina. Every appointment made by our Governor within the past three months indicates his entire sympathy and co-operation with those plotting to sever California from her allegiance to the Union, and that, too, at the hazard of civil war. About three-eighths of our citizens are natives of slave-holding States, and are almost a unit in this crisis. The hatred manifested so pointedly in the South and so strongly evinced on the field of battle is no more intense there than here.*** Our advice, obtained with great prudence and care, shows us that there are about sixteen thousand Knights of the Golden Circle in the State."

The loading with arms and powder of the clipper ship J. W. Chapman; the plot to take Mare Island Navy Yards, have been fully stated in Bancroft's "History of California." The Department of the Pacific was then in the control of an experienced and loyal man who, when the situation would become serious, would issue an order that would make them consider well their actions. His orders were like this: "No Federal troops in the Department of the Pacific will ever surrender to rebels. E. V. Sumner."

In regard to the Secessionist movement in California, Kennedy, in his "Contest for California" says, using as his authority, "The Rebellion Records," and quoting from them: "The Secessionist continued defiant and seditious demonstrations occurred in many places, a common feature being the raising of the Bear Flag, accompanied by military ceremonies.''

In his first report to Washington, General Sumner said: ''There is a strong Union feeling with a majority of the people of this State, but the Secessionists are much the most active and zealous party, which give them more influence than they ought to have for their number. I have no doubt there is some deep scheming to draw California into the secession movement, in the first place as the 'Republic of the Pacific,' expecting afterward to induce her to join the Southern Confederacy.''

On the thirteenth, the General wrote to Assistant Adjutant General Townsend, at Washington, D. C.: ''I have found it necessary to withdraw the troops from Fort Mojave, and place them at Los Angeles. There is more danger of dissatisfaction at this place than any other in the State.'' On the seventh of May Captain Winfield Scott Hancock, commanding at Los Angeles, reported: ''The Bear Flag was raised at El Monte, twelve miles distant. The escort was say forty horsemen. I have, I believe, reliable evidence that it will be raised here on Sunday the twelfth inst. That is, the flag will be paraded through the streets under a strong escort.''

The coming of Brigadier General Sumner, as Commander to the Department of the Pacific Coast, had a wonderful effect in giving the Union people courage, especially in San Francisco. There were so many different factions and with E. D. Baker in the Senate at Washington City and Broderick dead, there were few strong and influential men left in California, but when Fort Sumter was fired upon, it seemed to make heroes of men everywhere, and a mass meeting was held in San Francisco and it has been said that fully fourteen thousand persons attended; and at this meeting under the influence of Rev. Thomas Starr King there were Union companies organized. The Catholic Archbishop Alemany, Sheriff David Scannell and many others were present. While the people of the Pacific Coast were holding mass meetings encouraging Union sentiment; the people in far-away New York were holding a similar meeting, and a voice from the Pacific Coast and California was raised in this meeting to give courage to the men to save the Union. That was the voice of Hon. Col. E. D. Baker, then United States Senator. The following is quoted from his speech on this occasion: ''The majesty of the people is here today to sustain the majesty of the Constitution, and I come a wanderer from the far Pacific to record my oath along with yours of the great Empire State and offer from the far Pacific a voice feebler than the feeblest murmur upon its shores may be heard, to give you courage and hope in this contest. That voice is yours today.***If Providence shall will it, this feeble hand shall draw a sword, never yet dishonored, not to fight for honor on a foreign soil; but for country, for home, for law, for government, for constitution, for right, for freedom, for humanity.''

This address was delivered just one week after the firing on Fort Sumter. The President of the United States called for volunteers on the fifteenth of April, and on May first a meeting was held at the Metropolitan Hotel, New York City, and was composed of former citizens from California and Oregon, one hundred of whom had paid their way from California to New York that they might be near the center of activities. At this meeting it was decided to raise a regiment and offer their services to the United States Government, and also tender Col. E. D. Baker the position as Colonel of the regiment. The chairman of the meeting wrote to Senator Baker telling him of the wishes of the men at this meeting and also wrote to the Secretary of War, Hon. Simeon Cameron, concerning the appointment. Men in all parts of the East were anxious to serve under Col. E. D. Baker, and they soon had a brigade which was known as ''Baker's California Brigade.''

President Lincoln issued a call for a special session of Congress. Senator E. D. Baker delivered a most eloquent speech upon a bill reported from the Military Committee. But he did the Pacific Coast honor when he spoke on the floor of Congress of the United States. While addressing that body he was so sincere in his desire to save the country that he forgot that he was addressing the highest body in the American nation, in the uniform of his regiment. There has never been before nor since been such an occasion as this. Mr. Breckenridge had made a speech that members of the House deemed demanded an answer immediately, since it was vital in its effect if permitted to go unanswered. They realized that Col. Baker was about the only member of that body that had the courage to give an immediate answer. A courier was dispatched to bring Col. Baker to the U. S. Congress. He was near by, drilling his regiment. Like a true soldier he did not wait to question the reason why, but, forgetting self, hastened to the Halls of Congress and addressed that body. It has been recorded as one of the most wonderful addresses ever delivered before that body in the most critical time of its history. After addressing Congress he returned to the drilling of his regiment. Shortly afterward his regiment was ordered to Fortress Monroe, and then fought the Battle of Ball's Bluff, where Col. Baker was killed, the first Union officer to lose his life in the Civil War in the cause of Freedom.

Hon. John Hay said of him: ''Edward Dickinson Baker was promoted by one grand brevet of the God of battle above the acclaim of the field, above the applause of the world to the heavens of the martyr and the hero.''

President Lincoln grieved greatly over the death of Col. Baker. Hon. Timothy G. Phelps, a member of the United States Congress, then representing California, in his tribute to Col. Baker delivered before the House of Representatives in December, 1861, declared: ''The whole country is indebted to him, in no small degree, that California is today in the Union.'' Congressman A. A. Sargent said: ''California is largely indebted to E. D. Baker that she is not today within the grasp of Secessionists.''

Can the reader doubt the reason the few pioneer Negroes were so courageous when they had such a man and soldier as their friend and counsellor in their struggles?

Hon. Theodore Hittell once told the writer that he had never heard a greater orator than was Col. E. D. Baker, nor one with a more musical voice; to hear him speak meant at once respectful attention

CHAPTER VIII

RIGHT OF TESTIMONY—GORDON CASE—A TRAGEDY WITH THE COLORED MAN

Several years previous to this tragedy, a colored family had moved to San Francisco, California, coming from Baltimore, Maryland. This family consisted of Mr. and Mrs. Gordon, together with several sisters of the wife. One of the sisters opened a millinery store and Mr. Gordon a barber shop in the basement room of the Niantic Hotel, corner of Bush and Samson streets, San Francisco, California. The proprietor of the hotel was a white gentleman by the name of Mr. Fink.

The tragedy in which Mr. Gordon lost his life occurred as follows: One evening before dusk as one of the young ladies who had the millinery store was going to her supper in the rear of the store, she suddenly turned in time to see a man robbing her cash drawer. She ran back into the store. When the man ran out into the street she continued to chase him, calling "Stop, thief!" She was not, however, successful in overtaking him. The next morning this white man, who was chased the evening previous for robbing the cash box of the millinery store, went into Mr. Gordon's barber shop and demanded that Mr. Gordon make his sister take back the name "thief" she had called him the night before, while chasing him. Mr. Gordon replied that he had not been at home, and had had nothing to do with the affair. The white man then began to abuse Mr. Gordon, finally shooting him at his barber's chair. When shot, Mr. Gordon ran to the street crying "murder!" The white man followed him, and, after Mr. Gordon had fallen to the sidewalk, shot him again and beat him with his revolver. The proprietor of the hotel was coming down the street and recognized the white murderer. There was, however, in the shop at the time of the shooting, a colored man of very light complexion, a Mr. Robert Cowles. This gentleman witnessed the whole affair, but in order to rule his testimony out of court as a witness, he was subjected to an examination by a corps of physicians, who decided that his hair showed he had one-sixteenth part of a drop of Negro blood, and his testimony could not be taken. There was, however, another witness to be dealt with, and that was the proprietor of the hotel, Mr. Fink, who had witnessed the tragedy. His testimony could not be disputed, resulting in this white murderer being sent to the penitentiary for ten years. Owing to the fact that the prisoner had tuberculosis, at the end of two years he was pardoned—dying soon afterward.

A white attorney by the name of Mr. Owens represented the colored family in court against this white murderer. This information, as stated, has been given to the writer by two different members of the Gordon family now living in California.

The Court's decision in the Gordon murder trial was depressing to the colored people then living throughout the State of California and resulted in a few public-spirited and justice-loving Negroes in San Francisco organizing the Franchise League. The object of this league was to do all they possibly could to have removed from the statute books of the State of California the law denying Negroes the "Right of Testimony" in the courts of justice.

The name "Franchise League," and the names of the members and officers were sufficient to inspire in all the Negroes in the State the confidence that it would be a genuine league. "I am resolved 'tis more than half my task, 'twas the great need of all my past existence." "The Franchise League was organized August 12, 1862. Remarks were made by Messrs. F. G. Barbadoes, William H. Yates, Symon Cook, I. G. Wilson, R. A. Hall, Peter A. Bell and J. B. Sanderson. It was deemed proper to organize a movement of the people which shall be responsible to them with a view to action among them in securing from the next Legislature our testimony in the State. Mr. Wilson submitted a paper proposing a basis. It was quite elaborate; the hour was too late to examine it in detail. A committee of five was appointed to examine this and secure other plans as might be proposed." The foregoing account is taken from the diary of J. B. Sanderson, with the permission of his family.

Aside from the workings of the Franchise League to secure the right of testimony in the courts of justice, the following named gentlemen solemnly pledged themselves to go to Sacramento and lobby until they were successful in having the Legislature pass a bill which would repeal those portions of the Civil and Criminal Practice Acts which had prohibited Negroes from the right to testify in the courts of justice in California where white people were parties to suits: Henry Collins, Alfred White, Rev. Peter Cassey, William Hall, William A. Smith, George W. Dennis, J. B. Sanderson, John A. Jones, James Brown,

Peter Bell, Mifflin Gibbs, David Ruggles, John Moore, Symon Cook, I. G. Wilson, R. H. Hall.

The reader will more fully understand the work to be done by the Franchise League if he first reviews that which had already been done in an effort to obtain the "Right of Testimony" in the courts of justice, and the privilege to own land. The struggle for the "Right of Testimony" was long and difficult, lasting from 1852 to 1863. During the entire time the colored pioneers never relaxed in their efforts.

In the Journal of the Assembly under date March 22, 1852, page 395, the writer has found the following: "Mr. Canny presented a petition from Free Negroes of San Francisco praying a change in the laws to authorize them to give testimony against white men. Mr. Hammond offered the following resolution: 'Resolved, that the House, having heard the petition read, do decline to receive it or entertain any petition upon such subject from such source.' The resolution passed by a vote of 47 to 1." In the same Journal (page 159) the following appears: "Mr. Peachy introduced a memorial from citizens of South Carolina and Florida, in reference to their removing to the State of California and bringing their (slaves) property. Mr. Miller moved to refer to the special committee of thirteen and that five hundred copies be printed." This resolution was enough to discourage almost any other body of men except the Negro pioneers of California, who were just as active the next year in the same cause as they had been the year previous.

In Bancroft's California History the following appears: "At the Legislative session of 1853 W. C. Merdith, a Democrat from Tuolumne, presented a memorial to the Assembly signed by Negroes, asking the repeal of the clause prohibiting the Negro persons from testifying in the courts of justice where white persons are concerned. Instantly one member moved to throw the memorial out of the window; another did not want the Journal tarnished with such an infamous document. The chair reluctantly ruled the motion out of order, and an appeal was taken finally in the greatest excitement. The petition was rejected and the clerk instructed not to file it." Even this did not discourage the Negro pioneers. They immediately proceeded to organize to fight it out and decided to call a State convention. The following is an exact copy of their call:

"State Convention of the Colored Citizens of California, Brethren:—Your state and condition in California is one of social and political degradation; one that is unbecoming a free and enlightened people. Since you have left your homes and peaceful friends in the Atlantic States, and migrated to the shores of the Pacific, with the hopes of bettering your condition, you have met with one continued series of outrages, injustices, and unmitigated wrongs unparalleled in the history of nations. You are denied the right to become owners of the soil, that common inheritance which rewards our industry, the mainspring of all human actions, which is to mankind in this world like the action of the sun to the other heavenly bodies. You are compelled to labor and toil without any security that you shall obtain your just earnings as an inheritance for yourself or your children in the land of your birth.

"The Statute books and the common law, the great bulwark of society, which should be to us as the rivers of water in a dry place, like the shadow of a great rock in a weary land, where the wretched should find sympathy and the weak protection, spurn us with contempt and rule us from their very threshold and deny us a common humanity.

"Then, in view of these wrongs which are so unjustly imposed upon us, and the progress of the enlightened spirit of the age in which we live and the great duty that we owe to ourselves and the generations that are yet to come, we call upon you to lay aside your various avocations and assemble yourselves together on Tuesday, the 20th day of November, A. D. 1855, in the city of Sacramento, at 10 A. M., for the purpose of devising the most judicious and effectual ways and means to obtain our inalienable rights and privileges in California.

"All of which is most respectfully submitted and signed.

"JAMES CARTER, Sacramento
"J. H. TOWNSEND, San Francisco
"PETER ANDERSON, San Francisco
"WILLIAM H. NEWBY, San Francisco
"D. W. RUGGLES, San Francisco
"J. B. SANDERSON, San Francisco,

"The Committee, San Francisco, September 27, 1855.

"Every Assembly District is recommended to send two delegates for every member of the Assembly in the said district to the convention."

The following is the California legislative records in the Negroes' struggles for the "Right of Testimony" in the courts of justice in this State. The legislative records for the sessions of 1857 show that the Negroes in California sent to the Assembly no less than seven petitions from as many counties. They were presented by the following Representatives: McCallen, Eldorado county; Goodwin, Yuba county; Johnson, Sacramento county; Crandall, Amador county; Cosby, Siskiyou county.

In a recent collection of papers discovered by the California Secretary to the Archives, and owned by John T. Mason, of Downieville, is the following letter, written by Rev. J. B. Sanderson to Mr. David Brown, of Marysville, in regard to the activities of the State Executive Committee in the fight for the "Right of Testimony" during the year 1856:

"Sacramento, March 20, 1856.

"Mr. David Brown:—

"Dear Sir:—I have today received a letter and petition from you with eighty-four names. It is the second letter I have received from you. It is also the second petition. We shall put the Sierra petition into the Assembly and, as no effort has been made yet to bring the matter before that branch of the Legislature, your petition is quite in time.

"On Thursday, the 13th, Mr. Flint, of San Francisco, presented to the Senate the petition for that county. The next day, the 14th, Mr. Fisk, of Eldorado, presented to the Senate our petition from that county. The San Francisco petition had five hundred signatures and the best men of the county. The Eldorado petition had sixteen hundred names, a fine array, presenting an effective appearance. Both were received respectfully and referred to the proper committee, the Judiciary. The Senator from Tuolumne, Mr. Coffroth, holds the petition containing eight hundred names for that county which he has promised to present early. We hope to get the Sacramento petition before the Senate immediately. Tomorrow I am to meet Mr. Ferguson, Senator from this county, and chairman of the Judiciary Committee. We do not control events, we hope Mr. Ferguson will favor the presentation of our petition; being chairman, he can greatly control the action of the Judiciary Committee in causing a bill proposing the specific change in the law to be drafted, presented and commended to the acceptance of the Senate. We cannot tell what will be done. The indications appear rather favorable and we hope for the best. I may mention that Mr. Fisk told me today that he was preparing a bill for presentation to the Senate which will embrace the subject of giving us the 'Right of Testimony' in the courts. I can only state the fact or language generally. I have not the time now to say as much as I would like. We are all equally interested in this matter, you as much as I; I no more than you, as a member of the State Executive Committee. I will do what I can. Each member feels the same way.***May success crown the effort we are all making for the 'Right of Testimony.'

"Very respectfully yours,
"J. B. Sanderson."

All these petitions were to repeal the law denying the Negroes then living in California, the "Right of Testimony" in the courts of justice where a white person was a party to a suit.

The California Statutes of 1861, (chapter 467, page 521) reads: "An Act to amend an act entitled an Act in Civil cases in the Courts of Justice in this State passed April 29, 1851. Approved May 18, 1861. The people of the State of California represented in Senate and Assembly do enact as follows: Section 422 of an Act to regulate proceedings in Civil cases in the Courts of the State, passed April 29, 1851, is hereby amended so as to read as follows: 'Section 422. A person for whose immediate benefit the action is prosecuted or defended, though not a party to the action, may be examined as a witness in the same manner and subjected to the same rules of examination as if he were named as a party. And a party to an action or proceedings may be examined as a witness in his own behalf the same as any other witness.***This section shall not be held to impair or in any way affect the existing provision of law by which persons of Indian or Negro blood are excluded from being witnesses.' "

The section of the law preventing Negroes from being witnesses or testifying in the courts of justice was known as Section 394—Witness—Persons incompetent. Section 394 of the "Civil Practice Act" provides: No Indian, or Negro, or persons having one-half or more Indian blood and Negroes or persons having one-half or more of Negro blood, shall be allowed to testify as a witness in action in which a white person is a party. Section 14 of the "Criminal Act" provides that, No Black or Mulatto person or Indian shall be allowed to give evidence in favor or against a white man.

DR. CLAUDIUS BALLARD
Awarded the Croix de Guerre in World's War.

ATTORNEY CHARLES D'ARDEN
Land Litigation Specialist.

EDITOR JOS. B. BASS
Editor of the *California Eagle*
of Los Angeles.

PROF. CHARLES ALEXANDER
Editor, Author and Lecturer.

SIDNEY P. DONES
Investment Broker.

The Negro was not the only person who was denied the "Right of Testimony" in the courts of justice; a case is recorded in California Reports, number 4, October, 1854, page 399: The People, respondent, against George W. Hall, appellant. The appellant, a free white citizen of this State, was convicted of murder upon the testimony of a Chinese witness, the point involved in the case is the admissibility of such evidence. The case was tried before Chief Justice J. Murry and J. Heydenfeldt. The following is a part of the decision: "No Black or Mulatto person or Indian shall be allowed to give evidence in favor of or against a white man. Held, that the word Indian, Negro, Black, and white are generic terms designating races. That therefore Chinese and all other people not white are included in the prohibition from being witnesses. The reader can readily see the great difficulty the Negroes as well as other races other than white, had to obtain a hearing in court in pioneer days in California.

It is gratifying to the writer to have been able to quote from the letter by Mr. J. B. Sanderson in regard to the number of names signed to the different petitions sent to the Assembly of California in the struggle. It is quite evident that he mentioned the number to give the reader of the letter the idea of the feeling of a large number of white people in regard to the Negro's right to give testimony in the courts of justice. There were not only a great many white people who were in favor of the "Right of Testimony" for the Negro, but they were not in the least backward in letting it be known that they were in favor of the same, as the following quotation from the writings of Hon. John Archibald, shows. He said: "Would to God my feeble words could have power to make my fellow citizens reflect that the difference between the Englishman and the Russian,***and the Chinese and the Negro is one of degree, not of kind. That to draw a line anywhere between them is to make a wholly unfounded distinction. Let us give each individual the treatment to which his character, his attainments entitle him, but let us never forget that they are all of them men endowed with like capabilities, like faculties, like feelings with ourselves. Let us make a beginning by restoring to them at once the 'Right of Testimony' and leave it to our juries to judge of the value of that testimony just as they do now.*** Finally, let us bring our State Constitution once more into accord with the glorious Declaration of Independence, to which we so often and so fondly appeal, yet which our fathers would have thought a monstrous abortion if it had contained any such clause as 'We hold these truths to be self-evident, that all white men are created equal, that they are endowed by their Creator with certain inalienable rights***.''

The quotation just given was a very strong plea in favor of justice for the colored people, and must have created a strong public sentiment which always helps members of the Legislature in deciding the way to vote on any pressing measure. And yet while it helped, still the efforts of the pioneer Negroes in blazing a trail for the present-day Negroes in California were not successful until after many more years of struggle for the "Right of Testimony" in the courts.

Hittell, in his "History of California" (vol. 4, page 340) says, in regard to the "Right of Testimony": "It was one of the glories of the Legislature of 1863 that it made the first break in the illiberal and disgraceful provisions of the Legislature of 1850, that no black or mulatto person or Indian should be permitted to give evidence in any court of the State in an action in which a white person was a party. These provisions reenacted in 1851 had been amended and enlarged in 1854, and in that shape they continued for nine years longer a foul blot upon the history of the country.

Two bills introduced into the Senate by Richard F. Perkins, of San Francisco, on January, 1863, had for their object the removal of this inhibition against Negroes and Mulattoes. They passed the Senate. In the Assembly Morris M. Estes introduced a similar amendment to the effect that the testimony of Negroes and Mulattoes shall be disregarded unless corroborated in some material particular.'"

The bill referred to by Mr. Hittell in his history in regard to the "Right of Testimony" was introduced by Senator Richard F. Perkins through the Franchise League, composed of colored people or, rather, colored pioneer men. The object of the bill framed and introduced by Senator Perkins was to repeal those portions of the Civil and Criminal Practice Acts which prohibited the "Right of Testimony" in the courts of justice in California where white people were interested. He presented the bill at two different sessions of the Legislature before he was successful in having it passed. Governor Leland Stanford, a Republican, immediately signed it.

The following is a copy of the bill as introduced by Richard F. Perkins, Senator and Member of the 14th session of the California Legislature: "An Act to amend an act entitled, An Act to regulate proceedings in Civil Cases in the Courts of Justice in this State, passed April 29, 1851. Approved March 16, 1863. People of the State represented in Senate and Assembly. Section I.***Section 394 of the said act is hereby amended so as to read as follows: 'Section 394. The following persons shall not be witnesses: (1)—Those of unsound mind at the time of their production for examination; (2)—children under six years of age who, in the opinion of the Court, appear incapable of receiving just impression of the facts respecting which they are examined or of relating them truthfully; (3)—Mongolians, Chinese, Indians or persons of one-half or more Indian blood, in an act or proceeding where a white person is a party***This act shall take effect and be in force on and after its passage. Section 14. No Indian or person with one-half or more Indian blood, or Chinese shall give evidence in favor or against a white person.' ''

There was great rejoicing among the colored people then living in California in regard to their success in securing the ''Right of Testimony'' in the courts of justice. The following is quoted from an old copy of the *Pacific Appeal*, of San Francisco, under date of March 21, 1863: ''The Executive Committee of the Colored Convention met immediately after the passage of the Testimony Bill, and passed resolutions of thanksgiving for their hard-earned victory. They met in the church building on Scott Street, San Francisco. Solomon Penelton, through the recommendation of Peter A. Bell, moved that a special committee be appointed. Mr. J. G. Wilson moved that a committee of three would be sufficient. The committee was elected by the house. The following gentlemen were elected: Alex Ferguson, J. B. Sanderson, Peter Anderson, F. G. Barbadoes and S. Howard. The name of Mr. Yates, who was President of the first State Convention in 1855, and a consistent, co-worker with the committee, upon the recommendation of Mr. Barbadoes, was added to the committee.

''T. M. D. Ward was elected as president of this committee and Peter Anderson secretary. The committee retired to the choir room to form the resolutions when Mr. James Brown moved the propriety of publishing Mr. Barstow's speech in the *Appeal*. Mr. Barstow delivered a forceful address in the California Assembly in behalf of the passage of the Testimony Bill, March 4th, 1863.''

After the adjournment of the Legislature the colored people living in San Francisco, through the Contraband Relief Society, held a public meeting, at which time they invited Senator Perkins to address them. The laws were not fully wiped off the Statutes until 1873.

In the California Reports, 1872-3; Tuttle No. 3372, People vs. McGuire: ''Testimony of a Chinese or Mongolian witness is not admissible under existing laws against white persons. After the first of January, 1873, when the codes take effect, no witness will be excluded in any case on account of nationality or color.''

HOMESTEAD LAWS

The few colored people living in California were anxious to obtain homes. It is true that a few were hustlers and had secured homes, but in every new country a few men and women are willing to pioneer and take up homestead land. Under the laws of California the colored people were not allowed homestead rights. There are people today who wonder why relatives of pioneer families of color are not wealthy.

The Homestead law was passed in 1851 and again February 4, 1860.

This bill, like all the others of its kind, was discussed among the people of color, resulting in their calling a convention. This convention debated especially the ''Right of Testimony,'' because if the word of a colored person would not be taken in court, they might purchase land and yet be defrauded out of it. Section 2 of the Homestead law reads:

''Whenever any white man or female resident in this State shall desire to avail himself or herself of the benefits of this act, such person shall make a written application to the county judge of the county in which the land is situated.''

This same bill was brought up in the Legislature of 1860, and the Senate and Assembly passed concurrent resolutions February 4th, 1860, which read: ''Resolved by the Assembly, the Senate concurring, that our Senators in Congress be instructed and our Representatives requested to use their influence to procure the passage of a law by Congress donating to each bona fide settler on the public agricultural lands within the State, being a free white person over the age of twenty-one years and a citizen of the United States; who shall have become such a homestead community of one hundred and sixty acres or more after a continuous residence and occupation thereof for five years.''

By the wording of the Homestead law a colored man could not acquire a homestead plot of land. He might even purchase a home and yet if a white person should claim the land, a colored person could not go into court and testify in his own behalf. The records in the following case will prove the statement, and also the necessity for the Negroes to fight for the ''Right of Testimony'' in the courts. This case will also explain that the persons of color did not often accumulate fortunes because of the fact that they spent about all they were able to acquire in fighting adverse legislation, that they might live in the beautiful, balmy atmosphere of California.

The papers published among the pioneer Negroes in California were of a high type and are really historical gems for their painstaking records of events of vital interest to the Negro. The following is quoted from a copy of the *Pacific Appeal,* San Francisco, May 30, 1863:

"An interesting land case. The colored man has rights which the Government respects. We publish a transcript of an interesting and important correspondence between the Register of the Land Office at Marysville and the Commissioner of the General Land Office at Washington, D. C. The Register appointed for the Marysville Land District, Mr. A. J. Snyder, finding that there were several cases in this jurisdiction of Negroes claiming rights on public domain, and believing that these ought to be allowed, submitted the following test case to the department at Washington, D. C.

" 'United States Land Office,
" 'Marysville, California, Feb. 3, 1863.

" 'Sir—Benjamin Berry, a colored man, settled upon the southwest quarter of Section No. 12, of T. 13, N. R. 4 E., has this day applied to me for advice and relief in certain matters pertaining to his claim to said land.

" 'The facts from his own statements and the enclosed affidavit appear to be that the claimant was originally a slave, born in Kentucky, taken to Missouri and then sold to a man by the name of Halloway, with whom he came to this State. This was about 1850. Here he performed services supposed to be equivalent to $3000 and obtained his freedom. He then settled on this land now claimed by him, erected improvements and has continued to reside there as an actual bona fide settler upon the public land. He is now old, being sixty-seven years of age. Within the last three years he has married. It appears from the file of this office that his settlement was made long prior to the survey upon unoccupied vacant public land. Since his settlement certain parties, taking advantage of his legal disabilities, have attempted to acquire title to the land claimed by him through the State as portion of the five hundred acre grant. Such claims have not as yet been perfected. It is feared that the parties now claiming adverse to Berry will proceed to eject him by an action in the State courts, and his application is made to your office for some mode of relief by which Berry, who has settled and improved this public land in good faith, may be protected in his improvements and occupancy.

" 'I have asked your careful consideration of the case and an equitable ruling at your very earliest convenience.

" 'I am, sir,
" 'Very respectfully your obedient servant,
" 'A. J. SNYDER.

" 'To the Honorable J. M. Edmonds, Commissioner.' "

Answer:
" 'General Land Office, March 12, 1863.
" 'Register of Land Office, Marysville, California:—

" 'Sir: Your letter of third of February last covering an affidavit of Edward E. Thurman and in relation to the case of Benjamin Berry, a free man of color, is received and in reply thereto I have to state that the Attorney General of the United States in an elaborate opinion published the 29th of November, 1862, upon the subject of rights of free persons of color to citizenship under the Constitution of the United States, declares: "The free man of color, if born in the United States, is a citizen of the United States." The administration of the business of this department will conform to the above opinion and you will therefore have no difficulty in disposing of the case in hand.

" 'The man Berry, upon making proper proof of his being a free man and born in the United States, will be entitled to the benefit of the Preemption Laws as also of the Homestead Laws. Of course he can purchase with money without regards to citizenship.

" 'Should there be adverse rights in the above case, you will give the parties due notice, and a full hearing.

" 'Very respectfully,
" 'Your obedient servant,
" 'JOSEPH S. WILSON, Acting Commissioner.' "

In commenting on this land case the editor of the *Pacific Appeal* said: "Under this straightforward and just ruling Berry will be able to secure his rights and maintain possession of the land he has improved and occupied for so many years. His place is near Johnson's ranch on Bear river and he will obtain a quarter section as a homestead. Heretofore colored men have been forcibly expelled from portions of the public domain which they had improved and paid taxes upon. In this district that class of our citizens being now assured of protection by a government which, even in the midst of a great civil war, finds time to do justice to the humblest individual, colored people should hasten to make themselves independent by entering on the unoccupied public lands where they can become independent.''

The above case will give the reader an idea of the greatest reason for the rejoicing of the Negro people in California in regard to the passage of the Perkins ''Right of Testimony'' bill. It was a sincere celebration because it meant much to them since, even if life in beautiful California was a constant struggle, they liked the climate and realized the possibilities of the then young State. But they also wished to own homes and, as they were pioneers, felt entitled to the homestead privileges which they could not enjoy like others coming to this faraway western land.

Elective Franchise

''I see the future rise before me,
The glory of the coming man.''

The colored people did not pause in their activities because of their success in securing the Right of Testimony. They were anxious to become full citizens and enjoy the Elective franchise, and issued a call for a convention to work for the passage of a legislative amendment to the Constitution of the State of California. The following is an exact copy of their call for a State Convention of the Colored Citizens of the State of California: ''The undersigned, believing at this time the wisdom, the virtue, the learning, the wealth and the prestige of our people should assemble in convention to deliberate on the political and educational intent, hereby request our leading men throughout the State to make arrangements to effect the same.

''A. Waddy,

''President of public meeting in May 26, 1864.

''George W. Dennis

''Wm. Burris, *Vice-presidents.''*

This call for a convention in the effort to secure the franchise was the very first made along that line and too much credit cannot be given to these few men. In this convention there was a committee named from every county in the State, whose duty was to have the Senator or Representative of the Legislature living in their district to present a petition to the Legislature praying for the Elective Franchise.

The law they wished amended so as to give them the right of suffrage read: ''Article 2, Section I, of the Constitution of the State of California. Every white male citizen of the United States and every white male citizen of Mexico who shall have elected to become a citizen of the United States under the Treaty of Peace exchanged and ratified at Quoritire on the 30th of May, 1848, of the age of twenty-one years who shall have been a resident of the State six months next preceding the election, and of the county and district in which he claims his vote thirty days, shall be entitled to vote at all elections which are now or hereafter may be authorized by law; provided, that nothing herein contained shall be construed to prevent the Legislature, by a two-thirds concurring vote, from admitting to the right of suffrage Indians or the descendants of Indians in such special cases as a portion of the legislative body may deem just and proper.''

In the Senate Journal under date 1865-6 the following appears: ''Petition and Remonstration presented by Benton Memorial to the Legislature of California from a committee on Elective Franchise, attested by the president and secretary of the colored convention, recommending an amendment to the Constitution of the State of California. In accordance with the above, Mr. Benton submitted a proposed amendment, which was placed on file and ordered printed:

'' 'The Legislature of the State of California at its sixteenth session, commencing on the 4th day of December, 1865, proposed the following amendment to Section I, of Article —, of the Constitution:

'' 'Article —, Right of Suffrage

'' 'Senate Bill Number 417, Section I. Every male citizen of the United States, of the age of twenty-one years, who shall have been a resident of the State six months next preceding the election and of the county or district in which he offers his vote thirty days, shall be entitled to vote at all elections which are now or hereafter may be authorized, to pass such laws for the registration of voters as may be necessary for the more effectual providing against frauds upon the Elective Franchise.

"'Read the first and second times and sent to the Judicial Committee.'

"The object of this bill was defeated by the introduction of a bill by Senator Haws asking for 'An act to provide for the registration of all the citizens of the State and for the enrollment in several election districts of all the legal voters thereof and for the prevention and punishment of frauds affecting the Elective Franchise.' Mr. Hager offered an amendment (page 228) Section 9: 'Before the word "County Clerk" in line six of the printed bill insert the following: "Provided, if any person claiming to be a native-born citizen, shall make affidavit or claim under oath that he was born in the United States, giving the time and place of his birth, such affidavit shall be received as proof of his citizenship."' Mr. Montgomery moved to recommit the bill with the following special instruction: 'Providing, if any person claiming to be an elector shall make oath or affidavit that he is a white male citizen of the United States of twenty-one years of age, and had been a resident of the State six months, next preceding, and of the county or district in which he claimed his vote, shall be sufficient to be registered.' Bill passed by vote of Ayes, 24; Noes, 7."

The Elective Franchise, like all the other rights obtained by the pioneers of the Negro race in California, was not obtained without a struggle. But they were equal to the task, and year after year sent petitions to the Legislature in an effort to secure the object of the passage of a bill giving them this right. The entire male population of colored residenters in the State were earnest and sincere in their desire to obtain the right of suffrage. In 1865 they organized what was afterward known as the Executive Committee of the Colored Convention. This committee became a permanent organization, the aim of which was published in the following Negro papers: *San Francisco Elevator* and the *Pacific Appeal.* The following is quoted from *The Elevator,* under date of January 24, 1865, Editor Phillip A. Bell: "The Executive Committee appointed at a meeting of the colored citizens of San Francisco on the 24th of January, 1865, presented the following address explaining the origin and object of their appointment: 'The difficulties which attended our celebration on the first of January and indifference too often evinced by the people generally in public affairs, induced many to believe that a permanent organization or an Executive Committee, appointed by the people for one year, and a similar committee elected each year, was necessary for the better conduct of public business, such as calling meetings on important occasions and to take a general supervision of public affairs. At a meeting held on the sixth of January, 1865, to hear the final report of the celebration committee, a motion was made to elect an Executive Committee of thirteen members. A nominating committee was appointed who reported at a subsequent meeting of which notice was given. That meeting confirmed the selection made by the nominating committee; object for which the committee was appointed, will need money. Hence they proposed establishing a permanent fund to carry out these objects. We therefore recommend that subscriptions be given by citizens generally to aid us in our operations. We also recommend that similar committees be organized throughout the State with whom we shall be in correspondence so that on important subjects, either political or moral, we might act in unison. The advantage arising from a connection between the different sections of the country is obvious.

"'A State Central Committee might be formed through whose agency the work of inviting the people in all important measures of reform may be consummated.

"'Executive Committee of San Francisco: W. H. Yates, Henry Collins, Wm. H. Hall, J. P. Dyer, J. Madison Bell, Edward W. Parker, D. W. Ruggles, John F. Meshaw, F. G. Barbadoes, President; S. Peneton, Vice-president; R. H. Hall, Corresponding Secretary; J. R. Starky, Treasurer; Shadrick Howard, Recording Secretary. Publicity Committee, Equality before the law: Wm. H. Yates, James R. Starkey, R. A. Hall, J. P. Dyer, F. G. Barbadoes, S. Hall, P. A. Bell.'"

The Executive Committee used every means within its power to obtain the passage of an amendment to the State Constitution, with success. In July there was another convention called. This call was issued by the Phoenixonia Institute of San Jose, California. This Institute was organized first as a private school December 22, 1863, by the Rev. Cassey for the religious, moral, and political improvement of the colored people of the State. Among the active members of this convention were mentioned the names of such well-known pioneers of color as the Honorable Peter Bell, of San Francisco, Andrew Bristol, also of San Francisco, James Floyd, A. J. White, G. A. Smith, S. J. Marshal, Rev. Cassey, Mrs. Wm. A. Smith, all of whom were residents of San Jose. Resolutions were drafted at this convention in regard to education, industrial pursuits and the Elective Franchise. These resolutions were intended to give courage to the colored people living in the State. The part in relation to suffrage was as follows:

"SUFFRAGE

"Resolved, that while the mind of every patriotic statesman is fully aroused to the question of impartial suffrage as the only guarantee of liberty, it is our duty and our privilege to make known our wishes and our claims to all that belong to American citizenship;

"Resolved, that an agent should be appointed to canvass the State, not only to solicit aid for the school, but to awaken an interest in political matters, the first of which will be to secure the right of suffrage;

"Resolved, that a competent representative gentleman, one who will worthily represent our people, be employed for the above mentioned purpose who shall receive a sufficient percentage to enable him successfully to perform his mission."

In October, 1867, the colored people of the State through the Executive Committee of San Francisco, drafted a petition and sent to the Legislature, praying the right of suffrage. The following is a copy of it as given in an issue of the *Elevator* of that date, although it was published in both the colored papers in San Francisco. The agents of the two papers were instructed to obtain the signature of all colored male citizens of voting age in every county and send them to the Executive Committee at San Francisco, who would see to the forwarding of it to the Legislature at the proper time. The call was issued Oct. 18, 1867, and the names of the signers to the petition were published every week in these two colored papers in San Francisco until the Legislature was presented with the same.

"THE PETITION

"To the Honorable Senate and Assembly of the State of California in Legislature assembled:—

"The petition of the colored citizens of California respectfully showeth that your petitioners are native-born American citizens of full age and of average intelligence. They are acquainted with the Laws and Constitution of the General State Governments and are noted for being a law-abiding class, respectful of all the statutes of the land, and rendering due obedience to the powers that be. They are taxpayers and willingly render all the aid and assistance in their power to support the Government and institutions of the country. But by the organic law of this State your petitioners are deprived of the rights of suffrage and we would respectfully pray that your honorable bodies recommend to the people of this State an alteration of the Constitution by the addition of a clause to the first section of Article 2 of the said Constitution, in the following words to-wit:—

" 'Provided, that nothing therein contained shall be construed to prevent the Legislature by a two-thirds concurring vote from admitting to the right of suffrage colored American citizens in such special cases as such a proportion of the Legislature may deem just and proper, and for the prosperity of the State, the perpetuity of our Government and institutions and for the health and happiness and harmony of your honorable bodies, your petitioners will ever pray.'

"Signed by the Executive Committee of the Colored Convention.

"San Francisco, Oct. 18, 1867."

Abraham Lincoln, while President of the United States, in a letter to Governor Michael Hahn, of Louisiana, in regard to the Elective Franchise for colored people, after congratulating the Governor as the "First Free State Governor of Louisiana," proceeded to say: "Now you are about to have a convention which among other things will probably define the Elective Franchise, I barely suggest, for your private consideration, whether some of the colored people may not be let in, as, for instance, the very intelligent and especially those who have fought gallantly in our ranks. They will probably help in some trying time to come, to keep the 'Jewel of Liberty' within the family of freedom. But this is only a suggestion, not to the public, but to you alone." The writer was especially happy to have discovered this letter, since it has been said that the Honorable Fred Douglass, the great Negro orator, ex-slave and a tireless worker for his race, at the time of the Civil War when the crisis seemed to be turning the wrong way for the Union Army, went to the President of the United States, Abraham Lincoln, and plead that he use Negro slaves and make them soldiers to fight for the salvation of the country and afterward reward them by giving them full citizenship.

The right of franchise for the Negro in California was won after years of earnest work not only by the Executive Committee, but by many others. The colored people in California did not obtain the right of suffrage until after the Constitutional Amendment to the Constitution of the United States, which read: "Constitutional Amendment to the United States Constitution, Article 15, Section I. The right of citizens of the United States to vote shall not be denied or abridged in the United States, or any other State on account of race, color or previous condition of servitude.   Section 2.   Congress shall have power to enforce this article by appropriate legislation.

"Received by the Department of State, Feb. 27, 1869."

Privileges to ride in street cars in California: The testing of the privilege to ride in street cars by persons of color was the most interesting occurrence in San Francisco in the year 1864.   In an issue of the *San Francisco Bulletin* of that year appeared the following article by a person signing himself "A Virginian:"

"I am not an Abolitionist, nor do I approve of the President's Emancipation Proclamation, but I do think that in a State pretending to be free the colored people should be allowed a few more privileges than they enjoy in a slave State, therefore I am surprised that such an outrage should occur as I read in last evening's *Bulletin*, where three women were ejected from the cars for no other offense than that of being colored.

"Who was contaminated by their presence, or who would have suffered if these three persons had been allowed to ride to their journey's end?   Now I claim to be a Christian and a southerner, yet I would rather sit near a decent black man in the cars (or anywhere else) than to have a big bloated white fellow sit near, breathing his whiskey and tobacco in my face.   But such people are free, white American citizens and use up so much liberty that there is none left for anybody else***It is this class who think they can only show their own liberty by encroaching upon that of others.

"In conclusion I sincerely hope that the liberality and common sense of this beautiful, free and Christian community may prevail in this matter and that all respectable colored people may be allowed to avail themselves of the cars whenever desired.

"Signed, A VIRGINIAN."

This letter demonstrated the spirit and feeling of a large number of white people of that date living in California.   In the writer's research work in the interest of this history, she had the pleasure of talking to one of the three women mentioned in this article, a Mrs. Louise Tyler.   She is now an inmate of the "Home for Aged and Infirm Colored People," located at Beulah, California, near Oakland.   She said that she, together with Mammy Pleasant, Mrs. Bivins and Laura Clark, were coming home from church one Sunday and, becoming very tired of the tramp over the hills and sand dunes to their homes at North Beach and Baker street, they decided to walk in front of the street cars, whereupon the car stopped and Mrs. Tyler, being a Mulatto and looking much like a foreigner, was allowed to ride; but the others of the party were dark and the conductor pushed them off the car.   This was no new occurrence for the conductors to treat colored people thus.   They had been compelled to suffer such treatment for years.   There was in the party a woman who was not afraid to go into the courts with a grievance.   That person was "Mammy Pleasant."   She immediately sought counsel and then attempted to ride in the street cars, whereupon she was again pushed off.   Through the advice of her counsel she had a hack following the car with her attorney in it and some white people in the car to act as her witnesses to the treatment accorded her by the conductor.   She was pushed off the street car to the street and the hackman who was following the car immediately quickened his speed and stopped and through the assistance of her white friends on the street car they lifted her into the hack and drove away.   "Mammy Pleasant" entered suit against the street railroad company and won damages.

There were many occurrences afterward against the colored people riding in the street cars until a suit was brought against the street railway company by a Mr. Brown and his daughter, Miss Charlotte Brown, who afterward became Mrs. Riker.   This suit, through their attorney, Mr. Burnett, was won.   Judge Owens in his decision was very severe and settled for all time the rights of colored people to ride in street cars in any part of California.

CHAPTER IX

SLAVERY IN CALIFORNIA. THE BEGINNING OF SLAVERY

The subject of "Slavery in California" is far reaching, and to be fully understood the reader will have to review California under Spain. The Crown of Castile governed through conquest or discovery many colonies in the Western Hemisphere, namely: South America, Hispaniola, Mexico and California, which at one time was considered Mexican territory.

The King of Spain had very liberal slave laws governing the Negro slaves. A splendid history of these has been given by Sir Arthur Helps in his "Slavery in the Spanish Colonies," in which he says: "The Royal Historiographer, Herrera, speaks of the King having informed the Admiral Don Diego Columbus, in 1510, that he had given orders to the officials at Seville that they should send fifty Negroes to work in the mines of Hispaniola. In June, 1511, there is a sentence in one of the King's letters addressed to a man by the name of Sampler, who held office in the colony about the Negroes***'I do not understand how so many Negroes have died. Take much care of them.' In October of the same year there is an order from the King to his officials at Seville authorizing them to pay Ledesma, one of the Royal Pilots, what was due him for the last voyage he had made at the King's command to carry Negroes to Hispaniola.

"The Jeromite Fathers had also come to the conclusion that Negroes must be introduced into the West Indies. Writing in January, 1518, they recommended license to be given to the inhabitants of Hispaniola or to other persons to bring Negroes there.*** Zuajo, the Judge of the residencia and the legal colleague of Las Casas, wrote to the same effect. He, however, suggested that the Negroes should be placed in settlements and married."

The reader will find it of interest to review the colonization scheme of Las Casas. This has been quoted from Sir Arthur Helps, in which he said: "Las Casas prepared his memorial taking for his basis the plan which the Jeromites had carried out to Hispaniola and which they had partially acted upon. He added, however, some other things, among them, that of securing to the Indians their entire liberty. And he provided a scheme for furnishing Hispaniola with laborers from the mother country.***The King was to give to every laborer willing to emigrate to Hispaniola his living during the journey from his place of abode to Seville at the rate of half a real a day throughout the journey for great and small, child and parent. At Seville the emigrants were to be lodged in Casa de Construccion and were to have from eleven to thirteen maravedis a day. From thence they were to have free passage to Hispaniola and to be provided with food for a year. If the climate should try them so much that at the expiration of this year they should not be able to work for themselves, the King was to continue to maintain them. But the extra maintenance was to be put down to the account of the emigrants as a loan which they were to repay.

"The King was to give them lands of his own lands, furnish them with plowshares and spades and provide medicine for them. Lastly, whatever rights and profits accumulated from their holdings were to become hereditary. They were certainly most liberal plans of emigration and, in addition, there were other privileges held out as inducements to these laborers in connection with the above scheme***added another provision, namely, that each Spanish resident in the island should have license to import a dozen Negro slaves. The origin of this suggestion was, as he informs us, that the colonist had told him that if license were given them to import a dozen Negro slaves each, they (the colonists) would then set free the Indians and so, recollecting the statement, he added this proviso."

Sir Arthur Helps further states in regard to laws affecting free Negroes and Negresses: "The earliest laws that declared the ground on which the Negroes could demand their liberty dates from 1528.***That many Negroes did obtain their liberty may be inferred from the fact of there being several laws having reference to free Negroes enacted, for instance, what tribute they should pay and with whom they should live, and commanding that free Negresses unless married to Spaniards, should not wear gold ornaments, pearls or silks." This will illustrate how the Spaniards in every instance honored their blood. They married their Negresses who happened to be slaves, thereby legalizing their children, as will be seen by the following law enacted in regard to children born to Spaniards with Negresses as wives. This law reads: "Provision is also made that in the sale of the children of Spaniards and Negresses, their parents shall have a right of pre-exemption.''

''In later times under the admirable administration of Count Florida Blanca, during the reign of Charles the Third, of Spain, it is evident that Negroes were treated humanely and were cared for by the government, being taught to read and write and having the privilege of purchasing their freedom, and also the power of getting themselves transferred to another master if their own had been guilty of cruelty to them.'' These laws in regard to slavery in the Spanish colonies were applicable to the West Indies and Mexico. California was a part of the territory of Mexico, hence these laws controlled the slavery of California. It is now that we come to the subject of ''Slavery in California.''

The reader will readily say ''California was always a Free State. It was free territory when purchased by the United States from Mexico.'' It can perhaps be more clearly understood why it was free territory if you first survey the struggle carried on by England for thirty years to abolish the slave trade throughout the world. ''During the period between 1814 and 1845, there were many conventions held and treaties signed between England and the different slave countries. There was one treaty signed in 1817 with Spain, the Treaty of Madrid, engaging that slave trade shall be abolished throughout the entire dominion of Spain on the 30th of May, 1820, restricting the Spanish trade in the meantime to the south of the Equator and also confining it to the Spanish Dominions. Spain promised, by the treaty of September 30, 1817, to abolish the slave trade entirely October 31, 1820, in all Spanish territories, even south of the line.''

This treaty did not abolish slavery in the Spanish colony of Mexico. In after years this colony declared her independence from Spain and, in 1829, Guerrero, the President of Mexico, issued the following decree: ''Desiring to signalize the year 1829, the anniversary of our independence from Spain, by an act of national justice and beneficence that may turn to the benefit and support of such a valuable good; that may consolidate more and more public tranquility; that may co-operate to the aggrandizement of the Republic, and return to an unfortunate portion of its inhabitants those rights which they hold from nature and that the people protect by wise and equitable laws, in conformity with the 30th article of the Constitutive Act.

''Making use of the extraordinary faculties which have been granted to the executive I thus decree: 'Slavery is forever abolished in the Republic!***And, in order that the present decree may have its full and entire execution, I order it printed, published and circulated to all those whose obligation it is to have it fulfilled.'

''Given in the Federal Palace of Mexico, 15th of September, 1829.''

''In 1835 England made another treaty with Spain, the treaty of Madrid, abolishing slave trade henceforth on the part of Spain, totally and finally in all parts of the world, and regulating right of search reciprocally.'' There was still slavery in parts of Mexico and California, which resulted in England succeeding in abolishing it through a treaty signed at Mexico City. In a few years after the signing of this treaty, Texas, which was a part of Mexican territory, seceded and was known as ''The Republic of Texas.''

''In 1845, by a joint resolution of both houses of the United States Congress, a portion of the United States Army under General Taylor was, early in the spring of 1846, moved down to the east bank of the Rio Grande del Norte, claimed by Texas as her western boundary, but not so regarded by Mexico. A hostile collision ensued resulting in war between the United States and Mexico. It was early thereafter deemed advisable that a considerable sum should be placed by Congress at the President's disposal to negotiate an advantageous treaty of peace and limits with the Mexican government. A message to this effect was submitted by President Polk to Congress August 8, 1846, and a bill in accordance with its suggestion laid before the House, which proceeded to consider the subject in committee of the whole. The bill appropriated $30,000 for immediate use in negotiating with Mexico, and placing $20,000 at the disposal of the President to be employed in making peace.

''Mr. David Wilmot, of Pennsylvania, offered the following proviso in addition to the first section of the bill: 'Provided, that an express and fundamental condition to the acquisition of any territory from the Republic of Mexico by the United States, by virtue of any treaty which may be negotiated between them and to the use by the Executive of the money herein appropriated, neither slavery nor involuntary servitude shall exist in any part of the said territory except for the punishment of crime, when the party shall first be duly convicted.' This proviso was carried in committee by a vote of 84 to 63, but was lost in the Senate. A similar resolution was introduced by a Mr. Putnam, of New York, on February 8, 1847, at the session of the 30th United States Congress. The resolution said: 'Whereas, in the settlement of the difficulties pending between this country and Mexico, territory may be acquired in which slavery does not now exist, and whereas, Congress in the organization of a territorial government at an early period of our political history, established a principle worthy of imitating in all future time forbidding the existence of slavery in free territory, therefore; Resolved, that in any territory that may be acquired from Mexico over which shall be established territorial government, slavery nor involuntary servitude, except for the punishment of crime, whereof the party shall have been duly convicted, shall be forever prohibited, and that in any act or resolution establishing such government a fundamental proviso ought to be inserted to that effect.' ''

The reader has but to refer to the above quotation in regard to the different treaties made by England with Spain to fully understand that the territory of California, as it was then known, was free soil for nearly nineteen years before its cession to the United States Government in 1848. It was this knowledge that gave the pioneers, who came to California and were opposed to slavery, the courage to fight to oppose and forever keep California free soil.

The greatest question with the Spaniards and Mexicans was to extend commerce. ''Cortez, when he discovered California, immediately transported three hundred Negro slaves to build ships.'' The following pages will prove that there was slavery in California, although it has been a great surprise to many persons to learn that slavery in any form ever existed in this State. There never were plantations of Negro slaves, but slavery was carried on here up to the early Seventies. The military rulers and a large number of the residents were opposed to slavery and did not fail to give their views to the public through the press and in every available manner open to them in those pioneer days in California. The following extract which has been quoted from one of the very first newspapers issued in California, and also the proclamation issued by the Commander-in-Chief of the port of Yerba Buena (now known as San Francisco) both speak in the strongest terms against the introduction of slavery. And yet immediately following these published statements, the writer will give abundant proof that slavery did exist with all its horrors, by court records of slaves being returned to slavery, and by Freedom Papers issued by the courts, after the Negro slave had paid the price for his freedom. These records will also show that they paid more for their freedom in California than would have been demanded of them elsewhere. The proclamation was as follows:

''A Proclamation to the Inhabitants of California

''It having come to the knowledge of the Commander-in-Chief of the district that certain persons have been and still are imprisoning and holding to service Indians against their will and without any legal contract for service;

''It is therefore ordered that all persons so holding or detaining Indians shall release them and permit them to return to their own homes unless they can make a contract with them which shall be acknowledged before the nearest Justice, which contract shall be binding upon both parties. The Indian population must not be regarded in the light of slaves. But it is deemed necessary that the Indians within the settlement shall have employment with the right of choosing their own master and employment. Having made such choice they must abide by it, unless they can obtain permission in writing to leave, or the Justice in their complaint shall consider they have just cause to annul the contract, and permit them to obtain another employer.

''All Indians must be required to obtain service and not be permitted to wander about the country in idleness in a dissolute manner. If found doing so they will be liable to arrest and punishment by labor on the public works at the direction of the Magistrate. All officers, Civil or Military, under my command are required to execute the terms of this order and take notice of every violation thereof.

''Given at headquarters in Yerba Buena.

''Signed, John Montgomery.

''September 15, 1846.

''Published for the Government for all concerned.

''Washington A. Bartlett,

''Magistrate of San Francisco, California.''

The following appeared in the editorial department of the *California Star* (B. R. Buckley, Editor) under date of March 15, 1848:

''We have recently heard it intimated that an effort would be made in the United States Congress to introduce California into the American Union as a slave-holding territory. We do not believe that such should be the case, and we cannot think that a slave institution will unceremoniously be transferred to our soil by the people who profess to be friends of California. We have not heard one among our acquaintances in this county advocate the measure, and we are almost certain ninety-nine out of a hundred of the present population are opposed to it. We entertain reasons why slavery should not be introduced here.

"First—It is wrong for it to exist anywhere. Second—Not a single instance of precedent exists at present in the shape of physical bondage of our fellow-man. Third—There is no excuse whatsoever for its introduction into this country. But very few sections are unhealthy at any season of the year and none so much but that hardy white population can soon eradicate all causes of climatic diseases. Intermittent fever or fever and ague is the only disease that prevails during any part of the year and only in the San Joaquin Valley and some sections of the Sacramento, and this, with the settling of dense population, proper drainage and cultivation will effectually remove. We have often seen Negroes shake as heartily as the whites and precisely as we did during a six months' siege in the days of our childhood in the vicinity of a stagnant pond in healthy Long Island, in the State of New York; which is proof sufficient for us to decide that neither Negroes, whites, Californians nor Long Islanders require any labor comparison to justify slavery here on account of climate or physical endurance. Fourth—Negroes have equal rights to life, liberty, health, and happiness with the whites, and if slavery is ever introduced here we hope the law, at least the rule, will be established to have the whites and the blacks to serve one another year about. Reciprocity could not be anything but fair. Fifth—It is every individual's duty to self and to society to be occupied in useful employment, sufficient to gain self-support.***Eighth—We left the slave States because we did not like to bring up a family in a miserable 'Can't-help-one's-self condition,' which fate would be inevitable to a family of any kind of self respect surrounded by slavery. In conclusion, we dearly love the Union, but declare our positive preference for the independent condition of California to the establishment of any degree of slavery or even the importation of free blacks."

The reader has been given the proof that slavery was not encouraged in California, and yet when the evidence in this chapter is read it is difficult to understand the situation except as a result of the determination of the Southern slaveholders to extend slavery.

The reliable California historian, the late Theodore Hittell, when questioned as to the reason why he had stated in his history of California that the first slave in California was brought here in 1825, when the wife of Antonio Jose de Cot, a Spaniard, brought with her a slave girl named Juana, aged 14 years, from Lima to San Francisco, he doubted even then that this was the first slave. Mr. Hittell arose from his chair and replied: "Well, there were some gentlemen who brought to California their slaves and allowed them the privilege of working for their freedom and should be commended for it." The writer then read from her manuscript of the Mulatto slave, Ignacio Ramirez, who died on the San Antonio, and whose funeral was the first Christian burial, according to the Holy Catholic Church, in all of California. This slave was buried in the cemetery at San Carlos Mission, and the President, Father Junipero Serra, with a community of twenty-three Friars officiating. If the reader will consult the chapter on the "First Settlers on the Pacific Coast" he will find the names of many Negro slaves. The greatest number of slaves were brought to this coast after the discovery of gold in California.

The following quotation will give a true attitude of the slave when told he could come to California and work for his freedom:

"Behind I left the whips and chains,
Before me was sweet Freedom's plains."

The poor Negro slaves, as they started with their masters to California, thought only of the opportunity to work for their freedom. They were used to hardships. What did it matter if the road be long, full of dangers and obstacles? The one thought that fired their brains was that on the other side of the mountains were "sweet Freedom's plains."

PERSONAL SKETCHES OF SLAVES

"Mr. George Washington Dennis arrived in San Francisco, California, September 17, 1849. He came with the gamblers who opened the Eldorado Hotel, which was a tent 30x100 feet, brought from New Orleans. They ran a Faro Bank and a Monte Game. Ten tables were going night and day. The tables were played during the day by men and at night by women. The hotel was located at the corner of Washington and Kearney streets, the present Hall of Justice now occupies this place. Mr. Dennis was brought here as a slave by Green Dennis, a slave trader from Mobile, Alabama. Joe and Jim Johnson, coming from Ohio, were in the party of gamblers and another man by the name of Andy McCabe.

"Previous to coming to California, unable to obtain accommodation from New Orleans to Colon, they were compelled to row up the Chagress river to Panama. While en route these gamblers won and lost Mr. Dennis three different times. It cost them $350 fare for him from Panama to San Francisco, because he was a Negro slave. It was after arriving and establishing the Eldorado Hotel that Green Dennis made the proposition to George Dennis that if he saved his money, he could buy his freedom.

"The gamblers employed Dennis as a porter in the Eldorado Hotel, and at the end of three months, from the sweepings of the floor he had saved, in five and ten-cent pieces $1,000, which he paid for Freedom Papers for himself from Green Dennis, who was his own father and also his master.

"He again saved the sweepings and when Joe Johnson, from Ohio, who was one of the party owning the Eldorado Hotel, told him that he was going back east to bring out some graded cattle and would bring Mr. Dennis's mother with him to his former master, Mr. Dennis paid $950 for his mother, and she returned with Mr. Joe Johnson to California. She lived many years afterward and died in San Francisco at the age of 105 years. After Mr. Dennis's mother arrived in San Francisco he rented one of the gambling tables at $40 a day with the privilege of his mother serving hot meals in the gambling house on it. Boiled eggs sold for $12 per dozen, apples 25 cents apiece, and a loaf of bread $1. But she also paid $25 for a sack of flour containing one hundred pounds. These prices were during the early Fifties."

The case of Alvin Coffey was very unjust and has been commented on by Historian Bancroft. It has been the custom of the writer, if possible, to secure original information pertaining to every case mentioned, and this account of the subject was given by a Mr. Titus Hale, a lifelong friend of Alvin Coffey, who came from the same part of the country. He said: "Alvin Coffey was born in 1822, in St. Louis County, Missouri. He came to California with his master, a Mr. Duvall, landing in San Francisco September 1, 1849. His master was sick and they did not remain long in this place, but went to Sacramento, October 13, 1849. During the next eight months Alvin worked in the mines and made for his master the sum of $5,000, and by washing and ironing for the miners after his workday ended, earned for himself the neat sum of $700.

"After staying nearly two years in California the master, continuing in poor health, decided to return to his home in Missouri. Alvin had nursed him tenderly and now was to care for him on the return trip. When they reached Kansas City, Missouri, the master sold Alvin Coffey to Nelson Tindle, after first taking from him the money earned for the master by working in the mines and also the money earned by working at night in washing for the miners.

"Nelson Tindle took a great liking to Alvin and in a short time made him overseer of a section of slaves. Alvin, however, longed to return to California and, in order to earn his freedom, bought his time from his master and took contracts to build railroads.

"One day Nelson Tindle said to Alvin that he was too smart a man to be a slave and ought to try and buy his freedom; whereupon Alvin told him if he would let him return to California he could easily earn enough money to purchase his freedom. Nelson Tindle replied: 'But when you reach California you will be free and then I will lose the money that I paid to purchase you.' Alvin replied: 'If I tell you that I will send you the money, I will do so. What do you wish for me?' He was told $1,500. Alvin made the return trip to California and in a short time sent his master the money to pay for his freedom.

"He then went to work to earn the money to pay for the freedom of his wife and daughters, who were slaves of Dr. Bassett, of Missouri. He earned the required sum and then went back in person to pay it over and, after securing the freedom of his family, started with them to Canada, where he left his daughters to be educated, he and his wife coming to California. It cost him for the freedom of himself and wife, Mahala, and his two daughters, together with their education and trips to California, something like $7000. He earned this money through placer mining in California in and around Redding and Red Bluff.

"After the arrival of his wife Coffey located in Red Bluff and opened a laundry. He also made a small fortune making hay at $16 per day, and in a few years was worth $10,000. Then a friend of Alvin's, a white minister, who owned a farm in the Sacramento Valley, borrowed a few thousand dollars from Alvin until his crops were harvested. But floods destroyed his crops and Alvin, not holding a note against him, of course lost his money.

"About this time his wife died and, as his daughters were married and he still had a few hundred dollars left, he became the prime mover in organizing the 'Home for

Aged and Infirm Colored People,' located near Beulah, California, where he spent the remaining days of his life.''

Daniel Rodgers came to California across the plains with his master in 1849, coming from Little Rock, Arkansas. He worked in the mines in Sonora, California, during the day for his master and at night for himself, earning and paying for his freedom by giving to his master the sum of $1,100. Soon afterward the master returned with him to Little Rock and sold him. This time a number of the leading white gentlemen of the town raised the money and paid for him and gave him his Freedom Papers. Copies of both his Freedom Papers and an extract of his wife's will be found with the collection of other Freedom Papers.

Cooper Smith told the writer that he worked in the mines two years after coming to California to pay for his freedom.

Sowarie Long worked in the mines of California, earning the money to pay for the freedom of himself and wife. They had come to California in 1849 with their master. After securing their freedom, they located in San Jose, California.

Henry Valle, coming with his master from Fredericktown, Mississippi, to California, worked in the mines, paying $2500 for himself and $2200 for his wife. This was paid three years before the Civil War. He afterward earned enough money to enable him and his wife to return to Ironton County, Missouri, and ever afterward live comfortably on the money thus earned in the mines of California.

William Pollock and wife, coming to California with their master from North Carolina, located in Cold Springs, Coloma County, California, paid $1000 for himself and $800 for his wife. This money was earned by his washing for the miners at night, and his wife making and selling doughnuts to the miners. After obtaining their Freedom Papers they moved to Placerville and earned their living by acting as cooks in taking party and wedding work from those able to secure their services.

Jacob Johnson came to California with his master from St. Louis County Missouri. He worked in the mines and paid for his freedom, afterward sending a large sum back to pay for the freedom of his family, but never received any word from either his money or family.

Mary Ann Israel-Ash, of Sonoma County, California, mortgaged her home in 1852 and then begged to enable her to raise the sum of $1100, and paid the same to the master of a family of slaves who were being returned to the South and into slavery.

Basil Campbell worked ten years to pay for his freedom after coming to California with his master. After obtaining his freedom he located in Woodland, California, where he engaged in ranching. When he died he left property valued at $80,000.

Ellen Mason, coming to California with her master in 1849, under contract to pay for herself at fifty cents a week, not only paid for her own freedom but that of her sister. After securing her Freedom Papers, she then worked to secure herself some good clothes and celebrated the event, so they say, by an outfit costing a hundred dollars. Afterward she sent for her brother Benjamin, and was paying for his freedom in California when he, learning that the State was a Free State, ran away from the master, who did not compel Ellen to finish paying the bill of sale. Mrs. Mason afterward lived many years and died in the ''Home for Aged Colored People'' in Beulah, California.

Nathaniel Nelson came to California with his master, William Russell, from Cook County, Tennessee. He worked in the mines and in four years paid for the freedom of himself and his family of several children and his wife. Afterward he earned enough to bring them to live in California in 1854, and located in Marysville. He died leaving his family well provided for.

Mrs. Langhorn and family, who were slaves, came with their master, a Doctor Langhorn. She earned the price of her own freedom and that of her husband, daughter and three grandchildren by working at night. After obtaining their freedom they located in San Jose, California.

Joseph Bathelome, coming to California with his master, hired his time and worked in the mines and procured enough gold to buy his freedom and that of his wife and four children. He continued to work and save his money until 1861, when he returned to Missouri and moved his family to Sparta, Illinois, where he bought a home and forever afterward lived happily. The following are the names of his children: Christian, Joe, Henry and Frank.

The history of the Samuel Shelton case was given to the writer by one of the members of his family. She said: ''Samuel Shelton came to San Francisco in 1840, which was before the Indians had been driven out of the country. He was his master's offspring by his little African girl, whom he had stolen from Africa. He came to California with his master and the first thing he did, after the purchase of his own freedom, was to earn the money to purchase the freedom of his wife and that of his son Frank. He earned the money in the mines in California. After securing their freedom he worked to pay for the freedom of other members of the family, namely, Moulton Shelton, Moses Brown and Lucy Shelton. The Irish kidnaped Moulton Shelton in New York and when Lucy Shelton arrived in San Francisco and related the news to Samuel Shelton he held a lawsuit between San Francisco and Washington City, for the sale had been recorded in Washington City. This suit lasted months, but finally Moulton Shelton was given his freedom and landed safely in San Francisco, California. Samuel Shelton spent thousands of dollars in purchasing the freedom of himself and immediate family and their families and bringing them to live in California.''

AUCTION OF SLAVES IN CALIFORNIA

In the remarkable book by Mr. George Tinkham, ''Men and Events,'' he says, in regard to slavery in California: ''In 1849 a slave owner brought his slave to California. Then, not wishing to take the Negro back to his native State, Alabama, he concluded to sell him by auction. An advertisement was put in the papers. The boy was purchased at $1000 by Caleb T. Fay, a strong Abolitionist, who gave the boy his freedom.

''A Mississippi slave owner brought several slaves from that State. He promised to give them their freedom in two years. They all ran away save one, Charles Bates, when they learned that they were already free. The owner finding that mining did not pay started east, taking Charles with him. On the Isthmus of Panama Charles was persuaded to leave his master. He returned to Stockton, California, with his new-found friend. On the street one day he was recognized by a party who had loaned money to Charles' master. The debtor got out an attachment for the former slave as chattel property, and in accordance with the State law, the Negro was put up and sold by auction. A number of anti-slavery men bought the boy for $750. He was given his freedom.''

The following has been copied from the same book (p. 157): ''Under the provision of the law in May, 1852, Justice of the Peace of Sacramento returned a Negro to a Mr. Lathrop. He claimed that he brought the Negro to California in 1849. The boy ran away later in 1851 and his owner, learning of his residence, had him arrested in June, 1852. Three more runaway slaves were arrested. This case was taken to the Supreme Court on the ground that the law was unconstitutional. The Supreme Court at this time was comprised of Hugh C. Murry, Chief Justice, and Solomon Hydenfelt and Alexander Anderson, Associates. They gave their decision July 30, 1852, that the law was constitutional and the slaves were given to their owners immediately without cost. They were returned to the South and slavery.''

''Another case more cruel was that of a Mulatto woman as reported September, 1852, in the *San Francisco Herald*: 'Yesterday Justice Shephard issued a warrant for the arrest of a Mulatto woman as a fugitive slave claimed by I. J. Smith, of Missouri. She was brought by him to California in 1850 with other slaves and a few months ago married a free Negro man and ran away from Smith. Her owner learned that she was secreted on the Clipper Ship ''Flying Cloud.'' She was arrested, given into his possession and taken back into slavery.' ''

''The following advertisement appeared September 12, 1852, in the *San Joaquin Republican*: 'Escaped, a fugitive slave. Mr. O. R. Rozier called upon us yesterday and stated that his slave, Stephen, whom he brought with him from Sonora and was taking back to Alabama, made his escape from the steamer ''Urilda'' while in San Francisco. Mr. Rozier is still in the city at the St. Charles Hotel, where he will be pleased to receive any information of his fugitive slave.' ''

On page 158 of Mr. Tinkham's book the following appears: ''The Negro was not the only person subject to slavery, for the same Legislature, that of 1852, passed a law permitting the slavery of the Indian man, woman or child and compelled them to labor, the only condition upon the party being a bond of a small sum given to the Justice of the Peace of the county where he resided, that he will not abuse or cruelly treat the Indian. Under the provision of the same law, Indians could be arrested as vagrants and sold to the highest bidder within twenty-four hours after arrest, and the buyer had the privilege of their labor for a period not exceeding four months. An Indian arrested for a violation of the law could demand a jury trial, yet could not testify, either in his own behalf or against a white person. If found guilty of any crime, he could either be imprisoned or whipped, the whipping not to exceed twenty-five lashes. A. G. Stakes was the Judge of San Joaquin County, California.''

All the above has been quoted from the same book, which is the only work giving an account of the enslaving of the Indian. Slaves being returned to slavery is also made note of in the California Reports, No. 2, page 424-5-6, which says: "The owners of slaves in Mississippi brought them voluntarily into California before the adoption of the Constitution by the State. The slaves asserted their freedom and for some months were engaged in business for themselves. Afterward the Act of April 15, 1852, was passed by the Legislature, the fourth Section of which in substance enacts that slaves who had been voluntarily introduced into the State before the adoption of the Constitution and who refused upon demand of their owners to return to the State where they owed labor, should be deemed to be fugitives from labor, and gave the owner the same remedies for their reclamation as are provided for the recovery of such fugitives. The owners, under the provision of the above act, brought them before the Justice of the Peace, who allowed the claim of the owners and ordered them into his custody. The slaves then petitioned for a writ of habeas corpus, which came before the Supreme Court and, after hearing the case, the Court ordered that the writ be dismissed and the slaves remanded to their owners."

California Report, No. 2, Carter Perkins and Robert Perkins, (p. 426): "This case was brought before Judge Wells of the Supreme Court by the petition and affidavit of the prisoners, Robert and Carter Perkins and Sandy Jones, July 1, 1852, which set forth that about the first of June, 1852, they had been seized without process of law and taken before B. D. Fry, a Justice of the Pease, of Sacramento, upon a pretended claim of one C. S. Perkins, of the State of Mississippi, for a certificate to remove them from the State of California to Mississippi, under act of California, respecting fugitives from labor and slaves brought into the State prior to her admission into the Union, passed April 15, 1852. It is further stated that Fry granted the certificate and they were advised that the said act was wholly unconstitutional and void and that the Justice had no jurisdiction.*** Each for himself said that he was not a fugitive from labor and owed no service to the said Perkins, but that they had been brought by the said Perkins into this State prior to its admission into the Union and that they had resided here ever since, and that for several months prior to their arrest they had been engaged in business for themselves. They stated further that they were held in confinement under the said certificate upon the claim of the said Perkins and under the said act of the Legislature, and prayed for a writ of certiorari to the Justice to certify the proceedings to the Supreme Court.***

"The petition of Moses Jackson in behalf of the prisoners was also presented and a writ of habeas corpus ordered returnable before the Supreme Court at the July term, 1852, at the opening of the court. The Sheriff made return and produced the prisoners in court and Harden Scoles answered to the writ and said that he had held the prisoners as agent of C. S. Perkins by virtue of the certificate of Justice Fry, issued under 4th Section of the act entitled 'An Act respecting fugitives from labor and slaves brought into the State previous to her admission into the United States,' they having been held to service in the State of Mississippi, by the laws thereof, by C. S. Perkins. The answer also states that the said Robert and Sandy had been taken before Judge Aldrich of the Sixth Judicial District, by habeas corpus, who remanded them to the possession of the respondent June 11, 1852, and Scoles showed his authority as agent of the said C. S. Perkins, also the proceedings before the Justice and the District Judge, Morris and Brown for the petitioners***Murry, Chief Justice, and Anderson, Justice, severally delivered opinions."

California Reports, No. 2, p. 424: "By the act of April 20, 1852, the power of hearing and determining writ of habeas corpus is vested in the Judge of every court of record in the State. The final determination is not that of a court, but the simple order of a Judge, and is not appealable from or subject to review. The State, in the exercise of her police power, may expel from her limits slaves brought here voluntarily by their owners before the State was admitted into the Union. The act of the 15th of April, 1852, is not an ex-post facto law. It impairs no right, nor does it constitute the refusal to return to service a crime. It simply provides for the departure of slaves brought here before a certain period. Nor does it impair the obligation of contracts. The State has entered into no contract with free Negroes fugitives or slaves by providing by her Constitution that slavery, or involuntary service, shall not exist within her limits, which would prevent her, on proper occasion, from removing them. Nor does the act impair the constitutional rights of trial by jury. The rights of slaves are not determined by the arrest and commitment, nor by the examination on writ of habeas corpus. The right of trial by jury is secured in all cases involving questions of liberty, property or punishment."

There were many similar cases brought before the highest court in the State, but the one which the writer will now quote is quite unique in that it was a case brought concerning a slave and property rights after the Civil War, when the emancipation had already gone into effect. It is quoted from California Report, No. 51, page 120: "Statement of facts (No. 4500): Adelaide Pearson vs. Laura Pearson; Manumission of a slave.—

Marriage of master with his female slave amounts to a relinquishment of rights to hold her as a slave and manumits her. The Court below gave judgment for the plaintiff for an undivided one-seventh of two-thirds of the demanded premises. There were seven children. The plaintiff and six others were born to the testor and defendant Laura and under our statute of descents and distribution, the wife by whom there is more than one child, inherits one-third and the children two-thirds. The action was brought to recover all the land of which the testor did seize.

"W. F. Good; P. Van Claff and Beaty & Denison for the appellant.

"Currans Evans & John T. Harrington for the respondent."

The decision of the Court was: "The action is ejectment and was brought by the appellant, Adelaide Pearson, as heir-at-law of Richard Pearson (deceased) to recover of the defendants certain premises situated in the County of Colusa.

"The appellant was born in the year 1850 and is a daughter of said Richard Pearson, a white man (lately deceased) by Martha Powers, a white woman with whom he inter-married in the year 1848, in the State of Iowa, and from whom he was divorced in the year 1854, by a valid judicial decree rendered in the courts of the State of Missouri.

"The defendant, Laura Pearson, is a woman of African descent and claims a distributive share in the estate of the said Richard Pearson, as his surviving wife. The other defendants are the children of Richard Pearson by said Laura and were born after the alleged inter-marriage between said Richard and Laura, presently to be mentioned, and during the subsequent cohabitation between said Richard and said Laura in the assumed relation of husband and wife. It appears that in the year 1847 the defendant Laura, being at the time a slave in the State of North Carolina, was purchased by the said Richard Pearson, who immediately moved her to the State of Missouri, where he held her as a slave until the year 1854, during which year and after the entry of the decree in the courts of that State divorcing him from Martha Powers. He moved her to the Territory of Utah, reaching the Territory in September of that year, where he remained engaged in business pursuits until the year 1855, when he moved to this State and settled in the county of Colusa, in which county he continued to reside until his death in the year 1865.

"The Court below found the facts to be that in the fall of said year, 1854, and while residing in the Territory of Utah, the said Richard and Laura inter-married and' thence, until the death of said Richard, they lived and cohabited together as husband and wife and that during such cohabitation there were born to them the defendants, Theodora, Harry, Mary, William, Richard and Jefferson, the oldest of these children being born in the year 1856 and the youngest shortly before the death of the said Richard. Judgment was thereupon rendered to the effect that upon the death of said Richard, his estate descended to and became vested in the plaintiff and defendant in all respects as though the defendant Laura had been a white woman, and the lawful, surviving wife of the said Richard, and from this judgment, an order having been subsequently entered denying the motion of plaintiff for a new trial, she prosecutes this appeal.

"At the new trial the defendant, Laura Pearson, examined as a witness for the defendants, having testified that she had been at one time the slave of Richard Pearson, in the State of Missouri, but that she had subsequently been emancipated by him by certain judicial proceedings had for that purpose, of which a record was duly made in a court in the city of St. Louis. The plaintiff duly objected to oral proof of Laura's alleged emancipation, but the objection was overruled and an exception was reserved. The views we entertain upon other points involved render it unnecessary to notice this exception further. It is argued for the appellant that the alleged marriage between said Richard and said defendant Laura, even if solemnized in due form, was void because she was at the time a slave and therefore incapable of contracting marriage. But we see no force in this position. Conceding that she had been a slave in the State of Missouri, in 1854, she was such only by force of the local law at the time prevailing in that State, and, conceding that her removal by her master to the Territory of Utah did not of itself change her status in that respect, and that Pearson might hereafter lawfully hold her in slavery in that Territory, it certainly cannot be denied that he might, if he chose, manumit her there by any act evidencing a purpose on his part to do so. His general authority, as master, to manumit his slave was not taken away nor limited in its exercise by the local law of Utah, and we think that his inter-marriage with her in that Territory amounts to a relinquishment of his claim to further hold her as his slave. At common law, if a man bound himself in a bond to his villein granting him an annuity, or gave him an estate even for years it was held to be an implied manumission for his dealing with his villein, on the footing of a free man. There being no law or regulation at the time prevailing in

HON. JAMES M. ALEXANDER
Six years Internal Revenue Cashier for the Sixth District of California.

MISS VIRGINIA STEPHENS
Sponsor for the name Jewel City for the Panama Pacific
International Exposition.

the Territory of Utah inter-dicting inter-marriage lawfully had there between a master and his female slave, neither party being otherwise incapacitated to contract marriage, operated by analogy to the rule of the Common Law already adverted to and resulted in the manumission of the slave woman, since such manumission was indispensable to her assuming of her new relation of wife to her former master. She certainly could not in contemplation of the law be both the slave and the wife of Pearson. The marriage of these parties, being valid by the law of the place where it was contracted, is also valid in this State.

"The Statute of this State provides in terms that all marriages contracted without the State, which would be valid by the laws of the country in which the same were contracted, shall be valid in all courts and places within the State. Marriage between master and slave—If one, holding a female slave of African descent in Missouri, removes with her to the Territory of Utah and there marries her, the marriage was legal, there being no law in Utah prohibiting such marriages.

"Validity of marriages—A marriage contracted with-out this State which is valid by the law of the place where contracted, is valid in this State, if the parties subsequently remove here, even though the marriage would have been invalid by the laws of this State if contracted here.

"Appeal from the District Court, Tenth Judicial District, County of Colusa; October, 1875.

"Adelaide Pearson, the plaintiff, was the legal child of Richard Pearson and his former wife from whom he was divorced, and was born in Missouri on the tenth day of October, 1850. The defendant, Laura, claimed to have been the legal wife of Richard Pearson. But the plaintiff denied that she became such.

"Richard Pearson made a will, just before his death, in which he bequeathed all his property to Laura and her children. No provision was made for, and no allusion was made to his daughter, Adelaide, the plaintiff. Under our statutes of wills the daughter, Adelaide, having been permitted in the will, was entitled to the same share of the estate she would have received if her father had died intestate. If Laura was the wife of Richard, then Adelaide was only entitled to share the estate with Laura and her children. But if Laura was not the wife of Richard, then Adelaide was entitled to the whole. This case was once before this court (California Report, No. 46, p. 609) and everything in regard to the rights of the parties had been fully settled and determined, except the question as to whether Laura was or was not the wife of Richard. The Court below held, on the second trial, that Laura Pearson was the lawful wife of Richard, and this appeal was taken by the plaintiff to test the correctness of the decision in that regard. The only question raised was in relation to that point.

"The statute accords with the general principle of law theretofore prevailing. 'The validity of a marriage (except it be polygamous or incestous) is to be tested by the law of the place where it is celebrated. If valid there, it is valid everywhere' (Story, on Conflict of laws, Section 113). We discover in the records no error committed against the appellant. Judgment and order denying a new trial affirmed.''

The following is an extract from the arguments offered by the counsel first for the appellant, in which W. F. Good, P. VanClif and Beatty Denson are quoted as saying: "A slave is incapable of contracting marriage, and if Laura remained a slave up to the time she reached California, in 1855, certainly she could not have been married to Richard Pearson in the Territory of Utah, in the year 1854 (Bishop on marriage and Divorce, vol. I, Sec. 154-56; Jones, North Carolina 235-6). If Laura was a slave in Missouri, she remained a slave whilst passing through the Territory of Utah.''

The following is an extract from the argument offered for the defendant by Curry & Evans and Jno. T. Harrington, for the respondent: "Laura's emancipation prior to the marriage is to be inferred from Pearson's acts and conduct. If it could be held that Laura was a slave in Utah, notwithstanding Pearson's failure to make and file the proof required by the statute, then we maintain that she ceased entirely to be a slave upon her marriage with Pearson. In New York it has been held that when a man bought a woman and her child for the purpose of marrying the mother and with the intention that they should be free, that his declaration on the subject and the fact that he married the woman, were sufficient evidence of emancipation of mother and child. Emancipation will be inferred wherever the master's conduct toward the slave is inconsistent with the continuance of the condition of slavery. (Wells v. Lau, 9, Johns 144; La. Grand, v. Darnell, 2, Peters, 664.)''

FIRST CALIFORNIA LEGISLATURE—FREE NEGROES—COURT TRIAL OF THE SLAVE ARCHY LEE.
The first session of the California Legislature met December 28, 1849, and lasted until March 22, 1850. The first State Governor, Peter Burnet, was duly inaugurated, and in his

first message to the Assembly, he recommended the exclusion of ''Free Negroes.'' A bill was introduced in the Senate, but was indefinitely postponed.

This bill was in keeping with the Fugitive Slave Law, and claimed that Negroes brought into the State previous to its admission into the Union were fugitives (See Journal of the California Legislature, page 1232, 1850). Previous to the admission of the State into the Union, there were many Negroes brought to California. Some, coming with their masters, by working in the mines paid for their freedom. There were other colored people who had come on trading ships and, aside from earning the money to pay for their freedom, had purchased good homes. There were still others, who had come who were already free, and who, after reaching California, had gone into business. This was especially true in and around San Francisco, Sacramento and Stockton.

The colored people realized the joy of living in California and were preparing themselves to become useful citizens when they were startled by the sudden passage of a bill by the California Assembly known as House Bill No. 395, which was introduced by a Mr. Stakes, a Democrat, from San Joaquin County, during the session of 1858. The object of this bill was to prevent Negroes from immigrating to or residing in California. The wording of the bill was very harsh and sent terror to the hearts of the colored people living throughout the State.

In the meantime gold was discovered on the Frazier river, British Columbia, and Governor James Douglass, of British Columbia, sent his harbor-master, James Nagel, to San Francisco, California, to invite the colored people to come to Canada to make their home and work the Frazier river gold discovery. This resulted in a large number of the best families of colored people going to British Columbia. Among the number were the following: Mifflin Gibbs, George Dennis, Stone Wall Jackson, Ezekil Cooper, John Upsheer and a Mr. Carter, together with many others. One ship with a passenger list running into the hundreds was lost in a storm en route.

The bill that was the means of frightening so many colored people away from the State was not so easily passed. But year after year there had been similar bills introduced, until they finally became panic-stricken and left the State in large numbers. Many, however, returned to the beautiful State of California. This bill introduced at the first session of the California Legislature in 1858 and known as House Bill No. 395, read as follows: ''An Act to restrict and prevent the immigration to and residence in this State of Free Negroes and Mulattoes.'' The bill was amended, or an additional section was added as follows: ''Nothing in the act provided shall prevent the immigration to this State of any member of the family of any Negro or Mulatto who may be a resident of this State at the date of the passage of this act, nor of the arrival in this State of any who may be the owners of any real or personal estate at the date of the passage of the act, nor of any person who may be a resident of this State and temporarily absent therefrom at the date of the passage of this act.'' The bill passed, ayes 21, noes 8. The bill was repealed in 1859. There had been similar bills passed in regard to free Negroes leaving the State, from the first session of the first Legislature. The time for them to leave the State would be extended every year.

The climax was reached when a Mr. Stovall came to California in 1857 from Mississippi, bringing his slave boy, Archy Lee. Mr. Stovall opened a private school in Sacramento and, after teaching for a year, decided to return to Mississippi and take the slave boy, Archy Lee, with him again to slavery. His effort to carry out his intention of returning to Mississippi with his slave boy was the means of furnishing the courts with a case that became one of the most famous in regard to the Negro in California. The decision of the case has been recorded in the Constitutional United States slave laws. It is highly interesting to the present day Negro in California, because its success was due mainly to the united action of all the Negroes then living in California. They were guided in their actions by the Executive Committee of the Colored Convention, who saw to the raising of the necessary funds. They fully recognized that the right to live in California of every Negro would be affected by the decision of this case.

The following is quoted from Hittell's History of California in regard to this celebrated case (vol. 4, p. 244): ''The Archy case: One Charles Stovall, a citizen of Mississippi, had, in 1857, come to California overland from that State and brought along his slave, a Negro boy called Archy. After hiring Archy out for some time at Sacramento, Mr. Stovall thought of returning to Mississippi and, as a preliminary put the slave on a Sacramento river steamboat with the intention of sending him to San Francisco and thence to Mississippi in charge of an agent. But the boy, who had attracted a great deal of attention as a slave brought voluntarily into the State, refused to be taken back and escaped from the vessel. Stovall, therefore, for such escape had him arrested as a fugitive slave and he was taken into custody by the Sacramento Chief of Police, who, however, refused to deliver him over to his master. Stovall immediately had issued a writ of habeas corpus for his possession and the matter came up for adjustment before the Supreme Court. The decision and opinion of that tribunal was rendered by Peter Burnett, formerly Governor, who had been appointed a Justice of that Court by Governor Nealy Johnson in 1857, and filled the office until October, 1858.''

The following is from the proceedings of the California Supreme Court, January term, 1858, p. 147: ''Supreme Court and the Archy case, Habeas Corpus: Charles A. Stovall, a citizen of Mississippi, petitioned this court for a writ of habeas corpus for the recovery of his slave, Archy. The writ was issued and, on the return thereof, the following argument of counsel was made. The facts appear in the opinion of the Court. James Hardy, counsel for the petitioner, Stovall.

''There is no question from the return of the writ and evidence in the case that the boy, Archy, was a slave owned and held to service by the petitioner in the State of Mississippi, nor is there any pretense of any voluntary or actual emancipation of the slave by his master. Counsel for the slave, however, have argued that he was voluntarily brought to this State by his master and he is thereby manumitted. In reply I contend that there is no proof in the case that Archy was brought voluntarily into the State by his master. This whole evidence shows that he owed service in Mississippi; that about the first of January last he was in this State with his master, and that when about to leave the State, he escaped from him. In support of the petitioner's right to remove the slave, I contend: That the eighteenth section of the first article of the Constitution of this State is inoperative and requires legislative aid in the shape of penalties and manner of proceedings to give it effect; that for the purpose of transit or journey in or through the State, he has full and complete guarantee of the courts of the United States that even if the eighteenth section of the first article of the Constitution be operative upon our citizens it has no effect as against travelers or sojourners by reason of the constitutional provisions both of this State and of the United States, and that no emancipation of the slave can be had or preserved without due process of law. This is the very doctrine Judge Murry declared in the matter of Carter (California Rep. No. 2, p. 44). Now in determining how far under our seemingly absolute and uncompromising Constitution restraint of the principle of comity should (within the constitutional restraint) be allowed, the Legislature passed the Act of April 15th, 1852, entitled an 'Act respecting fugitives from labor and slaves brought into this State prior to her admission into the Union in which they provided for the reclamation of fugitives escaping into the State.' ''

The counsel for Archy was equal to the occasion and he was ably defended by Mr. E. Winans. His argument: ''Conceding that Stovall left Mississippi with the intention of returning in eighteen months, that would have allowed him a year's residence or sojourn in this State. If he desired to be a sojourner during that time and to carry on business and let out his slave during that time for hire, he would be acting in violation of the spirit and meaning of the constitutional prohibition of slavery. But after his arrival here he appears to have entertained nothing but a remote, undeveloped intention of leaving the State at some future, unascertained, undeveloped time. If we judge from his acts, he appears to have invested himself with all the rights, attributes, and characteristics of a continuing citizenship. He made his advertisement for scholars and announced his school as permanent, not transitory. The business is one which for its success looks for permanency. He also hired out Archy from time to time and told the parties hiring him that they could keep him as long as they chose, saying nothing about intending to leave the State. This question is not to be settled in his favor by simply proving that he retained the *animus reverteudi*. If that alone was the criterion, he might preserve the *animus* for years, continuing here and enjoying all the rights, immunities and advantages of citizenship the while. The doctrine criterion is this (if the doctrine of comity be sustained), was he simply engaged in actual passage or transit through the State and were the circumstances which detained him of such an unavoidable character that they still preserved him in a condition of actual transit? The case of Julia V. McKinney, 3 Miss. 270, is a leading authority on the subject: Wilson v. Melvin, 4 Missouri, 597. The doctrine of Lord Stovall is favorably cited.

''The court says: 'The principle above stated, in which a slave brought here becomes free in that he is entitled to the protection of our laws, and there is no law to warrant his arrest and forcible removal, and also for the immediate transportation from the State of slaves brought here before the adoption of the Constitution and the entire concession and provision of the Act, and in section five it is provided that even in the case of a slave brought here before the Constitution, if his master seeks to reclaim or hold him in servitude in the State except for the purpose of his immediate removal.' This Act was to continue in force for only twelve months and was renewed for another twelve months by the Act of 1853. After and since which time even these priveleges were and have been denied to citizens of this State. By this Act the Legislature established their conclusions of the sovereign will that recognized the constitutional prohibition of voluntary servitude.

"They did not consider such prohibition as preventing them from allowing by comity the reclamation of slaves brought here before the adoption of the constitution and were willing therefore to carry the diction of comity so far and of course, by necessary implication, no farther, and even this concession was but temporary and designed to be withdrawn after a brief period by the express provision of the Act. In upholding the institutions of other governments, we cannot carry the doctrine of courtesy so far as to subvert our own, and whatever violates the spirit of our laws, the policies of our government, and the rights of our citizens has a tendency to subvert our institutions. The Dred Scott case, of which so much has been said, does not conflict with the principle here contended, for it only declares that, slaves being property, the master has a right to hold them in servitude in any portion of the Federal territory, but it does not attempt to conclude or pass upon the right of sovereign States in this behalf, and if it had so done, it would have laid the cherished doctrine of State Sovereignty—a doctrine no less dear to all sister States than slavery can be to these who own it as their institution—completely prostrated in the dust. (See the opinion of Judge Burnet in Nougees v. Johnson, 7 California; R. Somerset, 20; Howell's State Trial 79; Story in Conflict of Laws, 96-244, edition 1846, p. 371-2).

"But this court has heretofore passed upon this question in the matter of Perkins 2 California, 441, and it is then held that while the slave, by being taken upon free soil does not become *ipse facto* free—yet that the master's control over him ceases and he becomes thereby virtually free. Now if this court recognizes the doctrine of the Star decision, for this is not a mere diction, then the application of the claimant must be denied. (See also Landsford v. Conquillion, 24, Martin's Rep. 413, and Expartra Simmon, 4 Washington, C. C. Report, 396, and see Butler v. Hoffer, 1 Washington.)"

Judge Burnet, after listening to the arguments, decided the case as follows, which has been quoted from the California Reports No. 9, Expartra Archy: "In the matter of Archy on habeas corpus. The right of transit through each State with every specie of property known to the Constitution of the United States, and recognized by that paramount law, is secured by that instrument to each citizen and does not depend upon the uncertain and changeable ground of mere comity. The character of immigrant or traveler, bringing with him a slave into the State, must last so long as it is necessary by the ordinary modes of travel to accomplish a transit through the State. Nothing but accident or imperative necessity could excuse a greater delay. Something more than mere ease or convenience must intervene to save a forfeiture of property which he cannot hold as a citizen of the State through which he is passing. But visitors for health or pleasure stand in a different position from travelers for business, and are protected by the law of comity. It is right for the Judiciary, in the absence of legislation, to determine how far the policy and position of this State will justify the giving a temporary effect within the limits of this State, to the laws and institutions of a sister State. To allow mere visitors to this State for pleasure or health, to bring with them, as personal attendants, their own domestics, is not any violation of the end contemplated by the constitution of the State. The visible acts of a party must be taken as the only test of his intentions in deciding whether he is entitled to be considered a mere visitor, of which fact his declaration constitutes no evidence. The privileges are extended to those who come for both business and pleasure or health, and who engage in no business while here, and remain only for a reasonable time. If the party engages in any business or employs his slave in any business except as a personal attendant upon himself or family, then the character of the visitor is lost, and his slave is entitled to freedom. This rule admits of no exception upon the ground of necessity or misfortune, or it would introduce uncertainty and complexities and lead the courts into profitless investigations. The peculiar condition of the party is difficult of proof, and will not be inquired into nor will the rule be relaxed to meet the hardships of a particular case."

"BURNETT."

The concluding remarks of the learned Trial Judge were as follows: "From the views we have expressed it would seem clear that the petitioner cannot sustain either the character of traveller, or visitor, but there are circumstances connected with this particular case that may exempt him from the operation of the rule we have laid down. This is the first case that has occurred under the existing law, and from the opinion of Justice Anderson and the silence of the Chief Justice, the petitioner had some reason to believe that the constitutional provision would have no immediate operation. This is the first case, and under the circumstances we are not disposed to rigidly enforce the rule for the first time. But in reference to all future cases it is our purpose to enforce the rules laid down strictly according to their true intent and spirit. It is therefore ordered that Archy be forthwith released from the custody of the chief of police and given into the custody of the petitioner, Charles Stovall.''

TERRY, C. J., *Chief Justice:* ''I concur in the judgment and in the principles announced in the opinion of my associate, while I do not entirely agree with his conclusions from the facts of the case. I think the delay of the petitioner was unavoidable and that the facts of his engaging in labor in order to support himself during his necessary detention did not divert his rights under the laws of comity as laid down in the opinion.''

In Hittell's History of California, he says in regard to the decision: ''James G. Baldwin, author and wit who succeeded Burnett upon the Supreme bench, characterized the decision as 'Giving the law to the North, and the nigger to the South.' It may be added that Archy, after being delivered over to Stovall, was taken to San Francisco for the purpose of being sent back to Mississippi, but his friends sued out a new writ of habeas corpus, this time for his liberation instead of for his redelivery into slavery. He was taken before Judge Thomas W. Freelon of the County Court, of San Francisco. But while the case was pending before him, Stovall saw fit to swear to a new affidavit which did not correspond very well with the one he had sworn to in Sacramento. In the latter he made oath that Archy had escaped from him in the State of Mississippi, and procured a warrant from George Pen Johnson, United States Commissioner, for his arrest as a fugitive slave from Mississippi. Upon this state of facts and at the request of Stovall's attorneys, James H. Hardy and George F. James, Archy was discharged by Freelon. But he was immediately re-arrested and taken before George Pen Johnson, who on April 14, 1858, after full consideration, decided that Archy was in no proper sense a fugitive slave from Mississippi, and therefore discharged him finally, much to Archy's own relief and to the satisfaction of the larger part of the community.''

Bancroft, in regard to the Archy case, says: ''Burnett was appointed to fill the vacancy caused by the resignation of Terry. Stovall took Archy on board the steamer for the States. But when outside the entrance, Stovall was arrested for kidnapping and Archy brought back by writ of habeas corpus. E. D. Baker was counsel for Archy and J. H. Hardy, afterwards impeached for treasonable utterance, pleaded Stovall's case. George Pen Johnson, United States Commissioner, heard the case impartially and ordered Archy liberated.''

The reader has been given not only the police and Supreme Court proceedings of this case, but that part of the proceedings as considered of historical value by the two greatest California historians, namely, Hittell and Bancroft. During this period in California, the colored people who were here lived in constant fear of the Fugitive Slave Law and the various interpretations that could be and were given to it by those in authority. They were not allowed to testify in the Courts of Justice in their own behalf, owing to the workings of the fugitive slave laws. They were not allowed the benefits of the Homestead Law, notwithstanding through it all they clung to California.

The few members of the race living in the State at the time were most admirable, because they acted as one family in whatever concerned the welfare of the Negro Race. Through the greatest struggles a few had acquired homes and good paying businesses. They owned good churches and several private schools, and strove to improve themselves and be fit for citizenship whenever it should come to them. They had among them an effective organization which was known as ''The Executive Committee of the Colored Convention.'' All the colored people throughout the State were members of this organization and contributed of their funds to aid in covering the cost of different court trials. The duty of this committee was to be on the constant watch to defend the interest of the race in every part of the State. They had what corresponded to a secret service or code of transmitting news to one another, since there was neither a rapid mail service nor telegraphic communication. They transmitted the news by the way of the barber's chair. The barbers at the time throughout the State were colored. It was through this channel they learned of any move for or against the Negro made in the legislative halls or elsewhere. Word came to a few colored gentlemen living in Sacramento, that Mr. Stovall was intending to send Archy, the Negro slave boy, back to Mississippi to again become a slave.

A number of Negroes had already been taken back into slavery after coming to California and working to pay for their freedom, and the few who were free when coming to California had had a difficult time to acquire anything like a home. The word of a Negro would not be taken in the Courts of Justice, and if the Negro, Archy, was allowed to be returned into slavery after a residence in the State for one year, the day might come when other colored people would be returned to the South and into slavery, if a white person should make affidavit that they were their slaves. Many had been returned by the courts. In view of these undeniable facts, the colored people realized that Mr. Stovall having taught school for a year in Sacramento would give weight to his actions. They also were aware of the fact that California was admitted to the Union as a Free State, and that the Constitution of the State also forbade slavery.

The Executive Committee of the Colored Convention decided to make the Archy case a test case as to the rights of Negroes to live in beautiful California. They staked their all upon the outcome and decided that if they lost and had to leave the State, they would not do so without a struggle. California's admittance as a Free State did not give them any more peace of mind than a Free Negro would have enjoyed in the heart of the Southland.

The officers of the Executive Committee living in Sacramento soon sent word to those living in San Francisco, Red Bluff, Marysville and other places throughout the State. They decided to fight the case to a finish, not in holding meetings and protesting, but to arm themselves with the best counsel available on the coast. The services of such an attorney required money and a lot of it. There were white people living in the State who believed that the Negro was human and entitled to the treatment of a human being, though such views always made the person unpopular among other white people. Hence to secure a good attorney they knew that they would have to pay a good fee. They secured a man who, while he valued his future career, was a deep, dyed-in-the-wool Abolitionist and a personal friend to the immortal Abraham Lincoln. The writer refers to Col. E. D. Baker, who conducted the second trial in San Francisco.

The first trial they employed a Mr. Winans, who came to California in 1849, after graduating in law from Columbia college. He was very popular and influential in organizing the San Francisco Bar Association. George Wharton James says: "His word was worth more than the biggest bond his richest client could give." What a splendid selection the Executive Committee made in employing such reliable counsel!

The second trial was held before Judge Freelon, and Archy was dismissed. Mr. Stovall immediately boarded a steamer for the States, carrying Archy with him. The colored people and the members of the Executive Committee sued out a writ of habeas corpus before George Pen Johnson, United States Commissioner. But who would serve the writ for them? One of the Executive Committee, a Mr. George Dennis, living in San Francisco, learning that ex-Judge Terry, an old friend of his, who, while a Democrat, still would do a kindness for those whom he liked, went to him and explained the case. He replied that if given the proper authority he would go out into the San Francisco bay and arrest Stovall. The Executive Committee of the Colored Convention chartered the tug "Goliath," paying the sum of three thousand and fifty dollars for the use of it. The tug being secured, ex-Judge Terry went out into the San Francisco bay and, as the steamer was about to pass through the Golden Gate, he hailed it and went on board and arrested Mr. Stovall for kidnapping Archy and returned to San Francisco, with both Stovall and the Negro slave-boy, Archy. The case was then tried before George Pen Johnson and Archy was defended by E. D. Baker, a lawyer of wonderful oratorical ability and a staunch friend to the Negro Race. E. D. Baker's pleading of the case was so forceful that George Pen Johnson, notwithstanding he was a southern man, granted Archy his liberty.

The Executive Committee spent altogether the sum of fifty thousand dollars in these different court trials in the interest of the Archy case. The money to defray the expense of the chartering of the tug "Goliath" was raised through the assistance of "Mammy Pleasants," Afterward the colored men and women begged, mortgaged their homes and gave concerts in an effort to raise the money to pay the cost of these trials. The battle was not for Archy alone, but because of the vital interest of the matter to all the people of color then living in California.

The few Free Negroes then in the State, with few exceptions, had earned their freedom after coming here and working in the mines after a long, hard trip overland by ox-team. If they were free when arriving in California, they used almost all their money in making the trip and were compelled to start life all over. Even so they handled this case as one would handle a great financial deal or adventure. They secured the best available attorneys, pledged themselves to the raising of the money to pay the cost and then opened battle, showing unity of purpose and marshalling of forces. Let the reader consider the thousands of miles lying between California and the men and women of the East who were using their voices, pens, money and time in an effort to influence public opinion in behalf of the Negro Race and the cause of freedom, trying, if possible, to convince the public mind that the Negro was actually made of flesh and blood, with a soul and with feelings the same as other human beings. These few Negroes and the loyal white persons in California who assisted the Negroes in this case are greatly to be admired.

After the final decision of the case it has been told the writer that San Francisco was on the verge of a riot, and that Mammy Pleasants hid Archy Lee in her home until the Executive Committee could secure him passage to Canada. In after years he came back to California and died in Sacramento. His demise was the cause of a revival of the case through the daily press. The following is from the Sacramento Daily Union, November 7, 1873, and which was republished in the Pacific Appeal of San Francisco under date November 10, 1873: ''Archy Lee was found buried in the sand, with only his head exposed, in the marsh-lands of Sacramento. He was ill and claimed to have buried himself thus to keep warm. He was taken to the hospital where he died.***Archy Lee arrived in Sacramento October, 1857.***He was arrested in the Hackett house kept by colored people on Third, between K and L streets. Judge Robinson, who locked him up in the city prison, turned him over to James Lansing, Chief of Police, who issued a writ of habeas corpus directed to Dansing and Stovall, and on petition of Charles W. Parker, for whom Crocker and McKune appeared as attorneys. Smith and Hardy, opposing Judge Robinson, heard the case and it was continued a day or two. Meanwhile Stovall filed a petition with U. S. Commissioner George Pen Johnson, calling on him to enforce the Fugitive Slave Law. Winans and Crocker appeared for the slave in reply and moved to dismiss the petition. H. Johnson took time to consult M. Hall McAllister, United States Circuit Judge, and in a few days referred the case back to the State Courts. For two weeks the slave lay in prison when Judge Robinson released him and held that his master could not retake him. But Lansing detained the Negro, and refused to deliver him to Stovall, who petitioned the Supreme Court for a writ of habeas corpus for the recovery of his slave. In that case Stovall would be protected in his property and the chief was required to surrender the Negro to his master. He was escorted by a strong force of police from the court house to prison and three times tried to escape into the crowd surrounding him. The next day Officer O'Neal was detained to accompany Stovall and the Negro, heavily-ironed, was taken in a wagon out of town, a rescue being anticipated. The next heard of the matter was when Stovall and the Negro were in a boat in the San Francisco bay, ironed to a yawl and his master trying to get him on the steamer, while an excited crowd was on the wharf. A writ of habeas corpus was sworn out and an officer sent in a boat and the slave taken from his master and carried to the city hall, an immense crowd following him, The writ was heard before Judge Freelon a week later. Judge Hardy and Col. James appeared for the master, and Col. E. D. Baker, E. O. Crosby and W. H. Tompkins for the slave. On a motion to dismiss the warrant of arrest as fugitive slave, Judge Freelon denied it, whereupon Stovall set the Negro free and at once had him rearrested by U. S. Marshal, as a fugitive slave and George Pen Johnson heard the case. Meanwhile the Negro sued Stovall for $2500 damages for imprisonment and beating. The case lingered for weeks exciting greater interest all the time. Witnesses were brought from this city and the trial was attended by an immense crowd. Finally, early in April, Johnson decided the case and released Archy Lee, holding that he was not a fugitive slave.''

A portion of this chapter has been published in an article of the writer's under the title ''Slavery in California'' in the Journal of Negro History, January, 1918. Later the editor of this journal received a letter from a relative of the slave boy, Archy Lee. In the next issue of the magazine he published the following short sketch: ''Mention of the slave boy, Archy, in Miss Beasley's 'Slavery in California' has called forth from a relative the following sketch:

'' 'Archy's mother was named Maria. Maria had four children, Archy, Candace, Pompey and Quitman. (I am the daughter of Candace.) At the time Charles A. Stovall took Archy to California, Maria, with her other children were with Simeon Stovall, the father of Charles Stovall. Charles A. Stovall had been graduated in medicine and had returned home to begin practice, but his health having failed him, he went to California, taking Uncle Archy with him. My grandmother Maria heard through the relatives of Stovall of Archy during the time Stovall remained in California, but near the close of the Civil War, Charles Stovall returned to Mississippi and remained there until his death a few years later. After Stovall came back from California, my grandmother never heard any more of her son, Archy, except when she once heard that he was with the Indians who were treating him for some kind of sickness. Whether he died or whether this rumor was put out to keep the Stovalls from trying to steal him and bring him back to Mississippi, I have never been able to learn. My grandmother Maria continued to search for Archy, by writing several times to San Francisco, but without success. She died in 1884. Pompey and Quitman continued to live near Jackson, Mississippi. When Quitman died some time ago, Pompey was still alive when I last heard from him.'

'' 'Signed, MRS. R. A. HUNT, Marshall, Texas.' ''

FREEDOM PAPERS.

STATE OF CALIFORNIA,
    COUNTY OF MARIPOSA.

Know all men to whom these presents shall come, that I, Thomas Thorn, of the State and County aforesaid, being the rightful owner of the Negro man, Peter Green, and entitled to his service as a slave during his life have this day released and do by these presents release him from any further service as a slave.

And I do by these presents from myself, my heirs, executors and administrators declare him, the said Peter Green, to be free to act for himself and no longer under bonds as a slave. Provided, however, that the said Peter Green shall pay to me the sum of one thousand dollars, good lawful money or work for the service, from the present time until the first day of April, A. D. 1854.

In Testimony whereof, I have hereunto affixed my hand and Scroll for Seal, at Quartzburge, this 5th day of February, A. D., one thousand eight hundred and fifty-three.

THOMAS THORN. (Seal)

In the presence of Benjamine F. Cadell, Jr., Joseph A. Tiry, I hereby notify that the above obligation has been complied with and that Peter Green was legally discharged.

Given under my hand at Quartzburge, this day of August, A. D., 1855.

JAMES GIVENS, *Justice of the Peace.*

ELDORADO COUNTY RECORDER'S OFFICE

RECORD BOOK ''A'' (Miscellany, p. 541).

JOHN A. REICHARDT,

TAYLOR BARTON
        to
NEGRO BOB

EMANCIPATION.

STATE OF CALIFORNIA,
    COUNTY OF ELDORADO.
    COLD SPRINGS PRECINCT.

Know all men to whom these presents shall come: That I. Taylor Barton, lately a citizen of the State of Missouri, and owner of slaves, do here by this instrument, under my hand and Seal, given this ninth day of October, in the year of our Lord eighteen hundred and fifty-one, set Free from Bondage to me and all men, my slave Bob, and do declare him forever hereafter his own man, wherever he may go. Nevertheless, I make this condition that the said Bob shall remain with me as my slave, faithful and obedient unto me, until the twenty-fifth day of December next, commonly known as Christmas.

Witness my hand and seal on the day and date aforesaid.

TAYLOR BARTON. (Seal)

In the presence of
    WILLIAM F. EMERSON.   December 25, 1851.

I do hereby declare my slave Bob, to be forever free from and after this date.

TAYLOR BARTON. (Seal)

In the presence of I. G. Canfield, Justice of the Peace.
    Filed for Record, January 5, 1852, at 4 P. M.

JOHN A. REICHARDT,
Recorder of Eldorado County, California.

SAMUEL GRANTHAN
        to
ALECK LONG.
STATE OF CALIFORNIA, ELDORADO COUNTY.

DEED OF MANUMISSION.

Know all men by these presents that I, Samuel A. Granthan, of the county and State aforesaid, acting by Power of Attorney vested in me by Oliver Granthan, of St. Louis, State of Missouri, acting for and in behalf of said Oliver Granthan, and in consideration of the sum of four hundred dollars to me in hand paid, the same to receive to the benefit of the said Oliver Granthan, have this day liberated, set free and fully and effectually manumitted Aleck Long, heretofore a slave for life, the lawful property of the said Oliver Granthan.

The description of said Aleck Long, being as follows to-wit: About fifty-seven years old, five feet, ten inches in height, gray hair, dark complexion with a scar on the inside of the left leg above the ankle. The said Aleck Long to enjoy and possess now and from henceforth the full exercise of all the rights, benefits and privileges of a free man of color, free of all or any claim to servitude, slavery or service of the said Oliver Granthan, his heirs, executors, and assigns, and all other persons claiming, or to claim, forever.

In testimony of this Seal of Manumission, I have this day signed my name and affixed my seal this second day of March, 1852, at 4 P. M.

SAMUEL A. GRANTHAN,
Attorney for Oliver Granthan.

STATE OF CALIFORNIA,
COUNTY OF ELDORADO.

Personally appeared before me, William Palmer, who makes oath and says that Samuel Granthan, whose name appears in the accompanying Seal of Manumission as a party thereto, did freely, voluntarily and of his own will, execute to and subscribe the same for the use and purpose therein contained.

Witness my hand and seal this 2nd day of March, 1852, A. D., at 4 P. M.

GAVIN D. HALL,
Judge of Eldorado County.

J. A. REICHARDT,
Recorder for Eldorado County, California.

Recorder's office, Eldorado County, Record Book "A" (Miscellany, p. 545).

E. H. TAYLOR
to
DENNIS AVIERY.

SLAVE RELEASE.

To all whom it may concern: This is to certify that Dennis Aviery has been my slave in the State of Georgia for about the term of eight years, but by virtue of money to me in hand paid, he is free and liberated from all allegiance to my authority.

Coloma, Eldorado County, California, February 8, 1851.

Witness, GEORGE SCALL.

STATE OF CALIFORNIA,
ELDORADO COUNTY.

On this day, the eighth of February, A. D., 1851, personally appeared before me, the Recorder of said county, E. H. Taylor, satisfactorily proven to me to be the person described herein who executed the foregoing instrument of liberating his negro slave by the oath of George Scall, a competent witness for that purpose, by me duly sworn, and the said E. H. Taylor, acknowledging that he executed the same freely and voluntarily for the use and purpose therein mentioned.

In testimony thereof, I, John Reichardt, Recorder for the said county, have hereunto signed my name, and affixed the seal of said office at Coloma, this day of year first above written.

JOHN A. REICHARDT,
Recorder of Eldorado County.

Filed for Recording, February 8, 1851, at 9 o'clock A. M.

JOHN A. REICHARDT.

Recorder's office, Record Book "A" (Miscellany, p. 335).

This indenture made and entered into this 14th day of August, A. D., 1860, between A. J. Houstis, as County Judge of Humboldt County, for and in behalf of a certain Indian boy, called and known by the name of "Smokey" of the first part, and Austin Wiley of the said county, of the second part. That whereas, the said Austin Wiley had in his possession and under his control a certain Indian boy named "Smokey," and whereas, the said Austin Wiley avers that he, with the assistance of James Frint, obtained said Indian of his parents in Mattole Valley of this county, by and with their consent; and whereas the said Austin Wiley does now apply to me as County Judge, to bond and apprentice the said boy "Smokey" to him according to law to learn the art of household duties about his premises, and in this respect to hold the relation of an apprentice until he shall arrive at the lawful majority, the age of twenty-five years, or for the term of seventeen years next following this indenture, the boy being now considered eight years of age; and whereas, it appears to me that the second party in this agreement has obtained this boy in a lawful manner without fraud or oppression, and that the boy ''Smokey'' therefore comes justly under the first provision of the law providing for apprenticeship approved April 8, A. D., 1860.

Now, therefore, I, A. D. Houstis, County Judge aforesaid, in consideration of the premises and acting for and on behalf of the aforesaid Indian boy ''Smokey,'' do by these presents bind and apprentice as above stated the said boy ''Smokey'' to Austin Wiley for and during the term of seventeen years next following this indenture; entitling him according to law to have the care, custody, control and earnings of said boy during said period and all other advantages and responsibilities growing out of this indenture and apprenticeship that the law contemplates.

And the said Austin Wiley, the second party, in this agreement doth hereby agree, obligate and bind himself that he will truly and faithfully discharge all obligations on his part growing out of this indenture, according to law. That he will suitably clothe and provide the necessaries of life for the said boy, during his term of indenture. That he will in all respects treat him in a humane manner. That he will not take him out of the State, nor transfer him to any party not known in this agreement without the consent of legal authorities endorsed thereon, and that in all respects he will carry out every provision of law that contemplates the safety, protection and well being of said boy.

In witness whereof, the parties to this indenture hereunto set their hand and seal this day first above written.

A. J. HOUSTIS, *County Judge*, First Party.
AUSTIN WILEY, Second Party.

STATE OF CALIFORNIA,
HUMBOLDT COUNTY.

And now comes Austin Wiley and deposes as follows: ''The statements made by me in the preamble to this indenture referring to the age of the Indian boy 'Smokey' and the manner in which I obtained him are true to the best of my knowledge and belief.

AUSTIN WILEY.

Sworn to and subscribed before me on this 14th day of August, A. D., 1860.

A. J. HOUSTIS,
County Judge of Humboldt County.

This is one paper from a collection of 105 in the Court House at Eureka. Austin Wiley, whose name appears in the document, was later appointed Superintendent of Indian Affairs for California, and, during his term of office, did much to bring to a satisfactory termination the trouble then existing between the settlers and the natives. These above Freedom Papers were kindly furnished the writer by Dr. Owen Coy, California Archivest. The following papers were obtained by the writer:

History of Butte County, California (p. 199), reads: ''Subscribed and sworn to before me at this office at White Rock, this, the nineteenth day of April, A. D. 1853. The first document in the records of the County of Butte is the Deed of Manumission by Franklin Stewart to the slave, Washington, a copy of which we give below. Another instrument of the same nature appears on the records of 1851, in which William Compton sets free his slave, Joseph Compton, for two years of faithful service, a curious feature of this document being the inability of the master to sign his own name, making his mark instead.

'' 'FREE PAPERS OF THE SLAVE.

'' 'Washington, from Franklin Stewart.

'' 'State of California,
'' 'County of Butte.

'' 'Know all men by these presents, that Franklin Stewart, of the County and State aforesaid, do for and in consideration of seventeen years of faithful service of my slave, Washington, rendered by him in the States of Arkansas and Missouri, do hereby set free and emancipate him, the said slave; his age about thirty-three years, color slight copper; and fully relinquish all rights in the said slave, Washington, which I might be entitled to in law or equity.

'' 'Given under my hand and seal this 4th day of May, A. D., 1852.' ''

The following is quoted from a copy of the *Pacific Appeal* of 1863: ''Benjamin Berry, who was born a slave in Kentucky, taken to Missouri and then sold to a man by the name of Halloway, with whom he came to this State in 1850. Here he performed services supposed equivalent to $3,000, and obtained his Freedom Papers.''

The following is quoted from Bancroft's "History of California": "On May 23, 1850, a colored man named Lawrence was married to a colored woman, Margaret, who was hired out to service by a white man named William Marr, who claimed her as his slave. Early the following morning Marr forced the woman, by threats and showing a pistol, to leave her husband and go with him. He afterwards offered to resign her on payment of $1000. (Placer Times, May 27, 1850).

"A white man, named Best, brought a colored woman (Mary) to Nevada, California, in 1860, from Missouri. He was a cruel master, but she remained with him until he returned in 1854, when she borrowed money to purchase her freedom. Soon she married Harry Dorsey, a colored man, and lived happily ever afterward."

Daniel Rodgers came to California with his master in '49, and worked in the mines, and at night for himself, earning the sum of $1000 which he paid to his master for his freedom. He was not given either a receipt or his Freedom Papers. He returned with his master to Arkansas and in after years decided to return to California and bring his family, whereupon his master auctioned him off to the highest bidder. A number of white gentlemen who knew him raised a purse of money and bought him; afterwards giving him a certificate to prove that the person by the name of Daniel Rodgers was a free man of color.

One of Mr. Rodgers' daughters, now living in Oakland, gave the writer the privilege of making the following copy of the original certificate, for its reproduction in this book:

"Dardanell, Yell County, Arkansas, April 30, 1859.

"We the undersigned citizens of Yell county, Arkansas, having been personally acquainted with the bearer, Daniel Rodgers, a free man of color, for many years past and up to the present time, take pleasure in certifying to his character for honesty, industry and integrity; also as a temperate and peaceful man; and one worthy of trust and confidence of all philanthropic and good men wherever he may go.

"Signed by: Robert E. Walters, George Williams, Joseph Miles, W. H. Spirey, L. D. Parish, George L. Kimble, Samuel Dickens, Haunis A. Hawill, A. Ferril, James A. Baird, William A. Ross, C. M. Mundock, A. H. Fulton, Joseph P. Williams, B. I. Jacoway.

"BURKE JOHNSON,
"County Judge."

The daughter permitted the writer also to copy an extract from a paper, which was given to Daniel Rodgers' wife, whose maiden name was Miss Artimisa Penwright. She was forced to produce her Freedom Papers before she could accompany her husband on the trip to California. This extract states: "Artimisa Penwright was the daughter of her mistress by a negro man, and neither she nor any of her children were to ever be slaves."

The United States slave laws were so strict, and the fugitive slave laws so far-reaching in their interpretation that this was not the only person who was compelled to have Freedom Papers before starting to California, as will be shown by the following, which is quoted from a copy now in possession of Dr. Owen C. Coy, California Archivest, and which he copied from page 95 of an old scrap book owned by John T. Mason, at Downieville, California:

"Virginia, Hampshire County, to-wit:

"David Brown, a black man, aged twenty-two years, five feet, eight inches high, with pleasant countenance, a scar on the forefinger of the left hand, a scar on the shin of each leg, and was born free.

"Registered this day October, 1834.

"In testimony whereof I, John B. White, Clerk of said County Court of Hampshire, have hereto set my name and affixed the Seal of the said Court this 27th day of October, 1834.

"JOHN WHITE,
"Clerk of Hampshire County.

"Attest:
"JOHN BRADY, a Justice of the Peace for the said county."

"Whereas, by reason of the anxiety of various persons residing in and near Lancaster, Ohio, to emigrate to Marysville, in California; and the difficulty of procuring passage by water, Thomas Sturgeon and Samuel Crim, of Lancaster, Ohio, have agreed to unite themselves together as partners for the purpose of transporting from Lancaster to Marysville, aforesaid by land, a company of emigrants; it is therefore agreed between the said Sturgeon and Crim and David Brown, (written in) as follows, to-wit: Agrees to pay the said Sturgeon and Crim one hundred and fifty dollars, fifty dollars of which is paid in hand and the balance is to be paid before said Sturgeon and Crim start to California, which shall be between the first and fifteenth of April next.

"(2) Should the said David Brown fail to make payment as above stated he thereby agrees to forfeit the amount paid on this contract.

"(3) Full payment being made as aforesaid, the said Sturgeon and Crim to transport the said David Brown from Lancaster, aforesaid, to Marysville, aforesaid, and clear of all expenses, or charges (board included) except as aforesaid but they are not bound to furnish clothing or to pay doctor's bills.***

"In witness whereof the parties have hereto signed and sealed duplicate this 28th day of February, A. D., 1852.

"Received MacLurin's obligation for $50.00.

"THOMAS STURGEON. (Seal)
"SAMUEL CRIM. (Seal)
"DAVID BROWN. (Seal)"

"Fugitive Slave. The following appeared in the *Alta Californian*, April 20, 1853: 'A person by the name of Brown attempted to have a negro girl arrested in our town a few days since as a fugitive slave, but was taken all a-back by the girl's lawyer, F. W. Thomas, producing her Freedom Papers. Brown's father set the girl at liberty in 1851, and it is thought by many that the son knew the fact, and thought to catch the girl without her Freedom Papers but fortunately for her he did not.'—Placer Times. (*Auburn Herald*.)"

"The Isthmus in '49" appeared in the *Century Magazine* and, among other things, said: "Fremont and '49 Saunders was to return with the Fremonts, happy in having gained enough money to buy the freedom of his family, enough to buy a home as well; one successful '49er. at least."

"STATE OF CALIFORNIA, }
"COUNTY OF LOS ANGELES. } ss.

"Before the Hon. Benjamin Hayes,
"Judge of the District Court of the
"First Judicial District State of California,
"County of Los Angeles.

"In the matter of Hannah and her children, Ann (and Mary, child of Ann), Lawrence, Nathaniel, Jane, Charles, Marion, Martha, and an infant boy two weeks old; and of Biddy and her children, Ellen, Ann and Harriet, on petition for habeas corpus. Now on this nineteenth day of January, in the year of our Lord, one thousand, eight hundred and fifty-six, the said persons above named are brought before me in the custody of the Sheriff of said County, all except the said Hannah and infant boy two weeks old(who are satisfactorily shown to be too infirm to be brought before me), and except Lawrence, (who is necessarily occupied in waiting on his said mother Hannah) and Charles (who is absent in San Bernardino County, but within the said Judicial District) and Robert Smith, claimant, also appears with his Attorney, Alonzo Thomas, Esq. And after hearing, and duly considering the said petition for habeas corpus and the return of said claimant thereto, and all the proofs and allegations of the said parties and all the proceedings previously had herein, it appearing satisfactory to the Judge here that all the said persons so suing in this case to-wit: Hannah and her children, and Biddy, and her said children are persons of color, and that Charles, aged now six years, was born in the Territory of Utah, of the United States, and Marion (aged four years), Martha (aged two years), Mary, daughter of the said Ann, and aged two years, and the said infant boy aged two weeks, were born in the State of California, and that the said Hannah, Ann, Lawrence, Nathaniel, Jane, and Charles as well as the said Biddy, Ellen, Ann, and Harriet have resided with the said Robert Smith for more than four years, and since some time in the year of our Lord one thousand, eight hundred and fifty-one in the State of California; and it further appearing that the said Robert Smith left and removed from the State of Mississippi more than eight years ago with the intention of not returning thereto, but establishing himself as a resident in Utah Territory, and more than four years ago left and removed from said Utah Territory with the intention of residing and establishing himself in the State of California, and has so resided, in the last mentioned State, since some time in the year of our Lord one thousand eight hundred and fifty-one. And it further appearing by satisfactory proof to the Judge here, that all the said persons of color are entitled to their freedom and are free and cannot be held in slavery or involuntary servitude, it is therefore argued that they are entitled to their freedom and are free forever. And it further appearing to the satisfaction of the Judge here that the said Robert Smith intended to and is about to remove from the State of California where slavery does not exist, to the State of Texas, where slavery of Negroes and persons of color does exist, and established by the municipal laws, and intends to remove the said before-mentioned persons of color, to his own use without the free will and consent of all or any of the said persons of color, whereby their liberty will be greatly jeopardized, and there is good reason to apprehend and believe that they may be sold into slavery or involuntary servitude and the said Robert Smith is persuading and enticing and seducing said persons of color to go out of the State of California, and it further appearing that none of the said persons of color can read and write, and are almost entirely ignorant of the laws of the state of California as well as those of the State of Texas, and of their rights and that the said Robert Smith, from his past relation to them as members of his family does possess and exercise over them an undue influence in respect to the matter of their said removal insofar that they have been in duress and not in possession and exercise of their free will so as to give a binding consent to any engagement or arrangement with him. And it further appearing that the said Hannah is thirty-four years, and her daughter Ann, seventeen, and all of her children, to-wit: Lawrence (aged from twelve to thirteen years), Nathaniel (aged from ten to eleven), Jane (aged eight years), Charles (aged six years), Marion (aged four years), Martha (aged two years) and said infant boy of Hannah, aged two weeks, as well as Mary (aged two weeks), daughter of said Ann, are under the age of fourteen years and so under the laws of the State of California, are not competent to choose a guardian for themselves; and it further appearing that the said Biddy is aged thirty-eight years, and the said Ellen is aged seventeen years, and the other children of said Biddy, to-wit: Ann (aged from twelve to thirteen) and Harriet (aged eight years), are under the age of fourteen years), and so by the laws of the State of California, are not competent to choose a guardian for themselves. It further appearing that the said infant boy two weeks of age of Hannah is of tender age and must be kept with his said mother, Hannah, the same is accordingly ordered and said infant boy is entrusted to his said mother hereby, and is ordered to appear with him before the Judge—here at the Court House, in the City of Los Angeles, on next Monday, January 1, 1856, at ten o'clock, a. m., of said day, if her health should permit and if not, as soon thereafter as may be practicable, of which the Sheriff of Los Angeles is thereby notified to notify her, the said Hannah, and whereof the said Robert Smith, being now in the Court, has notice, it appearing that she resides in his house and is under his control, and the said Mary, child of Ann, appearing to be of tender age, is entrusted to the said Ann, to be brought before the Judge here at the time and place aforesaid, to be dealt with according to law of which the said Ann and the said Robert Smith have notice here and the said Martha, being of tender years, is entrusted to the said Ann, her sister, to be brought before the Judge here at the time and place aforesaid to be dealt with according to law of which the said Ann and the said Robert Smith here have notice and the said Hannah and Ann, are appointed Special Guardians respectively of the children so hereby entrusted to them, and notified that it is their duty to obey all lawful orders of the Judge here or of some competent Court touching the premises, and the further hearing of this case as to the said Hannah, and the infant boy and her children, Lawrence, Charles, Mary and Martha, is adjourned until said last mentioned time at the Court House of the City of Los Angeles, and it is further ordered, that the said Nathaniel (aged from ten to eleven years), Jane (aged eight years), Marion (aged four years), all children of the said Hannah, and said child Ann (aged seventeen), and Harriet (aged eight years), are committed to the custody of the Sheriff, of Los Angeles County, David W. Alexander, Esq.; as Special Guardian until the further order of the Judge, here or of other Judge or Court of competent jurisdiction to appoint General Guardians, of aforesaid children last mentioned and the said Sheriff will leave in full liberty and discharge the said Biddy and her child Ellen, (aged seventeen years), and the said Ann, only being required to obey the said orders hereinbefore made to appear before the Judge here in manner and form aforesaid, and it further appearing that the said Charles is absent in San Bernardino County, within said Jurisdiction District. It is ordered that Robert Clift, Esq., Sheriff of said county, be and is hereby appointed Special Guardian of said Charles, and as such duly authorized and required to take said Charles in his custody, and him safely keep in such manner that said Charles shall not be removed out of the State of California, but shall abide the further order of the Judge here or other Judge or Court of competent Jurisdiction touching his Guardianship. And it is further ordered and adjudged that all the cost accrued in the case up to the present date and in executing the present order of the Judge here as to the production of said Hannah and her said infant two weeks old, and said Lawrence, Martha and Mary, before the Judge here as aforesaid, shall be paid by the said Robert Smith.

"Given under my hand as Judge of the first Judicial District of the State of California, on the 19th day of January, A. D. 1856, at the City of Los Angeles.

"BENJAMIN HAYES,
"*District Judge.*

"On this 19th day of January appeared the said Robert Smith by his attorney, Alonzo Thomas, Esq., and moves the Judge hereto the cost in this case which is taken under advisement until Monday next at 10 o'clock a. m.

"BENJAMIN HAYES,
"*District Judge.*

"On this Monday, January 21st, 1856, the said Smith and the said parties so ordered to appear as aforesaid do not appear and this cause is continued until tomorrow at 10 o'clock a. m.

"BENJAMIN HAYES,
"*District Judge.*"

SLAVES EMANCIPATED IN CALIFORNIA THROUGH THE COURTS AND FRIENDS OF THE NEGRO RACE BEFORE THE ISSUING OF PRESIDENT ABRAHAM LINCOLN'S EMANCIPATION PROCLAMATION.

All white persons who lived in California during its pioneer days were not in favor of slavery. They disliked it, and more than one has proven their dislike to the institution of slavery by assisting in securing through the courts the emancipation of Negro slaves held in California. Slaves did not, however, always tell when they were thus held, for fear of not being able to prove their freedom with the Freedom Papers, which they were given after working for the master a given period in the mines of California. The ensuing records will prove the statement.

The record of the following case was given to the writer by the daughter of the subject. She said: "Biddy Mason came to California with her master, Robert Smith, coming from Hancock County, Mississippi, to Salt Lake, and as the Mormons were going to San Bernardino, California, and since Mr. Smith's wife continued in poor health, he decided to also go to California. Robert Smith and his party of slaves reached San Bernardino, California, in 1851. Their trip from Mississippi was by ox team. Biddy Mason drove the livestock across the plains into California. There were three hundred wagons in the ox team.

They remained in San Bernardino from 1851 to 1854, when the master decided to take the slaves and his family to Texas. En route, they journeyed through Los Angeles County, and camped in a canyon near Santa Monica, where they had spent only a few days when the news reached Los Angeles, through a Mrs. Rowen, of San Bernardino, that these slaves were leaving California to go back into slavery in Texas. The Sheriff of Los Angeles County, who, at that date (Jan. 19, 1854), was a Mr. Frank Dewitt, issued a writ against this slave-master, preventing him from taking his slaves from the State of California.

Mrs. Biddy Mason, the subject of this sketch, was one of the most wonderful of all the colored pioneers coming into California in this history. After securing her freedom, she and her family went from this Santa Monica Canyon to Los Angeles. She secured employment as a confinement nurse with Dr. Griffin. The first resolution she made to herself was that she would secure a home for her children, and she began to save her money for that purpose.

The first piece of property she purchased was one that was considered on the outskirts of town. After obtaining the deed to this property, she told her children that this was always to remain as their homestead, and it mattered not what their circumstances, they were always to retain this homestead. Elsewhere will be found a full sketch of the useful life lived by Mrs. Biddy Mason, the leading trail blazer in finance of the Negro race.

Robert Anthony came with his master to Sacramento, California, in 1852, from St. Louis, Missouri, by ox team across the plains. Two years to pay for his freedom he worked in the mines by day for the master. At night he worked for himself and with the money thus earned he purchased and built two quartz mills at Horncutt, California, which is located between Yuba and Dry Cut.

While working his mills he heard of a colored girl at Hansonville, in the mountains, who was being held as a slave. She was working as a sheepherder. He drove out to the place and asked her if she did not wish her freedom. She replied: "Yes." He requested her to get into his wagon and he drove with her to Colusa. Some time afterward this slave girl became his wife. The writer interviewed the subject a few years ago at the poor farm in Marysville, and he made the following remark in regard to his marriage: "The marriage of Miss Addie Taylor to Robert Anthony was witnessed by Allen Pinkard and Thomas Scott.'' He further stated that he had an only son, who worked on one of the Hearst papers, but who had forgotten his old father.

Mary Ann Harris, a young colored girl, came with the family of Dr. Ross from Richmond, Virginia. She worked as a nurse girl for $4.00 a month to pay for her freedom. The doctor and family were stationed on the Island of Alcatraz, in San Francisco Bay. This girl was held virtually as a slave, so she told the writer, until an old colored woman by the name of Aunt Lucy Evans stole her off the island and gave her her freedom.

Rev. Thomas Starr King went to a ranch near Napa, California, and emancipated a number of slaves. Among the number were the following named persons: Aaron Rice, Old Man Sours, Wash Strains, Old Man Sydes. Their names were given to the writer by a Mr. Grider, who was a member of the Bear Flag Party. He said that these persons were the slave-property of a gentleman in Walnut Creek, and had been taken to Napa to continue as slaves, when the word reached Rev. Thomas Starr King, who proceeded to go to this place and emancipate them.

The emancipation of Mrs. Jane Elizabeth Whiting and family is another interesting event in the emancipation of slaves through the efforts of the colored people of San Francisco. The subject of this sketch came from West Virginia with her mistress and family, a Mrs. Thompson, whose oldest son acted as guide for the party. These slaves were being taken to work on Mr. Thompson's ranch in Petaluma, California.

Howard Thompson, together with his mother and her children, and the party of slaves, consisting of Mrs. Jane E. Whiting and her three children, and his mother's five children, made an interesting party to manage from Kanawa, West Virginia, en route to California. They left their home in Virginia on a Sunday morning, June 1, 1856, going to New Orleans, where they boarded a steamer sailing to Aspinwall, Isthmus of Panama. It was while at this port they first realized they were going to a new world, where there was no slavery. The children in the party, both those of the mistress and the slave woman's, decided to go on a sightseeing party after they had been comfortably located in a hotel. The natives, seeing this party of children, began to question them as to where they were going. The children innocently told the truth, whereupon they were asked where they were stopping, and as to whether the mother of the colored children was slave or free.

After learning where they were stopping, the natives went to the hotel and asked to see the colored woman. When she appeared they asked her if she was free and to produce her Freedom Papers. Since she was not free, she did not return to talk with the party. Her actions aroused the suspicion of the natives, since it was the law of their country that a slave could not cross it and remain a slave. They spread the alarm among themselves, that slaves were being carried through the country. This resulted in the forming of a mob on the outside. It was several days before Mr. Thompson could convince the people that the colored people were his servants and were willingly going to California with him.

The party, however, met the same conditions upon reaching Panama City. The feeling at this place was so strong against them that they left before the next morning. Mr. Thompson hired some strong natives to carry the party out to the boat on their backs, since the water was shallow. A party of small launches met the party and finished the journey to the steamer, but the launches were compelled to go up stream five miles and then out and across to the steamer, in an effort not to arouse suspicion of kidnapping the party of colored people. The ladder of the steamer was lowered to admit of their boarding the ship. When the captain saw that there were colored people in the party, he drew his revolver and commanded them to halt. Mr. Thompson, upon being questioned, stated to the captain that these people were his private servants and were quite willingly accompanying him and his mother to California. The captain was still in doubt as to the truthfulness of the statement and demanded to know the reason why they were coming to the steamer at such an early hour, since the steamer sent for its passengers at ten in the morning. Whereupon Mr. Thompson told of the natives' suspicion that the colored people were slaves and he feared trouble, since he could not make them understand. After a long parley the captain finally allowed them to board the steamer.

Aboard the ship there were several Abolitionists from Boston, and a colored man by the name of David Johnson, from New Bedford, Mass. This gentleman became very much interested in the colored people and readily secured their confidence, and learned that they were going to a ranch in Petaluma, California.

This newly-made friend and the white Abolitionist on board the steamer decided that, since the laws of California did not permit of slavery, they must plan some way to liberate these colored slaves after they reached California. They decided to tell the colored woman that she and her children must be the first to land when the ship docked, and that these newly-made friends would look out for their safety. They took them to a colored boarding house, at the corner of Kearney and Clay streets, San Francisco, which was known as the "Harper & West Boarding House."

The news soon spread that a family of slaves from Virginia had arrived on the steamship "John L. Stevens." The colored people in San Francisco held a mass meeting and decided to protect them in every way possible. They decided that the first thing to do would be to change their names from Whiting to Freeman, and then secure for the mother some day's work. They instructed the children to keep the shutters to their room always closed. But one day the children went out to play, and a passenger who was on the ship that brought them to San Francisco recognized and questioned them and afterwards wrote to Mrs. Thompson and told her where to locate her slaves; Mrs. Thompson did not attempt to reclaim them. Strange to relate, fifteen years afterward "Aunt Jane" and her former mistress met on the streets of San Francisco, and recognized each other and talked together, learning that for five weeks, while Mrs. Thompson was in search of these slaves, that they were boarding within a short distance of them all the time, and yet she never located them.

There was a number of slaves liberated in San Jose, California, through the combined efforts of Rev. Peter Cassey, Mrs. Harriett Davis and a Mrs. White. Among the number of slaves were a Mr. and Mrs. William Parker.

The colored people were united in their efforts to liberate slaves whenever they heard of such on California's soil. Prominent among those who were ever watchful for such were Rev. J. B. Sanderson, Mr. Minor and Robinson, of Stockton, who, together, went armed into San Joaquin County and liberated slaves. In many instances the slaves refused to talk to them, since they had been told that the colored people would harm them. These men, after a struggle in many instances, succeeded in convincing them that they were their friends and finally rescued them.

The following case will illustrate some of their work, and is quoted from the diary of Rev. J. B. Sanderson, with the permission of the family: "Monday, June 3, 1872—Dismissed school at nine o'clock; went out to Mr. Durham's ranch with Sheriff T. Cunningham after Annie Randall. I interviewed Mr. Durham; rode into town with Annie Randall; called upon Mr. Durham; took dinner at Mr. Cunningham's; attended court before Judge Bonker. Annie Randall released, and at my house. Attended meeting this P. M., an enthusiastic meeting." The ranch where this slave girl was found was near Stockton.

Through the efforts of Mr. William Robinson, of Red Bluff, a Miss Hester Anderson and Miss Belle Grant were liberated during the last of '68 or '69.

The following is quoted from Bancroft's "History of California": " 'Charles, a colored man, came to California as the slave of Lindall Hays. He escaped and was brought before Judge Thomas on a writ of habeas corpus and was discharged. The Judge maintained that under the laws of Mexico, which prevailed at the time of Charles' arrival, he was free. The Constitution of California forbade slavery, and the man, having been freed by the Mexican laws, could not in any case be seized as a slave. On the twenty-fourth of May Charles was brought up for breach of peace, charged with an assault on Hays, as resistance to a sheriff. It turned out that the sheriff had no warrant, and that Charles, having been declared a free man, was justified in defending himself from assault by Hays and the unauthorized officer who had assisted him. Counsellor Zabriske argued the law, also J. W. Winans. Justice Sackett discharged the prisoner.—*Placer Times*, May 27, 1851.' "

Fay's statement:

"In August, 1850, one Galloway, from Missouri, arrived in California with his slave, 'Frank,' whom he took to the mines, from which the slave escaped in the spring of 1851, going to San Francisco. Galloway found him in March and locked him up in Whitehall Building on Long Wharf. A writ of habeas corpus was issued in Frank's behalf by Judge Morris. The Negro stated that he believed Galloway meant to take him on board a vessel to convey him to the States. Bryne and McAlgay, Halliday and Saunders were employed in the interest of the slave, and Frank Pixley for the master, who alleged that he was simply traveling with his attendant and meant to leave the States soon. But the judge held that Galloway could not restrain Frank from his liberty as he was not a fugitive slave, but if brought at all to the State by Galloway, was so brought without his consent. He was allowed to go free."—Alta, California, April 12, 1851. *San Francisco Courier*, March 31, 1851 (Borthwick, 164-5), Hayes Scrap Book (Hughes Ms. I-28).

ATTORNEY E. BURTON CERUTI

MME. SADIE CHANDLER-COLE
Musical Instructor.

MME. FLORENCE COLE-TALBERT
Diamond Medalist and Lyric Soprano.

MISS JUANITA ALICE PATTON
Lyric Soprano.

DR. RUTH J. TEMPLE
First Colored Woman Physician in
the State.

Cases like the above just quoted were paid for through the efforts of all the colored people throughout the State, who contributed freely to the expense of the employment of lawyers.

While speaking of slavery in California, and the numerous laws to prevent Free Negroes from coming to or residing in the State, and the number of colored people who left the State and went to live in Canada, and afterward returned to fight it out in California, there was one Negro woman who left the State also to go to Canada. Any of the old pioneer colored people, when asked concerning her, immediately begin to tell all sorts of queer stories about her, and usually end by saying: "She always wore a poke bonnet and a plaid shawl," and "she was very black, with thin lips." Then sometimes they will also add: "She handled more money during pioneer days in California than any other colored person."

It will not interest the average colored person of today, in California, whether this strange woman was a witch or a great financier, but the following story concerning her activities with the hero, John Brown, of Harper's Ferry, will interest more than one. While the general public may have criticized her life, as they thought they knew it, nevertheless, if the story which I am relating be true, she was in disguise a modern "Queen Esther." A colored lady once told the writer that the mysterious woman—who was her personal friend—had said to her that she had no respect for white people because of the way they had treated her when she was a slave, and that she purposed to rule them with an iron hand. From the different stories told concerning her, she knew the morals of pioneer California, and if history be true, more than one pioneer man and woman did things that they would rather the court records did not mention. Yet the world passes over their faults and says that they were pioneers, and had made it possible for the State to become such, and that they had developed its resources. Charity is thrown over the faults of these pioneer empire-builders; then why may not a little charity be spared to this black slave woman, who was really a pioneer character of early San Francisco?

This story was given to the writer by a Mr. William Stephens, of Oakland, California (now at Del Monte), who said: "While on the private car of Mr. Crocker, and while the car was at one time in the railroad yards at Point Levy, Quebec, Canada, I was engaged in conversation with the foreman of the yards, who, after learning that we were from San Francisco, asked if I had ever seen 'Mammy Pleasants.' I said I had, and he then told me that his father had been a Canadian Labor Commissioner before the Civil War, and also had been connected with the Underground Railroad (a society organized to assist Negro slaves to escape to Canada). When the slaves reached Canada, his father, as Labor Commissioner, had seen to their securing work, that they might not become public charges."

This foreman of the railroad yards further told Mr. Stephens that his father had seen "Mammy Pleasants" give John Brown a large sum of money, and that this money was used by John Brown in financing his raid on Harper's Ferry. Mr. Stephens said that he paid no attention to this story because of the fact that he had never heard anyone in California say that "Mammy Pleasants" had been to Canada. But a number of years afterward, at the death of "Mammy Pleasants," there appeared in the *San Francisco Chronicle and Call* a wonderful biography of the woman which Mr. Stephen saved, and from which the writer was permitted to make the following copy:

San Francisco Call, January 4, 1904: "Her epitaph is written; the tombstone of 'Mammy Pleasants' will express her loyalty to the hero of Harper's Ferry. Tribute to John Brown, remains of woman who gave him financial assistance are borne to last resting place. The remains of 'Mammy Pleasants,' who died early Monday morning at the home of Lyman Sherwood, on Filbert street, will rest tonight under the soil of the little cemetery in the town of Napa, to which her body was taken this morning. One last request of 'Mammy Pleasants' was that there be placed above her grave a tombstone bearing her name, age, nativity, and the words: 'She was a a friend of John Brown's.' One of the many interesting stories of her eventful career, told by Mrs. Pleasants, was her experience during the exciting times preceding the outbreak of the Civil War. With the money inherited from her first husband, she came to California, and was here in 1858, when the first news of John Brown's efforts to free the slaves of the South were conveyed to San Francisco. Being in full sympathy with the movement, she conceived the idea of lending him financial assistance for the undertaking, and April 5, 1858, found her eastward bound with a $30,000 United States treasury draft, which had been procured for her through the aid of Robert Swain, John W. Coleman and Mr. Alford.

"Reaching Boston, Mrs. Pleasants arranged for a meeting with John Brown in Windsor, Canada. Before leaving Boston, Mrs. Pleasants had her draft exchanged for Canadian paper, which she converted into coin and finally turned over to Brown. After a conference in Canada, it was agreed between them that he should not strike a blow for the freedom of the Negro until she had journeyed to the South and had aroused the feelings of rebellion among her people. Disguised as a jockey, she proceeded to the South, and was engaged in her part of the plot when she was startled by the news that Brown had already made his raid on Harper's Ferry and had been captured. Learning that the authorities were in pursuit of Brown's accomplices, Mrs. Pleasants immediately fled to New York, and, after remaining in hiding for some time, assumed another name and made her way back to California.

"When Brown was captured, there was found on his person a letter reading: 'The ax is laid at the root of the tree. When the first blow is struck, there will be more money to help.' The message was signed 'W. E. P.' For months the authorities vainly searched for the author of the message. In later years it developed that Mrs. Pleasants had written the letter, but in signing it she had made her first initial 'M' look like 'W.' Mrs. Pleasants always blamed Brown for hastening his attack at Harper's Ferry, which she claimed cost her in all over $40,000. Among her effects are letters and documents bearing upon the historical event in which she played a secret and important part."

It may interest the reader to know that in 1864, about the first of October, the family of John Brown, of Harper's Ferry fame, reached California. They came across the plains and reached a meadow near Red Bluff, California, on the above-named date. They spent the fall on the meadow and afterward removed into Red Bluff upon the approach of winter. One of the daughters, "Sara," accepted a position in the public school at Red Bluff, teaching for a number of years, during which she had as a pupil a colored student by the name of Miss Clara Logan, who today lives in San Francisco, and is the widow of the late Mr. Albert Frazier. Miss Sara Brown later in life moved to the Santa Cruz Mountains, between Los Gatos and Saratoga, where she recently died. Another daughter, Mrs. Ruth Brown-Thompson, located in Pasadena, California, as did also their brother, Owen Brown.

Returning to the subject of "Mammy Pleasants": If reports be true of her activities as financial adviser to distinguished white gentlemen in California, she must have come into possession of the cold facts that men were selling Negro slaves and were making great fortunes from their labor in the mines of California. She realized that after the Negroes had worked sufficiently long to pay the price asked for their freedom in California, and with the crude manner of living then in the State, there soon would be a race of free Negroes in California, with neither health nor government protection. She had great confidence in John Brown's sincerity, and believed that, together with her help, he would start a bold dash for freedom for all slaves. The mere fact that she went to Boston before starting on this history-making and daring undertaking will readily recall the fact that Boston was the home of the great Abolitionists, and that all the workings through the Underground Railroad were directed from there. It was the home of the immortal William Lloyd Garrison, Sumner and our own Hon. Fred. Douglass. The sincere friends of the Negro slaves were in Boston. This California black woman may have spent her remaining days, for all anyone knows, in an effort to repay the money given to John Brown, notwithstanding the following, which appeared in the *San Francisco News-Letter* and was republished in the *Oakland Tribune*, September 3, 1916:

"The true story of 'Mammy Pleasants': The recent sale of oil lands of the Bell estate for $1,800,000 has created a flutter in oil circles. Not many years ago this same land was hawked about San Francisco by parties who had the option on it for $15,000, and there were no buyers. It seems a queer thing, that while there was oil on three sides of the land, no one could be persuaded into the idea that it was to be found in that particular tract. Some twenty or more of San Francisco's capitalists are now metaphorically kicking themselves for their lack of venture, when they had such a chance to admit opportunity knocking at their doors.

"In this connection, some papers have stated that Thomas Bell was induced to buy this land by old 'Mammy Pleasants,' his housekeeper and servant, when she was with him in the old 'House of Mystery' on Octavia street. As a matter of fact, Mrs. Pleasants built that house and owned it, and never was Tom Bell's servant or the servant of anyone else while she lived in San Francisco. She was his personal friend and business advisor, and for years was supposed to exercise some uncanny power over him.

"Mrs. Pleasants was a wonderful woman, with a dominating mind, and bent everyone about her to her will. She was born a slave in Georgia, and worked as a cotton picker on a plantation. One day a planter named Price stopped to ask the way, as he was riding past on horseback. Her ready reply and bright mentality so attracted his attention that he told her owner that she was too smart to be a slave and purchased her freedom for $600. He sent her to Boston to be educated, but the family to whose keeping she was entrusted failed to keep faith and merely made her a drudge.

"She came to San Francisco in 1849, with $50,000 in gold from the sale of Cuban bonds from her first husband's estate. His name was Alexander Smith. His home in Boston was a resort for such men as William Lloyd Garrison, Wendell Phillips and the coterie of men who advocated the abolition of slavery. On his deathbed Smith made his wife promise to use his legacy in the liberation of slaves. When she came to San Francisco, California, she loaned out money at 10 per cent per month and accumulated a fortune.

"She had a stormy life. In 1858 she carried out her husband's wishes by meeting John Brown in Chatham, Canada, and giving him $30,000 to start the Harper's Ferry fight. He bought 15,000 condemned government rifles with the money, at $2 apiece. After Brown's capture letters from her, signed 'M E P.,' were found upon his person. The detectives, however, read her rough signature as 'W. E. P.,' and thus she evaded them and reached California on a ship that came around Cape Horn. She escaped detection by giving her ticket to a white woman, and sailed in the steerage under an assumed name.

"When the famous divorce case of Sharon v. Sharon went to trial in this city, Mrs. Pleasants backed the plaintiff to the extent of $65,000. It was claimed that Tom Bell advanced the money to get even with Sharon, but such was not the case. She had a way of taking sides with the under-dog, and every cent advanced was her own.

"Mrs. Pleasants was locked out of the 'House of Mystery' after the death of Bell. At the time he fell over the bannisters in the night and was killed, it was claimed that 'Mammy Pleasants' threw him over to get several hundred thousand dollars that he left her in his will. When the will was probated, however, it transpired that she was not even mentioned. The motive, therefore, fell to the ground and the case was dropped. Those who knew her intimately declared that her name was omitted from the will at her own request. She argued that if she were remembered in the will, some people might think the legacy was hush money, given her by Bell to preserve silence over some dark spot in his life.

Thomas Bell and she were rare, warm personal friends, and that was all there was in the story. She was on friendly terms in the old days with most of the men in San Francisco worth knowing—W. C. Ralston, D. Q. Mills, Newton Booth, Lloyd Tevis, David Terry and a score of other prominent men.

"It is claimed that she went into a trance and saw the future of the oil land wealth, and induced Bell to buy. This story is all moonshine, as he was a practical and matter-of-fact man and despised everything connected with the occult. Mrs. Pleasants probably saw in this land a good place to raise beans, such as she used to cook in Boston, and was governed in her choice solely by this idea.

"What irony there is in fate! After Bell's death she was locked out of the 'House of Mystery' and died in poverty in a little place on Baker street, where friends had given her an asylum. So ended the old colored woman who for years was a power in San Francisco's affairs and who so largely aided in precipitating the crisis that started the Civil War by furnishing John Brown with the funds to start his historical raid at Harper's Ferry.

"Before her death she made a transfer of all her property to Sam Davis, of Carson City, on the ground that he was the only person who came to her assistance when she was thrown into insolvency and supposed to be in want. She also furnished him the data with which to found the story of her life."

CHAPTER X

FIRST COLORED SETTLERS OF CALIFORNIA

Historians, in their research work for material to write a true history of California, have found it necessary to quote often from documents found in the Archives of Mexico and Spain. One of the best and most scientific works published by the University of California, covering years of research work by the assistant Professor of history, Mr. Charles Edward Chapman, is a book called "Spanish California." The writer of the "Negro Trail-Blazers of California" has also found it necessary to consult documents found in the Archives of Spain and Mexico.

There are a great many names given in the pioneer list of the Bancroft histories which have been quoted from the Archives of Spain. Some of these are those of families which have been registered as a mixture of the Spanish and Negro races. The writer spent fully a year in research work in an effort to find the reason for this register. In consulting with Professor Chapman, of the University of California, as to the advisability of quoting the references in the Bancroft histories, Professor Chapman stated that he had seen the originals in the Archives of Spain while making research for his book, and that they were absolutely accurately quoted. In further study and research work, especially after attending a course of lectures by the greatest living historian, Hon. Henry Morse Stephens, who gave an interesting course of lectures on Spanish California at the University of California, the writer was convinced of the advisability and justice of giving these names. This belief was further strengthened after reading from the reliable historian, Sir Arthur Helps, who, in his "Slavery in the Spanish Colonies," gives the slave laws governing the colonies. A portion of these slave laws is quoted in this chapter and also the chapter on "Slavery" in this book. The quotation is as follows:

"In a lengthy quotation from the Royal Historiographer, Herrera, who speaks of the king having informed the Admiral Don Diego Columbus, in 1510, that they should send fifty Negroes to work in the mines of Hispaniola * * * Zuajo, the judge of residence and the legal colleague of Las Casas, wrote to the same effect. He, however, suggested that the Negroes should be placed in settlements and married." Sir Arthur Helps further states, in quoting Las Casas's colonization scheme and the laws affecting free Negroes and Negresses: "Free Negresses, unless married to Spaniards, should not wear gold ornaments, pearls and silk. Provision was made that in the sale of children of Spaniards and Negresses, their parents should have the right of pre-emption."

There was another clause in the king's colonization scheme that fully explains why these names were recorded in the Archives of Spain. That clause said: "The king was to give them lands of his own lands; furnish them with plowshares, spades and provide medicine for them; lastly, whatever rights and property accumulated from their holdings were to be hereditary." The last quotation is very clear and should be sufficient for the most prejudiced mind to fully understand the reason many Negro families had Spanish names.

The writers of California history have also found that the early population of California was composed of persons who migrated from Mexico and settled in California. It has also been found that many were of the direct descendants of pioneer families who had gone to Mexico under the colonization scheme of the king, as just quoted; hence, under the Spanish slave laws, they were registered in the Archives of Spain, and also their children, that they might enjoy the hereditary benefits of the holdings and accumulations of their foreparents. As the king permitted the Spaniards to marry the Negresses, their children were protected by the slave laws of that period. This was sufficient reason for Mr. Bancroft, as a true historian, to include their names as he found them in the Archives of Spain. It is the only reason that the author has thought it worth while also to include them in the beginning of the pioneer list of this book. In doing so she also suffers a pang of regret that the United States government did not have such slave laws in the days when slavery was permitted in the United States. Had there been such there would not today be so many people with more white than Negro blood—people who all their lives must endure the stigma of having come from an unlegalized union between the white slave-master and his Negro slave-woman.

Mr. Bancroft, realizing that the people of today are prejudiced against the Negro race or anyone with Negro blood, had the following to say in volume 1, page 4, of his "History of the Native Races of the Pacific Coast States": "Anatomically there is no difference between the Negro and European. The color of his skin, the texture of the hair, the convolutions of the brain, and all other peculiarities, may be attributed to heat, moisture and food. Man, though capable of subduing the world to himself, and of making his home under climates and circumstances the most diverse, is none the less a child of nature, acted upon and molded by these conditions which he attempts to govern; climate, periodicities of nature, material surroundings, habits of thought and modes of life, acting through a long series of ages, exercise a powerful influence upon human physical organization, and yet man is perfectly created for any sphere in which he may dwell, and is governed in his conditions by choice, rather than by coercion; articulate laying, which forms the great line of demarcation between the human and brute creation, may be traced in its leading characteristics to one common source. The differences between races of men are not specific differences. The greater part of the flora and fauna of America, those of the circum-polar region excepted, are essentially dissimilar to those of the old world. While man in the new world, though bearing traces of high antiquity, is specifically identified with all the races of the earth. It is well known that the hybrids of plants and animals do not possess the power of reproducing; while in the intermixture of races of man no such sterility of progenity can be found; therefore, as there are no human hybrids, there are no separate human races or species, but all are of one family. Besides being consistent with sound reasoning this theory can bring to its support the testimony of the sacred writings, and an internal evidence of a Creator divine and spiritual, which is sanctioned by tradition and confirmed by most philosophic minds. Man, unlike animals, is the direct offspring of the Creator, and as such he alone continues to derive his inheritance from divine source." This is indeed a fine tribute to pay to the Negro race and Negro people, not only of the Pacific Coast but of the entire world.

Sir Harry Johnston, in his "Negro in the New World," said: "But although the Negro still possesses pithecoid characteristics long since lost by the Caucasian and Mongolian; although he comes of a stock which has stagnated in the African and Asiatic tropics uncounted, unprogressive milleniums, he has retained dormant the free attributes of sapient humanity. He has remarkably ungaugeable capabilities."

Both of these masterful quotations are from the best known white writers of history. The following is one from the pen of the greatest Negro historian, George W. Williams, who says in his "History of the Negro": "And yet, through all his interminable woes and wrongs, the Negro on the West Coast of Africa, in Liberia and the Sierra Leona as well as in the southern part of the United States, shows that centuries of savagehood and slavery have not drained him of all the elements of his manhood. History furnishes us abundant and specific evidence of his capacity to civilize and Christianize." This last quotation, coming from a great Negro writer, shows that great minds are about the same in their opinion in regard to the Negro race.

The writer, having given positive proof that the California historians have all traced the beginning of the settlers in and of California to persons who had migrated from Mexico and Spain, the following will give an account of the first Negroes on this coast, beginning with the mention of the Negroes in the North Mexican States.

The following quotation is from Bancroft, who, in his "History of the North Mexican States," says, in speaking of the struggles of the Jesuits in establishing the Mission of Loretto: "Having to wait for a craft promised by Sieppe, Salvatierra made a visit to the scene of his former labors in the mountains, and later a revolt in Tarahmara Alta required his presence, so that he was delayed till the middle of August. Back at the Yaqui he found the 'Lancha' and 'Galliot,' and was greeted by the commander with harrowing tales of perils escaped by 'Our Lady's' aid on the way from Acapulco. The vessel was kept in waiting for nearly two months longer, and, after all, was then greatly disappointed, chiefly because Father Kino was prevented by Indian troubles from joining the party, as he had intended, and also because, for the same reason, only a small quantity of persons could be obtained. Francis Maria Piccolo had been appointed in Kino's place, but was not waited for. With a military escort of six men, a motley army with which Cortez himself might have hesitated to undertake a conquest, Father Juan resolved to embark without further delay, a step characteristic of the man."

In a footnote of the chapter quoted, the names of the military escort are given and also the Spanish references. It reads as follows: "The force was composed of Barteloma de Robles Figuro, a Creole of Guadalajara; Juan, a Peruvian Mulatto; also three Indians from Sinaloa, Sonora. Jalisco Romero commanded the vessel, and there were six sailors on the 'Lancha.' "

Bancroft further states (vol. 5, p. 572): ''There is little to be said of the Jesuit Mission in the last years; their expulsion from the Provinces, and American statistics, from the Bishop's visita, the descriptive list and the Jesuit catalogue, corresponding to those already given from Pimeria Alta and appended in a little note in which I include the Province of Sinaola proper and Ostimuri, and to which I add Tamarep's statistics of the southern coast provinces of Culican to Rosario. From the items thus represented we learn that in the territory corresponding to modern Sinaloa and Sonora, during the last years of the Jesuits' era, there was a population of **gente de razon** of Spanish, Negro and mixed blood, amounting to 30,000 souls.''

After the return of Portola from the trip through Northern California, in search of the Bay of Monterey, shortly after he reached San Diego, the supply ship ''San Antonio'' hove in sight, thereby saving California from being deserted by the expedition. The entire party afterward set out again to try to locate the Bay of Monterey. They divided; part went by a land route, and the remaining members sailed on the ''San Antonio.'' When the ship finally cast anchor in the Santa Barbara Channel she had many sick from scurvy; some were dying. She left part of her crew, and Father Junipero Serra sailed with them to Monterey. After being convinced that the bay was Monterey, and establishing a Mission, the reader is told in Palou's Noticias that ''The President Father celebrated the feast of 'Corpus Christi' with a community of twelve friars.'' The historian, Bancroft, makes mention of the Negro when he says (vol. I, p. 175): ''The 'San Antonio' anchored at Monterey, May 21, 1771. On board with the President Father, Junipero Serra, were twenty-three friars, who, after the founding of the Mission San Carlos, celebrated the feast of 'Corpus Christi.' The first burial was on the day of the founding, June 3, when Alezo Nuno, one of the San Antonio's crew, was buried at the foot of the cross.'' In Palou's Noticias (vol. I, p. 401): ''The first interment in the cemetery was that of Ignacio Ramirez, a Mulatto slave from the 'San Antonio,' who had money to purchase his freedom.''

The reader will readily recall that Palou was the lifelong friend of Father Junipero Serra, having come with him from Spain to Mexico and hence to California. He was associated with him during all his work on this coast in establishing missions and Christianizing and civilizing the Indians. There can be no doubt whatever of the truthfulness of a statement coming from Palou, who is considered an eminent authority concerning the struggles and work of the Franciscans on this coast, especially in California. According to this writer, the first Christian burial in California, according to the rites of the Holy Catholic Church, were the remains of a Negro slave, who had money to pay for his freedom. It is indeed a strange coincidence that the last burial in this same cemetery was of the bones of Friar Junipero Serra, which, after laying for a hundred years or more in the burial ground connected with the Mission of San Carlos, near Monterey, were removed, in 1913, under the auspices of the Young Men's Institute, to the burial ground of the Mission Carmel, which is located at Carmel-by-the-Sea, and was the first ground consecrated for a burial place in all of California.

The historian, H. H. Bancroft, in speaking of the founding of Los Angeles, said: ''The governor, Neve, issued his instructions for the founding of the Pueblo of La Reina de Los Angeles from San Gabriel on the 26th day of August. While agreeing with or literally copying the clause of the regulation which I have translated in the preceding note this document contained many additional particulars respecting the survey and distribution of lots. Of subsequent proceedings, for a time, we only know that the pueblo was founded September 4, 1781, with twelve settlers and their families, forty-six persons in all, whose blood was a strange mixture of Indian and Negro, with here and there a trace of Spanish.'' The names of the settlers, as given, the writer will quote when either the wife or husband is registered as a Mulatto or Mulattress.

''Joseph Moreno, Mulatto, 22 years old, wife a Mulattress, five children; Manuel Cameron, Mulatto, 30 years old, wife Mulattress; Antonio Mesa, Negro, 38 years old, wife, Mulattress, six children; Jose Antonio Navarro, Mestizo, 42 years old, wife, Mulattress, three children; Basil Rosas, Indian, 68 years old, wife, Mulattress, six children.''

Bancroft also mentions that: ''From a later padron of 1785 (Prov. St. Pap-Ms. xxii-29), it appears that Navarro was a tailor.'' The following named colored settlers appeared in the pioneer list of vols. 2-4 and 6 of Bancroft's ''History of California.'' They are registered as coming to California after 1790: ''Bob, or Cristobal, 1816, the pioneer Negro, left by Captain Smith of the 'Albatross'; Norris, 1818, Negro of Bouchard's force, captured and became a cook at San Juan Capistrano (vol. 4, p. 755; vol. 2, p. 230-248-393); Anderson Norris, 1843, Negro deserter from the Cyan, killed by the Californians (vol. 4, p. 400-565); Hood Frisbe, 1848, Negro steward on the Isaac, Mokelumn Hill, 1852 (vol. 3, p. 787); Frances LaMott, 1845, Negro deserter from Bouchard's force or expedition, remained in California (vol. 2, p. 237-293; vol. 4, p. 768); Francisco, Negro of Bouchard's force (vol. 2, p. 237-746; Fisar, 1825, Negro from Pennsylvania, who came to Santa Barbara on the steamer 'Santa Rosa' in 1829; at Los Angeles, a farmer, 35 years old, without religion, but of good conduct, mentioned by Coronel, for whom he worked in 1846-47, and perhaps by Foster in 1849. It is possible, however, that this Fisar and the following were the same Fisar in 1846 of the California Battalion, said to have been attacked by Indians near Los Angeles in 1847. Fremont court-martial, Fisar, 1847, member of the Californians (vol. 5, p. 576). Fisar, 1847, at Sutter's Fort, for the quicksilver mines, also (vol. 3, p. 739). Allen B. Light, 1835, Negro who deserted from the 'Pilgrim' or some other vessel and became an otter hunter (vol. 3, p. 413). He was known as Black Steward, his encounter with a grizzly bear in the Santa Barbara region being mentioned by Alfred Robinson and other adventurers. According to Nidever, he was one of Graham's men, 1836-8, and in 1839, being a naturalized resident of Santa Barbara, he was appointed by the government agent to prevent illegal otter hunting (vol. 4, 6, p. 91). At Los Angeles in 1841, and in 1846-8 at San Diego, still a hunter.''

In the history of Santa Clara County, by J. P. Monroe Fraser (p. 62), he says: ''The soldiers of the San Francisco district were divided into three cantonments, one at the Presidio, one at Santa Clara Mission, and one at the Mission of San Jose. We here append a list of soldiers connected with the Presidio in the year 1790, which has been copied from the Spanish Archives in San Francisco. Here will be found the names, position, nativity, color, race and age of the soldiers, as well as those of their wives, when married. Justa Altamarino, Mulatto, from Sonora, 45 years old; Maria Garcia, Mulatto, 18 years old. There was a half-cast race between the white Castilian and the native Indian, very few of the families retaining the pure blood of Old Castile. They were consequently of all shades of color, and developed, the women especially, into a handsome, comely race.'' The writer has quoted the names that were given as Mulattoes.

Father Engelhardt says in ''Missions and Missionaries of California'' (p. 151): ''It seems that when Friar Kino and Salvatierra arrived, the natives lived in precisely the same manner as when Cortez appeared on the coast 160 years before. Physically these Indians, as a rule, were tall and robust. Their color was dark chestnut, approaching black. The men had no beards, but their hair was straight and black. Their features were somewhat heavy; the forehead was low and narrow; the nose thick; the inner corners of the eyes were round, instead of pointed, and the teeth were white and regular.''

In Bancroft's ''Native Races'' (vol. 5, p. 328), he says: ''The Northern Californians around Klamath Lake and the Klamath, Trinity and Rogue Rivers are tall, muscular and well made, with complexions varying from black to light brown. About Redwood Creek, Humboldt Bay and Ell River they are squatty and fat in figure, rather stoutly-built, with large heads, coarse, black hair and repulsive countenances, and are of much darker color. * * * At Crescent City Mr. Powers saw some broad-faced squaws of almost African blackness.''

Bancroft, in giving native characteristics of the people in the Northern Mexican States and Texas, says: ''The intermixture of races in Colonial Days was much slower in the North, owing to the inferior culture of the Indians and the later entry of settlers. For a long time after the independence Creole families sought to resist the inevitable but rapid influx of settlers, and the allurement of mineral wealth tended to overcome hesitancy, partly by bridging the chasm. Nevertheless, the Spanish element remained strong and the mixture has been little varied by the admission of Negro blood.''

The following is quoted from a Historical Sketch of Los Angeles, which was published by the Centennial Committee, J. J. Warner, Benjamin Hayes and J. P. Widney, in 1876: ''Peter Biggs was the first barber. As a slave he was sold to an officer at Fort Leavenworth. At the close of the war, left on California territory, his freedom was necessarily recognized. He lived here many years thereafter. In the spring of 1850 probably three or four colored persons were in the city. In 1875 they numbered 175 souls, many of whom hold good city property, acquired by industry. They are farmers, mechanics or of some one or other useful occupation and remarkable for good habits. They count some seventy-five voters. Robert Owen, familiarly by Americans called Uncle Bob, came from Texas in December, 1853, with Aunt Winnie, his wife, two daughters and a son, Charles Owen. They survive him. He was an honorable, shrewd man of business, energetic and honorable in his dealings, made money by government contracts and general trade. He died well esteemed by white and colored, August 18, 1865, aged 59 years.

''Of the Society of Mexican Veterans are five colored men: George Smith, George Diggs, Lewis G. Green, Paul Rushmore and Peter Byers. The last named was born in Henrico County, Virginia, in 1810, and served with Col. Jack Hayes, Gen. Z. Taylor and Capt. John Long. He was at the Battle of Monterey. Rushmore was born in 1829 in Georgia, and served on Taylor's line. He drove through the team of Col. John Ward and James Douglass from Chihuahua to Los Angeles. Smith and Diggs (the first born in New York, the second in the District of Columbia), both served on the ship 'Columbus,' under Commodore Biddle and Captain Selfridge. Green, born in North Carolina in 1827, was a seaman on the 'Portsmouth,' Capt. John B. Montgomery, and in the navy nine years and eight months on the ships 'Erie,' 'Cyane,' 'Constitution,' 'Pennsylvania' and 'Vermont.' ''

The following list of the names of Negro pioneers, many of whom have members of their families still living in California, has been copied from papers published by colored people during pioneer days in San Francisco. The issues quoted date from 1857 to 1875. Other names have been added through interviewing old pioneer persons in different parts of the State, and the *Western Outlook,* published at this writing, in San Francisco. The list will begin with those coming in 1849, and is as follows:

''George Washington Dennis, Mifflin Gibbs, Daniel Seals, Dixie Beard, Charles Gibson, Edward Harper, Mrs. Ellen Tooms, Charles Woods, George Toogood, John Peters, Rev. Stokes, Henry Williams, Abraham Cox, John Anderson, William Stacey, James Marshall, Abraham Lewis, Thomas Detter, Charlotte Detter, Albert Brevitt (gentleman's nurse), Miss Mary Coleman, William Moses, William Davis, J. H. Townsend (editor of the Mirror of the Times), James Wiseman, Moses Gibbs, Joseph Usher, George Haigler, Ezekiel Cooper, Mrs. Angeline Pickett, Sam Waters, Alvin Coffey, George Lee, Henry Collins, Samuel Shelton, '46; J. J. Moore, Hank Jones, Adolphus Goodman, James Moody, Harriett Washington, James E. Whiting, David Johnson, Sarah Mildred Freeman, Mr. McDowell, Rhoda Adams, Mary Ann Campbell, Mrs. Virginia Simmons, Mary and Ann Groves, Henry Marryat, Mrs. Jane Dove, J. M. Flowers, Ellen Seith, Aunt Lucy Evans, Rev. Adam Smith, Mr. and Mrs. Alex Taylor, William Pallier and wife, Mrs. Priscilla Moore, George Jamison, William F. Harris, Mrs. M. Godfrey, Daniel Carmack, Lige Hare.''

''Pioneers of Sacramento, California: B. A. Johnson, Aaron L. Jackson, A. S. Hopkins, Nathaniel Christopher, '49; Ella Segui, George Segui, '50; Albert Grubbs, '49; J. B. Handy, H. Yantes, George Booth, '52; Elige Booth, '52; Edward Booth, '48; Miss Booth, '52; H. Cady, Jessie Slaughter, Arthur Christopher, Mrs. Penny, '49; Mrs. Coger, Mrs. Russell, S. P. Hyer, '49; Mrs. Brice, '49; Reuben Johnson, '49; Mary Jane Bellis, '49; Mrs. Barbara N. Christopher, '49, and many others which space will not permit giving.''

''Pioneers of Marysville: James Churchill, '49; Samuel Brown, '49; Texana Breeden, '49; James Monroe Breeden, '48; Bill Huff, '49; Nimrod Jones, Bill Vaughn, Robert Chandler, Sarah Thompson (first colored woman in San Jose. Her husband, Mr. Thompson, was the body-servant to Gen. Wade Hampton. She lived for forty years in Grass Valley and later in Marysville, and at this writing is a resident of Pacific Grove, California). Joseph Edward Hatton, '49, from Norfolk, Va.; Hester Sewall Hatton, via ox team, '57; Major Breeden, '49; Richard Breeden, '52; John Gains, Sandy Clark, Bob Mitchell, Mrs. Mary Churchill, '49; Mrs. McGowan, '49; Rev. Randolph, '49; Mrs. Ellen Clark, '56, via ox team from Polk County, Missouri. There were sixty souls in the party and 2000 head of cattle. The party located at Honey Lake Valley, hence to Santa Rosa, hence to Petaluma, where Mrs. Clark became the wife of Mr. Piper. The remaining members of the family that came across the plains were her mother, Abigail Clark, and uncle, Bacchus Clark, who came in '58; Henderson Clark, the father, and one daughter, Matilda Clark, and a Mrs. J. N. Williams, came in 1856. They all finally located in Marysville, after having come to California through the influence of one John Loney, who had come in '49. Mr. Grant Smith, '47; Rev. J. H. Hubbard, J. B. Johnson, W. W. Moulton, Mrs. Carpenter Williams, '49; William H. Baily, cousin of Hon. Fred Douglass, '49.

Grass Valley—Joseph Thomas, Jordan Ousley, Joseph Baltimore, J. Jones, Isaac Bulmer, George Jenkins, James Miller, William Smith, Jacob Saunders, Robert Norton, John Thomas, John Hicks, Isaac Sanks, Jacob Harris, Green Ousley, John Hicks, John Allen, Abner Kinnie, George Seville, Henry White, Ed. Miller, Evans Walker. George H. Clay, Robert Allen, Mrs. Segee, William Kinkage, T. Detter, Rev. Peter Green, Rev. William Hillary, Catherine Baily, John Astor, Isaac Pickett, Dennis

Carter, S. E. Cuney, J. C. Mortimer, Peter Powers, '51; Abraham Freeman, '49; Albert Holland, '49.

"Beaver Valley: Mrs. Sara Branna, Frances Brown. Rough and Ready: Robert Sharp, Martin Mawy, Jennie Mitchell, Henry Smith. North San Joaquin: Samuel Dudley, Archibald Fisher, Mr. McLeMar. Mud Springs: John Buckner. Woodland: James Scott, S. S. Jones, Mrs. Reno. Fiddletown: William Smith. Sutter's Creek: Stephen Truax, Mrs. Anthony, Mrs. M. Tenny, C. G. Hawkins, Wm. Bird, J. W. Whitfield, Dr. H. H. Holland. Cash Creek: Basil Campbell. Folsom: Henry Gibson, Wm. Ford, Wm. Serrington. Mariposa: James Duff, John Peters, L. A. Monroe (stage driver). Suisun City: T. Cooper, W. E. Town. Placerville: Jack Perkins, '49; J. Johns. Gold Hill: James Moore, porter of the bank. Sonora: Mr. Jackson. Truckee: Mrs. Ann Wielrich, died, leaving twenty-five thousand dollars in the bank. Her only heir was found one year afterward in Farmersville, Va. Downieville: Mr. Callis and Mrs. Callis, '49; William Moore, Mrs. Campbell, Mrs. Scottall, '49. Strawberry Valley, Eldorado County: Mr. Roderick McGains and Miss May Wood. Colusa: George Suggard, Giles Gresdan, Joshua Jones, Ben Franklin, A. Pincard, Chas. Lansing, Thomas Banks, Thos. S. Scott, I. M. Wiley, Henry Luell, James Oliver. Princeton, Colusa County: Ed Harris, Joshua Samuel, Z. Copeland, M. T. Tidball. Chico, Butte County: Samuel DeHart, Jas. Low, Samuel Childress, Josiah Jackson, Peter Jackson, '57, from Brooklyn, N. Y.; Samuel Jackson, Edwin Holmes, Benj. Maulbine, Lewis Roberts, C. M. Day, Mrs. Williams, '49; Peter Pogue, Chas. McGowan, Moses Talchan, Richard Lewis, A. J. Anderson, fruit buyer, Roseburg Packing Co.

"Stockton: Moses Rodgers, '49; William Robinson, '48; Emanuel Quivers, '49; S. B. Serrington, Rev. E. L. Tappan, I. B. Barton, Anderson Robinson, W. R. Brown, Isaac Rodgers, George Johnson, Mrs. Catherine Callis, Joseph McKinney, Henry Hall, '49; James Fountain, '49; Wm. O. Saunders, '49; Elizabeth Miller, John Burrows, '55; Miss Amy Burrows, Rev. Jessie Hamilton, Capt. Pierson, E. W. Vesy, Samuel Elliott, Chas. Gray, Jno. Blackstone, S. M. Jackson, Henry Miles, '53; Mrs. Elizabeth Scott, '59; Elizabeth Barnett, Mrs. Polly A. Barton, '49; Mr. Barton, 49; Mrs. Forney, '49; Alfred Collins, Wm. Hutchison, '53; Susie Hutchinson, '49; Wm. Robertson, '49; Barbara Potts, '49.

"Petaluma: Mrs. Barnes, '49; Aunt Peggie Barnes, '49; Miss Wilson, Edward Chandler, '49; Mrs. Mary E. Gross, '54; Elizabeth Miller, '53; Bell Bowles, Isaac Mull, '52. Oroville: Mrs. Cannon. Coloma: Rufus M. Burgess. Red Bluff: Mrs. Sarah Parker, P. A. Logan, Wm. Robinson, Charles Christopher, Charles A. Delvicchio. San Jose: Alfred White, H. E. Speight, Wm. Whiting, Mrs. Harriett Smith, James Williams, '49 (first colored person to settle in Santa Clara County); Mrs. Ella Hawkins, Jacob Overton, Sarah Massey Overton. Santa Cruz: R. C. Frances, James Smallwood, Albert and Amanda Logan, George A. Chester. Salinas City: Wm. Miller, Thos. Cecil, Geo. Gray, Robert Johnson. Watsonville: Daniel Rodgers, '49; R. Campbell, Mrs. Riley, John Derrick, Emeline Smith. Santa Barbara, Santa Cruz Islands: Sarah Lewis. Vallejo: John Grider, George Van Blake, Dr. Rodgers, Geo. Courtney. Visalia: Wiley Hinds. Redlands: Isaac Beal, '49, miner, owns orange grove; Mr. and Mrs. Whiteside, Henry Beal, Mr. Mendenhall, Mrs. Appleby, Horace H. Harold. San Bernardino: Walter and Byron Rowen, Mrs. Lizzie Fake-Rowen, Mr. Ingraham, Mason Johnson. San Diego: Dr. Burney, John Moore, '49. El Cajon Valley: Shephard Waters, '50; Henry Hunter, Albert Robinson, Isaac Jackson, '50, Charles Frederick Easton, coming to California in 1850 by the way of Cape Horn from New York to San Francisco, opened a barber shop with Jerry Bowers, a '49er.''

CHAPTER XI

Negro Miners of 1849, and Home for Aged and Infirm Colored People at Beulah, Cal. Negro Miners

A history of the Negro people of California would be incomplete without mention of the mining men who came in 1849. The writer has the pleasure of recording the name of the first colored miner in California, in the person of Waller Jackson, who came (via the Horn) from Boston, and located at Downieville, California.

There were at one time several hundred Negro miners working claims on Mormon and Mokelumn Hill, at Placerville, Grass Valley and elsewhere in the California mountains. The writer has failed to find a single instance where there was any rioting among the Negro miners, notwithstanding there were so many working one claim that they called it Negro Bar.

Nearly all the mining in the early days in California was placer mining. It will perhaps be better understood by calling it surface mining. The men used a pan, a pick and a rocker, or sieve. They picked only surface dirt, and when they found "pay dirt" they threw it into the rocker, which was made like a box with holes in the bottom, covered with a piece of netting or sieve-like wire, if handy. They turned, or rather poured, water on this, and the dirt and gravel would run out while the gold would remain in the rocker. This they placed in a pan, which caught the gold-dust while being washed. Later on hydraulic mining was employed until the United States government stopped the practice, since it was clogging the rivers. There has recently been organized a company which is dredging over the waste from this kind of early-day mining in California on the Yuba River, in the Sacramento Valley.

Tuthill's "History of California" (p. 67), in speaking on mining, says: "Almost everybody bought stocks. Nothing but war news could check the perpetual talk of 'feet,' 'out-croppings' and 'indications of sulphurets and ores.' No profession or class, age or sex was exempt from the epidemic. Shrewd merchants, careful bankers invested the property of their legitimate businesses, sometimes infringing upon their invested capital. Sharp lawyers sold their homesteads for shares; clerks anticipated their salaries; laborers salted away their wages and washerwomen their earnings in promising mines."

The colored miner rarely took a chance in buying mining stock. He had more sacred duties to perform with his money. He either used it to pay for the freedom or liberty of himself, his family or other loved ones in faraway "Dixie-Land." If not that, then he contributed largely from his diggings to assisting the Executive Committee of the Colored Convention in their struggles to secure legislative enactments in the interest of the Negro race in California.

The Negro miners came to California with the one thought of having better days. The allurement of gold was for the white men. The privilege of working in the mines that they might earn their freedom was to the colored men more precious than gold. There is no record of their rioting after they had purchased their freedom, notwithstanding the Negro miners were not given the protection of the California laws, in that they could not legally own claims. The writer has been told by pioneer Negro miners that the white miners had laws of their own and were often fair and kind to Negro miners.

Hittell's "California," in speaking of the history of Tuolumne County, says: "A vein was discovered by a Negro known as Dick, but the richness was so great it proved the ruin of its discoverer. Dick first sold out several shares, and then went to work on what remained and the outcome was that in a comparatively short time, carrying about one hundred thousand dollars, he left the place for Sacramento, with the intention of having a good time. It did not require long at that place for one in his circumstances to lose all his money. Afterward he committed suicide." The writer has been told that the location of this rich vein was near "Tuttletown" in the mountains.

There was another mine discovered by Negro miners who were of a different caliber from the above-mentioned person. The discovery of this mine was in Brown's Valley. The men immediately organized a company of Negro miners who worked the claim. The names of the men were as follows: Gabriel Simms, Fritz James Vosburg, Abraham Freeman Holland, Edward Duplex, James Cousins and M. McGowan. They called their mine "The Sweet Vengeance Mine." Judging from the title, it would seem to indicate that they were bent on proving to the world that colored men were capable of conducting successfully a mining business, even in the pioneer days in California.

In after years there were still other mining companies organized by colored men. *The Pacific Appeal* of San Francisco, after listing a number of mines with Negro owners, says: "'Rare, Ripe Gold and Silver Mining Company,' located in Brown's Valley, Yuba County, an incorporated company; capital stock is represented by 1,200 shares and they are now offering three hundred shares for sale at $10 a share. The board of trustees, John H. Gassoway, president; E. P. Duplex, secretary and treasurer; G. W. Simms, J. H. Johnson. The offices of the company are located at Marysville, California." The officers of this mining company were all "Forty-niners," notwithstanding the company was not organized until 1868.

Moses Rodgers was a mining expert and was considered one of the best mining engineers in the State. He was also a metallurgist and owned a group of mines at Hornitus. Even to this day his family still owns a few mines in this locality.

Robert Anthony owned the first quartz mill in California. It was located at Horn-cut, between Yuba and Dry-cut. The following is a list of some of the Negro miners of 1849, in California, who in after years became identified with every interest of the race: "Waller Jackson, Moses Rodgers, mining expert and metallurgist; Emanuel Quivers, Henry Hall, Daniel Seals, Samuel Shelton, Rev. Randolph, Rev. Stokes, Isaac Dunlap, Robert Small, James Stanley, Macklin Ford, James Buchanan, Daniel Blue, John Wilson, Aaron Jackson, Thomas Dunlap, James Cole, Cooper Smith, Hampton Whittaker, James Penny, Carter Jackson, Simon Emory, Edward Booth, John Shipman, Dennis Carter, John Adams, John Rymus, Abraham Freeman Holland, Benjamin Young, Preston Alexander, Edward Mills, John Allen, Henry Dorsey, Green Ousley, Jordan Ousley, John Loney, William Price, William Hart, Alfred Collins, Alvin Coffey, Major Breedon, Ruben Johnson, Joseph Hatton, John Wesley, John Haley, John Peters, Nathaniel Nelson, Robert Anthony, Mifflin Gibbs, George Washington Dennis, George Seville, John Adams, Isaac Sanks, Isaac Mills, Peter Lombard, Jack Perkins, Jessie Hughes, Sandy Clark, Charles Breedon, Peter Powers, William Williams, William Burns, Edward Wysinger, Daniel Hart, William Price, Perkins Bettis, Isaac Caulwell, Franklin Howard, Isaac Jackson, Henry Miles, Sandy Clark, George Booth, Elige Booth, Charles Graffells, John T. Johns, Edgar Johnson, Cloyd Brown, John Haley, John Grider." These men mined at Murphy's Diggings, Diamond and Mud Springs, Grass Valley, Negro Bar, Mokelumn Hill and elsewhere in the mining districts throughout the State.

HOME FOR AGED AND INFIRM COLORED PEOPLE.

This is one of the creditable institutions conducted by and for colored people in Northern California. It is located at Beulah, a suburban town of Oakland. It was founded by Mrs. Emma Scott, September 16, 1892. The corner stone was laid August 22, 1897. Mrs. Stanford was the first president and Mrs. Harriett Davis the first matron. Mr. Alvin Coffey, the first inmate, gave money to help found the institution, a Mr. Montgomery giving the ground for a home and orphanage and a Mr. Pollard, the windmill.

The institution has an ideal location about a block from the Mills College street car line, on the brow of a low hill overlooking the Piedmont Hills, with a broad, sweeping view of the sky-line boulevard in the distance. When the home was first opened, the lady managers decided to charge $500 for life membership, but the steady advance in the price of food has made it most difficult for the home to sustain itself. The officers are untiring in their struggle to prevent this worthy institution from closing its doors. Too much credit cannot be given to the following named officers who have, at a great personal sacrifice, worked, through public solicitation, to keep the institution for the Negro race in Northern California: Mrs. Julia Shorey, president; Mrs. Grasses, financial secretary; Mrs. Withers, recording secretary; Mrs. Morey, treasuer. The board of directors are: Mesdames Tyler, Scott, Dugar, Stanford, Warren, Jackson, Mattie Cohn, Mary Humphry, Harriet Davis and Purnell.

A few of the inmates of this home are real California pioneers, and brief sketches of their lives follow. Mrs. Harriett Davis came to California in 1854 from Philadelphia by the way of the Isthmus of Panama. She was educated in a private school in that city, and told the writer many interesting things pertaining to the "Underground Railroad," and its activities. She was educated an Episcopalian, and, after coming to San Francisco, immediately identified herself with the colored church pastored by Rev. Peter Cassey. She was active in the choir and literary work of the parish.

Her first husband, William Smith, came to California in 1857. He was prominently identified with all activities of vital interest to the race. He gave freely of his time and money, especially in the fight for "The Right of Testimony" in the Courts of Justice in California. He was employed for a number of years as an officer in the custom house of San Francisco. Mrs. Davis, appointed as the first matron of the home, retained the position for several years. She has a wonderfully retentive memory and an amiable, sweet disposition which endeared her to all. The writer was very much benefited by her many visits to Mrs. Davis and especially by the conversation concerning the colored people in California who paid for their freedom after coming to the State.

The second matron in the home was a Mrs. Theresa M. Thompson who came to California in early pioneer days from Camden, N. J. Her father, Mr. William Brown, who came to California in 1849, was a sea-faring man. After coming to California he decided to leave the sea and followed the laundry business in Sacramento. Mrs. Thompson has been an inmate of the home for fourteen years.

Mr. George Seville was an inmate of the home two years before he was called to his reward. He came to San Francisco from Key West, Florida, in 1858. It was his intention to go to Victoria, British Columbia, but, changing his mind up reaching California, he went to Grass Valley where he engaged in mining. He was an entertaining gentleman and gave the writer many interesting accounts concerning colored miners of pioneer days. Many of the names he gave are recorded in the chapter on mining. Shortly after beginning his career as a placer miner, he married and the union was blessed by the birth of three children, namely, Isabell, Stella and James. He was a widower thirteen years before deciding to enter the home.

Two other interesting inmates are Mrs. Louise Tyler, born in Shasta County, California, during pioneer days, and Mrs. Flowers, who came from Niles, Michigan, when four years old, reaching the State in pioneer days.

Mrs. Lane came from Clay County, Mississippi, forty-eight years ago. Her mother, coming to California in 1852, sent back for her son and daughter. They lived for a number of years in Benicia, California.

Mrs. Edinburg, the third matron, who retained the position for a number of years, had a charming personality and was well suited for the position. She came to California in 1880 from Middleport, Ohio, and located first in Redlands where she left a community of warm friends to accept the position at the home.

The following persons have been inmates of the home: Mrs. Margaret A. Murray, Mrs. Allen Washington, Willim H. Davis, Mrs. Ellen Mason, Mrs. D. Washington, Mrs. Marie White, Mrs. Annie Johnson, B. W. Johnson, Fanny Foggs, Theresa Thompson, Jacob Williams, Annie Baker, Eva Reeder, Zora Flowers, Eliza Miller, Emilie Phelps, Mrs. Duvall, Mrs. Allen Fletcher, George Seville, Emily Thompson, Mrs. Stewart, Phillips Jenkins, Annie Purnell, Margaret Wilson, Mrs. E. Barnett and Mr. Abe Lee.

There is a home similar to this one located at Albia, California, which has been founded through the united efforts of the Colored Baptist Ministerial Association of Southern California.

CHAPTER XII

BIOGRAPHICAL SKETCHES OF DISTINGUISHED NEGRO PIONEERS

In early days of California, the United States Government sent its prize graduate soldiers from West Point to this coast; men who in after years became prominent figures, showing that California even at that early date developed the possibilities in men. Stockton, Folsom, Sherman and Larkin were all young men in those days and began their career in Monterey, California.

Some, satisfied with their appointment, remained. Others soon asked to be relieved and went back to the East, but they always expected to return and make California their home. Of these latter was Commodore Sloate who was relieved of his command on this coast. Commodore Stockton was appointed as Military Governor of California and it was under his rule that Consul Larkin appointed as Vice-Consul to Mexico Captain Leidsdorff, who became the first distinguished Negro under the United States rule.

William Alexander Leidsdorff was the most distinguished Negro of pioneer San Francisco and of the State of California. It may be a great surprise to a large number of people to know that in early San Francisco's history, the then Governor of the State of California was the guest of the city and the banquet given in honor of his visit, was given at the residence of a Negro. This Negro at the time owned and lived in the largest house in all San Francisco.

This Negro also owned the first steamship sailing the beautiful bay of San Francisco. He was a prominent business man, a member of the City Council, treasurer and a member of the school committee. Men thought it a distinguished honor to have the pleasure of meeting Captain Leidsdorff. H. H. Bancroft, in his History of California, said: "While he was Vice-Consul of Mexico Captain Leidsdorff's correspondence with Larkins was a source of valuable information." There are few men whose lives have been spoken of so much in early San Francisco as that of Captain Leidsdorff. Even in death he commanded the very highest respect of all, notwithstanding they all knew he had Negro blood in his veins, and the same is mentioned in different summaries of his life.

When the United States Navy sends vessels to sail through the Golden Gate in visiting San Francisco, the Negro race can proudly say that Don Gaspar de Portola, when looking down from the Berkeley Hills, may have discovered the San Francisco Bay and the Golden Gate; Balboa may have brought the first sailing ship through the Golden Gate, but the first steamer to pass through the Golden Gate was owned and mastered by a Negro. Bancroft in his history gives very clear and convincing proof that William Alexander Leidsdorff, a Negro, owned the first steamer to pass through the Golden Gate.

Mrs. Annie Peters, a pioneer of early California, who came to San Francisco with Rev. Flavel Scott Mines, told the writer that she came from the same island as did Mr. Leidsdorff, the Island of Santa Croix, Danish West Indies. She said that she knew his mother, who was a Negress. His father was a Danish sugar planter.

Jacob Wright Harlan, in his book "California from 1846 to 1888," speaking of Mr. Leidsdorff having sold him some shingles, closes by adding: "Mr. Leidsdorff was a native of the Danish Island of Santa Croix and I believe he had a dash of Negro blood in his veins." While he says, "I believe he had a dash of Negro blood in his veins," he also says many complimentary things of Mr. Leidsdorff.

In Bryant's "What I Saw in California," the author mentions that Captain Leidsdorff's residence was selected by the committee as the place in which to hold a banquet in honor of Governor Stockton. There are many instances in which the Negro has done credit to the race in early days, but none have reached the heights this man did. It is a source of great pleasure to note that, notwithstanding he was a Negro, the California historians have written of him as befits a man of his position and influence in the community.

The following is an account of his life as given by H. H. Bancroft (vol. 4, p. 711): "William Alexander Leidsdorff, a native of Danish West Indies, son of a Dane by a mulattress, who came to the United States as a boy and became a master of vessels sailing between New York and New Orleans, came to California as manager of the 'Julia Ann,' on which he made later trips to the Islands, down to 1845.

"He is prominent among a number of about sixty-seven classed as prominent residenters (p. 279, 566). Engaging in trade in San Francisco he got a lot, in 1843, at the corner of Clay and Kearney streets, and, in 1844 or '45, built a warehouse on the beach at California and Leidsdorff streets (669-78), in '46 building the city hotel on his first lot, and in '47 buying from Ridley the cottage at the corner of Montgomery and California streets where he passed the rest of his life. (Vol. 4, p. 678-680.) In '44 he obtained naturalization papers and a grant of the Rio Del Americano Rancho (vol. 4, p. 673), and from October, 1845, served as United States Vice-Consul by Larkin's appointment (vol. 4, p. 188, 557, 599, 665). His correspondence of these years, especially with Larkins, is a most valuable source of historical information. In 1846 he had a controversy with Forbes, Ridley and Hinkley, who were not intensely American enough to suit this Danish citizen of Mexico who was visiting New Helvetia and Monterey. In 1847 he had a California claim of $8,740 (vol. 5, p. 462), and launched the first steamer that ever sailed the San Francisco Bay (vol. 5, p. 577-8). He was not only one of the town's most prominent business men but a member of the City Council, treasurer and a member of the school committee, taking an active part in local politics (vol. 5, 455, 648, 652-6). He was educated, speaking several languages, active, enterprising and public-spirited, honorable for the most part in his transactions, but jealous, quick tempered, often quarrelsome and disagreeable. His estate, burdened heavily by debt at the time of his death, after the gold excitement became of immense value. The State laid claim to it but yielded after long litigation.

"Leidsdorff was buried at Mission Dolores with imposing ceremonies befitting his prominence and social virtues. Warm of heart, clear of head, sociable, with a hospitality liberal to a fault, his hand ever open to the poor and unfortunate, active and enterprising in business and with a character of high integrity, his name stands as among the purest and best of that sparkling little community to which his death proved a serious loss.

"It is necessary for the living to take charge of the effects of the dead, but it smells strongly of the cormorant, the avidity with which men seek to administer an estate for the profits to be derived from it. We have many notable examples of this kind in the history of California, in which men of prominence have participated, sometimes in the name of friendship, but usually actuated by avarice. The body of William A. Leidsdorff was scarcely cold before Joseph L. Folsom obtained from Governor Mason an order to take charge of the estate in connection with Chas. Meyers. The indecent haste of Folsom was checked by the appointment of William D. M. Howard as administrator. The estate was administered by him with the assistance of C. V. Gillespie, and was for years the subject of complicated litigation. But the title of Captain Folsom, who had found the mother and other heirs of Leidsdorff at Saint Croix Island and had bought their interest, was finally adjudged to be valid."

The historian further says in the footnotes of vol. 6: "Vice-Consul Leidsdorff died in 1848, leaving property then regarded as inadequate to pay his liabilities of over $40,000, but a year later its value had so advanced as to give to the heirs an amount larger than the debts, while agents managed to make fortunes by administering the estate.

"The first steamer in San Francisco Bay. In the maritime annals of this period the appearance of the first steamer in California's waters merits a passing notice. The steamer had no name but has since been called the 'Sitka.' Her dimensions were: length, 37 feet; breadth of bow, 9 feet; depth of hold, 3½ feet; drawing 18 inches of water and having side wheels moved by a miniature engine. She was built by an American at Sitka as a pleasure boat for the officers of the Russian Fur Company and was purchased by Leidsdorff, being brought down to San Francisco in October, 1847. She made a trial trip on November 15 and returned later to Santa Clara and then to Sonoma. Finally, on the 28th of November, she started on the great voyage of her career to Sacramento, carrying ten or a dozen souls, including the owner, Geo. McKinstry and L. W. Hastings as far as Monterey. She returned to Yerba Buena and was wrecked at her anchorage in a gale, but was saved, hauled inland by oxen and transformed into a launch or schooner.

"As the 'Rain-bow' she ran on the Sacramento river after the discovery of gold. A notice of the arrival from Sitka is found in the San Francisco, California, Star, October 23, 1847, also a notice of the steamer at Sonoma, November 25, when there was a celebration with toasts to the rival towns of Sonoma and San Francisco, California, December 1, 1847, S. F. Dictionary, 1852, p. 197; Hutchings Magazine, vol. 4, p. 4; Secramento Directory, 1871, p. 153; Sacramento newspaper, May 19, 1858; S. F. Bulletin, February 26, 1868, and many other newspaper articles, some of which say she was 60 feet long and 17 feet wide."

BIDDY MASON

The subject of this sketch was born in Hancock County, Georgia, and was the most remarkable pioneer of color coming to California. She came under the most trying circumstances as has been related in another part of this book under "Slaves Emancipated in California."

After the Courts of Los Angeles County granted Biddy Mason and her family their freedom, she took her family to the home of Robert Owens, in Los Angeles. Then she went in search of work which she readily secured at two dollars and fifty cents per day, as confinement nurse, Dr. Griffin having engaged her services. The securing of work meant to her the great boon of acquiring not only the money for the support of her dependent family, but also an opportunity of securing a home. With the first money she could save she purchased two lots, located from Spring street to Broadway, between Third and Fourth streets in Los Angeles. There was a ditch of water on the place and a willow fence running around the plat of ground which was considered quite out of town at that date, but which today is the most valuable piece of property in all of beautiful Los Angeles.

Biddy Mason had a splendid sense of the financial value of property and such great hopes for the future of Los Angeles that she continued to buy property and retain it until after the city began to boom, when she sold a forty-foot lot for twelve thousand dollars. She then gave her sons a forty-foot lot which they sold for forty-four thousand dollars.

The world never tires of speaking of the late Hetty Green and her great financial ability. But think of this slave woman coming to California in 1851 by ox-team which consisted of three hundred wagons, and, at the end of these wagons, Biddy Mason driving the cattle across the plains, notwithstanding she had her own three little girls, Ellen, Ann and Harriett, to care for en route!

Biddy Mason was a devoted mother. Her most remarkable trait of character was her ability to teach her children and grandchildren the value of money and property. So thorough were her teachings that her vast holdings have been retained by her children and grandchildren, who have never sold a piece of property unless they were positively sure that they were making great gains by so doing. The greater part of her purchases of property in early days they have retained, and these have grown in value at least two hundred or more per cent since their first purchase by Biddy Mason.

The name of Biddy Mason is reverenced in the City of Los Angeles where her kindness to the poor is fresh in the minds of the public. In an issue of the *Los Angeles Times*, under date of February 12, 1909, in a special feature article by the late Mrs. Kate Bradley-Stovall in regard to the Negro women of that city, among other things was said in regard to Biddy Mason: "Biddy Mason was well-known throughout Los Angeles County for her charitable work. She was a frequent visitor to the jail, speaking a word of cheer and leaving some token and a prayerful hope with every prisoner In the slums of the city she was known as 'Grandma Mason' and did much active service toward uplifting the worst element in Los Angeles. She paid taxes and all expenses on church property to hold it for her people. During the flood of the early eighties she gave an order to a little grocery store which was located on Fourth and Spring streets. By the terms of this order, all families made homeless by the flood were to be supplied with groceries while Biddy Mason cheerfully paid the bill.

"Her home at No. 331 South Spring street in later years became a refuge for stranded and needy settlers. As she grew more feeble it became necessary for her grandson to stand at the gate each morning and turn away the line which had formed awaiting her assistance." But the best part of Biddy Mason's work is seen in the charming family she reared which shows her careful training and counsel.

The Courts of Los Angeles County granted to her and her children their freedom January 19, 1854. There were only eight white families living in the town at the time. The doors of the home of Robert Owens were thrown open to Biddy Mason and her children. Mr. Owens was a livery-stable keeper. Two years after the Mason family came to Los Angeles, the oldest daughter, Ellen, married Mr. Robert Owen's son, Charles. She named her first son in honor of the grandfather, Robert C. Owens, and the second child, Henry L. Owens. It seems strange, but true, that Mr. Robert Owens, the father-in-law of Biddy Mason's daughter, Ellen, was the same type as the girl's mother in regard to acquiring and holding property, and he taught his son the value of both money and property and the greatest possible necessity of a good education.

Mrs. Ellen Mason-Owens, as a slave girl, had not been allowed the advantage of an education. After the birth of her second child, her husband decided that she must have an education. When his sons were old enough, he sent them and their mother to be educated in the public schools of the city of Oakland, California. After the sons had completed the course of study, he sent them to the public schools of Stockton to receive a business education under the then greatest colored educator on the coast, J. B. Sanderson. They boarded in the home of the teacher. After finishing under the instruction of J. B. Sanderson they returned to Los Angeles and, owing to the prejudice against colored persons attending the public schools, they were compelled to enter business college at night. This splendid foundation of a good education, especially the business education, has been an example to this day through the surviving son, Robert C. Owens, who is considered among the most level-headed capitalists, either white or colored, in all of Los Angeles.

Charles P. Owens and Ellen Mason were married October 16, 1856, in Los Angeles, California. He died September 12, 1882. Long years afterward his widow married Mr. Huddleston. She is one of the most charming ladies the writer has been privileged to interview, a perfect inspiration, she kindly furnished the facts in regard to the family history. Her son, Henry L. Owens, married Miss Louise Kruger, December 3, 1884, at Denver, Colorado. He has since passed beyond.

Mrs. Huddleston kindly allowed the writer to copy the following from the family Bible pertaining to the family records: "Biddy Mason was born August 15, 1818, in Hancock County, Georgia. Ellen, her daughter, was born October 15, 1838, in Hinds County, Missouri." The dates of the birth of Harriet and Ann were not given but the record of their deaths were as follows: "Died, Miss Ann Mason, August 1, 1857; Biddy Mason, January 15, 1891; Louis L. Owens, August 5th, 1893; Mrs. Harriet Mason-Washington, June 9, 1914; Charles Owens, September 12, 1882."

The senior Robert Owens came to Los Angeles in 1852 with his family, which consisted of his wife, Winnie Owens, two girls and one son; namely, Sara Jane, Martha and Charles. He bought lots on San Pedro street and opened a livery stable. When he died, his son, Charles, took charge of the business and opened a livery stable on Main street near First. At the death of Charles his sons, Robert C. and Henry L. Owens, took charge of the business, and following the death of Mrs. Biddy Mason, they opened a livery stable on Spring street between Third and Fourth streets, the property on Main street having become too valuable to hold for a livery stable.

During pioneer days Charles Owens purchased on Olive street between Sixth and Seventh twelve lots each sixty feet front by one hundred and sixty feet deep. The Owens estate still retains them at this writing. The following additional data pertaining to the Owens family history is quoted from a historical sketch published in 1876 by the Los Angeles Centennial Committee, J. J. Warner, Benjamin Hays and J. P. Widney, in which it says that "In the spring of 1850, probably three or four colored persons were in the city. In 1875, they numbered 175 souls, many of whom hold good city property acquired by industry. They are farmers, mechanics, or some other useful occupation, and remarkable for good habits. They count some seventy-five votes, . . . Robert Owens, familiarly by Americans called Uncle Bob, came from Texas in December, 1853, with Aunt Winnie, his wife, two daughters and son, Charles Owen. They survive him. He was a shrewd man of business, energetic and honorable in his dealings, made money by Government contracts and general trade. He died well esteemed by white and colored people, August 18, 1865, aged 59.''

A COLORED PIONEER.

"Mifflin Gibbs, of Little Rock, in town. From blacking boots to the Bench; Remarkable career of one of San Francisco's early Negro citizens.

"One of the guests now registered at the Grand Hotel is Judge Mifflin Wister Gibbs, of Little Rock, Ark. The Judge is a colored gentleman and one of California's pioneers of 1849. He arrived here on the 'Umatilla' last Wednesday from Victoria, B. C., in which town he laid the foundation of his fortune. The Judge has had a wide and useful as well as checkered career. From a bootblack stand in San Francisco he rose to the Judicial bench in the State of Arkansas. He is 72 years of age, but is as compactly built and free from ills as the most model athlete.

"The Judge was born of poor parents and at the tender age of eight years was thrown upon his own resources, his father having died at that time. When he reached the years of manhood he had not accumulated much of the world's goods, but his years brought him experiences and he had a pretty fair share of worldly knowledge. He was a porter, and blacked boots in front of the Union Hotel, where the old City Hall now stands. The facade of the old hall, in fact, still bears the name of the historic caravansary. Afterward he was partner in the boot and shoe firm of Peter Lester and Gibbs at 636 Clay street. The shop will be remembered by 'Forty-niners.'

MRS. BIDDY MASON (deceased)
Nurse and a Great Financier.

MRS. A. H. WALL
Treasurer California Federated Colored
Women's Clubs, and Founder of the
Colored Orphanage in Oakland.

MISS GLADYS REO HARRIS
Supervisor of Charities, Los Angeles
County.

MRS. LYDIA FLOOD-JACKSON
Originator Flood Toilet Creams.

MR. AND MRS. J. H. SHACKELFORD
Furniture Dealers.

"When the Frazier River excitement broke out, in 1858, young Gibbs, full of grit and ambition, determined to try his luck in the North. He went to Victoria and there established the first general merchandise house excepting that of the Hudson Bay Company. Being an enterprising and progressive young fellow, he became quite a factor in the infant city. He was elected Councilman from the James Bay district, the most aristocratic portion of the town. In 1867 he entered into a contract to build a railroad from Queen Charlotte coal mine to Skidgate harbor. He was made superintendent of the road when it was completed and he shipped to San Francisco the first cargo of coal mined on the Pacific Coast.

"Gibbs remained in British Columbia until 1869, when he went to Little Rock, Ark. While in Victoria he had studied law with an English barrister, and a year after he arrived at Little Rock, he was appointed by President Hayes, Registrar of the United States Lands for the Eastern district of Arkansas. He held this office for eight years, being reappointed by President Arthur. Under the last administration of Harrison, he was appointed Receiver of Public Moneys, at Little Rock.

"While in San Francisco, Judge Gibbs was always prominent in every movement which tended to the elevation of his race. He was one of the publishers of the 'Mirror of the Times,' the first paper devoted to the interests of the Negro on the Coast. He made a determined stand against the collection of poll tax from men of his race. He took the ground that his fellow colored men should not be compelled to pay the tax, as they were denied the right of suffrage and as their oath would not be accepted in court. His goods were seized and offered for sale to pay the tax, but not a man could be found who was mean enough to bid on the store. He was afterwards sent to Sacramento on the first committee which was appointed to petition for the 'Rights of American Citizenship for Negroes.'

"When the Judge was in Victoria this time he was treated with every mark of consideration. The Speaker of the House of Parliament escorted him to a seat and he was the recipient of many other marks of distinction at the hands of the leading citizens.

"During his stay in San Francisco, Judge Gibbs has been the guest on several occasions of Robert Brown, editor of the *Vindicator*. 'I knew Bob, as a boy,' said he last evening, 'and I remember well the time when his father and I bought a fifty-vara on the corner of Market and Stockton streets, which was then in the midst of sand hills. Truly the change in the city has been wonderful. . . .' " The above is quoted from the *San Francisco Chronicle*, February 2, 1895.

Judge Gibbs recently died at his home in Little Rock, Ark., having lived a useful life up to the last. He has written his autobiography and other writings. The time referred to in the above article when he left San Francisco was during the introduction of a bill in regard to Fugitive Slaves, which had for its object the coming to or residing in California of Free Negroes. There were many other prominently-connected colored men who also left the State about that time, going to British Columbia, but the charm of California was too great and they returned to the State deciding to fight it out. Their opportunity soon came through the attempt to return to slavery the Negro boy, Archy. The decision of this case forever settled the question of "Fugitive Slaves in California."

The following is quoted from "Who's Who of the Colored Race:" "Mifflin Wister Gibbs***born in Philadelphia, Pa., April, 1823***graduated, Oberlin (Ohio) College, 1870.***Admitted to Arkansas Bar, 1870; began practice in Little Rock. Elected City Judge, 1873***Registrar U. S. Land Office, 1877-81, and Receiver of Public Moneys, eight years; U. S. Consul to Tamatara, Madagascar, 1897-1901."

MOSES RODGERS.

The subject of this sketch was a wonderful pioneer and it affords the writer great pleasure to give the biography of such a useful citizen. Mr. Rodgers came to California in 1849 from Missouri. He was born a slave, but by a great effort, close study and application seized every opportunity that might come to him along educational lines. He finally acquired an education as a mining engineer and was very successful in California. His knowledge soon made him one of the most distinguished miners in all California. This statement will be borne out by the following facts in regard to his mining career in California: He succeeded in working claims successfully, and thereby was soon able to purchase several mines at Hornitos, Mariposa County, California, located twenty-five miles from Merced.

In the Sixties he married Miss Sara Quivers of Snelling, California, building a beautiful home for her at Quartsburg not far from his mines. The marriage was blessed by the birth of five daughters, to all of whom he gave the very best education California afforded. One daughter graduated from the State University at Berkeley.

Moses Rodgers was one member of the race whose color the pioneers of the opposite race never for a moment stopped to consider. He was at all times treated as a distinguished citizen. The esteem with which he was held can be better understood from the following quotation which appeared in a pioneer paper, *The Merced Star:* "A carload of machinery arrived at the depot last Friday, consigned to the Mount Gains Mine, Mariposa County. Moses Rodgers, of Hornitos, than whom there is no better mining man in the State, has been engaged as its superintendent. The standing and known energy of the men backing the enterprise are a guarantee that the mine will be carefully handled and worked on a paying basis. The Mount Gains Mine is well known among mining men to be good mining property, and the new arrangement and its undoubted success will mean a great deal for mining in the vicinity of Hornitos."

Moses Rodgers was not only actively engaged in mining, but was interested in and contributed liberally to every movement that was of benefit to the race. In order that he might give his daughters the advantage of better school facilities, he removed his family to Stockton, and built an elegant home which even to this day is attractive and is located on one of the best residence streets in the town. There was no gas at that date in Stockton and he was the first to bore for it. He did not give up his efforts until he had spent thousands of dollars in boring a well and a flow of gas was finally reached, but his partners were not satisfied and there was nothing made of it.

A bank cashier of Merced, for whom he acted as bondsman, was accused of a discrepancy in his accounts. The accusation grieved the bank cashier so that, before the trial, he committed suicide and his bondsmen had to make good the funds. Mr. Rodgers' bond for this cashier was thirty thousand dollars. The Court ruled that he, together with the other bondsmen were compelled to pay their bonds. Notwithstanding such heavy losses, he was such a good financier that he left his family comfortable, and they still retain the homestead in Stockton, together with a few of the mines.

At his death he left a host of warm and appreciative friends in both races who fully valued his worth to the community, irrespective of color. An idea of the many kind expressions concerning his death will be given by the following clipping from the *Merced Star*, under "Mariposa Items," October 25, 1890: "Saturday morning Moses Rodgers died at his home in Stockton. He was well-known through the Southern Mines, having arrived in the early fifties from Missouri, where he was born a slave. He entered actively into mining pursuits and followed mining the balance of his life. He was an expert in his line and his opinion was always sought by intending purchasers of mines. He was a man of honor and his word was as good as his bond. He was energetic in his younger days and took a great interest in helping along any good enterprise."

The following is one of many kind letters of condolence:

"San Francisco, California, Oct. 22, 1900.

"Mrs. M. L. Rodgers, Stockton, California.

"Dear Madam: A card was received this morning notifying me of the death of Mr. Rodgers, of which I am sorry to learn. I have known Mr. Rodgers a long time and knew him only to respect him. It is true he was a colored man, but I always regarded him as the whitest man in all my acquaintance of Mariposa County.

"In all his dealings and business relations in every way he was as honorable, high-toned a man as I have ever met. When with him I never had the feeling that he was a colored man. It never seemed to occur to me. I have sat at his table many times and he at mine, and the reflection that he was a colored man never entered my mind. He was a gentleman in every sense of the word. But he has gone and many others of his day are dropping out. The time will soon come when all of that generation will have passed. I must put him down as one of the friends who is forever gone.

"Very respectfully yours,

"WILLIAM S. CHAPMAN."

Mr. Moses Rodgers, at his death, left a widow and the following daughters: Miss Adele Rodgers, a professional nurse in Stockton, California; Mrs. Elinor Harrold, of Spokane, Washington; Miss Lulu Rodgers, who for a number of years has been assistant Postmistress at Hornitos, California. She is also an artist with the needle. She sent to the Panama-Pacific International Exposition, held in San Francisco, 1915, two exquisite pieces of handiwork, one of embroidery and the other Mexican drawn-work. An idea of their beauty and value may be had from the fact that the ladies who had charge of collecting the exhibit for San Joaquin County carried the highest rate of insurance on her work of any of the exhibits of embroidery, and the pieces were kept on display in a glass case during the entire exposition.

Miss Vivian Rodgers, another daughter, graduated with the class of 1909 from the University of California, majoring in Science and Letters. She afterward accepted a position as teacher in the public schools at Hilo, Hawaiian Islands. While there she contracted the tropical fever, and after months illness on the island, she returned to the United States and to her home in Stockton. She never regained her strength and finally passed away. The writer had the pleasure of meeting her and it seemed more than sad that one so young, amiable and beautifully educated should have to pass from the stage of action.

Miss Nettie Rodgers is a modiste and is kept busy by the very best families in Stockton who wish advanced styles. The entire family shows clearly that they are well-born, and, if their father was so grand, noble and good, the mother was equally so. She has left her imprint on the daughters whom one has only to meet to realize their superior womanhood and their gentleness of manners.

The Booth family are descendants of Edward Booth, from Viriginia, and Clarice Rodgers, from Baltimore, Maryland. Edward Booth was of free parentage, but Clarice had been a slave, owned by Jacob Rodgers. She remembered seeing George Washington and noted it because he wore knee breeches and handsome buckles.

In after years Clarice married Edward Booth, and the union was blessed by the birth of several children. They lived two blocks from the monument of George Washington, which is at the head of Channel street, in Baltimore. In the early Forties the oldest son, Edward, decided to go to the West Indies and then to the Trinidads, where he made considerable money in trading. In 1848, he was in Baltimore and, hearing of the discovery of gold in California, decided to cross the plains in quest of gold. He arrived in California in the early part of 1849 and was successful in mining claims.

In a year or so he decided to return to Baltimore and bring the remaining members of the family to California. On his way home he stopped at Oberlin College, in Ohio, and bought shares in the college; and also made arrangements to send his nephew, James H. Hubbard, to be educated in this college, the young man's father having died.

Mr. Edward Booth left Baltimore on his return trip to California in November, 1851, accompanied by the following members of the family: George W., Samuel, J. Elijah, Ann-Maria Booth-Hubbard and Harriett Booth-Gale. Before they could leave Baltimore they were compelled to prove that they were free persons of color. They secured the testimony of a Mr. Owens, a white gentleman who had a wholesale grocery at the corner of Calvert and Lombard streets, in Baltimore, but who lived at the Benzinger Hotel opposite Light Street Methodist Church. The locating of his residence on a Sunday morning, just as they were about to leave Baltimore, was the beginning of their troubles. When about to go aboard the ship they had to be measured, notwithstanding the testimony of Mr. Owens. Mr. Edward Booth protested against allowing them to take his measure but was forced to submit to this humiliation.

They finally sailed from New York via Panama to Virgin Bay, and from there to the mouth of the Chagres river, where they obtained the services of some Spaniards to row them up the river in a canoe, stopping at night on the shore of the river, using for beds dried hides. Owing to Edward Booth's speaking the Spanish language, he was enabled to save the life of a man and a woman en route. They finally reached the town of Chagres.

From this town they took a pack train of mules to cross the Isthmus of Panama. As there were others who wished to cross, the muleteers decided to make the Booth family wait over. This they did not wish to do, but, when they began weighing their freight, they found they had so much that the rate of ten cents per pound made their bill more than they could pay. They decided that they would have to do as others had done—throw away some of their stuff. They were still heavily loaded. As a last resort they decided to open the trunk of one of the sisters and discard some of her belongings. Then they found the cause of the extra weight. She was carrying a set of sad irons to California. Notwithstanding the fact that it would be difficult and perhaps impossible to buy a set at that date in California, still she was compelled to give them up or not continue the journey.

They finally reached Panama City and had to wait three weeks for a steamer to go to San Francisco. The steamer arrived and it was discovered that they had sold more tickets than they could accommodate. Just then Mr. Edward Booth discovered that he had had a previous acquaintance with the captain of the steamship, having met him in Pittsburg, Pa. Through this acquaintance he and his sisters were able to sail on the ship to San Francisco. During the interval a sailing ship came into the harbor. The Booth boys, Sam, George and Elige, engaged passage on this vessel which was called "Sailing Ship Cabargo." They left port on the 24th of December, 1851. The captain sailed south to catch the trade winds. In doing so he lost his route and, when he had taken his bearings, found that he was in the region of the equator. It was so hot that the pitch used in sealing the vessel began to melt. They finally reached Acapulco, Mexico, instead of San Francisco. From there they started on the right course.

After a time the supply of fresh water began to run low and they were only allowed a pint a day for each passenger, which resulted in mutiny on board. A colored passenger, a Mr. Barney Lee, who understood navigation, stood ready to "Man the Boat" had the captain deserted, as he threatened to do. Another passenger, who was acting as cook, also understood navigation. A voyage of several months finally brought them to California.

Mr. Edward Booth and sisters had arrived in San Francisco and had sailed on the Sacramento river boat "New World" to Sacramento. The Booth boys were so long in arriving in San Francisco that their brother had instructed every employee on the Sacramento river boats to be on the lookout for them and to direct them to Sacramento. They arrived in San Francisco in 1852 and immediately sailed on the steamer "Sydney Stepp" for Sacramento. Arriving in that city they were met by a flood from the American river which was coming in torrents down "J" street. This flood had washed down a large number of river rats which were so large and so many they frightened the Booth boys more than the flood.

The boys, after becoming accustomed to their new surroundings in California, decided to go to the mines. Mr. Elige Booth went to Nevada City, California, and his brothers to Grass Valley. Mr. George Booth, however, decided to return to Sacramento and look after their sisters. By so doing he was enabled to keep in touch with every movement for the betterment of the condition of the race in this State. He became active as a member of the first Colored State Convention, held in Sacramento in 1855, in the interest of the "Right of Testimony" for colored people in the Courts of Justice. The other male members of the Booth family were just as interested in the welfare of the race, and, whenever they came down from the mines, they contributed heavily of all their diggings to aid in such movements and to give encouragement to the other members of the race in the struggle.

In after years Mr. George Booth, married a Mrs. Ferguson, who had come to California in 1861 from Port Gibson, Mississippi, with the intention of spending three years with her sister, a Mrs. Harriett Page. Mr. George Booth made his living as an expressman. He was successful and saved his earnings, and, in his old age, enjoyed all the comforts of life. After a happily-married life covering eighteen years, he passed to his reward, leaving his widow securely protected from hardships. She lived in comfort until her death which but recently occurred. Mrs. George Booth was a delightful lady to converse with, a devoted church member and actively engaged in the various church societies.

Mr. Edward Booth followed mining all his life and was successful. He was very unselfish both with his family of sisters and brothers and their families, contributing to every movement of interest to the race. He enjoyed traveling, making extensive trips. Upon hearing that gold had been discovered in Alaska, he decided to leave California and go in quest of it. He took up a claim in Alaska and was a successful miner, remaining in that country until his death, which occurred in 1900.

The following is quoted from an address made by Mr. Edward Booth before the Second Annual Convention of the Colored Convention of California: "Mr. President and gentlemen. I am happy to meet you on this occasion and to respond to the call on behalf of this convention. The object for which we have met is a good one and I feel deeply my want of language to express my feelings in relation thereto, but I will endeavor briefly to present a few facts respecting the condition of our people in my county. There are about five hundred colored people residing there, variously employed. A few are farmers and mechanics; a small number are engaged in trading, but the majority of them are miners. It is with pride I say, we are showing to our white fellow-citizens, that we have some natural abilities.

"We are resolved to let them see that all we want is an equal chance, an open field and a fair fight. . . . We intend to disprove the allegation that we are naturally inferior to them. The colored people of Nevada County possess property to the amount of $3,000,000 in mining claims, water, ditch stock and some real estate. We have one church, but no permanent school-house. A company is forming to build one."

Mr. James H. Hubbard, a nephew, whom Mr. Booth sent to Oberlin College to be educated, after his graduation came to California to live with his mother and the remaining members of the family. He was ordained under Bishop T. M. D. Ward of the A. M. E. Church, and soon became one of the distinguished colored ministers in the State. He remained in the California Conference until 1905, when he joined the Colorado Conference, continuing in the Ministry of the Afro-American Methodist Church until his death, which occurred in 1912, in Denver, Colorado. He left to mourn his passing three daughters and four sons, respectively: Mrs. Ida Williamson; Mrs. Esther Morrison, of Denver, Colorado; Mrs. E. Gordon, of Furlong Tract near Los Angeles, California; Messrs. James and Joseph and the Rev. Edward Hubbard, a minister in the A. M. E. Church.

Mr. Elige Booth, a brother, who graciously furnished the biography of the family, the writer found to be a delightful and intensely interesting gentleman. He was dignified and reminded one of a gentleman of the old school of aristocracy. His mind was clear in relating details of the trip to California and in regard to matters of interest to the race during pioneer times. When questioned concerning the treatment accorded to Negro miners during pioneer days in California, he replied: "There were often disputes concerning miners jumping their claims," and then he told of a meeting held by miners to protect his claim. He said: "A man was a man, even if he was a colored miner. There were some sections where the colored men were not treated as they should have, been, but the minters had a rule that everybody's claim should measure alike, "fifty feet front running back one hundred feet." It was highly interesting to listen to him tell of the methods used in mining and also something of the life of the miners of pioneer days in California.

Robert Anthony, who came to Sacramento, California, from St. Louis, Mo., by ox-team in 1849, was a slave, and worked in the mines for two years to pay for his freedom. After obtaining his freedom, he mined for himself, owning the first quartz mill in California. Later he purchased another. His mills were located at Horn-Cut, between Yuba and Dry-Cut. One mill was worked by horses, the other by water. All the mining previous to the establishment of these mills was placer mining. By the aid of the mills men were enabled to go down into the bowels of the earth and bring forth pieces of mineral-bearing rocks or those showing mineral deposits, and to break these rocks, securing the gold, silver or other valuable deposits.

Mr. Anthony, in after years, removed his mills to Brown's Valley. One day, while he and the team of dogs which he had been driving were far in the mine, one of the chambers caved in and crippled him. He worked as a miner until 1905, when, owing to poor health, he was compelled to give it up. Mr. Anthony was the means of emancipating a young colored girl who was working as a sheep-herder in the Santa Cruz Mountains, an account of which will be found in the chapter on "Slavery," under the department entitled, "Slaves Emancipated in California."

Daniel Rodgers came to California in 1849 with his master from Little Rock, Arkansas. He worked in the mines and in other ways earned enough money to pay his master $1,100 for his freedom. This money was earned after the work of the day, which ended at sundown. After a couple of years in California his master decided to return to Little Rock, Arkansas.

Daniel Rodgers was never satisfied again to live in the South, and decided to try and return to California with his family. When he was about to start back west, the master, to whom he had paid the money for his freedom in California, began to make arrangements to sell him again into slavery, as he had not given the Negro his Freedom Papers, although he had received the thousand dollars for them. A few white gentlemen, hearing of the intentions of this slave master, raised a purse of money, paid for his freedom and gave him his Freedom Papers, signed by the best men in the county. A copy of the papers may be found in this book.

Daniel Rodgers again started with his family for California, but was again stopped because his wife did not have her Freedom Paper, an account of which will also be found in chapter on Slavery. He then made another attempt to reach California with his family, crossing the plains with an ox-team, spending one year in coming. They arrived in 1860, locating at Watsonville, where he secured a tract of eighty acres of land and began life as a farmer.

The following are the names of his children: John, Martin, Sam, James, Carrol, Redmond, Jessie, Julia-Ann, Martha and Sallie Rodgers. They were only children and, as the children of slave parents, had not enjoyed the blessing or advantage of an education. The first thing to be done for them was to apply to the school board of the township for a school and a teacher. The board was slow in securing a teacher. In the meantime the oldest daughter decided to marry a colored gentleman who had previously moved to Watsonville, a Mr. John Derrick. The union was blessed by the birth of several children, which in time opened the school doors to both the children of the Rodgers and of the Derrick families, who still lived in Watsonville and were anxious for an education.

The Board of Education secured the services of a young white girl of northern parentage, a Miss Knowlton, who because of her own home influence and education, which was of the spirit of the Abolitionist, gave so much of her personal interest to the welfare of the children that they became devoted to her. It has been the writer's privilege and pleasure to interview this teacher, who, among other things, said that she recognized the excellent talent of the children of these two colored families, the Rodgers and the Derricks. She spoke of how she had urged their parents to move to San Francisco, where the children could advance in a higher education and in the struggle in life's battles. This teacher further said that it was gratifying to her in after years to learn that they all had made a success of life.

John Derrick came to California in 1859 and located in Watsonville. The next year the Rodgers family also located in the same town, which resulted in the meeting and marriage of Mr. Derrick and Miss Martha Rodgers. The union was blessed by the following children: John, Lincoln, Nellie, Andy, Jake, Artismisa and Eva Derrick. These children were given the best education that California afforded. They have lived creditable lives, filling positions of responsibility, both in the United States Government and also local appointments. They are distinguished members of the St. Augustine Episcopal Church for colored people, located in Oakland, and are actively engaged in every movement of interest to the race in California. Mr. Lincoln Derrick is an associate editor of the *Western Outlook*, of San Francisco, published for the benefit of the race in all of the State, and is considered thoroughly reliable. Daniels Rodgers died at the home of his daughter, Mrs. Derrick, in Oakland.

Albert Grubbs, senior, was born in Lexington, Kentucky, and came to California in 1854. He was the body servant to the Honorable Henry Clay, traveled with him during his public life, and closed his eyes in death. After coming to California, Mr. Grubbs located in Sacramento and, after spending a number of years in the laundry business, began teaming, and took an active part in every movement for the uplift of the race. He had one son born in Sacramento, to whom he gave a good education. After the boy had completed the course in the public schools, he was sent to the private school conducted by Rev. Peter Cassey, in San Jose, California.

Mr. Grubbs, junior, has always been an active Episcopalian, at the present time being a vestryman and church clerk of the St. Augustine Episcopalian Mission, located at Oakland, and an active participant in any movement of interest to the race. While quite young he joined the Sacramento Zouaves, a military company of colored men. At the time he joined he was too young to become a regular cadet, and was made a "marker boy." He remained with the organization for many years, retiring from it as second lieutenant.

Mr. Grubbs has been employed a great many years by the Southern Pacific Railroad company. Something of an estimate of the high regard in which the gentleman is held can be given by the following letter sent to the home offices by the head of the San Francisco office after the great earthquake and fire of 1906:

"Temporary Office of Secretary, Southern Pacific Railroad Company, 72 San Pablo Avenue, Room 8, Oakland, California.

August 13, 1906.

J. L. WILLICUTT,   MR. E. E. CALVIN,
    Secretary.   *Vice-President and General Manager,*
C. P. LINCOLN,   Southern Pacific Company,
    Assistant Secretary.   Ferry Building.

"Dear Sir: The recent published reports that employes of the Southern Pacific Company who had been rendered destitute by the fire are to receive financial assistance from the company, and the later reports that money is already being paid to some of its employes, while others have but just heard that there was such a plan on foot, has led two of the latter, both of whom are old and most deserving employes, to call upon me with the view of learning if I had been notified of the plan or knew whether or not their names were under consideration, to which I was obliged to make a negative reply.

"The first is Albert Grubbs, who is now and for the past six years has been employed in my office. He entered the service of the company in May, 1870, as massenger in the telegraph office at Sacramento, and was engaged in that and General Manager Town's office for some two or three years, then went into the Sacramento shops and learned the trade of cabinet-maker. From there, on account of ill health, he was placed on the pay-train, at the suggestion of Secretary Miller, in which capacity he continued for nine years.

''He was then transferred to a position in the Auditor's and Secretary's offices, having the charge and care of the paid coupons, in which line of work he has now been especially employed for nearly fifteen years, and a more correct, carful, painstaking man it would be difficult to find.

''The coupon records in my department have been gradually increasing through the consolidation of various roads, which, together with the new issues of bonds, has required of Albert constant application to his duties and many extra hours of service. He lost all of his furniture and personal effects by the fire, for which he received $300 insurance money, which is all he now has to show for his life's work. . . . During the respective thirty-six years' service . . . not a coupon has been mislaid or a dime unaccounted for, . . . nor has anything occurred to attract him from his direct line of duty to the company, and I therefore feel that I am called upon to present such worthy and meritorious cases to your attention in the belief that it is your desire to learn of such instances of remarkable care and devotion to the company's interests.

''Yours very truly,

(Signed) ''J. L. WILLICUTT, *Secretary.*''

The person acting as copyist was so delighted over the letter that he asked permission to give Mr. Grubbs a copy, and thus the writer has been able to reproduce it here. One of the largest dailies in Oakland, *The Oakland Tribune*, as a special feature in its issue of December 24, 1910, published a full-page article commenting on the services rendered by Albert Grubbs to the Southern Pacific Company. The article was headed, ''Handled Millions in Coupons,'' and in every way spoke in the highest terms of the subject of the sketch.

Mr. Grubbs married young and the union was blessed by the birth of one son, to whom was given the best education possible. He was ambitious to learn a trade, and chose to become an electrician. He secured work as errand-boy in a ladies' tailor shop and studied at nights and mastered a correspondence course in the California Electrical Works. He then secured employment with Charles Person & Co., located at 102 Powell Street, San Francisco, the only electrical store in San Francisco owned by a colored man, and had been employed here for two years when Mr. Persons died. He then secured employment as foreman in a white store. Afterward, for a while, he was employed at the Union Iron Works, learning to be a machinist. Finding the color prejudices so great a hindrance to securing work, he studied and mastered the Spanish language and sailed for Buenos Ayres, South America.

He married Miss Carrie Phelps, of Chicago, who in time joined him. He now has regular employment in one of the largest shops in the South American city.

GEORGE WASHINGTON DENNIS.

This sketch, which portrays the struggles in the life of the late Mr. George Washington Dennis, is both interesting and valuable. It carries with it a grand lesson to those of today who think they are handicapped because of their color. It should be inspiring because the subject, even with his handicap, never for a moment lost his great ambition to better not only the condition of his mother and himself, but that of his race.

In after years he was a prime factor in all the struggles of his race against adverse legislation. He reared a most interesting family which is a credit to the community. He was a loving father and a devoted husband, a highly respected citizen of San Francisco and the State of California. His life stands out in bold relief in proof of the fact that if a man wills, he can make his life represent something to the world for the betterment of mankind.

The following facts in the life of George Washington Dennis were given by his son, Edward Dennis, who said:

''George Washington Dennis came to California September 17, 1849, with the gambling party that opened the 'Eldorado Hotel' in San Francisco. This party of gamblers was from New Orleans and was composed of the following persons: Green Dennis, a slave trader, from Mobile, Alabama; Joe and Jim Johnson, from Ohio, and Andy McCabe. When they reached Colon, the only passage they were able to obtain was a row-boat, which they used up the Chagres river to Panama.

''While en route from Panama to San Francisco, the gamblers lost and re-won Mr. Dennis three different times. He was their slave and therefore chattel property. When they engaged passage on the steamr at Panama for San Francisco, the captain charged them $350 for the Negro, since it was not certain that he was a slave, and the laws did not permit the carrying of slave passengers. This was done presumably to protect the captain from a fine if Mr. Dennis was a slave.

"The entire party in due time reached San Francisco and opened the 'Eldorado Hotel,' a tent measuring 30 by 100 feet, which they had brought from New Orleans. They located on the corner of Washington and Kearney streets, on the site which is now the home of the Hall of Justice. The Eldorado Hotel ran a faro bank and monte, ten tables going night and day. They were played during the day by men and at night by women. Green Dennis made the subject of this sketch the proposition that if he would save his money he could purchase his freedom. George W. Dennis was given the position of porter of this hotel at a salary of $250 per month. Mr. Dennis, very anxious to secure his freedom and at the same time to start life with a little money, saved the sweepings from the gambling tables and at the end of three months he paid, in five and ten cent pieces, the sum of $1000, and received a bill for himself from Green Dennis, who was his father and also his master.

"Shortly afterward Joe and Jim Johnson, who were of the party of gamblers, decided to give up gambling and return to Ohio and bring to California some graded cattle. Joe Johnson told Mr. Dennis that if he wished he would bring back Dennis's mother, whereupon the subject of this sketch paid to Green Dennis the sum of $950 for the freedom of his mother, and Mr. Johnson returned to California with her. She lived in San Francisco with her son many years afterward, dying at the advanced age of 105 years.

"Upon the arrival of his mother in San Francisco, Mr. Dennis rented one of the gambling tables at $40 per day for the privilege of his mother serving hot meals in the gambling house on it. Eggs were selling at $12 per dozen, apples 25 cents apiece, and a loaf of bread $1. While her expenses were heavy, she averaged $225 a day. After working here two years he decided to start out for himself and went with the 'Frazier River Mining Company.' He staked two or three claims, but was not successful, and returned to San Francisco, going to work for the same parties at the 'Eldorado Hotel' at the same salary, making money rapidly. Mr. Dennis and Mifflin Gibbs decided to purchase, in partnership, a piece of property on Montgomery between Jackson and Pacific, paying eighteen thousand dollars for the same. After holding it for six months they sold it for thirty-two thousand dollars. In 1856 Mr. Dennis bought the block bounded by Post, Geary, Hyde and Larkins streets, paying one thousand five hundred and fifty dollars for the same. He built a homesite on this property for his children, four of whom were born at this place. Later he purchased a block on Post, Sutter, Scott and Divisidera streets, paying three hundred and fifty dollars. He sold the greater part of this at a good margin, but retained until his death the beautiful home and homestead, notwithstanding he passed through seven fires in San Francisco. Each time the city was destroyed he lost all, with others.

"Mr. Dennis opened the first livery stable in San Francisco. It was located at Sansome and Washington streets, on the site now occupied by the Custom House. Later he had a partner, a Mr. James Brown. The British government wanted five hundred cavalry horses, and Mr. Dennis secured the contract to furnish them. He bought the horses and, after breaking them, shipped them to the British govrnment. This was not done without its hardships of jealousy. Mr. Dennis had in his employ an Irishman who poisoned ninety head of these horses. It was proven that he did it, and resulted in his conviction before a court of justice, the judge giving him a sentence of fourteen years in the penetentiary. After Mr. Dennis disposed of his horses to the British government he gave up the livery stable business and opened a wood and coal yard on Broadway near Montgomery street, in San Francisco.

"Mr. Dennis then decided that he needed a helpmate, and was fortunate in marrying Miss Margaret A. Brown, the daughter of James Brown, who had come to San Francisco, with his family, from Baltimore in 1845. The marriage was celebrated June 21, 1855, Rev. Thomas officiating and the Hon. Mifflin Gibbs acting as groomsman. The bride was attended by her sister, Miss Charlotte Brown, as bridesmaid. The couple lived to celebrate their golden wedding in San Francisco, a privilege granted to but few. Many years afterward Mrs. Dennis passed away. The union was blessed by the birth of eleven children, all of whom were given the best education obtainable in California. The following are the names of the children: Margaret L. Benston, Mrs. C. R. Downs, William E., Andrew, Alexander, Julian, Joseph, George, Carlisle, Edward and Link Dennis.''

This family is remarkable not only because they won honors in school as great scholars, but their children have followed in their footsteps and have won the same distinction. Mrs. Margaret L. Dennis-Benston, for instance, was the first colored girl to graduate from the San Francisco High School, graduating with honors in a class of fifteen hundred students. She was most efficient in the Spanish and Chinese languages, and afterward taught in a private school for Chinese. Se had been offered a position as interpreter for the courts of San Francisco, when she suddenly decided that she would rather marry Captain Benston.

The daughter by this union is now Mrs. Margaret Benston-Evans. She graduated with a class of seven hundred from the Commercial High School, in San Francisco, as the valedictorian of her class. She speaks and translates the Spanish language and is a stenographer of ability. Aside from these accomplishments, she has been trained in elocution and short-story writing, which has resulted in her writing ten or more plays, many of which she has produced for charity. She married young to a United States Naval steward, a Mr. Evans, who has the distinction of being the steward of the Pacific Fleet of the United States Navy. Since it will be impossible to give a sketch of each of the eleven children, the writer will only give a short review of the interesting lives of a few members of the family.

Mr. George Dennis studied law at Hastings Law College, of San Francisco, and took a business course in Heald's Business College. He was very prominent in politics, and was a member of the Democratic State Central Committee, representing Alameda County. He took a prominent part in Mr. Hasting's nomination and election, and seconded the nomination of Governor Budd, at the Convention held in the Old Baldwin Theatre, San Francisco, and stumped the State in the interest of the election of Governor Budd. He was a member of the Y. M. I. (Young Men's Institute) and the Knights of Columbus. He was employed as solicitor for Hamburg Bremen Insurance Company at a salary of $150 a month for twenty-seven years, and, although he was in poor health for fully two years before his death, they retained him on the pay-roll at half-pay. The night before his death the priest and the order of Y. M. I. came in a body and offered for and with him "The Holy Viaticum," or prayers for the dying.

Carlisle Dennis worked for Mark Hopkins' family for eleven years as butler, and for five years as secretary to the widow, Mrs. Mark Hopkins, who was a stockholder of the Southern Pacific railroad, associated with the late Governor Stanford, Mr. Crocker and C. P. Huntington. Mrs. Hopkins died leaving forty-two million dollars.

Mr. Link Dennis for a number of years was a clerk for the Standard Oil Company. Mr. Edward Dennis was a policeman, the first of the race in San Francisco; Joe Dennis, an altar boy in St. Dominica's Catholic church. Miss Elsie, who is the daughter of Mr. and Mrs. Joe Dennis, is a violinist and pianist and gives great promise as an artist with the brush.

Mrs. Annie Peters, a most charming lady, and the oldest living pioneer of color in California, came to the State in 1851, with the family of Rev. Flavil Scott Mines, the first Episcopal minister on the Pacific Coast, who founded the Trinity Church of San Francisco, brought the church around the Horn and rebuilt it in San Francisco. Mrs. Peters, who was then Miss Garrick, was just fourteen years old when she landed in New York from her home in the Island of St. Croix, West Indies. She was most thoroughly educated in a private school on the Island. She was a keen observer of things and events that were making California history. She has been a great assistance to the writer in many talks with regard to pioneer days in San Francisco. The writer has many scrap-books filled with newspaper clippings given to her for use in this book by Mrs. Peters. Her patriotic instinct, race pride and love of the beautiful, even when a very young girl, would do credit to any man or woman of today.

The writer is very much indebted to Rev. David R. Wallace for a letter of introduction to Mrs. Peters. She was a member of the First Mission established for colored people in San Francisco, and in this way Father Wallace knew of her and the value she could be to the writer in telling things of vital interest concerning the Negro race and its early history in California. After being convinced that the material was to be used for the best interests of the race, her face lit up like the halo around the painting of a Madonna. She said: "Thank God, my prayers have been answered. I have saved these clippings and data all these years, and now that I am going to make a change I am glad to give them to you."

The first visit of the author to this grand old lady was a perfect literary feast, one to live in the memory the same as the recollection of a first visit to California fields of wild flowers after the winter rains in the land of Sunshine, a feeling indescribable. Such was the great inspiration secured from every visit to Mrs. Peters. She would pour out her soul like the music of a great organ, as she would tell of the struggles of the colored people in pioneer days in California. A favorite expression of hers was: "The events are painted upon my memory and brain," and many an event that historians had forgotten to mention as of value to the Negro she would recall, together with the truth about the same, and why some white persons were mistreated, even today, by writers ''because they defended the Negro and his rights even against their own best interests.'' Mrs. Peters was still living in January, 1918.

Nathaniel Pointer, the subject of this sketch, came to San Francisco, California, in 1852. He went into business with Mifflin Gibbs, opening the Philadelphia Store. Later he was joined by other relatives, who came from Mississippi via Panama. In the party was his mother, grandmother, two uncles, four cousins and two aunts.

In 1863 Miss Mary Pointer, another member of the family, came to California, and, after living in San Francisco for three years, sent back east for her father and mother, William and Julia Ann Pointer; her brothers, John, Nathaniel and Charles; her sisters, Mary and Ellen Pointer. After coming to California, Miss Mary Pointer married Mr John Callander, and they opened a boarding house for sailors at No. 5 Broadway, San Francisco, May, 1866.

Mr. Frank Shelton, the subject of this sketch, came to California from Orange County, Virginia, with his mother, in 1847. His father, Samuel Shelton, came to the State in 1840, and followed mining.

Frank, the youngest son, was given a fair education by private teachers until the organization of a colored school which was taught by Rev. J. J. Moore. When the gold craze was at its height and men were going to British Columbia, he joined the crowd and spent several years there as a miner. He was very successful.

Previous to his going to British Columbia he helped to organize a Baptist church in San Francisco, purchasing with his own money an old warehouse which was converted into a church. He had two daughters, Lizzie and Julia, to whom he gave the best education then attainable. They were sent to a private school conducted by Rev. Peter Cassey and located at San Jose, California. The Misses Shelton graduated from this institution with honors.

In after years Mr. Frank Shelton returned from British Columbia and, locating in San Francisco, became a successful furniture dealer in new and second-hand furniture. He died leaving his family well provided for, with many pieces of valuable property. His wife was left in full charge of the estate until her death, which did not occur until a generation afterward. She was very liberal and gave heavily to charitable institutions. Several years previous to her death, which occurred at the ripe old age of ninety years, she made a gift-deed to her daughters whereby they secured the rental of some of the property before her death.

Miss Julia Shelton became the wife of Captain Shorey. She has an interesting sketch in the department devoted to Distinguished Women.

Few people are blessed with a long life which passes the century mark, as has been the subject of this sketch, Mrs. Susan Wilson, who came to California in 1853 from Wayne County, Missouri, going first to Texas and from there to California by the way of the ox-team. She had three children of her own with her. It was most interesting to hear her tell of the long, tedious journey across the plains, and how the Indians would frighten them, and how, at one time, they came near being massacred by the Indians. There were one hundred wagons in the ox-team. They started on their trip to the coast in March, and reached Miles Creek, Mariposa County, California, three weeks before Christmas. This lady is now more than one hundred years of age. Her daughters have all married and have interesting and highly respected families. One daughter married Mr. Edward Wysinger. Mrs. Wilson makes her home in Oakland with another daughter, a Mrs. Quinn, while a third, Mrs. Allen, and Mr. Reuben Wysinger, a grandson, live at Fowler.

Mr. James Segee, his wife, Elizabeth, and young daughter, Emma, coming to California from Jacksonville, Florida, via the Isthmus of Panama, arrived in San Francisco in 1852. Later they moved to Marysville, where they decided to open a laundry, and afterward were joined by the other members of the family, Mary and Julia Hermandez, who came from Florida in 1853. When the Frazier River gold excitement reached California the aunts decided to go to British Columbia and cook, at a wage of $100 a week. Mr. and Mrs. Segee sent their daughter, Emma, to Canada with them, that she might be educated in the public school of that place. She remained there for seven years, when she returned to Marysville, where she married Mr. Washington and was given a position as the first colored public school teacher in that city.

''Peter Powers, the subject of this sketch, was born in Missouri, of slave parents, in 1828. His mother died a few months afterward. He was reared by his mistress, being well liked, and was placed in charge of the farm and the ferry, which he managed with success for a number of years. When his mistress died she said he should be free, which wish her husband carried out at his death. But the laws were that, on becoming free, he had to leave the State, which he did in 1857. Before leaving he married Miss

Rachel Seals, daughter of Frank Seals, of Kentucky. Leaving Warsaw on April, 1858, he crossed the plains. When at Gravelford, on the Humboldt river, they were attacked by Indians, whom they put to flight, having only one man wounded, but many redmen's scalps. At this place a Mr. Martin lost three hundred head of cattle. Peter Powers engaged in mining and at the same time kept a boarding house and laundry, which he continued for three years. He then moved to Grass Valley, spending an unprofitable year there, after which he moved to Marysville, where he soon accumulated property and first learned to read and write. He continued his studies until he, at length, was able to attend to all of his own affairs. Afterward he became a teacher in the public school for a number of years. Later on, in 1865, he and his family moved to Tehama County, where he took up land. In 1866 his wife died. It was at this place he began building a church. In 1870 he went to Chico and bought property and planned and built a church on two beautiful lots belonging to colored citizens. This was known as the A. M. E. Church. He was elected to represent his County in a school convention.''
—The Souvenir of Prominent Colored People of the Pacific Coast.

Mr. William Robinson, coming to California and locating in Red Bluff in 1859, came from West Virginia across the plains. He engaged in the restaurant business and invested heavily in mining stock. He owned a group of mines at North San Juan, Nevada County, California. He married Mrs. Logan in 1861, a widow who had come to California with three children from Arkansas, and locted in Red Bluff. The union was blessed by the birth of three additional children. Mr. Robinson believed in acquiring property and owned property wherever he lived. He was fortunate to be able, when his children were old enough to attend school, to employ a private teacher, and opened a school for his children at North San Juan, Nevada County, California. He then began a movement to establish a public school for all colored children, and was joined in the movement by his wife, Mr. A. J. Logan, of Palocedro, Shasta County, California, and Mr. and Mrs. P. D. Logan, who all worked in unison to establish a colored school in Red Bluff. They also worked to collect the money to build a church for the A. M. E. denomination in Red Bluff. Mr. Robinson kept the pastor for years free of cost.

Miss Clara Logan-Robinson in time became too advanced for the colored school, whereupon her father, Mr. Robinson, again took steps to fight for her admission into the public High School of Red Bluff. This resulted in this daughter graduating in the pioneer class. She was the first colored girl to receive a certificate to teach. She taught in one of the Red Bluff public schools. Mr. Robinson sent his sons to San Francisco to be educated under the instruction of J. B. Sanderson.

Mr. William Robinson believed in fighting the battles of the race through politics without the hope of personal gain. He rescued from slavery, long years after the Emancipation Proclamation, two young colored women in Red Bluff, Miss Hster Anderson and Miss Bell Grant. Mr. Robinson was a valuable member of the race, and shared their struggles throughout the State, giving liberally of both time and money in assisting the members of the Eexecutive Committee of the Colored Convention. He died at the age of sixty-eight, much beloved by all who knew him.

Mrs. Cloye Burnett Logan-Flood came to the Pacific Coast with some white people, crossing the plains in 1853 into Umicano Valley, Oregon, where she lived until eleven years old. The people were unkind to her and one day she decided that she was going to California. She proceeded to mount a horse and ride to Shastatown, and afterward to Red Bluff, where she secured work. In after years she married Mr. Griffin Logan and moved to Tehama County.

Mr. Logan was engaged in farming and sheep-raising and was very successful. The union was blessed by the birth of five girls and one boy, Byron Logan, who was an upholsterer by trade. The girls are: Mrs. Hickerson of Guinda, California; Mrs. Houston, of Los Angeles; Mrs. Edward Johnson, of Berkeley; Mrs. William Stephens, of Del Monte, California, and Mrs. Blick, of New York City.

After the death of Mr. Logan his widow moved to Berkeley, where she followed professional nursing. After her children were grown, she married Mr. Flood, a member of the old pioneer family of that name in Oakland. She is a delightful lady, much loved by all who know her.

Mr. James Churchill came to California in 1849 with a party of white people. He had an interesting experience shortly after the party crossed the mountains into California. Mr. Churchill met a bear and succeeded in killing it. His experience in killing this bear he told in after years to a colored school-boy in Marysville, by the name of James Allen, who wrote a good story concerning it and published it in the Marysville High School paper. Mr. Churchill, after locating in Marysville, became a teamster in the mountains, and owned a ranch in the northern part of the State. He was the proud father of fifteen children, nine of whom were living at the time of his death. He lived in California fifty-nine years, the greater part of which was spent in Marysville. His wife, Mrs. Mary Churchill, came from Missouri in 1853. The remaining members of his family now living in Marysville are: Sons, William, Phillip, Albert and George; daughters, Mrs. Ellen Breeden, Mrs. W. G. Holland, Mrs. Annie Breeden, Mrs. A. B. Davis and Mrs. Ida Churchill.

Mr. William Hart, the subject of this sketch, came to California in 1849. He drove and cared for race horses from Richmond, Virginia, to Little Rock, Arkansas, and thence to California. Upon his arrival in California he immediately went to work for himself. Since he was free-born all his earnings were his own. He successfully mined at Angel and Chinese Camps. He gave liberally to every movement of interest to the race in its struggle for the right to live in California. He was painstaking and saving, which resulted in his leaving his family, at his passing, comfortably provided against a rainy day. He left a ranch on the Mariposa Road, which still yields a good income. He left a widow and twelve children, seven of whom were boys. All of the children were given the best education possible. His son, Daniel Dabney Hart, who graduated at the age of nineteen years, was, up to 1914, the only boy of the race to have graduated from the public high schools in San Joaquin County. He took the civil service examination and received an appointment as clerk in the San Francisco post-office. Charles Hart is employed in the street department of Stockton, California. The daughters, Alice, Helen and Ruth Hart, are exquisite needlewomen. Miss Helen Hart sent a perfectly wonderful piece of French hand embroidery to the Panama-Pacific International Exposition, in San Francisco, in 1915. It was so daintily done it was impossible to tell it from a piece of imported handwork. The mother of this family is a thoroughly gentlewoman and most interesting. She showed the writer a rocker and cart used by her husband when he did placer mining in Angel and Chinese Camps.

Dr. Fletcher, coming to California from the Island of Saint Christopher, Danish West Indies, arrived in San Francisco in 1860. He joined the Navy and served until 1865, when he returned to San Francisco and for three years practiced in the Hamman Baths, afterward moving to Sacramento.

Mr. John Gryder came to California in 1841, with Major Burney, Dick Gardner and Major Wyeth, owners of fine horses. They came from Silver County, Tennessee, through Mexico to California. He acted as horse-trainer for the party. After reaching California Mr. Gryder decided to follow mining. He worked in the mines at Murphy's Diggings, which was located seventy miles from Stockton. He was very successful and paid Major Wyeth $800 to bring his mother to California. Upon her arrival he purchased her a home in Marysville, where Mrs. Caroline Gryder spent the remaining days of her life. Mr. Gryder has practiced as a veterinary surgeon in Vallejo almost continuously since 1851. He was a member of the Bear Flag Party and, at one of the celebrations of the Native Sons and Daughters, he rode in state through the streets of Vallejo in their procession.

Mrs. Addie Stanley came to California with her parents, Mr. and Mrs. John Raimus. They came across the plains by ox-team from Galena, Illinois, to Nevada City, Nevada County, California, arriving September 20, 1852. She married Mr. John Stanley in Sacramento in 1872. He had come to California during early pioneer days, and at his marriage was acting as valet to Governor Booth, filling the position with credit for eleven years.

"John A. Barber, born of free parents in Nantucket, Massachusetts, in 1834, immigrated to this State in 1853 and entered upon a business career as a contractor and builder. He won for himself a world-wide reputation as an orator and an agitator. He associated with others in drawing up many petitions which were sent to the legislature in behalf of colored people.

"Mr. Barber was Grand Marshal of the procession that commemorated the adoption of the Fifteenth Amendment to the Constitution of the United States. As Past Grand Marshal of the colored lodge of California and Grand Lecturer, he exercised a potent influence. Mr. Barber, though not a politician, was a delegate and represented the Thirty-third Assembly District of San Francisco at the Democratic State Convention at San Jose, California, being the first of the race in the State to receive such a distinction."—*Prominent Afro-Americans of Pacific Coast.*

Henry Miles, the subject of this sketch, came to California in 1853 from Baltimore, Maryland. He immediately went to the mines and was very successful, purchasing several mines in Calavares County, California. He also purchased five hundred acres of land fourteen miles from Stockton. His family did not reach the State until 1857, the sons, William Blake and John, having come earlier. The daughters, Silvia, Sara and Josephine, came with their mother, Mrs. Miles. The family then moved to San Francisco, and Mr. Miles took a contract to do the grading of the city, employing a large number of teams. He gave his children the best education possible. William Blake became an instructor in music and also the leader of a band. One daughter, Sara, is a finished vocalist. She married Mr. Alexander Taylor, who was an excellently educated musician. They went east and, after spending considerable time in study under the best instructors in music, both vocal and instrumental, they decided to make a tour, first in the United States and then of the European countries. While in Prague, Germany, a son was born to them, which was the first colored child ever born in the country, and for that reason the ruler of the place and his wife acted as god-parents of the child and gave it what would amount in our money to the sum of two hundred and fifty dollars. Silva, another daughter, married a German carpenter who was very successful and invested heavily in property, at one time owning ten or more good two-story, modern houses. They still own a ranch down the peninsula. The writer refers to Mr. and Mrs. Bennett, of Oakland. William Blake, a son, was not only a splendid musician, but he mingled freely in every movement that was of interest to the race. He was an active member of the Young Men's Beneficial Society of San Francisco, and of the Executive Committee of the Colored Convention.

Joseph McKinney, the subject of this sketch, came across the plains with Captain McKinney from Missouri to California in 1854. He engaged in stock-raising and farming in Merced County. He afterward owned 1,700 acres of land.

Captain William T. Shorey was born in the Island of Barbadoes of the British West Indies. The son of a sugar-planter and a beautiful creole lady by the name of Miss Rosa Frazier, he was the oldest of a family of eight children. When quite young he learned the trade of plumber, but, like many of the boys living on the island, preferred to follow the sea. He shipped on a sailing vessel to Boston, where he learned navigation from Captain Whipple A. Leach, of Vermont, who, at the time, was residing at Provincetown, Cape Cod. He afterward applied and was accepted as a seaman on the sailing bark "Emma H. Herman," a whaling-vessel sailing for Boston. During this cruise they touched several points along the South Atlantic, west coast of Africa, sailing around the Cape of Good Hope and calling in at Australia and Tasmania, and thence around to the west coast of South America, touching at Chili, Valparaiso, Peru and Panama, and from thence to San Francisco. This cruise lasted three years, during which time Mr. Shorey was promoted from third officer to first officer of the vessel. After this voyage the vessel was sold to McGee and Moore, of San Francisco, whereupon Mr. Shorey sailed on the same vessel as second officer with a new crew, en route to the Arctic Ocean. On the next cruise he sailed as first officer and had a very successful voyage; on the third cruise he sailed as master of the vessel. Previous to sailing he married Miss Julia Ann Shelton, of San Francisco, and they went on this cruise, during their honeymoon, to Mexico and the Hawaiian Islands. Shortly before they landed the volcano Mt. Pelee became active and, shortly after the lava flowed down the mountain-side, the waters of the ocean were so heated that the fish were killed for miles around the harbor.

Mrs. Shorey was a keen observer and a great lover of nature, aside from being a sea captain's wife. While on the island she gathered considerable valuable information and sent an interesting letter to the editor of the *San Francisco Elevator*, who published the same in a weekly issue of the paper. The party afterward landed at Honolulu, where Captain Shorey left the party and continued his cruise to the Arctic region. Mrs. Shorey, accompanied by other sea-captains' wives, returned to California. It was not the custom then for sea-captains to be accompanied to the Arctic coast by their wives. The captain was gone about one year, returning to San Francisco after a successful cruise. After being on the "Emma Herman" for several years, he was transferred to the "Andrew Hicks." After several successful voyages on this vessel he transferred to the "Alexander," making two successful voyages on her, but on the third voyage he lost her in an Arctic ice pack, without the loss of life. The captain and entire crew returned by a Government vessel to San Francisco, sailing the next year in the whaling-bark "Gay Head." Captain Shorey was accompanied on this cruise by his wife and daughter, Zenobia. When they reached the Hawaiian Islands the daughter fell ill, and Mrs. Shorey was compelled to return home, where the child died. Captain Shorey continued on the voyage to the Arctic region, returning as usual in the fall after a successful cruise. The captain attributed his wonderful and amazing success to his happiness in having his wife and daughter accompany him part of the voyage.

During the many years Captain Shorey was cruising as whaling sea-captain in the Pacific Ocean he had many thrilling experiences. They were often prominently mentioned in the daily press. The vessel which Captain Shorey then mastered left the port of San Francisco February 9, 1901, and returned November 3, 1901. So many vessels had been wrecked during the season no one expected the return of this bark. When she was sighted the Examiner sent a reporter out in the pilot boat with the pilot who was bringing the bark into port. The following appeared in the paper the next day with the headlines: ''Whaling bark passed through two typhoons. Only vessel on the coast having a colored captain safely reached harbor after trying experiences.— Battered about in two terrible typhoons, the whaling bark 'John and Winthrope' arrived yesterday in a bedraggled condition, having lost four of her boats and davits and being otherwise damaged by the storms through which she passed during her voyage from the Okhotsk Sea. While coming across, the little vessel had a narrow escape from being wrecked in a thick fog which hung over Rocky Point in the Boscell Channel.

''The 'John and Winthrope' with the only colored captain on the Pacific Coast in command, left here in February and while in the Okhotsk Sea, secured four whales. The voyage back was begun October 13. When in latitude 8 degrees north and longitude 168 degrees east, a terrible typhoon swept down on the vessel. All sail was taken down at the first indication of the approach of dirty weather and the typhoon caught the whaler under bare poles.***The ship was laden down and all hands, as far as possible, remained below. The wind and sea increased in fury, smashed the davits and carried away one of the boats besides sweeping everything off the deck. For thirty long hours the tempest lasted, during which time no one on board ate nor slept. The man at the wheel when the storm was at its height was blown against the bulwarks and severely bruised and shaken.

''Another and more fierce typhoon caught the whaler on November 11. The wind, which blew with tremendous velocity, carried away all the sails. Hugh seas swept the decks as one mighty comber carried away two more of the boats from the starboard davits. The davits themselves were shattered, as was likewise the raft. The storm lasted forty-eight hours.***Many of those on board who had many years' experience say that never in their time had they seen such frightful weather.

''When near the Boscell channel, the 'John and Winthrope' ran into a thick fog and, when it lifted, she was only twenty feet off the rocks. The men on board say that nothing but Captain Shorey's coolness and clever seamanship saved the vessel. The 'John and Winthrope' visited the wreck of the 'Carrie and Ann' and brought down her cargo of bones. The vessel brought two hundred barrels of oil and 2,500 pounds of bones.''

In conversing with Captain Shorey concerning his life and success in following the sea, the writer was impressed with his high ideals as to right and wrong. He was reared an Episcopalian and is an active member of the Odd Fellows Lodge, Golden Gate No. 2007, also the Foresters No. 1704 and was Past Grand Master of Council 54, Patriots 93. He is on the Advisory Board of the Home for Aged and Infirm Colored People located at Beulah, near Oakland, California. He was master of sailing-vessels from 1887 to 1909 and at the present time holds a license to man a vessel of unlimited tonnage for sailing- or steamship in any ocean. He has retired from the sea and holds a position as special police officer for the Pacific Coast Steamship Company.

The wonderful success of many of Captain Shorey's trips was in a measure due to his happy marriage, and, unlike other sea-captains, he often was accompanied by his wife and daughter. Mrs. Shorey has a wonderful, calm personality and the following account as quoted from a San Francisco paper will show that often ''Love guided the wheel'' while Captain Shorey mastered the vessel: ''With Baby Shorey at the wheel. Commanded by Baby Shorey and the baby's father, Captain Shorey, the whaling bark 'Andrew Hicks' came down from the north this morning. She is the third vessel to return from the Arctic cruising this year. The baby and the whaler have been at sea since February, most of the time in Okhotsk waters. The baby is only three years old and it is considered creditable to so young a navigator that she and her father steered their bark further to the north than any other whaler ventured this year. Victoria is the name of the three-year-old child that has been engaged in hunting whales all summer while most other children have been engaged in less venturesome occupation.

''In an ice-drift off the coast of Siberia trouble was picked up.***'On a wild, stormy night we were driven into an ice-drift at Shanter Bay, and when daylight came we found ourselves caught by ice on every side,' said Captain Shorey today, using the plural pronoun with evident reference to himself and the baby. 'There was nothing in the world we could do but wait for the ice-fields to break up, and for eight days we lay wedged in the drift while the tides carried us back and forth, ever threatening to carry us on rocks or dash us on the shore.' This did not alarm the baby. Finally the ice was carried out to the open sea and the drift released the whaler.***During all the cruises of the whaler, Baby Shorey and the captain were accompanied by Mrs.

Shorey. 'Victoria is a remarkable sailor,' said the mother. 'She knows all the ropes, and has perfect command of her father.' ''

Mr. and Mrs. George W. Mitchel were natives of Virginia and relatives of Mrs. Rebecca Averett and Mrs. Ford, well-known citizens of Oakland. Mr. Mitchel was the oldest of the three and was their much-loved brother. It was on account of his living in California that they moved to the State. Mr. Mitchel's life is most interesting, because, while he accumulated thousands of dollars' worth of property during his residence in California, he also had the distinction of having been one of the few slaves, who, during their bondage, purchased property. This was an unusual occurrence, because the majority of them first desired their freedom and did all they could in hiring out their time to earn a little to apply to their manumission papers. Mr. Mitchel was born a slave in Halifax County, Virginia, and, when two years old, was sold from his parents and carried into Richmond, Va., where he remained until manhood. It was then that his thrift enabled him to buy property through the acquaintance of a charitable white lady, whose advice he followed. Evidently she realized that emancipation would some day come and this Negro would have a home to begin with. The laws of the country did not permit slaves to own property. She was honest and purchased it for him and held the same in her name until after President Lincoln issued the Emancipation Proclamation. She then deeded it to the rightful owner, Mr. George Mitchel. The property cost a small fortune. Mr. Mitchel paid $2,300 for a lot and $3,000 for a house and lot, but it was paid in Confederate money, which was not worth its face value.

After paying the purchase price for these two pieces of property the great desire came over Mr. Mitchel to become a free man, and somehow he made the acquaintance of a member of the "Underground Railroad" who assisted him, in 1862, to make his escape to Culpeper Court House Va,, where the Union Army was stationed. After answering many questions, he was given a position in the War Department, being accepted as steward on the Government steamship "Russia" that was engaged in taking the Government officials to Savannah, Ga., and to Charleston, S. C., to look after the cotton that had been taken from the rebels and stored in these towns. This voyage was so important that it was made with many cabinet officials such as Secretaries Wells and Stanton; Generals Sherman and Dodge, and also Senator Chandler.

After the close of the war Mr. Mitchel returned to Richmond, Va., and married Miss Mary Parsons, who had also been a slave. This union was blessed by the birth of one son who was named for the father, George (junior). Mr. and Mrs. Mitchel were both thrifty and desirous of advancing in life. They never allowed a chance to escape whereby they could better their condition. This led to their accepting an opportunity to come with the crew that opened the Palace Hotel in San Francisco in 1875. In this hotel Mr. Mitchel was given the position of bellman for the first floor. The tips alone for this position in those days were worth while. This enabled Mr. Mitchel, in a few years, to purchase property in San Francisco and Oakland. He retained this position for twenty-five years, when he was offered a better position in the mint, located in San Fancisco during President Harrison's administration. He retained this position during this Republican administration, but with a change of parties he was removed and again went to work for the Palace Hotel proprietors, as head bellman. He retained this position until the house changed to a Caucausian crew. Mr. Mitchel was then employed by the State Board and Harbor Commissioners for eight years, resigning owing to failing health.

During his long years of residence in San Francisco, he purchased many pieces of property, one was within a block of the Fairmont Hotel. He owned a two-story house at 2583 Sutter street; one at 292 Second Ave., another at 1665 10th street and 1022 Twenty-fourth street, corner of Linden in Oakland. Mr. Mitchel was a great lodge man, being a High Mason and serving as treasurer of his lodge for twenty-four years. He was Past Eminent Commander of Saint Bernard Commandery, having been in the Masonic Lodge in good standing for forty-five years. He was also a member of the Omega Chapter of Royal Arch Masons. He was reputed to be worth, at his death, between thirty and forty thousand dollars. He was practically a pioneer in the purchase of property for the Northern part of the State. He and his estimable wife enjoyed the confidence and respect of the community. He was ill for three years and passed away, leaving to mourn his passing his wife, one son and two sisters.

Mr. Alexander Averett, a distinguished citizen of Oakland, California, the subject of this sketch, is one of the pioneer citizens of the San Francisco Bay district of Northern California. He came to San Francisco from Virginia with his wife, Mrs. Rebecca Averett, over thirty years ago. He readily secured employment and with little interruption has been steadily employed ever since.

Through his industry and economy he has accumulated considerable property. Previous to the great fire of 1906, he resided in San Francisco where he was identified with the Odd Fellows and other organizations of help and uplift to the race. He was the prime mover in the organization of a Building and Loan Association among the colored citizens of San Francisco, the object of which was to encourage the Negro renters to acquire homes. Since moving to Oakland, Mr. Averett still retains his interest in the lodge and other organizations in San Francisco.

Mr. Averett, after moving to Oakland, became interested in the North Oakland Baptist Church, which was established by the late Richard Clark. He can be considered a pillar of this church, where he is untiring in fulfilling his duties as an honored and trusted officer. He is an intense race man and the weather is never too inclement for him to go either to his church or to any meeting which has for its object the uplift of the Negro race. Would that the race had a few more such conscientious workers! He and his wife are highly respected citizens, both among their own race and with the best white citizens of the Bay cities.

The Honorable Beverly A. Johnson was born of free parents in Washington, D. C. He has the distinction of having attended both the inauguration and the funeral of the martyred President Abraham Lincoln. He came to California in 1868 via the Straits of Magellan. He has lived in California ever since, spending his first four years on a ranch in Placer County, and the remainder of the time in Sacramento where he has lived an intensely active life for the best interest of the race. Mr. Johnson married, in 1870, the daughter of William and Hester Sanders, who came to California in 1857 from New Bedford, Mass., via the Isthmus of Panama. The union was blessed by the birth of three daughters and one son to all of whom he has given the best education obtainable in California, his son, Mr. Earnest Johnson, graduating with the pioneer class of Leland Stanford Junior College, of Palo Alto, California. During his college days he was active and prominent with the student-body and on the editorial staff of the student paper. He also assisted in setting the type and editing the same. He graduated with honors, majoring in law.

Mr. Johnson's daughters have all graduated with honor from the public schools of Sacramento and were among the first to enter the high school of that city. Mrs. Harper since has graduated with honor as a trained nurse from one of the training schools of that city, the first of the race to receive this distinction. Mrs. McCard is an excellent scholar and a delightful lady as was Mrs. Butler, now deceased. A son of Mrs. McCard at this writing is attending the University of California in Berkeley. Mr. Beverly A. Johnson is a thorough race man and did much in the fight for equal school privileges for the Negro children of California. He spent both time and money first in making a fight in Sacramento for this just privilege and then he joined hands with the men in San Francisco Bay district who finally carried their fight to the highest court of the State where they won a favorable verdict. A finer Negro gentleman and truer race advocate for equal citizenship does not live on this plane of human existence. He is an active member of the National Association for the Advancement of Colored People and will come from Sacramento, which is something less than a hundred miles from Oakland, to attend the executive Board meeting, or any public meeting that will aid in stimulating interest in the affairs of the Race. He is an active member of several fraternal lodges in the State, in many of which he has the distinction of being a charter member. He is a devoted Episcopalian, thoroughly reliable and has done much for this Church.

He is the best-informed man living today concerning the struggles of the Negro in California. It was through the Rev. Father Wallace that the writer had the privilege of meeting this delightful gentleman many years ago, while securing data for this book. His review of the history and struggles of the Negro in California was very valuable in after years when the creative work of the book was begun. Would that California and the Negro race throughout America and the entire world had just a few more such men! But, alas, he belongs to the Fred Douglass, Bishop Arnett, and Bishop T. M. D. Ward age of grand men who were great warriors in the cause of the race; men with sterling personality and executive ability.

Mr. James E. Grasses, coming to California in 1868 from New York City, was a splendidly educated gentleman and readily found employment as clerk with a mining company. He was for a number of years with Haggins and Travis, Capitalists, after which he was employed as Secretary to Judge Hastings and Judge Lake. He went to Virginia City as secretary and time keeper of the Jestice Mining Company. This mine was near the Mackey, Flood, Fair and O'Brien Mine.

Mr. Grasses in after years was employed as deputy county assessor and tax collector of Alameda County, California, for a great many years and died at his desk. He was a devoted husband and a delightful Christian gentleman. He left to mourn his passing

MRS. KATE BRADLEY-STOVALL (deceased)
Founder of the Southern California Alumni for the Colored.

MRS. EVA CARTER-BUCKNER
Poetess.

MRS. BEATRICE SUMNER-THOMPSON
Social and Civic Worker.

MRS. WILLA STEVENS
Modiste.

MRS. ELOISE BIBB-THOMPSON
Author and Writer.

one daughter to whom he had given a splendid education. She is a clerk in the San Francisco post office. Mrs. Grasses, the widow's sketch, will be found under "Distinguished Women."

The Honorable Wiley Hinds came to California in 1858 and, for a few days, located in Stockton. He met at this place some white men who were going to take up land in the San Joaquin Valley and do ranching. They spoke to him concerning accompanying them, stating that if he wanted to make money and have something when he was a man, the country would be the place to go. After thinking over the matter for a few days he decided that he would go and work for them and learn the lay of the land in California. He saved his money and soon bought a small plot of land and each year added to his holdings until he felt able to return home and marry. The lady whom he married was a delightful person and has made him a wonderful housewife. The union was blessed with a family of children. During their childhood days they lived on the ranch, the mother teaching them their letters until they were old enough to enter the public schools in Visalia, which they attended until sufficiently advanced to move to Oakland where the schools were better equipped. In Oakland Mrs. Hinds saw that all of her children were given the best education possible, at the same time making trips back to the valley to do whatever she could to encourage her husband in his great undertaking. This sustained him until his sons were older and he could call on them to assist in managing his ranch of several thousand acres. Mr. Hinds, in his day, has employed many of the colored ranch-holders in Fowler, who owe their success in farming in California with its scientific irrigation, to the experience they secured from working on Mr. Hind's ranch. He has thousands of acres which he divided up into ranches some of which are devoted to the raising of cattle, hogs and poultry. Another portion he has planted in vines and deciduous fruits, such as peaches, apples and prunes. He still retains this great ranch at Farmersville, California. One son, Mr. John Thomas Hinds, has in late years relieved his father of the heavy responsibility of the ranch. A sketch of one daughter will be found in the "Music" chapter. He has sons who have served in the Spanish-American War and another who is now serving in the National Army now in France.

There are a few other Negro people who have large, successful ranches in that district of whom the people seldom hear. One such ranch is located on an island in the King's River and is owned by Mr. and Mrs. Lewis Washington Brunson, who came to California from Sumpter County, Ga., in 1906. They first located in Los Angeles where Mr. Brunson engaged in peddling vegetables. When he had a little cash saved, he bought a ten-acre ranch in King's County, King's river, nine miles from Lamoore Township, and fifteen miles from Hanford. They planted this ranch in garden-truck and, during fruit season when others were cutting fruit, they were selling their garden-truck. They had a hard time of the adventure for a season, but were determined to not give up. The next year they purchased another fifty-acre plot, and planted it in grain, corn and potatoes. They continued until last year's crop, in June, 1917, they harvested a prosperous crop of barley, yielding $3,000 off of thirty-one acres; a crop of Egyptian corn yielded $2,000 from twenty-one acres. Eight or ten acres planted to potatoes yielded a good crop. They killed one hog in the fall, and after saving enough meat to last them for two years, they rendered from this same hog ninety pounds of lard. Mr. Brunson is happily married to Miss Mary Calbert, who is of great assistance to him. He owns a Buick auto of the latest model, five head of horses and all the latest models of farm implements. This is a fair example of what many persons of the race are doing all over California.

Mrs. Mary E. Crawford, on the same island as Mr. Brunson, owns a ranch of forty acres planted to Egyptian corn, grain and potatoes and has always had excellent crops. This lady makes a specialty of raising poultry for the market. She has a family of five children. One daughter, Mary, has recently graduated from the high school of Hanford, and another daughter is married to Mr. Welsher, of Hanford, California.

Mr. Isaac Jackson arrived in California in 1850, locating in Sacramento. Later he went to the mines until 1853 when he returned to Pittsburg, Penn., staying until 1887, when he returned to El Cajon Valley, San Diego, Cal., where he owned a ranch. He successfully managed the same for ten years, when he died. He left a wife and four children who still own the ranch and keep it stocked with cattle and hogs.

Dr. Burney also owns a ranch near San Diego which yields him a handsome income. Also John Moore, who came to California in 1850, located in the mountains nearby where he did successful ranching, as did Shephard Waters, who came in 1850, from Pennsylvania and did successful ranching in San Diego County.

Mr. Henry Hall came to California in 1848 with a half-brother, riding horseback all the way from Missouri. He was just a boy of fourteen years and was employed as a teamster, hauling freight in Tuolumne and Mariposa Counties, where he made his home. He died, leaving a homestead in northern California, near Stockton. A daughter, Mrs. Potts, and her husband live on this place and are successful ranchers. She is a devoted Christian woman and a great worker for the cause of temperance. At one time she traveled all over the State and organized societies for the advancement of the cause of temperance work among the race.

James Monroe Bridges, the subject of this sketch, was born in Hickory County, North Carolina, receiving his education in the rural schools. During the summer he worked in the tobacco factories to help earn a living for the family, since they were dependent upon the small wages the father was able to earn in that district. He came to California with his father in 1889, and first located in Fresno and later Bakersfield, where he was instrumental in organizing the well-known business firm of furniture-dealers known all over the State as the "Winters, Bridges and Simpson Furniture Dealers." The success of this company has been great. About ten years ago Mr. Bridges moved to Oakland where he opened a branch store. Later he purchased the Oakland Sunshine, a race paper, published and founded by Mr. John Wilds. Mr. Bridges is an active lodge man, beloning to the Ancient Order of Foresters and is president of the Oakland Literary and Aid Society. He also belongs to the Occidental Lodge and the Grand United Order of Odd Fellows and is one of the promoters of the Oakland Negro Business Men's League.

The colored citizens of Pasadena are thrifty and own many beautiful homes. The writer was greatly surprised to find that a great deal of the landscape gardening has been done by Negro workmen who still retain their positions. Among the leading and successful gardeners is Mr. Weatherton, who, after working for one family over thirty years, has been retired on a pension.

The late Henderson Boon, who for over twenty-five years conducted a blacksmith shop in Pasadena, was killed a few years ago in an automobile accident. His wife and son still conduct the business. They own a beautiful home and other properties. A son, Henderson Boon, is in the employ of the city and a daughter, Mrs. James Miller, has a daughter who is a great singer and is called the "Canary Mocking-bird of Southern California."

The Prince Family of Pasadena is another fine family and is interested in every movement for the best interests of the race. They have lived in that city for over thirty years. There are three brothers.

Mr. J. W. Oatman, a gardener, owns considerable property which has increased in value until it is now worth at least five figures. Also Mr. Bodkyn owns valuable holdings. Mr. Thomas J. Pillow also owns a beautiful home in Pasadena and reared all his children there previous to moving to Los Angeles. One son learned his trade in Pasadena in Hodge Brothers' machine shop where at the age of fourteen he made a machine and gas engine. Mr. Pillow is now demonstrator with the Western Motor Car Company on Olive street, Los Angeles.

Pasadena is the home of Mrs. Corrine Hicks and also of Miss Marie Ford whose families are among the pioneers of this city, which is also the home of Captain Reynolds, and many others too numerous to mention but who are good citizens and race-loving, enterprising persons. They have several churches, the Friendship Baptist Church having sent more boys to the front in the first draft than any other church in Southern California.

Los Angeles, California. It will be impossible for the writer in this book to fully describe the enterprise and thrift of the citizens of this city. They had the first Fire Department in the United States manned by Negro firemen. At one time they had two companies. They have many patrolmen, one detective, substantial business enterprises and lovely, modern homes. The story of Los Angeles is like the gold thread in paper money to ensure that it is genuine currency. Thus it is with this city. There is not a chapter in this book that has not a sketch of one or more citizens of this beautiful city.

They have wonderful apartment houses, modern in every appointment. The first to build were Mr. and Mrs. Fern Ragland who were followed by Mr. and Mrs. Lewis, McDowell, Robinson, Alexander and Chrisman. They have one successful home for working women, namely "The Sojourner Truth Home," which was founded through the influence of the late Mrs. Sessions who has left a lasting memory in the hearts of the people. There were others who worked for the founding of the Sojourner Truth Club, namely, Mrs. James Alexander, Mrs. Shackelford and Mrs. Scott. The friends furnished it free of cost to the club and the writer, while not a member or even a resident of Los Angeles, gave a mahogany book-case and writing-desk, together with fifty books by colored authors and many others of value to girls without employment since she believes that a good book is the kindest thing to give to an idle person and is next to work or a home. There is another institution of great value located in Los Angeles and that is the Y. M. C. A. which was founded many years ago and has been successfully managed by that grand gentleman, Mr. T. A. Green, who is a well educated Christian gentleman. Mr. Green is an Alumnus of Rust University, and, at various times, has held professor-ships in Rust, Walden, Alcon and the New Orleans Universities. He is an old news-paper-man, having edited and published *The Enterprise* in Mississippi and California. Mr. Green is a fine executive and has brought the Y. M. C. A. from nothing to the present comfortable quarters and, had not the World War drawn the United States into its meshes, they would have built a large building. Instead they have built a ground-floor auditorium with all the necessary equipments of a modern Y. M. C. A., with baths and everything else. Mr. Green is discreet, of high principle, reasonable and a good man to have as a friend, and every man in the Association feels and knows that Professor Green has a deep interest in his personal and spiritual welfare.

Mr. Theo. Troy, another highly respected citizen of Los Angeles, comes from the distinguished and highly respected family of Theodore Troy of Cincinnati, whose father for a number of years was a messenger in one of the largest banks in that city and who was one of the founders of the Zion Baptist Church of Cincinnati. This son, Mr. Theo. Troy, was educated in the public schools of Cincinnati, graduating from the old Gains high school. After graduating he went to Tennessee where he was employed in the Government service as letter-carrier for a number of years. While living there he married and decided to come to Los Angeles to live. He did not succeed in getting anything to do immediately, so he decided to polish shoes for awhile. Later he took the civil service examination and received an appointment as letter-carrier in the city of Los Angeles, being the first of the race to receive such an appointment. After filling this position for a number of years he purchased a corner lot and improved the same. It is located at San Pedro and East Twelfth streets where he has a residence and a second-hand furniture store. Mr. Troy in late years has invested successfully in mining stock. He has a wife and one son whose sketch will be found in the "Music" chapter. The writer is grateful to Mrs. Troy who several years ago furnished her with a copy of the *Los Angeles Times,* February 12, 1909, which contained the historical accounts of the race in that city.

RIVERSIDE, CALIFORNIA, a most beautiful city, numbers among its residents some of the most enterprising colored people in the State. They are not so numerous, but they have the executive ability to have something. Several years ago they built a block and opened a dry goods store, grocery and a butcher-shop. These stores occupy the ground floor and the second floor is given over to an auditorium, or hall, which has been named "The Mercantile Hall," the leading citizens of color forming a company and sharing the expense of this hall.

Mr. Bob Stokes has lived in Riverside for forty year. There are many creditable citizens living in this city, among whom are the Rev. Frank Cooper, the Rev. Simpson, Jerry Wiley, Mr. and Mrs. D. S. Stokes and Mr. and Mrs. Chas. Gordon.

There is another man in California who has been extremely enterprising and that is Mr. Winters of Bakersfield, who many years ago built the Winters block, valued at fifty thousand dollars, and has located in the block, many successful businesses oper-ated by members of the race. On the second floor is a large hall, which is used for fraternal organizations.

Mr. Jordan Young came from Columbia, South Carolina, December 21, 1891, locat-ing at Fowler, California at the suggestion of his sister, Mrs. Julia Bell. He passed the station going to Fresno, which was ten miles away. It cost thirty cents to return to Fowler and he only had thirty-five, so he walked. He soon secured work and in a few years sent back for his family which consisted of a wife and seven children. After this he began to save and buy property. He bought a city block for four hundred dollars, retaining the same until the town began to grow, when he sold twenty-two lots for $2,500 and bought eleven more for $700. He then made a vow that none of his children should marry until they owned a home. At this writing Mr. Young owns a ranch of 160 acres of well-improved property, aside from valuable city holdings. His daughters, Mrs. Reuben Wysinger and Mrs. Abernathy, of Bowles, all own valuable holdings as also does one son, Dr. Benjamin Young, who has graduated from both the University of California and a University in Chicago, recently locating in Fowler to practice medicine.

Modesto, California, lies midway between Stockton and Fresno. Many of the old pioneers of the race live there. It is the home of Mr. and Mrs. Joseph Bishop, well-educated young people who have made their presence felt in the community with all races. Recently Mr. Bishop, who for many years has been steadily employed at the head of the carpet department of a large store in Modesto, decided to open a store of his own, and is doing well.

Mr. and Mrs. Knox are also progressive citizens of this town and own considerable ranch property. She is a former school teacher and her husband is a retired Baptist minister.

Mr. Walter Archibald Butler, the subject of this sketch, was born in Baltimore, Md., being the youngest and seventh son of the late John and Martha Butler, who brought him to California in 1878. He attended the public schools of Oakland for ten years and then entered a large law firm in San Francisco to read law. This firm soon dissolved partnership, and, while waiting to enter another law-office, he accepted a vacation position in a fire insurance office and has remained there for twenty-eight years. In addition to holding a position in the office of the Liverpool, London and Globe Insurance Company, he has conducted a loan and insurance office at 251 Kearny street, San Francisco, for ten years. This office being managed until the date of his marriage by his future wife, Miss E. Ardella Clayton. In his early manhood Mr. Butler resolved that the interests of the race could be best cared for by organization. Therefore, he identified himself with those organizations that to him held out the brightest future for the race, particularly in which the Caucasian and the Ethiopian met and fraternized on an equal basis. The doors of that great English fraternal order, "The Ancient Order of Foresters," were opened to the race about this time and Mr. Butler became a member and has labored assiduously therein for a quarter of a century, receiving all the honors that "Court Bournemonth" could give him. At the session of the Subsidiary High Court of the A. O. G. held in San Francisco in May, 1918, he was elected to the office of High Court Junior Woodward, thereby becoming a member of the Executive Council for two years. This is the first time in twenty-five years that this exalted honor has been conferred on one of the race.

Mr. Butler is also a member of Knarsbourgh' Circle, C. O. G. P. N. G. of Occidental Lodge G. N. O. O. F., Past President of Planet Lodge No. 1, A. R. E., President and one of the founders of the Northern California Branch of the National Association for the Advancement of Colored People. Secretary and treasurer of the Afro-American Co-Operative Association; secretary and treasurer of the Waiters' Employment Association. In politics he has long been identified with the Republican Party and at the last State Convention of the party held in Sacramento, in August, 1918, he was elected a member of the Republican State Central Committee. Mr. Butler was married to Miss E. Ardelle Clayton, on April 19, 1916, at "Wrest-Acre," the home he had built the previous year. His home-life is ideal and he takes much pleasure in showing his friends his pet hobbies, to-wit: his gardens and his thoroughbred poultry. For recreation, when time permits, the Butlers are enthusiastic motorists.

Hon. James M. Alexander. An appreciation, by E. I. Chew, in the June, 1910, *Cactus Magazine.* "James M. Alexander is a bright example of our young western manhood and thoroughly typical of whatever is good and admirable among the best of our race. Of the elements which go to make up a strong, good man he has a full and varied store, being industrious, law-abiding, intelligent, sagacious, whole-souled, sympathetic, manly and thoroughly honest and courageous. His civic spirit is shown not only by passively refraining from the infraction of law, but by his active influence to help his fellow men to a higher plane and there to assume and retain the right attitude toward the law and performance of civic duty. He is the product of our system of public schools, to which he later added a business course and a law course, broadening his horizon by a systematic study of our best literature. History, as influenced by great moral and industrial questions; statecraft, to meet and control these issues to the betterment of the whole people; political parties, as the engines to perform the tasks as directed by the statesmen—these questions early took hold of him. To them he gave much study and thought. They made him a republican. They strengthened his love for his race and indicated his duty to him. The growth of the scope and power of the organization of which he is the head is the outcome of his meditation and reveals his sagacity.

"If he were not chock-full of whole-souled human sympathy he could not attract to him so many men of diverse character and rivet them to him with fetters strong as steel. The trouble, whether whipped by adverse fortune or paying penalty of indiscretion, vice or sin, have in him a sympathizer and willing helper to secure for the one consolation, for the other, a chance for reformation and rehabilitation. Mr. Alexander is a manly man, lives a clean, home-centered life. Frivolous, boyish, foolish, questionable actions, speeches, assumptions, ambitions and ideas never come from him; they are not in him. Grave yet simple, sincere and kindly in manner and speech, his character gives added force to what he says and does. You instinctively acknowledge when you come into his presence, 'This is a Man.'

"That element which more than any other has contributed to the wonderful growth of the Afro-American Council in this State, is the personality of Mr. Alexander, its head. That element in his character which appeals most to the people is his unswerving and inflexible honesty; you can always know where to find him, for he is never on the fence. The goddess of his early boyish love is the divinity of his ripened manhood. The recognition given him by the Chief Executive of the Nation in placing Mr. Alexander among her financial agents was well bestowed and well deserved. His position is and will continue to be well-filled. It is a great inspiration to any boy to look at the life and character of Mr. Alexander and realize that it is in his power to do as well. Mind has no color. That honor, integrity, high principle and clean-living are the inalienable right and privilege of every American. The color of skin nor texture of hair must not count, and, if we are true to ourselves, shall not mean inferiority in intellect, conscientiousness, sense of responsibility or possibility of achievement. Unquestionably he is one of the foremost Negroes of the West."

"Mr. Cyrus Vena was born in North Middleton, Kentucky, April 4, 1829. He was married to Sarah J. Wernell in 1849; moved to Xenia, Ohio, in 1851, taking an active part in every movement for the uplift and encouragement of the Negro race. The union was blessed by the birth of seven children, five girls and two boys, only two of whom are now living, James M. and Miss Sing A. Vena. They are residents of Los Angeles. The son for a number of years has been employed as a clerk in the city post office. Mr. Vena was distinguished while a resident of Xenia, Ohio, by being elected for two different terms as a member of the City Council and the Board of Equalization. He was also a member of the board of trustees of Wilberforce University. Mr. Vena was a contractor and builder by trade. During his residence in Ohio he contracted for and built many notable buildings at Wilberforce and Xenia. He erected many handsome residences for distinguished persons in the race, namely, Bishops Payne, Shorter, and Arnett; also the Ohio Soldiers' and Sailors' Orphan Home, located at Xenia.

Mr. Vena and his family moved to Los Angeles over thirty years ago, and he immediately identified himself with all the activities of value to the race. He joined the historic Eighth and Towne Church, which at the time was located on Azusa street. Shortly after coming to Los Angeles he and his wife celebrated their golden wedding, and less than three months afterward Mrs. Vena passed to her reward."

Since the above data was given the writer, several years ago, by the son of the subject, Father Vena has passed to his reward. He was employed for thirty years as head janitor of the Hall of Records in Los Angeles, and at his passing, which occurred Monday evening, September 23, 1918, the flag of the City Hall was kept at half mast until after his funeral. The Board of Public Works and the City Council adopted resolutions of respect. *The California Eagle*, in speaking of the funeral, said: "Father Cyrus Vena, at a ripe old age, crosses the divide. No prince or potentate ever received greater homage than was the lot of Father Vena, over whose body the last sad rites were held on last Thursday at Eighth and Towne Avenue A. M. E. Church. The large edifice was filled to pay their last respects to the memory of this venerable patriarch. The city officials and the Mayor, represented by his secretary, were at the funeral. Father Vena was ninety years old at his passing and had been a member of the A. M. E. Church for sixty years."

Mr. David Cunningham, the subject of this sketch, was the first colored bricklayer to work on any important building in the City of Los Angeles. He assisted in the construction of the Douglass and Stimpson blocks. Later, as a contractor, he erected Bekin's warehouse and the East side cannery, and many others. Mr. Cunningham married the daughter of Mrs. Harney, who is the widow of the pioneer Sheriff of Hinds County, Jackson, Mississippi. The union was blessed by the birth of several children, to all of whom they gave the best education California afforded. Since then the children have honored their parents and the race by filling places of responsibility and dignity. Their daughter, Miss Mamie, who recently married Lieutenant Journer White, was employed, previous to her marriage as clerk in the main Los Angeles postoffice. She was very popular socially. During spare time she assisted in editing *The New Age*, a splendid race paper published in Los Angeles. A son, Harvey, is with the Los Angeles Trust and Savings Company of that city. David, another son, is employed by the Don Lee Automobile Company as a mechanic; Lawrence, another son, is special messenger of the United States mail from the main postoffice of the City of Los Angeles, California; Miss Edna is a student at the Jefferson High School, and Master Russell is a student at the Fourteenth Street Intermediate. Mrs. Cunningham-Slaten is one of the distinguished women of Los Angeles, an active worker of the Sojourner-Truth Club, and a member of the Soldiers' and Sailors' Welfare Commission. She is kind and a sincere co-worker in every movement for the betterment of the race.

Mr. Louis M. Blodgett, the subject of this sketch, is the son of Albert and Amanda Blodgett, of Augusta, Georgia. He was educated at Miss Laney's school, in his home town. Among other things, he learned the trade of tile-setting and brick mason. He was at one time secretary of the Bricklayers' Union of Augusta, Georgia, and was elected by them as a delegate to the convention of Bricklayers' Union which met at Trenton, New Jersey. He came to Los Angeles with his brothers about thirteen years ago. They found the prejudices so great that in order to get work they were compelled to do their own contracting, which they were competent to do, thereby giving work to many Negro workmen. Later, Mr. Louis Blodgett decided to not have any partners, but continued to do contract work. By careful attention to business, he has built up a business that has enabled him to have a weekly payroll of from $500 to $1,800, an amount sufficient to insure that he employs a large force of Negro mechanics, bricklayers and other workmen, thus opening a door for our men who hitherto were unable to secure employment at their trade on buildings. Mr. Blodgett is busy the year round. During the past winter he built a large hotel in Brawley, in the Imperial Valley of Southern California.

Mr. Louis M. Blodgett is a member of the Contractors' Association of Los Angeles. He is on the board of directors of the People's Realty Company. He has acquired much valuable property, including his own modern home on Dewy avenue, Los Angeles. He married Miss Nella Allensworth, the daughter of the late Colonel Allensworth. The union has been blessed by the birth of two children, Allensworth J. and Josephine L. Blodgett. Would that the race had a few more such men who were capable of and would open the door of opportunity for the workmen of our race!

Mr. and Mrs. Hal Pierson and Mrs. Ellen Jacobs, coming to California from Tennessee in 1845, located in Vallejo. Mr. Pierson, working in the Navy Yards at Mare Island, learned the trade of building light houses, and afterward moved to San Francisco, where he owned stock in the California street railroad. There were several children to bless the union. They were educated in the public schools of San Francisco. Their names are Alonza, who for twenty years was employed in the custom house, in San Francisco; Thomas Pierson, who was admitted to practice as an attorney at law in Chicago; Mrs. Henry Weimer, a successful cateress at Pasadena, and Mrs. Cassandra Louise Jacobs, a great songstress of San Francisco. Her husband, Nathaniel Jacobs, is a chauffeur and mechanic in San Francisco, California.

Hon. T. B. Morton was a great race man and a leader among the people. He was employed as a messenger to District Judge Morrow, of San Francisco, and was a distinguished member of the Afro-American League and many other helpful organizations in San Francisco and throughout the State of California. He has left a memory well worthy to inspire others in an effort to assist the race in sincerity.

Mr. Abraham Butler Brown and wife, Mary Robinson-Brown, came to California, from Philadelphia, Pa., in 1852. They were blessed with two children, Mary and Julia, who were native daughters of California. Miss Julia became the wife of Mr. William Nell Saunderson and Miss Mary became the wife of Mr. Morey, a successful business man of Oakland. She was for years, the Treasurer and earnest worker of the Home for Aged and Infirm Colored People at Beulah, Cal.

Mr. A. J. Jones came to California over thirty years ago from Emporia, Kansas. He located in Los Angeles and built the first hotel owned by colored people in that city. It was located at 109 San Pedro street. This section of the street at this writing is called Wilmington. Mr. Jones made a specialty of hot biscuits and was always well patronized by the tourist trade. He was more than successful and about ten years ago retired to enjoy a well-earned rest. He has reared several orphan children and has done other good charitable work throughout Los Angeles. Mr. Jones was for thirty-five years a member of the Christian Church, but after the organization of the People's Independent Church of Christ he became identified with it and is a Deacon of the Seventh District. He is a member of the Y. M. C. A. and a charter member of the Men's Forum. About ten years ago he married Mrs. Billingsley and they are very happy and vitally interested in all movements that have for their aim the advancement of the race. They are both active members of the Ohio State Club.

Mr. Richard H. Dunston, the owner of the Los Angeles Truck and Storage Co., has lived in Los Angeles over thirty years. He has been in this business over twenty-five years, building, in 1905, his first warehouse, which covers one hundred feet by one hundred and twenty feet and is two stories high. He owns seven vans and six open wagons which he uses in moving, packing and shipping furniture. Aside from this he also owns his residence, his barn, and several other valuable pieces of property. He and his wife are highly respected citizens of the city of Los Angeles.

Mr. and Mrs. J. H. Shackelford, who own the Canadian store of new and second-hand furniture, have been in business about fifteen years, starting with comparatively nothing. She clerked while Mr. Shackelford delivered the goods to customers on a bicycle. They were determined to make a success and at this writing they own their own delivery-wagons and have a store valued at ten thousand dollars, besides their own seven-passenger touring car and other valuable property. Mrs. Shackelford is a prominent club worker and has done much for the success of the building of Sojourner-Truth Home. She was an enthusiastic worker and furnished a beautiful room in this home when completed. She stands for all that is good and clean in advancing the race. She is a devoted worker in visiting the sick and needy and is practical and reliable, without pomp or self praise. She is one of the pillars of the Independent Church of Christ, and the head of the deaconess board, a delightful Christian lady who is well known and highly respected. Mr. Shackelford is an officer of the same church and a good conscientious Christian gentleman, a graduate of Corning Academy and Simpson College.

Mr. Andrew J. Roberts came to Los Angeles, California, from Chillicotha, Ohio, over thirty years ago. He was accompanied to the coast by Mr. Dunston and they together organized the Los Angeles Van, Truck and Storage Company. Several years afterward they built or had built two of the largest vans in the city.

After fourteen years Mr. Roberts, finding the work did not agree with his health, resigned from the business and later opened the Roberts Undertaking establishment. This is the pioneer establishment in the State. Mr. Roberts has been very successful and is assisted in the business by his sons, Frederick Madison and William G. Roberts, the latter being the business manager of the firm. About two years ago Mr. Roberts, together with his sons, built a modern block for the housing of the undertaking establishment and also the *New Age*, a race paper owned and published by his son, Hon. Frederick Madison Roberts. This is the most up-to-date building of its kind owned by colored people in the State of California. The second floor is used for an auditorium and has perfect acoustics and will seat fully five hundred persons. Mr. Andrew J. Roberts has been most fortunate in having a family of sons who have worked for and with him in building up a good business in both the undertaking business and the race paper. This has enabled him to invest money in land, both in the San Joaquin Valley, where he owns eighty acres, and in Lower California. His son-in-law, Mr. Izan E. Saunders, is an expert embalmer, and, aside from caring for all his father's business, does much work in that line for the Japanese undertakers of Los Angeles. His wife, Mrs. Myrtle Estelle Roberts-Saunders, is a great musician and a joy to her family and friends.

Mr. John Wesley Coleman, the distinguished and well-known real estate and employment agent of Los Angeles, was born at Columbus, Texas, March 12, 1865. He is the son of Sam and Mattie (Green) Coleman and was educated in the Tilleston Institute of Austin, Texas, graduating in 1884. He married Miss Lydia Lee of Austin, Texas, in 1885. The union has been blessed by four children. Mr. Coleman was active in church and Sunday school work in Texas until 1887 when he moved to Los Angeles, Cal. Since locating in that city, he has distinguished himself by becoming an active member of the Texas State club, the Y. M. C. A., the Forum, Odd Fellows, Knights of Pythias and is a thirty-third degree Mason. When first locating in Los Angeles he followed landscape gardening and contracting, later serving the Pullman Company for twelve years, after which time he was proprietor of Hotel Coleman for five years. He has served as deputy constable of Los Angeles County and township for the past fifteen years.

Mr. Coleman is reliable and highly-respected by all citizens of the State. Because of this he was employed to travel throughout the State in advertising and developing the cities of Venice and Santa Monica Bay district. After two years he accepted the position as assistant superintendent of Dr. Burner's chain of sanitariums located throughout the State. Mr. Coleman has successfully conducted in Los Angeles a real estate and employment agency for the past twelve years, during which time he has placed in good positions in the State and elsewhere over twenty-five thousand colored people. He is noted for his kindness to the needy and distressed. He is public spirited and was selected to make the presentation speech when the Second Negro Drafted boys gave an American flag to the People's Independent Church of Christ of Los Angeles. He is an active member of the Forum Club of Los Angeles, and his name has been mentioned for the presidency of that well-established club.

In speaking of the Forum, the following by Theodore W. Troy, is quoted from the *Los Angeles Times* under date of February 12, 1909: ''This large body was organized February 1, 1903, at the First African Methodist Church for the purpose of encouraging united effort on the part of Negroes for their advancement and to strengthen them along lines of moral, social, intellectual, financial and Christian ethics. Any man or woman of good character is eligible to membership and no fees are charged. Its meetings are held every Sunday afternoon at four o'clock at the Odd Fellows' Hall, corner Eighth and Wall streets, and the public is always welcome. Thus the humblest citizen has access to those meetings and can state his grievance before this body. The following are its recently-elected officers: president, Thomas A. Cole; vice-president, Morgan T. White; recording secretary, Harvey Bruce; corresponding secretary, J. L. Edmonds; treasurer, J. Edwin Hill; critic, Mrs. Eva Queen.

''In our work along moral lines the permanent issue has been the suppression of the vicious element. To this end we have worked in harmony with the pulpit, the press, the Chief of Police and especially with our Negro officers, for the closing of dens of vice. The Forum has, from time to time, appointed committees on strangers to keep new-comers to our city in the proper channel for its moral uplift. These strangers are introduced to the Forum and a chance given them to meet the best class of our race and become useful members of society. We believe in the Good Samaritan principle of life and hope to win into our ranks every good citizen. Our organization teaches race-love, race-pride and declares a good character to be the highest social credential. It looks with pride upon those who are smilingly taking up the responsibilities of life in helping to uplift our race and only asks those who are dodging these responsibilities not to be stumbling-blocks to us.

''The intellectual food for the Forum is derived from the various lectures and papers read from time to time by some of America's brainiest thinkers and scholars. The current topics clipped from the daily papers are read and discussed at our meetings. These discussions form one of the most instructive and entertaining features of our organization. Financially the Forum takes the position of a philanthropist. All of its monies except the actual current expenses are given to charity. To its members it especially advises the utmost frugality and warns them that the price of land in this vicinity now within reach of the ordinary laborer will not always remain so. It strongly advocates the purchase now of real estate in this section. There is nothing in the solid financial world offering greater inducements to small investors. The Forum was instrumental in the settling of a small colony on government land in San Bernardino County, California, near Victorville.***

''From the civic standpoint the Forum declares for the majesty of the law and advocates its respect. A knowledge of the supremacy of the law and of the justice of the judiciary of this fair land has in the greatest measure led to our presence here. The Forum stamped its approval on President Roosevelt's 'Door of Hope,' 'The Square Deal' and 'All Men Up.' It declares Booker T. Washington our greatest benefactor and insists that we can only rise in proportion as we are useful in our respective communities. It advises its members to conduct themselves in such a manner as to win the respect of the people of their communities and thereby to create favorable race sentiment.

''The Forum does not regard the giving of menial positions the fulfillment of patronage due Negro tax-payers. We believe the governing powers of this city should take the lead in fairly treating Negro citizens. In the ethics of Christianity, the Forum, born as it was under the shadow of God's altar, can only point to Christ as the exemplary life. It classes the church as the highest institution.

''The Forum has met every deserving appeal for charity with a substantial donation. Among its beneficiaries might be named the San Francisco earthquake sufferers, the Atlanta riots sufferers, the Florence Crittenden Home, the Helping Hand Society, The Sheltering Arms Home, the Day Nursery and many deserving individuals.***It has always worked in harmony with the Church and has been especially active in work with the colored Y. M. C. A.''

The Forum has educated the first colored lady doctor on the Pacific Coast in the person of Dr. Ruth J. Temple of Los Angeles. It has also contributed to scholarships for many others studying in the East for law and other professions. The writer regards it as one of the greatest clubs since ''The Underground Railroad'' because of its actual help to individuals and the community.

Mrs. Lucy Caulwell-Disard arrived in San Francisco, California, in 1855, coming from Bowling Green, Kentucky, with her parents, Isaac and Maria Caulwell, together with her sister, Margret, and brothers, Charles and Zackariah. The father, as a boy, was purchased his freedom by his mother (who was also a slave) and sent to New York to be educated; instead he shipped as a cabin boy on the first ship leaving for Africa. The ship was wrecked and he was the only survivor. He was held as a captive for five years by the natives, during which time he learned five different lingoes. He arrived in Africa in 1820, and after five years made his escape and reached Liberia, Africa, where he met President Roberts, who was the first President of the Republic of Liberia. Mr. Caulwell remained in Africa three additional years. He took up considerable land in Africa and a town located forty miles from Liberia was named after him. In time he returned to New York and to his home at Bowling Green, Kentucky, where he married Miss Maria Barnett. He then decided to go to California and engage in placer mining and earn enough to take his family to Africa. When he returned to his home in Kentucky he found that his wife's health was very poor, and for fear that she could not stand the trip he changed his plans, and, instead, moved to California. He reached Kentucky on his return trip in 1853, and returned to California by ox team in 1855. The family for a while lived on Leidsdorff street, San Francisco, afterward moving to Sacramento, California.

In two years he returned to Kentucky and brought to California his mother, Mrs. Lucy Titus, his mother-in-law, Mrs. Sophia Barnett, and also his sister, Sophia Schofield. During the flood of 1861 in Sacramento the family lost everything they had, and was compelled to step from the second-story window into a boat to save their lives. They finally reached San Francisco where they afterwards lived.

Mr. Caulwell gave his children the best education possible, one daughter, Lucy, graduating at the head of her class, receiving a silver medal. In after years she married Mr. Luther Disard, who had come to California in 1863 from Topeka, Kansas, with a company of soldiers as far as Idaho, and thence across the plains into California. The union was blessed by the birth of ten children, eight of whom are still living. They were given a thorough education in the public schools of Oakland. The daughters were musical and one son was for a number of years book-keeper for the San Francisco Jockey Club. Mrs. Lucy Caulwell-Disard is a prominent church and club worker in Oakland, a beautiful Christian lady with a winsome personality.

Mr. Louis G. Robinson came to California in January, 1904, from Barnsville, Georgia. He was in the senior class in Payne Theological School, Augusta, Ga., when he decided to leave for California. Upon his arrival he located in Pasadena, where he was one of the founders of Scott Chapel (M. E.) and served as pastor for three successive terms. Later he served as porter in the Pasadena Hospital. In 1907 he moved to Los Angeles, where he was appointed as janitor for Los Angeles County buildings and in 1912 was appointed by the Supervisors Chief Janitor and Custodian of the County Buildings, having under his immediate supervision fifty-five men and one woman. He employs many colored men. This is the first time the position has been held by a colored man. Mr. Robinson has on his force two white men who were chief janitors prior to his appointment and who highly respect him. Mr. Robinson has been entrusted to the supervision of all the County sales under $50. He is a thorough race man and well respected by all citizens.

CHAPTER XIII

JUST CALIFORNIA

JUST CALIFORNIA.

'Twixt the sea and the deserts,
　'Twixt the wastes and the waves,
Between the sands of buried lands
　And ocean's coral caves,
It lies not East nor West
　But like a scroll unfurled,
Where the hand of God hath hung it,
　Down the middle of the world.

It lies where God hath spread it,
　In the gladness of His eyes,
Like a flame of jeweled tapestry
　Beneath the shining skies;
With the green of woven meadows
　And the hills in golden chains,
The light of leaping rivers,
　And the flash of poppied plains.

Days rise that gleam in glory,
　Days die with sunset's breeze,
While from Cathay that was of old
　Sail countless argosies;
Morn breaks again in splendor
　O'er the giant, new-born West,
But of all the lands God fashioned,
　'Tis this land is the best.
Just California stretching down
　The middle of the world.

The poem above-quoted is from the pen of Mr. John Steven McGroarty and is one of the most charming ever written concerning California. It is a new world so unlike any other; its climate is so varied. A stranger coming into the State can hardly believe the different statements told him concerning its joys and delights. The old residenters will tell him that immediately after the rainy season, spring in all its beauty without a pause will greet him. They will also say that the more rain, the greener the grass and the greater the abundance of fresh vegetables. The stranger will think it unbelievable that the thermometer will register 114 degrees in the San Joaquin Valley during the months of July and August and yet at night one can sleep under blankets.

People invariably remove to California either for health or business reasons without first finding out the particular part of this far-away western land is best suited for their interests. It does not require long for one to rest from his trip to the State and then realize he is far away from old friends. Immediately he lays the state of his feelings to the weather, forgetting that he should have first found out all about the climate in that part of the State before coming. No other State in America has such a variety of climate and business possibilities as this State, yet it is of the greatest value to learn all the truthfulness concerning both before locating. If people would only do this, they would not only save themselves the feeling of depression, but often their success in business would be assured by such knowledge.

The Sacramento Valley lies less than a hundred miles from San Francisco. It is one of the greatest agricultural belts in the State, producing the finest asparagus in America. All the canned asparagus shipped to the eastern markets is grown in the Sacramento Valley of California. It is white, large and full and is grown in such quantities that the poorest family can feast on it for months.

They also raise oranges and lemons in this valley. It used to be considered an impossibility to raise these fruits outside of Southern California, but, through the valuable aid furnished by the University of California, oranges are raised and marketed within less than a hundred miles from San Francisco. The first Valencias of the season are raised and shipped from the Sacramento Valley and bring the highest price. They are delicious, especially those grown in Pengrin and Oroville, showing plainly that the soil of every section of the State is productive. The University of California will gladly furnish anyone with an analysis of the ground and will explain just what it will produce, thereby enabling the farmer to secure the best results.

The first luscious cherries of the season are grown in the Sacramento Valley. The greatest industry of this valley is the raising of rice. Last year's yield was a million bushels, not a bad crop for an infant industry. Nearly all kinds of deciduous fruits are grown in this valley in such quantities that they supply not only the home markets but are shipped to the eastern markets. Any of the Sacramento Valley ranches can be reached in less than a day's ride from San Francisco.

The largest city in the valley is Sacramento, which is also the Capital of the State of California. It is a beautiful city, with well-paved streets, homes and business blocks planned with the object of adding to the beauty of the city. The shade-trees of the city are especially attractive, consisting of every variety grown in California. They are especially beautiful in the Capitol grounds. This city, like Washington, D. C., radiates from the Capitol grounds and the streets are designated in the same way— that is by letters. All the railroads lead to Sacramento which is really the gateway to the San Joaquin Valley. There is a line of steamers plying on the Sacramento River making trips from San Francisco to Sacramento. Such a trip carries the passenger through the waters of the San Francisco Bay, the San Pablo and Suisun Bays into the Sacramento River and is often spoken of as equal to a trip in Switzerland or down the Rhine River—it is so picturesque. The climate of the Sacramento Valley is very hot in summer with a refreshing breeze in the evening. They suffer with tule-fogs during the winter months, fogs which are produced from the tule-lands and invariably pass down to San Francisco. They are at present working these lands over into profitable rice fields, and in other ways and it is a possibility that in time these fogs will disappear.

The San Joaquin Valley is the longest in the State and one of the greatest producers of deciduous fruits. It lies between the high Sierras and the Coast Range. The climate of California can be divided into Coast and Valley, and while the State has many picturesque valleys still the climate of them all is about the same.

The climate of this valley is very hot which enables the raisin-growers and dried-fruit men to supply the markets with the delicious dried fruit and raisins. It is also a great agricultural belt. The first field of alfalfa in the United States was grown in this valley. The largest dairy-farms in the State are located in Modesto, from which city butter was on exhibit at the Panama Pacific International Exposition and can be bought in any city of the State. Sugar-beets are raised in this valley, especially in Allensworth. The largest oil fields in the United States are located in and around Bakersfield.

The charm of this valley is that while it is hot enough to dry thousands of tons of raisins and other dried fruits, even so in the evenings there is always a refreshing breeze and one can usually enjoy a refreshing night's sleep. The soil of all California is watered by irrigation because there is only a rain-fall during the winter months. The San Joaquin Valley has been blessed with plenty of water through the eternal snows of the high Sierras. (See under Fresno, Fowler and Bowles, the part colored people take in living and producing from the soil in this valley especially during the drying season.)

The Tehachepi range of mountains acts as a gate closing the San Joaquin Valley against destructive desert sand-storms and winds. It is on this mountain that one of the greatest feats of civil engineering for railroading has been successfully carried out. The road loops the loop going to the summit of the mountains and then down and around finally making a level grade that they found impossible to make in any other way. The mountain is unattractive in appearance looking much like a large sand-dune with little vegetation.

Los Angeles County, its climate and beauty is considered one of the most choice in all of California. The climate has a warm, balmy joyousness, giving to the people living there great business enterprise. The reader will often hear the people living in other parts of the State say that Los Angeles has a climate too relaxing; it seems to the writer that if they did not have a relaxing impulse, judging from the heights from which the city, and county, has reached during the past few years, they would soon work themselves to death, if we believe the statistics of this wonderful city. The greatest charm of this city is that the people work in unity. Their one aim is to make this city the most beautiful, successful, healthful, morally and physical in the world.

They aim to build their prosperity upon an enduring foundation into the hearts of the people, which will make it more enduring than stone.

The climate of Los Angeles, during the morning hours, is cool and gradually grows warmer until mid-day, when it is quite hot, and then it again grows cool until it finally reaches a difference of thirty degrees between night and day. The morning hours remind one much of Cincinnati, Ohio, which has a high fog lasting often until nearly noon, when the sun appears. During the winter season Los Angeles often has heavy night fogs lasting until nearly noon the next day. These fogs are just as dangerous to weak lungs as the San Francisco winds and fogs. The person coming to California for his health must always use precaution during the first year's residence in the State, it matters not what part. He cannot with safety do the things persons who have lived in the State for a longer period may do. One must become acclimated. He will then find the climate the best in the world, with all the healing properties claimed for it. There are, of course, some sections better suited for some diseases than others, and one should be governed by the statement of the doctor consulted. It has always been a puzzle to persons living in the East to believe that while one can eat luscious, fresh strawberries during the last of December, he can also be reminded that he is not living in the tropics by a keen frost, and while the frost rarely kills the citrus fruits, still one is conscious of the need of more clothing. The fruit-growers in the southern part of the State have more to fear from frost than those living around the San Francisco Bay, because it is never hot, and usually cool even in summer. The frost in the southern part of the State is rarely destructive, but the growers are always on the alert and the weather bureau sends out reports to the ranchers, who immediately burn their smudge pots to protect their crops, often burning them for many nights. It requires a whole year to grow an orange crop; hence the growers, since the destructive frost of 1912, have a society that studies the weather conditions, and they, too, send out additional warnings to all members, thereby protecting themselves, since the State laws require them to allow the fruit to ripen on the trees.

Los Angeles is tropical enough to grow every kind of tree, shrub and flower which can be raised in any other part of the world. It is not an uncommon sight to look from the street-car window and find that one is passing homes with great hedge fences of blooming poinsettias and pepper trees with their red berries and lacy foliage. In the district in which are located the boulevards, beautiful homes and parks, one can see banana, magnolia, palm and rubber trees. There are few days in the year in which these districts are not a perfect riot of color with the bloom of beautiful flowers.

The climate of Los Angeles is especially fine for heart and lung trouble, and also asthma; the weather is just warm and dry enough not to over stimulate the heart. The only danger to weak lungs is the sand-storms in the winter months, which occur sometimes once and not more than twice during the season. They are off from the desert and, aside from being disagreeable, they are also destructive to more than weak lungs. Had not Los Angeles its periodic winter frost and high sand wind-storms, it would have no way of purifying its atmosphere of the deadly germs of all kinds brought into the city through its annual influx of tourist-travel. It has been given as a truthful record that the railroads coming into and going out of Los Angeles handle, on an average, twenty-six thousand persons a day, a good record for one city. Los Angeles, like San Francisco, has many nearby cities, that are easily reached, where the climate is different. These cities near Los Angeles are often much easier to reach than one's own home. The greatest draw-back to the city is its congested street-car service, whereas San Francisco has excellent street-car service to all parts of its vastly larger city. But if one is fortunate enough to own an automobile, he will find the finest roads in the world in beautiful Los Angeles County, California, and they are comparatively dustless.

Pasadena, the home of millionaires, lies just eight miles from Los Angeles. It has a much different climate. It is warm all during the winter, and in the summer is very hot. It is a valley with an elevation of one thousand feet, and is near the mountains of Mount Lowe, Old Baldy and the Casa Verduga Range. This gives the atmosphere of this beautiful city a crispness not found elsewhere, with a temperature reaching the height it averages. Aside from the beautiful homes of the wealthy, it can boast of more beautiful homes of the middle-class than any other city in the State, added to the natural beauty of its location. The climate of Pasadena makes it an excellent place in which to lose rheumatism, being dry and high and seldom having any kind of fogs.

If the reader would wish a real joyful street-car trip, he can have it by taking a trolley trip from Los Angeles through Oak Knoll to Pasadena any day in the year. This trip will lead through winding orange groves, with their fragrance either of blossoms or the ripe fruit. One feels that it is a mountain in a faraway country he is climbing, the scenery changes so often, and at each bend in the road becomes more beautiful, until finally there comes into view the imposing Huntington hotel which crowns Oak Knoll like a castle in a faraway land. Then drive or ride on the street-cars through the town of Pasadena with its broad streets, its shade-trees of palms, pepper trees and rubber plants, with numerous other tropical shrubbery and flowers, before beautifully-kept lawns. There is a civic pride running through all the town, making it a city of beauty and harmony.

The business section has numerous skyscrapers and is bustling with activity, but always with that air of *noblesse oblige*, realizing that one may be a stranger within the city and that it is the little courtesies extended by every one that makes the city so delightful, aside from its wonderful climate and beautiful homes and gardens. Colorado and Orange Grove avenues are spacious boulevards with tropical trees, flowers and the palatial homes of the wealthy, with their enchanting Roman and sunken gardens giving to the eyes of the humblest passer a feeling of harmony, rest and peace. These places are built so that the general public can enjoy the sight as well as the owners. This is especially true of Busch's sunken gardens and his rose gardens, which have been so well described in magazines and pamphlets.

An attempt will be made to describe to the reader the impression of a rose parade viewed in Pasadena the first day of January. The writer had just arrived from the East on December the first, and the bloom of the poinsettia in Los Angeles was so abundant that it did not seem possible anything else could equal its beauty. The climatic condition in the East on January the first were too fresh in mind to believe that even California could produce a real flower-parade on that date with anything else but paper flowers. But when the writer actually saw the rose parade with real cut flowers, vehicles covered with violets, horses blanketed with fresh violets, a four-in-hand covered with sweet peas, and with each part of the parade displaying an even more lavish use of actually fresh flowers, and requiring hours to pass a certain point, it did not seem possible that one could be in America. To the writer's surprise, when attempting that day to walk to the Busch sunken gardens with a winter coat, she became exhausted, not from the weight of the coat, but from the climate.

The greatest surprise was when, in after years, the writer was visiting Pasadena in quest of material for the book concerning the colored residents of the place, she found that these beautiful gardens, with few exceptions, were the work of Negro land-scape-gardeners. It was more than interesting to listen to their description of these grounds twenty-five years ago. These same grounds today are considered the most picturesque landscape gardens in America, and yet they were the product of Negro handiwork. Some of these gardeners have now grown to old to work and enjoy a pension from their former employers.

Riverside, California, lies south of Los Angeles and enjoys a charming climate, free from fogs or excessive heat. It is in a great orange belt and is sheltered from the cold of the ocean by the surrounding mountains, namely Mt. Rubidoux and Old Baldy. Riverside abounds in tropical vegetation and flowers, with numerous drives and a profusion of magnolia, pepper and palm trees.

The beautiful Glenwood Mission Inn is located in Riverside, California, with its beautiful gardens, old Mission settings and Mission relics brought from abroad, together with its priceless paintings and wonderful pipe-organ located in the chapel, make this one of the most unique hostelries in all America. It was the proprietor of this hotel who suggested and encouraged, together with other gentlemen the writing of that beautiful historical play by Mr. J. S. McGroarty, the "Mission Play." It was also the proprietor of this hotel, Mr. Frank Miller, who was the father of the idea of holding sunrise Easter service on Mt. Rubidoux. It was at one of these services that the Hon. Henry Van Dyke read his poem, "God of the Open Air," which is characteristic of the people of all California, who live out-of-doors during the day and sleep out by night.

Redlands, a beautiful Southern California city, lies at the foot of Old Baldy, or rather Mt. San Antonio. It is much higher than any of the other California cities, with a more tropical climate. It would be an excellent place for persons suffering with lung trouble or asthma. It is a picturesque city and, aside from its numerous orange groves, it is the home of "Smylie Heights." Mr. Smylie, coming from the East in search of health, finally regained it in Redlands, and afterward gave to the city a large mountain acreage which he had beautified with drives and every specie of flowers, plants and trees. It is one of California's show places. He gave this beautiful park to the city of Redlands without money, to be used for the enjoyment of all, perpetually free, having endowed it and also a large library. Mr. Smylie also owned the hotel and grounds at Lake Mohonk, New York. "Smylie Heights" overlooks the San Timoteo Valley, where they successfully raise cotton.

The homes of the wealthy in Redlands are somewhat similar to those in Santa Barbara, with large acreage, but the flowers and trees are ten times more tropical. It is in Redlands you see the beautiful Virginia crape myrtle, growing in all its glory beside all the tropical trees of the rest of the world. In the distance one can see the Arrowhead Hot Springs, with their Indian legends.

San Bernardino is one of the cities which was created as a supply station during pioneer days. It is a beautiful city, lying very high up in the mountains which surround it with their snowy peaks. This city would be very bad for any one with a weak heart. The few colored people living there are contented and happy. It is the home of Mr. and Mrs. Mason Johnson, who are reputed to be worth fifty thousand dollars in real estate. It is a railroad center, and many colored people find employment in the Santa Fe shops.

Imperial Valley, California, embracing the towns of Brawley, El Centro and Calexico, has a climate hot and dry enough to raise cotton for the markets. The first cantelopes of the season in the United States are grown in this valley. Colored people live in great numbers in this valley and are producers from the soil. They have their own churches and schools and apparently are happy and prosperous.

The deserts of California, namely the Mohave and at Victorville, are government lands, and quite a few colored people have taken up homesteads on this land and are improving them. Some sections have been found to contain oil. Many of the colored people have bought this land and afterwards sold it for a good margin.

San Diego, California, the first settlement of civilized men on the Pacific Coast, contains the first Mission in California, which was established here and was used as headquarters by Friar Junipero Serra until after the discovery and return of the party from San Francisco. Notwithstanding its age and all of the early romance connected with San Diego, it has been more than slow in developing. It was given its first boom at the completion of the Panama Canal, at which time it was decided to celebrate this great engineering feat with an exposition. San Diego tried to convince the United States Congress that it was the logical city to receive the honor, since it would be the first port of call after the ships leave the Panama canal. They were not successful in winning the honor, but decided that they, too, would hold an exposition, and to that end enlisted all of the home-loving citizens of wealth to join them in the enterprise. These citizens used their private fortunes and did hold a creditable exposition. Seeing their courage, the Counties in the southern part of the State built a beautiful building on the grounds.

It was the pleasure of the writer to review the grounds in company with one of the commissioners, who, after learning her mission as historian of the Negro in California, showed her special courtesies. The writer viewed for the first time the Bay of San Diego from the balcony of the California building on the exposition grounds. The atmospheric conditions were such that she turned to the commissioner, who was explaining to her the surrounding country, and said that the sight of the very blue, glistening waters of the San Diego Bay, with its expanse of waters joining the Pacific Ocean far beyond, made a sight to be remembered as much as the Bay of San Francisco, because both were historical. It was on this bay that, coming around what is now called "Point Loma," the ship "San Antonio" was first sighted by the missionary fathers who were about to abandon California as a hopeless place. Mr. McGroarty calls the bay the "Harbor of the Sun and the Bright Shores of Glory."

San Diego has the most equable climate in all of America. It is said that there are only six degrees difference between winter and summer, with neither fogs or blighting winds. It is quite tropical in both vegetation and flowers, without the excessive heat.

The Panama-California Exposition, held there for two years, was truly a great blessing to this beautiful city. Men, seeing the confidence the people had in themselves, decided to invest their money, and soon there were great skyscrapers and business blocks and many other businesses which had been much needed for many years.

The name of San Francisco, like that of California, carries with it a charm that has aroused in the breast of civilized men in all parts of the world a desire to see and know the city for themselves. The early Mission fathers were from the Franciscan College, San Fernando, Mexico City. They were given instructions to establish missions in honor of certain saints. Junipero Serra was very much surprised when he was not told to establish a mission for Saint Francis. We are told that Galvez, who was governor-general of the expedition, replied, "If San Francisco wants a mission, let him cause his port to be discovered." This statement showed clearly that Galvez did not regard seriously Drake's discovery of a bay under Point Reys and at the time called San Francisco. It has been proven in a recent publication that Drake's voyages were in the interest of the English crown. This statement is quite valuable because of the fact that the Mission fathers did not consider seriously that Drake's Bay was the real Bay of San Francisco. If it is true that Sir Francis Drake made voyages in and by the instruction of and at the expense of the English crown, and had he found the large land-locked Bay of San Francisco, it is strange that the English Government did not claim California hundreds of years before the United States purchased it from Mexico. In a work covering years of careful research, Mrs. Zelia Nuttall has fully proven the claim that Sir Francis Drake did make discoveries in the interest of the English crown. There are writers who claim that when Sir Francis Drake landed in the bay under Point Reys a heavy fog closed the Golden Gate so that he did not see it during the thirty-six days of his stay. A more recent writer says that at the time the bay was discovered under Point Reys there was no bay of San Francisco, but that later an earthquake made a bay. Either of the last-named statements would be difficult to prove, but history does record the fact that Portola, on his trip of exploration, failed to recognize the Bay of Monterey and journeyed on up and through the Santa Clara Valley and over the hills of Berkeley, and from the "treeless slopes" of these hills he did discover the beautiful, large, land-locked Bay of San Francisco. In the language of Viceroy Mendoza: "So that as well as in the chusing of the entrance as well as in not being able to find the way it seemed unto all means that God has shut up the gate to all those who by human strength (force) had gone about to attempt this enterprise and hath revealed it to a poor and barefoot friar."

Since the days of the Mission fathers men have been willing to undergo all kinds of hardships if at the "end of the trail" it led to San Francisco. Men during the gold craze were willing to take their chance with fate. The trip was difficult, long and fraught with many dangers, whether by ox-team or by the way of the Isthmus of Panama, or the longest way round "the Horn" to California. It will never be known the number of persons losing their lives in an effort to reach San Francisco, California. Those who did not come and remained on the other side of the Rocky Mountains were anxiously awaiting a chance to come, heeding not the hardships if the trip led to San Francisco, California.

In pioneer days San Francisco was not very much of a city, consisting of sand dunes and a number of hills without streets. Even the houses were only shacks and tents. A few wooden houses were brought around the Horn and afterward rebuilt. Rev. Flavil Scott Mines brought from New York the first Episcopalian church to San Francisco around the Horn, and rebuilt it afterward.

The climate of San Francisco is like perpetual spring, never very warm either in summer or winter, although it is a better winter climate than it is usually given credit for. The fogs are very much over-advertised, and while they are at times disagreeable, still they are, in a measure, an advantage because of the purifying effect on the air. There are several different kinds of fogs that appear around the Bay of San Francisco. Mr. George McAdie, who for years was the weather forecaster for the Bay region and lived in San Francisco, has a book in which he has given to the public his study of "Fogs and Sky of San Francisco," which gives the reader a wonderful idea of the great amount of good done through the fogs. This book also describes the various kinds of fogs and the wonderful sky effects, especially during the spring months. The nearby cities have more fogs during the winter than the City of San Francisco and are much colder. The heaviest San Francisco fogs occur during the summer.

There are many near-by cities within easy communication from San Francisco, namely, Sausolita, Mill Valley, San Raphael, Oakland, Berkeley, Alameda, Elmhurst, Richmond, and down the peninsula to San Mateo and Burlingame.

San Francisco of today is a city of beauty and cleanliness. Few cities in the State have more natural beauty. There are lovely vistas from the many hills overlooking the Bay and ocean, and from the mountains in the different sections of the city, namely, Lone Mountain and Twin Peaks. It has many parks, the largest being "Golden Gate," which contains hundreds of acres of beautiful landscape gardens and a memorial museum given to the city by Mr. Mike de Young, editor of the *San Francisco Chronicle*, a daily newspaper. In the center of this park rises majestically a small mountain called "Strawberry Hill." To some Californians there is only one city in all the State. and that is San Francisco. It is a real city, with as many skyscrapers and business blocks (with the distracting noise left out) as either Chicago or New York. It has all the eastern styles and displayed at the same time they are in the East.

San Francisco has been destroyed seven times by fire and rebuilt as often. The last destruction was by the earthquake and fire of April, 1906. They say that it has been rebuilt more beautiful than ever. It seems almost unbelievable that a city could be reduced to ashes, aside from the earthquake shocks, and yet the people would love it so that they would rebuild more beautiful homes and greater businesses than ever. The writer visited this city just three years after the fire of 1906, spending the winter studying the people, climate and the spirit of San Francisco, and left, returning to the East so filled with its spirit that ever afterward she has only spoken of it as ''The City of Inspiration.'' The name, its spirit and atmosphere, seemed to carry with it an inspiration to do great things. In pioneer days it developed the spirit of adventure and possibilities of greater manhood in the individual. It had the same effect upon colored pioneers as it did upon other persons. Notwithstanding the numerous laws against the Negroes living in peace in California, he seemed to catch the spirit of San Francisco which enabled him to walk through his obstacles and to do the things that developed manhood in members of the other races then living in California.

To prove the statement just given, the writer will cite one instance. The white citizens had their newspapers, *The Californian, The American Flag, The Alta,* and later *The Bulletin;* the colored people had also papers to champion their rights before the public, and we find among these early-day Negro papers such papers as *The Mirror of the Times, The Pacific Appeal,* and *The San Francisco Elevator.*

The majority of the colored people during pioneer days lived in the City of San Francisco and the northern part of the State, namely, Sacramento, Marysville, Stockton and Red Bluff. They were the fighters against adverse legislation, giving their time and money, rarely ever calling on the few colored people living in the southern part of the State for assistance. The colored people now living in the northern part of the State and around San, Francisco remind one much of persons living around Boston and other New England towns; they are so fond of their own little corner of the world; they are so self-satisfied. A portion of them, however, did move to Los Angeles after the great fire of 1906. The colored people living south of the Tehachapi mountains and farther south are such that you wonder in which part of the State the colored residenters are the most admirable, because they are all so loyal to their end of the State.

The colored population living in San Francisco have several well-established churches, modern structures, often with a pipe organ. The largest churches are the Third Baptist and the Bethel A. M. E., and the church which is often called the old ''Thomas Starr King Church,'' and known as the A. M. E. Zion Church. It was in the last-named church that during pioneer days all the business of the ''Franchise League'' was transacted and the meetings of the executive committee of the Colored Convention were often held during those strenuous days. There was also another colored church whose pastor and flock were great workers in the fights for an opportunity to live in California, and that church was the Episcopalian church and its pastor Rev. Cassey, who spent much time and money in the meetings.

The colored people of San Francisco now have several well-established and patronized lodges, many coming from the east Bay cities of Oakland and other places. San Francisco has a community of delightful colored citizens who have modern homes. They are descendants of pioneer families and have grasped every opportunity for a higher education for themselves and children.

The following list of the businesses conducted by pioneer persons of color during early days in the City of San Francisco has been copied from a file of old newspapers loaned to the writer through the courtesy of Mr. G. W. Watkins, author of ''Prominent Afro-Americans on the Pacific Coast,'' and editor of the *Pacific Appeal,* of San Francisco; ''Jonas H. Townsend and William H. Newby, editors of the first colored newspaper published on this coast, *The Mirror of the Times,* which was published in 1855 in San Francisco; Phillip A. Bell and Zadock Bell, editors of *The San Francisco Elevator,* which made its first appearance in the late fifties; Peter Anderson, editor of the *Pacific Appeal,* published in San Francisco from 1857 to the late eighties.

''Fritz James Vosburg and James Riker organized a company and manufactured 'Cocoanut oil soap' in San Francisco; George Dennis, proprietor of a large livery stable; James P. Dyer, manufacturing 'Queen Lily Soap,' wholesale and retail dealers; Henry M. Collins, capitalist and owner of the steamship 'Princess Ann,' also a heavy stockholder in the 'Navigation Company of Colored men'; Daniel Seals, capitalist and a miner; Avenden Frances, wholesale merchant in dry goods; Monroe Taylor, proprietor of the ferry boat lunch counters; G. W. Waddy, laundryman; C. Harris, locksmith; S. Long, drayman; George Davis, livery stable; William H. Blake, musician and leader of band, dealer in band instruments; Gibbs & Pointer, proprietors of the Philadelphia store; C. Griffin, barber on the Panama steamers; Albert Bevitt, herb doctor, office corner Stockton and Powell streets, San Francisco; Mrs. Charlott Callander, sailors' and seamen's boarding-house; James Richard Phillips, hair-dressing parlors and bath house, employing ten barbers and having twenty bathtubs; John Jones and James Riker organized the 'Brannan Guards,' with the assistance of Alexander G. Dennison. Captain Alexander Ferguson was connected with the 'Richmond Blues' and was considered

MRS. ELLEN HUDDELSTON
Financier and Investor.

MRS. MAMIE CUNNINGHAM-WHITE
First colored girl clerk in Los Angeles
Postoffice.

MISS GERTRUDE CHRISMAN
Teacher of Spanish in Los Angeles
City Schools.

MRS. LOUISE CHRISMAN
Owner Chrisman Apartments.
Los Angeles.

MRS. SALLIE RICHARDSON
Social Worker.

a great orator; Anthony Loney, manufactured cigars and smoking tobacco; Lester & Pointer, conducting the Philadelphia store of clothing; Mifflin Gibbs & Pointer conducted a wholesale and retail shoe-store and the only store of its kind in San Francisco during that period. They decided to open the shoe-store after turning over to Lester & Pointer the Philadelphia store. Mr. Whitfield, author of a work on the 'History of Masonry'; R. C. O. Benjamin, a distinguished lawyer and writer; Ellen Spach, fashionable dressmaker.''

It is to be regretted that the writer cannot give even a greater list for this present period of the history and life of the Negro in San Francisco, but there are but few colored people in business of any kind today in the City of San Francisco. One of the reasons is that common labor, upon which the business man must depend for his trade, is not very remunerative for the Negro race in this city. With but few exceptions, all the avenues of trade are closed to the Negro workman through the powerful influences of the trade unions who rule San Francisco. During the past year business men, realizing that the trade unions were ruining San Francisco, decided to try, if possible, to force an open shop. To that end the Chamber of Commerce and business men all over San Francisco subscribed to a fund which soon reached over a million of dollars to be used to fight for an open shop. Negro hotel waiters were employed for a while in all the first-class hotels, cafes and elsewhere. This lasted just long enough to make the Negro happy and hopeful that the pioneer days of good work and good pay were returning to the city and the Negroes could again earn a good livelihood. But, alas! their dream was soon over and before winter returned they were all out on the cold bricks hunting for a job, with good references from the men who had recently employed them, but were forced to manage their business at the dictation of the labor unions. There was a time when all the help in the Palace Hotel was colored, and many of these men served for years and today have good homes in other parts of California. They were not let out because of lack of efficiency, but on account of the labor union's demands. Hence they have gone to make their homes in Los Angeles, where there is open shop and a chance to make a living through the fight made for years by the late General Harrison Gray Otis of *The Times*.

The Chinese and Japanese laborer is employed almost exclusively in many avenues in San Francisco. Some of these foreigners are more than the equal of white labor for the same purpose, having been trained in the schools of their native homes for general and special service, and they fill the exacting demands for the highest kind of service in whatever line they may desire to enter. It is an imposing sight to visit a home of those who employ Japanese cooks and see them in their white frocks, aprons and caps. They dress the same, whether washing or cooking, and the writer has even seen window-washers dressed in the same way. They have their own Y. M. C. A. and employment agencies. Help sent from these places work for the money and nothing else; they will not give you a minute over the time for which you employ them; they ask no favors and give no extra time; it is strictly business with him and nothing else.

There are many colored graduates from the late Booker T. Washington's school who have acquired the highest point of efficiency of service, and who have told the writer how they have been forced either to move to other parts or give up the idea of finding employment at their well-fitted trades in San Francisco.

Oakland, California, it has been said, was produced from the fire and calamity of San Francisco during 1906. This resulted in a large number of persons moving to Oakland and other east Bay cities to live, where they found a climate that was very different from the city of Saint Francis, which still was easily accessible, and they decided to build homes. At first men established temporary businesses which were so profitable that they have increased the same until today the future of Oakland does not depend upon the left-overs from San Francisco, notwithstanding, according to the records furnished by the Key system of ferries and railroads, that they transport together with other roads something over forty thousand commuters daily who make their living in the City of San Francisco. There is such a large number who do not contribute a penny to the maintenance of the City of San Francisco that there has been, for the past few years, a strong movement to annex the east Bay cities and call them "The Greater San Francisco," as has been done in New York State.

Oakland is fast growing into an independent manufacturing city and, with the deep water harbor, bids fair to rival any city in the State. It is a beautiful city, especially around Lake Merritt, upon whose shores fronts the beautiful million-dollar municipal auditorium, which is the most complete and thoroughly fireproof auditorium in the United States.

Lake Merritt is a large body of salt water in the center of the city. Its shore-line has been beautified by numerous drives and parks, together with a public tennis court and a municipal boat house. The lake at all times can be plied by pleasure craft with perfect safety. There are many beautiful homes along its shores with their hanging and Roman gardens. In one of the numerous parks which make the immediate shore-line is located a band stand and music is rendered throughout the greater part of the year on Sunday afternoons for the pleasure of all who may wish to enjoy it. On the lake-shore boulevard, aside from the homes of the wealthy, there are a number of artistically designed flats and apartment houses. This boulevard runs back into the hills, in which are located the beautiful suburban homes of the City of Piedmont. Adjoining are the Crocker Highlands. The location of the land makes this one of the most attractive suburbs in the State.

Oakland and the east Bay cities do not have exactly the same kind of fogs as San Francisco. During the winter months they suffer with ''low fogs,'' which drift down from the ''tule lands of Sacramento.'' These fogs are most dangerous to traffic, especially on the San Francisco Bay, yet few serious accidents occur. The east Bay cities also suffer during the winter months with northwest winds. Oakland and Berkeley especially suffer with the disagreeable winds. The climate is considered more equable than any outside of San Diego.

The colored population have beautiful homes and own them. They also own more businesses of their own than the colored people do in San Francisco. They have several prosperous lawyers and two dentists and furniture stores, the business of which would be creditable to any community.

Santa Cruz, California, is a city and also a summer resort with a most wonderful climate for the nerves. It lies between the ocean and the Santa Cruz Mountains, resulting in the air being always filled with the fragrance of the pine, madrone and redwood, mixed with the sea-air, making a restful and healing tonic for the nerves. It is just far enough from the smoke and annoyances of a large manufacturing center to give the air from the sea real saltiness and invigorating freshness.

Santa Cruz has a manufactory for making cement and a deep-water pier extending about a mile out from land. The climate here is always mild, with little low fogs, but considerable high fog during the summer months, which makes it a summer resort for people living in the San Joaquin valley. Santa Cruz lies so near the mountain ranches that few people cultivate gardens. This makes it a city with considerable business, beautiful homes, modern in every appointment; up-to-date business blocks and cleanly-kept, large streets, well-paved. There are few colored people living in Santa Cruz. Mrs. Albert Logan owns and keeps a hotel for colored tourists which is always filled during and out of season. The largest apple orchards in California are located less than fifty miles from this resort, which is in the Pajaro Valley, the largest town of which is Watsonville.

Monterey and Pacific Grove lie south of Santa Cruz and are two very picturesque places. They are located about four miles apart, and one usually speaks of both at the same time, notwithstanding they are very different in every appointment except the climate, which is always warm and balmy. During the summer the climate is very much like San Francisco's, cool and refreshing, with high fogs, which makes the places a resort for those living in the Sacramento and San Joaquin Valleys. They are like Santa Cruz in that they are a powerful nerve tonic and lie between the beautiful Bay of Monterey and the wonderful forests of Del Monte.

Monterey Bay, with its beautiful blue waters and massive cliffs, together with the historical settings, makes it all very attractive. The first custom house, the first wooden house, and the first theater in all of California were located at Monterey. It was here that the headquarters of Consul Thomas O. Larkins and Lieutenant W. Sherman were located. It was also at Monterey that the much-beloved poet, Robert Louis Stevenson, made his home and enjoyed its beauty and inspiration. As if to add to its romantic and historical setting, there is located only a few miles from the town of Monterey the beautiful, large, picturesque grounds of the Del Monte Hotel, the gardens of which cover some four hundred acres and, aside from being planted with the most tropical plants and flowers, are beautifully landscaped in every appointment. They are located far enough away from the bay and sheltered from the ocean by the massive forest of Del Monte to be protected from cold, blasting winds and frosts, which enables them to raise with ease these beautiful tropical plants and the most beautiful flowers. These gardens and grounds of the Del Monte Hotel are one of the show places of all California, and no one should ever consider that he has seen California until he has viewed the blue waters and cliffs of the Bay of Monterey and these wonderful gardens.

A few miles south of the Del Monte Hotel grounds is located a colony of writers and artists at a village called ''Carmel by the Sea;'' a little villa or rather several villas, the homes of great minds who wish to be alone, believing ''there is pleasure in the pathless woods and the music in the distant shore.'' They long for that quiet the poet meant when he wrote, ''Come, and let us go into the woods where none but God will be near, for I hate the sound and to breathe the thoughts of other men.'' But they are seldom alone, for, in spite of their desire and their determination not to improve either the roads or their homes, still, even so, the writer has been told that nothing less than eight hundred vehicles a day wend their way to Carmel by the Sea during the summer months. The people go there not only to see what a village of great minds would look like, but also to view the first Mission established in Upper California, and, while the first Christian burial in all of California was performed at this Mission, it also is the last resting place for the bones of Friar Junipero Serra, which were re-en-terred in 1913, through the Native Sons and Daughters and with an escort of the Young Men's Institute, a Catholic society with branches or chapters all over the State. The sands of the bay of Carmel by the Sea are the whitest sands in all of California and, it has been said, in all the world. One must return to Monterey to reach the rest of the world, and, while resting from the drive, it is interesting to note that while this town is one of the first Spanish settlements in California, and the first capital of the American California, it has grown up with the times. The people, however, reverence its historical setting and memory, and have destroyed not one land-mark for more modern structures.

The Presidio, established during the pioneer days by the Padres, is still standing and in use today, with but seemingly few changes, as United States army post, or Presidio. A short distance from here is located a little town called New Monterey, which is the home of retired Negro G. A. R., some of whom are ex-army officers. They are living comfortably and have a good church and are quite a factor in the community, especially Mr. and Mrs. Washington and Mr. Rodgers, a veteran of the Ninth Cavalry.

Paso Robles, California, lies south of the town of Monterey and is farther down the coast. The climate is considered fine for rheumatism. The famous sulphur springs and mud baths are located here, a statement which is not doubted for a minute after one leaves the train, because the smell of sulphur is so strong it reminds one readily of Mt. Clemens, Michigan. The town is quaint and has an atmosphere of contentment. The municipal bathhouse is a modern structure. There is also a bathhouse operated by a colored gentleman, a Mr. Wathington, which is patronized by the public.

Santa Barbara, California, is where the wealthy people from the east come for rest and perfect climate to restore their nerve and brain fag. It has been said that no better climate in all the world can be found for such than at this beautiful seaside resort. Like Santa Cruz and Del Monte, it lies between the mountains and the sea. The St. Inez Mountains are located at the back of the town, and the ocean and the Santa Barbara channel on the southern exposure give the climate a wonderful mixture for healthfulness.

The drives around the town are picturesque, with the settings of beautiful homes and the large, well-kept grounds which, it has been said, are more like the great estates in England than any other in America.This, they say, is especially true of the homes at Montecito with the landscape gardens and houses so like English manor houses. The flowers are more beautiful because of the tropical climate of California, and they can be grown during the entire year.

The stately, palatial Potter Hotel is located here with its wonderful rose and geranium gardens overlooking the ocean. Santa Barbara, with its soft, balmy, restful atmosphere, free from fogs and blighting winds, is also the home of the only monastery on the coast, the historical Santa Barbara Mission, which, of all the missions established by the Mission fathers during early days, has never been allowed to go to ruin and has been in constant use for over a hundred years, with its wealth of beautiful sacred paintings brought from Spain during the last century, and readily makes Santa Barbara the most delightful place on the coast for a home.

There are few colored people living here, but the few are progressive and their businesses consist of establishments for cleaning and dyeing and auto stages. The pastor of the colored Baptist Church, Rev. Thompson, has a social settlement in connection with his church that would add to a larger community pride for the successful management of the same.

Fowler, California, is one of the most interesting districts in the San Joaquin Valley. The holdings of the colored people in the district prove beyond a doubt that they are capable of pioneering. This progression was really started through the enthusiasm of Mrs. Julia Bell, who came to Fowler, California, nearly thirty years ago. She and her husband worked for the family of Mr. Curby, who moved to California from Charlotte, North Carolina, bringing their servants with them. The town of Fowler, at that date, was only a wheat field, and Mrs. Bell planted the first tree in the townsite.

After living in California for several years, she sent the price of a railroad ticket to her brother Jordan Young, who was living in South Carolina and desirous of coming West. She was so hopeful of the possibilities of Fowler that she wrote to every one she knew to come to the town. She also invested heavily in property, using about every penny she could possibly spare for the purchase of real estate. In after years she sent for her father, Mr. David Jennings, who readily came to the State, and although he was ninety years old at the time, he made the trip safely and lived to be one hundred and five before passing.

Mr. Reuben Wysinger, a native son, owns a good ranch of fifteen acres planted in Muscat, Tompkins and seedless raisin grapes. These grapes yield, on an average, a ton to the acre and are marketed for $50 to $100 an acre. He also has a peach orchard of the "Muir" and "Alberta" peaches which yield two tons to the acre and sell all the way from $100 to $150 an acre.

Mr. Wysinger and two other colored gentlemen, realizing the possibilities of this section of California in the fruit industry, decided to procure a plot of land while the price was within their reach. They purchased a plot of eighty acres, paying $100 down and in five months paying another hundred dollars, which entitled them to a deed, with five years in which to pay the remaining indebtedness at 10 per cent interest. They paid twenty dollars an acre at the date of purchase, some fifteen years ago. Today one could not buy the same ground for several hundred dollars an acre. After securing the deed to the plot each man settled on his share and began the cultivation of the land. It will be impossible to give the experience of every one of the gentlemen, but that of Mr. Wysinger can safely be taken as an example of them all. His experience and perseverance show what one can do with a will. He was employed during the day. After night, with the assistance of his wife, he planted his peach orchard and vineyard. Owing to their lack of experience, it required years of hard work before they were able to secure a crop of anything. They never faltered and finally conquered, and today they have a wonderful ranch that any one in the valley would be proud to own. The best part of it all is, they own a beautiful, modern home and an automobile from the products of a well-paying ranch. They have a family of three children, to whom they are giving the best education that the State affords. They are also giving them actual experience in ranch life, so that, if they wish, they can remain on the ranch and be independent.

Mr. and Mrs. W. W. Eason own eighteen acres in Bowles, which is another settlement of fruit growers just four miles from Fowler. Their ranch is planted in peach orchards and vineyards for producing raisins. They also own fifteen city lots. They moved from Atlanta, Georgia, less than fifteen years ago. When Mrs. Eason reached Fowler, she learned that through an error in checking her baggage she had lost all her belongings en route, and had only five dollars to her credit. Her husband had preceded her to California. They had left their daughter to finish her education at Clark's University, Atlanta, Georgia. Mrs. Eason soon secured work as a laundress, following the same with success for nine years, and with Mr. Eason working as a ranch hand, they together saved enough to buy a ranch from the earnings of which they purchased the city lots.

Jeremiah S. H. Ellard owns twenty acres in Monmouth planted in peaches and grapes, owning the same for the past eight years. They came from Atlanta, Georgia, about thirteen years ago with, as they told the writer, "money enough to buy a pair of shoes." Today his ranch is valued at $6,000. Mrs. Ellard, who was Miss Elizabeth Eason, has been a wonderful help-mate. She told the writer that during the fruit season she has picked, day after day, three hundred trays of grapes, each tray averaging twenty-two pounds. At another time she has cut seventy-five boxes of peaches in one day. They are paid five cents a box for peaches and two and a half cents a tray for grapes. It is considered a good day's work to cut fifty boxes of peaches a day. A box will yield fifty pounds.

Mr. and Mrs. J. E. Abernathy, coming from Pulaski, Tennessee, own a ranch of one hundred and sixty acres. This ranch is very attractive, with its wonderful farm houses and modern home. It is planted as follows: Twelve acres in peaches, twenty in grapes, six in alfalfa, and eight in young peach trees, forty unimproved and eighty acres as a pasture for a dairy farm. Mrs. Abernathy was Miss Mary Young, a daughter of Jordon Young of Fowler. She thoroughly understands the managing of a ranch and showed the writer many points of interest. Especially interesting were the large stacks of drying trays which, she said, were worth at least $500. The sulphuring and drying of fruit was all thoroughly explained to the writer, who could scarcely believe the dried fruit of which we are so fond requires so much care before it is ready for the markets of the world. Mr. Abernathy also cares for the forty-acre ranch of Dr.

Lowe, who lives in Mt. Pleasant, Tennessee, which is under cultivation, twelve acres planted in peach trees, eight in vines, and twenty in alfalfa.

Mr. and Mrs. George Clark, moving from San Francisco three years ago, have purchased twenty acres, starting a dairy farm.

Mr. and Mrs. Lee Crane own a ranch of five acres. They came from El Paso, Texas, a few years ago and first located in Allensworth, California, but, learning that Fowler would be a better place to carry on truck gardening, they decided to retain their holdings at the first place and moved to Fowler, where they decided to purchase a plot of land on which they have placed every available convenience, even their own motor engine for the pumping of water. Mr. Crane has the distinction of being the only colored man in Fowler who has a truck garden. He also successfully raises for the market chickens and hogs. He enjoys a modern home and a charming wife.

Rev. Riddle owns five acres in Fowler planted in peaches and deciduous fruits, and has a large, modern home. Messrs. Willie, John, Thomas and George Smith, all brothers, own thirteen and a half city lots in Fowler and eighteen acres in Bowles. These boys, together with the sister, came to California from Grand Bass, Liberia, Africa.

William Bennett owns three city blocks in Fowler. C. L. Brown owns twenty acres in Bowles. The following are the names of a few families and their real estate holdings in Bowles: William H. Boatman, twenty-two acres; Mr. Walker, one hundred and sixty acres; Marshall Sutter, William Asken, Hayes Patrick, John Maxey, S. P. Phillips, and H. Simmons own twenty acres each. The two last named live in Monmouth.

Chapel Henry Nelson, living southwest of Fowler, owns a ranch of twenty-two and a half acres in peaches and vines and a flourishing poultry farm. He also owns his own ice plant, horse and buggy, and has an interesting family. He is an officer in the Odd Fellows lodge and a prominent member of the A. M. E. Church of Fowler.

Mr. Clarence C. Orr owns a ranch of seventy acres. He has a modern dairy farm and also raises hogs for the market. His place is one of the show places of the settlement, with its modern home and barns. Adjoining this ranch is one of twenty acres owned by Mr. A. M. King.

Hanford, California, is the center of the fruit industry. The largest vineyards in America producing wine grapes are located there. They are owned by Japanese. The colored people, however, own good paying ranches and large holdings in city property. It is in this little inland city that the late Mr. Alex Anderson established, owned and managed the largest livery and feed stables in central California. Since his death his widow manages the stables, which are known as the "Seventh Street Stables." She owns between thirty and forty head of horses, besides race horses. All the leading stores and hotels board their horses at this stable, which employs never less than seven men. Mr. Anderson had been in business over thirteen years when he died. He had come to California from Council Grove, Kansas, about twenty-five years before. He was happily married to Miss Mary Dobbins from Huntington, Virginia, a college graduate and a music teacher of ability, who thoroughly understood business and was a great helpmate to him. She has a charming personality which readily endears her to everyone. They were married twenty-four years.

Another interesting person in Hanford is Mrs. Ishour, who owns a ranch of one hundred and sixty acres on which she successfully cultivates alfalfa and grain. It has been said that one winter she marketed five tons of turkeys and a good crop of fruit. She is an active member of the A. M. E. Church and also owns, aside from her ranch, at least four houses in town. She has lived in California for twenty-seven years, coming from Saulsbury, North Carolina.

The only amusement park in Hanford is owned and conducted by a colored man, Mr. George Smith. It contains an acre filled with tropical plants and wild animals. It is called "The Kings County Zoological Garden."

Mr. J. W. Moulden, coming from Rentville, Tennessee, over twelve years ago, owns town property, a concrete house, and an interesting family of two girls and two boys, who have graduated from the public high school of Hanford. The gentleman is employed as city scavenger.

Mr. and Mrs. John Welshar came to California from Council Grove, Kansas, thirty years ago. Mr. Welsher has been the janitor of the public school of Hanford for over twenty years. He has two children, a girl and a boy. He owns eleven town lots and thirteen and three-quarters acres one and one-half miles from town.

Mrs. Cornelia Mason, coming from Tyler, Texas, owns her home and four town lots, and has two sons.

Mr. Wyatt, coming to California from Kansas City, Kansas, over twenty-six years ago, owns two dwellings and twelve lots. There are many colored ministers living in

Hanford who are well situated. Among them is Rev. McEachen, who, a few years ago, conducted a colonization party from North Carolina to California. Rev. G. W. Ayers, from Richmond, Virginia, living in California some twenty or more years, and connected with the Second Baptist Church, owns a home and four city lots. Rev. Blakney, an A. M. E. minister, coming from Saulsbury, North Carolina, owns valuable town property. There are many others of the race living in Hanford who are doing well and own good ranch and town properties

Mr. and Mrs. Gordon own good property. They are both well educated and a factor in the community. Mr. Gordon is head porter of the City Hotel.

Allensworth, California, is a settlement of colored citizens located south of Hanford in Tulare County. It was founded by the late Colonel Allensworth, who, together with a number of other colored gentlemen, in 1908 organized The California Colony and Home-Promotion Association. It was officered as follows: President, Colonel Allensworth (retired), chaplain of the Twenty-fourth Infantry of the United States Army; secretary, Professor W. A. Payne, formerly principal of Grant County colored school of West Virginia. The remaining members of the company were: Dr. W. H. Peck, J. W. Palmer, a Nevada miner, and Harry Mitchel. The company received its state corporation papers in 1908 and immediately began to find a suitable location for a tract of land for colonization. Mr. Oscar O. Overr was one of a committee of five gentlemen sent out to look over the present tract with regard to colonizing the same. Mr. Overr was so impressed with it that he purchased twelve acres immediately, but soon sold his holdings for a handsome margin, which enabled him to make another purchase of twenty acres. From this beginning has grown the prosperous town of Allensworth, California, which is destined to be one of the greatest Negro cities in the United States.

The company of colored gentlemen who had made it possible for this colony, almost immediately placed the land on the market. They met with encouragement, colored citizens not only purchasing, but locating and building good homes. They were not only settlers, but pioneers in spirit and deeds, willing to toil and hustle for development.

The rapid settlement of the colony necessitated the establishment of a school for the colored children of the colony. Through the county superintendent of schools, a Mr. Walker, of Visalia, in 1910 they secured a county school for the colony of Allensworth, California, and a school house was built. The following are the names of the members of the first school board of the colony of Allensworth, California: President, Mrs. Allensworth; secretary, Mrs. Oscar Overr, and Mr. W. Hall, member of the board.

In 1912, Allensworth was made a voting precinct school district, and in 1914 a judicial district, covering an area of thirty-three square miles. The school is a regular County school, the district being known as Allensworth school district, and ample funds are furnished to carry on the work. A State fund of $550 for every teacher employed, also a County fund of $120 per average attendance, and, when occasion demands, there is available a district or special fund. The work of Allensworth school, which has been equipped with all modern apparatus for school work, including a good piano, is on a par with that of any other district school in the State of California. The building is so arranged that it can be thrown into an assembly room. It is truly the Allensworth social center. Services are conducted there on Sabbath, while a stage with two dressing rooms make it possible to hold entertainments in it. When the school was first established, through the influence of Mr. O. Overr the Pacific Farming Company donated enough lumber to build the school-house, the Alpaugh school district supplying the money for its teacher. To the surprise of this district the colony selected a colored teacher, Mr. William A. Payne. Later, when the school warranted, another teacher was appointed in the person of Miss Whiting from Berkeley. The rapid growth of the colony soon made it necessary to erect a large school-building to accommodate the children of school age. The colony having been declared a school, voting and judicial district by the County Board of Supervisors in 1914, the citizens of Allensworth voted bonds to the amount of $5,000 for a new school-house and furnishings. Upon the completion of the building, Mrs. Allensworth donated the old building for a library. She remodeled it and dedicated it to the memory of her mother, Mary Dickinson, and the building is now known as ''The Mary Dickinson Memorial Library'' and reading room of Allensworth, California.

Colonel Allensworth immediately gave his valuable private library of books to this library. Others of the race have followed his example, namely a Mrs. S. M. Ballard, of Fresno, giving a set of encyclopedia consisting of five volumes and a set of four volumes of Universal English Language and a number of other valuable books; a Mr. Greek, of North Dakota, a set of books on agriculture; Mr. Jerry Williams, San Francisco, two volumes of Dunbar's works; Mr. Welsher, of Hanford, ten volumes of the Encyclopedia Brittanica, and the writer, sending twenty-five standard works. The

County of Tulare, seeing the effort made by the colony to have a library and reading room, decided to make it one of its circulating stations, sending them fifty books every month. The books are called for and delivered free to the station and, in addition, they also pay the current expenses of the library, the chief expense being that of the custodian, a young colored girl, Miss Ethel Hall, who is a resident of the colony. The library, as a branch of the free library of Tulare County, is quite a help and pleasure to the settlers in Allensworth, especially the periodical room, which carries all the latest magazines and papers. In a recent copy of the Visalia Delta occurred the following: ''Allensworth Folks Great Readers. From all branch stations have come requests for books dealing on questions of political economy and civic and other reform movements, the warring nations of Europe and a variety of technical books upon draughting and a score of other subjects. Particular interest is attached to the nature of books wanted by the Allensworth colony. Chief of reference books asked for by this branch library are those dealing with problems and interests of the colored race in America and elsewhere. According to Miss Herman, the librarian, the first people to take advantage of the University of California's extension course were residents of the Allensworth colony, who formed a club expressly for that purpose.'' The above quotation is quite gratifying to all race lovers, and, like the colony, cannot help but be inspiring to others to do likewise.

Much has been said about water in Allensworth, and the following statements have been furnished the writer by Professor Payne, a gentleman who has been connected as secretary of the colony from its formation and who ought to know the conditions better thany any one else: ''The land is excellent, water-bearing land, as subsequent facts will show. The main irrigation system is under the Allensworth Rural Water Company, a State corporation, owned and controlled by Negroes, with a capital stock of $45,000 all paid in. There are three artesian wells, two of which are 1,200 feet deep and another is 300 feet. Two of these wells are pumped by gas engines. Contracts have been made for the placing of three electric motors. There are three large reservoirs for the storage of immense quantities of water. Water for the town-site is supplied by an excellent artesian well and water mains have been laid throughout the residence district during and since 1912. Storm waters have no more fear or terror for the inhabitants of Allensworth than is experienced by persons living in the Sacramento Valley or Southern California. This town is included in the Deer Creek storm-water district and, with Alpaugh, Spa and other communities, is protected from any possible damage by an excellent system of dykes which is maintained by the County. The development of the County, with the increase of the use of water for irrigation and the establishing of new enterprises make possible the use of all water that may accumulate. These dykes were built during 1910 and 1911.''

While hundreds of race men all over the State are anxious about employment, Allensworth citizens are given all they can do. Were there a larger population they could secure many contracts. Their steadiness, honesty and integrity make them much sought after in Tulare and adjoining counties. Not only are they given ordinary employment, but they have secured valuable contracts, to-wit:

George Johnson, carpenter, has built many excellent houses in the vicinity, and was given the contract to build the school-house in the colony; Travis & Hedges, plasterers, keep in their employ continually four men, and at present are completing the building of a forty-room hotel at Corcoran, doing the brick work and plastering; John Morris is a well driller and a driver of traction engines. He has continuous employment on large ranches; John Heitzig, a wealthy farmer, continually employs a force of Negro workmen; W. H. Dodson, formerly of Oakland, is manager of several acres and is king of the poultry business in that district; W. H. Wells constructed more than $6,000 worth of irrigation ditches for the Pacific Farming Company; Oscar Overr is general manager of the Lambert-Detwiler interests and has a force of men continually under his supervision. A number of others find profitable employment in harvesting grain and sugar beets and in the gathering of fruits. Elmer Carter, a young man of business foresight, readily siezed the opportunity to open a livery barn in Allensworth. He has a number of excellent horses, good-looking vehicles and a good barn to keep them in. He takes care of the rapidly-growing traffic between Allensworth and vicinity.

Mr. Zebedee H. Hinsman conducts a general merchandizing store. He has thoroughly prepared himself by studying and graduating from the National Co-operative Realty Company of Washington, D. C. He was appointed notary public for Tulare County by ex-Governor Hiram Johnson, and is the Allensworth agent for the Home Insurance Company of New York. Mr. Hindsman places the value of his stock in the general merchandise store at $7,000. He also conducts a coal and feed yard and owns four town lots. Mr. G. P. Black, coming from Cleveland, Ohio, owns twenty acres of land, ten of which he has planted in alfalfa and eight in grain which averages about twenty-five bushels to the acre. He also has raised twenty-nine turkeys from two turkey hens and has three cows, a beautiful span of horses, a modern home and a charming wife.

Mr. Hedges, coming from Cleveland, Ohio, owns a modern cement house and has a chicken ranch with every modern improvement. It is not only the most sanitary the writer has ever visited, but is a gem in its uniqueness. Mr. Hedges does cement work and is also a member of the Allensworth Water Company. Mr. Powell, coming from Pueblo, Colorado, has ten acres in grain. He has a son who graduated from the high school of Alpaugh, California.

Mr. Anderson Bird, formerly a member of the Twenty-fifth Infantry, U. S. Army, Company D, having been retired, moved his family to the town of Allensworth and purchased five acres of land. He is a very successful raiser of sugar beets. Mr. George Archer, coming from Logan County, Kansas, owns five acres on which he cultivates sugar beets and which yield three tons to the acre. He also owns a larger number of chickens and pigs and a' modern home. Mr. John and Mrs. Vena Ashby were among the first inhabitants of the colony, coming from Pueblo, Colorado. He is employed as section boss on the Santa Fe railroad, and is also a member of the Allensworth Water Company. Sergeant James Grimes, from the Twenty-fourth Infantry (retired), U. S. Army, owns eleven and a half acres. Mr. Wallace Towne came from New York City because of poor health, never expecting to regain it. After a residence of three years in the colony of Allensworth he has fully regained his health and owns and manages a forty-acre ranch. He has planted one-half in wheat and the remainder in barley and hay. He has sold as high as one hundred and fifty sacks of wheat from twenty acres, at two dollars a sack. He owns six horses, eight cows, four heifers, four pigs, and one hundred and fifty broilers, thirty-five hens (he usually keeps two hundred hens), one hundred young ducks and four old ducks. Previous to coming to Allensworth he married Miss Annie Wanter, of Washington, D. C., who is truly a helpmate, so cheerful, kind and helpful to all in the colony. Mr. Towne is actively engaged in every movement for the interest of the colony and is a prominent citizen of the County.

Mr. William H. Wells, coming from Shelby, North Carolina, was the second person to locate in Allensworth, landing with ten dollars, a sick wife and three children. At the time the writer visited the colony his holdings were one hundred and eighty-two and a half acres, six head of horses, farm implements valued at four hundred dollars, two town lots with two developed wells. He was a most interesting person and thoroughly understood the art of pioneering. When asked for a statement as to his success with so small a beginning, he replied: "I am trying to prove to the white man beyond a shadow of doubt that the Negro is capable of self-respect and self-control." He has a charming wife who, the writer thinks, has added much to the confidence and success of the farm, because she is from the great State of Ohio, having been Miss Anderson, of Xenia, Ohio, a town where the colored people know nothing else save thrift and no limit to their aim in life to advance.

Mr. and Mrs. Frank and Miss Laura Smith located in Allensworth in 1910. There were only seven persons then living in the colony. They own two city lots and the best truck garden in the district, also raising Belgian hares for the market.

James Coleman owns five acres and is a dealer in oil, gasoline and ice. Mr. Dunlap, coming from Erlanger, Kentucky, owns seven and one-half acres and two town lots. He and his wife conduct a successful laundry. G. W. Hicks, sergeant of the Twenty-fourth Infantry, U. S. Army(retired), owns three city lots and a ten-acre ranch in alfalfa. W. L. Perkins, coming from Buxton, Iowa, is the president of the Young People's Society and the leader of a brass band. He owns thirteen acres planted in grain.

There are many other property-holders living in the colony, and others who have vast holdings but do not live in California. Would that space permitted giving a sketch or the names of the same! Sufficient to say that the colony is a success, and a greater success than one living away from the State can imagine, especially since the Negro race is not given to pioneering.

It would not be just to close this chapter without mentioning something concerning two gentlemen who, from the founding of the colony, have been untiring in their efforts to build the place up to the standard it has now reached. The first of these is Prof. W. A. Payne, who was secretary of the California Colonization Home Company, and is the principal of the Allensworth public school. He is actively engaged in assisting in any movement for the betterment of Allensworth and is untiring in his efforts. He has been well prepared for the responsibilties he has assumed. He is a graduate from the Dennison University at Grandville, Ohio, having received the degree of B. A. and B. S. His Normal training was secured at the State Normal school, located at Athens, Ohio, and for seven years he held the position of assistant principal of the school in Rendville, Ohio. He married Miss Zenobia B. Jones, a niece of Professor James McHenry Jones, of the West Virginia Colored Institute of Virginia. He has a large and interesting family, owns ten acres under cultivation, carrying on truck-gardening during his spare time; and also a modern home located on a plot of one acre of land. He worked untiringly in an effort to have a polytechnic school located in Allensworth. Too much praise cannot be given to this untiring and unselfish worker.

Mr. Oscar Overr is another person of whom too much cannot be said concerning his devotion and earnest work for the advancement of Allensworth. He owns twenty-four acres in the colony and is also taking up Government land and has a claim of six hundred and forty acres located two and one-half miles east of Allensworth. He came from Topeka, Kansas, having lived in the State less than fifteen years. He has the contracting and developing of water for irrigation, four wells and one pumping-station or plant valued at $2,000. He has under his supervision thirteen hundred acres of land, four wells and two pumping stations, and other things necessary for that line of work which he values at $2,500.

Mr. Overr owns a modern home located in a plat of land consisting of twenty acres. He raises in abundance chickens, turkeys and ducks and has several cows. He is quite enthusiastic concerning Allensworth, and, when asked for an opinion, replied: "It has passed the experimental and pioneering period, and, while it is still in its infancy, for many reasons it is the best proposition ever effered to Negroes in the State." Mr. Overr was the first colored person in California to be elected a justice of the peace, having been elected to that office several years ago in Allensworth. In his untiring efforts to locate a polytechnic school in Allensworth he freely spent both his time and money and, while he did not succeed, still the people of the State after his lectures were more fully informed as to the conditions and future of the colony of Allensworth, California.

The question will naturally appeal to the reader, how do the people of Allensworth entertain themselves after the day's work is over? The following organizations are their source of mental and physical relaxation: The Girls' Glee Club of the public schools, a brass band, the Women's Improvement Club, and the Singleton orchestra. The Girls' Glee Club donated a set of four assembly-room brass swinging lamps for the public school house. The civic business of the community is conducted by the Allensworth Board of Trade. Allensworth being a judicial district comprising thirty-three square miles, they hold town elections and elect by vote a justice of the peace and constable, both of whom are colored.

There are many districts in California where there are well organized Negro settlements, namely: Furlong Tract and Albia, but Allensworth is the only one governed by Negroes, and it is destined to become a real city.

CHAPTER XIV

SOMETHING OF THE COLORED CHURCHES

All the movements for the uplift of the Negro race during pioneer days in California were strongly supported by all the ministers of the A. M. E. Church. It is befitting that a short survey of these trail blazers be given in this history. In view of the same, the writer is quoting from the Semi-Centennial Conference minutes held in Oakland during 1917, a copy of which was kindly furnished the writer by Rev. J. M. Brown, then pastor of the Fifteenth Street Church, that city. The sketch is as follows:

"The California Conference was organized in what was then known as the Union Bethel African Methodist Episcopal Church, San Francisco, California, April 6. 1865, Bishop Jabez Pitt Campbell, presiding bishop. The membership roll contained the following names: Rev. Thomas M. D. Ward, missionary elder; traveling preachers, Peter Green, Edward Tappan, James Hubbard, Charles Wesley Broadley, Peter Kilingworth, James C. Hamilton, John T. Jenifer; local preachers, Barney Fletcher, J. B. Sanderson, the last named was the secretary, with James Hubbard, the assistant.

"At the time we numbered: Missionary elder, 1; local preachers, 2; traveling deacons, 3; traveling preachers, 3; in full membership, 350; number of churches, 10; total valuation of church property, $29,600. How or when we lost the two years in reckoning our age, I know not, but today our records make us fifty years old, when, as a matter of fact, we are two years in excess of the half-century mark, and as the result of fifty-two years of organic life we have presiding elders, 1; traveling elders, 16; traveling deacons, 2; licentiates, 3; local elders, 3; local preachers, 10; full membership, 2,202; probationers, 376; Sunday-school pupils, 1,239; number of churches, 27; number of parsonages, 19; total valuation of church property, $368,049.

"Seeing California as it is today, her metropolitan cities, her well-settled country, her factories, shops, schools, and stately churches, with her wonderful railway system, all but incapacitates one for the task of looking backward over a period of time, although short as fifty years, and properly realize from whence we came. For the darkest hour, for the task most difficult, to the lands most distant and for a people most needful, God has never lacked for the man who would say, 'Here I am, send me.'

"With a population, in 1860, of 4,086 free people of color in the State, to elevate them and develop their manhood came Rev. Charles Stewart, preaching the fatherhood of God and the brotherhood of man. He sailed from New York December 1, 1851, on board the steamer 'Brother Jonathan,' arriving in San Francisco Bay February 11, 1852. The Sunday following, in company with his son who had come with him, a prayer meeting was held in the home of Edward Gomez, a West Indian, owning a rooming house, whom they met at St. Thomas. Present at this first service were Brother James Wilkerson, Henry Butler, James Barton and Henry Lewis. On the next Tuesday they met again at noon and for two hours prayer and discussion occupied their time, concluding with arrangements for a permanent place of worship. A vacant house was secured at a rental of $45 per month. Sixteen benches and a small pulpit comprised the furniture, and February 22, 1852, the First African Methodist meeting house on the coast was dedicated by Rev. George Taylor of Boston, Mass. Rev. Joseph Thompson, who had been ordained in England in the Wesleyan Methodist church, arrived in March and soon was installed as pastor.

"He, with the assistance of Brother Stewart, employed a lawyer, secured articles of incorporation, presented them to the Mayor of San Francisco for his signature, who signed the document and pledged $100 for the erection of a new church. April 29, he left for Sacramento, the capital, to secure the signature of the Governor. Here he met the Rev. Barney Fletcher and other brethren, to whom he made known his mission. He preached for them on the Sabbath and received a collection of $50. On Monday he met the Governor, who signed the papers and gave him $100. He visited the Adams Express Company and the Townsend Banking Company, receiving from them $100 each, and from other various amounts, so he was able to return to San Francisco with $450. Here the sum was increased by $900, the church built, and on August 8 was dedicated by the Rev. George Taylor.

"N. B.—To Rt. Rev. B. T. Tanner, D. D., in his 'Apology for African Methodism,' are we indebted for the historical data herein presented.

"(Signed)   J. H. WILSON, *Presiding Elder.*"

The A. M. E. Church has been the leading spirit in the building of California for the Negro, notwithstanding the other denominations, such as the Episcopalian church and their pastors have worked shoulder to shoulder. The other denominations were not so ably represented on the coast in pioneer days. Those who were in California united their forces for the good of the race in those strenuous days of the transition period. It has been the object of the writer to secure sketches of as many pioneer ministers as possible. Hence the sketches that follow should, because of the self-sacrifice of these men and the great good they have done, be considered really the Honor Roll of all the pioneers in or of California, regardless of the '49ers.

The following is a short survey of the Episcopalian Church of Northern California. There seems to have been no record kept of the work done among the colored people in San Francisco until after the coming of Rev. Peter Cassey. Rev. Flavel Scotts Mines came to California in 1851 and soon afterward established a mission for colored people. It has been impossible to obtain any definite data concerning the same, except from a few old pioneers who could not remember the date sufficiently exactly to record. The following concerning the Episcopalian Church for the colored has been kindly submitted by Rev. David R. Wallace, who, like Rev. Peter Cassey, is intensely interested in the uplift of the race:

"St. Augustin Mission, Twenty-seventh and West streets, Oakland, California: Work of the Episcopal church among the colored people of the Bay region of San Francisco, California, is no new thing, as an attempt was made forty years ago to establish 'Christ Church Mission' in San Francisco; but the effort failed then, as it would now for lack of members. Then there were but few people, because they had not yet begun to migrate to California in sufficient numbers. Now there are but few in San Francisco because the former residents have, since the fire of 1906, become successfully established in other cities, especially Oakland, because of difficulty in securing employment. Oakland next to Los Angeles, has a population sufficient to warrant the establishing a mission and was wisely selected for that purpose.

"St. Augustin's Mission was begun by the Rev. E. C. Gee, then Rector of St. John's Church, Oakland, on the last Sunday in July, 1910, Bishop Nichols being present and preaching. Each Sunday evening at six o'clock from that time evensong, with sermon, was sung in the Sunday-school room and classes for confirmation were prepared in the same place on Wednesday night. After the coming of the present Vicar the 'Holy Eucharist' was celebrated each Sunday, Wednesday, and Friday morning and on holy days in the chapel. The first fruits of the mission, eleven persons were presented to the Bishop of San Joaquin, May 18, 1911, by the founder of the mission and since that time the Rev. David R. Wallace, who was called to be Vicar in August, 1911, has presented, up to 1916, to the Bishop of California, 86 persons. Fifty others have been added to the communicant roll. Seventy-seven have been baptized, seventeen couples married, and fifty-one persons buried.

"A building fund was started and some $600 accumulated in addition to moneys raised for missionary, benevolent, salary and other purposes. The mission could not, however, have passed its first stage successfully without assistance, and we gratefully acknowledge free lights, heat, janitor service, vestments, and furnishings from St. John's altar and linens from the women's auxiliary; a monthly contribution from the Rev. Dr. Bakewell and a substantial sum from the convocation of San Francisco toward the building fund.

"So well satisfied were the Bishop and Archdeacon with the results achieved and so convinced were they that the mission needed a plant of its own, which it could not itself provide, that, in February, 1913, it was decided to make St. Augustin's a Cathedral Mission and purchase a lot and building for its use at the southwest corner of Twenty-seventh and West streets, Oakland. The lot cost $3,000 and is forty-five by ninety feet, with a high basement cottage across the back thirty-two by thirty-six feet. The congregation undertook to meet all expenses incidental to acquiring property and making the necessary alterations to the building thereon, which it has done to the amount of $4,600. A chapel has been provided thirty-two by twenty-five feet, with vestry, and kitchen in the rear and seating about eighty-five people. St. Paul's, Oakland, aided with benches, pulpit, Bible, gifts and memorials from the people. Trinity Parish will cede the necessary territory when the mission becomes organized.

"A fund for a new and permanent building was immediately started and now has reached $650 (1917). Now, after almost four years of combined success with the present inadequate equipment, the Archdeacon has authorized the drawing of plans and the starting of a campaign to raise six thousand dollars. The plans provide for a church seating two hundred people, with basement containing an auditorium, seating two hundred people, stage, kitchen and store room. It is planned to raise $1,000 more from the colored people, then to secure twice as much from the parishes of the diocese, and, finally, to appeal to wealthy individuals for the balance.''

The A. M. E. Zion church was founded August, 1852, in Stockton street, between Broadway and Vallejo streets, San Francisco, with Rev. J. J. Moore as pastor. From there they moved to Pacific street, where they built a brick chapel. In 1864 they bought the Rev. Thomas Starr King Church property. This church has been carefully pastored by Rev. J. J. Moore, D. D. (now Bishop), Rev. Lodge, Walters, Hector, A. B. Smith, W. H. Hillary and C. C. Pettey.

The first A. M. E. Church established in California was in San Francisco and was known as St. Cyrian A. M. E. Church. It was located at the corner of Jackson and Virginia street. In 1854 the pastor raised the building and a school for the colored people was opened in the basement. The public school board leased it for one year, with the privilege of two years, at the monthly rental of $50, payable monthly in advance. Mr. J. J. Moore (colored) is the teacher.

In Grass Valley Township, Nevada County, an A. M. E. Church was established in 1854. "The trustees, during the past year, erected a small but complete school house on the church lot, the trustees of the church forming a society for the purpose of erecting this school. Rev. Peter Green, pastor, and the following named persons: Isaac Sanks, James Thomas. John Hicks, Harry Blackburn, and Isaac Bulmer."—Grass Valley Directory.

Peter Powers, in Tehama County, began the building of a church in 1866. In 1870 he went to Chico and bought property and planned and built a church on two beautiful lots owned by colored people. It was known as the A. M. E. Church.

Mr. William Robinson, of Red Bluff, was one of the prime movers in building and organizing a church in Red Bluff, and boarded the pastor free for years.

The first Baptist Church in the State was organized in 1854, in San Francisco. A Mr. Samuel Shelton purchased an old warehouse and personally paid for having it fitted for a church.

Rev. Randolph, Mrs. Segue, Mrs. Blue, Mrs. McGowan and Mrs. Bland, were the founders of Mt. Olivet Church of Marysville, California. Mrs. McGowan was the treasurer for thirty years.

Rev. Stokes organized a church at Rozenville Junction, with Mrs. Smith and Mrs. Scott, Mr. C. Alexander, Rosa and John Alexander, of Nevada City.

"Religious Life of Los Angeles Negroes," by Rev. G. R. Bryant, in the Los Angeles Times, February 12, 1909: ". . . There are three distinct branches of the Methodists in this city—African Methodist Episcopal, African Methodist Episcopal Zion, and the Colored Methodist Episcopal. The African Methodist was the first of these to organize. . . . They started out with a small membership and labored under many disadvantages to pay for the old church property on Azusa street. They were at one time in such straitened circumstances for the payment for the property that one of the bishops advised the officials of the church to give up the property, but some of the faithful band held on until all could see the possibilities of paying the debt, which was done in 1902, under the pastorate of the Rev. J. E. Edwards. A new and better location for a church on the corner of Eighth and Towne Avenue was purchased and a large and beautiful house of worship was erected at a cost of over $20,000. In 1907, the pastor, Dr. W. H. Peck, and his official board sold the old Azusa street property for enough money to finish paying for the new church on Eighth street and Towne avenue. They have almost nine hundred members, with two mission churches in the city. Some of the wealthiest Negroes in Los Angeles attend this church.

"The African Methodist Episcopal Zion Church was organized soon after the African Methodist Church, with less than twenty members. In 1906 dissension arose which resulted in the removal of the pastor and the division of the church. Many of the communicants went to the African Methodist Church. Three years ago the talented Rev. W. D. Speight of Arkansas was appointed to this charge. He has been able to restore harmony and the church is in a prosperous condition, with one of the finest church edifices for Negroes in the State.

"The Colored Methodist Church was organized in this city January 8, 1906, with eight members, by Rev. J. W. Reese. They have forty-five members and a parsonage and a lot on which a church is soon to be erected. Rev. S. L. Harris, of Texas, has recently been appointed pastor of this flock. May 4, 1888, the First Methodist Church, of which Dr. R. S. Cantine was pastor, on request of the few Negro members that belonged to it, and by appointment of the Methodist preachers' meeting, through Dr. Hugh, a superannuated preacher, organized Wesley chapel with eight members. Dr. Tubbs, a white man, was the first appointed pastor. He was succeeded by Rev. D. Mucker, a Negro.

"September 14, 1892, a lot on the corner of Sixth street and Maple avenue was purchased at a cost of $2,520. In 1904 this lot was sold for $24,000, with which the present location was purchased and a building erected at a cost of $32,000. The lots, buildings and furnishings cost $45,000. After releasing a number of members to organize a church at Long Beach and Mason chapel in this city, Wesley chapel has more than 500 members.

"Mason chapel, organized 1903 through the assistance of the City Missionary Society, has a neat church and a parsonage, with a membership of less than a hundred. It is in a prosperous condition Rev. G. W. Pinkney, a graduate of Howard University, is pastor.

"The Second Baptist Church was the first of the Negro demoninations to organize in this city. For more than eighteen years Rev. C. H. Anderson was pastor of this flock. Three other congregations were formed from this organization, Tabernacle, Mt. Zion and New Hope Baptist Church. In 1908 the Rev. McCoy, a graduate of Howard University, an able preacher and experienced pastor, was called to this church. His success has been great. There are five hundred members. Their church property is valued at $40,000.

"Rev. J. D. Gordon, a graduate of Atlanta Baptist College, is the pastor of the Tabernacle Baptist Church. This congregation has a membership of 300, with a beautiful church edifice valued at $10,000.

"The Mt. Zion Baptist Church has a large building on Third street and Stevenson avenue, worth $20,000. Rev. J. T. Hill, A. M., D.D., one of the ablest men of his denomination is pastor. They have about two hundred members.

"December, 1907, Rev. C. H. Anderson resigned the pastorate of the Second Baptist Church and organized the New Hope Baptist Church with one hundred members who went with him from the Second Baptist Church. They have one hundred and seventy-five members and a building near Sixteenth and Paloma street suited to their needs worth $5,000, with very little debt on it. Rev. Anderson is a wise and successful pastor.

"On request of some of the Negro communicants, the Presbyterians of this city organized the Westminster Presbyterian Church for the Negro people, October, 1904. Rev. Dr. Baker, an able man and a friend to the Negro people, was appointed pastor. He was succeeded May, 1908, by Rev. R. W. Holman, a graduate of Willingsford. Dr. Holman is a great preacher. His beautiful church of forty members, situated on the corner of Thirty-six and Denker streets, the only Negro church west of Main street, is a blessing to the West Side. The Presbyterian board is making no mistake in helping to sustain this church.

"The Negro constituency of the Christian Church is grateful to Mr. Coulter, proprietor of Coulter's dry goods store, this city, for the gift of a neat church on East Eighth street near Central avenue.

"The Mission of St. Philip the Evangelist, the last of the Negro churches to organize in this city, with less than a score of members, is worshipping in Scott's Hall. They are soon to have a house of their own in which to worship. E. L. Chew is in charge of this mission. He has a class to be confirmed at an early date. Mr. Chew is eminently fitted for this work. He is a graduate of Mississippi State College and of the Gammon Theological Seminary at Atlanta, Georgia. He was dean of Turner Theological School in Atlanta four years. He served as principal of Gray street public school in Atlanta for ten years. He owns considerable property in Los Angeles. He is deputy assessor and tax collector, the only clerical position held by a Negro in this city's government. Negroes are to be found in almost all the other Christian denominations in Los Angeles. There are a large number of Roman Catholics, most of whom are members of the Cathedral parish, and their numbers are constantly increasing."

The following are some extracts from the great mortgage burning of the historic Eighth and Towne Church, which took place in March, 1918. This is quoted from the *California Eagle*. The first is from an address delivered by Rev. Mrs. D. R. Jones on that occasion. She said: "The month of August, in the year 1893, was an eventful one in the annals of African Methodism on the Pacific Coast. The Twenty-ninth Annual Conference was held at Marysville, August 9 to 13, and was visited by two distinguished prelates, Bishop B. F. Lee, the presiding bishop, and Bishop James A. Handy, also a prospective bishop in the person of Dr. L. J. Coppin, and an aspirant for financial secretary, Dr. Phillip A. Hubbard. Both reached the goal to which they aspired. Bishop Coppin is at present serving the Fourth Episcopal district. Dr. Hubbard passed from the financial chair to his final reward, many years ago.

"The conference was also graced by the presence of three prominent women, Sister Bishop Handy vice-president, W. M. M. Society; Sister Fanny Coppin, noted educator, and Sister Hannah Hubbard. From San Francisco, our former parish, after a few days' delay occasioned by the publication of the conference minutes, husband, daughter and myself proceeded to Los Angeles, our new charge, arriving Sunday, August 27, about 1 P. M. We went to my mother's home on Azusa street, near the church.

"It being the custom to hold class immediately following the morning service, the meeting was soon dismissed and a number of the members came to the house to greet us, among them Father Cyrus Vena and Mother Norris (Elvira). The people were apparently pleased and received us gladly. The membership, composed of about 125 persons, including probationers, scattered far and wide over the city noted for its vast area and its inclination to include in its corporate limits every pebble and stone between the mountains and the sea. Some members lived as far distant as Santa Monica, Long Beach, Pasadena, Monrovia, San Gabriel and Pomona. Though scattered from one end of the city limits to the other and beyond the limits, there was solidarity of thought and action, a unison of spiritual power and alertness, that made Stevens A. M. E. Church, as it was then known, a potent factor in the religious, moral, educational and civic life of the community. The people were in a receptive frame of mind, they seemed to be hungering and thirsting after righteousness. A revival was started at once. At the first meeting, Sunday evening, Sister Carrie McClane held up her hand for prayer and was converted. A number of others followed and the interest grew until a score were converted and added to the church.

". . . I recall some of the splendid men and women who were active in the church at this time. I will name them as they come to my mind, without comment: Cyrus Vena, Charles Clarkson, John Banks, John Sanders, Abraham Curtis, B. T. Talbot, Harry Franklin, Charles Parker, J. W. Marsailes, L. F. Fanner, Julius Maxwell, H. W. Spiller, A. B. McCollough, Jackson Harris, William Wells, Elvira Norris, Nancy Fulgen, Harriet McNeil, Bessie Owens, Eliza Posey, Eliza Warner, Fannie Warner, Emily Clarkson, Jennie Lewis, Mary E. Bronson, Mary Harris, Ellen Keen, Sarah Thompson, Virginia Nelson, Sarah Thompkins, Emma Anderson, Amanda Spiller, Fannie Seals, Hattie Lewis, Ellen Huddelston, Mary Harney, Harriett Brown, Maria Duncan, S. W. Calvin, Rebecca Sanders, Rachel Lee, Polly Smith, Alvain Murphy, Nannie Buford, Minnie Cunningham, Mamie Newman, Emily Baker, Nannie Reynolds, Julia Maxwell, Core E. Finney, Carrie White, and a host of others, enough to fill many pages, whom I found ready and determined to wrestle, fight and pray, 'the battle ne'er give o'er.' These by their sacrifices and labors of love made it possible for us to be here tonight. . . .''

The following is an extract from an address delivered by A. H. Wilson, trustee and steward: ". . . In November, 1903, we moved into this grand old building. Our congregation was small because only a few people were in Los Angeles. The church began to grow. After Rev. J. E. Edwards left, Rev. Peck was appointed to this charge, and he went to work and put in this great pipe organ. He finished his work; then came to us Rev. Jessie F. Peck, the great pastor of the day. He built up this great choir of ours, which stands as one of the greatest choirs in the United States.

"The city put a great debt on us of $6,000. When Rev. J. F. Peck left us the indebtedness was upon us for $3,975. He built up a great congregation and left us. The next pastor found us in debt. He stayed with us two years, paid $815 on the debt and borrowed $300 from the Mutual Aid Association. When he left us we were in debt $3,460. Now the church of today, as we now stand: This great pastor, Rev. J. Logan Craw, came to us on the third day of October, 1915. He found the church in a very bad condition. You can see it today. He did not complain of anything, but went to work. Interest was due. He went to work the first Sunday and raised $121, which was $11 over the amount that was due. He found the basement in a very bad condition. You can see it today. It is nicely fixed up and we call it our banquet hall. The pastor saw that $3,460 was upon the church, and said to the people: "Let us pay off this debt.' We said 'Yes.' This great pastor has done a great work, with the assistance of his dear wife. I have never seen her equal as a pastor's wife. May God bless both of you.''

The following is an extract from the financial report of Rev. Craw, as he was leaving for conference, August, 1918. It is taken from the *California Eagle*: "Dr. Logan Craw, successful pastor and financier of historic Eighth and Towne Avenue Church (First A. M. E.), this city, with his accomplished, Christian wife, wound up their third conference work here Sunday night and left on Monday evening for the annual conference, which meets with Rev. G. L. Triggs, pastor of Stockton, California. Three years ago, when Dr. Craw came to this metropolitan charge from Portland, Oregon, he found First Church here in a turbulent condition. The membership had split. A mortgage debt of $3,160 to the Security Bank and $300 to the Mutual Aid Society, and several other little outstanding debts confronted him. . . . Today the mortgage debt has been burned, all debts paid; . . . The church entirely beautified at nearly a cost of one thousand dollars; the membership brought back where it was before the awful split, and every vestige of trustee indebtedness wiped out. This church sings now in truth 'Free at last.' and Dr. Craw's annual report read for this year amid thanksgiving and joy Sunday night. . . .''

It is impossible to give in full this lengthy report, which shows that none of the obligations to the general conference was neglected, but, on the other hand, was liberally supported. ''Total money collected for all purposes, $8,120.59. Value of church and Sunday school property, $90,000. Indebtedness on the charge, none.'' It is gratifying to quote these extracts concerning this church. Well do they call it ''Historic,'' for in the list of names of the bishops and lay members the writer has found many who were ''Trail Blazers'' in the ''Pioneer History'' of the State. It was through their suffering and sacrifices that the Negro of today is able to live comfortably in this State.

The next sketch will contain the work of a notable ''Trail Blazer'' in the fight for the full citizenship of the Negro and his spiritual uplift. Rev. Bishop T. M. D. Ward, tenth bishop of the A. M. E. Church, was born in Hanover, Pennsylvania, September 28, 1823. He was converted in 1838 at Philadelphia and joined the A. M. E. Church; was licensed to preach in 1843 at Harrisburg, Pa., by Rev. Lewis Lee, and, in 1846, was admitted to the New England Conference; was ordained deacon, 1847, and elder in 1849. After being ordained he was appointed missionary for the Pacific Coast, where he remained several years, organizing churches in, that section, then but sparingly settled.

''In 1868 he was elected bishop, ordained in Lexington, Virginia, and the rural schools; was licensed to preach in May, 1868, and returned as bishop to the Pacific Coast, where he remained four years. He was afterward assigned to Alabama, Florida, and Mississippi, and other districts in the, South, while he did much to build up the church and distinguish himself as pulpit orator of the first class. The degree of D. D. was conferred upon him by Wilberforce University. He died June 10, 1894, and was buried in Washington, D. C.'' (From the A. M. E. Centennial Review). Bishop Ward's name appears in every movement for the betterment of the race in California. He was instrumental in Rev. J. B. Sanderson coming to this coast, as the bishop came direct from his home town, New Bedford, Massachusetts. After Bishop Ward was ordained as bishop he returned to San Francisco and, on the occasion of the celebration of the Emancipation Proclamation, he delivered one of the greatest orations ever delivered since or before in California by a Negro on the subject of ''The Aspects, Prospects and Retrospects of the Negro Race.''

Rev. Jeremiah Burke Sanderson, the subject of this sketch, was born in New Bedford, Massachusetts. He was the son of a full-blood Gay-head Indian woman and a Scotchman. He came to California from New Bedford, Massachusetts, in 1854. Sailing from New York to Aspinwall, stopping en route at Key West, Florida, crossing the Isthmus of Panama, he boarded the steamer ''Sonora,'' sailing to San Francisco, California. All the help on the steamer were colored. A Mr. Cowles, who was storekeeper, afterward became a distinguished pioneer colored citizen of San Francisco. Mr. Sanderson, upon reaching San Francisco, soon learned that the greater number of the colored people then living in California were located in Sacramento and the mining districts in the mountains. He soon left and, located in Sacramento, where the colored residents, learning that he was an educator, extended him a call to conduct a school for their children. After a careful consideration, he decided to open a day and evening school for the education of the colored race. He met with great encouragement and, in time, decided that his school was not equal to the needs, being supported through private subscription from the colored people. Acting upon his own initiative, he wrote a letter to the board of education asking them to establish a colored public school. A, copy of this wonderful letter will be found in the chapter devoted to ''Education.''

The board of education of Sacramento erected a new school house for the colored in May, 1855. Mr. Sanderson was appointed as teacher and filled the position with credit until he received a call to a position as principal of a colored school in San Francisco. He accepted the position and retained it for eight years. Learning that the colored children in Stockton were without a school, he resigned his position in San Francisco and went to Stockton, where he established a school for colored children. Mr. Sanderson was the father of schools for colored children throughout California. It was while teaching in Stockton that his fame as an educator became so well known throughout the State. The following press notice from a (white) daily paper of that period will give the reader an estimate of his position as an educator: ''We accompanied Mayor Orr, city superintendent of public schools; Mr. Randall, principal of the grammar schools, and Mr. Nelson, teacher of the intermediate school on Fremont Square, on a short visit to the colored school on Elk street, between Market and W streets.

"Many professional teachers might be benefited by paying a short visit to the same place and noting the thoroughness of instruction given to the colored pupils by Mr. Sanderson, the colored school teacher. We hazard nothing in saying that he is one of the best teachers in the county; and it is only the prejudice which so extensively prevails against a sable skin that prevents him from occupying one of the highest positions as a teacher in one of the public schools. There are few men if any in the County who can excel him."—(*Stockton Independent.*)

The above quotation is self-explanatory and readily gives the reader the key as to his superb leadership among the race people then living in California. Mr. Sanderson was an active figure in every movement for the betterment of the race in the struggle against adverse legislation. He was a member of the first and subsequent Conventions of Colored Citizens, an active member of the "Executive Committee," the Franchise League, Educational Convention and the Young Men's Beneficial Society of San Francisco. He assisted in organizing many churches throughout the state. It has been said of him that "He was a delightful Christian gentleman."

Mr. Sanderson's family did not accompany him to California owing to the lingering illness of his mother-in-law. Immediately upon her passing Mrs. Sanderson and the children came to California, arriving in San Francisco in 1859. The steamer arriving late, there was no one to meet them, whereupon Mrs. Sanderson remarked that it was prayer meeting night, and if shown to the colored church she would find her husband there. She was escorted to the church and the family reunion was such a happy one the prayer meeting was soon dismissed. Rev. Sanderson had not forgotten God and was found at his post of duty after an absence from his family of five years, while living in the "Wild and Woolly West."

Neither time, money, position nor anything else counted with Mr. Sanderson if he could serve the best interest of the race by giving either, as will be seen from the following: While he was teaching in Stockton he heard of a colored girl being held as a slave on a ranch near by. Several of the colored people had at various times tried to liberate her, but in vain. The moment Mr. Sanderson heard of her, he dismissed school and, going to the sheriff of the County, together they drove out to the ranch and brought the girl into town. After a court trial she was liberated.

It was while he was teaching in Stockton that the colored people throughout the State began to fully realize his worth as a teacher and sent their children from all parts of the State to be tutored by him. The thoroughness of the foundation he laid for their future education can best be judged if the reader is told that the greatest Negro financier of the United States was educated under Mr. Sanderson. This refers to Mr. Robert Owens, of Los Angeles, California, who was a pupil and boarded in the home of Mr. Sanderson when he taught in Stockton; also Mr. Byron Rowen of San Bernardino was a student under this same teacher.

Previous to coming to this coast Mr. Sanderson often filled the pulpit in his home town. The following quotation from William Nell's book, "The Black Man," says: "New Bedford, Massachusetts, has produced a number of highly intelligent men of the doomed race, men who by their own efforts have attained position intellectually which, if they had been of the more-favored class, would have introduced them into the halls of Congress. One of them is Mr. J. B. Sanderson, an industrious student and an ardent lover of literature. . . . He has mastered history, theology and the classics.

"Mr. Sanderson, although not an ordained minister, in 1848 preached for one of the religious societies of New Bedford on Sunday and attended to his vocation (hair-dresser) during the week. Some of the best families were always in attendance on these occasions. . . . In stature Mr. Sanderson is somewhat above the medium height, finely formed, well-developed head and a pleasing face, an excellent voice, which he knows how to use. His gestures are correct without being studied and his sentences always tell upon the audience. Few speakers are more happy in their delivery than he. In one of the outbursts of true eloquence for which he is noted, we still remember the impression made upon his hearers when he explained 'Neither men nor governments have a right to sell those of their species. Men and their liberties are neither purchasable nor salable. This is the law of nature which is obligatory on all men, at all times, in all places.' "

One need not wonder at the unity of action of the pioneers of color in California, when you consider such leadership among them as the subject of this sketch. He never tired in the fight for justice for the race. In the East he had worked with those of the "Underground Railroad." Rev. Sanderson was not only interested in the education and betterment of the race, but he saw to it that his own children were well-educated. This resulted in his daughters teaching in the public schools of California, one in Oakland and another in Visalia and also Red Bluff.

MRS. ARDELLA C. BUTLER
Social Leader.

HON. WALTER A. BUTLER
President Northern California Branch
National Association for the Advance-
ment of Colored People.

Wrestacres, suburban home of Hon. Walter A. Butler, of Oakland

MRS. J. M. SCOTT
Distinguished Club Woman.

MRS. HETTIE B. TILGHMAN
President California Federated
Colored Women's Clubs.

MRS. ALBERT LOGAN
Proprietor Tourist Hotel at
Santa Cruz.

MRS. A. C. HARRIS BILBREW
Elocutionist and Poetess.

Rev. Sanderson was ordained as elder of the A. M. E. Church by Bishop T. M. D. Ward, March 1, 1872, at Stockton, California. He was appointed pastor of the Shiloh A. M. E. Church of Oakland in 1875. While returning home from prayer meeting one evening, in crossing the Southern Pacific tracks he was killed by a local train. The sudden taking away of so useful a colored citizen as Rev. Sanderson resulted in the people throughout the State holding memorials in his honor and memory. The one held in San Francisco was in Bethel Church, and Mr. William H. Hall, the silver-tongued orator, was selected to give the oration. The L'Overture Guards turned out in a body and were officered by Captain R. J. Fletcher; first lieutenant, Joseph Harris; second lieutenant, Charles H. Whitfield; secretary, W. J. Summers; treasurer, T. M. Watson; financial secretary, J. T. Abrams.

The memorial exercises held in his memory in Oakland were at the Shiloh A. M. E. Church. The following persons were appointed to draft resolutions of respect, a copy of which were sent to the bereaved family. Abraham Gross, Cornelius Frances, Isaac Flood, John Johnson, I. N. Tripplett, chairman protem; Isaac H. West, secretary. The sketch and eulogy was delivered by William Powell. He left to mourn his passing a devoted wife and a mother who lived to see the fourth generation of children of the family. Rev. Sanderson also left the following children: Mary Sanderson-Grasses, who is mentioned in "Distinguished Women"; William Nell Sanderson, the only son, who was given an excellent education aside from learning the trade of plasterer and also barber. He was messenger to the sergeant at arms of the California Legislature in 1884. He married Miss Julia Brown. Unfortunately his wife died, leaving a family of six children, all small, but which he carefully reared and educated. His son Jeremiah B. Sanderson, is a clerk in the postoffice of Oakland. Harry B. Sanderson is clerk in a hotel at Martinez. Arthur Sanderson, another son, was the first colored policeman of Oakland.

Florence Sanderson-Wilson, the youngest daughter of Rev. Sanderson, was a delightful lady, true and sincere, and as good as pure gold. She was an active worker in the Fifteenth Street Church, a deaconess and superintendent of the Sunday-school primary department for a number of years, a practical, Christian lady. She looked much like a full-blood Gay-head Indian. She left a husband and daughter to mourn her passing, which came suddenly in the summer of 1916.

Mrs. Sara Sanderson-Collins, another daughter, has the distinction of being the only colored girl to graduate from the kindergarten school of San Francisco during pioneer days. She graduated with honor from the Silva street school. Miss Kate Douglas, or rather at that time Miss Kate Smith, who is now Mrs. Kate Douglas-Wiggins, was her principal. The closing exercises were held in Dashaway Hall, Post street, San Francisco. After her graduation she was given a position as assistant teacher in the same school. She also taught school in Visalia and Red Bluff. She afterward was married to an eminent divine, the Rev. A. A. Collins, of California, a native son, born in San Francisco. The union was blessed by the birth of several children, to whom he gave the best college education as doctors of medicine and dentistry. The above statement was received through the courtesy of Mrs. Wilson.

Rev. J. H. Hubbard, the subject of this sketch, was the son of Mrs. Ann Maria Booth-Hubbard. He was educated at Oberlin College by his uncle, Mr. Edward Booth. After his graduation he came to California and joined the ministry of the A. M. E. Church, under Bishop Ward, remaining in the California Conference until 1905, when he went to Colorado, where he continued in the ministry until his demise in 1912, leaving to mourn his passing three daughters and four sons: Mrs. Ida Williamson, Mrs. Ethel Morrison, Mrs. E. Gordon, of Furlong Tract, near Los Angeles; Mr. Edward Hubbard, an A. M. E. minister, and also James and Joseph Hubbard.

Rev. Simpson, coming from Clark University, Atlanta, Georgia, to Riverside, California, for twenty-five years was missionary preacher of Southern California, during which time he organized and built many churches in Redlands, San Bernardino, Pomona and Riverside. At the last named place he and his wife bought the lot for the church. Rev. Simpson is a real "Trail Blazer." While organizing and building these different churches, he reared and educated a family of two girls and one son, namely, Walter J., Azalia, and Gussie. Mr. Simpson was elected by the Council of Riverside to the position of head scavanger and contractor, having under his control three wagons. He has filled this position with satisfaction for a number of years. He has a large, comfortable, modern home situated at the foot of Mt. Rubidoux and fronting on Magnolia avenue, one of the most picturesque drives in Riverside. His son, Walter J. Simpson, during the past ten years has been engaged in farming at Blythe, Palo Verde Valley, California. Owning forty acres and acting as foreman in contracting and leveling and cleaning up land for the owners, having under his control at one time fifty colored men working the delta country, contracting. A daughter, Mrs. Gussie Simpson-Bacon (see Music chapter).

Rev. T. A. McEachen, the subject of this sketch, was educated at Whiten's Normal school, Lomberton, North Carolina, and at Biddle University. He left school in 1886, his eyes failing him, and in the spring of 1887 he came to California and united with the A. M. E Church at San Francisco Conference. In 1888 he was licensed to preach by the lamented Bishop Petty. He is one of the best known ministers on the Coast. When the church was as yet in its infancy in this State, undaunted he traveled from one end to the other of the San Joaquin Valley, zealously laboring for the uplift of the cause. He was the organizer of the first colored church in the San Joaquin Valley, at Fresno, California. For a number of years he was at the head of a colonization party and would go into the heart of the South and conduct parties of colored people to California and the San Joaquin Valley.

Rev. J. Logan Craw was born in Navasota, Texas, November 21, 1874. With his parents he left the State of Texas when scarcely five years of age and located in Parson, Labetto County, Kansas. Here he received a high school education and graduated as valedictorian of his class from Hobson Normal Institute, May 24, 1894. In September, 1895, he was elected as a teacher in the McKinley school in his home town, and for several consecutive years held this position of honor and trust. In May, 1902, against the will of the Board of Education, Professor Craw resigned as teacher to accept the high calling of the ministry, having been thoroughly converted in the A. M. E. Church at Parsons, Kansas, with the Rev. J. R. Ransom as pastor, at the age of nineteen years. Some three years were devoted to preparations for the work of the ministry and under Bishop Grant, at Omaha, Nebraska, September, 1904, he was admitted on trial to the Kansas Annual Conference at Hutchinson. Rev. Craw was ordained by Bishop Grant and began his active work in the pastorate assigned to the Olathe Circuit, Topeka District, Kansas Conference. On October 3, 1909, Rev. Craw was ordained elder by Bishops Grant and Lee, at Bethel A. M. E. Church, Leavenworth, Kansas. On July 1, 1911, Rev. Craw was married to Miss Lillian Jeltz, of Topeka, Kansas, a most successful teacher and a consecrated Christian lady.

After having pastored very successfully two years in Emporia, the seat of Kansas State Normal school, and two years in Lawrence, the seat of Kansas State University school, Rev. Craw was transferred by Bishop H. B. Parks, presiding bishop of the Fifth Episcopal District, in October, 1911, from the Kansas Conference to the Puget Sound Conference, and stationed at Bethel A. M. E. Church, of Portland, Oregon. Here Rev. Craw, aided by his brilliant wife, paid to the Church Extension Society in October, 1913, the largest amount ever paid at any one time in cash, viz., $2,085, a loan which had been standing for sixteen years. The membership was tripled during the three years of Rev. Craw's pastorate and one of the most modern and beautiful churches in the Pacific Northwest nearly completed. Rev. and Mrs. Craw are now at Los Angeles, where he is pastor of Historic Eighth and Towne Avenue Church.

The Declaration of Principles of the People's Independent Church of Christ reads as follows:

"Rev. 21:3.—'And I heard a great voice out of heaven saying, Behold the tabernacle of God is with men and He will dwell with them, and they shall be his people and God, himself, shall be their God.'

"Now whereas, We, the members of the First Independent Church sincerely devoted with the warmest sentiment of Christian affection and duty, with minds deeply impressed with duty first to God, deploring the present and impending misfortunes of our former associations in the church militant, and having considered the same as naturally as time will permit, do esteem it our duty to make the following declarations:

"(1) When in the course of human events it became necessary for the people to dissolve the bands which have connected them with a certain religious dnomination and to assume a separate and equal station in Christian work to which the laws of God and man entitle them, a decent respect to mankind requires that they should declare the cause which impelled them to the separation:

"(2) We, the adherents of this Christian movement, divorced of human potentates, rules and regulations repugnant to the best interests of our Christian lives, believe that all governments instituted among men derive their just powers from the consent of the governed, that whenever any form of religious denominational government becomes destructive to these ends, that it is the right of the people to alter or abolish it and constitute a reformation, laying its foundation on such principles and organizing its powers in such form as to them is believed the safest vehicle to affect their Christian growth and happiness:

"(3) We declare that we are actuated by the dictates of prudence, after long suffering of abuse, of power, position or station assumed by church potentates who disregard the will of the people who created them, and upon whom they are dependent for support, and we further declare that this act is prompted by no light or transient cause, but from a long-increasing train of disregard of the will of the people by men in high places, and that it is our religious right and duty to throw off such yoke for our Christian growth and for the benefit of present and future generations, thereby freeing ourselves from the greed and avariciousness of church despots.

"(4) First of all, we invoke the blessing of Almighty God on this movement for church freedom. We pray unto God for us and our successors forever, who have confirmed that this church shall forever be free from all demagogic or political rule whatsoever and shall keep its rights intact and its liberties uninfringed upon, that there shall be freedom of the communicants in prayerfully directing the affairs of the church.

"(5) Inasmuch as for the sake of our God, and for the betterment of our Christian lives, and for the more ready healing of the discord which has arisen between us and the earthly church masters we have been serving, we here and now grant them our forgiveness, wishing and praying that they may have peace and Christian growth, working faithfully in the Master's vineyard for the salvation of the souls of men, such as is the will and purpose of this congregation of men and women who believe in the saving grace of our Lord and Master. We believe in the sovereignty of the will of the people; that all preachers and officers are the servants of the people who have honored them with posts of duty in the house of God.

"Whereas, therefore, we have herein published our action and the cause leading up to the same, and having invoked the blessing and favor of Almighty God upon us, pledging our allegiance, and our love and faithfulness to His service, with abiding faith in His promise that where a few of His believers are assembled in His name He would be in their midst, to own and bless them, we do declare ourselves the 'Independent Church of Christ of Los Angeles, California,' and pray God to have mercy upon our souls.

"We here and now make known to all Christians and to the people at large that we welcome you to services in which there shall be no discrimination against those who profess to love and serve the one living and true God, everlasting, without body or parts, of infinite power, wisdom and goodness; the maker and perserver of all things visible and invisible and in unity of this God-head there are three persons, of one substance, power and eternity—the FATHER, the SON and the HOLY GHOST.

"We believe in God, the Father Almighty, Maker of Heaven and earth, and in Jesus Christ His only Son, our Lord, who was conceived by the Holy Ghost, born of the Virgin Mary, suffered under Pontius Pilate, was crucified, dead and buried; the third day He arose from the dead. He ascended into heaven and sitteth at the right hand of God, the Father Almighty, from thence He shall come to judge the quick and the dead.

"We believe in the Holy Ghost, the Holy Catholic Church, the communion of Saints, the forgiveness of sins and the resurrection of the body and the life everlasting.

"The foregoing declarations were unanimously adopted by the congregation assembled Sunday, October 23, 1915.

"Resolution: Be it Resolved, That the chairman and secretary be, and they are hereby authorized to tender the Pastorate of the First Independent Church to Rev. N. P. Greggs, of the City of Los Angeles, California.

"Adopted:

"J. H. SHACKELFORD,
"*President of Organization.*

"Respectfully submitted:
    "P. J. Alexander
    "Mrs. B. B. Prentice
    "F. H. Crumbly
    "G. W. Whitley
    "Mrs. L. E. C. Shaffer,
            "Committee."

This church represents the members who left the Historic Eighth and Towne Avenue Church of Los Angeles in 1915. For a while they were known as "The Faithful Forty-nine," since there were just that number who united and finally organized. For two years they worshipped in halls, but finally erected a church edifice at Eighteenth and Paloma streets. They have annual conference meetings at which the presidents of the different boards report to the people the spiritual and financial condition of the church. Each section of the city has been divided into districts to look after the spiritual and financial growth of the church. They have a membership of many hundreds and a splendid choir. It is a united, live, spiritual, working church of the people and for the people. The services are always refreshing, in that Rev. Greggs is evangelical, has a wonderful command of language, is a splendid orator and a Christian gentleman.

Rev. N. P. Greggs, pastor of the People's Independent Church of Christ, was reared and received his high school education in Columbia, Tennessee. It was while he was attending the A. and M. College, located at Normal, Alabama, that the Rt. Rev. Charles Todd, quintard bishop of Tennessee Episcopal Church, discovered that the subject of this sketch was an exceptionally fine student, and would, as he thought, make a great Episcopalian priest. Through the recommendation of this bishop the diocese decided to educate this colored lad. They paid all his expenses and sent him as a day student first to Fiske University and then to Hoffman Institute, to study theology. The latter school is located in Nashville, Tennessee, and represents the Episcopal Church.

After his graduation he served for a time in the Episcopal Church in the South, but finding that his work was not reaching the masses of the people, whom he believed he could save, he resigned his charge. Notwithstanding he had been reared and educated in the Episcopal Church, his determination was so great to serve the masses that he joined the A. M. E. Church Conference of Tennessee, in 1903. He pastored for a time in Tennessee, East Tennessee and the California Conferences. It was because of his desire to serve where the harvest would be great and the fields full and ready for the word of the Master that he subordinated the will of the bishop of the California Conference and refused the appointment to go to San Diego in 1915. The People's Independent Church of Christ extended him a call to serve as pastor in October, 1915. Since his acceptance of the pastorate of this flock they have built a great edifice at a cost of $35,000 and in one single collection at a recent rally they collected in money the sum of $4,200.

The Rev. W. T. Cleghorn is a native of the Islands of St. Kitts, British West Indies, where he received his earliest education. Winning a scholarship in St. George's School, of that Island, he entered Lady Mico College, St. John, Antigus, and graduated there in 1899. He was successively appointed principal of St. John's and St. George's Schools, and later served as assistant principal in the Frederiksted high school (1902-1905), in the island of St. Croix, Danish West Indies, now owned by America. Here he entered the ministry, and came to the United States in 1905, taking his A. B. degree at Oskaloosa College, Iowa.

He was ordained deacon in 1908 and priest in 1909 by the Rt. Rev. William N. Brown, D. D., bishop of Arkansas, in which State he organized several missions, chief among them being St. Mary's, Hot Springs, and St. Andrews, Pine Bluff. He came to the diocese of Los Angeles, under orders of the Rt. Rev. Joseph N. Johnson, D. D., and organized a mission and erected the first church edifice west of Denver for colored churchmen. He is now priest in charge of this church, and is also actively interested in the National Association for the Advancement of Colored People as an executive member, and in the Y. M. C. A. work as one of the directors, as well as in other institutions for the progress and welfare of his people.

The following additional history concerning the organization of St. Phillip's Church (Episcopal) is quoted from *The New Age Magazine:* ''St. Phillip's Church had its birth about three years ago in the house number 1428 East Fourteenth street, this city (still standing). When Archdeacon Marshall organized a Sunday-school and asked Mr. E. S. Williams of the Brotherhood of St. Andrews, a man entirely without race prejudice, to lend his support in reaching the colored people of the city, a conference was soon called at St. Mark's Church. Among others interested in the missionary work of the church as well as in these people were Mrs. Janivier, Mrs. Burr, Rev. F. N. Bugbee, Archdeacon Marshall presiding and Mr. Williams acting as secretary. Scott's Hall, 564 Central avenue, was rented, and services were held every Sunday morning and evening as a result of this meeting. This arrangement continued for a year or more, and to secure the permanence of the work the bishop, after several months of inquiry and deliberation, called the present clergyman, the Rev. W. T. Cleghorn, who arrived February 1, 1910, to be priest in charge. With wide experience in the work, he quickly took hold of the situation, negotiated for a valuable lot, and by prompt action and systematic plans secured a loan of $1,000 from the bishop and enough in subscriptions from members and friends to erect the present church (chapel). On October 9, 1910, the first choral mass with vested choir was sung. The outlook for this church among our people is very bright. The priest in charge says: 'It is a star in its ascendancy.' ''

There is one ministerial Trail Blazer to whom the writer must not forget to give befitting mention, namely, the late Rev. John Pointer, who came to San Francisco, California, in the early sixties. He secured a position on the Sacramento River boats as steward. In 1877, he became united with Bethel Church, of San Francisco, and served as leader of the choir in this church and superintendent of the Sunday-school in Zion Church, that city. In 1887, he became a local preacher in San Francisco, and took charge as pastor in the A. M. E. Church, at Los Angeles, under Bishop Grant, thence to St. Andrews, of Sacramento, for five years, building the parsonage and paying for it, after which he was promoted to presiding elder by Bishop Wesley Gains. He held charges at various times in Oakland, Fresno, Stockton and Marysville.

He was superannuated in 1909, and passed to his reward, well beloved and highly respected by all who knew him, on the morning of January 2nd, 1917. The funeral was held the following Sunday and lasted four hours. Ministers from all over the State of California attended and paid homage to this grand saint of God.

There are many Baptist ministers who have been ''Trail Blazers'' in this State. Among this number Rev. Allen leads the list as having served as missionary worker for the Baptist faith for over thirty years, during which time he has done some very good work. Rev. Hawkins, of Oakland, and also Rev. Dennis, of San Francisco, have done some wonderful work in the State for the development of the race as well as the saving of souls.

The Rev. David R. Wallace was born in Cleveland, Ohio, September 30, 1878. He attended the schools of Cleveland, Milwaukee, and Chicago. After graduating from the old South Division high school, Chicago, he entered the summer school of the University of Chicago. The inspiration to study for the ministry came to him at this time as a fulfillment of the wish of his deceased mother, and he entered the Western Theological Seminary, Chicago, from which he graduated in 1901. He was ordained a deacon in July of that year and, going to Nashville, Tennessee, where he was proctor of Hoffman Hall and in charge of the local church, was ordained priest in 1902.

He was called to Boston shortly thereafter to assist the Cowley Fathers at St. Augustine's Church, where he remained until 1908. Going again to Tennessee, he started a mission in Chattanooga, and took charge in Columbia. He then was called to assist at St. Thomas' Church, Chicago, where he remained a year. In July, 1911, he was called to St. Augustine's Mission, Oakland, California, where he is now engaged in leading a splendid congregation of 145 souls in the building of an edifice to cost $6,000. So efficient has been the work of this congregation that the bishop has just paid the mortgage on the property as a token of appreciation. Rev. Wallace has always found time to aid in all community activities, and was four years vice-president of the Northern California branch, N. A. A. C. P.

CHAPTER XV

EDUCATION

While statesmen were passing laws to retard the progress of the pioneer Negroes of California, they never for a moment considered that the Negroes were planning and striving to improve their mentality and become good citizens when the time came for them to be admitted as such. This calls to mind an editorial the writer once read in the *Los Angeles Times* from the pen of Mr. John Stevens McGroarty, author of the "Mission Play." The paper is the largest published on the Pacific Coast, and, as a special feature commemorating the hundredth birthday anniversary of the martyred President, Abraham Lincoln, on February 12, 1909, devoted eight pages of the paper to colored writers. Each article was written by some one who was a master in his or her line, and would tend to show the progress of the colored race in Southern California. Mr. McGroarty at the time was on the editorial staff of the *Los Angeles Times*, and was assigned the duty of writing an introduction to this special feature, explaining it to the reading public. It is with a great degree of pleasure that the writer quotes from this just and humanitarian editorial, which is as follows:

"When out of chaos earth was hurled
    And God's great mandate spread;
When he made the races to fill the world,
    Yellow and white and red,—
There was one made black, and the other three,
    Seeing him, asked to know
Whence from what darkness cometh he
    And whither doth he go?

"What is the destiny of the American Negro? Whither does he go? Is he to survive, or is he to be ground between the upper and nether millstones of time to be blown as dust by the winds of fate; to disappear as the American Indian is disappearing, and as many another race has disappeared since the world began? It is a timely question to ask on this the one hundredth anniversary of the birth of Abraham Lincoln, the great emancipator. . . . Men will answer this question each in his own way, according to his faith in the Negro or his prejudices against him. No one ever seems to think it worth while to ask the Negro himself for an answer. The *Times*, however, does think it worth while, and has accordingly invited the Negro people of Los Angeles and Southern California and the great Negro leader, Booker T. Washington, to speak for themselves. This they have done through the columns of the *Times* this morning. . . . As a rule the white man's knowledge of the Negro is superficial. We know our brothers in black only from meeting them on the highways or the jokes that are printed about them in the comic papers. Some times our impressions are gained from none too friendly sources, from those who hate the Negro blindly and without reason."

What a world of thought this editorial arouses in every self-respecting Negro, for we know better than any one else. We are more often judged unjustly than otherwise. We are hated, as Mr. McGroarty says, "blindly and without reason." It was thus when the pioneer Negroes were struggling to obtain an education in California. The struggle was difficult, but they believed in the saying of Daniel Webster, who said: "Were I so tall that I could reach from pole to pole and grasp creation in my span; I still must be measured by my soul. The mind's the standard of the man." In order to develop the mind one must have an education.

The First public school in California was made mention of as a public school in San Francisco, and is recorded in Bancroft's history of California, which reads: "The first public school after the American occupation was established in San Francisco. The number of persons in June, 1847, under twenty years of age were 107, of that number 56 were of school age. On the 24th of September of that year the town council appointed a committee consisting of William A. Leidsdorff, William Clark and William Glover to take measures for the establishing of a public school. A school house was erected on Portsmouth Square dignified by the name of Public Institute, and on the 3rd of April, 1848, a school house was opened by Thomas Douglass, a Yale graduate, who received a salary of $1,000 a year. From this beginning has grown, with some interruptions, the public school system of California."

Mr. Bancroft, in another chapter, in speaking of the life of Captain William Leidsdorff, says: "He was a mulatto, the offspring of a Dane by a mulattress." Jacob

Wright Harlan, in his "California from 1840 to 1888," in speaking of Captain Leidsdorff, says: "He had a dash of Negro blood." Thus the first public school in California had as a committeeman in its organization a person with a dash of Negro blood in his veins. The dash of Negro blood did not in those days count against a man, for more than one writer of pioneer times in California mentioned Mr. Leidsdorff in the highest terms, never failing to mention the "dash of Negro blood."

The colored population in San Francisco did not attend the public schools until 1854, notwithstanding the annals of San Francisco, in recording the census for the State of California for the year 1853, gives the number of Negroes as 2,000, and of that number 1,500 lived in San Francisco. The State had been admitted into the Union as a free State. The colored people, however, were anxious for an education. Through the courtesy of the family of Rev. J. B. Sanderson, who was a teacher of pioneer days in San Francisco, the writer has been permitted to quote from his diaries concerning the history of the colored schools in San Francisco for the year 1854.

"Something of the history of the colored schools in San Francisco for the year 1854. This school was first opened May 22, 1854; under the superintendency of William O. Grady. It was located on the corner of Jackson and Virginia place in the basement of the St. Cyprian A. M. E. Church. The annual report of the school board of education in San Francisco, for the year 1854, presented to the Common Council September 1, 1854, the following: 'A school for the colored population of our city has been established. It is located at the corner of Jackson and Virginia street, in the basement of the St. Cyprian Methodist Episcopalian Church. The patrons of the church have raised the building and fitted it up for a school. The lower room, which is eleven feet high and fifty by twenty-five feet surface, is well lighted, ventilated and has its walls hard-finished. This we have leased for one year, with the privilege of two years, at the monthly rental of fifty dollars, payable monthly in advance. Mr. J. J. Moore (colored) is the teacher. The school commenced on the 22nd of May, with 23 pupils. It now has 44 pupils registered. It has been thus far conducted quite satisfactorily and bids fair to be prosperous.' (N. B.)—Mr. Moore had taught a private school. Mr. William O. Grady was principal of the Rincon Point school one year and a half. He was appointed superintendent of the public schools of San Francisco October 25, 1853.''

The writer has been unable to find a record of the colored school after the one just quoted until the report as recorded in the Municipal Reports of San Francisco, beginning 1859 and 1860. In the school reports for this year the following appears: "J. B. Sanderson, teacher; number of pupils, 100; average attendance, 39. Primary report for 1861: The same teacher; 88 pupils; daily average, 42; primary class, 60; grammar, 50 pupils. The board of education in its report for 1863-4 and 5 speaks of a new building for the colored children.

"During the year three new school buildings have been erected in San Francisco; one on Broadway, for the colored children. The lot on which the colored school stands has 693¾ feet on Broadway and a depth of 91¼ feet. The lot cost $600. The building is frame, one-storied, and divided into two recitation rooms each 28 feet by 32 feet, with ceiling 15 feet in the clear; separate halls and clothes rooms are provided for each sex. The building is well lighted and ventilated. The building and fence cost $4,435, and the furniture, which is of the improved style, $498. The colored children richly deserve their present comfortable and neat school-house after having continued unmurmuringly for many years in their former squalid, dark and unhealthy quarters."

This new school required the appointment of an additional teacher, and in the report for the year 1864 and 1865 the following appears: "J. B. Sanderson, principal; Mrs. Precilla Stewart as teacher." The report for the year 1861 showed the method employed by the school board of San Francisco to obtain the very best teachers for the schools of that city. "The board of education strives by subjecting candidates for positions as teachers to a rigid examination of their natural and acquired abilities and by offering a fair pecuniary compensation for services rendered to secure the best professional talent in the State for the education of the youths of the city." In the report for the year 1863 and 1864, the following appears: "By an act of the Legislature, Negroes and Mongolians and Indians are excluded from the public schools, although the penalty for admitting them to the schools for the whites has recently been abolished and a more ample provision has been made for their education in separate schools." The report for 1865 and 1866: "The Broadway school was taught by S. D. Simmonds, with Mrs. Washburn primary assistant. Fifth street school, J. B. Sanderson, teacher; length of time in the department, eight years. Colored school in San Francisco for the year 1868 and 1869: One principal, one assistant and one probation teacher; first grade pupils registered, 161; attendance, 98; Mrs. Georgia Washburn, Mrs. H. F. Byers, Miss Adrianna Beers. The report for 1869, colored school, located northeast corner Taylor and Vallejo streets: Pupils registered, 68; average attendance, 26; Miss Georgia Washburn, teacher."

The first colored class to graduate in the colored schools of San Francisco was under J. B. Sanderson. This class began its first instruction under the same teacher during his term of teaching in Sacramento and previous to his accepting the position in the San Francisco schols. The names of the first San Francisco colored graduates were: Mary Whittaker, Cornithea Johnson, Ella Dorsey and Lucy Caulwell. The last named afterward married Mr. Dizard and still lives in Oakland, California. This class while in Sacramento was taught, after Mr. Sanderson, by J. B. Handy and Peter Powell.

The following is a partial list of names of pupils of J. B. Sanderson while he taught in San Francisco, some of whom are still living and are the heads of highly respected families: Bell Freeman, M. A. A. Drew, William Nell Sanderson, Addie Hall, M. E. J. Bolmer, M. A. Alberger, William M. Blake, Madge Vosburge, A. Grubbs, Alice Reams, Louise Bryant, Eveline Evans, Elsie Brown, Lucinda Bryant, Lenna Haws, Sara Brown, Josephine Miles, Mrs. M. J. Johnson, Ella Wells, Mary Groesbeck, Lauretta Southers, Florence Brown, Laura Millen, Clara Shorter, Claress Waters, George Shepard, Sara Carroll, George Fletcher, Henry Undly, Mrs. Keithly, Frank Ewing, Martha Green, Edward Yantes, Isaac Washington, Frederick Sparrow.

The first colored school in Sacramento was commenced by Mrs. Elizabeth Thorn Scott, May 29, 1854. Through the courtesy of her daughter, Mrs. Lydia Flood-Jackson, the following has been copied from her school register: "Elizabeth Thorn Scott commenced school for the promotion of colored children, May 29, 1854, Second street between M and N streets, Sacramento, California. Names of the pupils were George Booth, Lauretta J. Bryson, Edward Yantes, Mrs. Mary Ann Burns, Laura M. Luckett, Richard Brown, Thomas Allen, Cornelius Campbell, George Waters, Reubin Johnson, Alice Mitchell, Chesterfield Woodson, Abraham Goodlow, Frederick Sparrow."

Their teacher, Mrs. Scott, after the first year, became the bride of Mr. Isaac Flood. The school was then for months without a teacher. The colored people in Sacramento on August 7, 1854, organized the first public school established for colored children in Sacramento in the A. M. E. Church on Seventh street, and employed Mrs. Scott as the teacher at a salary of $50 per month.

"The colored school committee for school number one: Dennis Brown, Abraham Simpson, John L. Wilson, William Hall, Moses Rodgers, William Robinson, Mrs. Yantes and J. B. Sanderson, raised through subscription the money with which to purchase the lot and house in which Mrs. Elizabeth Thorn Scott opened the first private school for colored children and dedicated it to the education of colored youth."

Some time after Mrs. Scott married, the school committee decided to employ Mr. J. B. Sanderson as the teacher and re-open the school. The following has been quoted from his diaries: "Sacramento, California, April 20, 1855. Today I opened a school for colored children. The necessity for this step is evident. There are thirty or more colored children in Sacramento of proper age to attend school and no school provided for them by the board of education. They must no longer be neglected, left to grow up in ignorance, exposed to all manner of evil influences, with the danger of contracting idle and vicious habits. A school they must have. I am induced to undertake this enterprise by the advice of friends and the solicitation of parents. I can do but little, but with God's blessing I will do what I can."

Mr. Sanderson, realizing that the colored children were entitled to a public school, sent a letter to the board of education of Sacramento, asking them to assist in maintaining or establishing a school for the colored children. His letter is really a history of the struggle the colored people were then making in an effort to have a school for their children. The letter is as follows:

"To the Honorable Board of Education of Sacramento, California.

Gentlemen: Allow me to call your attention to the subject of the school for colored children in Sacramento. This school has been operated now about thirteen months, having been commenced on the eighteenth day of April, 1855. I will briefly state its history: At the time it was commenced no provision whatsoever had been made by our city authorities for the education of colored children, so that this school was started necessarily as a private school. In March, 1855, the grand jury recommended the establishing of a fund for the support of a school for colored children. In consequence of that recommendation and the advice of several friends of education, the undersigned presented a communication to the board of education, soliciting the attention of the members to the subject. They at once took the matter under advisement, favored an appropriation and laid the question before the Common Council for its action and approval. After some delay, on the 21st of October, 1854, the Common Council passed an ordinance authorizing the board to make such appropriation as they might deem necessary for the support of one school or more for the colored children in Sacramento. Funds were exceedingly scarce; it was only with great difficulty the board could meet the expense of their own schools; they could do nothing for us.

"But in February, 1855, the board voted to appropriate $50 toward the support of our school for the last quarter of the term in office. Besides this, for the last three months, a few of the colored parents, seeing the difficulty surrounding the school, have resumed the responsibility of paying the teacher of the children $40 per month, which sum they have raised by contribution among themselves. This is briefly the history of the colored schools in Sacramento. Mr. Edward Knight, the school census marshal, stated in December, 1854, that in taking the census of school children in Sacramento (though not authorized to include colored) he had ascertained incidently that there were over eighty colored children in Sacramento. The school kept by the undersigned has numbered 30 pupils during the past two months, and twenty-two has been the lowest number of children at any time for the last month. The number of children is increasing; the necessity for a permanent public school grows more imperative.

"Gentlemen, you have just been elected the board of education for the City of Sacramento. The parents of the colored children appeal to you; they respectfully and earnestly ask your attention to the school for their children. They ask you to take it under your protection and patronage and to continue such appropriation for its support as in your wisdom and liberality may seem required to make it permanent and efficient for the training of their children's minds, than whom they know none need instruction more than those children that they may become upright and worthy men and women.

Respectfully submitted in behalf of the colored parents of Sacramento, California, by the teacher of the colored school.

"J. B. SANDERSON.

"July 10, 1855."

The board of education acted upon the letter sent to it by Mr. Sanderson and decided to take over the colored school, whereupon the teacher, Mr. Sanderson, sent them another letter. The board of education at that date was composed of the following gentlemen: F. Tucker, superintendent; ex-Mayor R. P. Johnson, John F. Morse, H. Houghton, J. N. Hatch, G. W. Wooly and G. Wiggins.

Mr. Sanderson's second letter to the board of education was to ask permission to stand the examination for the position as the teacher of the colored school. He was examined and having met the requirements was employed as the teacher. The board of education of Sacramento built for the colored children a new school house in May, 1856, The writer has no record of the colored school from that date until 1865, but an old history of Sacramento of that date gives the following account of the colored schools: "Sacramento, 1865. Colored boys and girls of school age, 92; colored school teacher, Mrs. Julia Folger, principal. School located on Fifth street between N and O (brick), 47 pupils. Sacramento, 1868. Colored school, William H. Crowell, principal; Miss Annie M. Yantes, assistant; located between H and Tenth streets; number of pupils, 55. Sacramento, 1869. The following pupils passed a satisfactory examination and were recommended to the high school: Mary Owens, Ernest Small, Robert Small, Tiracy Mooris, Natty Christopher, Hiram Jones; the teacher, Miss Aubury.

"In August, 1873, Miss Sara Jones was given a position as teacher in the colored schools (M street school). Shortly afterward, when the schools became mixed, she was appointed as the principal and retained this position until her retirement in 1915. Miss Jones is a graduate of Oberlin College, in Ohio."

The colored people in San Jose were anxious to obtain an education and, like all the other cities then in California, they had to struggle to have schools for the colored children. Nothing daunted the courage of the colored people in the fight for an education. They at all times were able to accomplish their desires. There were only a few colored people then living in San Jose. Even so they were desirous of educating their children. Through the efforts of Rev. Peter Cassey a private school was opened, but it needed money for furnishings. It seemed that the colored people were always able to solicit the assistance of some loyal white person in any undertaking. Their friend on this occasion was Professor Higgins, the music teacher of the white school. He offered to teach the colored children music and give a concert in the town hall. Among the pieces he taught the children was "Marching Through Georgia." The city band, at the hour of the concert, was playing on the plaza and caught the strains, resulting in the town hall not being able to accomodate the crowd. The sum of two hundred dollars was raised at the concert.

This school was organized by Rev. Peter Cassey in 1861. The gentleman was the rector of Christ Episcopal Church for colored, located in San Francisco. Many of his parishioners sent their children to his school, which was private boarding school for the higher education of colored youths. The following statement by Rev. Cassey setting forth the object and aim of the school has been copied from an old copy of *The Elevator* of that period: ''The design is to establish a high school for colored children. This is a public good which all must acknowledge is one of the necessities of the age. I ask the assistance and co-operation of all. Board and tuition per term of four weeks, $16 to $20. All the English branches and vocal music without extra charge. Piano or melodian, with the use of instrument, per month, $6.''

This school afterward, through the organization of a convention of colored citizens, was given prestige and financial support of a large number of race-loving people living in the San Joaquin Valley. It was given the name of ''Phoenixonia Institute of San Jose, California.'' This convention met in San Jose December 11, 1863. The names prominently mentioned in connection with it were the following: Rev. Peter Cassey, William Smith, James Floyd, S. J. Marshall, A. Bristol, A. J. White and G. A. Smith. This convention met every year, and at one of their meetings held in San Jose, July 31, 1867, the following resolutions were passed setting forth their position in regard to the education of colored youths on the Pacific Coast:

''Whereas, The convention of colored citizens of California, called by The Phoenixonia Institute, having assembled in San Jose, July 31, 1867, to consider the subject of education, industrial pursuits and the elective franchise; and Whereas, Education means improvement; improvement is the guiding of the Deity; to whom is improvement more desirable or more necessary than to those who from long oppression are just merging into the light of liberty; and Whereas, The education of our people as a man has been sadly overlooked, owing to a variety of causes, and as this convention has for one of its objects the educational interest of the rising generation, therefore, be it

''Resolved, That we endeavor by every means within our reach to carry out its designs, that we devote our time and our means and be prepared to make any sacrifice consistent with our circumstances to elevate our people in this particular. Resolved, That the facilities for the education of the colored children on the Pacific Coast are not in proportion to our necessities; and with a view to elevate them we will build upon the foundation already laid in this city, San Jose, until its educational advantages shall be fully equal to our necessities and will compare favorably with the best.''

The Stockton colored public school was taught by J. B. Sanderson. He resigned from the San Francisco colored schools at the spring term, 1868, and went to Stockton, where he established, through the assistance and co-operation of other race-loving men, a school for colored children. Mr. Sanderson's reputation as a teacher was so well-known that colored people sent their children from all parts of the State to be tutored by him. Among the out-of-town pupils who attended the colored Stockton school was Robert C. Owens, of Los Angeles, and Byron and Walter Rowen, of San Bernardino. These students today are a fair example of the careful instruction given by Mr. Sanderson, because they are both successful business men, well respected by all. Mr. Owens is one of the very best financiers of the race in California, if not the wealthiest.

The colored people were sincere in any movement that would assist them to improve their mentality. While the members of the race were perfecting plans for the success of the institute in San Jose, those living in San Francisco were organizing a plan by which at some future date they hoped to have even a better institution or college. They planned not to have their project spoiled for the lack of funds, hence they decided that they would not open this college until they had a certain sum of money. They aimed so high that they were never able to carry out their plans and, after a period of ten years, they had a meeting and returned to the stockholders their money. The following quotation from an old copy of the *Elevator* will more fully explain their workings:

''The meetings to organize the Livingston Institute were held in the vestry of the A. M. E. Church, in San Francisco. Among the names prominently mentioned in connection with the project were: Barney Fletcher, who was elected president; J. J. Moore, financial secretary and traveling secretary. The trustees were John A. Barber, William Hall, James Sampson, William Ringold, D. W. Ruggles, and W. H. Carter. At a special meeting of the board of trustees of the Livingston Institute held at number 54, Merchants Exchange, San Francisco, January 7, 1873, they decided to return the money to the stockholders, since the conditions had so changed the Institute was no longer needed. They returned the money contributed with 132 per cent interest. N. Gray, H. H. Collins, R. T. Houston, Peter Anderson, R. F. Houston, John A. Barber, S. D. Simmonds, trustees.''

The Marysville colored school was established by Rev. Randolph, who was assisted by Miss Washington, who was the first colored child born in Marysville and had been sent by her parents to Canada to be educated.

Chico colored school was organized by Peter Powers.

Nevada County, California, colored school, as given in Bean's History of Nevada County: "A building was purchased last fall on Pine street for the colored school, and has been fitted up for the purpose. This school was opened on the first of January, 1860; G. A. Cantine, teacher; number of pupils, 18; average attendance, 14."

"Grass Valley Township, Nevada County. There is made mention of an African Methodist church in 1854, and speaks of the trustees during the past year erecting a small but comfortable school house on the church lot, the trustees of the church forming a society for the purpose of erecting this school. Rev. Peter Green, the pastor, and the following named persons: Isaac Sanks, James Thomas, John Hicks, Harry Blackburn, Isaac Bulmer."

The Red Bluff colored school was taught by Miss Sara Brown, daughter of John Brown, of Harper's Ferry fame, and a Mr. Craven taught a colored school in the country out from Red Bluff. It was very difficult for the children to drive out from Red Bluff during the rainy season to attend school. Through the united effort of the well-known colored citizens of Red Bluff, Mr. A. J. Logan, William Robinson, and P. D. Logan, they succeeded in calling the attention of the school board to that section of the State school laws which read: "Section 58. Where there shall be in any district any number of children other than white children whose education cannot be provided for in any other way, the trustees, by a majority vote, may permit such children to attend schools for white children, provided that a majority of the parents of the children attending such school make no objection in writing to be filed with the board of trustees." The board recognized this law and, there being no objection, Miss Clara Logan, a colored pupil, was enabled to continue her studies in the Red Bluff high school, graduating in the pioneer class.

Afterward she stood the county examination and passed, and the board of education appointed her to teach in the school with Miss Sara Brown. This student today is a well-known society matron and charity worker among her people in San Francisco. The writer refers to Mrs. Frazier. Attending the Red Bluff colored school at the same time Miss Clara Logan attended were her sisters and brothers, namely, James and Thomas Logan, Clara, Will and Ella Robinson; also Miss Laura Robinson, who today is Mrs. Albert Tooms, a prominent lady in San Francisco.

The first colored school in Alameda County, California, was organized as a private school by Mrs. Elizabeth Thorn Scott-Flood. She opened a school for colored children about 1857, in the old Carpenter school house, corner of Seventh and Market streets, Oakland. This school had been used for white children, but, becoming crowded, they built them a new building, after the completion of which this colored lady was allowed to use the abandoned building for a colored school. Among her first pupils was a lady by the name of Miss Lyncholm, who lived in Oakland and still is a resident of the county. Her present name is Mrs. Walter Edmonds.

The first public school for colored children was opened under the California statutes of 1865 and 1866, page 398, which read: "An Act to provide for a system of common schools, Section 56. Any board of trustees or board of education, by a majority vote, may admit into any public school half-breed Indian children and Indian children who live in white families or under guardianship of white people.

"Section 57. Children of African or Mongolian descent and Indian children not living under the care of white people shall not be admitted into public schools except as provided in this act, provided that upon the written application of the parents or guardians of at least ten such children to any board of trustees or board of education a separate school shall be established for the education of such children, and the education of a less number may be provided for in separate schools or in any other manner. The same laws, rules and regulations which apply to schools for white school children shall apply to schools for colored children." Under this law the trustees of the public schools of Oakland opened a school for colored children in the old Manning house, located in Brooklyn. This district is now known as East Oakland. This house is now owned by Mr. Wilds.

The first public colored school had as its first teacher Miss Mary J. Sanderson. She was considered a very good and kind teacher, much beloved by her pupils. The writer had the pleasure recently of reviewing a program rendered by her pupils at the closing exercises held at Shattuck Hall. It seemed that nearly every child in her school was on the program, and, as she told the writer, she could not bear the thought of slighting any little one. This lady is just as thoughtful of others today and still manifests the same kindly spirit. Miss Mary J. Sanderson taught the colored school in Oakland until the parents of the colored children began to move from the district. They were compelled to go where the heads of the families could make the best living. The distance usually was too far for the children to attend the colored school. The law required that there must be at least ten children attending any colored school to remain open. After the removal out of the district of the families of Lewis Whiting, J. P. Dyer, and Isaac Flood, they practically emptied the district and forced the closing of the colored school. But it also robbed their children of the privilege of attending another school, on account of their color, and the distance compelled them to give up the idea of even trying to attend the colored school.

The parents of these children were not desirous of raising their children in ignorance, and appealed to the board of education of Oakland, asking the admittance of their children into the Oakland school nearest to the different families. The following is quoted from the *San Francisco Bulletin*, under date of October 5, 1871:

"Oakland public school matter. Colored school room wanted. A breeze has been sprung in peaceful Oakland on the question of admitting colored children into the public schools. There is no school set apart for them. A few have been admitted to one of the schools, and some of the parents of the white children have withdrawn their children on that account. The superintendent of the schools has brought the matter before the board of education to have the matter settled. The board discussed the matter and finally refused to adopt the following resolution which was presented by one of its members:

" 'Whereas, The parents of certain colored children residing in Oakland ask that their children be admitted to the public schools of this city, and whereas, there are not within the bounds of the city a sufficient number of such colored children to require the establishment of a separate class for colored children as required by law of this State; and whereas, the school laws of this State expressly prohibit the admission of such children into the classes as now organized in the department; Resolved, That the superintendent be instructed to refuse admission to any colored children applying for admission to the schools as now organized in conformity with the law of this State.' This refusal to adopt goes for nothing, however, as the next action of the board was to instruct the superintendent to furnish to all the teachers a copy of the new manual, with instructions to have it strictly followed: Section 97 of the Manual reads: 'The education of children of African, Mongolian or Indian descent shall be provided for in accordance with the California school laws.' "

In commenting on the action of the board of education in regard to admitting colored children to the public schools the editor of the *Pacific Appeal* said editorially: "We will here state that the colored citizens will be compelled ere long to take this whole public school question before a State or United States court; to have their children driven from the free schools in each county for which they are taxed in common with other citizens to suport is becoming unbearable, and the sooner a test case is made in one of the courts of some county the better, even if it has to be followed up to the Supreme court of the United States for a final decision. There is no State in the Union which has such mean proscriptions against school privileges for colored children as at present exist in this State, where, at the best, nothing higher has been allotted to them than isolated primary schools."

The colored pioneers were very patient in their suffering, but when they finally did decide to act, they organized, and no army of soldiers ever worked in more unison than they. They decided to call a convention, the proceedings of which are quoted from the *Pacific Appeal*:

"District Educational Convention, Stockton, November 20, 1871. Pursuant to previous notice, colored citizens met at Second Baptist Church (colored) to take into consideration their educational interests; Rev. Peter Green, temporary chairman; I. B. Barton, secretary pro tem; the following committee on credentials: Messrs. George Johnson, William Robinson, Thomas Hutchingon; on permanent organization, Phillip A. Bell, J. B. Sanderson and Emanuel Quivers. They recommended the following permanent officers: President, Rev. Peter Green; vice-president, J. B. Sanderson; secretary, Peter Powers; I. B. Barton, J. H. Hubbard.

"The evening session was opened with prayer by Rev. J. B. Sanderson, after which the following resolution was adopted: 'Resolved, That a petition be sent to the Legislature of California at the ensuing session, praying that Section 56 of School Law of this State be annulled by striking out the words "Children of African descent" from the said section, and that said children be allowed educational facilities with other children.

" 'Resolved, That an educational executive committee be appointed by the president of the convention; that the executive committee be empowered to bring test cases before the United States court and to make collections throughout the State to defray the expense thereof.

" 'Resolved, That the members of the educational committee residing in Sacramento be appointed to attend to the printing of the petition.'

" 'Resolved, That the members of the executive committee in San Francisco be required to have a bill drawn up in accordance with the proposed resolution.'

"The following are the names of the executive committee living in different parts of the State: San Francisco County, Phillip A. Bell, Henry M. Collins, S. Peneton, E. A. Clark; Sacramento County, A. J. Jackson, J. H. Hubbard, C. M. Dougal; San Joaquin County, J. B. Sanderson, R. H. Munn; Santa Clara County, Peter Cassey; Yuba County, E. P. Duplex; Sierra County, John Johnson; Eldorado County, James Price; Shasta County, William Johnson; Merced County, A. E. Tally; Mariposa County, S. A. Monroe, Perkins Bettis; Nevada County, Isaac Sanks; Tuolumne County, W. Suggs; Amador County, C. Hawkins; Solano, G. W. Miller; Tehama County, N. Balsh, C. A. Delvechio; Santa Cruz, Joseph Smallwood.

"Whereas, The colored citizens of California are being deprived of educational rights for their children equal to those granted to other children, we, therefore, represented in convention assembled, passed the following: 'Resolved, That we declare that the Amendment of the Constitution of the United States and the Civil Rights Bill give us full educational privileges, which we cannot obtain in the caste schools as now organized, and unless these privileges are granted us we will appeal from the unjust public sentiment to the highest tribunal in the land.'

"The executive committee of the Educational Convention held in Stockton was successful in having introduced in the State Senate and also the Assembly bills to enable colored children to enter the public schools. The bill provided that where there are less than ten colored children to constitute a separate school they shall be admitted to white schools.

"Mr. Thompkins added a few words in support of the bill. He did not consider ignorance as a bar to improvement; it was the highest interest and the highest duty of every other citizen in advancement and especially to aid the humble and the poor. He hoped there would be no voice in the Senate against so just a proposition.

"Mr. Vanness said that whenever he was willing to vote for the education of white children he was willing to vote for the education of colored children. Mr. Wheaton presented a similar bill in the Assembly. *The San Francisco Bulletin* said: 'Mr. Wheaton has, in compliance with the petition of a convention of colored people held in Stockton, introduced a bill providing that all school children, regardless of color, shall be admitted to the public schools. This bill was presented to the Assembly February, 1872.'

"The evening following the day this bill was introduced by Mr. Finney for the education of colored children, the board of education of the City of Oakland held a meeting and decided to allow colored children to enter the public schools. The members of the educational committee of the Colored Convention living in Oakland were very anxious to have their children enter the schools, and had, previous to the introduction of this bill, made a second appeal to the school board for their admission. The following account of their meeting appeared in the *Pacific Appeal*: 'Educational committee met in Oakland at Shiloh A. M. E. Church, Seventh and Market streets, president, Isaac Flood; secretary, R. Wilkerson. The committee appointed to wait upon the board of education on petition in compliance with resolution of the last meeting, praying that our children be admitted to the public schools of Oakland subject to no other restriction than those imposed upon white children, was received and acted upon and had been presented to the school board by Mr. Fred Campbell. It was resolved by the board that after the commencement, on the 7th of July, all children of African descent who may apply for admission to the public schools shall be received and assigned to such classes as they may be fitted to enter.'

"The following resolutions were offered by the educational committee of the Colored Convention, living in Oakland, Isaac Flood, R. Wilkerson, Peter Anderson, committee: 'Resolved, That this meeting tender our thanks to the superintendent and the board of education of the city of Oakland for their independence in conceding to us our rights.

" 'Resolved, that this meeting tender our thanks to the committee for the able manner in which they performed the duty assigned to them. Resolved, That a special vote of thanks be tendered to Mr. Peter Anderson for his kindness and assistance as a member of the committee that waited on the board of education and for devoting his time in coming over to Oakland to attend our meetings.' "

The Legislature was not so favorable to the colored people educating their children as the school board of Oakland. The two bills introduced in the Legislature were defeated. Phillip A. Bell, the editor of the *Pacific Appeal*, said editorially in an issue of the paper under date of April 6, 1872: ''The colored citizens of this State made a test of the Legislature by the introduction of two bills relative to the schools in both houses. The democratic Senate choked them both to death, but the colored citizens are not dismayed. They have done their duty in respectfully asking the Legislature to allow the colored children equal privileges and admittance to the public schools. It is now at the pleasure of the colored citizens whenever they choose to seek the remedy in the State and United States courts, under the Fourteenth and Fifteenth Amendments to the Constitution of the United States and the Civil Rights Bill.''

The school laws of California will more fully explain the necessity for legislative enactment to remove this caste. The seventh proviso of the California school laws of 1855, in regard to establishing schools, reads: ''Seventh proviso. Provided that the Common Council on the petition of fifty heads of white families, citizens of the district, shall establish a school or schools in said district and shall award said schools a pro rate of the school funds. An Act amendatory of and supplementary to an Act to establish, support and regulate common schools and to repeal former acts concerning same. Approved May 3, 1855. Approved April 28, 1860.'' The California school laws of 1860 reads: ''Section 8. Negroes, Mongolians and Indians shall not be admitted into the public schools; and whenever satisfactory evidence is furnished to the superintendent of public instruction to show that said prohibited parties are attending such schools, he may withdraw from the district in which such schools are situated all share of the State school funds; and the superintendent of common schools for the county in which such district is situated shall not draw his warrant in favor of such district for any expense incurred while the prohibited parties aforesaid were attending the public schools therein; provided, that the trustees of any district may establish a separate school for the education of Negroes, Mongolians and Indians and use the public school funds for the purpose of the same.''

The school laws for 1866 read: ''Section 53. Every school, unless otherwise provided by special law, shall be open for the admission of all white children between five and twenty years of age residing in that school district, and the board of trustees or board of education shall have power to admit adults and children not residing in the district whenever good reason exists for such exception.''

School laws for 1865-66, page 398: ''An Act to provide for a system of common schools. Section 56. Any board of trustees or board of education, by a majority vote, may admit into any public school half-breed Indian children, and Indian children who live in white families or under guardianship of white people. Section 57. Children of African or Mongolian descent and Indian children not living under the care of white people shall not be admitted into public schools except as provided in this act; provided, that upon the written application of parents or guardians of at least ten such children to any board of trustees or board of education a separate school shall be established for the education of such children, and the education of a less number may be provided for by the trustees in separate schools or in any other manner. The same laws, rules and regulations which apply to schools for white children shall apply to schools for colored children.'' The statutes of 1869-70 read: ''The education of children of African descent or Indian children shall be provided for in separate schools; upon the written application of the parents or guardians of at least ten such children to any board of trustees or board of education a separate school shall be established for the education of such children, and the education of a less number may be provided for by the trustees in separate schools or in any other manner.''

The Californians classed the Indian, Mongolian and the Negro all together and legislated so as to include them all. The colored people were not willing to have their children go through life ignorant of educational advantages. They decided that they would make a struggle for their education. The pioneer Negroes were fortunate in that their leaders were all men who had been blessed with a good education previous to coming to the West. There were, however, others who came with their masters and were not so fortunate, but were willing to aid in the struggle by contributing money. Their leaders, with few exceptions, came from either Canada or Massachusetts. Their one great wish was to come to California to help those living in this far-away land who were members of the Negro race. The most of the men were ministers of the gospel. They were sincere in uniting the people, and had a wonderful effect by their own lives in shaping the destiny of the Negro race in California.

The trustees of the public schools in Oakland, realizing the injustice of either forcing the colored children to walk miles to attend a colored school or do without an education, said, ''Let the children enter the schools.'' The executive committee of the education colored convention, grateful for the independent stand of these trustees, still realized that the same conditions existed in other parts of the State, notably in

Sacramento. Mr. B. A. Johnson was making the fight to have his children enter the nearest school. The Negro pioneers were determined to educate their children and decided that if they could not be permitted to enter the nearest school they would make a struggle to have the doors of all the schools opened to them. Let the reader review the struggle the Negro children had in an effort to secure an education in San Francisco.

The board of education closed the Broadway street school, not because there were not enough colored children attending to keep it open, but because, as one member of the board of education said: "It was a nuisance." When asked to explain more fully his remark, he said "It was too close to a white school on the same street." The school was ordered closed and another school for colored children was also ordered closed, resulting in all the colored children living in San Francisco having to go to the school on "Russian Hill" or do without an education. Although the schools furnished the colored children were ungraded, still they were better than nothing; but the reader will remember that the years this struggle for an education was being waged by the colored in San Francisco there were neither street cars nor jitneys. The only way to traverse the hills was either to own a horse and vehicle or walk. One can imagine school children trying to climb "Russian Hill" during the rainy season. They were very anxious for an education, and more than one colored child climbed it, notwithstanding they often had walked miles before reaching the hill.

The colored people tried to fight out the issue in the legislature, but were not successful. They were determined to educate their children. Mr. John Swett, in his "History of Education in California," speaking of the education of the colored children, says: "The first legal recognition of the rights of colored children is found in the revised school laws of 1866." The author then gives a section of this law, and adds: "Under this provision most of the colored children in the State were admitted to school privileges, though in a few outlying districts, notably the City of Oakland, they were excluded from white schools and were not allowed a separate school." The Legislature of 1870 repealed Section 56.

In September 28, 1872, a test case was entered in the Supreme Court of the State for the admission of colored children into the common schools of the State of California. The following is an account of the case as reported in the *Pacific Appeal* of that date:

"Mary Frances Ward, by A. J. Ward, her guardian, against Noah F. Flood. Please take notice that upon papers, with copies of which you are herewith served, I shall move the superintendent of the schools of California at the court room in the capitol at the City of Sacramento, on the second day of October, A. D. 1872, at the opening of the court on that day, or as soon thereafter as counsel can be heard in the same, for a writ of mandate commanding and enjoining you as principal having charge of the Broadway grammar school described in said papers, to receive and act upon my appointment to be received as a pupil in the said school. Also to examine me as such pupil and if found qualified to enter said school as a pupil to receive me as such. Also for such further or other mandate as I shall be entitled to in the premises.

"Dated, September 24, 1872.

"MARY FRANCES WARD,
"By A. J. WARD, Her Guardian.

"J. W. Dwindelle, 509 Kearney street, San Francisco, California, Attorney for Counsel.

"It appears that the plaintiff, her attorney, and counsel and the defendant all reside in the city and county of San Francisco. It is ordered that the witness of application for writ of mandate in this action be shortened to fifteen days, September, 1872.

"WALLACE, C. J.

"Argument of J. Dwindelle before the Supreme Court of California on the right of colored children to be admitted to the public schools." After a statement of the case, the learned counsel gives the following:

" 'These colored children of African descent who are citizens have the right to be admitted to all the public schools of the State and cannot be compelled to resort to separate schools for colored children. We shall discuss this point solely and shall not address ourselves to questions of ethnology, political or poetical justice, nor to any sentimental question whatsoever.' He then referred to the constitutional provisions, statutes and regulations, citing the Fourteenth and Fifteenth Amendments to the Constitution of the United States; also citing the Civil Rights Bill. He also in this connection quoted the school laws of California on the subject of the education of children of African descent, Section 56-7-8, and the following regulation of the board of education of the city and county, Section 117, 'Separate schools. Children of African or Indian descent shall not be admitted into the schools for white children, but separate schools shall be provided for them, in accordance with California school laws.' The learned counsel referred to eight cases before the Supreme Court of the State of Ohio; also cited the case lately decided in the State of Nevada in which a mandamus was granted.

"His closing argument: 'But we are told that by a just exercise of the police power of the Legislature these distinctions of color may be lawfully made and enforced. The police power! Gracious heavens! this is the power always invoked in desperate cases. Just as the Hindu convert prays to his Christian God for rain and, failing to receive the genial showers, then invokes the god of his ancient idolatry. The police power—the last resource of tyrants, the last weapon for the assassination of written constitutions and of free institutions! Urge it in Russia, or to the despot who simulates republicanism in France, but here it is not worth an attempt at argument!'

"Decision. Separate schools for colored children. The act of the Legislature providing for the maintenance of a separate school for the education of children of African or Indian descent and excluding them from schools where white children are educated, is not obnoxious to the constitutional objection. Rights of colored children to attend schools with white children; but unless such separate schools be actually maintained for the education of colored children, then the latter have a legal right to resort to schools where children are instructed, and cannot be legally excluded therefrom by reason of race or color.

"Application of Writ of Mandamus. The facts are stated in the opening John W. Dwindelle, of the petitioner. William H. Thornton, for contra. Mary F. Ward versus Noah Flood, principal of the Broadway grammar school of the city and county of San Francisco. No. 3532. Filed February 24, 1874. This decision was pursuant to the provision of Subdivision 14, of Section 1617 of the Political Code, Writ of Mandamus.

"WALLACE, C. J.

"We concur.

"NILES, J.
"CROCKET, J.

"I concur in the judgment on the ground first considered in the opinion of the Chief Justice.

"McKINSTRY, J.' "

This case was argued September 22, 1872. The decision was rendered February 26, 1874, just two years after it had been submitted to the judge for a decision, which resulted in the following law being passed by the Legislature of the State through the recommendation of the code commissioners of the Political Code of the Reversal Laws of the State of California (1872-74, page 246), which reads: "Schools for Negroes and Indian children. Section 1669. The education of children of African descent and Indian children must be provided for in separate schools (Section 1670) upon the written application of parents or guardians of at least ten such children. The education of a less number may be provided for by the trustees in separate schools or in any other way. If the directors or trustees fail to provide such separate schools, then such children must be admitted into schools for white children."

The decision of Chief Justice Wallace caused great rejoicing among the colored people, especially in San Francisco. The editor of the *Pacific Appeal*, the leading organ of the colored race at that time in the State, said editorially, in commenting on the decision: "The Federal court secured to all children the right to attend public schools." The editor then quoted a section of the Fourteenth Amendment to the Constitution of the United States.

The executive committee of the Colored Convention did much in every county to aid in securing for the colored children better educational facilities. The colored citizens of Marysville held a meeting of rejoicing after the decision of Chief Justice Wallace rendered in the school case brought in San Francisco. The Marysville committee was composed of the following colored gentlemen from the educational convention: Rev. Thomas Randolph, Rev. J. B. Handy, E. P. Duplex, Robert Saline and others. In speaking of the Supreme Court decision of the San Francisco colored school, Rev. Thomas Randolph, among other things, said: "They worked with a oneness of purpose and a unity of action until the object was accomplished."

The colored schools throughout the State were closed in 1875, and colored children were supposed to attend the schools in the district in which they lived. Nevertheless, we find Mr. Wysinger making the fight in behalf of the education of his children in the schools at Visalia. He was the proud father of six boys and two girls, and was determined not to allow them to grow up without an education. He went before the school board of that county and asked them to established a school for his children. After a struggle they opened a school for the education of colored children, and a Miss

MME. ELLA BRADLEY-HUGHLEY (deceased)
Vocal Instructor, Lyric Soprano.

MALCOLM HARVEY PATTON
Lyric Tenor.

PROF. WM. T. WILKINS
Wilkins School of Music

PROF. ELMER BARTLETT
Pipe Organist.

Sara Sanderson was appointed as teacher. When Mr. Wysinger's oldest son, Arthur, was ready to enter the high school, he was refused admission, resulting in his father being compelled to enter suit against the county school board of education in the Supreme Court of the State before he was finally admitted into the high school. Mr. Cady, of Sacramento, on March 31, 1877, had trouble in entering his children in the school in the district in which they lived instead of the colored school.

There are many colored people living in California today who, in consideration of the deep prejudices of pioneer days against the Negro, the harsh legislation, and the long, bitter struggle to reverse these laws, and because the California schools are considered among the very best in the United States, believe it will be the best for the future of the Negro race to maintain mixed schools as a powerful medium in erasing lines of prejudices. But there are others of the Negro race living in the State today who would like to teach and wish to have colored schools. Their desires have been the means of the introduction before the State Legislature, during 1913-4-5, bills to create separate schools for colored children. The one introduced by Senator Anderson, January 20, 1913, was fought vigorously by the colored people throughout the State. The one introduced by Mr. Scott, of Hanford, in 1915, was at the request of a colony of colored people at Allensworth. The colored people also fought this bill because of its framing.

The colored people all over the State reverence the name of the founder of the town of Allensworth, who was Colonel Allensworth of the Twenty-fourth Infantry, U. S. Army, a man beloved over all the world by the race, and while the colony is a credit to the Negro race, still they were unwilling to allow the passage of a bill which would require all the colored children desiring to attend a polytechnic school to go to Allensworth.

The town of Allensworth is very near Visalia, the county seat, was another argument used against the bill, because of the bitter fight made by that county against the admission of colored children into the public schools long after other counties throughout the State had admitted them. The town of Allensworth some day will be one of California's great centers for the raising of sugar beets and poultry. It is no longer a colony, having been made a voting and school district. The people interested in the passage of this bill, giving Allensworth a polytechnic school, argued that because of the high standard and efficiency of its citizens it favorably compared with Wilberforce University for the colored, located at Wilberforce, Ohio. In their argument it was forgotten that this institution was founded by the African Methodist Episcopal Church of the entire United States and maintained by them, by the giving of the prestige and financial support of that body for nearly a quarter of a century before the great State of Ohio gave it an appropriation for an industrial or polytechnic department. It was also not mentioned that this institution was the home of the late Bishop Arnett, the father of a bill to abolish colored schools in the great State of Ohio. This bill was framed and introduced by the then Mr. Arnett who, as a plain minister of the gospel, entered politics for the one purpose, and that was to reduce racial lines of prejudices through abolishing colored schools throughout Ohio. The next general conference of the African Methodist Episcopal Church, recognizing the great value to the race of Rev. Arnett, raised him to the dignity of a bishop of that body. He was a thorough race man and at his first opportunity he used his influence to secure an appropriation for Wilberforce Institution for industrial training in the school. The great body of bishops in electing him did so with the perfect confidence that he would not forget the race in its struggle, but that his influence would be greater to the race of his true worth. The writer is proud to state that she comes from the great State of Ohio and knew personally the late Bishop Arnett, who more than once told her of the men of prominence who had come to his home seeking his advice, and that he never forgot his race while giving his advice to such men as the late President William McKinley and others of like prominence of that date in Ohio.

Allensworth has a creditable colored school, since it is principally a colored colony with a few white residents. It is also a voting district, and in order that Allensworth might build a larger and better school, it was made a school district. The school trustees of the county gave the residents of Allensworth permission to issue school bonds for that purpose. Their new school cost $5,000. They employ two colored teachers, Mr. William Payne and a Miss Prince, who have complied with the laws governing the public schools of California requiring a course in the State Normal school. The town of Allensworth is a judicial as well as a school district, and bids fair to become a great city some day not far distant.

There are several schools taught by colored teachers in California, namely, the one at Furlong Tract, near Los Angeles, another colored colony. The names of the teachers employed in this school are Miss Bessie Bruington and Miss Sinola Maxwell. In the Imperial Valley there are two schools taught by colored teachers, one at El Centro and another at Brawley. The following teachers, graduates of the State Normal schools have taught in these schools, namely, Mr. G. W. Simms, Miss Ella Kinard, Mrs. Davis Mrs. Lorena Hunter-Martin, Miss Eva Whiting, Miss Gertrude Chrisman, and Miss Baber. The Rev. J. A. Stout of the C. M. E. Church has been a strong factor in securing positions for colored school teachers in the various districts where their services were needed.

The principal products of the Imperial Valley is the raising of cotton, tobacco and cantaloupes. A large majority of the settlers are colored people coming from Louisiana and Texas, and, while they are not enough to really make separate colonies, still with the Indians, Spaniards and Mexicans they manage to establish separate schools. The temperature of this part of California is very much like that of Mexico, since it is near the border line.

The schools of the State of California are classed among the best in the United States, both in scholarship and equipment. They maintain this standard by demanding the teachers to take a course of two years training in the State Normal schools before being permitted to teach. The student who wins laurels in the California schools wins not because of favoritism, but purely on scholarship, after a rigid test. The reader, in reading of the following honors won by colored students, may feel proud of their achievements.

In pioneer days colored children were only permitted a primary education in isolated schools. The moment that they were permitted better advantages they not only seized them, but never stopped until they graduated from the high schools with honor. The writer records the name of Emanuel Quivers, the first colored boy to graduate from the San Francisco public schools. The first colored girl, Minnie Dennis, in a class comprising fifteen hundred white students, was not daunted because she was the only colored member of the class, but graduated with honors, mastering Spanish and the Chinese languages. She taught for four years a class in a private school for Chinese, teaching them the English language. She was afterward offered the position as court interpreter but decided instead to marry. Her daughter by this marriage in after years graduated from the San Francisco commercial high school as the valedictorian of the class, and was the only colored member in a class of several hundred, Margaret Benston, who is now Mrs. Evans. Miss Sara Sanderson had the distinction of being the only colored girl in a class to graduate in kindergarten at Silva street school in San Francisco. Miss Kate Smith was the principal. The closing exercises were held in Dashaway Hall on Post street, San Francisco. Miss Sanderson was afterward employed as an assistant teacher. The first colored boy to graduate from the high school of San Joaquin County was Daniel D. Hart, of Stockton. His father was a ''Forty-niner.'' Daniel Hart afterward moved to San Francisco, stood the civil service examination and received an appointment as clerk in the San Francisco postoffice. The first girl to graduate from the Fresno high school was Miss Elfleta Chavis. The first boy to graduate from the same school, William Bigby, is now studying pharmacy. Arthur Wysinger was the first colored boy to graduate from the public high school in Visalia.

The colored pupils attending the California public schools are constantly winning honors, thereby adding to the laurels for the advancement of the education of the Negro race. The following is of especial interest because it shows the ability of a colored girl, a pupil in the Santa Monica Polytechnic high school, located at Santa Monica, California. The school offered a prize to the pupil who could design a seal for the new high school. This seal was to be made from the school's initials, S. M. H. S. There were three hundred and seventy competitors and the honor was won by a colored girl, Miss Hazel Brown, who, aside from her design, which was artistic, made from the initials the words, Sincerity, Manliness, Honor and Service, words that are worth remembering, for if all scholars who attend school were sincere, manly and honorable the service they would render, both to the community and State, would not only be honorable but wide in its effect for good to mankind. Miss Hazel Brown is modest, unassuming, and has great ability in wood-carving. She bids fair to win a place for herself along those lines, if not in the literary world, having during the past year edited with credit and satisfaction the *Federated Clubs' Journal.*

Miss Victoria Shorey won a gold medal for speed on the Remington typewriter, writing sixty words a minute, making only four mistakes. She also won a certificate for efficiency on the Underwood machine. These contests were held while Miss Shorey was a member of the Commercial high school of Oakland.

University graduates among the Negro race in California are frequent, few, however, leave the State for an education except in music. The first colored university graduate in the State was Ernest H. Johnson, of Sacramento, who graduated from the Leland Stanford Junior University located at Palo Alto, California. Ernest Johnson graduated in the pioneer class of that institution, majoring in law after completing a course in social science and economics. The University of California, located in Berke-ley, has also had many Negro graduates. The first colored boy to matriculate in this university was Mr. Dumas Jones, who entered to study civil engineering. Dr. Lytle, graduating from the College of Dentistry, is successfully practicing in Oakland. Mr. Benjamin Young, of Fowler, graduating from the College of Pharmacy; Miss Grace White, graduating in science and letters, is now teaching in the East. Miss Vivian Rodgers, graduating in the class of 1909, majoring in science and letters, afterward taught in the public schools of Hilo, Hawiian Islands. Miss Beatrice Rice, majoring in science and letters; Mr. Raymond Maddock, from the College of Agriculture and Natural Science; Leonard Richardson, from the College of Law, majoring in science and letters; C. E. Carpenter, from the College of Law. The University of Southern California has many who have won degrees. Among the number has been a lady dentist, Mrs. Vada Somerville. The writer has been told that there are over twenty-five women in Southern California who have graduated for teachers from the Normal school. The first to grad-uate was Miss Alice Rowen, and the second, Miss Bessie Bruington. She was in a class of five hundred and held sixth place with a general average of ninety-seven.

CHAPTER XVI

DEPARTMENT OF LAW

In introducing this department to the reader, it has been with the object of giving some idea of the great legal battles fought by the pioneer Negroes in California, and the splendid legal talent of the present day Negroes in the State. The pioneer Negro fought all of his legal battles through the service of white attorneys. The race had many legal battles of harsh prejudices to fight for the privilege of living in beautiful California. This required the services of attorneys who had both exceptional talent and great moral courage to defend the Negro at that period of his history in the State. This was due to the slavery question, which made it most unpopular for a white person to be considered a friend to the Negro. The State law did not permit the testimony of either a Negro, mulatto, Chinese or Indian person in any of the courts of justice in the State. Notwithstanding these harsh restrictions, the pioneer Negroes fought and won some of the greatest court trials known in the pioneer history of the State of California. This is especially true in the celebrated Archy Lee case (see "Slavery in California").

The pioneer Negroes at this period had a most effective organization among themselves which was known as the "Executive Committee of the Colored Convention." All the colored people then living in the State who were free were members of it. They contributed freely of their "diggings," thereby raising funds to aid in covering the expenses of court trials. The executive committee was formed at the first Colored Convention, which was held in Sacramento, California, in 1855. The duties of this committee were not alone to raise the necessary funds, but to be constantly on the watch and report discrimination and cruelty to any member of the race. There was a member of this committee in every county of the State. There was no rapid mail or telegraph service in those days in California, hence it was difficult to transmit news from one part of the State to another. The Negro members of the executive committee formed a secret code and transmited their news by the way of the barber's chair. This was accomplished because all the barbers in the State were Negroes. The general method of transportation was by the river or ocean-going vessels. It was an easy method to give to some customer going, say, from San Francisco to Sacramento and on up into the mines, a message to give to the best barber in the town upon his arrival. This method was most successful in transmitting news all over the State. It really corresponded to the "Underground Railroad" of anti-slavery days in the eastern part of the United States. This was a secret organization pledged to defend escaping slaves to the North and other free Negroes who might be again returned to slavery. So, like the "Underground Railroad," the "Executive Committee of the Colored Convention" learned of any movement for or against the Negro settlers, whether it was introduced in the State Legislature or on the local streets. They readily learned of it through this effective channel, the executive committee secret code.

The Executive Committee of the Colored Convention employed, in the celebrated Archy Lee case, the services of Attorney Winans in the first court trial. This gentleman came to California in 1849, after graduating in law from Columbia College. He was very popular and influential in organizing the San Francisco Bar Association. George Wharton James says of him: "His word was worth more than the biggest bond his richest client could give." What a splendid selection the Executive Committee of the Colored Convention made in employing such reliable counsel. In the second court trial of this same case they employed the late Col. Edward E. Baker, a personal friend to the immortal Abraham Lincoln. He was a deep, dyed-in-the-wool Abolitionist, and was the first officer to lose his life in the Civil War, dying at the battle of "Ball's Bluff." It has been told the writer that the Archy Lee case cost the executive committee the sum of fifty thousand dollars.

There were other victories to the credit of this Executive Committee of the Colored Convention. They were "The Right of Testimony," the "Homestead Law," and the fight for equal public school privileges for Negro school children. The "Right of Testimony" was won through a bill which was introduced at the request of this committee by Senator Perkins in the California State Legislature. This was followed by every member of the Legislature receiving a petition from the executive committee asking his support of these different measures. These different members of the Legislature were asked and did make speeches favoring the legislation asked for. This was especially true in the fight for the "Right of Testimony," which was kept before the public and the Legislature for years, when it finally became a law, whereby the Negro was given the "Right of Testimony" in all the courts of the State. (See Right of Testimony, and Ward vs. Flood.)

The present day Negro of California, like the pioneer, does his greatest fighting against discrimination through an organization. This is one similar to the Executive Committee of the Colored Convention. It is known as the National Association for the Advancement of Colored People. It was organized in New York City during 1911. It is officered by influential white and colored citizens, with headquarters in New York City. They have branches in nearly every city of importance in the United States. They publish a magazine monthly called *The Crisis*. This magazine chronicles the activities of the Negro race throughout the world, together with the different persecutions and proscriptions against the race in every part of the world.

The National Association for the Advancement of Colored People is very influential in California. This State is so very large that for convenience it has been divided by this organization into a northern and a southern branch. The active organized branch in Oakland acts as headquarters for Northern California; and the branch in Los Angeles for the southern district of the State. Both branches are governed by laws issued from the National headquarters in New York. The organization is supported by a membership fee of one dollar per year, one-half of which goes to the National headquarters and the other half remains with the local branch to create a fund to fight discrimination in the local districts against the Negro race or an individual of the race.

The Northern California branch has fought and won many legal battles of discrimination. They have, in a measure, been fought out in the council chamber of the cities of Oakland and San Francisco. This has been accomplished through the members of the executive board having appeared before the councils of these cities and personally plead the cause and justice of their demands. They have rarely been known to lose a fight, either preventing an ordinance of discrimination from becoming a law, or blocking its passage by the city council.

The Northern California branch is a live organization having over a thousand members. The executive board has as their most efficient secretary, a Mrs. Hattie E. DeHart, a lady whose heart, energy, time and money are in the work. This secretary is so earnest and sincere that she has in a manner so organized the forces that it has not been necessary for the branch until very recently to employ an attorney. Mrs. H. E DeHart is untiring and irrepressible in her fearlessness. Her enthusiasm has brought to the organization the working support of many white ladies of prominence around the Bay cities.

The Northern California branch is a well balanced organization. It was organized by Mr. Roy Nash, the former secretary of the National Association for the Advancement of Colored People. The first president of this branch was a Mr. Christopher Reuse who at the time was a truant officer of the City of Oakland. During his administration there was advancement of the branch in membership and subscribers to the *Crisis*. The branch, however, did very little active work, as it was a new feature for the people, who, for a long time, thought it only necessary to pay their money, but did not take any interest in the monthly meetings. Mr. Reuse was hopeful and encouraged the few who did attend the public meetings to hold on, and after a season the colored people would awake to their own interest and attend. They were thoroughly aroused when the branch was addressed by Major Lynch (retired) of the United States Army. His address was clear and convincing as to the foundation and the great necessity for such an organization. There were no more dull meetings from that night. They were convinced that it was not a political organization for the scheming politician of old, but that its only political aim was to see that only men who were friends to the Negro were elected with the aid of the Negro vote.

Previous to the coming of Major Lynch the branch had elected to the office of president a colored gentleman by the name of Mr. Walter A. Butler, a man of education, a race lover, true and loyal to the cause of justice and the advancement of the Negro race, a man of wonderful executive ability; a man who commands the confidence and respect of the white and Negro population of the Bay cities, where he has been reared from early boyhood. He has by his conduct, careful study and attentiveness to business won for himself a position of great trust in the financial world among both the white and Negro races of the Bay cities. With such a man to guide the ship of destiny of the Northern California branch it has accomplished wonders for the Negro people. It has also won for Mr. Butler the hatred of all the politicians who had been in the habit of using the Negro vote as they chose. These politicians did not become interested in the organization until there was a thousand members working in unison.

The first test of Mr. Butler's ability as a race lover and president of the Northern California branch of the National Association for the Advancement for Colored People, came with the first appearance of the photo-play, ''The Clansman,'' or better known as ''The Birth of a Nation.'' The moment it was billed to open at the McDonough theater of Oakland Mr. Butler called a public mass meeting, at which meeting resolutions were passed condemning this race-hating, mischief-making film. As a result of this meeting, and the respect with which the president of the organization was held by the influential white citizens, there was immediately a campaign launched against the play's showing in the City of Oakland. The daily papers were constantly filled with letters of protest from citizens of influence showing the injustice to the Negro people of California in allowing it to appear in any city of the State. The writer, at the time, was a special feature writer on the *Oakland Tribune,* and this paper, more than any other, published both editorials and special letters against the play, thereby creating sentiment in favor of the Negro race.

Father David R. Wallace, rector of the St. Augustin Episcopal Mission, and also vice-president of the Northern California branch and a strong defender for the rights of the Negro race, personally organized a vigilante committee, who succeeded in having a restraining order issued by the mayor of the City of Oakland, which compelled the play to stop in the midst of a performance. Through some technicality of the law, the order was rescinded the next day. But Father Wallace did not stop the fight until he had succeeded in having some objectionable parts removed from the film before it was again permitted to show.

Another event in stimulating confidence in the Northern California branch was the reception given by it to and in honor of Hon. George Cook, dean of the law department of Howard University, of Washington, D. C., and his distinguished wife, together with the widow of the late Senator B. K. Bruce, all of whom are members of the National executive board of the organization. Mr. Walter A. Butler personally invited many white persons of distinction, as well as out-of-town distinguished colored people to attend this reception. He also acted as personal guide to these persons of distinction, while they were in the northern part of California. His efforts were rewarded by an overwhelming attendance at this public reception, which was held in the historic Fifteenth Street A. M. E. Church of Oakland. There have been few affairs more enjoyable and inspiring to the Negro race and the public in the City of Oakland. Hon. George Cook delivered one of the best addresses, up to that date, ever delivered on the organization in the city. He told of many hard-fought battles won, hitherto unknown by the average member of the organization. Also the talks by Mrs. Bruce and Mrs. Cook were all great. Mrs. Corline Cook is so pleasing in her manner that all were sorry when she had finished, for her message was well received and inspiring. On this occasion the former president, Mr. Christopher Reuse, who had resigned his position in Oakland and had entered the ministry and was holding a charge in Fresno, California, several hundred miles away, readily responded to Mr. Butler's telegram, and arrived in time to attend the reception and introduce Mrs. Bruce, since her son was a class mate of his at Harvard University. His introduction was a masterful address that helped to add many new members to the already increasing roll. Among others things, Mr. Reuse said on that occasion was that while it was deplorable the ''Clansman'' had been permitted to show, still it had acted like a slap in the face to the colored citizens who had been awakened to their responsibility to fight to maintain their rights as citizens of the United States and to secure full justice in any community.

Since then the Northern California branch of the N. A. A. C. P. have succeeded in having removed from the windows of restaurants discriminating signs and the preventing of photoplay houses from discriminating in the seating of colored patrons. A notable case of the kind was won by a member of the executive committee of the northern branch, a Mr. Leonard Richardson, who had but recently graduated from the law department of the University of California. It was his first case after being admitted to practice. It was against discrimination being shown by the management of the handsome photoplay house known as the T. and D. in the City of Oakland. One of its attractions is that it has the largest pipe organ on the coast. They began segregating colored patrons.

The Northern California branch also succeeded in securing a stay of vote in the Oakland city council in regard to an ordinance introduced by the Santa Fe Tract. This ordinance was drawn similar to the Baltimore and Louisville land segregation laws in regard to Negroes purchasing property in white neighborhoods. After securing a stay of vote, the executive committee, acting upon the advice of the president, Mr. Walter A. Butler, and through the untiring efforts and time devoted to the cause by the secretary, Mrs. H. E. DeHart, they traced the origin of the trouble to an alien enemy of the United States Government. This man was a German salesman in one of the large stores that was well patronized by colored people. He was an unnaturalized resident of the United States. Mr. Butler and Mrs. DeHart were told by officials that if they wished they could have this man interned for the duration of the war. The activities and bitterness of the Santa Fe people were such that it was feared that there would be in Oakland a repetition of the East St. Louis massacre. In view of the same, the executive committee, acting upon the advice of the president, went in a body to the store and told the proprietor of their findings. The committee consisted of Mr. Walter A. Butler and Mmes. Gilbert, DeHart, Tilgman and Brown, Father Wallace and Mrs. Tob Williams. The last named, like Mrs. DeHart, is a thorough race woman and fearless in any fight for the uplift of the race. This alien was brought face to face with the proprietor and this committee. It is needless to say that the Negro people of Oakland rested more peacefully after the report of this committee. There were some who feared that Mrs. DeHart and Mrs. Tob Williams would, by their fearlessness, make martyrs of themselves before it was through. Mrs. DeHart solicited influential white ladies of Berkeley and two of our own race (near white) to attend the secret meetings of the Santa Fe Tract people and report the minutes to her. She then had Mr. Butler, the president, call a public meeting and plan a reception in honor of a distinguished guest in the city, Hon. S. W. Green, chancellor of the K. of P. lodges of the world.

The meeting lasted way beyond the time usual for closing such meetings. Mrs. DeHart appeared before the people and asked them if they would not wait just a little longer, as there was an important report to be made. During the long wait there were many voluntary speeches made as to preparedness and unity of action. Mrs. Tob Williams made one that would have done credit to a warrior of old. This Committee arrived and made their report and, coming directly from this Santa Fe tract stormy meeting, gave the facts in such a convincing manner that when the secretary, Mrs. DeHart, made an appeal for new members, the people came in such droves to sign and register their names that Mr. Ricks had to be called in to assist. In less than a half-hour over thirty-six people had paid their membership fee and they were after midnight still coming to register.

Mr. Butler commented on the seriousness of the occasion and what unity meant if a crisis should come, and, if it did, what the home office in New York would do to assist them in their struggle to protect their homes. He made this speech while every one was anxiously awaiting the arrival of the committee. He was cool and dignified in making these statements and every one felt that his ruling during the entire evening had been as a warrior leading a mighty host to battle, and that we had actually reached the firing line. This speech instilled confidence in the people in his ability to truthfully guide them in any dark hour and with an organization that would do the things he had said they would do with such leadership, there would never be an East St. Louis repetition in Oakland, and that we would not surrender without a sacrifice if necessary. He was both eloquent and inspiring. All were proud of his conduct of the meeting, for every man in the audience was, by his coolness and plain words, brought face to face with the issue—that they were American citizens and therefore did not believe that they had a right to consider the politics of any man. They were not currying favors, but simply asking for what was due them. This meeting was pronounced the greatest meeting ever held in Oakland since the celebrated Archy Lee case of 1858. It was great and inspiring for race unity.

The executive committee of the Northern California branch of the National Association for the Advancement of Colored People, after this meeting, finding that the whole work was that of an alien enemy, succeeded in securing a stay of vote by the city council. To their surprise the ordinance was again introduced on the morning the first Negro drafted boys were leaving Oakland to offer their lives as a sacrifice for democracy. This was indeed the severest blow of all because, just a few evenings previous, the branch had held a public reception for the boys. On this occasion the mayor of the city and a member of the city council who had opposed the Negro fight and had encouraged the members of the Santa Fe tract in their persecution, was a speaker at the reception for these boys. He spoke of his surprise at the appearance and the intelligence of the audience. We had all hoped that the patriotic address delivered by Father Wallace would impress this councilman and, if not, then that the one by Mrs. Hettie Tilghman, who was the promoter of the reception, would finally win him over to the Negro's side in the fight. But nevertheless while the mayor was bidding the Negro boys God-speed and an honorable return to Oakland, and nearly every Negro man, woman and child in Oakland was at the depot bidding the boys goodby, this ordinance was again introduced to the city council at this same hour.

Father Wallace, who is really the watchman on the wall, left the depot the moment the boys departed, and on his way home stepped into the council chamber. He was in time to hear the ordinance read before council. When the crowd returned from the depot, the first issue of an evening paper had head lines stating the news to the public. That evening the branch received a telegram from Washington, D. C., stating that the Hon. Morefield Story had won a favorable decision before the United States Supreme Court with a full bench in "vetoing segregation as it affected property rights of Negroes as American citizens." It was welcome news to all throughout the Nation, and none welcomed it more than Mr. Walter A. Butler, president of the Northern California branch of this organization which, as a National body, had made the fight for the good of the American Negro.

It has been said that the time produces the man for the occasion or event. If the pioneer Negroes in California were compelled to employ white attorneys to fight their battles of discrimination, the friend and counselor-at-law of the present day Negro of California is one of their own blood, well educated and an active member of the Southern California branch of the National Association for the Advancement of Colored People. Notwithstanding, he is a naturalized citizen, having been born in the beautiful island of Nassau, the Bahama West Indies. He was educated and then came across the continent from New York to California before beginning his career as an attorney. This refers to the Hon. Edward Burton Ceruti of Los Angeles. He is the official attorney for the Southern California branch of this National organization and recently has been elected to represent the Pacific Coast as a director on this National board. He is the leading criminal attorney among the Negro people in California.

He was of great assistance to the Northern California branch of this National Association for the Advancement of Colored People in their struggle to save the life of a race prisoner who had been sentenced to death. The people and the warden of the penitentiary did not believe him guilty. Mr. Ceruti worked earnestly on the case for weeks in an effort to secure a reversal of sentence or a new trial. He was unsuccessful. Nevertheless the earnestness with which he conducted his efforts was quite satisfactory to the Northern branch who immediately wrote him for his bill for services rendered. To the great surprise of the executive committee, he donated his services, only allowing them to pay for the telegrams sent during his research and the typing of his briefs in the case. This amounted to practically nothing compared to the vast amount of work done by Attorney Ceruti on this case. Such acts by him in many instances have endeared him to every race lover in California. He is like Mrs. DeHart in that he is so unselfish in his work for the branch.

His work with the Southern California branch of the National Association for the Advancement of Colored People, has been principally in fighting discrimination in the refusal of moving picture houses and cafes to serve patrons of the Negro race the same as they would any other American citizen. He is so thorough and sincere that he has thoroughly established the facts in the courts of Los Angeles and Pasadena; that Section 51-2-3-4 and 5 of the California Civil Code can and will be enforced. His last case of this kind was won in Pasadena where he plead before a mixed jury.

Aside from these suits of discrimination won by Attorney Ceruti, he has won some remarkable criminal court trials, that have attracted the attention of the bar of the entire state. Among these trials was the one of "People vs. Burr Harris." The reader's attention is called to the second trial for murder of Burr Harris, in which Attorney Ceruti attempted to prove the insanity of the prisoner through hereditary influence and an irresistible impulse to commit crime. The learned trial judge allowed the evidence, yet, when instructing the jury, it was ruled out (see "Notes on the Text"). Attorney Ceruti, being convinced that if the laws of California did not recognize such evidence, then the laws for the criminally insane were faulty, anxiously awaited an opportunity to prove to the courts, and to the public that it was wrong to hang a criminally insane prisoner. His opportunity came when he was called to defend Thomas Miller at Santa Barbara, California, at the second trial for murder (see "Notes on the Text"). Santa Barbara is the home of many retired millionaires with large and magnificent estates similar to England. They are owned by many who are descendants of pioneer California families. Because such remembered that during pioneer days the Negro people fought for ten years through the courts to gain the "Right of Testimony" in the Courts of Justice, they considered it a joke and treated it as such when challenged as to their fitness to serve on a jury to try a Negro murderer. They gave neither the Negro murderer nor his attorney any consideration except to frankly express themselves as to their willingness to hang the Negro. But ah, when the Negro attorney, week after week against such terrible odds, stood before the bar of justice and whose pleadings equalled that of any attorney, black or white, his arguments meant more to the aristocratic residents of Santa Barbara than the flow of mere oratory. It caused them to pause and consider, not only in this city, but all over the State, for even while the trial was in progress, petitions were being circulated by club women to abolish capital punishment, in California. Notwithstanding no mention was made of the forceful arguments of this Negro attorney, or the case he was then pleading in beautiful Santa Barbara. The truth had been sent home to them that California has more criminally insane murders than any other kind. It is the firm belief of the writer who followed the case with continued interest, that the sincere and intelligent pleadings of this Negro attorney, Edward Burton Ceruti, was the direct means of arousing the great humanitarian minds of the great State of California, to pause and begin to think that after all he was right. The way to wipe out crime, is to remove the cause for producing criminally insane, or else legislate to treat such persons as human beings with defective minds. The greatest reforms the world has ever known have been started by men who had the power to cause the great minds to stop and think. We all move in groups, and when a thought is once grasped by any one group it does not require a very long time before it becomes a fixed fact, and leads to a successful execution. John Brown, of Harper's Ferry, did not succeed in emancipating the Negro slaves; but he started the minds of the great humanitarians to thinking in the right way. He found his own group and in time the thoughts of that group crystallized in the final emancipation of the Negro slaves of America.

The heroic legal fights made by Attorney E. B. Ceruti in these two murder trials in an effort to prove that the California laws for the criminally insane conflict with the laws of humanity, and cannot be strictly just although legally right, in time resulted in a member of the Legislature introducing a bill which was, however, defeated. It was introduced just one year from the beginning of this history making second trial of Thomas Miller of Santa Barbara. This bill was introduced in the California Legislature by Senator Rominger of Los Angeles, California. Its aim was to reduce the percentage of alcohol in wine and all liquors to the extent that it will not cause drunkenness. Dr. Hatch, superintendent of the State hospital, and also head of the lunacy commission, in commenting on the bill, among other things said: "Whatever we do to prevent the excessive use of alcohol, personally I place my greatest hope on the proper education of the young of the dangers accompanying the use of alcohol. They should be taught to look on it as a drug, a poison without which they can get along in life; that partaking of it is an acquired habit that often grows until it enslaves.***Nowhere are the bad and lasting effects of alcohol on the individual shown more clearly than in our hospitals for the insane. There you find young inebriates whose purpose in life has been side-tracked by drink, also the chronic alcoholic whose life is hopelessly wrecked; and men and women with actual mental disease due to excessive use of alcoholic stimulants." During all these court trials Attorney Ceruti had the moral support of the entire colored population of California and especially the Southern California branch of the National Association for the Advancement of Colored People.

The Southern California branch of the National Association for the Advancement of Colored People has done some very effective work through the leadership of Attorney Ceruti. For two years they earnestly worked in investigating conditions affecting the admission of colored girls to the training school for nurses connected with the county hospital, of Los Angeles County, California. At the psychological moment they asked the various societies and clubs of the county, representing the best interest of the Negro race, to co-operate with them, in presenting a petition to the board of supervisors, to ask for the admission of Negro girls to train for nurses on the same terms as white girls. These various organizations held a joint meeting with the Southern California Branch of the N. A. A. C. P. and they presented the findings after their two years of earnest work. This joint committee voted to employ Attorney Edward Burton Ceruti, to introduce the petition to the board of supervisors, asking for the privilege of colored girls' admittance to train for nurses on the same terms as white girls. The writer by chance heard of the meeting and attended in time to hear Attorney E. B. Ceruti make his masterful plea. He was voluntarily followed by Judge Forbes, who, upon hearing of the object of the meeting, had followed the crowd, and made a speech that was astonishing to the writer. He fully explained every possible reason why in justice to the negro girls, as American citizens, they should be admitted to train for nurses. The gentleman told of being a descendant of an old Abolitionist family who fought for the freedom of Negro slaves. No one doubted his statement after listening to his address. He was followed in a closing argument by Mr. Ceruti who gave the technical points of law as to the justice of their admittance and closed by adding that if they had been admitted five years ago, today we would have Negro girls trained nurses in France caring for our boys who are giving their lives for democracy. The supervisors granted the request without a dissenting vote. This was a great victory, not only for the Southern California branch of the N. A. A. C. P., but for the Negro race women throughout America. *The Los Angeles Times,* one of the largest daily papers published in the United States, the next day paid the speaker and the colored people of Los Angeles a great tribute in their victory and repeated Edward Burton Ceruti's remarks concerning our girls caring for soldiers in France. It is a strange coincidence, but in less than ten days afterward the War Department, through Captain Emmitte Scott, announced that they were sending Negro nurses to the cantonments in the United States through the influence of the Red Cross National organization. The writer wonders if, after the constant pleadings of the Negro people for years to win a place as trained nurses, the earnest pleadings of Attorney Ceruti had not caused them to stop and consider if they were treating the Negro women squarely when they were not even given a chance to nurse the Negro soldier, whose life was just as dear to him as is the white soldier's. In less than a month from the masterful plea and argument advanced by Edward Burton Ceruti favoring Negro trained nurses, the National Counsel of Defense issued a statement to all the local boards in the different cities of the United States, asking that they use their influence wherever there was a county hospital to admit Negro girls to train for nurses, thereby releasing the nurses who were already trained for service in France. When the writer read this statement she wished that the late General Harrison Gray Otis, could have lived to have seen this day for he had done so many things of value to the Negro race, and having served in the Civil and Spanish-American Wars with Negro soldiers, would have rejoiced to know that after years the nation was awakening to judge the Negro for what the individual represents and not by the worst in the race. The paper which he founded and which is still owned by his heirs, *The Los Angeles Times,* published this address of Attorney Ceruti, calling the attention of the board of supervisors to the fact that had Negro girls been admitted to the training schools five years ago, today they would be in France nursing wounded soldiers. The eastern readers of the *Times* are as numerous as the Californian, and weigh whatever it says. The writer sincerely hopes that some day the Negro race will be benefited by the able counsel of Edward Burton Ceruti in the halls of the United States Congress, for he is so sincere and honest in his desire to see the race have justice that he carries the force of his arguments to the heart and consciousness of the American people. Would that the race had many more of this old school of losing self in the interest of the race.

The present day Negroes in California have many good lawyers who have won history-making cases. There is one who won a favorable verdict in regard to the purchase of land by Negroes against segregating. He won this case February 4, 1915, which was identical to the Louisville case which the National Association for the Advancement of Colored People carried to the United States Supreme Court, through the able consul, Hon. Morefield Story, and won a favorable verdict in 1917.

The present day Negro of California can boast of a foreign consul and a justice of the peace whose duties in the Negro township of Allensworth, Tulare County, is on equal footing with a judge. He has never had a decision reversed.

All of the above men have been admitted to practice law in California. Many of them have studied and graduated from the law departments of the universities, the one at Berkeley and the Southern California in Los Angeles. During pioneer days the prejudice was so great that a Negro boy could not be admitted, notwithstanding he had read law under good instructors who had previously examined and considered him qualified for admittance, as was the case of James Wilson, the first Negro boy to apply for admittance to the bar in Alameda County, California. He lived to see afterward others of his race admitted to the bar and he was appointed and served as deputy sheriff of Alameda County, California, for years.

There is one branch of the law represented by the present day Negro, and it is worthy of more than a passing notice. That is, the Negro foreign consul for the Republic of Liberia, at the port of San Francisco, a Mr. Oscar Hudson, whose practice is among the best Spanish families in San Francisco. He is intelligent and speaks and writes Spanish, Italian and English. He is an active member of the National and Local Northern branch of the National Association for the Advancement of Colored People, a distinguished member of the Sixth Christian Science Church of San Francisco. The list, dear reader, may be long but there are many more who could be cited from the list in Los Angeles alone, who have had history-making cases and have been an honor and credit to the race and the betterment of humanity, as will be found in the life of the first Negro boy to matriculate in a law school in California, in the University of Southern California, a Mr. James M. Alexander, whose sketch will show the kind of men that have mastered the science of law in the State.

The pioneer Negro attorney in California was a real Trail Blazer in that he was the first Negro attorney to practice in the courts of the State and shared an office with a well-known white firm. The following sketch has been quoted from his career, as given by Dr. W. J. Simmons in his book, "Men of Mark," who said: "Mr. Robert Charles O'Hara Benjamin was born on the Island of Saint Kitts, West Indies, March 31, 1855. Education being compulsory on the island, he was sent to school while very young, and at the age of eleven was sent to England under a private tutor who prepared him for college.

"While yet a boy he entered Trinity College, Oxford, where he studied for three years and left without taking a degree; * * * visiting Sumatra, Java and the Islands in the East Indies. He then returned to England after a two years' tour. He next took passage on a vessel coming to America and arrived in the city of New York, April 13, 1869. Ten days after he shipped as a cabin boy on the bark Lepanto, Captain Cyrus E. Staples, and made a six months' cruise to Venezuela, Curacoa, Demara and other West Indies ports.

"Returning to New York in the fall of the same year he concluded to abandon the sea and settle there, working at anything he could get to do. In the meantime he took an active part in public affairs which brought him in close association with such prominent politicians as Dr. Highland Garnett, Cornelius Van Cott, Dr. Isaac Hayes, the Arctic explorer, and Joe Howard, the well known newspaper man.

"Mr. Howard, then editor of the New York Star, employed Mr. Benjamin as a solicitor and agent. When not at his work he was assigned to office duty. In the course of a few months business led him into the acquaintanceship of Mr. J. J. Freeman, editor of the Progressive American, who made him city editor of his paper. In the same year (1876) he appeared before the Court of Common Pleas and was naturalized. Soon after he was given a position of letter carrier in the New York postoffice, but, finding the work too laborious, after nine months' trial he was compelled to give it up. He then went south and engaged in school teaching. It was while engaged in this business that he took a notion to become a lawyer. In Kentucky he read law with County Attorney David Smith, afterward State Senator, also ex-Congressman Reid, and in Alabama with Judge Sineral Clark. He finally placed himself under Hon. Josiah Patterson, an eminent lawyer of Memphis, Tenn., through whose influence he was admitted to the bar, January, 1880. Mr. Benjamin's achievements as a lawyer, journalist and lecturer are unrivaled. The territory over which his legal services have extended aggregate twelve different States. * * *

"He is highly esteemed by the members of the California bar and is regarded by both black and white citizens of the State as an able scholar and an honorable Christian gentleman. At Los Angeles Mr. Benjamin was a member of the well-known law firm of Barham and Stewart. This might be regarded as an honor when we consider that the firm is among the most prominent on the Pacific Coast. * * * Mr. Benjamin is the only Negro lawyer on the Pacific Coast. At the same time Mr. Benjamin filled the position as city editor of the Los Angeles Daily Sun, the first Negro in the United States, so far as we know, to hold so prominent a position on a white paper.

"Soon after the inauguration of President Benjamin Harrison the members of the bar of Southern California, with whom Mr. Benjamin came in contact daily, the Judges of the Supreme Court, the mayor of the city of Los Angeles and the members of the city council, together with the city officials of superior ability, petitioned Senator Stanford and the congressional delegation, asking that Mr. Benjamin's name be sent to the President of the United States for an appointment. Accordingly the entire delegation indorsed and presented his name for the position of United States Consul of Antiqua, West Indies. The State Department, not caring to make a change of officials in that particular consulate, offered him, several months later, through the congressional delegation another equally prominent position which he declined; preferring to remain at the editorial helm of the San Francisco Sentinel which he then edited and which he made one of the brightest race journals in the United States.

"Mr. Benjamin is an intense race man, and his manly stand and eloquent speech in behalf of the race before the Republican convention at Sacramento, his fearless editorials in his newspaper demanding recognition for the race, and the able manner in which he defended his race before the courts have all tended to endear him to the colored people of California. * * * Mr. Benjamin has been an earnest member of the church for some years, but some months ago he concluded to give church work and book-publishing more of his attention. He therefore resigned the editorship of the Sentinel and turned over the major part of his lucrative practice of law to a San Francisco attorney, appearing himself only in the criminal courts, and has entered actively into the ministry. * * * He is presiding elder of the California conference of the A. M. E.

Zion Church, his territory covering the State of California, Oregon and Washington.''

The office of Foreign Consul stands alone and distinctive. It is comparatively little understood by the average person, but is strictly an appointment made by the President of the United States. The person selected to fill the office must be of more than average intelligence, must know something of law and the different languages and must possess great diplomatic abilities.

The duty of a Foreign Consul is not only to represent the country for which he has been appointed in every social function, but he must listen to every complaint of any of the citizens who may come to the port where he is located. It is his duty to adjust any differences coming between a citizen of the country he represents and a citizen of the country where he is located. It is his duty to adjust these differences cautiously lest he cause a diplomatic break between the two countries.

The Foreign Consul is often called upon by the country he represents to attend to the purchase of large supplies for their home use. If a citizen from a foreign government should find himself in distress by lack of funds, or require identification, he immediately applies to the Foreign Consul representing his government at the port where he might be at the time.

There are few Negro Foreign Consuls at the present time because of the fact that the Republic of Liberia is the only Negro-governed country now in existence. In view of the above the writer considers it a pleasure and honor to be permitted to present the sketch of a Negro Foreign Consul, Mr. Oscar Hudson, who is the consul for Liberia at the port of San Francisco.

Hon. Oscar Hudson has been well-qualified through education and travel to fill the office with credit to himself and honor to the Negro race. He is a splendid example of what a boy can make of himself if he but tries and wills to be somebody. Mr. Hudson was born in Missouri, January 4, 1876, and attended a country school until he became an orphan at the age of eleven years, at which time he was forced to shift for himself. He went to Mexico where he again attended school and secured a good education with a splendid knowledge of the Spanish, Mexican and many other foreign languages. So thoroughly did he master these languages that when the United States Government was at war with Spain, he was selected as Spanish and English translator in Cuba.

After the Spanish-American War he located in Albuquerque, New Mexico, where he lived for several years, during which time he was owner and editor of a paper called the "New Age" which voiced the interest of the Negro race. He was elected delegate at large to the Republican State Convention, of New Mexico, in 1911. This was the first Republican State Convention ever held in that State. Hon. Oscar Hudson was appointed a delegate to the Negro National Educational Congress held in St. Paul, Minnesota, in July, 1912. This appointment was conferred upon him by the then Governor, William C. McDonald, of the State of New Mexico.

During all the years he lived in New Mexico he had a great desire to master the profession of law, and, thinking he saw an opportunity to study in California; he removed to Los Angeles during the winter of 1907-8. During his stay he established and published the "New Age," a paper whose policies were for the uplift of the Negro race in California. He published it for a year when he sold out and moved back to New Mexico.

The charm of California was so great, notwithstanding he had many honors conferred upon him after his return to New Mexico, still, even so he returned to California and stood an examination and was admitted to practice law in 1911 by the Appellate Court of the First District of California. Since then he has been granted the right to practice before the United States District Court for the Northern District of California.

Mr. Hudson decided to locate in Northern California and was for sometime engaged in the real estate business in Alameda County, during which time the Governor of the State appointed him notary public for Alameda County. It was while serving as such that the Hon. President Woodrow Wilson appointed him as consul for Liberia at the Port of San Francisco. The 1917 annual edition of the *San Francisco Daily Chronicle*, the largest paper published in San Francisco, devoted one page to ''Foreign Consuls holding important places in the life of the community.'' In speaking of Mr. Hudson, among other things, it said: ''Many honors have come to Oscar Hudson in his chosen profession, the law. Not only does he enjoy a splendid and successful practice in all the courts having jurisdiction in California, but he is also consul for the Republic of Liberia at the Port of San Francisco. He is the first and only Negro to hold a membership in any bar association in the State of California, and he has the respect and esteem of not only the bench and bar but of the public at large. * * *''

The writer considers the above quotation a fine tribute to the subject of this sketch, for Mr. Oscar Hudson is not only the Liberian Consul at the Port of San Francisco, but he is also the greatest public-spirited Negro in Northern California. He has the bearing of a king without being haughty. The writer, in studying him, often recalls a remark made to her by the late Hon. Theo. Hittell, in referring to the late Col. E. D. Baker, in which he said: ''His very presence commanded attention.'' Mr. Hudson aims high in everything he undertakes for the uplift of the race. This was particularly true in his earnest work to try and secure a Negro regiment in California.

Shortly after the United States Government declared war on Germany, Mr. Hudson, realizing that the Negroes of the Pacific Coast were without a military organization, immediately began to try and stimulate an interest in his fellow racemen to obtain a regiment. This required upon his part a personal sacrifice of both time and money in traveling over the State and preparing an appeal which he personally presented to the California Legislature, asking for permission to organize this Negro regiment. It was at a tremendous sacrifice that he succeeded in arousing the Negro men and in organizing four companies in Los Angeles which were officered by ex-United States Army officers who had served in the Spanish-American War. In the northern part of the State many men signed up for a unit of two companies. So confident was Mr. Hudson that he would have the required number that he told the glad news to Mayor Rolph of San Francisco, who, like a true San Franciscan, wishing to distinguish the ''City of Inspiration,'' hastily donated a beautiful silken United States flag to the First Volunteer Negro Regiment of California. After this enthusiastic act on the part of the Mayor of San Francisco, every Negro who had enlisted for this regiment wished to be chief boss. Before they finally settled their differences the order came from Washington, D. C., stating that no more such regiments should be organized, as it would interfere with the operation of the Draft Law. Thus a great opportunity to give the brave men in these different companies an opportunity to distinguish themselves was lost.

It is also gratifying to note that a number of the men who did sign their names to serve in this volunteer regiment were not content to wait for the draft and secured assignment to the separate training camp for the training of Negro United States Officers and graduated from the same with honor and now hold commissions in the Officers Reserve, and are at this writing serving with the National Army in France.

Mr. Hudson is happily married and his wife is a registered Christian Science Practitioner. She has been a great aid to the subject of this sketch in his struggle for distinction. She has a winsome personality and wonderful executive ability.

The following is quoted from *The Bench and Bar of California,* edited by J. C. Bates, who, in speaking of Attorney Willis Oliver Tyler, said: ''Residence 831 San Pedro street, Office 325-26 Germain Building, Los Angeles. Born July 19, 1880, in Bloomington, Indiana; son of I. and Mary Jane (M. S. Caw) Tyler; moved to California in January, 1911. Graduated from the University of Indiana in 1902, received the degree of A. B., and from the Harvard Law School in 1908 with the degree of L. L. B. Admitted to the Bar of Illinois, October, 1908. Commenced the practice of law in association with B. F. Mosely at Chicago, April 24, 1911. Attorney for the Robert C. Owens Investment Company since October 1, 1911. Corporal of Company ''B,'' Indiana Colored Volunteer Infantry, from July, 1898, to January, 1899. Practices his profession alone in Los Angeles to date. Member of the Harvard Club of Chicago, Illinois.''

Charles Darden, the subject of this sketch, is the son of Charles H. and Dianah Darden, a large and most prominent family of Wilson, North Carolina. His father is the pioneer undertaker of that city. Their son, Charles, was educated in the public schools of his home town. After graduating from the high school, was sent to Wayland Seminary, and later to Howard University, at Washington, D. C., where he graduated in law. He afterward traveled extensively throughout the United States, Hawaiian Islands and the Orient. Attorney Charles Darden located in Los Angeles, California, where he was immediately admitted to practice in all the courts of the State. During a visit east in April, 1915, and while in Washington, D. C., he had the honor of being presented and admitted to practice before the Supreme Court of the United States. The motion conferring this honor upon him was made by a former teacher, a Professor Hart, who holds the chair of Criminal Law, Procedure and Corporation in Howard University.

Attorney Darden is socially popular and is a distinguished member of the Knights of Pythias lodge, also the Masons and Elks. He is reserved, rarely ever giving an opinion in conversation on any subject. His evasive attitude has caused many to wonder at the great court trials he has succeeded in winning, the most noted of which was the one in regard to segregation or race restriction in the purchase of land by Negroes. Attorney Darden has made a specialty of land litigation. This case will show his thoroughness in such matters because he is persistent in carrying all his cases to the court of last resort in the State for a final decision. He has the honor and credit of winning a favorable decision in regard to race restriction clauses in the sale of property to

Negroes almost two years before the Hon. Morefield Story won a favorable and final decision from the United States Supreme Court on the same subject. It is strange to relate that while Attorney Darden was the first attorney in the United States to secure such a verdict it has not been commented upon except in few papers beyond the Rocky Mountains. The race papers of California proudly acclaimed his success, realizing that in due time other men of the race all over the United States would win such vital verdicts.

The following is quoted from a race Los Angeles paper in regard to this great victory for Attorney Darden: "Restriction against race holders of title to lands in this State has been declared void by John W. Shenk, who rendered a decision in favor of Mr. Benjamin Jones and Mrs. Fannie Guatier, plaintiffs against the Berlin Realty Company. Announcement of this decision so far-reaching to the Afro-Americans of America is made by Attorney Darden, able counsel, who handled the case for Mr. Jones and Mrs. Guatier. The decision obtained is so direct in its effect and consequences upon the much-mooted question of the validity of such race restriction that it establishes a real precedent, it being the first decision obtained directly upon the question involved in a Court of Justice in the United States, and was rendered by Judge John W. Shenk, ex-city attorney, and former candidate for mayor of Los Angeles City."

The California Eagle then further states the proceedings of the case in such a clear and impartial manner the writer has deemed it correct that it be quoted. It said: "Mr. Jones and Mrs. Guatier purchased of the Berlin Realty Company one acre of land in the tract known as The Moneta Garden Land Tract, in the city of Los Angeles, by mailing to the Berlin Realty Company their check as the initial payment, which was accepted by the Berlin Realty Company. The company then mailed a contract to Mr. Jones and Mrs. Guatier containing the following covenant and restriction: 'Said property shall not be sold to or be occupied by any person not of the white or Caucasian race.' Immediately upon receipt of the contract by Mr. Jones and Mrs. Guatier, and their discovery of the restriction above set out, Mr. Jones notified the Berlin Realty Company that such was objectionable to himself and Mrs. Guatier and demanded a new contract with the elimination of the restriction. Then the Berlin Realty Company discovered that Mr. Jones and Mrs. Guatier were persons not of the white race and the company immediately returned the check to Mr. Jones and repudiated the contract.

"Mr. Jones and Mrs. Guatier at once consulted Attorney Darden, an expert on the law of real estate, who has instructed and guided them to final victory through the courts. Mr. Darden immediately filed suit in specific performance, and reformation of the contract demanding that a deed be delivered without the objectionable restriction, claiming that there was no authority in the law warranting a refusal to issue the deed demanded and that the restriction in question was a violation of the Fourteenth Amendment to the Constitution of the United States and contrary to public policy of the State of California and the United States, which contentions were upheld by Judge Shenk.

"The Berlin Realty Company is a company composed of Jews organized for the purpose of subdividing and settling people on land in California and said company in its brief contended that the plaintiffs were merely attempting to extort money and in answer to that contention we quote from Mr. Darden's full and exhaustive brief the following: 'The plaintiffs in this case are persons of high integrity and are, as the court must have observed, quite intelligent; that from their reputation in this community they would not have entered into a scheme or any scheme to extort money from any person or people whose condition and circumstances in many places, particularly in Russia, are similar to the Negro, and the plaintiffs are unable to understand how a corporation composed of Jews, who are almost universally similarly circumstanced as the Negro could enter into or become a part of any iniquitous scheme such as the Berlin Realty Company had entered into to further degrade the Negro.'

" 'A leopard cannot change his spots, and the said quotation is not only an axiom but a truth well-known in human nature that Negroes cannot change their skin; they cannot be assimilated into the white race and nature did not intend the two races to intermingle.' This last quotation is from Ingall W. Bull's brief as attorney for the Berlin Realty Company.

"In further reading the brief prepared by Mr. Darden, the paragraph which more than any other in the brief was far-reaching in its effect and consequences upon the mind of Judge Shenk is the following: 'If the defendant in this case were to prevail, it would be possible for large land owners of the State of California and the United States or for large syndicates to buy up or acquire all the land in the United States, and then make an arbitrary selection of the residents who are to occupy and settle the same. They could even say, with the same authority of the law to support them, that no white man could own or acquire title to any land in the State of California or the

United States and absolutely supplant the Caucasian race, if they felt so disposed. That is the reason the State of California and the United States have adopted constitutions and made laws and rendered judicial decisions protecting property rights of the citizens.'

''In prosecuting the case Mr. Darden relied upon the broad ground of public policy and in his brief is found relative thereto the following: 'The only authentic and admissible policy of the State upon any given subject are its constitution, laws and judicial decisions. The public policy of a state of which courts take notice and to which they give effect, must be decided from those sources and not by the varying opinions of laymen, lawyers and judges as to the demands of the interests of the public. (U. S. vs. Tran. Miss. Freight Association, 166, U. S. 290.)' The brief continues: 'All persons born or naturalized in the United States and subject to the jurisdiction thereof are citizens of the United States and of the States wherein they reside. No State shall make or enforce any law which will abridge the privileges or immunities of the citizens of the United States.

'' 'This Court being an officer and representative of the State of California and acting in judicial capacity for said State in the case at bar cannot construe and declare valid the restriction in question or refuse to eliminate the same for the reason that such a holding and declaration or refusal to eliminate would have the effect of enforcing a law which would abridge the privileges and immunities of citizens of the United States, and would therefore be void as in violation of the Fourteenth Amendment of the Constitution of the United States and against the public policy of both the State of California and the United States.

'' 'Even if the law was not discriminating in terms, yet if it were even applied, administered or enforced by public authority so as practically to make unjust discriminations between persons similarly circumstanced in matters affecting their substantial rights, the law should be held invalid as being a denial of equal protection of the law, coming within the prohibition of the constitution of the United States; that our contractual rights and guarantees would amount to nothing, and that is the reason why the Fourteenth Amendment to the Constitution of the United States was made a part of the fundamental law of the land.'

''Attorney Darden concluded his able brief with the following: 'The defendant, Berlin Realty Company, will freely sell to whoever will buy, providing the buyer be not of the Negro race. The vendee may be a gambler, pugilist, his hands may be stained with human blood, and he may have committed every crime only that of suicide; he may be so densely ignorant of our form of government that if asked concerning same to answer that a kingdom is ruled by a king and a republic is ruled by a notary public, and the purchase of such one will be viewed with delight, while that of an educated and refined colored man devoted to his country and venerating its flag will be subject to the machinery of the law. It needs no argument to show that this is an instance of narrow race prejudices, born of intolerance, opposed to good citizenship and finds no support in the law.'

''Judge Shenk, in rendering his decision, declared that the brief filed by Mr. Darden in the case was as able and exhaustive as any he had ever seen or read in any case.''

The case just quoted is one of many similar cases won by Attorney Darden in land litigation. *The New Age* of Los Angeles had the following to say concerning this attorney: ''Mr. Darden, the first of his race to go before the Supreme Court of this State, has three victories before this court of last resort to his credit.''

Mr. Charles Darden has won another important decision the first time ever won by any attorney in the State of California. This case and verdict will affect the rich even more than the poor Negro people in that it establishes a precedent that ''A married woman can sell community property without the consent of her husband, especially when the title to same is vested solely in her name.'' The race papers in the entire State were elated over the victory. *The New Age* had the following, in which it said: ''This decision or procedure secured by Mr. Darden's legal ingenuity is not only far-reaching in its effect, but sets precedence for the organic law of the State, and it will enter into the pleadings of every attorney in the State who goes before the Superior courts of the State with similar questions to be litigated touching upon that peculiar phase.''

The case involved in winning this verdict was as follows: ''Case of M. Randall vs. Jane Washington and Samuel Washington her husband. The facts in the case are as follows: Mrs. Washington purchased three lots from a married woman by the name of Delcia Donnelson, whose huband, at the time of the sale, was confined in the county jail charged with embezzlement. The money from the sale of the property was to be used in the defense of the husband. Subsequently Donnelson secured his liberty and went back to the family dwelling-place, and refused to vacate, claiming that he had not signed or joined with his wife in the deed of conveyance of the property. As a matter of fact the property was community property, and Mr. Donnelson had not signed the deed.''

Mr. Darden brought suit in the Superior Court, charging ''unlawful detention of premises,'' and at the trial secured judgment, and Donnelson was subsequently evicted from the premises. Donnelson then regained possession and it became necessary for Mr. Darden to file his second suit in ejectment. This suit resulted in a second judgment in Mr. Darden's favor. The Donnelsons then jointly made a deed to ex-Judge M. Randall, who is himself an able attorney, who, they claim, paid them a fair market price for their interest in the property. Mr. Randall immediately brought suit against the Washingtons, Mr. Darden's clients, to quiet title. That suit came on for hearing about July 8, 1909, and judgment was rendered in favor of Mr. Darden's clients, making it a victory of magnitude for Mr. Darden, for it was the third winning of suits at law on the same property, covering a period of nearly two years' hard litigation. From the Superior Court an appeal was taken to the Supreme Court of the State, which court, on the third day of October, rendered an opinion in favor of Mrs. Washington, which opinion, being rendered by the Supreme Court of the State, is absolute and final. The whole time covered in hard and fierce litigation upon the property above mentioned was nearly five years.

Attorney Darden has won many cases in the criminal courts. One attracting considerable attention was the Edward Silva case, which Attorney Darden carried to the Supreme Court three different times and, while not winning a reversal of the verdict, succeeded in having his sentence changed to life imprisonment instead of the death penalty.

Attorney Darden has also won many cases of discrimination against the race in Los Angeles, the most notable of which was the one against the Ralphs' grocery store, a large retail store in that city. The one here referred to is one of their stores located at 631-35 South Spring street. These stores serve light lunches at the soda fountains. A white lady and her colored maid, together with the chauffeur, all entered the grocery for their lunch, since they were downtown at lunch time. The grocery lunch counter refused to serve the colored maid. Whereupon the lady, who was Mrs. Briggs, feeling humiliated and embarrassed, brought suit against the store, and Attorney Darden was employed to prosecute the same. He won a favorable verdict for his client.

Attorney Edward Burton Ceruti, the subject of this sketch, was born in faraway beautiful Nassau, of the Bahama West Indies. When he was four years old, his parents moved to the United States, at which time the father became a naturalized citizen, that his son and namesake might have a career under the Stars and Stripes. This son was given the best education possible. ''He took a course in the St. Augustine Normal and Industrial Institute. He also studied at Shaw University, Raleigh, North Carolina; Howard University, Washington, D. C.; the Brooklyn Law School, Brooklyn, N. Y., and the St. Lawrence University at Canton, N. Y. From the latter institution he was graduated with the degree of bachelor of law.''

After graduating from this institution, he came across the continent to Los Angeles before beginning his career as a criminal attorney. ''At the beginning of his career he trained for the ministry in the Episcopal church, served a congregation as catechist for a season and even now, while deeply engrossed in a rapidly increasing business, he finds time to serve as lay reader of St. Phillip's parish of Los Angeles, California.''

Edward Burton Ceruti was admitted to practice law in Los Angeles County, California, January 12, 1912, and in the United States District Court, March 10, 1912. It was then that he began his career as an attorney. He has distinguished himself and won a conspicuous place in the legal profession along the Pacific Coast because of his notable achievements.

''He is essentially a criminal lawyer. In criminal cases he has won for himself a standing second to no other criminal lawyer in California. He is a man of pleasing personality, of generous impulse and has been equipped for his work as a lawyer. Attorney Ceruti has demonstrated in many instances that his preparation for the practice of law has been most thorough. His versatility evinces wide reading, profound study and an intimate comprehension of human life and psychology of human action. He is considered the most competent attorney among the colored profession in California * * * and has won the respect and confidence of the leading attorneys and courts of the State. * * *

''Attorney Ceruti's first famous case was that of People against Burr Harris, a murder case, in which the defendant, a Negro, was charged with having killed Mrs. Haskins, a white woman of this city. It was by his ingenious management of the

MRS. OWENS-BYNUM
Real Estate Dealer and Investor.

HON. THEODORE W. TROY
Investor and Promoter of Mines, and
Furniture Dealer in Los Angeles.

ATTORNEY HUGH E. MACBETH
(Harvard)
Member of the Executive Committee of
the Morals Efficiency Association
for Southern California.

defense that Burr Harris was acquitted of the crime. But about two years later this same Burr Harris was again arrested charged with a more horrible murder than that of Mrs. Haskins. Under the most brutal circumstances, it was discovered that Mrs. Gay, a white woman and a Christian Science practitioner, was found murdered. Harris confessed to this murder and many other crimes, including the Haskins tragedy and was finally convicted.

"This case became one of national interest. It attracted the attention of alienists throughout this section of the country, some of them firm in their belief that Harris was afflicted with some strange form of recurring insanity. Attorney Ceruti waged a bitter fight in the Supreme Court in defense of Harris, attacking with great severity the existing law respecting the criminal insane. His conduct of this case was one of the most remarkable exhibitions of legal knowledge that has been witnessed in the courts of California for a number of years. * * * The most notable of the recent cases handled by Mr. Ceruti was the Thomas Miller case, recently concluded at Santa Barbara, California. This case has gone down into history as one of the greatest criminal trials that has ever taxed the courts of the State. The elements which conspired to make it a great criminal case were these: First, Thomas Miller did kill a man and a woman in Santa Barbara. Second, he was tried and convicted and sentenced to be hanged. Third, an appeal was taken for a new trial. Fourth, Miller's acts created intense feeling among all the people of Santa Barbara. The feeling was so bitter that not a single man or woman, white or black, could be found who would tell anything he or she knew about Miller and his eccentricities that would aid in any way the defense in its plea of insanity. Fifth, by diligence, by painstaking effort on the part of Attorney Ceruti, Thomas Miller was finally given a life sentence.

"It was without hope of reward that Attorney Ceruti seized this opportunity to demonstrate his thorough knowledge of criminal law. * * * He took what appeared to be an absolutely hopeless case, * * * which promises neither remuneration, praise nor commendation, and when the odds were overwhelmingly against him. But so convincing were his arguments, so skillful his examination, so painstaking his selection of jurors that he was able to break down the thick wall of prejudices against his client and secured the verdict above mentioned. * * * Three hundred and eighty men, many of them prosperous business men representing the progress and advancement of Santa Barbara County, were examined to serve on the jury. * * * Twelve men finally qualified. One man, engaged in a popular business, * * * stated frankly to the court that he believed Miller guilty simply because he was a Negro, the inference being that all Negroes are criminals. * * * This frank admission brought forth the rebuke of the court. * * *

"Mr. Ceruti deserves the heartiest praise of every member of the race for the manner in which he conducted this history-making case. For embodied in this man are social feelings and hopes for the Negro race which are rare in professional characters. * * * Mr. Ceruti made a great sacrifice of time, energy and money to save the life of this poor Negro man who, under a fit of insanity, committed the terrible crime with which he was charged.

"A verdict was rendered which reflects great credit upon the legal skill of Attorney Ceruti * * * The vigor, the courage, the persistence, the undaunted devotion of Attorney Ceruti in this instance marks him as one of the greatest criminal lawyers in the State. * * * In July, Thomas Miller, weak-minded from his youth, suffering some strange mental aberration at all times, on this fatal morning attacked with an unaccountable turn in his mental troubles, shot and killed, for no known reason, a man whose name was Bert Baker, in Santa Barbara. He wounded the same morning, while in his fit, a companion by the name of Smith, and later went to his rooming-place and killed his landlady, Mrs. Howard, by shooting her six times. These acts created great excitement in the beautiful little city by the sea, and racial feeling ran high on account of the fact that Miller belonged to the Negro family.

"In September Miller was placed on trial. He was found guilty and sentenced to be hanged. He was carried to the State penitentiary to await execution. In the meantime pressure was brought to bear. Attorney Ceruti was urged to appeal the case and secure, if possible, a new trial. * * * Sentiment was violently opposed to Miller. He had no friends among the people; both races were against him. * * * The brief period of time between Miller and the gallows could be counted in short hours. But Attorney Ceruti, * * * moved by the noble Christian impulse that values human life above everything else, consented to defend this poor, unfortunate, condemned man. No one believed that he could save his life.

"The appeal was granted, Miller was given a new trial. For six weeks this trial engrossed the serious attention of the people of Santa Barbara. Both races were interested in the outcome. Attorney Ceruti became the chief attraction each busy day, and while sentiment was clearly against his cause, he was, nevertheless, regarded by all who visited the court as a great lawyer and a noble hero. The plea of insanity was made. Testimony was brought to bear on this issue. Witnesses were called from all parts of the State. The argument made by Attorney Ceruti was one of the most eloquent and convincing ever heard in Santa Barbara. He proved clearly that Thomas Miller was not a sane man; that his acts were without reason or motive; that he did not know at the time he committed them that he was committing unlawful acts. Few lawyers have so unremittingly given themselves to so hopeless a task or have sacrificed as much in behalf of a client. Attorney Ceruti won a victory when he secured the verdict of life instead of death. He saved a life and, considering all the circumstances in this case, he accomplished a wonderful thing indeed.

"Beside these great criminal cases, Attorney Ceruti has been very successful in the handling of discriminating suits in California. Just recently he won the case of Williams versus New China Cafe. In this case the New China Cafe refused to serve Williams and his wife. He also won the case of Conners versus Clune's Theater, the largest and most attractive in Los Angeles. Conners and his wife were refused seats, for which they had purchased tickets, in the main body of the house.

"The most recent success was the case of Columbus versus La Petite Theater at Santa Monica, on November 1, 1916. The case of Mrs. J. Columbus versus La Petite Theater was tried in the justice's court in the township of Santa Monica. Justice Frank Shannon, of Sawtelle, presided. This was a suit for damages in which Mrs. Columbus alleged discrimination on account of her color at the company's theater on the Ocean Front avenue, Santa Monica, in that the theater people refused her seats on the main floor of the auditorium. On Monday, November 13, 1916, the justice rendered his decision against the defendant company for the sum of $50 and costs, the amount demanded by Mrs. Columbus. Attorney E. Burton Ceruti represented the plaintiff in this action. In speaking of this case, Mr. Ceruti said: 'This decision is another stone in that foundation on which rests our confidence in the courts generally and in Justice Shannon particularly. The justice allowed the full amount prayed for in the plaintiff's complaint. This amount was small; in fact, the minimum sum allowed by law. Unless the circumstances are aggravated or there be substantial injury incurred, no excessive or speculative damage should be sought in these cases. It is not proper that we should make capital of these offenses. An insult to our honor or dignity cannot be measured in dollars and cents; money does not heal a wound. The end or aim of these actions is to stop discrimination; to convince the wrong-doers that the law can and will be enforced. This can be just as effectively accomplished with small judgments as with larger ones. The compelling force lies in the certainty with which such offenses will be punished. No good business man will subject his enterprise to a series of expensive and vexatious lawsuits, especially when his chances of success are slim.' "

Since the above cases cited were won by Attorney Edward Burton Ceruti, he has been called to Pasadena, California, to fight a suit of discrimination in that city. *The California Eagle* had the following, in which it said: "California made safe for the Negro." Again it has been established that discrimination in this State will not and should not be tolerated. On Tuesday, May 14, 1918, in the Superior Court, before Judge Paul J. McCormick, Attorney Ceruti scored a victory over the apostle of discrimination. A mixed jury awarded his clients, Mrs. Banton and Mrs. Steward, damages in the aggregated sum of one hundred dollars. On January 1, 1917, Mrs. Banton and Mrs. Steward, prominent residents of this city, visited the Crown City Theater in Pasadena. Despite the fact that the regular admission fee was ten cents, they were forced to pay twenty-five cents. After entering the theater they learned on inquiry that, every one else had paid a dime, and that all seats were ten cents. They were convinced that they were the objects of discrimination. This they resented by filing suit for damage for the sum of five hundred dollars. Thus began the long and bitter legal controversy which ended in their favor.

"The case is noteworthy because it is the first of its kind ever tried before a mixed jury. But it is of a yet more vital significance because it proves that Sections 51-2-3 and 54 of the Civil Code can be enforced and that all who dare restrict the privileges of citizens on account of race, creed or color must expect adequate and just legal punishment.

"Mrs. Banton and Mrs. Steward, together with their intrepid attorney, are to be congratulated on the perseverance and courage they have shown in the fighting of this long and perhaps disheartening struggle. They have, through their efforts established a judicial precedent favorable to the race, and thereby 'Made California safe for the Negro.' "

William Lenton Stevens, the subject of this sketch, is a native of Texas, coming to California in August, 1903. He was appointed patrolman after taking the Civil Service examination on April 25, 1905. As soon as the detective department of the city was placed under civil service, Mr. Stevens took the examination and was appointed October 16, 1912, being the first colored man placed in this department on the Pacific Coast.

He has made some of the most important arrests and assisted in the prosecution of some of the greatest criminals that the city and State have known. Having been highly commended for bravery and efficient work in *The Police Bulletin* on different occasions, Mayor Alexander, during his administration, recommended that Mr. Stevens be given a medal for bravery.

Detective Sergeant Stevens is a thirty-second degree Mason, Shriner and Forester. He enjoys the highest respect of all the leading citizens of both races for his dutifulness, integrity and progressiveness.

Mr. Sidney P. Dones, the subject of this sketch, has a life filled with inspiration for those who think that poverty is a bar to success. He is practically a self-made man, and, while young in years, for he was born in Marshall, Texas, February 18, 1887, he attended the rural public schools until he was fifteen years old, when he decided that he wished a better education. To accomplish this meant to attend some preparatory department of a race college. He worked nine months in the year, picking cotton or anything else on the rural farms, and attended school the remaining three months. The small sum he was enabled to earn did not equal enough to supply him with the luxury of a coal oil lamp, whereby he could study at night. Nothing discouraged him and he studied by night, using a pine torch.

Mr. Sidney Dones by the time he was sixteen years of age had by hard study prepared himself to stand an examination and to be admitted to Wiley University at Marshall, Texas. Entering the academic department, he later graduated after mastering an English course. He then entered the college department and studied for two years, when, on account of his father's death, he had to assume the responsibility of the family, and gave up college.

Later he came to Los Angeles, and worked as a plain day-laborer, which enabled him to further assist the family. It was while thus working that he fully realized that he had sufficient education to go into business for himself. He wished an office of his own, but his business was not sufficient for him to pay rent. Not being too proud to work, he did the janitor work for the building, thus paying for his own office rent. He was determined to climb. This has resulted in that today he is considered the leading young real estate dealer in Los Angeles, having a suite of offices in the Germain building.

While he was climbing in the real estate business, he read law for six years. This prepared him so that today he is the head of the Bookertee Investment Company, dealing in real estate and insurance.

On June 18, 1913, he married Miss Bessie Williams, a musician of prominence. The union was blessed by the birth of a daughter, Sidnetta. He owns a beautiful home and a touring car. He was a candidate for the City Council of Los Angeles during the spring of 1917, but was defeated. He has been an active worker for all of the Liberty Loans, and untiring in his efforts to fully explain to the people the advantages of the Loan. It is the wish of his friends that some day he will represent the race in the legislative halls of the State.

CHAPTER XVII

A Song of Old Dreams in the Musical Life of the Pioneer and Present Day Trail Blazers

"Sometimes amid the tumult and the throng.
We hear an old sweet song,
A broken strain from one we used to hear
Back in some yester year;
A melody borne through the drifting haze
Of life's forgotten days.
The tumult dies around us, strangely thrilled
With roar of traffic stilled;
Our eyes are dimmed—our hearts turn back—and then
We dream old dreams again.

"Sometimes beneath Love's new-found, smiling skies
Remembered perfumes rise;
An incense from the violet or rose,
Where summer's south wind blows;
Lost fragrance from old lanes of mignonette,
That love cannot forget;
And in the twilight or the dawn we turn
To where old altars burn;
And new-found love must bide its moments; then—
We dream old dreams again."
                                                    —Anonymous.

Thus we of today in beautiful California, as we study the history of the pioneer colored people, with their trials and discouragements; and, as we review the sketches given of their children in the musical world and in letters and science reaching such great heights, we truly feel like singing with the poet just quoted that "We dream old dreams again." We measure a man's success in life by the distance he has climbed to the position he wins for himself and thereby honors his race.

Let the reader review the musical career of Madam Sara Miles-Taylor and her brother, William Blake. They are children of an early-day Negro miner. The life of a colored miner was filled with numerous hardships, but more than one endured it all that they might give to their children a good education. These two persons just mentioned were given the best education then possible in California, after which they went east and builded upon the foundation laid in California. In after years they became renowned musicians in the several branches they decided best suited to their liking. Mr. William Blake became a great band master and instructor of musical instruments in San Francisco, while his sister, Sara Miles-Taylor, was acknowledged a great singer and artist in the musical world of two continents. She married Mr. Alex Taylor, who was an excellent performer on the piano. They realized the value of thorough training and went east to better prepare themselves for a musical career.

After becoming sufficiently trained, they toured the United States, and then England, France and Germany. While in Prague they were blessed by the birth of a son. The first colored child to have been born in that city, whereupon the ruler and his wife acted as the child's godparents, and gave it for a christening gift a sum of money that would equal two hundred and fifty dollars in United States currency.

There were others who distinguished themselves in the musical world in pioneer days. They, in after years, returned to California, crowned with honors, to spend the remaining days of their lives. The writer has in mind the "Famous California Vocalists," who, after touring the world, returned to the United States and to the State of California, with all the laurels that a critical musical public showered upon them. In a book by Mr. James Monroe Trotter, called "Music and Some Highly Musical People," in referring to these singers, among other things said: "The Famous California Vocalists, Anna Madah and Emma Louise Hyer, made their debut before an audience of eight hundred people at the Metropolitan Theater on April 22, 1867, at Sacramento, California. On this occasion, as on others afterward in San Francisco and other places in California, their efforts were rewarded with grand success. The musical critics and the press awarded them unstinted praise and even pronounced them wonderful."

The author then quoted from the *San Francisco Chronicle* of that date, which said: "Their musical powers are acknowledged and those who heard them last evening were unanimous in their praises, saying that rare natural gifts would insure for them a leading position among the prima donnae of the age. Miss Madah has a pure, sweet soprano voice, very true, even flexible, of remarkable compass and smoothness."

These words of praise can be more fully appreciated when the reader learns that her program was a "Wagnerian one." The critic's comment on her rendition of a selection from the "Rhine Maidens" said: "Her rendition of a selection from this number was almost faultless and thoroughly established her claim to the universal commendation she has received from all lovers of melody who heard her."

In commenting upon the voice of her sister, the critic said: "Miss Louise is a natural wonder, being a fine alto singer and also the possessor of a pure tenor voice. Her tenor is of wonderful range, and in listening to her singing it is difficult to believe that one is not hearing a talented young man instead of the voice of a young girl." These criticisms were made, as the reader will note, without a single reference to the singers being of the African race, which is conclusive evidence that they were judged according to their merits. The singers thereby established their claim as musical artists of that period to sing such high-class music and win critical musical favor.

While the writer was traveling over the State in quest of data for this book, she had the unexpected pleasure of meeting in Sacramento one of the singers, Miss Madah, who is now the wife of the well-known and highly respected Dr. Fletcher, located in that city. The writer immediately told the lady her mission and attempted to interview Mrs. Fletcher, but, like most great artists, she was retiring and did not care to talk. But after convincing her of the good she could do for struggling musicians by telling that many years ago there lived in Sacramento, California, a young colored girl, scarcely in her teens, who had given a "Wagnerian" program in the city theater, in which she had won unstinted praise from the musical critics of the daily press, Mrs. Fletcher consented to tell the writer of her travels all over the world, and showed some highly interesting newspaper clippings which spoke in the highest terms of her artistic singing and the wonderful range and sustaining tones of her voice. It was interesting to listen to her tell of her trip across the continent with her parents to Boston for additional training. While in Boston she sang before the world renowned Madame Adelina Patti.

After spending years in training, the sisters toured the United States, and then they joined the late Sam Lucas in "Out of Bondage" and toured Europe, and later joined John W. Isham's "Famous Octoroons." While members of this company they went to the Hawaiian Islands and Australia. It was while in this company that the papers spoke of Miss Madah as the "Bronze Patti." Mrs. Fletcher has a charming personality and is a delightful conversationalist.

After the interview the writer was introduced to Mrs. Fletcher's mother, who, in speaking of her daughter's career, said that on their first appearance in the Metropolitan Theater in Sacramento she sang with them. Her maiden name was Miss Cryer and she married Mr. Sam P. Hyer, who came to California before forty-nine.

Mr. Denis Carter, a pioneer musical artist on musical instruments, came to California before forty-nine. He followed mining for a short time, when he decided to return to the profession he practiced at his home in Philadelphia. He was a musical instructor on musical instruments. Mr. Carter readily formed classes in a circuit of cities, beginning with Grass Valley and ending in San Francisco. Mr. Dennis Carter was a master of the bass viol, and among his pupils he had the distinction of having Mr. Markus Blum, who in after years become a distinguished band master in San Francisco. The pioneer persons remember and tell with pleasure of the Blum Band which was the joy of old San Francisco before the fire of 1906. A Professor Mueller acted as pianist in Mr. Dennis Carter's school of music. Among Mr. Carter's colored pupils the following names have been given: Preston Alexander, John Adams, William Cantine and Abraham Holland.

John G. Coursey, another music teacher of pioneer days, had the distinction of being a member of the Pacific Board of Musicians of San Francisco, in 1866. Among his pupils are the names of Miss Ophelia Randall and Virginia and Louise Campbell, who were considered fine singers. He had other pupils who in after years were internationally distinguished. In this list occurs the names of Cyrus Smith, the Purnell Sisters and Mr. and Mrs. Sampson Williams, all of San Francisco. The last-named were no less persons than Madam Selika and her husband, who had the best and most wonderful baritone voice of any Negro singer in America.

There were many organizations doing good work in those days to encourage the study of music among our people. The Pacific Musical Association was organized in 1877, and met every Monday night in the West Indian Benevolent Society hall, on

Pacific street, San Francisco. The following named persons were officers and members: President, William H. Carter; vice-president, Harry Givens; treasurer, J. S. Kipwith; Secretary, George W. Jackson; musical director, D. E. Jackson; members, J. H. Smith, Sara E. Miles, prima donna; Mary Josephine Miles, contralto; piano, William Blake; tenor, D. B. Jackson; baritone, Sampson Williams; soprano, Mrs. Sampson Williams; baritones, Mrs. Perkins, and M. S. Sampson; mezzo-sopranos, Fanny Master, Mary Appo, Ophelia Randall and Miss Tennie Edmonds.

There are many others who might be added to this list of organizations and persons who distinguished themselves in a musical career during pioneer days, but it will be impossible to continue this period of the musical life of the ''Negro Trail Blazers;'' and yet it cannot be closed with justice and not mention an account of the musical career of one who distinguished himself long after that period, and yet was of that period. This refers to Mr. Joseph Green, who had the distinction of being the only trombone player in the Alphia Orchestra of San Francisco. He served with them for thirty-five years, during which time he played in the celebrated Palm Court of the Old Palace Hotel before the fire of 1906. Mr. Green's trombone playing was one of the attractions of the orchestra, and, like the Palace Hotel of San Francisco, was loved over the world. The popularity of this hotel and the continuous playing of this Negro musician for so many years recalls to mind an expression made to the writer through a letter from the distinguished white musical director of Oakland, California, Professor Alexander Stewart. The writer had extended an invitation to the different musical directors of the white race around the Bay cities to attend a concert given by the great Negro musician, Professor Robert Jackson, director of music of the Western Reserve University of Kansas City, Missouri. The concert was given in Oakland, and, after its rendition, one of the directors sent the following letter, in which he said: ''It is very gratifying to me to find the colored people doing so much in music that is worth while. We certainly owe them a debt of gratitude already for their contribution to musical art. I honestly believe that music is to play a very important part, if not the most important part, in the future development of the colored people toward higher ideals. * * * Yours sincerely,—(Signed) Alexander Stewart.''

Coming down to more recent date, we find the ''La Estrella Mandolin'' club playing for the millionaires on ''Nob Hill'' before the fire of 1906, and a Mr. D. W. McDonald, a leader of an orchestra likewise employed. Mrs. Laura Logan-Tooms, who was not only a good musician and teacher, but an organizer of church choirs, especially during her residence in San Jose, now has a daughter recently graduated from the girls' high school of San Francisco who has a wonderful voice and is having it trained. There was another lady of that period who was an excellent musician and won fame throughout the United States, and that was a Miss Jose Morris.

In connection with music, there was another line that sent out to the world many persons who won distinction in the dramatic art, Miss Cecilia Williams, who was a Shakesperian tragedienne. She also wrote good verse, as will be seen from some of her poems in the literary chapter. The Bay Cities Dramatic Club, of San Francisco, did much to encourage the young colored men and women in California. It was this club which discovered and did much in developing the possibilities of Mr. Bert Williams, of Williams and Walker. Mr. Williams has long won the distinction of being the greatest comedian on the American stage.

The above, giving an account of the activities of the ''Pioneer Musical Trail Blazers,'' is no less interesting than ''The Present Day Trail Blazers'' in the musical world. The present day musician has not allowed any of the advantages gained by the pioneers to slip from his grasp. He has gone even further and has won distinction in conservatories while competing with white students. In this particular, one girl won a diamond medal. There will not be found in this department one single sketch except of those who have spent time in actual study to make finished artists of themselves. One of the conditions to admit a sketch in this department has been that the person be a real musical student. The writer realizes that far too many persons call themselves musicians who have never trained a single day and have never even had their work criticized by persons capable of giving an opinion of value. Such persons are not much to encourage the study of the art of music. Hence the writer is heading this department with a sketch of one who recognized the necessity of such training from a scientific standard. The first sketch, as the reader will note, is that of Professor William T. Wilkins, who deserves great credit. He is the greatest pianist and teacher of the same in California.

The next sketch is that of Professor Elmer Bartlett, the greatest pipe organist of California. His sketch shows plainly what one can do and the reward coming from such thorough study. He is the best trained Negro organist, in the writer's idea, of any

Negro in the United States. There are other men who may be better known, but none who have had better training in the art of pipe organ playing and instruction.

The next sketch is of Mrs. Corrine Bush-Hicks, who studied in London, England, and then Mrs. Florence Cole-Talbert, who won a diamond medal. This one is followed by one from Miss Pearl Hinds, who won distinction in music at Oberlin College and at the Conservatory of Music in Boston Massachusetts.

Then Mrs. Gertrude Pillow-Kelley, who has been wonderfully trained, both in Canada and in Los Angeles. Then there must be made special mention of Mrs. Teat, who has the distinction of being the only teacher in California who has been trained in Boston to teach the Fletcher Copp method for beginners; also Miss Marie H. Ford, who has won distinctive training at the Conservatory of Music in Chicago, and has successfully promoted concerts for the race in Los Angeles, taxing the capacity of the Trinity Auditorium. Mention could be made of each contributor in the chapter, but the reader perhaps would not care to read these interesting sketches.

The writer considers it a privilege to present to the reader this sketch of the Musical Trail Blazer, Professor William T. Wilkins, of Los Angeles, California, a man of whom the race can feel justly proud. We often read of musicians as geniuses. The writer calls the subject of this sketch an artist. The word ''genius'' too often is used, especially in speaking of colored persons in the musical world, to denote their supernatural gifts in the art of music, without the hard and careful study which is absolutely necessary to produce a real musician. This man has won his right to the title of artist or professor, in that he has been willing, at the advanced age of twenty years, to begin at the very beginning to learn music by note. He had the determination to win for himself a place in the musical world and considered it a pleasure to surmount any difficulties to accomplish this aim.

Professor Wilkins is the son of a musician and leader of a band in which he had all three of his children play. His father is a musician of the old school and taught his children to play by ear. Young William at the age of three years, was placed on a box and taught to play a bass drum in strict time. When he was older he played the snare drum in his father's fife and drum corps.

His father is a tinner, sheet-iron and hardware worker and was anxious that his son William learn the trade also. He was ambitious to advance his children's opportunity in life, and for that reason moved with his family from Little Rock, Arkansas, to Oklahoma. Later, finding the schools not as advanced as he would have liked, he moved to Los Angeles, California, where he entered his children in the magnificent schools of that place.

Before leaving Oklahoma he taught William how to play a few chords on the piano, and thus accompany him on the piccolo, and after this William learned to play the cornet. When they moved to Los Angeles, William's musical education was not given any more consideration. Instead he was taught thoroughly the trade of tinner and mechanic. This resulted in William, at the age of thirteen years, building a stationary engine which was so perfectly done that he readily sold it. The money thus obtained he used to further his studies in engineering. He invested the entire sum in a scholarship in the American Correspondence School of Electrical Engineering.

William readily advanced in his studies. When he entered the Polytechnic school, he spent his recess period in playing on the school piano. This attracted his teacher, and then the music teacher of the school, Mr. M. H. Grist, gave him a few private lessons in the art of reading music by note. During the years he attended the Polytechnic school he at the same time pursued a course of study through the American Correspondence school. When he received his diploma from the Polytechnic school he almost at the very same time received a certificate from this correspondence school for an electrical engineer. He readily found employment with the Edison Electrical Light and Power Company of Los Angeles.

His thirst for a musical education finally led to his consulting the well-known musical instructor, Professor Von Stein, head of the conservatory, by the same name. Having saved the money earned by working for the Edison Company, he was enabled to immediately begin the desired instruction. The long hours required for practice work on the piano compelled him to resolve that he would resign from his position, notwithstanding he was the first Negro boy to find employment with the Edison Light and Power Company. He worked for them as line inspector for ten months, when he resigned his position.

William, having saved his money while employed by the Edison company, thought this sum would see him through a course of music. But he was soon doomed to disappointment, since he had gone to the highest-priced teacher in the city. His father being determined that William should follow the trade of an electrical engineer, made no effort to assist him to study music by note. William, being equally determined to be a musician, thought long and seriously as to how he could earn the price of his lessons and also have time to practice. The only practical door opened to him was the cutting of lawns. He canvassed the fashionable residence districts of Los Angeles, and, securing enough customers, he retained them for years.

His faithfulness to duty soon won him friends among his customers, who, after learning of his ambition to become a musician, invited him to come in and play for them and their guests. It was then that William discovered that he had advanced to that place where he needed a good piano. His father was unimpressed, and William, still being determined, asked a friend, a Mr. Hill, to permit him to practice on his good piano. After this event William T. Wilkins won his father to realizing that he was sincere in his desire to become a great musician and purchased him a good piano. William, however, earned the price of his lessons by the cutting of lawns for over six years. After which Professor Von Stein gave him a certificate and advised him to teach music to his people or any one wishing his services.

Professor Wilkins had set his determination to not only teach, but some day become a great piano soloist. He secured a few pupils and immediately placed himself under the instruction of another well-known musician, Professor Brahm Van der Berg, also of Los Angeles. This instructor is the well-known Belgian solo pianist, who at one time was connected with the Boston Symphony Orchestra, and also associated with Emma Calve and Theo. Leschetizky.

Professor Wilkins' success as a teacher was so great from the very first that he felt safe on September 1, 1916, in opening a music school. This has been such a success that today he employs ten teachers, has five pianos and two of these are grand pianos. His school has departments where he has competent teachers in the giving of voice culture, the piano and violin. During the coming year he contemplates adding dramatic readings.

During the long years of his struggles to master the art of music he has won and retained the highest respect of the best members of both races in the City of Los Angeles. He has been shown the distinction of having the first Negro sketch accompanied by a photograph to appear in the oldest musical journal published on the coast, *The Pacific Coast Journal of Music*, having solicited and published the same in a recent issue. In the same issue appeared the pictures and sketches of white musical artists of international fame. Among this number was Mr. James Goddart, of Covent Garden, London, England, Royal Opera Company.

Professor William T. Wilkins gives a public students' and teachers' recital every May. After the one given in 1917 he received a letter from Mr. Carl Bronson, a musical critic for the largest daily papers of Los Angeles, and also director of the First M. E. Church Choir Association, which consists of one hundred and fifty voices, many of whom are world-renowned. In his letter to Professor Wilkins, Mr. Bronson said:

Los Angeles, California, May 24, 1917.

''My Dear Mr. Wilkins: After having inspected your system of teaching, I am thoroughly convinced that you are giving your people the exact science of music in a manner as simple as it is unaffected, and that every attentive student will acquire the principles of that art as laid down by the greatest standards of the world. I am amazed at your achievements and feel that somehow you are divinely endowed to carry life's greatest message to your people. May you ever prosper.

''Devotedly yours,

'' (Signed) CARL BRONSON.''

Professor Wilkins' recital for 1918 was given in the Lyceum Theater, which will easily seat a thousand persons. The admission price was fifty cents. A few hours before the recital came an unusual occurrence, the first in many years, when the City of Los Angeles was visited by a thunderstorm, rain, snow and lightning. This storm lasted all afternoon. The recital opened on time with standing room only. In the audience were recognized many white eminent musical instructors and their families. The pupils played a difficult program with ease and confidence. The class consisted of one hundred and fifty students, many of whom were white. The race people were thrilled with pride and delight over this acknowledgment of the ability of one who is genuinely representative of the Negro race. He has by his ability broken down a great barrier for the race. This recital was attended by Professor Carl Bronson, who, after the close of the program, addressed the audience and highly complimented Professor Wilkins and his students. Professor Ray Hastings also sent a good letter:

"RAY HASTINGS

"Organist, Temple Baptist Church, Clune Auditorium Theater
"2764 Roxbury Avenue, Los Angeles, California.
"Mr. William T. Wilkins. "May 16, 1917.

"Dear Friend: Your program last night was indeed a treat. The result of your teaching was astonishing. However, after attending two of such recitals, and when I remember your exceptional talent, splendid training and inclination to really 'do things,' I'll expect it always to be 'number one.' You are doing a great work.

"Success to you,

"(Signed) RAY HASTINGS."

"P. S.—Miss Wilson, in her absolute poise and masterful style, is certainly a 'wonder.'"

"Los Angeles Polytechnic School.
"Department of Music. Mrs. Gertrude B. Parsons, Head of Department.

"Los Angeles, California, June 18, 1917.

"Mr. Wm. T. Wilkins,
"1325 Central Avenue, Los Angeles, California.

"Dear Mr. Wilkins: I take great pleasure in expressing to you my appreciation of the splendid work done by your school music students at the recent recital given in Lyceum Hall. The assurance, precision and good taste exhibited in the work of the young people was delightful to witness, and the fact that they played and sang from memory was most commendable. I congratulate you upon the wonderful work you are doing with your people, and certainly the highest praise is due you for your years of indomitable perseverance—which are now bearing fruit. May success always crown your efforts.

"Most sincerely,

"(Signed) GERTRUDE B. PARSONS."

This lady was a former teacher of Professor Wilkins.

"Juvenile Court, Los Angeles.
"Sidney N. Reeve, Judge.
"Probation Department, Tenth Floor, Hall of Records.

"Los Angeles, California, June 21, 1916.

"To Whom It May Concern: Mr. William T. Wilkins has in his possession several very good letters of praise and recommendation from prominent people, and I am very glad to say a word in his behalf. I have known the young man, who is now twenty-nine years of age, since he was twelve years old. I have watched his career as he has climbed up step by step, working his way through high school and into his present position and musical attainments. He is worthy of every encouragement that the people of Los Angeles can give him, and I am sure that he will some day be recognized as a genius.

"Respectfully,

"(Signed) MRS. A. J. BRADLEY."

"Department 10, with the Juvenile Court."

The daily papers have been most kind to Professor Wilkins, as will be seen from the fact that, at the opening of the musical season of 1914, the *Los Angeles Tribune-Express*, October 14, of that year, appeared with the following head-line: "Los Angeles Negro Musical Genius. Concert season opens October 20." The article concerning this Negro musician appeared at the right of the page with a full two-column cut of the professor at the piano. Opposite his picture was that of Madam Olive-Fremsted, the soprano singer of the Metropolitan Opera Company of New York.

The *Tribune-Express* proprietor the following Christmas gave a dinner to a thousand newsboys. For their entertainment he invited the best singers and other musicians in the city. Among this number he included Professor William T. Wilkins. He was honored previous to his appearance with a two-column write-up which appeared in this paper. After the dinner, the following letter was sent to the professor by Mr. Noah D. Thompson, who is on the editorial staff of the *Tribune-Express*.

"*Tribune-Express* Editorial Rooms,

"Los Angeles, California, December 27, 1914.

"Dear Mr. Wilkins: I am sending you today under separate cover several copies of the *Express* and *Tribune* which speak of your excellent performance at the Christmas dinner given in honor of one thousand newsboys by Mr. Edward T. Earl, owner and publisher of the above daily papers.

"It is very gratifying for me to note that one thousand hungry newsboys stopped eating to listen to your compositions.Thanking you on behalf of the management of the papers for your contribution toward the success of the dinner to the local newsies, I am, yours truly,

"(Signed) NOAH D. THOMPSON."

The day will come when not only the musical public of his own race, but others, will acclaim Professor William T. Wilkins a great pianist. He has written several musical compositions that musicians say if published will be well received, especially "The Path of Destiny." At this writing he is studying under the greatest authority on Russian music in America, Professor Jaroslaw de Zielinski, who is so noted that he has already had his name given prominence in the Encyclopaedia of Music. He is spoken of as an author, composer and pianist. He writes for the *Etude* and is director of the Los Angeles Conservatory of Music, an institution which has been established for over thirty-five years.

Professor Elmer C. Bartlett, the subject of this sketch, was born March 18, 1887, at Galena, Cherokee County, Kansas. He was educated in the high schools of that city; came to Los Angeles in 1903; studied the piano under Professor Henry Amiraux, of Paris Conservatory, for three years. Professor Elmer C. Bartlett, after this foundation was so splendidly laid, decided that he would begin the study of his chosen life's work and began the study of the pipe organ under the best teacher in America, Professor Ernest Douglass, F. A. G. O. This teacher has founded a method of organ playing that is used in five leading colleges in America. He is at the head of the Douglass School of Organ Playing. Mr. Bartlett studied under this renowed teacher for five years, and at the present time is preparing to take the examination to become a member of the American Guild of Organists.

Professor Elmer C. Bartlett has held the position as pipe organist of the First A. M. E. Church since 1909, in Los Angeles, California. He is a successful teacher of the piano and pipe organ, and enjoys a large and intelligent class of pupils. He married, in 1910, Miss Gertrude Bruce and has a beautiful home and studio at 936 Pico street, Los Angeles.

There is not a sketch in the entire book that the writer enjoys more giving to the reader than the one concerning Professor Bartlett. He is, in her opinion, the best pipe organist of the Negro race. He understands and is able to get the soul of harmony from the instrument. He is a finished performer. The writer bases this opinion on the following knowledge: Having attended a summer session of pipe organ musical lectures given at the University of California through the American Organist Guild to stimulate and encourage an appreciation of the pipe organ, she afterward attended a fall and winter course of musical lectures and recitals by the world-renowed Professor Clarence Eddy, given on the pipe organ. This knowledge has enabled the writer, although not a performer, to judge and fully appreciate a good and soulful performer on that grand instrument, the pipe organ. Professor Bartlett may not be as well-known as a number of other Negro pipe organists, but the day will come when the world will acclaim his ability, thus adding another star to the glory of the Negro race.

The next sketch of interest is that of Mrs. Florence Cole-Talbert, diamond medalist, who comes from a long line of ancestors who were musicians. She is the daughter of Mr. and Mrs. Thomas A. Cole, who moved to Los Angeles from Detroit, Michigan, with their daughter when she was ten years old. Her father is a son of the well-known real estate holder, the late Hon. James H. Cole, who died leaving large and valuable real estate holdings in the City of Detroit, Michigan, having made his wealth as a blacksmith and carpenter. Her mother was a member of the Original Fisk Jubilee Singers and the daughter of Mrs. Hatfield-Chandler, who was the organizer and sang in the first colored Baptist church choir in Cincinnati, Ohio. Her grandfather, Mr. Hatfield, was associated with Levi-Coffin, of Cincinnati, as an active member of the "Underground Railroad."

The reader will note that Mrs. Florence Cole-Talbert was fortunate in having been born with a splendid foundation for a musical career. The mere fact of her grandfather having been an active member of the "Underground Railroad" would endow her with a spirit of undaunted courage to ever do the best for herself and the race. Her parents, coming from a long line of musicians, and being musical artists, early recognized their daughter's talent for music. They also recognized the value of a good education. Their daughter was thoroughly educated in the public schools and the University of Southern California.

Her musical training began with the best teachers available, placing her under the instruction of Madame Windsor, of Los Angeles. When she had advanced sufficiently, they continued her studies at the conservatory, after which she accepted a position as leading soprano or the prima donna of the "Midland Jubilee Singers." She filled the position less than six months when she married one of the managers.

Her husband is a son of the late Rev. Talbert, the former traveling financial secretary of Wilberforce College, Ohio. He readily recognized her wonderful voice, which resulted in her instantly leaving the stage to continue her musical studies at the Chicago Musical College.

While a student of the college she won a partial scholarship and was presented in student's recital during her first semester. She graduated with the class of 1916. In a public competition before thirty members of the faculty and judges, she won first place out of a class of sixty students, and was the only Negro member of the class. Her course at the Chicago Musical College consisted of Italian, composition, harmony, and vocal. She averaged one hundred in each subject. She also won the first prize, a diamond medal, the first time it was ever won by a colored student. The winning of the medal gave her the honor of singing at the commencement exercises accompanied by the Chicago Symphony Orchestra of one hundred pieces. Her selection on this occasion was "Caro Nome," from "Rigoletto," sung in Italian. The following are some of the musical criticisms she has received from musicians of both races:

"Chicago Musical College,
"624 Michigan Boulevard.
Chicago, Illinois, October 9, 1917.

"To Whom It May Concern: Mrs. Florence Cole-Talbert has studied in the Chicago Musical College in the voice and theory department and has accomplished highly remarkable results in her work. She won the diamond medal of her class and sang with the greatest success at the commencement exercises of the institution. There can be no doubt that she should become a very successful vocal artist.

"Yours very truly,
"FELIX BOROWSKI, President."

"Pedro T. Tinsley,
"Author of Tone Placing and Voice Development,
"6448 Drexel Avenue.
"Chicago, Illinois, October 6, 1917.

"Esteemed Mrs. Talbert: There are two things I wish to speak of concerning your art. First, your singing appeals to me because you seem to sing without trying. We all like to hear singers sing, and not work at it. Second, the most artistic thing about your work is the interpretation of the text. With good wishes, I am

"Sincerely yours,
"PEDRO T. TINSLEY."

"Andre Tridon,
"Lecturer and Critic.
"New York City, August 4, 1917.

"Dear Mrs. Talbert: One of the things I have enjoyed this summer (on Community Chautauqua) was the opportunity to listen day after day to your very luscious voice. A voice as well trained as yours, and with such an unusual range, should finally gain recognition outside of the very narrow circle to which barbarous superstitution is endeavoring to limit it. My friend Josef Transky and Modest Altschuler will hear about you as soon as I reach New York. Your day will come I am sure, and that day no one will feel happier than the man who has watched you closely doing your very best in things generally unworthy of your talent. That fact is a guarantee that you will succeed.

"Yours very cordially,
"TRIDON."

After receiving such wonderfully encouraging letters, Mrs. Florence Cole-Talbert decided to take the advice of the eminent vocalist, Madam Azalia Hackley, and tour alone. The following letter is self-explanatory:

"Mrs. Florence Cole-Talbert is my ideal of what a colored singer should be. She has arrived at an earlier age and with more musicianship and educational equipment than any artist the race has known. When she won the diamond medal in one short term at the Chicago Musical College, I was not surprised, for she has the combination of beautiful voice and musical intelligence that may only be found among the great artists of the country. I have known her all her life and have planned this tour for her that she may be heard by more of her own people; as heretofore her efforts have have been confined to the lyceum and Chautauqua circuits. I hope that every promoter and school will avail themselves of the opportunity of hearing Mme. Talbert. She is most worthy of your patronage.

"E. AZELIA HACKLEY."
(Eminent Vocalist, Directress and Author.)

Since receiving this sketch, Madame H. Talbert has been called by the daily press the "Bronze Galli Curci," and has received highly commendable letters from Mr. Harry Burleigh and many other high musicians.

Mrs. Corrine Bush-Hicks, the subject of this sketch, was born and educated in the public schools of Walnut Hills, Cincinnati, Ohio. Her mother discovered her musical ability when she was entering her teens, and immediately employed a celebrated vocalist to instruct her daughter, Madame Jennie Jackson Dehart, a former member of the First Fisk Jubilee Singers, whose own voice had been so well trained that she won the title of the "Black Swan." The mother of Miss Bush recognized the value of instruction in voice culture from a teacher whose own voice had been correctly placed. The success of her selection can be judged when it is known that she correctly placed Miss Corrine Bush's voice so that in after years she developed and retained all its qualities as a genuine lyric soprano.

It was while the subject of this sketch was in high school that Mrs. Dehart had the privilege of introducing her pupil to a Miss Henson, who, as an advance agent, was in America in search of a soprano voice to join the "Louden Fisk Jubilee Singers." This troop, at the time, was traveling under the personal direction of Mr. F. J. Louden, the celebrated bass singer. Mrs. Dehart convinced Miss Corrine Bush's parents of the advantage to their daughter of a tour abroad. The young lady signed a contract for a two-year tour through Europe. Her mother, Mrs. Bush, making one demand, that she continue her musical studies abroad under the best teacher available.

Miss Corrine Bush, upon reaching London, England, began the study of vocal music under the daughter of the late celebrated tragedian and writer, Miss Ira Aldridge, who had been named after her father Ira. The reader will readily recall that, notwithstanding his African descent, he was during his day, considered the greatest tragedian of England. During Miss Bush's stay in Europe she sang in all the cities, great and small, of Great Britain, Scotland, Ireland and Wales.

Mrs. Corrine Bush-Hicks has the distinction of having sang before the late Queen Victoria and her royal court, and afterward was again in London and was invited to sing at a memorial for the late Queen. This was held in the Spurgeon Tabernacle of London, England. It was at this time in London, England, she sang before the late S. Coldridge Taylor, whose musical writings have since been pronounced the greatest production of the age, especially his "Hiawatha Wedding Feast." While in England she was frequently asked to personally sing in the homes of titled persons.

The Fisk Singers, after a tour of two years in Europe, returned to the United States, and Miss Corrine Bush, remembering her pledge made some time before, became the wife of Mr. William Hicks, of Salem, Ohio. They immediately moved to Pasadena, California. They have lived there for the past fourteen years. Mrs. Hicks has meant much to the life of the clubs, both white and colored in Pasadena and Los Angeles. She is often invited to sing before these clubs. She sang for a season at the Chautauqua held in Monterey, California.

During the last visit of the late Booker T. Washington to Southern California, the people of Pasadena gave a reception to him in the auditorium of the Pasadena high school. Its seating capacity is rated as over two thousand, and was crowded. Mrs. Corrine Bush-Hicks on this occasion was the soloist. Afterward Mr. Washington personally thanked her for her delightful singing, which he said he thoroughly enjoyed. Notwithstanding all the honors Mrs. Hicks has had heaped upon her, she is as unassuming in telling about her success in singing in grand opera, as she is about telling of any other engagement. She has a wonderful and pleasing personality, is quite active in club life and has held many state offices in the Federation of Colored Women's Clubs. At this writing she is an active worker in both the colored and white Red Cross societies of Pasadena.

It is with pleasure that the writer is presenting to the reader the sketch of Miss Marie Hilda Ford, of Pasadena, who was born in Atlanta, Georgia, in 1895. Her parents moved to Pasadena when she was a year old, where she was reared and educated in the public schools. She was an apt student in music. Her parents, however, insisted that she continue her own study in music, notwithstanding she was capable of and did teach at the age of twelve years. This resulted in Miss Ford later taking a thorough course of several years' study at the Chicago Musical College.

Miss Ford entered this college in the beginning of 1914, and graduated in June 15, 1915, with the following honorable record, and was the only colored girl in the class studying the piano forte: She received a teacher's certificate or diploma with a general average of ninety-seven; piano, ninety-six; concerto, ninety-five; harmony, ninety-six; science of music, ninety-nine; history of music, ninety-seven. Her diploma was signed by President F. Ziegfeld.

The charm of this sketch is that our subject, while receiving such a high average, did not stop there, but immediately re-entered the same college the next term, and at the end of one year again graduated with the following excellent high record: Concerto, ninety-three; harmony, ninety-six; composition, ninety-six; general average, ninety-five. Her diploma was signed by Felix Borowski, president. It was at this time that another colored girl graduated with great honors from the same college in the person of Madame Florence Cole-Talbert. Each was the only Negro member of their respective classes.

After their graduation Miss Marie Hilda Ford and Madame Florence Cole-Talbert jointly gave a recital for their own race under the auspices of the Missouri State Club, at the St. Mark's M. E. Church of Chicago, Illinois. Upon this occasion Miss Ford played such difficult numbers as "Polonaise" (Opus 9), by Paderewski, and "Liebestraum," E major, by Liszt; Etude in F major, by Chopin. The Chicago daily papers and also the race papers spoke of her work in the highest praise.

While in Chicago Miss Ford was made a member of the "Ideal Bureau, Choir and Concert." This bureau acts as a clearing house for colored talent and those who seek them. Since her return to Pasadena she has received numerous calls through them to teach music in the East and Southern States. She is loyal to California and has steadily refused to leave the State.

Miss Marie Hilda Ford is very modest and unassuming concerning her work and the success she has met with since completing her course at the Chicago Musical College, but is more than generous in giving her services for charity. Recently she gave a recital for the benefit of the Second Baptist Church of Riverside, California. Among the many creditable press notices she received on this occasion was the following:

"Mlle. Marie Hilda Ford, of Pasadena, late of the Chicago Musical College, appeared in a piano recital last Friday night at Mercantile Hall, Riverside, for the benefit of the Second Baptist Church. Every available seat in the building was taken, many having to stand. This was in the face of inclement weather. Miss Ford proved her genius as a pianist upon this occasion. In the audience were musicians of high standing of the white race. Mrs. Porter (white), a teacher of music, was present and spoke of the accomplishments of Mlle. Ford. She said Miss Ford was the best she had ever heard. Mayor Horace Porter was also present, and spoke in glowing terms of Miss Ford's ability. Nearly one-half of the audience was white. This is the second time Miss Ford has appeared before the people of Riverside."

While studying in Chicago Miss Ford had the honor of being a member of the Chicago Treble Clef Club, which was a part of the chorus of the Lincoln Jubilee and Half-Century Anniversary Exposition, held in the Coliseum of Chicago from August 22 to September 16, 1915. This celebration was in commemoration of the Half Century of Freedom for the Negro, and there was gathered together during that one month the most talented and brainiest of the Negro race throughout the United States. Miss Ford at the present writing is teaching with great success, having large classes in both Riverside and Pasadena, California. She has also promoted some large concerts with success and has been solicited by artists in the musical world to secure them an audience in the State of California anywhere she might deem it profitable. The writer personally has great hopes for Miss Ford's future on a broader scale than heretofore attempted by one so young. She has our best wishes to mount upward and onward.

Mrs. Lillian Jetter-Davis, daughter of Rev. Henry M. Jetter, of Newport, Rhode Island, was educated in the public schools of her home town, after which she attended Neff College of Oratory, of Philadelphia, receiving a certificate in oratory and elocution; studied music under the widely-known Professor Frederick A. Fredericks, of Newport, Rhode Island. She mastered the piano forte.

Mrs. Davis, for a number of years has been recognized as a finished artist, both as an elocutionist and teacher of the piano. She has trained several large choruses and successfully directed large church choirs and presided at the pipe organ. She is internationally known as a promoter of entertainments, and has successfully given recitals in all the large cities of the United States, filling an entire evening's program with her music and elocution.

Mrs. Lillian Jetter Davis married Rev. Taylor Davis in 1904. The union has been blessed by the birth of five children, four of whom are living. Notwithstanding her large family, she keeps up her teaching of the piano. Recently her class of students at a recital in Fresno presented her with a wrist watch as a token of appreciation. Mrs. Davis has appeared on the program with nearly all the leading musicians of today who are identified with the Negro race.

Miss Pearl W. Hinds, daughter of Mr. and Mrs. Wiley Hinds, of Oakland, is a native daughter, and was born in Farmersville, Tulare County, California. She was educated in the public schools of Oakland, taking a literary course in the high school.

Her parents early recognized her musical ability and placed her under the instruction of the late Mrs. Pauline Powell-Burns of Oakland.

After her graduation from the Oakland high school, Miss Hinds attended a summer session of music at the Conservatory of Music of Boston, Massachusetts, making a specialty of the piano, after which she entered the Oberlin College of Music, connected with the college of the same name in Ohio. While attending this college she completed a course in harmony, the history of music and theory. She specialized in instruction on the piano, pipe organ and voice. This instruction fitted her for an instructor of public school music.

While in Oberlin, Ohio, she had charge of the M. E. Church choir of that city. Miss Hinds also wrote the music to one of Mr. Ricks's poems, "To a Bird," which was sung at a recital of original songs given in the Conservatory of Music of Oberlin College. After graduating, Miss Hinds accepted a position as director of the musical department of the State Normal College of South Carolina, located at Orangeburg. In connection with her work, she gave private instruction and did considerable work in the churches. At the present writing she has decided to remain with her parents in Oakland, where she will give private lessons, much to the delight of her friends.

"Mrs. R. C. Owens, the wife of the Negro capitalist, has devoted many years of ardent study to the cultivation of her remarkably strong, clear voice under the guidance of Mrs. Ben F. Thorpe. Ellen Beach Yaw, in a recent interview, declared that Mrs. Owens had a most beautiful natural voice and she firmly believed Mrs. Owens would meet with great success as a grand opera singer. Miss Yaw was very enthusiastic in her praise of Mrs. Owens devotion to the study of music, and hoped personally to see her appear in a well organized company of grand opera singers composed of the members of the Negro race.

"Mrs. Thorpe recently introduced Mrs. Owens as a singer to the Women's Monday Afternoon Club of Covina. Her rendition of 'Resignation,' by Caro Roma, and 'Spring Dreams,' by Schubert, and several other numbers, was much appreciated and heartily encored. Aside from her musical ability, Mrs. Owen is well-known for her charitable and loving disposition. She has encouraged and assisted several girls of her race through school. She is the social leader among her people in Los Angeles. Booker T. Washington and Mrs. Washington and most all of the noted Negro visitors to the city have been entertained by her. The appointments of her home proclaim her refined and artistic taste. She has carefully chosen an extensive library and with her two charming daughters spends a large portion of her time in study and travel."—(From *Los Angeles Times*, February 12, 1909.)

It is with pleasure that the writer adds to the above that she listened to Mrs. Owens sing shortly after this article appeared in the *Times*, but, not knowing Mrs. Owens, inquired if she was not a professional singer, her lack of self-consciousness and ease of manner, together with her sustained tones, readily gave one the impression that she had appeared before the footlights. It seems too bad that Mrs. Owens did not make a tour of the eastern cities as a "lyric soprano," for such talent should enrich others by its beauty.

Instead of a musical career Mrs. Owens has chosen, after all, the better part, for, while she has traveled extensively, it has always been with her daughters, that they might have the advantage of such knowledge aside from instructions in the best schools. There is no greater calling than to be a successful "queen of the home." This position Mrs. Owens has filled with all the simplicity of greatness, as will be seen in the sketch of her daughters.

Miss Manila and Miss Gladys were given all the advantages of the public schools of Southern California, after which they were sent to the Historic Fisk University of Nashville, Tennessee. Mrs. Owens choosing this high-standard colored school that her daughters, notwithstanding the wealth of their father, would not be autocrats. This school furnished them with a truly democratic education, aside from its excellent school system of imparting knowledge. In this particular Mrs. Owens is to be congratulated. She has left nothing undone to give her daughters every advantage, thereby she has given to the Negro race two girls who by careful training, travel and companionship of their mother will develop into well balanced womanhood.

Miss Manila has been given especial training in music. Previous to going to Fisk she studied music under Mrs. Newman, and, while attending Fisk, she mastered the pipe organ. Recently, since returning to Los Angeles, she appeared in public recital with Professor Elmer Bartlett, the greatest Negro pipe organist on this Coast. She has also appeared in recitals in Nashville, Tennessee.

Mrs. Ella J. Bradley-Hughley, the subject of this sketch, was born in Dallas, Texas, March 1, 1889; was reared under the discipline of Christian parents, receiving her college education in Bishop's College, of Marshall, Texas, graduating in the class of 1907. She was married in Dallas, Texas, in 1911, to Mr. David H. Hughley, shortly after which they moved to Los Angeles, where she lived until her sudden passing in February, 1918.

Madam Hughley was well and favorably known by every one in the City of Los Angeles. She was a favorite in the musical circles and had fully established her place as an artist upon her first appearance before the public in Los Angeles. Her first appearance was at a concert given by Rev. J. T. Hill at the Wesley Chapel. The concert was of an artistic nature, being the rendition of the beautiful oratorio, ''Stabat Mater,'' by Rossini. The beautiful but most difficult solo was given to Madam Hughley. One of the papers afterward, in speaking of the concert said: ''The solo of 'Inflammatus' was never sung by any one with more feeling and artistic temperament.'' Her rich, well-trained voice seemed to be suited for such high class work. She had trained for and did sing in the most pleasing manner the most difficult grand opera numbers. The critical music lovers of Los Angeles and Southern California from hence acclaimed her the ''Queen of Song,'' and she never gave them cause to regret the confidence bestowed upon her.

Madam Hughley was at the head of the voice-culture department of the Wilkins' Conservatory of Music, a position she filled with credit and satisfaction to all. Previous to coming to California she had studied voice culture. After locating in Los Angeles she immediately placed herself under the training of the best teachers of the voice in the city. She at one time studied under Professor J. Jurakian, vocalist and voice-placing, pure-tone production instructor, and also Professor George Carr, at his voice-production studio in the Mozart Theater building. Both of these teachers are well known in Los Angeles. Madam Hughley had made arrangements to study voice-culture under Constantino, director of the California Temple of Arts.

Madam Hughley often rendered to the delight of concert-goers many operatic selections which were always commented upon in the race papers and journals. An issue of the *Peace Guide*, a magazine at one time edited by Professor Biggers, had the following to say concerning her singing in an article under the head, ''In the Musical World'': ''Madam Hughley, of Los Angeles, most popular dramatic soprano. Madam Ella J. Bradley-Hughley is not only a leader of choir and chorus work but is a favorite as a soloist. She has a phenomenal voice of extra high range and extraordinary power.'' During the time she was at the head of the voice-culture department of the Wilkins School of Music it was such a great success that it became necessary to have a waiting list before a new pupil could be accepted. It is indeed sad that one so gifted should have to leave the world at so early an age. It is gratifying to those left that she still retains a sweet memory in the hearts of the public.

Mrs. Gussie Estell Simpson-Bacon, the subject of this sketch, is one of the sweet singers of Southern California, although she was born in Atlanta, Georgia. She came to California when a small girl with her parents, who located in Riverside, where she was educated in the public schools of that city. Mrs. Bacon from a child had a sweet, natural mezzo-soprano voice. Her parents early recognized the value of it and placed their daughter under the best vocal instructor then in California, a noted singer, in the person of Mrs. Agnes Overton Hall. The motto of this instructor was ''Self-Forgetfulness,'' which made her pupils always ready for any audience. After studying for several years under this noted instructor, who laid the foundation for her voice with sustaining tones, Mrs. Gussie Simpson-Bacon was sent by her parents to study voice-culture under the noted Canadian vocal instructor, Professor J. W. Gage. She filled some noted engagements under his direction, such as the ''Spring Carnival,'' at the Glenwood Mission Inn, the most beautiful and leading hotel in all of California, and also several of the leading white churches of Riverside. The M. E. Church (white) wanted to send her to Italy to be educated in voice culture. She had the distinction of having sung at the Booker T. Washington memorial services held at the Glenwood Mission Inn.

Mrs. Gussie Simpson-Bacon married Mr. Henry Bacon of Riverside, and they moved to Los Angeles to live. Since living in that city she has studied under Mme. Norma Rocka, a vocal instructor of note. Since coming to Los Angeles Mrs. Gussie Simpson-Bacon has sung on the program with noted colored musical artists such as Mme. Azalia Hackley and Mme. Patti Brown upon her first appearance on this Coast. Madame Hackley was very anxious that she return East with her to study for a concert singer, but Mrs. Bacon is happily married and the union has been blessed by the birth of three children. She and her husband own a beautiful modern home in Los Angeles.

Mrs. Gertrude E. Pillow-Kelley, the subject of this sketch, was born in Great Bend, Kansas, coming to California with her parents when an infant. They located in Pasadena, where their daughter was reared and educated in the public schools of that city, graduating with honors. After leaving school her parents sent her to Toronto, Canada, where she entered the Toronto Conservatory of Music and for five years she studied the art of music under Professor J. D. Tripp, the most noted Canadian pianist, at the end of which time she returned to California and married.

Mrs. Kelley longed to acquire a certificate to teach music and immediately made arrangements to enter the Von Stein Conservatory of Music of Los Angeles, where she studied the art of the piano forte and specialized in harmony. After two years of such study she received a certificate to teach the piano forte.

Mrs. Gertrude E. Pillow-Kelley is an accomplished musician and instructor, a delightful performer on the piano, with a pleasing personality, modest and unassuming. She immediately impresses one with her ability which has made her a great success as a teacher.

Mme. Catherine Marion Carr-Teat, the subject of this sketch, is one of the best educated teachers of music for children in the State of California, at least the writer has failed to find another who teaches the wonderful ''Fletcher-Copp'' method for beginners. She is the daughter of Mr. and Mrs. Joseph and Nancey Carr, of Nashville, Tenn. They moved to Topeka, Kansas, when their children were quite young. The subject of this sketch graduated from the Topeka high school, after which she immediately married Mr. Isaiah Allen Teat, of Silver Lake, Kansas. She entered the next term as a student of Washburn College of Music, attending the same for four years, when she received a diploma to teach the piano forte.

After graduating from this college she took a teacher's course at the Topeka Teachers' Institute, making a third-grade certificate to teach. Mrs. Teat accepted a position to teach in the public schools of Oklahoma, Kings Fisher County, teaching there for two years in a mixed school having fourteen white and seventeen colored pupils. Mrs. Teat, being anxious to advance in music, resigned her position and, with her husband, moved to Pasadena, California, where even the charming climate of this beautiful place did not change her determination to advance in music.

After residing there for a few years, she gave up her rapidly-growing class to go to Boston Conservatory of Music, where she studied ''The Fletcher-Copp Method'' for beginners, mastering that method together with harmony, counterpoint, technique and Spanish. Mrs. Teat then returned to Pasadena and again began teaching the art of the piano forte. Notwithstanding her high musical training, she is modest and unassuming in her manner, and quite gracious in playing for charitable purposes. She has played before many distinguished persons, among whom was ex-President Theodore Roosevelt when he was vice-president of the United States. The State Federation of Colored Women's Club of Kansas was holding their annual meeting in Topeka and the vice-president was in the city. He was extended an invitation to address the Federated Clubs at their annual reception. He accepted the invitation and Mrs. Teat was asked to perform on the piano as a part of the program for his entertainment. Upon this occasion Mrs. Teat played from memory Moskowski's ''Valse Brilliante.'' She afterwards was highly complimented by Vice-President Roosevelt. Mrs. Teat is happily married and has one son. She and her husband own a beautiful home, a modern cement house which sets in a plot of land of several acres planted in fruit trees, both deciduous and citrus, and also English walnuts and beautiful flowers. She has a large class in Pasadena and in Los Angeles, taking an active part in both church and club work, and is generally liked and is noted for her hospitality.

There are many persons who have developed great musical talent through inspiration. The following sketches will give the reader the value to children of parents who have a highly cultivated talent for music and the classics. This value is only estimated for good and lasting results if the parents are constant companions of their children. Too often parents withhold from their children the priceless boon of their companionship and expect the children to develop because of their inheritance in some particular art. This has not been the case with Mr. and Mrs. Malcolm Patton.

Mr. and Mrs. Malcolm Patton, formerly of Chicago, now of Los Angeles, California, are the parents of Juanita and Malcolm Patton. The father, Mr. Malcolm-Patton, was formerly a baritone singer of note and also an actor, having a strong voice previous to having it trained. He received his musical training at the Kimball Conservatory of Music and the Chicago Conservatory, both of Chicago, Illinois. The latter institution, with its reputation for correct placing and developing the voice, was the means of giving Mr. Patton a voice of artistic finish. He traveled for a while as a professional singer with several companies and quartets, and, while successful, after meeting Miss Alice Harvey, of Chicago, decided to marry. Mr. Patton selected for his life partner a lady of equally good musical ability whose education thoroughly fitted her for the

DR. JOHN S. OUTLAW
Physician and Surgeon.

DR. ALVA C. GARROTT
Dentist.

S. P. JOHNSON
Undertaker.

DR. HENRY W. BROWNING
First Lieut. Dental Reserve Corps,
National Army.

DR. WILBUR CLARENCE GORDON

DR. JOSEPH BALL

DR. JOHN ALEXANDER
SOMMERVILLE
Dentist.

DR. VADA SOMMERVILLE
Dentist.

mother of his children. This union was richly blessed by the birth of two children whose sketches will follow.

There are many children who acquire distinction in music among their own race, but it requires a real "Trail Blazer" to win distinction in both races. This is especially true in the public schools of California, where they have to compete with so much fine white talent. These musical sketches will plainly show to the reader the great blessing to a child of having parents who are both of such a strong type of what an educated and cultured parent should be that they reflect in their children the finished artist through constant and careful companionship and home training.

These children, Juanita and Malcolm Patton, began their musical careers at the age of four and six years of age. At a very tender age they made a public appearance on the theatrical stage, rendering a whole program. After entering the public schools they steadily advanced. Their ability was recognized by their teachers, notwithstanding colored children were not accustomed to appearing in festivities in music with their classes. The Patton children not only appeared with their classes but were always favorably mentioned in the weekly school paper.

Juanita began her career at the age of four and a half years, and from the beginning she had a strong, rich soprano voice. At the age of eight she could render the most difficult pieces, classical, religious or popular, with perfect ease and technique. She graduated from the Fourteenth Street Intermediate High School of Los Angeles and then from the Manual Arts High School, graduating with the class of the summer of 1917, at which time she was assigned a part in the play "Representatives of Nations" (white). The Manual Arts Weekly said: "Among the rich, melodious voices heard on the Manual Arts stage, Juanita Patton's voice can be classed as one of the finest, and those who had the joy of hearing her declared Miss Patton's singing exceptional." This quotation can perhaps be better appreciated when it is known that the stage in the Manual Arts school is one of the largest stages of any public school west of Chicago, and the auditorium in proportion.

The Patton children have been taught by their parents to give their best to the race for its pleasure and appreciation. Hence they have repeatedly appeared on the program of various organizations for charitable benefits of worthy causes. Miss Juanita was the youngest soloist in the rendition of "Fifty Years of Freedom," given for the benefit of the Young Men's Christian Association during the summer of 1915. Her voice, which is a strong, sweet lyric soprano, filled the immense Shrine Auditorium. She plays the piano and is fluent in both speaking and translating the Spanish language.

Dr. Wilber Clarence Gordon trained over one hundred voices to render "Hiawatha's Wedding Feast" for the benefit of the Old Folks' Home. It was rendered in the Trinity Auditorium September 5, 1916. Professor Jackson, superintendent of music in Quindara University, Kansas City, coming to Los Angeles to conduct the production. Malcolm Patton had been given the part of "Pau-pau-kee-wes," which is the most difficult and the leading role in "Hiawatha." After the concert, in commenting upon the singers, Professor Jackson said he had never witnessed a finer interpretation of the character than was given by Malcolm Patton. The city and race papers all spoke in the highest praise of his dancing, pronouncing it wonderful for a child.

Both the Patton children have graduated from the Fourteenth Street Intermediate High School of Los Angeles. When Malcolm Patton graduated he was on the editorial staff of the school magazine, The Blue and the Gold. He was assigned the class oration on the "History of Music." The principal of the school was asked to say a word in regard to the Patton children. The letter arrived after he had gone to attend a convention of the California Superintendents of the Public Schools at Riverside. Notwithstanding he held an important position in the convention, he found time to send the following letter to the Patton children for this book:

"Glenwood Mission Inn, Riverside, California, December 30, 1916.

"To Whom It May Concern: I take great pleasure in stating that Miss Juanita Patton and her brother, Malcolm, completed their work in the Fourteenth Street Intermediate school some two years ago. Both were eminently satisfactory students, and in addition showed marked musical ability, their services in this line were much appreciated by the school and community. Their voices showed the results of careful training and their numbers were always of a high order. It is to be hoped that they continue their musical work, both vocal and instrumental, and develop their talent to its fullest extent.

"(Signed) FRANK BOUELLA,

"Principal Fourteenth Street Intermediate School of Los Angeles, California."

Since the receipt of this letter Miss Juanita has graduated from the Manual Arts High School of Los Angeles. Malcolm has graduated from the Los Angeles High School in the winter class of February, 1919. During his many years attending the school he has won many honors for himself and the school. The most prominent of which is that he is the only Negro boy who is a member of the First Battalion Cadets of the school. He is a member of the High School Choral Club and assists the Glee Club on special occasions. He is a violinist in the High School Senior Orchestra. During the month of April, 1918, the combined choral and glee clubs, together with the Senior Orchestra, rendered in the high school auditorium the beautiful cantata of "Joan of Arc," by Gaul. The honor of singing the principal baritone solo was given to Malcolm Patton. The school paper, *The Blue and White*, in commenting on the rendition, said: "The entire composition was an ideal musical and educational event. It was presented with the same artistry which characterized all other concerts given by the two musical clubs. "The Ring Song," the vocal solo by Malcolm Patton, and the intermezzo by the orchestra were particularly effective." Malcolm Patton upon this occasion was accompanied by a thirty-one piece orchestra and an Italian harpist. His piece was Recitative and Aria. The successful rendition of the cantata was the means of an invitation from the Young Women's Christian Association deciding to invite the school to repeat it for their "Allied Market Day." One of the daily papers in speaking of the affair said: "The Third Allied Market Day of the Y. W. C. A. is being held today with an impressive program. It is designated as 'Lily of France Day' and the French atmosphere was intensified with an elaborate production of Gaul's cantata 'Joan of Arc,' produced by the music department of the Los Angeles High School." Among the names of the soloists appeared the name of Malcolm Patton. The race people of Los Angeles are especially proud of the Patton children in that they have been "Trail Blazers" in opening a door for the recognition of Negro children and their talent in the musical activities of the public schools of Southern California. It is a great advantage to a child to be given any prominence in these magnificent schools with so much fine talent to compete with and the prejudice which usually is ready to crush the ambition of aspiring Negroes everywhere. The *California Eagle*, a race paper, in commenting upon the solo by Malcolm Patton, in the cantata of "Joan of Arc," said: "Upon this occasion, as upon others when he appeared in this connection, he did honor to his school, parentage and the race."

The greatest work in the musical feature has been rendered by these children outside of the school room. They have made many public appearances before white churches and organizations. While singing for the Stanton Post, G. A. R. (white) they appeared on a program of artists at Sawtelle, California, the home for soldiers. On this occasion there was an audience of hundreds of old soldiers and several distinguished army officers on a tour of inspection from Washington, D. C. At this time and on another similar they were repeatedly encored and received a military salute. The race is looking forward to greater achivements by the Patton children in the musical world, especially if they have blazed a trail and lowered the bars of prejudice in competing with white school children. These children have been trained only by their mother.

Mrs. Bessie William-Dones, the subject of this sketch, is a native of Atlanta, Georgia. Coming to California with her parents at the age of five years, she attended the public schools of Riverside until graduating from the grammar school, when the family moved to Los Angeles and she entered the Los Angeles high school. During her attendance at the high school she was given instruction on the violin by Professor Meine, who, after two years of training, wrote a very commendable letter concerning Miss Williams' future outlook as a violinist.

After that period Miss Williams studied under the well-known instructor of the violin, Professor J. Clarence Cook, of Los Angeles Conservatory of Music, after which she traveled throughout the Middle West, giving recitals which were very successful. She later accepted a position as instructor of the violin in the Wilkins' School of Music in Los Angeles. She has the honor of giving the first instruction to the promising violin artist, Owen Troy, whose sketch will follow. Miss Williams, in 1913, became the wife of Mr. Sidney P. Dones, who is a successful real estate dealer in Los Angeles. The union has been blessed by the birth of one daughter, Sidnetta.

Master Owen Austin Troy, a native son, having been born in Los Angeles, is the son of Theodore Troy, formerly of Cincinnati, Ohio. He has been educated exclusively in the Seventh Day Adventist schools of this State. He graduated from the Academy of San Fernando, and also from the conservatory of music connected with the school, receiving a diploma from the music department covering theory, harmony and the history of music.

Master Owen Troy began his musical training on the violin with Mrs. Dones for two years, after which he was so advanced that he was immediately accepted as a pupil by the celebrated instructor, Professor Oskar Seiling. At this writing he is a student at the Pacific Union College located at Saint Helena, California, where he is studying to become an evangelist in the Seventh Day Adventist Church.

Leviticus Nelson Everell Lyon, the subject of this sketch, was born in San Francisco in May, 1894. He was educated in the public schools of Oakland, after which he took a course in general history and economics at the University of California in Berkeley. It was while attending the university that he discovered that he had talent for music, immediately placing himself for voice culture under the instruction of Miss Katherine Urner and Dr. George Bowdin, of the University of California. The last named was a former professor from London, England.

Mr. Lyon also decided to study the piano under Professor Emile Stinegger, a former pupil of Leschetizky. He also studied the piano under Mr. Guyla Ormay. His many years of training under these excellent musicians has produced in this young man a wonderful voice of real lyric tenor. The public some day will hear from him as one of the greatest Negro men-singers in America, because he has trained and fully prepared himself to fill the role of an artist, having mastered five languages.

The opportunity of living near the University of California and San Francisco has given him many advantages, which are seen in his repertoire covering the Italian, French, German and English schools. He specializes in sustained singing and particularizes in music of the ''Italian seventeenth century.'' This young man actually has a voice that can with credit be called a lyric tenor. The writer was charmed with his wonderful rendition of some old Italian ballads at a musical recently held in Oakland. She also attended a winter course of musical lectures by Professor Clarence Eddy on the pipe organ, and noted this young man's careful and critical attention at every lecture, and eventually located him, securing the material for his sketch. She hopes that he will favor the public ere long with a tour, that all may know of this California native son musician with the rich lyric tenor voice.

Soon after the above was penned and mailed to Mr. Lyon for criticism he was solicited by some friend to appear in a song recital at the Knights of Columbus Hall in Oakland. The following appeared in the *Oakland Bulletin* of April 17, 1918: ''Customs Employee in Singer's Role. An elevator operator with ambitions to become a concert singer has been discovered in the employ of Uncle Sam at the custom house in San Francisco. He is Leviticus N. E. Lyon, a Negro twenty-three years old, with a lyric tenor voice which he has cultivated in the face of many obstacles. He will make his first appearance with a program of his own at the Knights of Columbus Hall, in Oakland, on Saturday evening, April 27, 1918. His recital will be one of classic songs calculated to test his knowledge of the world's best music.'' Later, white friends of San Francisco to the number of forty, signed their names to buy tickets if he would give a recital in San Francisco, which he did in May at the Yosemite Hall, Native Sons of the Golden West Building, San Francisco. The *Oakland Sunshine*, in speaking of this concert, said: ''Mr. Leviticus N. E. Lyon's recital was given in San Francisco on Tuesday night. We went across the bay to attend the recital given by Mr. Lyon, assisted by Messrs. Walter Dyett, violinist, and Merrill Brown, accompanist. * * * On reaching the hall we found a pleasing audience sitting spellbound as these young men gave number after number from the fifteenth, sixteenth and seventeenth centuries.

''Their rendition was superb and the time sped by as in dreamland when the angels have sung a lullaby. Mr. Lyon has undoubtedly a future full of promise. We can say of a truth that all three of these young men, if they continue, will write their names among the stars and the world will lie at their feet. We shall do all we can to encourage them.'' The Hon. Oswald Garrison Villard has arranged to pay for the singer's training in New York City. He has accepted the honor and is now in the Eastern city studying.

There are many promising young persons in California who are preparing themselves for a musical career. Among this number the writer has discovered the following young man in Los Angeles: Mr. John A. Gray, who is the organist at the St. Phillips Episcopalian parish of that city. This gentleman was born in Norfolk, Virginia, in 1889. His father gave him his first lessons on the piano. These lessons were supplemented with a few by mediocre teachers until the death of his father in 1902. Since then he has been shifting for himself, coming to Los Angeles about nine years ago, during which time he has worked by day and attended night school, thereby earning his living. He has studied the piano, pipe organ, harmony, and counterpoint, also composition. He has also learned to read and write French, and is studying Spanish and Italian. He expects to master five different languages at least. His ambition is to become a teacher and composer, and he is fitting himself for a musical career. He is sincere and is willing to work for success. Mr. Gray served in the world war, winning a commission and distinction in the National Army.

The writer considers that too much attention cannot be given to teachers of beginners, because a musical career can be made or spoiled by a bad teacher. The subject of this sketch, Mrs. Pinkie Callender-Howard, is the descendant of a pioneer family of San Francisco, and has been thoroughly trained for a teacher of beginners. She was the first colored student who attended and won honors at the Lada Conservatory of Music, in San Francisco. She was considered the best sight reader in her class.

She has been before the public for years and has performed before large audiences of both races, displaying a thorough artistic education in music. She has given special attention to beginners and has been a successful teacher. Her success has been remarkable owing to special attention and good humor. At her last recital given in Oakland, her juvenile class showed wonderful training and played with exactness. The advanced pupils displayed great technic and great rapidity. She is very grateful for her musical education to her parents, Mr. and Mrs. John T. Callender, pioneers of San Francisco.

California has many persons of color living in the State who, while they may not be classed as Trail Blazers, nevertheless have lives filled with so much of interest that the writer has deemed it of value to give a sketch of at least one who, during the past few years, has been located in Los Angeles. This refers to Rev. Charles Price Jones, who has wonderful ability to write Gospel songs.

Dr. Jones was born December 9, 1865, in North Georgia and reared principally about Kingston. He was the son of Mary Jones-Latimer. She was a slave of William Jones, of Floyd County, Georgia, and was a God-fearing woman who prayed fervently for the salvation of the soul of her son and Divine guidance through life. Dr. Jones believes that God has so wonderfully blessed him in answer to her sincere prayers. The son of this slave woman was taught by his mother to be mannerly to all, which won him friends, among whom was a young man, a student from Talledgea College, named J. E. Bush, who gave him some school advantages.

Later he went to night school. Shortly afterwards his mother died. This caused the lad to shift for himself, which he did with success. He went to Chattanooga, Tennessee, where he found employment, and later to Arkansas, and thence to Cat Island, Arkansas, where he picked cotton. At this he was above the average; he believed in excellency in whatever he attempted to do.

While young Jones was on "Cat Island" he was converted, in October, 1884, and on the first Sunday in May, 1885, he joined Locust Grove Baptist Church on "Cat Island" and was baptized by Elder J. D. Petty. In the fall of the same year he went to preach the gospel of Christ. An impression now came upon Brother Jones to go to Africa and teach the Africans the way to God. He went to Helena, Arkansas, for counsel of Elder E. C. Mooris, whose counsel was that Brother Jones should first go to school. Accordingly Brother Jones went to Little Rock, January 3, 1888, and entered the Arkansas Baptist College. He worked his way most of the time. In the summer of that year he taught school in Grant County and paid back aid kindly received from Professor Joseph A. Booker, the president of the college.

Later he was ordained at Mt. Zion Baptist Church by Elder C. L. Fisher, D. D., and a committee of reputable men, white and colored. He soon became prominent and was elected corresponding secretary of the Baptist college from which he graduated in 1891. There was much talk of his candidacy for president of the Arkansas Baptist State Convention. He was elected editor of the *Baptist Vanguard*, the college and State organ.

Dr. Jones has held charges in some of the largest Baptist churches in the South. He has aimed to lead his people to a higher plane of living and in an effort to do this he conducted a publishing house and published a religious magazine called *Truth*. His plant was located at 329 East Monument street, Jackson, Mississippi. He was later burned out by a mob.

Dr. Jones believes in prayer, and it was through long prayer and fasting that he was blessed by the power of the Holy Ghost to write songs. It is most interesting to hear him tell of the outpouring of the Holy Ghost upon him. He first wrote songs without music, and then both words and music. His songs are sung throughout the civilized world. He has written and published five Gospel hymn books and a book of poems. His first song book was "One Hundred Hymns" (words only); his next book, "Select Songs," "Jesus Only" (words and music); "The Harvest Is Past," "O Israel, Return Unto the Lord," "Stretch Out Your Hands to God," "Deeper, Deeper," and many others.

Dr. Jones does considerable evangelical work, and always conducts the singing. This blessing of the gift to write songs led him to seek more spiritual uplift and finally led to his reaching a higher plane of service to God, which has been named ''The Holiness Body of Worshippers.'' ''In June, 1897, according to the leading of the Lord, the pastor called the first Holiness meeting in Jackson, Mississippi. This proved to be the most wonderful meeting in the Spirit hitherto held among the ministers and laymen in this section of the country. * * * And then after that the annual Holiness meeting at Jackson, Mississippi, and in many other places among the saints became an important part of the work among the saints.'' This meeting has grown until at this writing there is quite a demonination of churches that has grown out of this higher life ministry headquarters at Jackson, Mississippi.

Dr. Charles Price Jones came to Los Angeles to escape overwork. He is now overseer of Church of Christ and was given the honorary title of doctor of divinity by the Baptist College at Little Rock. He is at present associate editor of the *Citizen Advocate* of Los Angeles.

Rev. Jones is not the only song-writer among the race people living in Los Angeles. He will have to share the honors with the gifted and very talented daughters of Rev. Frowd. This gentleman needs no introduction to the average reader, for he is considered one of the best, if not the best, educated Negro Baptist minister in America. He has given to his daughters the best education possible, especially in music and languages, French and Spanish. Miss Lillian, the youngest daughter, is a writer of poetry and has written the words to many songs which her sister, Miss Ellen Consuello Prowd has set to music. These songs are popular and have met with ready sale. Their father, Rev. Prowd, is pastor of the Second Baptist Church of Los Angeles.

Professor W. T. Wilkins, of Los Angeles, has written several instrumental pieces which have merit, among them being ''The Path of Destiny.''

Mrs. Pearl Lowery-Winters, the subject of this sketch, is one of Los Angeles' favorite daughters. She has a voice and winsome disposition second to none. The following is quoted from the *California Eagle:* ''While touring the State and singing before some of the largest obtainable audiences in many of the white churches and high schools, Mrs. Winters was very favorably criticized by the Women's Harmony Club, of Bakersfield. The *Oakland Sunshine* and Rev. Coleman of the North Oakland Baptist Church presented Mrs. Winters but a few months past and were so highly pleased with her ability that they strongly recommended her to other audiences.''

''In 1912, while touring the East, Mrs. Winters sang in Convention Hall, Kansas City, Kansas, before twenty-five thousand persons, where she was loudly applauded, and before the National Federated Colored Women's Clubs at Hampton, Virginia, where she received the plaudits of Booker T. Washington, Mrs. Washington, Major Moton and Miss Armstrong. Other persons of note and musical ability who favorably criticized Mrs. Winters as an artist of ability are the following, whose criticisms we print in part:

'' 'My friend, Mrs. Lowery-Winters, has a rich contralto voice with organ-like depth which surpasses any other contralto of her race.'—Mme. Florence Cole-Talbert.

'' 'Mrs. Winters possesses one of the most beautiful natural contralto voices I have ever heard and is an artist of rare ability.'—F. Constantino (world's greatest tenor).

'' 'Mrs. Winter's voice as a contralto has sweetness, soul and power.'—Professor A. G. Jackson, Western University.

'' 'Having been a teacher of Mrs. Winters for three years, I find that she possesses one of the most beautiful natural contralto voices I have ever heard.'—Professor Wm. Jas. Clark.

'' 'Mrs. Winters has one of the best contralto voices I have heard.'—William Marion Cook.

''We have watched this young woman for a number of years. We not only consider her the race's best contralto in the whole West, but one of the best in the country, and one of the most unselfish artists we have ever been privileged to meet.''—*California Eagle.*

Mrs. Pearl Lowery-Winters, of Bakersfield, has written both words and music of songs which she has published.

CHAPTER XVIII

DISTINGUISHED WOMEN

Mrs. Josephine Leavell-Allensworth is equally as much of a worker for the betterment of the race as was her husband, the late Lieutenant-Colonel Allensworth. She has a very fine education and in every sense of the word is a Christian gentlewoman. She practically reared her two daughters in the army, having spent nearly if not twenty-five years in the United States Army with her husband, during which time she lived at the different forts with their children.

While Colonel Allensworth was serving in the capacity of chaplain, Mrs. Allensworth resumed the responsibility of furnishing amusement for the men and their wives. This would be an easy task were it not for the fact that the majority of the forts are located away from any large city. Nevertheless Mrs. Allensworth furnished the soldiers and their wives with good, wholesome and instructive amusement. Her faithfulness won a place in their hearts never to be effaced. Their confidence in Mrs. Allensworth was demonstrated when Colonel Allensworth and the Twenty-fourth Infantry were in the Philippine Islands. The wives of the soldiers made her their treasurer, and she received their moneys from their husbands, distributing the same to the proper persons. This money, on every pay day, amounted to thousands of dollars. She was always showing them acts of kindness. Neither did they forget her, for when Colonel Allensworth was retired and the Twenty-fourth Infantry returned from the Philippine Islands, the soldiers and their wives presented Mrs. Allensworth and her daughters with a handsome carved silver tray and candelabra.

After the plotting of the townsite of Allensworth, Mrs. Allensworth began the study as to what she could do to benefit the community. She was instrumental in organizing a Women's Improvement Club. This club was instrumental in establishing a children's playground and many other improvements for the town of Allensworth. When a new school house was erected, the old building was donated to Mrs. Allensworth, and she purchased the ground upon which it now stands, had it remodeled and fitted out for a public reading room. Later she solicited the Rural Free Circulating library, to furnish them books. Colonel Allensworth and many others, including the writer, gave many books. The custodian of the free reading room is a colored girl who is paid by the County. Mrs. Allensworth has named the reading room a memorial library in honor of her mother, Mary Dickson. Mrs. Allensworth is president of the school board, and spends a portion of the year in Allensworth doing whatever she can for the betterment of the race and community.

Mrs. Allensworth is a sincere club worker, but the greatest work she has ever done was when she reared, with all the simplicity of greatness, two daughters who reflect, with credit, the strong personality of herself and husband. The writer refers to Mrs. Harrie Skanks and Mrs. L. M. Blodgett, who were the Misses Eva and Nella Allensworth. They are thoroughly educated and are genuine gentlewomen of the old school of aristocracy, and have children whom they are rearing in the same delightful manner.

Mrs. John M. Scott, the subject of this sketch, was reared and educated in Atlanta, Georgia. During her school days she took an active part in church work. She was married at an early age to Mr. John M. Scott, who at the time was one of the leading successful oil dealers of Atlanta. After a few years of married life Mr. Scott, wishing to advance in business, answered to the "Call of the West" and he and his wife moved to Los Angeles, California, where he entered the business world by building the first hall for fraternal meetings in the State. It is still in use and is known as the "Scott Hall," located at 561 Central avenue. This hall was used by all of the race organizations in the City of Los Angeles until the erection several years later of the Odd Fellows Hall.

Mr. Scott for years has held the responsible position as mail clerk for the Santa Fe railroad division stationed in Los Angeles, having his own offices and handling thousands of pieces of mail daily. Through his decision to make Los Angeles his home the State and city have been richly benefited through the activities of his wife, who is untiring in her efforts to advance her race on a higher plane of living. This has been especially noticeable after she accepted the honor of an election to the presidency of the Sojourner Truth Club, of Los Angeles. The object of this club was to, at some future date, build a home for self-sustaining women. Mrs. Scott realized that such an undertaking, while noble in its purpose, could only be successfully done by beginning the work properly. Since much would depend upon her as president of the club to guide the ship through the journey, she decided to fully prepare herself by studying the work in other organizations. To do this she made a trip east, going directly to New York, where she registered at the ''White Rose Mission,'' stopping as any other traveler and stranger in the City of New York. This gave her a splendid opportunity to study the workings and the value to the community of such an institution.

En route back to her home, she stopped in Philadelphia and Chicago, visiting in these cities similar institutions for self-supporting women. Returning to Los Angeles, Mrs. Scott was so filled with enthusiasm as to her trip of investigation and study of institutions, it was not long before the club was convinced of the immediate need of such an institution in the City of the Angels.

This resulted in launching a campaign for funds which was very successful in raising $11,000, which enabled them to make their first payment on a lot. At the expiration of her term of office Mrs. Scott positively refused to accept the office of president, but the succeeding year she was again elected as president. She then immediately launched another campaign for funds which was a success to that extent the club completed paying for a lot costing $2,750. At the next election she began months in advance to state that she positively would not be a candidate for re-election. To show how the club appreciated her services, when the day arrived for election of officers, the following newspaper clipping will more fully explain. It is headed ''Sojourner Truth Club Election'':

'' 'Hoop-a-la, Hoop-a-la!
Who are we?
We are the members of the S. T. C.
Do we want a new president?
We do—not! Scott, Scott, Scott!
Hoop-a-la, Hoop-a-la! Scott, Scott!'

''With this yell, led by little Honore Moxley, Mrs. Scott was overwhelmingly re-elected president of the Sojourner Truth Club. This spirit of unity also elected the same day a splendid set of officers who, like the president, would support and work for success; it is well to give their names: President, Mrs. J. M. Scott; vice-president, Mrs. Offut; second vice-president, Mrs. M. Bates; Mrs. Ada Jackson, secretary; Mrs. Mary Smith, corresponding secretary; Mrs. Bernice Alexander, treasurer; Mrs. Lucy Carter, chaplain, and Mrs. Mary Hicks, pianist; executive board, Mesdames Shackelford, Moxley, Young, Campbell, Pool and B. L. Turner.''

With such a splendid set of officers and through the co-operation of the citizens and friends of Los Angeles, the club during that year built a clubhouse costing $5,200, consisting of nine bedrooms, two bathrooms, kitchen, dining-room, reception hall and library.

The appreciation of the citizens and friends of the building of this clubhouse for self-sustaining women was shown by their furnishing it throughout without cost to the club with new and substantial furnishings.

It must not be forgotten that no one showed their appreciation for the home more than the Negro press of the State, and their space was liberally used at all times for the good of the cause, as the following will show. When the club decided that they were about ready to build, one of the race papers in Los Angeles had the following to say: ''Few organizations have thrived as has the Sojourner Truth Club under the leadership of its present president, Mrs. J. M. Scott, and her noble corps of followers. When taking into consideration the fact that Mrs. Scott has marshaled the reins as president during the uncertain financial period, it is commendable. Her success has been such that the members have been steadily climbing from one summit to another in order to keep pace with her advanced ideas. The real work and what it means to the cause of noble womanhood has been the incentive, jealously guarded inspiration causing unceasing effort on the part of the members'' Another race journal said: ''The Sojourner Truth Club is forging to the front. The advisory board met last Monday night to discuss matters of importance. The society's financial affairs having increased so rapidly under the present president, Mrs. J. M. Scott, that an early investment for a home-site is anticipated.''

After the clubhouse was built and furnished and the club had taken full possession in May, Mrs. Scott's term of office expiring in June, she would not accept the office again. During the following three years the office was filled by three different members of her grand working board, namely, Mesdames Offut, Jackson and Campbell.

After having been retired for three years Fate decreed that Mrs. Scott should again be elected president, and the ''Star of Hope'' that had led her on in previous administrations brought the club to the realization of the cancellation of all indebtedness and a balance for future work. The club has always appreciated the sincere and valuable services given by Mrs. Scott. They tried to show a part of that appreciation at the burning of the mortgage on the lot, at which time one of the race papers said: ''Club presented to the president, Mrs. J. M. Scott, a beautiful diamond brooch; upon a plain but beautiful background rested a wreath of Victory composed of forget-me-nots. In the center glittered a beautiful diamond. Above the diamond was the year 1912; around the diamond were the initials 'S. T. C.' ''

Mrs. Scott, having seen the clubhouse built and paid for, has been able to give some of her time to other interests of equal value to the race such as being a member of the executive board of the local branch of the National Association for the Advancement of Colored People, and the Soldiers' and Sailors' Welfare Commission, which is doing a wonderful work in looking after the interests of the families of soldiers now fighting in France. Would that the race had many such grand, noble and self-sacrificing women as the subject of this sketch!

Mrs. Archie H. Wall is one of the most active workers in the California Federated Colored Women's Clubs. She has been elected for seven years as state treasurer. She is president of the city and district work of the Orphanage. Aside from that, she has been active along other lines in organizing the Spanish-American War Auxiliary, and at present holds the office of president in the organization. She was instrumental in organizing the King's Daughters' Circle, State vice-president of the S. M. T. and president of the Art and Iudustrial Club of Oakland, California.

Mrs. Wall is best known by her enthusiasm and work in building the Orphanage in Oakland. When the California Colored Women's Federated Clubs decided to federate, they also determined to do some monumental work of interest to the race, in both the northern part of the State and also the southern. The Sojourner Truth Home clubhouse was the work selected for the southern part of the State to assist in accomplishing. The northern part was undecided for years until enthused by Mrs. Wall, who worked long and untiringly with an uphill pull until she finally accomplished the desired result, which will ever stand as a great monument to her efforts.

Mrs. Hettie Blonde Tilghman is a native daughter, having been born in San Francisco, and is the daughter of the deceased and distinguished pioneers in the persons of Captain and Mrs. Rebecca Jones. She was their third daughter and was educated in the schools of San Francisco, living in that city until about fourteen years old, when her family moved to Oakland. She married in 1890 Mr. Charles F. Tilghman, the son of a California pioneer, Mr. Robert Tilghman, who came to the State in 1850. At the time of Mrs. Tilghman's marriage she was both secretary and organist of the Bethel A. M. E. Church Sunday school of San Francisco. She also taught a private school for Chinese boys, having been given permission by her mother to conduct the school in their home. She taught these Chinese students the English branches and language.

The union of Mr. and Mrs. Charles Tilghman has been blessed by the birth of a son and daughter; after which Mrs. Tilghman retired from active church and club life until the children were quite advanced in life, preferring to consider them as a gift from God which should receive the undivided attention of their mother. After they were advanced in school she became active in the club, church and lodges, as the following record will show, making up for lost time in her intense work to aid and build up a good, wholesome club life in which the community would be benefited.

Her first active club work was with the Fanny Coppin Club, and from that to an active worker in the Federated Clubs of the State, having served faithfully and conscientiously as an executive officer and assistant editress for two club journals, corresponding secretary, and also recording secretary of the State. At the present writing she is State president of the Federated Clubs of Colored Women in California. She is an untiring worker in the northern section of the State Federated Clubs' efforts to build and establish an orphanage.

The persons who have the pleasure of knowing Mrs. Tilghman admire her the most in the successful rearing and educating of two lovely children, Miss Hilda, who graduated from the Oakland Commercial high school with honors, having made a record ''A 1'' in stenography and bookkeeping; Charies (junior), who has graduated from the Oakland high school at an unusually young age, and before he was sixteen published and set his own type for a Directory of Distinguished Colored Residents of Oakland. He since has been called to the colors. It is sincerely hoped that because of the excellent work Mrs. Tilghman has done in rearing her own children she will be one of the board of directors for the Orphanage in Oakland.

The writer especially admires Mrs. Tilghman for the unselfish work she did in visiting all the exemption boards during the first draft for the National Army. During this time Mrs. Tilghman visited these boards, thereby securing the names of all the Negro boys who were drafted in the Bay Cities. After learning their addresses, she presented them to the executive board of the Northern California branch of the National Association for the Advancement of Colored People, who immediately called a public meeting and invited the public to a reception for the "First Liberty Boys," the like of which has never been equaled in Oakland. It was Mrs. Tilghman who afterward urged the club women of the State to send these boys a Christmas box of good cheer. The box was sent in the name of the Federation of Colored Women's Clubs. Mrs. Tilghman is very intense and an untiring worker in anything she undertakes.

Mrs. Eva Carter-Buckner, the subject of this sketch, was born in Washington, Iowa, and, when quite young, her parents moved to Des Moines, Iowa, and from thence to Colorado Springs, Colorado, where their daughter was educated in the public schools. It was while living in this city that the subject of our sketch won first prize in a contest instituted by the wife of the mayor of the city, a Mrs. J. D. Robinson. This contest was presented to the Paul Lawrence Dunbar Reading Class of Colorado Springs, of which Mrs. Buckner was a member. The lady instituting the contest selected for her judges prominent white persons. When the poems were presented to these judges, who were recognized as able literary critics, and their decision read, it was found that Mrs. Eva Carter-Buckner had won first prize. This decision rendered by judges of known ability immediately established Mrs. Eva Carter-Buckner's place as a writer of verse. Previous to this she had contributed verse to the papers.

Mrs. Eva Carter-Buckner has had the distinction of having her verse appear in such well-known and widely read papers as the *Denver Post, The Colorado Springs Sun* and the *Western Enterprise*. When she lived in New Mexico she was honored by having her poems appear in the *American* and *New Age*, papers published there. Since moving to California she has published poems in many of the race papers, especially the *California Eagle, New Age* and the *Advocate*. Among the white papers, *The Daily Tribune*, one of the largest white papers published in Los Angeles.

The greatest honor coming to Mrs. Eva Carter-Buckner was when some of her poems appeared in a book called "Gems of Poesy," a book of short poems by American authors. Mrs. Buckner is best known by her inspiring club songs, among which is the "Colorado and California State Federation" songs for Colored Women's clubs. She has written many interesting short stories and articles for the press. Her poems are soul inspiring appeals for the uplift and a square deal for the Negro race. She is sincere and quick to the defense of the Negro, as will be seen from her poem, "What Constitutes a Negro?" This poem was inspired in defense of Joe Gans, the prize fighter, when a white writer had published a poem in which he attempted to prove that Gans was not a Negro. The white papers refused to publish Mrs. Buckner's poem, but the *California Eagle* published it in full.

Mrs. Buckner has given much time to suffrage and the study of psychopathic and charity work. She is an artist of no mean ability, member of the local branch and a strong advocate of the National Association for the Advancement of Colored People. During the Morefield Story drive for new members, she secured a very large number of new members and penned a beautiful poem which she dedicated to Dr. Dubois. Mrs. Buckner is beloved by all who know her, and has a pleasing and winsome personality. Would that the world had a few more such women with such sterling character!

Mrs. Elizabeth Brown, the subject of this sketch, the daughter of John Glasgow and Jane Ferguson, was born in Sedalia, Missouri, where she lived until three years old. The family then moved to Kansas City, where their daughter was placed in the colored public school, which she attended until made an orphan at the age of fourteen years. She was self-supporting until she married Mr. John Brown at Fort Robinson, Nebraska, Chaplain Prioleau of the Ninth Cavalry performing the ceremony. When the Spanish-American War was declared her husband was given a commission in the Ninth Immunes as second lieutenant. When he left to participate in the Cuban campaign his bride, Mrs. Elizabeth Brown, remained with his relatives in Washington, D. C., until his return. She went to Fort Grant, Arizona, and then later, when the Philippine insurrection began, her husband was given a commission in the Forty-eighth Infantry Volunteers, a regiment of colored soldiers. While the regiment was preparing to be mustered into the United States service, Mrs. Brown joined her husband at Fort Thomas, Kentucky, and came across the continent with the regiment, which sailed from San Francisco, California, to the Philippine Islands.

While in California she visited Oakland and decided it would be a good place to buy a home. She purchased an elegant home on Thirty-fourth street. She immediately became an active worker in every movement for the betterment of mankind and the uplift of the race, in church, lodge and club work. She is a member of the Eastern Star, and has the honor of being the past grand matron of the jurisdiction of California. At the present writing she is grand treasurer, having served the office for the past eight years. She is also a member of the Household of Ruth, past most noble governess, 458, of Oakland; past daughter, Ruler of the Daughters of Elks of Mizpah Temple, and deputy of the State for five years; member of the Scottish Rite.

Mrs. Elizabeth Brown is a great club worker, as the following with show: She has served in every capacity of the California State Federated Colored Women's Clubs; as their second, first vice-president, and has the honor of being past president of the Federation and the sixth honorary president.

The honor of establishing the northern section for children's home-work must be given to this lady, who conscientiously worked for three years, which work has not yet reached its goal. Mrs. Brown is very proud of her work in the church, being a member and active worker of the Fifteenth Street A. M. E. Church, of Oakland; president of the Mite Missionary Society and vice-president of the Church Aid for years, during which time she has raised, through church fairs, hundreds of dollars to release the church mortgage. She is an active member of the Old Folks' Home board and a very much interested and active worker of the executive board of the Oakland branch of the National Association for the Advancement of Colored People. She is the mother of one daughter, Frances. It is hoped that she may grow to be as useful and distinguished as her mother and father.

Among the distinguished women of Los Angeles who have lived a life of service for humanity and the betterment of the Negro race stands out in bold relief the name of Mrs. Malcolm Patton (nee Alice Harvey), formerly of Chicago, Illinois. She has lived in Los Angeles, California, for over thirteen years. She is one of the best educated colored matrons in Los Angeles. Mrs. Malcolm H. Patton is one of the first colored graduates of the Chicago Normal schools, graduating with honors, and received a scholarship for special course in drawing at the Prang Institute of Boston, Massachusetts.

Mrs. Patton has the distinction of being the first and most efficient clerk of Provident Hospital, in Chicago, Illinois, having served as such for four years, during which time she was practically the superintendent. Her untiring efforts to place the institution on a firm foundation is a part of the history of Provident Hospital. The establishing of a hospital for the training of Negro nurses at the time was considered an experiment, hence the necessity for careful handling of both the management and the general public to instill confidence. While at Providence Hospital she attended the lectures and clinics in the institution, and also at the Northwestern Medical University, located in Chicago, Illinois.

Mrs. Alice Harvey-Patton's activities for the betterment of the race while a resident of Chicago were many. She was secretary of the Ida B. Wells Club, serving as such for many years. While a resident of Chicago she successfully passed two civil service examinations and was offered an appointment by the government, when she decided to marry.

Mrs. Alice Harvey-Patton, after her marriage, accepted the position as principal of the Normal department of Paul Quinn College, located at Waco, Texas. She also filled the chair of Geology in the college at the same time. While connected with the college she was appointed without an examination by the State Superintendent of schools of Texas, a Mr. James Carlisle, to do summer Normal institute work in Texas.

Since locating in Los Angeles she has been identified in active club work of the community, having served as president of the Sojourner Truth Club for self-supporting women. She was identified for eight years as the treasurer of the (white) Parent-Teacher's Association of the Fourteenth street intermediate school, and an active member of the (white) City and State Parent-Teacher's Association, thereby blazing a trail for the recognizing of the talent of colored school children.

Those who have the pleasure of knowing Mrs. Malcolm Patton in her home pronounce her truly a "queen of the home," as will be seen from the careful rearing of her own children as given in the music chapter, their sketches are a true tribute to the word "mother" and true womanhood. Mrs. Alice Harvey-Patton has filled these positions with honor and credit to the race, a pleasure to her immediate household and pleasing to Almighty God. Would that the race had many such women!

Mrs. Mary Sanderson-Grasses, the subject of this sketch, is one of the daughters of the late Rev. J. B. Sanderson, the pioneer minister of Oakland. She was the first colored public school teacher in Oakland, having taught a school in the part of the city which in pioneer days was known as Brooklyn, and at this writing is called East Oakland. The writer had the privilege of reviewing a program which was rendered by her class at Shattuck Hall, Oakland. It was quite evident that no little one was slighted. This same spirit still lingers with Mrs. Grasses, who is kind to everybody. None knew her but to love her.

Mrs. Grasses is active in church work, having sung in the choir of the Fifteenth Street Church (A. M. E.) for over thirty years. She has devoted many years of hard and unselfish work to maintaining the Home for Aged and Infirm Colored People. Few people ever realized how much she sacrificed to keep the home in the hands of the race. Recently she resigned from her position as vice-president and has given the work over to younger and we hope equally as self-sacrificing a body of women. Mrs. Grasses has one daughter, Miss Kate, to whom she gave the best education California afforded. She has traveled all over the United States as an elocutionist. At this writing she has the distinction of holding a position as the only colored woman clerk in the San Francisco postoffice.

Mrs. Kate Bradley-Stovall, founder and president emeritus of the Southern California Alumni Association, was an inspiration to the educational life of Southern California. A few years ago while the writer was making a trip over the State in quest of data for this book, she was greatly interested in a copy of the *Los Angeles Times* under date February 12, 1909, in which her attention was called to the eight pages devoted to the Negro in Los Angeles. Among these was a page edited by Mrs. Kate Bradley-Stovall. Unfortunately this dear one had just passed to the great beyond. Before the writer left Los Angeles she secured a copy of the *New Age* containing a complete account of her funeral, which we quote: "A most interesting obituary was read by Mrs. Thomas J. Nelson, president of the alumni. At Austin, Texas, on August 4, 1884, a little girl was born to Mr. and Mrs. Allan Bradley. Mr. Bradley was known to be one of the most prosperous business men of the community. This first little girl was named for a sister of Mr. Bradley's to whom he was much attached. Sister Kate grew up to be a great favorite of her aunt and, while quite young, came to Los Angeles to make her home with her. Carefully this aunt trained her for womanhood and with loving interest watched and encouraged the progress she made in her educational work. Upon her graduation, in 1903, from the Commercial high school, on account of her excellent record she was one of four chosen from her class to give orations. The commencement was commented upon in the *Los Angeles Times.* Among other things the paper said: 'Colored lass eloquent. Commercial high school's striking oration. It was a high compliment to Kate Bradley that she was chosen as one of the four orators to represent the graduating class of the Commercial high school, * * * and it was a distinguished honor the class conferred upon itself by its magnanimous action.

"'Kate Bradley in the execution of her trust did it with distinguished honor to herself and the class. She is a tall, lithe, good-featured colored girl; her oration was eloquent, concise and strong; and her topic, "The New South," was one that enlisted her sympathy and brought out the warmth of her nature toward her race, though no mention was made of any race.

"'Miss Bradley talked warmly of the progress in the South and its rapid strides toward a place of greater importance in the commercial world. "This progress," she said, "may be well termed wonderful, for it did not begin with the Constitution of the United States." This sentence brought the first applause and it was the nearest reference she made to the problem. Her summary of the industrial progress and coming commercial importance of the New South was worthy of a statesman, both in subject matter and manner of delivery.

"'Miss Bradley received no bouquets as she stepped back to her place, but the audience, perceiving the probable thoughtless omission, redoubled its applause, and no more fragrant nor complimentary bouquet could have been tendered her in the numberless masses of bouquets that banked the front of the stage. There no doubt were a goodly number for her as well as for the other graduates.'

"On November 1, 1904, Kate Bradley became the wife of William Stovall, a young man of excellent family and sterling worth, who has proven to the community his high qualities in the way in which he has stood up under the strain of illness and affliction. Two especially bright children, Wilalyn and Ursula, brightened the union of these young people. Mrs. Stovall became a factor in race progress in Los Angeles, being intensely interested in fraternal, religious and secular affairs.

"Her first thought was always toward the work of educational uplift among her people, and especially did she wish to inspire hope and enthusiasm in the minds of the young. Working on this line and acting upon the suggestion of her husband, she organized the Southern California Alumni Association, in 1909, and served that body as its very able president for four years, until forced by ill-health to resign. At the time of her death she was president emeritus of the organization and her thoughts and hopes were always for its progress.

"On August 5th, the morning after her thirtieth birthday her last sleep came to her. Though barely past her girlhood, her ambitious life has been so full of good and energetic purpose that her influence will ever remain, especially to the members of the Southern California Alumni Association to whom her life has meant much. This association passed beautiful resolutions of condolence and respect reflecting the great loss to the organization in the passing of their first president, Mrs. Kate Bradley-Stovall.''

Mrs. S. Wright, the subject of this sketch, came to California over thirty years ago, and has identified herself with every movement of interest to the race. She lives in Santa Monica, but takes an active part in fraternal organizations in Los Angeles. She was one of the charter members of the Ohio Club, president of Court of Calantha, S. M. T. worthy princess; most excellent queen of the Ancient Knights and Daughters of Africa; vice preceptress, Pride of Peace Tabernacle; a member of the Sojourner Truth Club, Day Nursery, and the Pioneer Club. She is a favorite and much beloved lady wherever she is known.

Mrs. Willa Stevens came to California in September, 1903, with her parents, Mr. and Mrs. George Rowland, from Georgia. Beginning a course in dressmaking when very young, she completed the course under one of the best modistes of the City of Los Angeles, after which she engaged in business for several years and made a phenomenal success, being the designer of some of the most gorgeous gowns worn by the elite of Los Angeles, planning throughout the most elaborate weddings of which the city can boast.

Mrs. Stevens has also finished the trades of millinery and tailoring. She is the wife of Detective Sergeant Stevens, and is at present the president of the Phy-Art-Lit-Mo. Club, which ranks as the leading culture club among colored women in Los Angeles. She is a member of the Eastern Star and Women's Day Nursery Association, and the Soldiers' and Sailors' Welfare Commission. She is active in all movements for the social and moral uplift of colored womanhood and the race in general.

Mrs. Mary I. Firmes, the subject of this sketch, is the wife of Captain Thomas A. Firmes and daughter of Elizabeth Wilson and the late J. B. Wilson of Oakland. Mrs. Firmes is a native daughter and a graduate of the Oakland high school. She is an expert stenographer, having been employed as stenographer by a large law firm in San Francisco for a number of years previous to her marriage.

When the government opened the Officers' Separate Training Camp at Des Moines, Iowa, Mrs. Firmes was the only colored girl employed as stenographer, the other two being white. While at the camp, Mrs. Firmes won the distinction of being the most proficient of the three stenographers. She is a devoted member of the St. Augustin Episcopalian Mission of Oakland.

The following is quoted from the *Western Outlook* and is a part of a very excellent letter that was written by Mrs. Sarah Severance, of San Jose, and published in the *San Jose Mercury* as a memorial on the death of Mrs. Overton, who was a distinguished citizen of that city and one of the distinguished women of the race in California. It said:

"August 24, 1914, passed to rest Sarah Massey Overton. She was born in Lenox, Massachusetts, in 1850, and, as a young girl, came to California with her family, living first in Gilroy and soon moving to San Jose. She was educated in the seminary of the Rev. P. T. Cassey, then located at Williams and Fourth streets. In 1869 she was married in Trinity Church to Jacob Overton, a native of Kentucky, who came to San Jose with Dr. Overton and for years was a trusted and highly esteemed employee of the Knox family.

"Both have filled a large place in the useful industries of San Jose. Mrs. Overton made a model home for her husband, her son, Charles, and daughter, Harriet. She was gifted in household arts, but she cared for all good things, such as peace and temperance. For years she was a member of the Political Equality Club of San Jose, and, in the campaign of 1911, at her own expense she went accredited by the club to several ities throughout the State to arouse the interest of the Afro-American voters, and doing more perhaps than any other member, as she was a good speaker.

"She was second vice-president of the San Jose Suffrage Amendment League. She was also president of the Victoria Earle Mathews Club, a branch of one founded in New York, designed to protect imperiled girls from those who prowl for their destruction, and she also worked to uplift Negro girls. When the Phoenixsonian Institute was planned, to give African children a chance for education, to be located where Christ Church now stands, Mrs. Overton canvassed California and Nevada with success, but probably through the sentiment she aroused, the California legislators passed a law giving the Negro children the right to attend the public schools, so the institution was not founded.

"Not only was our friend interested in public work, but she was a capable church member. The Rev. R. L. Mitchel wishes it recorded that she was an invaluable worker of that church, from which she was buried. The husband, daughter and son have our deepest sympathy, but this Christian woman liveth still; she has simply turned the corner a little ahead of us.''

Mrs. Julia A. Shorey, the wife of Captain Shorey, and mother of Miss Victoria, is a native daughter, coming from an old pioneer family. She is the daughter of Mr. Frank Shelton, who was one of the founders of the first colored Baptist Church in California. She was given the best education possible in pioneer days, receiving the same in Rev. Peter Cassey's boarding-school for girls located at San Jose. This school taught high school English branches and also music.

After completing her education in this school, she returned to her home in San Francisco. She had been thoroughly taught the art of French embroidery while attending boarding-school. This resulted in her readily securing employment with Miss Eldridge, who at the time had an establishment in the Samuels building in San Francisco. When Miss Eldridge had a display of handiwork at the ''Mechanics' Fair'' in that city, she selected some of the work of Miss Julia Shelton, which resulted in opening the doors for other colored girls to enter this school for the study of fine art French embroidery. For years, even after she became Mrs. Shorey, she would fill exquisite orders for Schowasher's, who have a shop across the street from the White House in San Francisco.

Mrs. Julia Shorey has lived an intensely active life for the benefit of the race. She is the most active officer and member of the organization known as the Home for Aged and Infirm Colored People of Oakland. She is past district grand most noble governor of California, holding the office of the district of California for two years; a member of the Household of Ruth; Good Samaritan; charter member of Knaresbourgh Circle, president of the Old Folks Home for sixteen years. Notwithstanding the active life Mrs. Shorey lives in the club and fraternal organizations, she must be given the credit of being an excellent mother and wife, and is directly responsible for the success of both her husband and daughter.

Miss Victoria Shorey, the subject of this sketch, has been given every educational advantage. During her student days at the Oakland Polytechnic high school she was the only colored girl member of the basketball team, playing with the team at all their games between the different high schools in the Bay cities, even with the fashionable private school of Miss Head, in Berkeley.

The students of the Oakland Technical high school have a special contest every term in typing. At one of these contests Miss Shorey won a gold medal from the Remington Typewriter Machine Company, her record being sixty words a minute. Previous to this contest she won a diploma from the Underwood Typewriting Machine Company, and also received a certificate of qualification for efficiency in typewriting, her speed in shorthand equalling one hundred and twenty words a minute. She graduated with the winter class of 1917, receiving her diploma in business and English.

It gives the writer great pleasure to present to the reader the following sketch of Miss Ruth Masengale, of Oakland, California. She is the daughter of the highly-respected citizens, Mr. and Mrs. John Masengale. She is a native daughter and has the distinction of being educated in the excellent public schools of California. The value of this statement will be appreciated as you review her sketch.

Miss Masengale is an accomplished musician. She graduated from the grammar school of Oakland in June, 1912, and, notwithstanding in poor health, she immediately re-entered school the following August, graduating from the high school December 2, 1914. After taking a two-year business course, consisting of English, Spanish, shorthand, typewriting, commercial correspondence, bookkeeping and gymnasium.

She returned to high school August, 1915, to continue her studies, took up algebra, English, history and Spanish. The last semester she worked in the office of the Spanish teacher, who was also the supervisor of Spanish in the public schools of Oakland. When she left school she had completed three and a half years of Spanish. The writer has in her possession a letter which was written by the supervisor of Spanish of the Oakland schools. In this letter he speaks of Miss Masengale's efficiency in the Spanish language, and also as his private secretary for six months. This was a recognition of her ability, because she was selected from a school containing many thousand white students. Miss Masengale is careful and thorough in anything she undertakes. The writer is glad to state that she has translated many very old Spanish documents for their use in the preparation of this book.

Afterward Miss Masengale was employed by Attorney Oscar Hudson, who, while he is consul for Liberia at the Port of San Francisco, is also an attorney who enjoys a large clientage among the Spanish people. She successfully served Mr. Hudson for over a year, when she took the civil service examination and passed with a high percentage, receiving almost an immediate appointment from Washington, D. C., and was ordered to the custom house in San Francisco, where she was engaged in making out passports. At this present writing she holds a position as stenographer in the county clerk's office of the City of Oakland, the first time the position has been held by a colored person.

Mrs. Ivah L. Gray came to Oakland, California, from Cheyenne, Wyoming, some twelve years or more ago. She is an active member of the Fifteenth Street Church; president of the Fanny Coppin Club, a social, literary and musical club of Oakland. She is the State organizer of the northern division of the Federated Clubs; an active member of the Ada Young Red Cross Auxiliary and a member of the Soldiers' Comfort Committee. Mrs. Gray is the mother of an interesting family of three children to whom she is quite devoted and a companionable mother. She is an artist with the needle, making fine laces and hand-embroidery. She has charge of this department of the Fanny Coppin Club. Many ladies have received instruction from Mrs. Gray. She is sincere and faithful in any undertaking she may engage in.

There are many colored ladies in California who are great artists in both oil and also the art of china-painting, but while the writer has solicited their sketches, the following is the only one received in time for this book: ''Patricia Garland was born in New York on March 17, 1882 Following her father's death, which occurred a few years later, she and a younger brother accompanied their mother to San Francisco, where they arrived in 1888, after a long trip down the Atlantic, across the Isthmus of Panama and up the Pacific Ocean to San Francisco Bay and city.

''Miss Garland attended the public schools of San Francisco and was graduated in 1899. Even at this early age she managed to master a trade through serving as an apprentice after school hours to Mrs. Phillip Johnson, from whom she learned the art of hair-dressing, manicuring and hairwork entirely.

''In 1903 the family moved to Oakland, and the following year Miss Garland took a nurse-training course in the San Francisco Foundling and Lying-in Hospital, under the direction of Dr. Harrison and Dr. Layne. She followed her profession of nursing for a number of years, but at the same time in conjunction with her mother, Mrs. Lyon, she maintained a model home for the care of young children, in which enterprise she has received the enthusiastic endorsement of prominent people and met with pronounced success. Her home for boarding children at present is under the State Board of Charities and Corrections of California.

''Not content with the usual amount of work she was able to crowd into her busy days, she decided through the medium of the Oakland evening high school to add bookkeeping, stenography, Spanish, French and typewriting to her other accomplishments. The night school work has been carried along with her other activities for several years. Previously she had been a member of an art and industrial club organized by Mrs. Mary Wilkinson, of Oakland, and had studied all the branches of handwork. Her entire outfit was presented to her by Mrs. Wilkinson. In October, 1908, this club was admitted into the National Federation of Colored Women's Clubs and Miss Garland contributed Spanish drawn-thread work, embroidery, crochet-work and many pieces of hand-painted china to its first exhibition. Later on she further perfected herself in this work through a course in the Arts and Crafts School under Professor Myers, of Berkeley.

''Through a fortunate chance Miss Garland was enabled to gain further valuable experience in the studio of Miss Alvira Miller, where she started work in the kiln-room and soon became so useful that she was often placed in charge of the entire studio and its valuable stock of china painting and gold coin during the owner's absence from town. She was a valued assistant in this work for four years, and during this period she took further lessons, covering the entire course in designing, realistics, conventional, raised paste, etching, enamels, semi-metallics, firing and the mending of china. She painted the designs on an entire set of one hundred and fifty pieces of china for one of the wealthy women of Oakland, California.

''An account of Miss Garland's varied life and talents would not be complete without referring to her love of music and her ability to play both the mandolin and violin, also the cornet. It would be difficult to say wherein lies Miss Garland's greatest ability, so varied and broad has been her training. But she is above all a credit to her race, in spite of the fact that in order to achieve the enviable progress she has been compelled to overcome many obstacles and has always been handicapped by lack of funds. It is the example of such lives which is helping more than anything else to break down the barriers.''

Mrs. Roberta Batie, the wife of the late Captain Henry Batie, comes from an old pioneer California family. Her mother was no less person than Mrs. Sara Johnson, who was a real ''Trail Blazer'' in opening a way for Negro people in Los Angeles to own homes in respectable neighborhoods. She purchased a piece of property in what was known as the Alexander Weild tract in pioneer days. The few white people then living in the tract entered a protest and threatened to burn her out, but she held her ground and today not only white but colored people live in the tract and in peace. The Negro residents own beautiful homes and many apartment-houses that are modern in every appointment.

Mrs. Batie is thoroughly educated and owns much valuable personal property. She has been an officer and active worker in the Sojourner Truth Home for Working Girls and in many other movements of value to colored women of California. Since the death of her husband she has studied and mastered the art of chiropody, being the first colored woman to scientifically study the subject in the State. She enjoys a large practice among the exclusive rich. She is a delightful lady whom everybody admires.

Mrs. Louise M. Chrisman is the widow of Lewis Edward Chrisman (deceased), Civil War veteran, and aunt of James Franklin Bundy (deceased), formerly secretary of Howard University Law School, of Washington, D. C.; pioneer "Trail Blazer;" holder of extensive timber lands in Idaho and Oregon and, with her daughters, owner and manager of the Chrisman Apartments of Los Angeles, one of our most modern and beautiful apartments for race families.

Mrs. Gladys Reo Harris, a native daughter, having been born in Pomona, is the daughter of Mrs. Lydia Harris, of Pasadena, graduating from the Pasadena high school in art and literature, in 1913. She entered the University of Southern California in 1914, majoring in sociology course. In March, 1918, she stood a county civil service examination for relief work. There were sixty-seven who stood the examination, seventeen passed, and Miss Harris, the only Negro, passed and received an immediate appointment in Los Angeles County for outdoor relief work among the colored people.

Mrs. J. Logan Craw is the daughter of Mr. Fred L. Jeltz, of Topeka, Kansas, one of the prominent settlers of that place and editor of the *Kansas State Ledger* for twenty-two years. He is the oldest Negro editor in Kansas. His daughter, Mrs. Craw, was given the best education possible. She graduated from the high school of Topeka and the Teachers' Normal school of the State of Kansas. During her school days she was an active member of the Philoihetorian Reading Club, after which she studied for four years in Mrs. Menninger's Bible School, of Topeka, Kansas. She graduated with honors from this school. Mrs. Craw is credited with organizing the first Bible class in Kansas. She is an enthusiastic Bible student wherever her lot is cast. For seven years she was a public school teacher in the Washington school of Topeka, Kansas.

When Mrs. Menninger's Bible school graduated the class of which Mrs. Craw was a member, the *Christian Herald* (white), in commenting on the different members of the class, said: "Among these pupils several teach Bible classes and several teach in the public school. Miss Jeltz, though young in years, has taught in the city schools. She is principal of the Sunday school primary department, and her intelligent encouragement and example were of great help to Mrs. Menninger."

Miss Lillian Jeltz was married to Rev. J. Logan Craw July 1, 1911. The *Centennial A. M. E. Review* had the following to say concerning Mrs. Craw: "* * * Most successful teacher and consecrated Christian lady, an ideal minister's wife, and has been president of the Puget Sound Conference Branch W. M. M. Society." During Rev. Craw's pastorate at Eighth and Towne A. M. E. Church, Mrs. Craw has produced two plays, products of her own pen. They were highly appreciated by the public. The first was "The Temple of Fame" and the other "The Kermisess of Brides." She not only wrote these plays, but staged them as well. She is an active member of the Sojourner Truth Club and the Harriett Tubman Red Cross Auxiliary, and is a delightful and lovable lady.

Mrs. Beatrice Sumner Thompson, the subject of this sketch, was born in Boston, Massachusetts, in 1880. Her parents moved to Denver, Colorado, where she was educated in the city schools. After graduation she received a clerical appointment in the County treasurer's office of that city, where she remained for ten years, during which time she held the position of assistant bookkeeper and other positions of trust in the office. Since then she has been actively engaged in educational work, especially along civic lines. Among other prominent offices, she has held those of secretary and president of the Women's Civic and Protective League, an organization of colored women having for its object the study of the intelligent use of the ballot and the making and enforcement of laws for the protection of colored citizens. She is an enthusiastic advocate of woman suffrage, especially as it affects the women of the race.

Mrs. Thompson is at present secretary of the Los Angeles branch of the National Association for the Advancement of Colored People and also secretary of the Colored Division of the Los Angeles branch of the California War History Committee.

Mrs. Rebecca Averett, the subject of this sketch, is known as one of the best educated colored ladies living in Oakland. She is a sister to the late George Mitchel, whose sketch appears in this book. Like her brother, she believes in accumulating property. She and her husband own many valuable pieces of property in Oakland, and their home in Oakland is both modern and elegantly but modestly furnished. Mrs. Averett has lived a life of usefulness for the benefit of the race. When a resident of San Francisco she was the leading contralto singer in the Bethel Church choir. After moving to Oakland she continued her church activities, but with the church of her husband's belief. She takes an active part in the choir and the giving of church entertainments. Some of the most spectacular entertainments ever given in Oakland have been staged by Mrs. Averett for the benefit of North Oakland Baptist Church. Previous to coming to Oakland, California, she taught in the public schools of Virginia, and until this day in whatever she does she uses the exactness and precision of a school teacher. She is sincere in all her dealings with others.

There is not an individual in this department more deserving than Miss E. Gertrude Chrisman, the subject of this sketch. This young woman is a real "Trail Blazer." She has a will second to none. She is of Indian extraction, and her parents came across the plains in pioneer days and took up two Indian claims in Idaho. Miss Chrisman was educated in the public schools and State University of Idaho. Later she attended the University of Puget Sound, of Tacoma, Washington.

After her graduation she stood the civil service examination and was given an appointment in the postoffice in Seattle, Washington. It was during her stay in this position that she attended the drawings for government lands held in Spokane, Washington, and secured a successful number for a homestead plot of land in Idaho. The government requires that one live on the land for two years to secure title. This did not daunt this young woman, who immediately resigned her position and decided that she would live on her plot, and with hammer and nails built her own shack. She stood all the hardships of homesteading for two years, during which time she discovered that the timber on her plot was very valuable.

In the meantime, the health of her mother becoming impaired, the family decided to move to Los Angeles, California. It was then that she was besieged by lumber dealers to sell the timber on her homestead plot. This she did by telegraph after the lumbermen decided to give her what she considered a fair market price. The family turned the money immediately into the building of a modern apartment house, after which she accepted a position where she worked at a fair wage and saved the same, attending the California State Normal school, from which institution she was graduated in March, 1916. Miss Chrisman was teacher, and then principal of the Brooker T. Washington school at El Centro, Imperial Valley, California, for two years. During the summer she returned to Los Angeles, where she spent the summer vacation with her mother and sister. She also attended the summer sessions at the University of California, where she continued the study of the Spanish language and other subjects. At the present time she is employed as teacher in the Palo Verde school, one of the Los Angeles city schools in the North Broadway district.

Miss E. Gertrude Chrisman is teaching in a school with eight white teachers. She is teaching Spanish and other languages. She is the most wonderful girl the writer has ever met. Several years ago, when she spoke of her intention to teach in the public schools of the State, the writer seriously advised against even the attempt, believing it would result in another race-issue concerning mixed schools, and remembering the struggle the Negro people of the State had made to obtain equal school facilities and the fight made against locating a Negro Polytechnic school at Allensworth; she could not in justice advise her differently. My motto is, "My race first and my best friend afterward." But I bow in proud recognition of the ability of this grand woman who has broken through the strong wall of prejudice in spite of the fact that at this writing the County Hospital nurses have defiantly refused to obey an order of the supervisors to admit colored nurses for fear of an equality of position and a possibility of just being human.

Miss E. Gertrude Chrisman is the honor "Trail Blazer" for education of the present day Negro people in California. Since the writing of this sketch the writer has been informed that the nurses at the County Hospital Training school threatened to strike because the superintendent of nurses has examined and placed on the eligible list Negro student nurses. They rank "eleven, twelve and thirteen on a list consisting of thirty, and in the ordinary course of events will be reached at or before the end of the year." (Quoted from the *Citizen Advocate*, as reprinted from the *Los Angeles Express*.)

MME. SUL-TE-WAN
Motion Picture Actress and Dancer.

HON. JOHN WESLEY COLEMAN
The Old Reliable Employment Agent of Los Angeles.

OF CALIFORNIA 239

The writer in giving this the history of the Negro in California has, by careful research, endeavored to secure the name of every "Trail Blazer," from the first Negro guide with an exploring party, to the having of Spanish documents translated for the truthfulness of statements made by other writers concerning the Negro in California. At great expense she has solicited and entreated persons of the race who have blazed a trail in any particular line to allow this history to give their experience for the encouragement of the race. Often the desired information has been withheld through a false pride as to the struggle and hardships encountered in their upward climbs. They seem to forget that they owe it to the future generation of Negroes to tell of this struggle that it might aid them to not lose heart. This has not been the policy of "Madam Sul-Te-Wan," who has secured her place in the motion picture world.

The motion picture, which we have all learned to appreciate as a mode of advanced entertainment, has but few Negro players who serve with white companies. In California it is a great industry. Many of our women make good wages serving motion picture actresses. There is one and only one Negress motion picture actress in "stock" on the Pacific Coast. She is employed at a good salary by Mr. D. W. Griffith, the producer of the film "The Clansman." This little lady, Madam Sul-Te-Wan, is a legitimate actress and her upward climb into the motion picture world is most interesting and worthy of the pen of a great writer. Nevertheless the author will attempt to give the reader some of the facts in her upward climb to this high position, for she is glad of the fact that she is a true representative of the race and her sketch will show that she has reached this position on merit alone.

There are some persons in the race who do not like to speak of their lowly birth because of the poverty of their parents, forgetting that honest poverty is no disgrace. Madam Sul-Te-Wan is proud of the fact that her mother was a washerwoman and, as a widow, washed for actresses that she might secure good prices and ready pay. This little lady, as a girl, would deliver the washing to the actresses at the stage door, and thereby was often permitted to remain and see the show. This was in Louisville, Kentucky. The next day she would rehearse the act at school and tell her classmates that some day she, too, would be an actress.

The mother was too poor to have her daughter trained either to sing or dance. But all the time she was delivering the washings to such well-known actresses as Mary Anderson and Fanny Davenport, two of the best teachers possible and who could not have been employed for any sum as a teacher. These renowned actresses and singers became very much interested in this nut-brown daughter of their washerwoman. So convinced were they that she had talent that they enlisted the assistance of the then Mayor of Louisville, a Mr. James Whalen, who had charge of the Buckingham Theater. He gave this little colored girl a trial, and used, as an attraction at his theater, twenty-five little colored girls who did singing and dancing. He offered a prize for the best "buck and wing dancer." The first prize was a granite dishpan and granite spoon. It was won by the subject of this sketch. This gave her confidence in herself. Her mother was very proud of the granite dishpan and spoon, and decided to allow her daughter to fill other engagements. After she was fully convinced that she did have talent she moved with her to Cincinnati, Ohio.

The move to Cincinnati was a good venture for this widow washerwoman, for it gave her daughter a broader field in which to develop her talent among strangers. This little dancing protege of Mary Anderson and Fanny Davenport readily found work for weeks at a time at the Dime Museum, located on Vine street, Cincinnati, Ohio. Afterward in the family theaters "Over the Rhine," as a section of that city is known. This led to her finally joining a company called the "Three Black Cloaks." She played under the title "Creole Nell" while in Cincinnati and won recognition. By assuming this title she soon again came in communication with Miss Fanny Davenport, who sent her a telegram to secure for her some colored players to take some minor part in a play she was playing, as she was coming to Cincinnati.

Her experience in Cincinnati, and the aid given to Miss Davenport, gave this little actress supreme confidence in her own ability, and she, too, decided that she could and did organize a company which was known as "The Black Four Hundred," which employed sixteen performers and twelve musicians. She traveled throughout the eastern States with this company, meeting with great success. The next season she organized and staged another company which she called "The Rair Back Minstrels." The success attending this adventure was so very great that she was besieged to marry and did marry.

But alas, the marriage of an actress or singer does not always spell success and happiness! The subject of our sketch came to the Pacific Coast and, after a residence in California of about two years, her husband deserted her with three little boys, the youngest being three weeks old. She became so reduced in finances that she was compelled to go before the Forum Club and beg for assistance, which they gave her three different times. She was presented to the Forum by Mr. J. W. Coleman, the employment agent. She was accompanied by her three children. When the time came for her to address that grand body of gentlemen, she began to cry, whereupon her oldest son, who was not yet seven years, looking up into his mother's face, said: "Mother you are not begging. We are going to sing and earn what they give you." He and his little brother sang as they had never sung before and greatly impressed the Forum Club.

Madam Sul-Te-Wan was living in Arcadia, and her husband not only deserted her with these three children, but he failed to pay the rent with the money she had sent home from her singing and dancing. She was left with ten months' back rent to pay. The Associated Charities of Los Angeles brought her into town and rented a place for her and her children. It is pitiful to hear how she then struggled to obtain work. Madam Sul-Te-Wan had never done anything else from a little girl but sing and dance. She knew nothing about housework, for she hired some one to stay with her children while she danced in the East and for a while in California. The first time in her life she was confronted with a mighty problem, how to become an immediate bread-winner for herself and three children. The white theatrical booking companies did not give her any engagements, claiming that they did not make independent bookings, and other excuses. She did not wish to become a charge on the charity of the neighbors and her children must have bread. She finally secured an engagement at the Pier Theater of Venice, California. This short engagement did not pay very much and it did not require long for her to use the money up. Then there was a long, long spell of idleness and tramping the streets to try and secure something to do. Finally, as a last resort, she decided to go to Mr. D. W. Griffith, who at the time was producing "The Clansman." She had heard that he was employing a great number of colored people. She personally went to Mr. Griffith and presented her card. He immediately hired her at three dollars per day, which seemed like a fortune to her at the time. After the first day's work he immediately gave her five dollars per day. He was so impressed with her acting that he immediately had written a separate sketch for "The Clansman" in which she appeared as a rich colored lady, finely gowned and owner of a Negro colony of educated colored citizens, who not only owned their own land, but she drove her own coach and four-in-hand. This scene was to show the advancement of the Negro from ante-bellum days to this present period. After the picture was made (and Madam was so proud of the money she had earned), the censor cut the part out in which she appeared as a rich colored lady, and other parts, leaving only the bitter-gall portions for the insults of the Negro race throughout the nation. Madam also appeared in the mob scene in "The Clansman," and carried a fan given her by Mary Anderson when she was a school child carrying the washing to the stage door. During her acting in the mob scene she lost the fan and stopped her acting, whereupon Mr. Griffith called through the speaking trumpet, "Go on; I will buy you another fan. Your acting is good; go on." After "The Clansman" was finished there was nothing else for her to do, and the three little children must have bread and rent must be paid. So one day she decided that she wanted the money that Mr. Griffith would give for the purchase of a new fan, as he had said on that particular day. She went out to the studio and asked him if he would not give her the money that he would give to purchase her another fan, as she needed the money worse than the fan, even if it was a keepsake gift from Mary Anderson, whereupon Mr. Griffith gave her a check for twenty-five dollars and placed her on the pay-roll at five dollars per day, work or play. He then went to New York with the picture, "The Clansman."

"The Clansman" at the same time began to play in Los Angeles and the Negro people proceded to have the censor cut out some objectionable features of the film. The next week's pay envelope contained a notice, "You are no longer needed." She inquired of the manager in charge why she was being discharged, and at first he would not give her a hearing. Then told her some white actress had lost a Christian Science book and thought that she had stolen it and that she was responsible for the colored people fighting the film, "The Clansman." Madam Sul-Te-Wan was very angry and replied that her struggle for bread for her three children had prevented her from coming in contact with the educated members of the race who had time to read and study as to whether the film was detrimental to the race. She came seeking an opportunity to honestly earn bread for her three little children, and the work in "The Clansman" was the only door open for her to earn it. Madam further replied to the manager in charge that she would immediately get in touch with some of the educated and influential Negro people of Los Angeles and ask them to defend her from the accusation of being a thief and the arousing of unpopular sentiment against "The Clansman" after it had given her bread. She knew that they would deal justly with her as they were able to do with the film "The Clansman."

She left the studio and decided to go to that great humanitarian and lawyer, Edward Burton Ceruti, who, without cost to her, defended her, sending a letter to Mr. Griffith in New York and the manager in Hollywood at the studio. This resulted in Madam being reinstated on the pay-roll and later was featured in "The Marriage Market," in the film "Intolerance." She was also featured in "Happy Valley's Oldest Boy" and "Up from the Depths."

Last Spring the thought occurred to her that it would not be a bad idea to ask for a letter of recommendation, which Mr. Griffith readily consented that she was entitled to and instructed his manager to write the same. Afterward he relieved Madam Sul-Te-Wan's fears that she might not secure work with other companies by introducing her to some of the leading motion picture film producers on the Pacific Coast, who have given her work in some of the best and most popular pictures made in the State. He also introduced her to Theda Bara and was the means of her employing Madam Sul-Te-Wan's middle son, John, to feature in "Madam DuBarry." The letter referred to is as follows:

"Fine Arts Film Company.
"Majestic Motion Picture Company Producers. Studio: 4500 Sunset Blvd.
"D. W. Griffith, General Manager, Frank E. Woods, Assistant to General Manager.
"J. C. Eppeny, Business Manager.

"Los Angeles, California, April 4, 1917.

"To Whom It May Concern: This is to certify that the bearer, Madam Sul-Te-Wan, is a colored actress of exceptional ability and has been a member of our stock company for the past three years. She has played a number of very good parts in our pictures and gave very good satisfaction. * * *

"Yours very truly,
"MAJESTIC MOTION PICTURE COMPANY.
"By FRANK E. WOODS."

Mrs. Sadie Chandler-Cole, the subject of this sketch, is the daughter of Abraham Washington Chandler and Sarah Hatfield-Chandler, of Cincinnati, Ohio. Her father was one of the founders of the Mound Street Baptist Church of that city and a conductor of the "Underground Railroad." Her mother attended the first high school for free colored people in Cincinnati, Ohio, and her grandfather bought a scholarship in Oberlin College, in Ohio. Her mother sang in the select choir of the Academy of Music established by the abolitionists and friends of free colored people. Her mother also attended school with Governor Pinchback, and many other persons who have since become notable.

Mrs. Sadie Chandler-Cole was given a fine education by her parents. She was especially trained as a singer and was a member of the Fisk Jubilee Singers, with whom she traveled for years. After her marriage she located in Detroit, Michigan, from where, after a residence of several years, she and her husband, Mr. Thomas A. Cole, who is a son of James H. Cole, the late wealthy real estate holder of that city, they moved to Los Angeles. They have lived in this city for the past eighteen years.

Mrs. Cole is a teacher of modern and vocal music and a great social worker. She is a thorough race woman, and has done much in Los Angeles to create favorable sentiment for the race. She was the first person to have removed an objectional sign, "Negroes not wanted." This was many years before the activities of the N. A. A. C. P. Mrs. Cole went into a lunch-stand on Broadway and asked for a glass of buttermilk. They first refused to serve her and then they told her it would cost fifty cents. They sold it to others for five cents. She told the writer that she was determined to break up the discrimination if she had to die, and proceeded to break up the man's place of business. They called the police and when he came and inquired the trouble he demanded that the proprietor serve her without extra charge. This was a direct opening wedge in removing objectionable signs.

Mrs. Cole, at the time, was engaged as deputy registrar for the City of Los Angeles, and a member of the executive board of the Dry Federation of the State of California. Her actions created favorable sentiment throughout the State and Nation for the Negro race. Mrs. Cole has always been a great race woman. While living in Detroit, Michigan, she framed a memorial and had the State Federation of Colored Women's Clubs send it to the Congress of the United States, asking them to give indemnity to Mrs. Baker, whose husband, Postmaster Baker, was assassinated in his home in South Carolina. This was during the McKinley administration, and before the late President McKinley could act upon it he, too, was assassinated.

Mrs. Cole is one of the first women to organize a club of women who have gone to the jails and prayed with unfortunate colored women. She has a wonderful personality and is the mother of four children. One son is now serving in France with the National Army, and her daughter, Florence Cole-Talbert, is the diamond medalist of the ''Music'' chapter.

Mrs. Sadie Cole's mother, Mrs. Chandler, lives with another daughter in Los Angeles, Mrs. Wildred Chandler-Williams, who has the distinction of being the first colored woman in Los Angeles to be recognized as a modiste by the exclusive rich. She is an artist in her line and has employed as high as ten colored women who were also artistic needle women. She has lived in the City of Los Angeles for thirty years and is fully recognized by the world of fashion as an artistic modiste. Her mother is past ninety, but with a mind very bright and has a keen interest in the passing events.

Mrs. Sadie Chandler-Cole has the distinction of having for a brother the leading Negro Baptist minister in the United States, Rev. Arthur Chandler, who has been wonderfully educated. He first graduated from Dennison University, at Granville, Ohio, and later at the school located in Ann Arbor, Michigan, finally going to Boston, where he studied and graduated in the Newton Seminary as a theologian. He, together with his interesting family, live in Detroit, Michigan. His daughter, Miss Anna, graduated last June from the Central high school of that city.

Mrs. Pool, the subject of this sketch, came to California some fourteen years ago from Leadville, Colorado, with her mother, who was then ill. She is a native of Leavenworth, Kansas, and, at the age of seven, became connected with the A. M. E. Church. Since coming to California she has identified herself with every movement which has for its object the betterment of the Negro race. She has been active in the building of the Sojourner Truth Home and has served that club as treasurer and, at this writing, is vice-president. Mrs. Pool is a member of the St. John Lodge Chapter (Electric) and one of the Forty-niners of the Independent People's Church of Christ of Los Angeles. She and her husband own many valuable pieces of property. Mrs. Pool is a staunch friend and an enterprizing race woman who is well liked and respected by all.

Mrs. Billingsley-Jones, a native of Greenville, Tennessee, came from Dayton, Ohio, to Los Angeles, California, sixteen years ago. She is a great worker in charity and benevolent societies. She has been a member of the M. E. Wesley Chapel for many years until the founding of the Independent People's Church of Christ, when she joined to be with her husband, who holds an office in this body. She is a member of the choir and an active worker in all the other branches of the church. She is also an active member of the Household of Ruth and is a well-respected and distinguished citizen of Los Angeles.

Mrs. Howard Skanks is another distinguished pioneer citizen who stands for enobled womanhood and is actively engaged in aiding all lone women who are struggling for an existence. She is modest and unassuming, giving freely of both time and money in any movement for the betterment of Negro women. She owns a beautiful home in the St. James district of Los Angeles and has entertained nearly all the distinguished colored people coming to the Coast. Mr. and Mrs. Shanks are New Englanders and are among the most reliable and highly respected people living in California.

Mrs. Fern Ragland is a great club woman, active in charity work and the Day Nursery. She and her husband came from Meridian, Mississippi, over thirty years ago and have built one of the first apartment-houses owned by colored people in Los Angeles. They have twelve apartments, with all modern improvements. They have three children, Reskin, Mary and Charlie. Mr. Ragland is a hotel man and a devoted husband.

Mrs. Amanda Shelton-Green, the subject of this sketch, came to California fifty years ago from Orange County, Virginia. She was one of four children whose mother had died, and their father, Mr. Edward Shelton, brought his young family to his father and mother, who at the time were living in San Francisco, California. Her father, Mr. Edward Shelton, followed blacksmithing and gave to all his children the best education possible. There were three girls and one boy, namely, Moulton, Amanda, Carrie and Julia. The oldest, Amanda, married Mr. Joseph Green, of Wilmington, North Carolina. Mr. Green was a great musician and for twenty-five years was a member of the Alphia Orchestra which played in the Palm Court of the Palace Hotel of San Francisco. The union was blessed by the birth of four children, two girls of whom are still living, namely, Cecil and Lauretta.

Mrs. Sallie E. Taylor-Richardson was born in Louisville, Kentucky. She is the daughter of Mr. Henry and Harriett Taylor. They moved from Kentucky when the subject of this sketch was quite young, locating in Woodlawn, Illinois, where the daughter was educated until ready to enter a girl's college. She was then sent to Extine Norton University, located at Caine Springs, Kentucky. She graduated from this institution as salutatorian of her class. After her graduation she married Mr. A. C. Richardson and for a while lived in Indianapolis, Indiana, later coming to Los Angeles, where she studied and mastered the science of Chiropody and received a certificate. She practiced in Los Angeles until she earned sufficient money to buy a large and valuable piece of property at Wilmington, near Los Angeles, which property, since the shipbuilding industry of the Great World War, has greatly increased in value.

She is a club worker, and an active worker for Sojourner Truth Home Club. The greatest work Mrs. Richardson has done was the benefit she gave for Dr. Bundy of East St. Louis, Missouri. She told the writer that she believed that he was trying to help the Negro race and for that reason was persecuted and should be befriended by every member of the race. She also said that she was from and old family in Kentucky who would die defending the race. Her grandmother was a conductor in the "Underground Railroad" and assisted many fleeing Negro slaves. Her grandfather was a blacksmith and also a member of the "Underground Railroad." A great uncle was a defender of his rights to that extent that he killed two white men whom he saw assaulting a Negro girl. He chopped them in the head with a garden-hoe. The court was so afraid of him that they put him in a cage and brought him to court to try him because he assaulted a white man. So, as she said: "My very spirit seemed to cry out to help Dr. Bundy, who had suffered so much on account of the East St. Louis riots."

She attended a course at the summer session of the Southern California University on "Current Events" and public speaking, and was invited to address the class on the Negro's part in the World's Democracy.

Miss Lillian Simpson, daughter of Mr. and Mrs. John Simpson, of Little Rock, Arkansas, came to California with her parents at the age of three years and located in Bakersfield, where she was educated. After leaving school she studied the art of millinery in an exclusive shop owned by Miss Eva Robinson. After finishing her trade and working up to the position as head maker and assistant trimmer, she filled an important position as such in Redlicks' department store, one of the leading stores in Bakersfield. After filling this position for three years, she resigned and accepted a similar position in the largest leading and exclusive department store of that city, Hockheimer & Company, serving as head maker and assistant trimmer for seven years.

This position required Miss Simpson's making annual trips to San Francisco and Los Angeles to the Wholesale millinery houses. This position was the only one of its kind ever held in California by a colored woman.

Mrs. Lula Russel, living in California for over thirty-two years and thirty years in Bakersfield, is one of the most successful colored women practitioners of the art of massage and hair dressing in the State. She has, because of her thorough training, succeeded in building up a practice in Bakersfield that has yielded her sufficient to purchase a city block and also her home, which is modern in every detail and valued at ten thousand dollars. This elegant home site is on a plot of land equal to one-fourth of a city block. She also owns three city lots at Point Richmond, California. Her husband, Mr. Barrington Russel, is a first-class carpenter and came to California many years ago from Austin, Texas. They are both well-respected and distinguished citizens of the City of Bakersfield.

Mr. and Mrs. Winters own valuable property, including the Winters block, in Bakersfield. He is the pioneer person of color in the State to conduct a good paying business in and for the race without asking members of another race to invest their money with him. He is considered the best business man in the race, possessing a keen idea of the value of co-operation and has made a success. Mrs. Winters has a sketch in the "Music" chapter. She is very popular.

Mrs. Ella Ardelle Butler, nee Clayton, the subject of this sketch, is a native of Richmond, Virginia. She came to California in 1893 to join her brothers, John and the late James L. Clayton, to make her home in San Francisco. Entering the high school of that city, she graduated in due season, subsequently taking a special course in stenography before engaging in a business career which terminated in the management of the insurance and loan office of her future husband, Mr. Walter A. Butler.

Miss Ella Ardelle Clayton was married to Mr. Walter A. Butler April 19, 1916. The wedding was one of the most elaborate social functions of its kind ever held in the Bay cities. It was solemnized in Oakland. The bride has, from her earliest arrival in California, been recognized as a social favorite, and as the writer has often remarked, "She wears well," for she is sincere and true to all who may enjoy her friendship, is affable and agreeable to every one, and possesses a charming personality. The groom has lived in Oakland for nearly forty years, and has always stood for everything that had for its aim the elevation of the race. He had by care and sacrifice built a most beautiful home for his bride which stands second to none in that district, and has few equals in the State. He did not marry until the home was built and furnished.

Miss Clayton, to show her appreciation of his forethought, said: "Then 'Wrestacre' shall be my marriage altar." She married in the home or rather "bride's nest" prepared by sacrifice and love for her to preside over as "queen of the home."

Their wedding presents showed the popularity of both the bride and groom. They received enough table silver to serve a meal for several persons without using any china, fully a thousand dollars worth of silver alone, besides Oriental rugs, fine imported china, and hand-painted pictures the work of celebrated artists. Mrs. Butler is very much interested in the N. A. A. C. P., being actively engaged on the membership committee. Since her marriage she has entertained many distinguished visitors in her palatial home.

Los Angeles, more than any other city in California, has many race women who have won distinction in unsual lines. This is especially true of Mrs. Harriett Owens-Bynum, who, together with her husband, Green Owens, and only son, John Wesley Coleman, and wife, located in Los Angeles on November 28, 1887, coming from Austin, Texas, where they owned a ranch of one hundred and sixty acres. The family having owned valuable land, knew the value to the race of being a taxpayer, and immediately purchased a twenty-five foot lot in the then new addition to Los Angeles which was known as Boyle Heights. They at intervals added to their holdings until they finally owned enough land to be given recognition by the real estate agent of the tract.

Mr. Owens followed expressing for a living, and his wife did day's work which required her walking miles back and forth to Los Angeles, since the street cars did not at that date extend to this suburb. After a year Mrs. Owens found that it was a disadvantage for her to walk so long a distance and opened a hand laundry and later a bakery, and finally a dairy. At different times she served as a sick nurse with some of the leading white physicians of Los Angeles.

These different adventures brought her into close contact with many families of the race, and she soon learned that few owned their own homes. Mrs. Owens consulted with the real estate agent of the Boyle Heights tract, and he appointed her agent among her people. This lady was anxious to see her people advance and made arrangements with the agent that they pay her a commission out of the sale price of the property, that she might sell and not add it to the original price. In this way the poor class of colored laborers were given a square deal in the purchase of homes. Mrs. Owens-Bynum sold over sixty-five houses and lots to colored families; some of these sold for thousands of dollars. Out of this number two families lost their property. She also succeeded in placing as renters in good property over a hundred families, and is still in the business. She trained her son to sell real estate, and they together invested their money thus earned in additional properties, building the "Coleman Flats" on Savannah street in Boyle Heights. This is a modern structure for colored families.

Mrs. Owens-Bynum is one of the founders of the Second Baptist Church of Los Angeles. She has been honored by having a sketch of her activities appear in many race papers and magazines. The author found the following tribute to the lady in *The New Age Magazine:* "She is a woman with great executive ability, a natural born financier and a good Christian worker of the old school. A wonderful career has been hers." In an issue of the *Eagle* of Los Angeles, under date of June 8, 1912, Mrs. Owens' picture appeared on the front page of an anniversary issue, and the article concerning this lady was headed "Mrs. Owens an Impetus. Such characters who present the lasting vitality, the stern qualities of a clean-cut business woman as Mrs. Owens cannot be overlooked, and certainly serve as an impetus for young persons who must tread the same paths as their forefathers. * * * The vigorous enthusiasm that characterizes her every sentiment is distinguishing in effect. * * * May her example be an impetus for those who must follow after her!"

Mrs. Louise Talbot-Young, the subject of this sketch, came to California with her parents from Chatham, Canada, where she had been educated. After locating in Los Angeles she was given additional educational advantages, taking a business course at Woodbury College; later she learned the trade as tailor and worked at the trade until married to Mr. Louis Wilburn Young.

After his death she went to Bakersfield where she was engaged in the tailoring business for five years. Mrs. Young then returned to Los Angeles where she was appointed Deputy County Recorder for Los Angeles County, California. She has held this position with credit to the race for twelve years. Mrs. Young's efficiency has proven a direct means of opening another door of opportunity for other colored women of Los Angeles.

CHAPTER XIX

DOCTORS AND DENTISTS OF THE RACE IN CALIFORNIA

The State of California has not been blessed by many colored doctors until recent years. During the past ten years Los Angeles has had some ten or twelve doctors to locate in the immediate city, after a period of over twenty-five years since the first colored doctor located in that city, and nearly if not fifty years since the first one located in San Francisco.

The first colored physician to locate in the State was Dr. W. J. O. Bryant, of San Francisco, an herb doctor, who was highly respected and successful. He was a ''Trail Blazer'' and came either in 1849 or the early fifties. Dr. Albert Bevitt, an herb doctor, with offices at Stockton and Powell streets, San Francisco, came in 1852 The next one to locate in the State was Dr. M. A. Majors, who came to Los Angeles in 1888. He was a native of Austin, Texas, and a graduate from a large Negro Texas college. He practiced in Los Angeles for a number of years and was very successful. Later he moved to Chicago.

Dr. Shadd, of Washington, D. C., was another physician who located in Los Angeles and practiced there for seven years, when he was suddenly called by death. He dropped dead at Santa Monica. He was followed by Dr. Melvin Sykes, who was a great success for twenty or more years, when death called him. He left an immense fortune, a widow and a host of friends to mourn his passing. About the same time the City of Los Angeles was highly honored by having another well-educated colored doctor locate there in the person of Dr. Taylor, and soon afterward Dr. Elmer Barr, from Chicago, but whose parents were forty-niners; and then almost a native in the person of Dr. Thomas Nelson, who was the first colored doctor educated at Stanford University of California. ''He graduated and received the degree of M. D. from the Cooper Medical School, in San Francisco, and during his last three years at that institution had the high honor of being assistant to the professor in chemistry, giving instructions to the classes under him.''

About five or more years ago Dr. Wilbur Clarence Gordon located in Los Angeles, coming from Springfield, Ohio, where he had practiced for eight years, He has been as successful in California as he was in the East. The following year there were at least seven or eight more colored doctors who located in California, and they are still coming. All seem to settle at this one place, when there are such rich fields all through-out the State for men in this profession, as well as in dental practice.

Dr. Purnell is the only colored doctor around the San Francisco Bay district. Only very recently a/ doctor has located in the San Joaquin Valley. Dr. Benjamin Young, who, after graduating in pharmacy from the University of Southern California, went East and studied medicine, graduated and returned home to Fowler, California, where he has located with his bride. The writer is adding a few sketches that the reader may form some idea as to the ability of the men practicing in California. The list could be extended to twice the length.

Dr. John Outlaw is the son of James Madison and Sarah Frances Outlaw, of Windsor, Bertie County, North Carolina. They were emancipated slaves and afterward became the proprietors of a hotel for tourist trade and were very successful and highly-respected citizens of that city. This was demonstrated when on May 2, 1885, their son John S. was appointed by the Hon. J. E. O'Hara, member of Congress, from Enfield, North Carolina, to represent that district as a cadet to West Point United States Military Academy. Master John S. Outlaw had decided that he wished to study medicine and declined the appointment.

Dr. John S. Outlaw graduated from the Lincoln University, of Pennsylvania, in 1888, receiving the degree of A. B., and the added degree through his high scholarship he made Cum Lauda. After graduating with such honors he immediately entered Howard University, at Washington, D. C., where he studied medicine, graduating with the class of 1891. It is such a rare occurrence to have a young appointee refuse to accept an opportunity to become a cadet to West Point Military Academy that the Government closely watched the educational progress made by young Outlaw. This resulted in the Government's offering him, before he graduated from the medical department of Howard University, the appointment as Mortality Statistician for the Census Bureau with offices in Boston and New York. After finishing his service with this appointment, he was given the appointment of Medical Examiner of Pensions in the Pension Department at Washington, D. C. This was the first time this appointment had been filled by a Negro physician. All these appointments were given to Dr. Outlaw, unsolicited, and speak well for the gentleman.

After ten years of service, he realized that he was not fulfilling the great desire of his life, to be an active physician and surgeon. He resigned his position in the Pension Department and, together with his wife and baby, moved to Los Angeles, California. He immediately began the practice of medicine in Los Angeles in 1901. Dr. Outlaw as a physician has been eminently successful. He has the confidence and respect of all the races and the best citizens of Los Angeles and the State of California. He is the Dean of colored physicians in the State. He has kept abreast of the times in medical research work. This has been made possible through his membership in the Los Angeles County and the State Medical societies, also the American National Association, together with the National Negro Medical, Dental and Pharmacist Societies of America. He is not only a member of these different societies but takes an active part in the proceedings, especially the clinics.

Dr. Outlaw married Miss Nannie Brown, a popular and beautiful reigning belle in the society of Washington, D. C. The union has been blessed by the birth of two children, a son and daughter. The son, Cornelius Harrington Outlaw, at the age of sixteen, graduated from the Los Angeles High School, and in June, 1918, graduated from the Williston Seminary at East Hampton, Mass., a preparatory school for entrance to Harvard University. Dr. Outlaw's daughter, little Miss Frances, although young, has already spent one year in the Los Angeles High School, and at the present is attend a school for girls in the east. She has been given the advantage of the study of French, Italian, Spanish and the English languages. She promises to develop into a good musician and has studied under Herr Thilo Becker. The writer has enjoyed the pleasure of hearing this little miss play on the piano some difficult classical pieces and was amazed at her technique, tone painting and phrasing, which, for a child, were most remarkable.

Dr. and Mrs. Outlaw thoroughly enjoy their home life with their children. Mrs. Outlaw is truly a "queen of the home." Her ease and grace of manner in her beautiful home with its rich furnishings reflect her personality and that of her husband by the elegance of simplicity. Their residence is on West Thirtieth street in the most exclusive and beautiful residence district of Los Angeles, and yet their love for their children and their advancement is the supreme effort of Dr. and Mrs. Outlaw. Dr. Outlaw's success has been very great and he has made some very good and paying investments, and yet is unassuming and modest in his everyday manner. He is gracious and kind to every one with whom he comes in contact.

Dr. Alva C. Garrott was born in the little town of Marion, Alabama. His early school-life was spent in that town, but he graduated from the Normal department of Talladega College, at Talladega, Alabama. Immediately after graduation he went to Texas, where he taught school until 1890, and then, through Civil Service, he was appointed to a clerkship in the United States Pension Bureau at Washington, D. C.

It was while working here that the subject of this sketch entered Howard University, first graduating from the Pharmaceutical Department in 1892, and then from the Dental Department in 1899. In 1901 Dr. Garrott resigned from the Government Service and came to Los Angeles, California, to practice dentistry. The field was new and uncertain and the difficulties numerous. By applying himself studiously to the task before him and giving efficient and painstaking service, the Doctor has built up a practice of which any one might be proud. He has identified himself with the social and financial uplift of the community and made himself felt among those with whom he has been associated. He has three children, two boys and one girl. The oldest boy, Alva C. Garrott (Junior), is now serving with the National Army in France. Miriam de J. will graduate in social science at the Fisk University. Robert W. is now in the Students' Training Camp at Fisk University.

Dr. Wilbur Clarence Gordon, the subject of this sketch, was born in Ironton, Ohio, May 9, 1880; graduated from the Medical Department of Howard University, Washington, D. C., May, 1904; admitted to practice medicine after an examination in Ohio, July, 1904. He located at Springfield, Ohio, where he successfully practiced from November, 1904, until July, 1912, at which time he moved to California. After passing the State medical examination held in San Francisco, August, 1912, he was admitted to practice in September of the same year. He then located in Los Angeles, California.

Dr. Wilbur C. Gordon immediately identified himself with the activities of the race in the City of the Angeles. He was instrumental in organizing the Ohio State Social Society and the Doctors, Dentists and Pharmacists' Association for Southern California. He was elected as special delegate to attend the National Doctors, Dentists and Pharmacists' Association in their National Convention, which was held at Raleigh, North

Carolina, in 1914. He was instructed on behalf of the Mayor of Los Angeles and the Doctors, Dentists and Pharmacists' Association of Los Angeles and Southern Calinia, to extend to that body an invitation to hold their next annual meeting in Los Angeles, California. He was unsuccessful in securing the convention, as Chicago was selected.

Dr. Gordon is a distinguished member of the National Doctors, Dentists and Pharmacists' Association, having frequently appeared on their programs. He was elected as a member of the executive board at the 1916 meeting, which was held in Kansas City, Mo. Since locating in Los Angeles he has purchased a centrally-located double corner lot, upon which he has erected a handsome residence and suite of modern offices. During the past year he has added three more rooms for electrical treatments.

Dr. Wilbur Clarence Gordon is quite musical and for a long time was the chorister of the Second Baptist Church of Los Angeles. He readily entered the musical activities of the community. He has trained several large choruses, the most notable of which was the one consisting of one hundred voices which rendered ''Hiawatha's Wedding Feast,'' a musical event of 1916, which was rendered in the Trinity Auditorium. This is considered one of the most beautiful auditoriums in all of Los Angeles.

In less than one year after Dr. and Mrs. Gordon moved to Los Angeles, his father and mother, Mr. and Mrs. J. Calvin Gordon, sold their farm in Ohio and joined him in Los Angeles. His mother is a wonderful Spanish scholar and his father a successful mechanic. Recently the Doctor has purchased a ranch of one hundred and thirty acres at Elsinore, California, and his father and mother will operate the same for him.

Dr. Gordon married in November, 1914, Miss Desdemona L. Valeteen, of Providence, Rhode Island. She is a graduate of Howard University, Washington, D. C., an ideal physician's wife, and, with her charming, winsome ways, has meant very much in shaping his success as a doctor.

Dr. Joseph W. Ball was born in a log cabin in St. Charles County, Missouri, having lost both parents when quite young. He was cared for in the home of his grandfather, Henson Scott. Joseph had the privilege of attending the rural school which, at that time, was open only three months during the year. At the age of thirteen the death of his grandfather compelled him to take the responsibility of the farm in order to earn a livelihood for the family. While thus engaged he never lost an opportunity to study at odd hours, cultivating the acquaintance of those better educated than himself that he might be assisted by them.

Believing that the city offered better opportunities for advancement, Joseph moved from the farm to St.Louis, Missouri, securing employment as porter in a barber shop, where, on account of faithfulness to his duties, he gained a friend who aided him in obtaining a much better-paying position in Albuquerque, New Mexico. How he raised the railroad fare to that city is indeed a most interesting story, showing persistent effort, in an attempt to better his condition.

Four years later, having saved enough money to buy a home and to make the necessary trips, he returned to St. Louis, and married Miss Alice Frances, a young woman well-beloved by all who knew her. Of this union the *St. Louis Post Dispatch,* one of the leading daily papers of that city, spoke in the highest terms. With his bride Joseph Ball returned to Albuquerque to their new home. This arrival being very different in every respect from the first, when, without money to pay for a room, he was permitted to sleep in the shop where he worked until he had earned enough to go elsewhere. His thrift from then on showed plainly that his determination to succeed was not in vain, and he proved the truth of the motto: ''Where there is a Will there is a Way.''

Still ambitious to advance beyond his present surroundings, in a short time from his wages of $10 per week they (Mrs. Ball becoming a helpmeet in deed as well as in words) saved $3,000 which, upon advice of friends, was invested in stock, with which they opened a first-class shoe store. Competition and lack of business training caused the store to be non-supporting, and it was sold. It had been opened to give employment to two Negro boot and shoe-makers who had been unable to find employment.

After selling the shoe store Mr. Joseph Ball gave work to the two above-mentioned men in a boot and shoe-shining parlor where he employed sometimes as high as six men. This parlor was the only first-class one of its kind in the State. Citizens, looking on, gained confidence in the man seeking to help himself by helping others and showed their appreciation of his efforts by nominating and electing him on the Republican Ticket for County Water Commissioner, in the fall of 1898. He ran ahead of his ticket a thousand votes.

While still in business in Albuquerque, he helped found the A. M. E. Church and was also a Thirty-second degree Mason and a Shriner. Having a little experience in the business world, and longing for further adventure, his next step led him to Chicago, where he studied and received practical training in the profession of chiropodist, under a well-known chiropodist. Completing his course, Dr. Ball returned to Albuquerque and opened a first-class parlor for the practice of this art.

The failing health of his wife caused him to close and move to California, where he soon found employment at Hamburger's, the largest department store in the city of Los Angeles. He filled the position as head of the department devoted to chiropody for eight years, when he again decided to go into business for himself. He opened a fine parlor where his work requires the services of two other doctors and a lady assistant.

Through careful investment, Dr. Ball has accumulated good properties among which are flats at Cimarron and New Orleans streets and his comfortable residence at Budlong and Twenty-fourth streets, a beautiful and exclusive residence section of Los Angeles. Dr. and Mrs. Ball have the respect of the community in which they live, and enjoy a host of friends and acquaintances. They represent a type of the American citizen whose thrift should be an inspiration to others. They have been willing to lift as they climbed. Dr. Ball and his wife are members of the Second Church of Christian Science, located on West Adams street, Los Angeles.

Dr. Leonard Stovall, the subject of this sketch, was born in Atlanta, Georgia, coming to Los Angeles with his parents when quite young. He was educated in the public schools of this city, having attended the Casco street school and the Los Feliz school of East Hollywood. He graduated in the pioneer class of the Hollywood High School in the class of 1906.

Dr. Stovall comes from a large and highly-respected family. Because of its size, it was necessary that those wishing a higher education than that of the public schools, would have to earn their way. This Leonard Stovall was perfectly willing to do. He did truck gardening and, at the same time, studied something about scientific gardening. In this way he earned the money to pursue a course in literary and scientific work for two years in the University of Southern California.

He afterwards decided to study medicine and save his money and entered the University of California, graduating with the closs of 1912, as a physician and surgeon. One of the Los Angeles race papers, in speaking of him, said: ''In 1908 Dr. Leonard Stovall entered the Medical College where his four years have won him the credit of being one of the most conscientious and able students of his class. * * * No physician could launch upon his professional career with greater promise of high success, nor with more of the confidence and kindly good will of the community.''

Dr. Stovall, after graduating as a physician, was appointed ''visiting surgeon, Selwyn Emmett Graves Dispensary, University of Southern California; attending physician, Municipal Child Welfare Station, 1914; grand medical examiner, U. B. F. of California; physician for Foresters, Odd Fellows, Knights of Pythias; president, Georgia State Society; corresponding secretary, State Societies of Southern California; Republican; Methodist; member American Medical Association; California State Medical Association; Los Angeles County Medical Association; Southern California Physicians, Dentists and Pharmacists' Association.'' Dr. Leonard Stovall entered the Separate Officers' Training Camp and graduated as First Lieutenant. He served with the National Army in France as a member of the Medical Reserve Corps, 365th Infantry. His friends anxiously await his return to Los Angeles and his fast-growing practice.

The writer is especially proud of this sketch, as it was sent from the battle ground of France. ''Dr. Claudius Ballard was born in Los Angeles, June, 1889. His parents were William L. Ballard, a native of Los Angeles, and Mary E. Ballard, who was one of the Tibbs family of Xenia, Ohio. The subject of this sketch was reared and educated in the Los Angeles public schools; graduated from the Los Angeles High School, after which he attended the University of Southern California (Los Angeles), studied medicine at the University of California (Berkeley) and graduated with the class of 1913. Took the State Board medical examination and practiced medicine in Los Angeles for four years. Dr. Ballard has won the Croix de Guerre, while fighting in France with the National Army. Notwithstanding his fast-growing practice, when the United States Government called for doctors to serve in the army, Dr. Ballard volunteered his services and received a commission as First Lieutenant Medical Reserve Corps, August, 1917. He was among the first colored doctors to go to France.'' Dr. Ballard then adds in his letter: ''I hope our efforts and sacrifices will mean something to our country and my race. I realize that the people are looking forward to many things from the old 8th Illinois, now 370th Infantry, and I can say they are making good in the great World War for Democracy.''

Dr. William H. Browning, the subject of this sketch, was born September 11, 1888, in Brenham, Texas; educated in the public schools and Wiley University; secured professional education at Meharry Medical College, Nashville, Tenn.; graduated 1915. He is the son of William and Fanny Browning, and practiced in his home town of Brenham, Texas, previous to locating in Los Angeles. He took the California State Board medical examination December 9, 1915, receiving a high percentage, and was licensed to practice dentistry. He has been very successful in a city crowded with men in the same profession.

Dr. Browning is socially popular, and is a member of the Knights of Pythias, Foresters, N. A. A. C. P., and vice-president of the Colored Doctors, Dentists and Pharmacits' Association of Southern California. He was commissioned by the President of the United States as First Lieutenant in the Dental Reserve Corps September 4, 1917, and was officially signed October 12, 1917. After receiving his signed commission, he rendered dental service to Negro-drafted boys as they were called to the colors from Los Angeles.

Dr. John Alexander Somerville was born in Kingston, Jamaica, West Indies. He is the son of Rev. Thomas Gustavius Somerville, an Episcopalian priest of that place. His son, the subject of this sketch, was reared and educated in Jamaica, West Indies, having graduated from Mico College. He came to California in 1902, and was the first colored man to enter the Dental College of the University of Southern California. He graduated with the class of 1917, receiving the degree of D. D. S. He made an especially high average when appearing before the State Board for examination. He then immediately began the practice of his profession in Los Angeles.

Dr. John Alexander Somerville has built up a good practice and has made many substantial friends. He is active in many movements for the good of the race. He was one of the founders and an officer in the Physicians, Dentists and Pharmacists' Assoation for Southern California. He was at one time president of the People's Realty Company, an organization of colored gentlemen. He has held for two terms the office of vice president of the Los Angeles branch of the National Association for the Advancement of Colored People. He is happily married and owns much valuable property. He and his wife are valued and much liked citizens of Los Angeles, California.

Dr. Vada Jetmore Somerville, the subject of this sketch, is the daughter of Mrs. Dora McDonald. She was reared and educated in the public schools of Los Angeles. After her graduation from the high school she won a Los Angeles Times Scholarship and entered the University of Southern California.

After leaving the University, she accepted a position at the "Hershey Arms" as telephone operator. Her employer soon recognized her ability and offered her the position of bookkeeper for the hotel. This high position of trust and responsibility can be better appreciated by the reader when told that the "Hershey Arms" is one of the most elegantly furnished and exclusive family hotels in Southern California. It is located in beautiful Wilshire Boulevard, right off West Lake Park. Miss Vada Watson held the position of bookkeeper and practically acted as assistant manager of this beautiful hostelry for the rich for six years, when she decided to marry Dr. J. A. Somerville.

Her marriage was one of the greatest social events ever held in Los Angeles. It was beautiful and lavish. The ceremony was performed in the Wesley Chapel, of Los Angeles; because Dr. Somerville's father is an Episcopalian priest, there were two ceremonies. The High Church Episcopalian ceremony was performed by Father Cleghorn, of St. Phillips Episcopalian Mission, of Los Angeles, after which the bride's pastor, Rev. Kinchen, performed the A. M. E. Church ceremony. A reception was held in the parlors of the church, after which the couple repaired to their home, a modern bungalow, built by Dr. Somerville for his bride on West Thirty-seventh street, Los Angeles. It had been elegantly furnished with wedding presents, the largest and most expensive coming from the bride's former employer, Miss Helen Mathewson, who gave a solid mahogany bedroom set. It was estimated that their presents amounted easily to twelve hundred dollars.

After a few years' practice with offices in the downtown district, the Doctor decided to build an office and residence on the "East Side." He built on the corner of Eighteenth and San Pedro streets a suite of offices and an old Colonial residence adjoining. It was after this that his wife decided to take up the study of dentistry. She has the distinction of being the first colored woman west of the Mississippi river to master the science of dentistry.

After attending the Dental College of the University of Southern California for three years, she graduated in a class of eighty-eight in June, 1918. She was the only woman and Negro in the class. Dr. Vada Watson-Somerville at the State examination made a record for efficiency. Fifteen of the class failed to pass. Dr. J. A. Alexander Somerville gave his wife, as a graduation gift, a complete office outfit of the most modern type. She is fast building a practice. She practices all the branches of dentistry.

She is socially popular and most happily married. Miss Louise Wilson, a niece of Doctor John Somerville, has come from Jamaica, West Indies, to finish her education in this country. She is at present learning to become a dentist's assistant to Dr. Vada Somerville. Would that the race had more such progressive and creditable citizens as Dr. J. A. and Dr. V. W. Somerville!

Dr. Fletcher, the subject of this sketch, came to California from the Island of Saint Christopher, Danish West Indies, arriving in San Francisco in 1860. He joined the United States Navy and served until 1865, when he returned to San Francisco. He practiced the art of chiropody for three years in the Hamam Baths of San Francisco, when he decided to go to Sacramento. He has lived in that town and successfully practiced the art of chiropody for over forty years. He has the distinction of being a member of the National Association of Chiropodists for a number of years. He is an active member of the A. M. E. Church and is happily married to Miss Madah Hyer, the distinguished vocalist, whose brilliant career will be found in the music chapter.

Dr. Rodgers, a chiropodist, located at Vallejo, coming to California in 1863, is a native of the West Indies and had followed the sea for years having been connected with the Navy. He learned his profession at his home in the West Indies, where the public schools teach both the trades and professions.

CHAPTER XX

LITERARY DEPARTMENT

In introducing to the reader this department, it is with the object of giving a small estimate of the literary ability of the pioneer and present day Negro of California. The greatest literary work done by the Negro is through his weekly papers. Hence the writer has deemed it correct that this chapter begin with a short review of the editors of race papers and special feature writers on white papers.

The reader's attention is called to the pioneer editors of papers published in San Francisco. These men you will note were internationally known. In view of the splendid services they rendered the race in California, it is quite evident that the Negro people could not have done so much for the good of the race, nor would they have attempted such great tasks, had they not been confident of the support afforded them through their race journals. The reader's attention is also called to the splendid collection of poems by pioneer writers. These poems were published on slips of paper and sold to raise funds to fight adverse legislation. The writer has the original copies in her possession, they having been given to her many years ago by pioneer Negro people for their reproduction in this book.

The poem by Mrs. Priscilla Stewart was written shortly after the passage of a bill demanding that all Free Negroes leave the State, at which time the Governor or Ruler of British Columbia sent his Harbor Master to San Francisco to extend an invitation to the Negro people to come to Canada and make their home. The writer of this poem recognized the call as coming from Queen Victoria, who has been quoted as saying that she would not be crowned with slavery in her crown.

The poem by William J. Wilson was written during the fight made by the Negro people for the "Right of Testimony." The poem by Miss Cecelia Williams was written and read at the Fourth Anniversary of the Fifteenth Amendment to the Constitution of the United States. This lady was a great reader, Shakespearean actor and writer.

"Forget-Me-Not" was written by Professor Edward Caine, who was a brother of Bishop Caine, and a great philosopher and lecturer, delivering many lectures for the encouragement of the race. He used the argument in all of his lectures that "God made of one blood all men of the earth." The reader's attention is especially called to a collection of short poems, beginning with "Crispus Attucks," "My Razor," and others. These poems, signed "Jeams," are from the pen of Captain Ferguson of the Brannan Guards. They are taken from an unpublished collection of his writings and were given to the writer for this book by his wife. The poems just listed constitute the pioneer contribution. There are many others in the book from present-day Negroes which are worthy of any race.

This brings us to the Pacific Coast Negro Newspaper Editors, Writers and Publishers, both pioneer and present-day. In pioneer days the Negro press in California was highly respected by the opposite race and much valued by the Negro race. The Negro press championed the race in all its severe fights for the privilege to live in California.

The first Negro paper published in California was the *Mirror of the Times*, which was published in 1855, at San Francisco, California. Hon. Mifflin W. Gibbs and Mr. James Townsend were owners and publishers. It was published for seven years, when it was merged with the *Pacific Appeal*. The editor of the *Afro-American Press*, in speaking of this paper, said: "*The Mirror of the Times* did much good work which cannot be denied by any one. * * * It nobly defended the race and fought for the common cause of Abolition until 1862. * * * The Times did excellent work and the *Afro-American* of today feels proud of its efforts.

"The next Negro paper published in California was the *Pacific Appeal*, which was established at San Francisco in 1862. *The Pacific Appeal* is independent in thought and in action. Its columns are open to all parties for logical discussion of every question pertaining to the welfare and progress of the people without regard to race, color or condition. With these characteristics, viz., its political attitude, extensive influence and wide circulation, it was regarded by the intelligent of all classes as the most desirable and readable newspaper ever published by Afro-Americans. As was the practice of every Afro-American journal, the *Pacific Appeal* had a motto: 'He who would be free, himself must strike the blow,' which it adhered to as best it could under existing circumstances." Thus it will be seen what was the vital principle underlying the contest this paper intended to make, in view of what was a common fight through the paper, that of Abolition or freedom to the enslaved.

Mr. Peter Anderson was the able editor for years and was untiring in his fight for the race, both through the columns of his paper and by attending every meeting of interest to the race. "He was assisted in the editing and publishing the paper by a Mr. William A. Carter. It was because of this paper that Mr. Phillip A. Bell left for the Pacific Coast to become its associate editor.

"During Mr. Bell's connection with the paper, he exercised his journalistic zeal for which he was so well and favorably known, and in this, as a matter of fact, did his part in enabling it to stand. It was a sprightly-looking sheet, a six-column folio and attractively printed. Its editorials were of a solid and sound character, which always indicated the power and makeup of the paper."

Mr. Phillip A. Bell served as associate editor of the *Pacific Appeal* until April 18, 1865, when he began the publication in San Francisco of *The Elevator*. This paper was the organ of the executive committee of the Colored Convention of California. The *Afro-American Press*, in speaking of it, said: "Mr. Bell, having had up to this time twenty-five years of experience in editorial work, of course, started the *Elevator* without any trouble either as a finished product or business enterprise. It was neatly printed, of four pages, with seven columns to a page. Its motto was 'Equality before the Law.' While an earnest and efficient writer himself, he had an able corresponding editor in the person of William J. Powers. His publishing committee consisted of William H. Yates, James R. Starkey, R. A. Hall, J. P. Dyer and F. G. Barbadoes.

"The life of Mr. Phillip A. Bell is one full of interest and sacrifice. Previous to coming to California he published the second Negro paper in America. The first one was *Freedom's Journal*, published in New York City by a Mr. Russwurm, making its appearance March 30, 1827. The owners of *Freedom's Journal* and the *Rights of All* were supposed to have been the same person. Rev. Cornish was the associate editor in the publication of *Freedom's Journal*, which was changed to *Rights of All* March 21, 1828. The *Rights of All* suspended publication in 1830, it having been conducted under more opposing circumstances than *Freedom's Journal*, owing, possibly, to the great amount of good it was doing for Abolition. Mr. Russwurm's career as an Afro-American journalist was soon cut short after the suspension of the paper. He was captured by the Colonization Society and sent to Africa.

"Afro-Americans, north and south, began to feel the need of an exponent of sentiment and thought. The road had been opened, if any one by dint of sacrifice and strength of effort, would lay all on the altar in the publication of another journal. Phillip A. Bell, the Nestor of Afro-American journalism, came forward and put upon the uncertain wings of journalistic time a paper which battled with unrelentless vigor for the right. In January, 1837, appeared the first issue of the second journal edited by Afro-Americans under the name of the *Weekly Advocate*. The editor was Rev. Samuel E. Cornish, and the proprietor Mr. Phillip A. Bell. It was published by Mr. Robert Seers, of Toronto, Canada, a warm friend of the race. * * * After two months it changed its name to *Colored American*. The money to aid in its publication was largely contributed by anti-slavery advocates. The proprietor, Mr. Bell, was known and respected for the work he did for the race in the newspaper field. He was one of those men who not only gave his literary ability to the cause, but his money also. * * * He longed to see Afro-American journalism a fixed thing in this country and he did not die without the sight."

A description of Mr. Bell has been given in "The Rising Sun," a book by William Wells-Brown, who said: "He is medium in size, dark complexion, pleasing countenance and very gentlemanly in his manners. Mr. Bell resigned from the *Colored American* in 1839 and later went to California. Mr. Bell had served in the school of experience before coming to California. He knew what it meant to sacrifice, and yet he came with no intention of shirking his duty to his race. He was well educated to that extent that previous to his identifying himself with any of the race papers he contributed to the daily white papers of San Francisco. He was a dramatic critic, and, during his time, criticized Keene, McReady, Forrest and others."

The Afro-American Press, in speaking of Mr. Bell and the publication of the *Elevator*, said: "Mr. Bell was often in very straitened circumstances, but he managed to continue the publication of the journal. It was always readable." The writer has seen many copies of the paper, which have been a source of great help in many departments of this book, and often regretted that more of our present-day journals were not as carefully edited.

Unfortunately Mr. Bell died April 24, 1889, in destitute circumstances. He sacrificed both time and money for the best interests of the race. He was a real "Trail Blazer" and the first Negro to write for white daily papers in California. At his passing the press throughout the land paid him the highest tribute. Would that space permitted giving extracts from all. The following is quoted from the *Gate City Press* of Kansas City, Missouri: ''Phillip A. Bell, the octogenarian journalist, is dead. In his death the Negro race loses the oldest and one of the ablest of American editors. Fifty-two years ago in New York, he flung to the breeze, as a menace to the slave owners and slave hunters, *The Colored American*. A quarter of a century ago he moved to San Francisco, where the *Pacific Appeal* was started in 1862. Mr. Bell launched *The Elevator*, a spicy, weekly, which continues to this day, the oldest secular Negro newspaper. Educated, original, capable of fine powers of analysis, he flung the sparkling rays of his imagination over the production of his pen and came to be regarded as the Napoleon of the colored press. For some years he has been too feeble to engage in newspaper work. Wednesday, April 24, at the age of eighty-one years, his spirit fled to his Maker. He died in the poor house. And this is the end of a great historic character.''

The *New York Age* paid him a fine tribute. It said: ''Phillip A. Bell has closed his eyes in death. * * * To all New Yorkers the fact opens a history of the past that is not only interesting but profitable to consider. It brings up previous memories; it recalls to mind when New York City would call her roll of fifty and more men, bighearted, self-sacrificing men, who publicly distinguished themselves and served the cause of the race, not selfishly, but for justice's sake; men upon whom each other could safely rely; sensible, considerate men, stirring energetic men, who were not simply active in efforts to free and enfranchise their brethren in bonds, but who were actively interested to forward the cause of morality generally, of education, of refinement and of the general weal. They were men of influence and inflexible character when principle was at stake. * * *

''To be restless and aggressive is the lesson his life presents to the individuals of today, to those who have the manliness to feel that their talents, character and citizenship are not properly respected. He was tall and prepossessing in appearance and manners. He had a fine address, was quick, impulsive and brave, with a keen sensibility as to honor, and those other amenities that mark a gentleman and refined society. He was open-hearted and genuine.''

The writer has in her possession a copy of the *Elevator* which was supposed to be an extra, and published under date of July 4, 1865. It is about seven inches long and less than ten wide. It contains the program for a procession and order of the exercises of a Fourth of July celebration, and the part of the parade in which the colored citizens would take part, together with the order of the exercises in the church afterwards. When we compare the large amount of advertisements contained in the program sheets for such purposes at this date, and the amount of money derived from their publication, one can readily understand how Mr. Bell went into bankruptcy through his devotion to the race. This program was delivered to the subscribers by him personally at four o'clock the morning of the parade. He may have died in the poorhouse, but all who knew him say that he left a priceless memory filled with rich inspirations for future generations of Negro men and women to be genuinely true to the race.

''In the early Eighties the *Elevator* passed into the hands of Mr. James Wilson and Mr. William Blake, two staunch race-loving men. Their sketches will be found in the biographical section of the book. While under their leadership the *Elevator* was published at 622 Clay street, San Francisco, and was a much larger sheet. During the Eighties there was another paper published in San Francisco by a Mr. Robert Brown. It was called *The Vindicator*. Mr. Brown was the descendant of a Forty-niner, and a personal friend of the Honorable Mifflin Gibbs. *The Sentinel* was edited by Mr. A. A. Collins at 1020 Powell street. Later a Mr. R. C. O. Benjamin became its owner and editor. He had edited and owned several newspapers in the east for the uplift of and defense of the race. Mr. Benjamin first located in Los Angeles, where he was employed as city editor of the *Los Angeles Daily Sun*, the first Negro in the United States, so far as we know, to hold so prominent a position on a white paper. Mr. Benjamin was widely known to the newspaper fraternity by the non de plume of 'Cicero.' As a newspaperman, Mr. Benjamin has been a marked success. He is fearless in his editorials, and the fact that he is a Negro does not lead him to withhold his opinion upon the live issues of the day; but to give them in a courageous manner. His motto is: 'My race first, and my best friend next.' '' (Extract from *Fair Play*, Meridian, Mississippi.)

Two Negro newspaper-writers of the present day, whose sketches the writer considers it a privilege to give to the reader, are the internationally-known Mr. and Mrs. Noah D. Thompson, of Los Angeles. They can be called pioneer, recognized writers for white daily papers. They have established themselves in the literary world and opened a door for other members of the race.

Noah D. Thompson is on the editorial staff of the *Evening Express* and *Morning Tribune* of Los Angeles, California. He is a special writer, featuring the best interests of the Negro race. He is a keen observer, never allowing an opportunity to escape whereby he can serve his people. Mr. Thompson's training and experience previous to coming to California well fitted him for his new position in the literary world, as the following will show: "Noah D. Thompson was born at Baltimore, Maryland, June 9, 1878, son of William P. and Sarah (Wood) Thompson; educated in the public schools of Baltimore; took course in Gregg's Business College, Chicago, Ill.; married Lillian B. Murphy, daughter of editor John H. Murphy, owner of the *Afro-American* of Baltimore, November 6, 1901. His first wife died March 31, 1905, and he was married to Eloise A. Bibb, of New Orleans, La., August 4, 1911. One child, Noah Murphy Thompson.

"For nearly twenty years Mr. Thompson was engaged in the money department of the United States Express Company of Chicago, Illinois. From 1909 to 1911 associated with the Booker T. Washington educational institution at Tuskegee, Alabama. Later moved to Los Angeles and engaged in the real estate business, handling mostly personal property, and was associate editor of *The Liberator* of Los Angeles from 1912 to 1913. Was offered the position of sergeant-at-arms of the Paris, France, Exposition in 1900. Member of the advisory council appointed by the Governor of Illinois for the National Half-Century Anniversary of Negro Freedom, Chicago, Illinois, 1915. Member of the Los Angeles Chamber of Commerce and the Soldier's and Sailors' Welfare Commission, also appointed by the United States Government as a 'Four-Minute Man' for the duration of the war.''

It is a rare instance in the literary world when both the husband and wife are a success in letters. The lives of Mr. and Mrs. Noah D. Thompson appeal to the writer with the same standard as that of Robert and Elizabeth Barrett Browning. If the reader will but recall the lives of these writers, it will be remembered that they were intensely in love with each other; and yet equally as much in love with their work in the literary world. Mr. and Mrs. Noah D. Thompson have a happy home life and are very much a success in the field of letters.

Mrs. Thompson is known best by her first name, Eloise Bibb-Thompson. For many years she has been special feature writer for the Sunday issue of the *Los Angeles Tribune, Morning Sun* of Los Angeles, and a contributor to the popular magazines. *Out West* and the *Tidings*. The last named is the official organ of the Diocese of Monterey and Los Angeles. Among her notable contributions to *The Tidings* was an article, "The Church and the Negro," and a beautiful, inspiring poem, entitled "A Garland of Prayer," which appeared in the November issue of 1917 and which, with Mrs. Thompson's permission, appears in the Literary department of this book.

Mrs. Eloise Bibb-Thompson and her husband are both Catholic; recently she addressed the Catholic Women's Clubs of Los Angeles in the Knights of Columbus hall. The daily papers, in commenting on her appearance, spoke of her as a "distinguished speaker," and, while her subject was an appeal for her race, in all the different daily papers her address was spoken of in the highest terms without the constant addition, as is often the case "as a colored woman." Too often a colored speaker before a white audience has had his subject overshadowed by the constant reference to the speaker's race. They wrote her up in a truly democratic fashion. The address did much good for the Negro race.

While Mrs. Eloise Bibb-Thompson is identified with the literary life of Los Angeles, she is not a Californian. But, as with her husband, her education and years of experience have splendidly fitted her for the position she now fills with honor to the race, as the following sketch will show: "Mrs. Eloise Bibb-Thompson, writer, born at New Orleans, La., daughter of Charles H. and Adel Bibb; father was inspector of United States Customs about forty years; graduated New Orleans University; student at Oberlin College, in Ohio; graduated from the Teachers' College, Howard University, Washington, D. C.; took special course in New York School of Philanthropy; head resident of the Social Settlement House of Howard University, Washington, D. C., from 1908 to '11; married Noah D. Thompson in Chicago, Illinois, August, 1911. Permanent address 1711 East Fifty-fifth street, Los Angeles.''

The following additional history has been made by Mr. and Mrs. Noah D. Thompson since the completion of their sketches: Mr. Noah Thompson has been appointed member of the official staff of the Soldiers and Sailors' Welfare Commission of Los Angeles, California; chairman of the National Colored Soldiers' Comfort Committee; member of the War Department's Special Committee of One Hundred Speakers; member of the editorial staff of the *Los Angeles Evening Express*, and frequent contributor to the *Los Angeles Times* and other periodicals. Mr. Thompson is a devout Catholic, who prays that his race will never lose its religious fervor.

REV. WM. T. CLEGHORN
Rector of St. Phillips Episcopal Church,
Los Angeles.

FATHER DAVID R. WALLACE
Rector of St. Augustine Episcopal
Church of Oakland.

HON. NOAH D. THOMPSON
Associated Editor on the Daily Express
and Tribune of Los Angeles.

REV. N. P. GREGGS
Pastor of The People's Independent
Church of Christ, of Los Angeles.

REV. CHARLES PRICE JONES
Overseer of the Churches of Christ.

Recognizing Mr. Thompson's ability and integrity, Congressman H. Z. Osborne nominated him to succeed the late James Curtis as United States Minister to Liberia. The nomination was endorsed by Senator Hiram Johnson and many others prominent in the affairs of the State and Nation.

As a "Four-Minute Man," in all his talks to his race, Mr. Thompson urges preparation in order that they may be ready to take advantage of present-day opportunities and still more opportunities that will come to them and all others that live in this progressive age and country.

When addressing white audiences, Mr. Thompson pleads for more encouragement to their colored employees by promoting them according to their merits. He especially urges that colored boys and girls, when not attending school, be given employment in office, shop and factory much in the same way that white boys and girls are given employment, and at the same time an opportunity to learn the business of the employer from the bottom up.

Mrs. Thompson is a staunch Catholic and deeply interested in the seven million or more of her race who possess no religion. Knowing the immeasurable benefit of Catholic training, she is very anxious to see this unfortunate group enter the bosom of the church, for she believes that, as she says: "You do not arouse the lethargic energies of a people seeking a newness of life by implanting information to the mind, or skill to the fingers, but by quickening of the spirit. Religion is absolutely essential, either as a solvent or as a salve."

The present-day persons of color in the southern part of the State have produced some wonderful race papers. Of these the reader's attention is called to the one published by the late Honorable J. L. Edmonds, who was the editor of the *Liberator*, a paper whose editorials were of great value in moulding sentiment for the race many years before the coming of the N. A. A. C. P. Mr. Edmonds has a most interesting sketch in this chapter. The next person to edit and publish a race paper in Los Angeles was Mr. J. Neimore, who came to California from Texas about twenty-five years ago and established the *Eagle*. Since his passing, a Miss Charlotta Spears, coming from Providence, R. I., has taken charge of the paper and has, by earnest and sincere work, succeeded in building up a first-class paper. After she had thoroughly established the paper on a paying basis, she enlarged the sheet, and about this time decided to marry. Miss Spears was such a perfect success and a great incentive for others to try and advance in the world, the public was fearful that she would retire from the editorial part of this great and most reliable race paper; but the lady has proven that she did not decide to take a life partner into the business without knowing that he, too, had been fearless and true to the race as an experienced newspaper editor. She married Mr. Joseph B. Bass. The writer is proud of the friendship of this lady, for she has encouraged her in the writing of this book by accepting articles from her pen for publication in her great paper.

Mr. Joseph B. Bass was prominent in public life in Kansas, teaching school until 1895. With Will Pope he established the *Topeka Call*. In 1898 he sold the same to Nick Chiles, who renamed it *The Plaindealer*. Went to Helena, Montana, in 1905, and established *Montana Plaindealer;* came to California in 1911; to Los Angeles in 1912 and joined forces with the *Eagle*, which was renamed the *California Eagle;* is prominent in church and fraternal circles; Grand Master of the Grand United Order of Odd Fellows   Editor Joseph B. Bass has succeeded in winning a powerful influence in politics, which carries with it a tremendous weight with the masses. He is a fearless writer and uncompromising in any fight for the best interest of the race. His influence in politics is recognized by politicians all over the State, until it is almost a foregone conclusion that whichever way Editor Bass is headed, "Just so will the ticket go."

Los Angeles has another race editor who wields a good influence in politics. He publishes the *New Age*, a paper whose tone and careful proofreading make it one of the most welcome papers in all homes, and he recently was elected to represent the Seventy-fourth District of the State of California in the Legislature. This refers to the Hon. Frederick Madison Roberts, who has the honor of having won an election in a district where two-thirds of the voters are white, and where his opponent circulated cards which said: "My opponent is a nigger." Mr. Roberts is the son of the well-known pioneer undertaker, Mr. Andrew J. Roberts of Los Angeles.

The Hon. Frederick Madison Roberts was born in Chillicothe, Ohio, coming to California with his parents when he was very young. He attended Los Angeles public schools, graduating from the L. A. High School, after which he immediately entered the University of Southern California, leaving before receiving a degree. Later he attended the University of Colorado, at Colorado Springs, and graduated, receiving the degree of Science and Letters. He afterwards graduated from Barnes School of Mor--

tuary and Sanitary Science. In 1910 he was deputy assessor in El Paso County, Colorado.

He returned to Los Angeles and purchased the *New Age*, a paper which had been but recently established in that city. He has successfully published it for years. Later, wishing to advance further, he accepted a position as principal of the Mt. Bayou public school, in Mississippi. He held this position for several years, after which he returned to Los Angeles and resumed his editing of the *New Age*. He is a true American and has worked unceasingly for the aid of the Liberty Loan and Red Cross, and is a member of the Soldiers' and Sailors' Welfare Commission of Los Angeles. Mr. Roberts has traveled extensively. This, together with his fine understanding of human nature, enabled him to become a ready writer, a firm and sincere race man. He knows how to fight for the race with that dignity and polish that comes from a knowledge of the science of understanding the mind of the masses. His writings, while convincing, are never abusive. His paper is thoroughly reliable, neat and well edited.

Professor Charles Alexander is another race editor located in Los Angeles. He is owner and publisher of the *"Citizen Advocate."* This paper is well edited and the proof is always carefully read. Mr. Alexander is an old newspaperman, having published many magazines and books, as his sketch will show. Mr. Alexander is actively interested in the N. A. A. C. P. and other movements for the advancement of the race. Recently he was on a committee of gentlemen who together accompanied Attorney Edward Burton Ceruti when he made a second plea before the supervisors of Los Angeles County not to rescind their vote to admit Negro girls to attend the Nurses' Training school. Mr. Alexander's address on this occasion will be found, together with Mr. Ceruti's, in this chapter, as they are both historical and in after years will show to coming generations the kind of men that were "Trail Blazers" in the fight for an equal opportunity in California for the Negro race.

The San Francisco district of California also has many good race papers edited by men who are sincere in the fight for equal opportunity for the race. Among this number is Mr. Joseph Francis and Mr. Derrick, editors and owners of the *Western Outlook*. It is a weekly paper and published in San Francisco. They have been very generous in donating space in their paper for worthy movements, such as the Sojourner Truth Home Club of Los Angeles, when a few years ago they were struggling to pay for the property. The paper is reliable for pioneer data and the writer has secured many names for the Pioneer List from the *Western Outlook*. Mr. Francis and Mr. Derrick at one time attended the University of California, at Berkeley. Their paper is a creditable race enterprise.

San Francisco also has a monthly paper edited and published by Mr. George Watkins, who came to California from Shrevesport, Louisiana, about thirty years ago. He owned a printing plant worth several thousand dollars which he lost through the earthquake and fire of 1906 in San Francisco. The paper he is now editing and publishing is called *The Pacific Appeal*. Mr. Watkins was personally acquainted with the late Peter Anderson and many of the pioneer race editors of San Francisco.

Editor Watkins enjoys the distinction of being the first colored person in California to publish a book on the Pioneer Negroes of the State. About twenty-five years ago he edited and published a small pamphlet which he called "A Souvenir of Distinguished Afro-Americans of the Pacific Coast." The work, contained a number of good and interesting sketches concerning miners and other pioneers who helped make California a good place for the Negro to live in. The editor kindly loaned the author the only copy of this valuable book now in existence, with permission to quote from these sketches in this history. He also generously loaned the author his files of old newspapers, many of which were issued before the earthquake and fire and contained valuable material which has been quoted, especially concerning San Francisco. Mr. Watkins is a sincere race man and owns valuable property in Oakland and the Imperial Valley.

Several years ago there was published in Los Angeles a race paper by a Mr. Buber Brown. This paper was known as *The Los Angeles Post*. He was a victim of the white plague, dying during the past year. The race has enjoyed at different times promising magazines by scholars and writers principally in Los Angeles. Among this number the writer has seen copies of *The Cactus*, *New Age* and *The Peace Guide*.

The following is quoted from the biographical sketch as written by the late Bishop Arnett concerning the "Poet of the Maumee," J. Madison Bell, as an introduction to the book of poems of the distinguished original poet and reader, which said: "The wealth of a nation does not consist alone in its bonds of gold, silver or land, but the true wealth consists in the intelligence, courage, industry and frugality of the men; the intelligence, culture and virtue of its womanhood. Each generation produces its men and women for the times in which they live.

"In war, warriors are produced. In case of law, judges and others are produced, so that the times, whether of an individual, family or race, very seldom call for a man that he is not to be found to lead on the armies, to teach its children, to encourage its people to renewal of energy and effort. Our race is no exception to the general rule of history. During all of our sorrowful and sad history we have had men and women when needed. * * * J. Madison Bell was born April 3, 1826, at Gallipolis, Ohio. He lived there until he was seventeen years of age. In 1842 he removed to Cincinnati, Ohio, and lived with his brother-in-law, George Knight, and learned the plasterer's trade. Mr. Knight was one of the best mechanics in the city.

"At the time of the arrival of Mr. Bell in Cincinnati, the subject of education was agitated among the colored and white people. The school question was one of the living and burning questions, and had been since 1835. Previous to that time the schools were privately taught by white men for white children, but Mr. Wing and a number of others allowed the colored youths to attend the night schools. Peter H. Clark, in speaking of the time that Mr. Bell came to Cincinnati, uses the following language: 'A number of young men and women, filled with the spirit of hatred to slavery and a desire to labor for the down-trodden race, came into the city and established schools at various points; one in the colored Baptist Church on Western Row, was taught at various times by Messrs. Barber, E. Fairchilds, W. Robinson and Angus Wattles. Among the ladies there were the Misses Bishop, Lowe, Mathews and Mrs. Merrill. * * * A part of the salaries of these teachers was paid by an educational society composed of benevolent whites, many of whom survived to witness the triumph of principles which they espoused amid such obloquy. A number of colored men co-operated heartily in this work, among whom may be named Baker Jones, Joseph Fowler, John Woodson, Dennis Hillis, John Liverpool, William O'Hara and others. These schools continued with varying fortunes until 1844, when Rev. Hiram S. Gilmore, a young man of good fortune, fine talents and rare benevolence, established the Cincinnati high school, which was in some respects the best school ever established in the city for colored people. Its proprietor, or rather patron, spared no expense to make it a good success. Ground was purchased at the east end of Harrison street and a commodious building of five large rooms and a chapel was fitted up. Good teachers were employed to instruct in the common branches of an English course, besides which Latin, Greek, music and drawing were taught.' * * *

"The subject of this sketch was a busy man; he worked by day and studied by night. He worked at his trade in the summer and fall and studied in the winter, each spring coming out renewed in strength and increased in knowledge. It was in these times that Mr. Bell entered school and at the same time was indoctrinated into the principles of radical anti-slaveryism. It was in this school in connection with Oberlin College that the sentiment of 'Uncle Tom's Cabin' was born in Walnut Hills, Cincinnati, Ohio, giving an impetus to the cause of human freedom. Thus imbued and thus indoctrinated, he desired a wider field to breathe a freer atmosphere where his sphere of usefulness could be enlarged, which could only be enjoyed under the British flag. In August, 1854, he moved with his family to Chatham, Canada, where he lived until 1860. Mr. Bell was a personal friend of John Brown, of Harper's Ferry. He was a member of his counsel in Canada, and assisted in enlisting men to go upon the raid. He was his guest while the recruiting was going on in Canada and was one of the last men to see John Brown when he left Canada for the United States. He only escaped the fate of many of John Brown's men by the providence of God. He assisted in raising money to carry on the work. * * * It was while in his twenty-second year that he courted and married Miss Louisana Sanderline, and to this marriage a number of children were born who became useful citizens. * * * February, 1860, he started for California and landed in San Francisco on the 29th of the same month.

"Upon arriving on the Pacific Coast he found the leaders of his race in an active campaign against the disabilities of the children and the race in that new country. He immediately became one of them, and joined hands, heart and brain to assist in breaking the fetters from the limbs of his race in California and giving an equal opportunity for the people to acquire an education.

"He was united on the Coast with a noble band of leaders; among them were Rev. T. M. D. Ward, Darius Stokes, John J. Moor, Barney Fletcher, J. B. Sanderson, Rev. John T. Jenifer, Richard Hall, F. G. Barbadoes and Phillip A. Bell, editor of the *Pacific Appeal.*

"Rev. James Hubbard, in speaking of the pioneers of the gold coast, said: 'They endured many privations, chief among which were the lack of home comforts and influences.' At the convention held by the ministers of the African Episcopal Church he took a prominent part in the convention, uniting his intelligence and moral forces with the people. A convention of ministers and laymen met in San Francisco Tuesday, September 3, 1863. Brother Barney Fletcher called the meeting to order and Elder T. M. D. Ward was appointed chairman. In this convention they discussed the subject of the Church and State. We find Mr. Bell participating in this convention, and he is reported as being a steward of the church at San Francisco. He was a member of the committee on finance and ministry and their reports gave the proper key-note for ministerial education. * * * While in California, some of his most stirring poems were written, among them the poems on 'Emancipation' and 'Lincoln.' * * *

"While living in Toledo, Ohio, J. Madison Bell was elected as a delegate from Lucas County to the State convention, and there he was elected as a delegate at large from Ohio to the National convention which met in Philadelphia, May, 1872. At this convention General Grant was renominated for the presidency of the United States. During the campaign his voice was heard in many portions of the State pleading for the re-election of the hero of Appomattox. * * *

"The honor of presenting an individual to a select company or to a distinguished audience is a privilege a man perhaps enjoys once in a life time, but the privilege that is now afforded is of a very high order, the privilege of introducing an author and his book not to a select company of friends or to a high dignitary, but to the commonwealth of letters, to the thinking men, women and children of the present and future generations. The honor carries with it a responsibility for the character of the individual and the character of the book, therefore I do not fear the consequences of the introduction of so distinguished an individual or so useful a book. * * *

"In 1884 the general conference of the A. M. E. Church adjourned its session in Baltimore and was received at the White House by the President of the United States, Chester A. Arthur. It was my pleasure to present the bishops, general officers and members to His Excellency, the President of the United States, an honor enjoyed by few. The privilege of introducing one of my own race, of my own church and political faith, a man whose poems will stand as his monument from generation to generation and will give light and joy to the laboring and struggling people for many centuries."

The above quotation is from the pen of one of the greatest Negro orators that ever lived and a delightful Christian gentleman. The writer is proud to say she knew the late Bishop Arnett, and will add that his estimate is valuable, for he was capable of judging the book and author.

William Edgar Easton (Senior) was born in New York City March 19, 1861, of Charles F. Easton, Sr., son of the American Revolution, and Marie Antoinette Leggett-Easton, a descendant of a hero of the Revolutionary War, of Haiti. There were three children, Marie A., born in Plymouth, Massachusetts; Charles, Jr., born in New Orleans, and the subject of this sketch. At the age of thirteen, bereft of his mother, William became the charge of his godmother, Baroness de Hoffman, who entrusted him to the care of a Catholic priest and he was entered in the Seminary de Troise Rivieres, Canada, afterwards entering the La Salle Academy of Providence, Rhode Island, and completing his education in a college of the Congregation de Saint Croix.

At the age of twenty-two he took up his residence in Texas, where he taught school, married and became prominent in the Republican politics of that State, having for twelve years served as secretary of the Republican State Executive Committee, chairman of the Executive Committee of the Republican party of the County Travis, the location of Austin, the capital of the State. With the assistance of Rev. I. B. Scott, afterward Bishop Scott, of the M. E. Church, and Rev. A. Grant, bishop of the A. M. E. Church, Mr. Easton organized the *Texas Blade* Publishing Company and became its editor, giving the race a fearless advocate and defender.

In the year 1895, Mr. Easton was appointed storekeeper of the bonded stores of the Galveston custom house. Prior to that, in 1886, he had been appointed, along with Rev. A. Grant, a commissioner to the New Orleans and South American Exposition. In the year 1895, Mr. Easton was appointed night police clerk of San Antonio, Texas, and served the administration with honor during his incumbency.

Though for many years a writer of short, humorous stories for weekly and daily papers, Mr. Easton elected to write his first book as a tribute to the magnificent courage and achievements of the Negro. Hence his first book, "Dessalines," came from the press, its theme the heroic struggles of the Haitians for independence. The late Judge Tourgee, "Bystander" of the Chicago *Inter-Ocean*, styled "Dessalines" the first evidence of a high order of literary excellence by the American Negro. The Haitian government attested its historical accuracy in a warm letter of appreciation. In the year 1910, Mr. Easton published his second book in Los Angeles, California, having been a resident of the State of California since July, 1901. This book was entitled "Christophe," a continuation of the heroic struggles for a stable government of the Haitian people. It was successfully staged in Los Angeles, having its initial performance in New York City by the foremost actress of the race, Miss Henrietta Vinton Davis. This lady had the leading character in the first performance of "Dessalines," afterward staging her own version of the drama in a Pennsylvania circuit. Mrs. Spear-Bass, editress of the *California Eagle,* and a lady of keen literary perception, wrote of Mr. Easton's books that they were a quarter of a century ahead of the race for whom they were written, and probably his literary work would not be properly appreciated in the author's life time.

Mr. Easton has been very active in public life here, editing a newspaper. He was the first of the race to serve as either a city or county deputy field assessor, and, at several tax collection periods, acted as a clerk in the county clerk's office. In politics Mr. Easton has always been found where he could do the most good for his race, and in the campaign of Mayor Harper, demanded and received for the race, in acknowledgement of its loyalty at the polls, an ordinance making the refusal to serve members of the race a misdemeanor with, as a penalty, loss of license to do business.

In the year 1915 Mr. Easton was appointed to the responsible position of custodian of the State offices, in Los Angeles, and, though furnished with white janitors at the start, he has succeeded in making the janitorial force of the State offices and Exposition Park partly colored. These positions pay ninety dollars per month. After serving seven months as custodian he entered into a competitive examination with sixteen others, all white but himself, and was reappointed under the State civil service. A short time ago Mr. Easton was appointed the manager of the Los Angeles branch of the State purchasing department and had an increase in salary.

Hon. Emmett J. Scott selected Mr. Easton as a member of the National Bureau of Speakers for the War Department, the first appointment of the race west of the Mississippi, and since, he was selected a member of the "Four Minute Speakers" by Hon. Marshall Stimson, the director for Southern California. The most recent honor to come to Mr. Easton has been his appointment as chairman historian for the race's war activities during the trying times of this great international struggle, worthy of a place in the volumes that will be published by the State Council of Defense.

Mr. Easton showed his appreciation of women's work by having Governor William D. Stephens make a forceful and sympathetic address to the California State Federation of Colored Women's Clubs, and escorting him to the rostrum, having himself the day before, in his capacity as a member of the National Speakers' Bureau, delivered an address that was received with marked attention and resounding applause. Mr. Easton believes in the good women of the race and tells me that he treasures, above all other testimonials (and they are numerous) the following letter, herewith reproduced:

"California State Federation of Colored Women's Clubs.

"Oakland, California, August 21, 1918.

"Mr. William E. Easton, National Represenative, All American League of California, Los Angeles, California.

"Dear Sir: We, as an earnest body of women striving for self-betterment and the betterment of all humanity, wish to congratulate you for the honor bestowed upon you as a member of the Special Speakers' Bureau of the War Department. We feel proud of you, and we know in selecting you to act in that capacity they have chosen one who is able to convey to the public the meaning and significance of this great and terrific conflict not for a world's supremacy and the murdering of innocent women and children, but a world's fight for democracy.

"We sincerely wish you continued success and attention with your able addresses and noble plea for justice for all humanity. You will overlook our delay in sending you our congratulations, for we have just returned to our homes from your beautiful city, where we had the pleasure of listening to your very interesting as well as instructive remarks during one of the sessions of our Federation.

"Yours for 'Deeds, not Words,'

(Signed) "MRS. HETTIE B. TILGHMAN, *President*

(Seal of Federation) "MRS. EDYTHE NICHOLAS, *Secretary.*"

In the department devoted to Speeches and Poetry will be found an interesting letter which Mr. Easton sent Hon. Emmett J. Scott and has since used as his four-minute speech when addressing the race. The writer considers it a masterpiece, as well as historical.

Mr. Jefferson Lewis Edmonds, the subject of this sketch, was a thorough race-loving gentleman. He was a resident for many years of Los Angeles. He was born a slave, having been the property of Dr. Jefferson L. Edmonds, and was reared where he was born on the plantation near Culpepper Court House, Virginia. He acquired an education after the Emancipation Proclamation issued by the martyred President Lincoln, and finally migrated to Los Angeles, California.

He immediately became an active co-worker and many times a leader in every movement of interest to the race. He was fearless and edited for years a weekly race paper known as *The Liberator*. He was one of the founders of the "Forum" and the "Afro-American Council," which extended its membership all over the State. A ready and forceful, polished writer, he did much for the race in Southern California, because he was an eloquent orator and one whose interest never lagged. He was often asked to deliver addresses by members of the other race, as on the occasion of the dedication of a monument to the memory of the late Owen Brown, a son of John Brown, of Harper's Ferry fame, and at the memorial services over the deceased daughter of John Brown, Mrs. Ruth Brown-Thompson, of Pasadena. His oration on these occasions were published in full in the daily papers. They are wonderful productions and, like his editorials, even to this day are inspiring to read.

This paper, *The Liberator*, was devoted to the cause of good government and the advancement of the Afro-American. Its title was one that the writer thinks was really one which the Liberator, John Brown, would have selected had he been privileged to do so. The combined issue of this worthy paper for January and February, 1904, was really of historical value because it gave a complete survey of the conditions and advancement of every activity of the race in Los Angeles.

In 1909 the *Los Angeles Times* issued a similar edition. Mr. Edmonds was invited to write the leading article, which was given prominence on the front page of this historical issue. Mr. John McGroarty, the great historian and writer, wrote the introduction which appeared opposite the article by the late Hon. Jefferson Edmonds.

Mr. Edmonds was happily married and left to mourn his passing a wife, Mrs. Ida Edmonds, and the following children: Jefferson L., Dorathea, Susie E. Warner, Ida, Elgin, Cordelia A., Blanchard K., Walter C., Willie and Lena M.; one daughter, Sallie, had died. Mrs. Edmonds' mother, Mrs. Sallie Moore, came to see her daughter after an absence of forty years, from Valdosta, Georgia, to California at the age of eighty years, traveling alone.

There were many beautiful testimonials written concerning the life of our subject upon his passing. Would that space permitted quoting from many, but this sketch cannot close without quoting from the *Western Outlook* of San Francisco, January 4, 1914, which said: "The death of J. L. Edmonds, editor of the *Los Angeles Liberator*, removes from the scene of action one of the most forceful writers of the race on the coast. He was a man who stood up for his convictions, and seemed to fear nothing. He believed in the right and stood up for the same and was a staunch advocate of manhood-rights for his race. He was an able thinker and a close reasoner and his editorials, though often keen and biting, always commanded attention."

The writer had the pleasure of looking over the files of Mr. Edmonds' papers and was surprised to find that he had every year bound in book form, leaving a historical record few men in any race would have taken the care and time to make, in order to preserve for future generations such valuable records as are newspaper files.

Mr. James B. Wilson, the subject of this sketch, came to California in 1863, from Wilmington, Delaware. He came as a cabin boy on the William Neil revenue cutter, and was in the waters of Hampton Roads during the battle of the "Monitor" and "Merrimac." The vessel was en route to Antwerp, Belgium, and Liverpool. On its return trip it called at the port of Baltimore and hence to California.

After Mr. Wilson's arrival at the port of San Francisco, he decided to remain. He readily secured employment in the Navy department of the Union Iron Works of that city. He served as messenger for the Union Iron Works of San Francisco for eleven years, during which time he studied the art of stenography and typewriting, being one of the first to master this trade in all of San Francisco's colored population. This knowledge was the means of opening the door of opportunity and he received a position in a white law office.

Mr. Wilson was ever ready to improve his condition, and during spare moments read law, qualifying himself to be admitted to practice, but owing to the prejudice existing in that period in California he was refused to opportunity to stand an examination. Having determined to advance in the world, he resigned his position and entered the newspaper world as an associate editor of the *Elevator*, together with Mr. Phillip A. Bell and William Blake. The writer has seen many copies of the paper during the time Mr. Wilson was associated as editor and was highly gratified over the clean, newsy, well-edited sheet, which had grown twice the size of the original paper.

Mr. Wilson was an intense race-man, was interested in and worked in every movement for the benefit and uplift of the Negro race in California. He was one of the organizers of the Afro-American Council, one of the most influential organizations in the State working for the welfare and uplift of the Negro. He was a member of the Grand Lodge of Odd Fellows, and for a number of years held the appointment as deputy sheriff of Alameda County, California, serving under Sheriff Frank Barnett

He was appointed by Governor Hiram Johnson as notary public for Alameda County, California. Mr. James Wilson was a valuable citizen not only of the City of Oakland, but of the entire State. His advice was often sought on many issues of the day. He was highly respected and has been greatly missed since his passing, leaving to mourn him a widow and one daughter, whose sketch will be found in "Distinguished Women."

Mr. John A. Wilds, the subject of this sketch, was born a slave in North Carolina, in 1845, and passed through the Civil War. He came to Oakland with his wife and four children in October of 1874, locating in the part incorporated as Brooklyn. He followed draying for a livelihood until 1879, when he was appointed night-watchman and janitor of the city hall. He retained this position under seventeen city administrations, and was retired under the new city charter in July, 1912. His faithfulness to duty won for him the highest praise from city officials and the public in general. Many commendable editorials concerning his diplomacy and faithfulness were published in the daily press and race papers at the time of his retirement.

Mr. Wilds has always been an active worker in the service to assist the race advance. He was associated with the men who made the fight for equal school privileges for the Negro children. He has been a member of the Fifteenth Street A. M. E. Church for over forty years. It has been fully thirty-five years since he assisted in the organization of the church aid and literary societies. He has been a trustee of the church for thirty years, and superintendent for the Sunday school for eighteen years.

Mr. Wilds is a member of the Odd Fellows Lodge and a leading member of the Afro-American Council. He found time to publish and edit the *Oakland Sunshine*, the first race paper published in that city. He had a paper that was well-edited, a clean, newsy sheet which aimed to inspire the Negro people to advance and contend for their rights as American citizens. During the past few years he sold the paper to Mr. Bridges, who still owns it. Rev. Coleman is editor and general manager. Mr. Wilds has lived a life for the good of mankind in general and is well-respected by all who know him, in both races.

Professor C. A. Biggers is the president of a commercial college by the same name located in Los Angeles. This young man is thoroughly educated and competent to give instructions in all the branches necessary for a business education. He deserves great credit for the courage he has in attempting to bring to the race such valuable knowledge. This war has demonstrated to the Negro race what a handicap it is to not be efficient in at least a business education, especially when the government has opened so many opportunities for advancement in the Army and Navy.

Professor Biggers has the distinction of being the only Negro whose sketch appeared in a book called "Men of Distinction." The subjects for this book were selected from men in California, Nevada and Nebraska. The work was well-known and highly recommended for its value in the commercial world, the Davis Commercial Encyclopedia, published in 1917. Since the date of its publication Professor Biggers had added much to the prestige of his record by the history he has made. Among the many the following is noteworthy of comment and credit to him:

"The manager of the *Labor Union Magazine* purchased a hundred-dollar scholarship and gave it away, as one of their first prizes, on Labor Day. A magazine publishing company known as the *California Delineator* purchased a hundred-dollar scholarship and gave it away as one of their Christmas prizes. Beside these commendable expressions of appreciation shown the Biggers Institute by white companies, fond appreciation has been shown by organizations of his own race. The B. Y. P. U. Federation, comprising the union of fifteen Baptist churches of Los Angeles County, purchased five and one-half scholarships and gave to four of their deserving members."

The following appeared in the "Davis Commercial Encyclopaedia": "C. A. Biggers, president of Biggers' Business College, located at 408 Germain building, Los Angeles, California, has been connected with the institution for the past thirteen years, during which time he has seen the college grow to gratifying proportions. The college offers instruction in all business branches, including higher English and gives individual instruction to all pupils, of whom there are a large number. In the time Mr. Biggers has been with the college he has had in his classes between four and five thousand students, three hundred and twenty-seven graduates, three hundred and twenty-two of whom were secured positions.

"Mr. Biggers was born in Oswego, Kansas, in 1882, a son of Phillip and Julia Biggers. His education was received in Kansas City, Missouri. He graduated in Pough-keepsie, New York; entered the George R. Smith College and graduated in 1903 with the degree of A. B. Moving to Oklahoma, Mr. Biggers was for three years in the government employ as court reporter in the deposition department concerning the allotment of Indian claims. Mr. Biggers was for two years principal of the Ardmore City schools, later opening his own business college in Muskogee, Oklahoma, where he remained for eleven years. He has lectured on various educational topics throughout Texas, Oklahoma, Kansas and Missouri in the interests of educational affairs. He won first prize in the Freedman Aid Colleges in the contest of writing poetry, and was offered a professorship in the commercial department of three of them. Coming to Los Angeles in 1913, Mr. Biggers has since conducted the present Biggers Business College, meeting with success in instructing and securing positions for his pupils.

"Mr. Biggers, in 1905, married Miss Trelawney Beatrice Dunbar, now dead, and has three children—Charles, ten; Earnest, eight; Willetta Mae, six years old. He is a member of the State Clubs, All American League and the Odd Fellows, and feels that this section is a place of great possibilities for all races, industrially and educationally. Truthful representation of the country will do much to assist in its advancement, and he himself is ever ready to support any movement which has for its purpose the dissemination of useful information regarding the community."

"Professor Charles Alexander, educator, author, literary critic and orator, was born at Natchez, Mississippi. He went to New London, Connecticut, when a small boy, and in that city received his literary training. He has been regularly employed on the staff of Boston (Massachusetts) and Philadelphia (Pennsylvania) daily newspapers; has traveled in Europe, the Island of Cuba and throughout the United States and Canada. He has served as teacher for four years in the Agricultural and Mechanical College at Normal, Alabama; two years at Tuskegee Institute, in Alabama, and four years at Wilberforce University, in Ohio. From 1893 to 1896 he published *The Monthly Review* in Boston, Massachusetts. From 1905 to 1909 he published *Alexander's Magazine* in Boston, and conducted a general printing business. He has contributed book reviews, short stories and poems to various newspapers and magazines throughout the country. He is the author of the following books: 'Evidences of the Progress Among Colored People' (1896), 'One Hundred Distinguished Leaders' (1897), 'Under Fire with the Tenth U. S. Cavalry' (1898), 'Making Printers at Tuskegee' (1900), and 'Battles and Victories of Allen Allensworth' (1914).

"As a platform speaker Professor Charles Alexander occupies a conspicuous place. He has lectured in eighty-six towns in California. In his work as lecturer on 'Paul Laurence Dunbar,' the Negro poet, there is subtle analysis and sincere appreciation of the poet's genius. The thought and feeling of the speaker find full expression in a voice of rare sweetness. Through his interpreation of the Negro dialect poems, the quaint picturesqueness of the Negro nature are vividly portrayed. After one hears the rich love stories, of how intensely and nobly the Negro strives to attain his possibilities, there is a heightened respect for the race. Professor Alexander is a fine writer, a poet of high ability and a platform orator of rare powers. He is a master of the Negro dialect so splendidly used in Dunbar's poems and short stories." (See Literary chapter for verse by Professor Alexander.)

The following is an exact quotation from letters received by Professor Alexander:

"First Methodist Episcopal Church.
"Charles Edward Locke, Pastor.
"Los Angeles, California, Sixth Street and Hill.

"It gives me great pleasure to speak in terms of heartiest commendation of Professor Charles Alexander and his unusually fine lecture on 'Paul Laurence Dunbar.' It is safe to say that Professor Alexander gives altogether the most exhaustive interpretation of the great Negro poet. He is an entertaining speaker and that audience is to be congratulated that has the opportunity of hearing him. The Methodist Ministers' Meeting of Los Angeles enjoyed a rare hour when Professor Alexander paid them a visit, as did also the Methodist Brotherhood of the First Methodist Episcopal Church.

"CHARLES EDWARD LOCKE."

"First Baptist Church.
"William H. Geistweit, Pastor. Fred D. Finn, Associate Pastor.

"San Diego, California, November 24, 1915.

"The best evidence I can give to the worth of such an evening as Professor Alexander gave our people in the White Temple is to say that we at once asked him to come a second time within the next six weeks. Personally, I want to say that it was one of the rarest evenings I have enjoyed for many a year. The Poet Paul Laurence Dunbar was truly a genius; I am inclined to say this ,'his interpreter, Mr. Alexander, is scarcely less a genius.'   ''WILLIAM H. GEISTWEIT.''

The following poems are the writings of Pioneer Negroes:

A VOICE FROM THE OPPRESSED TO THE FRIENDS OF HUMANITY
Composed by one of the suffering class.

MRS. PRISCILLA STEWART.

Look and behold our sad despair,
    Our hopes and prospects fled,
The tyrant slavery entered here
    And laid us all for dead.

Sweet home! When shall we find a home?
If the tyrant says that we must go
    The love of gain the reason,
And if humanity dare say ''No,''
    Then they are tried for treason.

God bless the Queen's majesty,
    Her sceptre and her throne,
She looked on us with sympathy
    And offered us a home.

Far better breathe Canadian air
    Where all are free and well,
Than live in slavery's atmosphere
    And wear the chains of hell.

Farewell to our native land,
    We must wave the parting hand,
Never to see thee any more,
    But seek a foreign land.

Farewell to our true friends,
    Who've suffered dungeon and death.
You have a claim upon our gratitude
    Whilst God shall lend us breath.

May God inspire your hearts ,
    A Marion raise your hands;
Never desert your principles
    Until you've redeemed your land.

COLUMBIA
By WILLIAM ROSS WALLACE.

Columbia stands forth as the Queen of the Nation,
With the diadem of Freedom radiant with the stars flashing
From her spotless brow.
Look up with proud and solemn joy unto our Flag,
That for the deathless right of man
Blazed over Freedom's threatening crag
When slavery's bolts were hurled,
For a million heroes made its stars
The hope-lights of the world.

Oh, see we not amid the joy
Now where the battle's o'er,
Our dear, great country, greater yet
On shouting chainless sea and shore,
All state hates from us hurled,
For a million heroes made our stars
The hope-lights of the world.

THE GLORY OF THE COMING MAN

By Miss Cecilia Williams, *Shakespearean Tragedienne.*

The one great act in Freedom's cause,
The act that now we celebrate,
That should uplift us man to man,
We still exist in name alone.

The iron hoofs of nations still oppress us.
I strove to penetrate the unknown future,
I look back on the dim and musty past,
And yet I feel it will not always last.

I rouse from apathy my sluggish self,
And shake the dust of bondage from my brow;
Until the Civil Rights in thundering tones be spoken
The task of freedom is but half-begun.

Let education fit us for the conflict
Let us be united both hand and heart together,
And then the sun will spread its rays before us
To cheer the glory of the coming man.

Those men that freedom has ennobled,
And men whose virtues are immortal,
So let our friend and statesman guide us,
Charles Sumner, from the spirit land.

And may his good deeds live within the Senate
Till with our fairer kindred
We shall be brothers hand in hand;
I see the future rise before me,
The glory of the coming man.

The following poem was written and recited by the author, James Madison Bell, on the occasion of a great public meeting held by the colored people in Sacramento, California, commemorating the death of the Martyred President, Abraham Lincoln, on Tuesday evening, April 18, 1865. The poem afterward was published in the daily papers and also the colored papers.

POEM

Wherefore half-mast and waving sadly,
And seeming ill-disposed to move,
Are those bright emblems which so gladly
Were wont to wave our homes above?
And why is this all glorious nation
Thus in her hour of hope bowed low?

Wherefore those marks of grief and sorrow
So visible on every face?
To what foul deed of bloody horror
Do all those gloomy signs retrace?
Aback to the walls and lofty spire,
Back to your country's bleeding sire,
Back to your dying Magistrate.

We know not why God has permitted
This tragic scene, this bloody deed;
An act so seemingly unfitted
In this auspicious hour of need.
Though none perhaps may the intention
Or the wondrous purpose tell,
Of this direful life suspension—
Yet God, the Lord, doeth all things well.

Our Nation's Father has been murdered;
  Our Nation's Chieftain has been slain
By traitorous hands most basely ordered;
  And we, his children, feel the pain.
Our pain is mixed with indignation,
  Our sorrow is not purely brief,
And nothing short of a libation
  From Treason's heart can bring relief.

And we, in spite of earth and heaven,
  On bended knee with lifted hand,
Swear, as we hope to be forgiven,
  To drive foul Treason from the land.
And that fair land so long polluted
  By the sweat of unpaid toil,
Shall be by Liberty uprooted
  And thickly spread with freedom's soil.

Thus we'll avenge the death of Lincoln,
  His noble principles maintain,
Till every base, inhuman falcon
  Is swept from freedom's broad domain;
Until from tower and from turret,
  From mountain height and prairie wide,
One Flag shall wave—and freedom's spirit
  In peace and love o'er all preside.

Among his poems is a collection of War poems, which were written in California, and are, namely, ''The Black-man's Wrongs'' and ''The Dawn of Freedom.'' Some of these poems contained as high as twenty-five verses and were full of music and a message that to the writer are classic. It is especially true of his poem upon leaving San Francisco.

THE COMING MAN

By WILLIAM J. WILSON.

I break the chains that have been clanging
Down through the dim vault of ages.
I gird my strength, mind and arms
And prepare for the terrible conflict.
I am to war with principalities, powers, wrongs,
With oppressions—with all that curse humanity.

I am resolved;
'Tis more than half my task;
'Twas the great need of all my past existence.
The gloom that has so long shrouded me
Recedes as vapor from the new presence.

And the light gleams. It must be life
So brightens and spreads its pure rays before
That I read my mission as 'twere a book.
It is life; life in which none but men,
Not those who only wear the form, can live
To give this life to the world;
To make men put off the thews and sinews of oppressed slaves.

FORGET-ME-NOT

By EDWARD CAIN.

To flourish around my native bower
  And blossom around my cot,
I cultivate a little flower
  That's called forget-me-not.

The ocean may between us roll,
    And distance be our lot,
I hope that we may meet again;
    I pray, Forget-me-not.

So adieu! Some happy day,
    When we shall meet again,
May the fragrant breeze of summer bear
    The fragrance of the glen.

May every bright-winged, singing bird
    Plume themselves in song;
So short would seem our summer's day,
    We wish it still more long.

Adieu, adieu! your little stars
    Are twinkling one by one,
When the moon comes out to take the place
    Left vacant by the sun.

When all the stars grow dim
    They cannot pierce her light;
How proud and beautiful she is,
    My dearest friend, good-night.

CRISPUS ATTUCKS

Black, and a man of might,
He struck, and fell for the right;
Tho' he himself was 'neath Freedom's ban,
He struck and died for his fellow man—
Not the black man; but the white.

History with hesitating pen has writ his name
But stealthily, as though in fear that fame,
In seeking out her heroes for her prize,
Might through her less discriminating eyes
See Black names 'mongst the White.

I saw him (in thought) as he stood,
And his glance seemed to say that he should
Yield up his own life though in unequal strife,
If 'twas only for Liberty's good.
And he struck, and how mighty the blow,
Though the Britons laid many lives low,
The blood of the Black and the blood of the White fomented a
Baptismal font for Freedom.   —JEAMS.

MY RAZOR

A thunderbolt from Heaven cast,
    When Angels warred against their God,
Fell on the summit of Mount Atlas,
    And Hercules tore it from the sod;
Vulcan, the mythological smith,
    From a small spark this razor made,
And Venus, who'd admired the work,
    Smiling sweetly, kissed the blade.

                              —JEAMS (1878).

LE BOUTONNIERE

Mignonette and Pansies, too,
    Pansies and sweet Mignonette,
Tell me that your love is true;
    Say that you will ne'er forget.
When Mignonette's sweet odor's lost
    And Pansies' purple hue is gone,
Then will I feel that hope is past,
    Your love forever from me flown.

                    JEAMS (October 15, 1881).

WITHERED FLOWERS

I have pressed in a book a pretty red rose
That oft-times reminds of a love I once knew,
And whenever I gaze on its delicate form
The leaves seem to say that love is still true.
When this sign of love's freshness no longer appears,
And the red, too, that told of a warm love is gone,
'Twill be then, not till then, I'll regret the past years
And feel that the love I once cherished is flown.

—JEAMS (May 9, 1881).

And now will be presented to the reader a few poems by the present day Negro.

A GARLAND OF PRAYER

BY ELOISE BIBB-THOMPSON.

Amid the stress of daily life,
Its cares, success, and its strife,
    I would repair
To Thee, O God, and at Thy feet
I'd lay, with all its perfume sweet,
    A wreath of prayer.

Today my only thought shall be
A zealousness in loving Thee—
    The Elder flower.
And to this chaplet I shall bind
The energy of soul and mind,
    Thus hour by hour.

Tomorrow, in my garland fair,
I'll twine Devotion deep and rare—
    The Heliotrope.
Though oft the tempter hover near,
In Thee, so faithful and so dear,
    Shall be my hope.

No virtue, Lord, is loved by Thee
More than a spotless Chastity—
    The Orange flower.
I'll weave my thoughts while I shall live
Without a stain, if Thou wilt give
    Thy grace and power.

And I would have my garland bear
The fragrant bloom of Meekness fair—
    The Lilac wild.
My soul shall then receive from Thee
A perfect peace, for I shall be
    Thy humble child.

And thus each day shall be my care
To add another flower of prayer,
    Until complete.
When fairest are my flowers all
Then may my spirit hear Thy call
    At Mercy's seat.

DO WE REMEMBER

BY WILLIAM NAUN RICKS, OF SAN FRANCISCO.

Full fifty years have passed away,
Yea, fifty years have day by day
Fulfilled the laws of destiny
And passed into eternity.
Hear you the drum throughout the land?

Old drums, which know the master hand,
Whose fervent practice for this day
Has swept the fifty years away?
These souls, whose darkened chambers keep
The key where memories lie deep
And break all the bounds this day,
To live this thirtieth of May.

With tattered flags and dream-fired gait,
(Impatient if the line should wait),
Come men who fifty years ago
Were flushed with manhood's healthy glow.
Not less today; but fifty years
Have brought conditions fraught with tears,
For some are poor and all are old;
But hearts as true, as brave, as bold
Beat underneath those coats of blue,
As when in youth they dared to do
The bidding of their soul for right.
How bravely now they face the might.

Do we remember why they fought?
Have we from them their vision caught?
Does Liberty stand out as clear?
Is Freedom to our hearts as dear?
If not, this thinning line of blue
Proclaims to us to our trust untrue.
If we forget their sacrifice
We stand disgraced before their eyes.
Let Freedom true our land embrace,
That we, like them, the grave may face
In conscious pride of work well done,
To keep Old Glory in the sun.

The following poem is also from the pen of Mr. Ricks, who is one of the most popular Negro poets today in California:

A GREETING AND A WISH FOR EASTER

I would that from out our lives
The winter of sorrow and sickness
And misunderstandings would pass;
That the marvel of the spring,
The resurrection of Light, perfect light,
And the sunshine of Love, perfect love,
For all God's creation would come
As the spring brings grass softly.

TO AN OLD FRIEND
By William Naun Ricks.

I did not know in long-past years
How full the way might be of tears—
How great the need before the end
Of one true heart like yours, my friend.

And joy of youth, all foolish, lies
Around our hearts to blind our eyes;
But time removes the gaudy veil
And shows the friend who will not fail.

Today I search the past years through,
Contrasting old things with the new,
And through each pathway to the end
I found your footprints, dear old friend.

And so, my friend, with faith secure,
What years may bring I can endure;
Because I know your loving heart
Of joy or pain will share a part.

IT MATTERS MUCH

By Professor Charles Alexander.

It matters little where I was born,
Or if my parents were rich or poor;
Whether they shrank at the cold world's scorn
Or walked in the pride of wealth secure.
But whether I live an honest man
And hold my integrity firm in my clutch,
I tell you, brother, plain as I am,
It matters much.

There is no more popular Negro poetess in the United States than Mrs. Eva Carter Buckner.

WHAT CONSTITUTES A NEGRO?

By Eva Carter Buckner, of Los Angeles.

When the first slave-ship was landed
With its cargo on this side,
There was then no vexing question
As to which race he's allied;
Just a Negro, pure and simple,
And as such might have remained,
But—well, here we drop the subject,
For there is nothing to be gained.

Years have passed, and now we see him
On him's turned the strongest light;
Every race is represented—
Black, brown, yellow, red, and white;
And they call him now a problem,
For there's One not been consulted
And in it He is involved.

There's rise and fall of Nations,
But, dispute it if you can,
There is just one God and Father
And the brotherhood of man.
Ten-tenths blood of pure Caucasian,
This it takes to make you white.
But one drop of Negro blood is
Just the same, as black as night.

For this stamp was put upon him
And so let it thus remain,
For what is the use contending?
All contentions are in vain.
It is said ten million Negroes
On this firm free land doth stand.
God inspires him to mount upward
Though chains bind both foot and hand.

Read his crimes in boldest letters,
Negro, and no question then;
And we own him, our heads bowing,
Grieved to know we have such men.
On the other hand turning,
We can point with pride to those
Who thought it worth while in striving,
And to fame and honor rose.

Dumas, known as the French nov'list,
He his Negro blood could trace;
Tanner, artist known so widely,
Who has won himself a place.
Yes, and there is the "Black Napoleon,"
Brace "Toussaint L'Ouverture,"
And the great Edmonia Lewis,
Sculptress, whose work will endure.

And we claim S. Coleridge Taylor;
    Dunbar, though he's dead still lives;
Booker Washington we all know,
    For the race his best thoughts gives;
Bishop Grant, in sermons, lectures;
    Dubois, John H. Jackson, true;
Chestnut, Vernon, trace 'em; Pushkin,
    Browning, many others, too.

Great Rome had her gladiators,
    And of them was very proud;
We care nothing for the prize-ring
    But, since it has been allowed,
Why not then applaud the winner,
    Whether white or dusky man?
The survival of the fittest
    Is the rule, and it will stand.

Call him Ishmaelite or Arab,
    Paraphrase him, if you will;
Say Egyptian, if more pleasing,
    But he is a Negro still.
This would be a grander Nation
    With the goodness that's innate.
It would be a perfect haven—
    But the prejudice—too great.

But, there, friends,
    Join us in life's great combat,
Though your skin be dark, what matter?
    You're a man, e'en for all that;
And we are using every effort
    To make good where e'er we trod,
One hand with the flag a-waving,
    And the other stretched to God.

Mrs. Buckner has also permitted the writer to publish her favorite poem:

IF LINCOLN COULD RETURN TODAY

If Lincoln could return today,
I wonder what he'd think and say
About this great and glorious land
O'er which he once had full command?
With all the progress he would see,
I know he would astonished be.

The lightning speed of which we boast,
A touch, a sound from coast to coast;
The clearly, distinct spoken words,
Ships sailing through the air like birds;
Numerous inventions, small and great,
Too many to enumerate.

With all these things so strange and new,
I'm sure he'd scarce know what to do.
And, like a wanderer on the strand,
A stranger in his own homeland—
Until he'd look around and see
That same old flag of liberty.

I wonder then if he'd recall
The greatest deed he did for all,
And that if he would sorry be
That he had set the captives free?
Ah, yes, the world knows it was he.

SERGT. CHARLES RAYMOND ISUM
365th Infantry, First Battalion, Medical Dept. 92nd Division,
National Army, World's War.

LIEUT. EUGENE LUCAS
Company A, 368th Infantry, 92nd Division,
National Army, World's War.

PERSONNEL INTELLIGENCE SERGEANT
HENRY M. BROOKS
350th Machine Gun Battalion, 92nd Division,
Map Maker, National Army, World's War.

But 'twas a mightier hand, you see,
Guided the pen. 'Twas so to be
That all his legacy might share
What you and I love best, free air;
And, too, his knowing eye could see
That, to advance, all must be free.

And Nature says, and it is true,
To crush the one we crush the two,
And all who love their country true
Love Lincoln's name, naught else to do.
And, O! could he take one survey—
I wonder what he'd think and say?

ONLY BE STRONG
BY JOHN H. ALLEN.
Reproduced from the *Pacific Appeal*.

In ancient days when Israel trod the way
    To God's promised land,
Temptations, sin and death strove night and day
    To cheat the band;
But God stood with them, 'gainst the heathen's ire;
    His presence kept them as a wall of fire.

And when the mighty host from Jordan's shore
    With rapturous gaze
Faintly beheld the promised land of yore,
    Through the thickening haze
Joshua, the Captain, stood gazing sad and long,
    And silent voices whispered:
"Only be strong."

O! Ethiopia, my own beloved race,
    Dispel thy fears,
Heed not the gathering mist, the dark disgrace,
    The gloom of years;
'Tis true, 'tis true, tho' I cannot tell thee why,
    But the battle's the hardest when the victory's nigh.

So, onward, upward to a higher plane,
    O'ercome the foes;
Forget old Egypt, her ways disdain,
    Her deadly throes;
And through the Jordan thou must go, O! valiant throng!
    But go like men, God whispers;
"Only be thou strong."
Marysville, California, August 6, 1903.

The following poems were written by Charles Alexander and were published in
The Los Angeles Times:

MY KIND OF MAN

I like the man who will go to the bat,
And will take of his coat, and throw off his hat;
Who will roll up his sleeves, and spit on his hands,
And hit at the ball just as hard as he can.
Hit at it, I say, never mind if he miss;
Never mind if the crowd will hollow and hiss.

I like the man who will enter the race
Unwavering, resolve shining out of his face;
Who will shirk not, nor falter, but will strive for the goal,
Showing courage and patience when nearing the shoal;
For courage and patience are big bits of grace,
And the man who will claim them may yet win the race.

I like the man who will pick up his load,
Who will start with a rush on his way up the road;
Who will risk every peril he finds on the way,
And say in his heart: ''Every debt I will pay.''
For that sort of a man unheeds the world's lust—
But that sort of man is worthy of trust.

I like the man who is gentle and kind,
Who will show by example the true master mind;
Who knows of the feeling of poverty's pinch
And will stand out for right, every foot, every inch.
For that sort of man is the man of the hour;
He has in his soul God's fire and power.

MY MOTHER'S CUSTARD PIE

You may talk about the cooking
    They do in Italy;
And the kind the Frenchman
    Sets before his company;
Of the German's toast and ''weinies,''
    Or the English mutton-chop.
But there is one thing to remember
    That will start you on the hop;
It's delicious, it is luscious,
    It will brighten up your eye;
It is like a view of heaven—
    That is mother's custard pie.

You have had poetic dreaming,
    With it's rapturous vision rare;
You have known the potent blessing
    Of that swiftly-vanished care;
You have felt ecstatic heavings
    In your big and noble heart,
And have felt the pangs of sorrow
    When your dearest friend would part.
But your joys are without number—
    You can stand the severing tie,
If you know you'll have a portion
    Of my mother's custard pie.

It will take one slice, I tell you,
    To dissipate the gloom,
And to start an agitation,
    Like the buzzing of a loom.
It will bring delights and pleasures
    You have never known before;
It will make you feel like hanging
    'Round about our kitchen door.
Yes, indeed, I know the feeling,
    You'll be ready then to die,
If, for once, you get a-plenty
    Of my mother's custard pie.

The following is quoted from an address delivered by Prof. Alexander before the Board of supervisors of the Los Angeles County upon the question of accepting the resignation of the nurses who had threatened to strike if Negro girls were admitted to the County Hospital. The speaker was one of the committee, and his address, as here given, is quoted from the *Citizen Advocate.* He said:

''Mr. Chairman: I am of the opinion that if this Board of Supervisors will maintain an inexorable position on this question, that the reformation will be of such weight and splendid character as to be beneficial to all classes of institutions all over the country. It is for some one community to take a stand like this, even though somebody has to suffer,—of course, in all these great movements, there is some suffering to somebody. When we close our saloons the bartenders are all put out of jobs—and if you engage in anything that is going to bring about a reformation for people, you are going to have some difficulty; and if these people really do walk out, it will probably be a very good thing for Los Angeles, in arousing the patriotism of the people here, and demonstrating whether or not they really want democracy. I think it would be a splendid thing for them to walk out. It certainly would not be a good thing for the Board of Supervisors to rescind its order for a few people at the hospital.''

An address was delivered by Hon. James M. Alexander of Los Angeles on the occasion of the visit of the then President of the United States of America, the Hon. President William Howard Taft, when he addressed the colored people of Los Angeles, California, at Blanchard Hall, Monday afternoon, October 16, 1911. This occasion was afforded the colored citizens through the combined efforts of Mr. Alexander, as president of the Afro-American Council, and Prof. E. L. Chew, together with a large and most efficient committee of representative professional and business men of the race living in Los Angeles.

On this occasion the master of ceremonies, on behalf of the colored citizens of Los Angeles, presented the then President of the United States, Hon. William Howard Taft, with a Gold Card in commemoration of the occasion. This address is now a part of the history of Los Angeles, and is herein quoted:

''Mr. President: In coming to this hall this afternoon you have highly honored the colored citizens of not only Los Angeles but the State of California, and the Nation. And we beg to assure you that in no place on your long trip will you find more loyal people.

''The colored people are interested in all of the problems that confront the Nation and are keenly watching the methods proposed for their solution. Your wise statesmanship has impressed us and we are looking to you to assist in bettering, as far as you can, the conditions surrounding us.

''We are aware of the fact that, in a great measure, our success depends upon ourselves, but we are forced to admit, that many obstacles in the shape of personal ostracism and discriminating legislation, lie in our pathway to full development. The best there is in us cannot be obtained under present conditions.

''We have learned that the Government is powerful enough to control offending corporate interests and we sincerely hope and fervently pray, that problems of social or political order, especially those problems affecting so large a portion of our people, may be so effectually worked out to the end that the humblest citizen in every section of this great Nation may enjoy every right and privilege guaranteed by the organic law of the land.

''Believing that your desire is to see us in the full enjoyment of all our rights, and that, whenever possible, you will give us the benefit of your assistance, the Afro-American Council of Los Angeles has commissioned me to present to you in their behalf this tablet, as a testimonial of its appreciation for your recognition of the attainments of the Negro race.''

It will be well to here state something of the Afro-American Council. It is an organization purely of California race men who, some twenty or more years ago, banded themselves together to fight for the advancement of the Negro race in this State. Once a year they hold a Congress, when representatives from the different Councils over the State meet in session. During these annual sessions the wives of the members of the Councils hold a fair, exhibiting their handiwork for the encouragement of the race, while the Congress is discussing the grievances of the race and also the advancements. They have their own charter and own property in Los Angeles to the value of fifteen thousand dollars. They intend some day to build a hall upon the plot of land for the use of the race.

''Los Angeles, April 4, 1918.

''Hon. Emmett J. Scott, Special Assistant Secretary War Department, Washington, D. C.

''Dear Sir: Kindly permit me to accept with thanks the honor you have vouchsafed me in tendering me the position on the Speaker's Bureau of the War Department, in your division. Every American citizen, be he of whatever race, creed or national derivation, should be a warm supporter of the United States in this great war for World's Democracy and no citizen more so than the American Negro. To him, in an especial manner, an appeal to arms for Liberty should have an especial significance and should possess all of the qualities of a command.

''The spirit of patriotism that actuated him to become a colossal figure in the Civil War which resulted in the manumission of four million of his brethern again should actuate him; a war equally as Holy and more sweeping in its results for Human Freedom. There can be no World Democracy which does not include the races of darker integument; there can be no World Democracy that fails to affect favorably the present status of the Negro in the American sun. This is so logical, that to deny or combat it would be irrational and, when Peace is attained by the Allies, will be its best argument for the perpetuation of a World's Democracy for which they fought and won.

"Out of this war will come new conditions, new lines of thought and a new spiritual direction. Every soldier who has been abroad fighting for Human Liberty; who, in the presence of death, communed with his soul and who has survived this great struggle for a World's Democracy, will return to his country a missionary for new conditions of faith and practice. There shall be no excuse, no shame for a Democracy charged with race discrimination; no carping criticism, no finger of scorn pointed at us by the Central Powers when we lay claim to be an exemplary Democracy for all the world.

"The world will be better because of this war, and if the white American be first to fill the trenches, first to sail beneath the seas, and first to soar through the starry night, it is not because the Blackman was reluctant, but because of restricted opportunity, and God takes cognizance of all these things. This war is educational; it has the conscience of men in training; it is drawing men closer to God and closer to each other, and when such time comes, He sees fit to give us peace, it will be a lasting and universal peace.

"Yours very sincerely,
"(Signed) WILLIAM E. EASTON,
"National Representative All American League of California."

"War Department, Washington, April 16, 1918.
"Mr. William E. Easton, National Representative All American League of California, Los Angeles.
"Dear Mr. Easton: Thank you for your letter dated April 4, expressing your views with reference to the great war for world democracy. The sentiment expressed by you is altogether worthy, and I am pleased to have you write me in this strain. Let me also thank you for your acceptance of the invitation to serve as a member of the Speaker's Bureau.

"Yours very sincerely,
"(Signed) EMMETT J. SCOTT,
"Special Assistant, Secretary of War."

The following address was delivered by Mrs. Lydia Flood-Jackson before the State Federation of Colored Women's Clubs at their session held in Los Angeles in 1918. It is really a historical paper and hence it is reproduced in this department:

"Madam President, Officers and Members of the California State Federation of Colored Women's Clubs, Greeting:

"Isolation will never develop a beautiful character, for character finds life and growth in contact with the world. After another year of conscientious striving up the path that leads to the higher walks of life we meet each other again in unity and friendship, bringing from our different homes, clubs and localities feelings of love and good cheer and recognizing God as our great protector and only source of supply.

"Dear ones, today we are standing on the threshold of a great era looking into futurity to the mid-day sun of Democracy. Democracy, the all-absorbing topic of the times, must hold our closest attention. We must advance to the firing line and stand shoulder to shoulder with our leaders and go with them over the top.

"Who can break through a phalanx of determined, noble-minded, upright women, backed by the power of the Holy Spirit? Suffrage stands out as one of the component factors of Democracy; Suffrage is one of the the most powerful levers by which we hope to elevate our women to the highest planes of life. None need be negligent or afraid to enter this great field of service that offers so much for the earnest, conscientious worker. The harvest is white. Women, what are we doing to glean this ripened field? What use are we making of the ballot? Lucretia Mott, Susan B. Anthony and Elizabeth Cady Stanton saw by an eye of faith this gleaming field sixty years ago, and their determination, true judgment and executive ability has made it possible for you and me to sit in the shade of the Suffrage Oak, a grand old tree, whose branches will soon top every State in the Union.

"And what are we doing, comrades? We are working with every increasing interest which is bringing us into recognition more and more in the political arena, which this year has especially encouraged us to work more ardently in our different clubs. A few weeks ago the club women of Oakland had an opportunity to test this fact of the importance of our influence and our vote, at a tea given by the Imperial Art and Literary Club at the home of Dr. Mehrman, the Public Administrator. We were pleased to have with us Superior Judge Quinn, District Attorney Ezra Decoto, Assessor Kelly, the Chief of the Detective Bureau and others, all of them recognizing the fact that every woman present had a voice for or against them at the polls on the 27th of August. In Union there is strength. * * * Our women all over the State are interested in all the departments of war work and are making good. The fight for Democracy has been a wonderful incentive to our women to work as they have never worked before. Let the good work go on, and look to the Father of all good and perfect gifts for results.

"(Signed) LYDIA FLOOD-JACKSON."

This lady is the daughter of the first colored school teacher in California, Mrs. E. T. S. Flood, who opened the first school for colored children in Sacramento, and later established a school for colored children in Oakland. Mrs. Jackson, like her mother, is actively engaged in every movement for the betterment of the race. She has traveled extensively, visiting Mexico and South America. She is the originator of the Flood toilet preparation now being manufactured in this State, a fine lady and one whom everybody likes and respects.

This paper is reproduced from an article which appeared in the *Citizen Advocate* under date of October 19, 1918. It said: "The Nurse Training School again. Special conference of Supervisors on Nurse Training problem. Noble attitude of Chairman John J. Hamilton showing him just. Attorney Ceruti makes strong appeal for Fair play. Dodge would dodge the issue." The article then gives in detail the address and fight made before the Supervisors on the question of the nurses striking if Negro girls were admitted. The part of special interest to the race is the wonderful addresses delivered by Attorney Ceruti and Prof. Alexander, which appear in this chapter. Mr. Ceruti's address is as follows:

"I want to first speak in defense of the Federal Government. I listened to the order respecting the training of nurses that came from Washington and I assume that if they are making calls for white volunteers to train as nurses, they have a sound reason and based on true principles. I am not willing to assume that the Washington Government is in favor of class privilege; that they are ignoring colored volunteers because they are colored. There might be some economical reason why the order reads that way. In further confirmation of that view doubtless, gentlemen, you have received a communication from the California Women's Committee of the Council of National Defense, of which Mrs. Seward A. Simons is secretary, and it is addressed to the Honorable Board of Supervisors, in which they urge: 'As colored men are being asked to serve the country as soldiers and as the Women's Committee has been asked to enlist women in the student nurse reserves, and as a number of colored women have already responded to the call, we urge that the training schools for nurses throughout the State be asked to accommodate colored women as student nurses.'

"Neither the sentiment of the public nor the Federal Government are in sympathy with that fine sense of discrimination which these nurses choose to exercise and which they try to bring to bear in the attempt to set up class privilege out at the county hospital. That is to say that no one has a right to train at that public institution, supported by the people of this county, unless he belongs to their class. No, that position is indefensible and should not be tolerated for a minute. I am a stranger to the institution and cannot be expected to know the conditions, nor to improvise nor to direct, nor to manage, such as either one of you gentlemen have. Each one of you has had more experience than I have had. There are—if I am mistaken in the exact number you need not correct me, because I am only assuming certain things not to be accurate—there are about one hundred and eighty nurses out there, we will say; and about one hundred of those have indicated that they will resign. It is my belief that they will not do so. Experience all over the country tells us that they will not do so. The most aristocratic institution in the country, perhaps, is Vassar College. Twenty years ago they had the same problem that you have here today. A young colored lady was admitted by the faculty and the student body, supported by their parents, indicated that they would go out. The college stood firm and not a student left. For twenty years after that the proudest girls' school in the United States has been accepting colored girls. The incident is duplicated and multiplied all over the country. It is a question of whether you are going to cowardly back down. If they win this, they will win in every other fight.

"Now let's see whether we have a real desire to solve the problem or not; that is the question. We can't expect people who are lukewarm and who really are antagonistic to the orders of the Board to devise means of carrying it out. Are the executive officers willing to carry it out? Now this is the question that perhaps these people ought to decide for themselves. If they find themselves out of harmony with the order and not able to carry it out for personal reasons, then it is up to them. It is a matter of professional conscience with them as to what they ought to do, but if this situation arose on any other question, what would this Board do? What would those executive officers of the hospital do? Suppose the girls had said: 'Now we have been receiving only $10 a month; we demand $50 a month, or we walk out.' Under such a condition the Board would receive and consider the proposition, measure it by the rule of reason, and, if that demand was unreasonable, this Board would say, 'Go.'

"Now we have a similar situation only it is more vital. It is a more sacred principle than mere dollars and cents. It is a principle that we are fighting for. It is worth more than dollars to us. It is the principle that we are fighting for in France, that we are fighting for at this table today. It is the same principle—democracy; and if we can sacrifice millions of lives in France for a principle, we can sacrifice a few inconveniences or perhaps even a few deaths in the county hospital, if they choose to walk out, for the same principle.

"Now that is the fair, honest, honorable attitude of this Board. These women who would walk out because colored girls come in and claim the same privilege as they, are Huns at heart."

Speech delivered by John Wesley Coleman, on the presentation of the American Flag to the Independent Church of Christ, Los Angeles, California, August 18, 1918:

"My dear Dr. Greggs, Officers and Members of the Independent Church of Christ and Friends: The regular religious services of this great edifice are permitted to be suspended this evening for a minute or two, while we give over to the care and keeping of this great membership the Colors of our country. This Flag was presented to those of our race who answered the call of their country in the Second Selective Draft, and who have gone forward to meet the discipline of the cantonment and the training of eye and hand and heart that they shall receive by way of preparation for the great struggle beyond the seas; whereupon a glorious battlefield the freedom of which this Flag is an emblem is to be saved from traitorous assaults of a ruthless and barbarous autocracy.

"Upon this Flag is to be enrolled the names of those of our brave boys who were called from Los Angeles and vicinity the first four days of August, 1918. This Flag was presented to them by John C. Cline, the High Sheriff of this great and prosperous County, and was accepted by them as a token of the unity of all the citizens of this great commonwealth in the preservation of the principles which underlie our institutions, and which make us a great and united people.

"This is the Flag of Freedom; it represents the most forward step in political and religious freedom that has ever been taken by any nation or any people in the known annals of the world; it represents every church of whatever denomination in the United States; it represents the right of all people to vote and choose their own leaders, officials and men of public affairs; it represents every school and college of our broad land, where enlightenment is widespread and free to the studious and energetic; this Flag represents all of the libraries, parks and playgrounds, the driveways, the boulevards, the mountain roads and the paths that wind through valleys and over hills of our great and glorious country; this Flag represents our great system of transportation running like a network across this broad continent, under the rivers and through the mountains, by tunnels, across canyon, by bridges that are feats in engineering; it represents the steamships, the lighthouses that guard them as they ply the inland waters and fight their way across the sea; it represents the massive and tremendous Panama Canal and all of the factories and shipyards and rolling mills and docks and foundries and business houses of the American people.

"What a glorious Flag indeed, indicative of the bravery that upheld it since the Battle of Bunker Hill! Indicative of the Freedom it brought to four million of our ancestors under Grant and Sherman, with Abraham Lincoln, the great Martyr, their Commander-in-Chief; indicative of the songs we have sung and of prayers we have prayed; of the determination that lies in the breath of every true American to uphold it forever and a day; for the realization of all the ideals of our republican institutions and that our Glory and Freedom may be enjoyed by us and handed down to our posterity unimpaired, on to remotest time; and that it shall be, we truly know, for it is unfurled and upheld by the Army of the United States, whose skins are red and white and black, but whose courage and devotion are as true and fixed as the eternal principles which flow from the throne of God.

"So we, the Pastor and Members of the Independent Church of Christ, and Citizens of Los Angeles City and County, accept this Flag with sincere gratitude, for we remember how a little more than fifty years ago, we having been in bondage for nearly two hundred and fifty years, God in his all-wise Providence, saw fit to look down and pity the suffering condition imposed upon us by our hard taskmasters and in answer to the prayers of our forefathers and mothers, He caused, by the stroke of the pen of Abraham Lincoln, to emancipate, under the colors of this Flag, and set free, breaking the shackles of four million slaves; turning us loose without, as it were, a penny in our pockets, and that God, having continued to hold the hand of mercy over us enabled us to begin to ferret out our own destiny. So we began at once to pattern after the white man until today we find ourselves in possession of houses and lands, schools and colleges, education and money that will compare favorably with a large percentage of the white people. And if we use the proper precaution in taking advantage of every opportunity that presents itself to us, we will, in the near future, be enabled, together with all other dark races, no doubt, to conquer the world, and then we shall remember that Biblical passage of scripture that says, 'Before the end of time Ethiopia shall stretch forth her wings over this broadcast land.'

''So let these few scattering remarks take root deep down in our hearts that they will cause us to get busy and take advantage of every opportunity that presents itself to us. and it will cause us to grow and flourish as a green bay tree, and that the roots will have grown down and taken such a deep hold that when Johnny comes home from the war and the floodgates of foreign immigration have poured into this country by the thousands from all over the world in the next few years, we will have risen so high in the estimation of those whom we are dependent upon for support, the soldier boy, or that foreign immigration, or any other will be unable to do us harm. And when all the battles of races will have been fought and victory won on our side we will be enabled to cry with a loud voice, as one of the prophets of old, and say, 'O Lord, we have seen Thy glory and now we are ready to be offered up.' 'Let us then be up and doing, With a heart for any fate, Still achieving, still pursuing, Learn to labor, and to wait.' So the 'Lives of great men oft remind us, We can make our lives sublime, and, departing, leave behind us Footprints on the sands of time.' ''

CHAPTER XXI

The Negro Soldier

The Southern Workman, under date of January, 1918, contained the following quotation from the *New York Times:* ''Like a pathetic romance runs the story of our soldiers in black. Too little has been told about them by the writers of American History. A better understanding between the races might have long ago materialized had a page or two here and there from the musty old Government reports and official war records, long buried in the dustiest corners of the big libraries, been inserted in the text books on American History, giving the Negroes' part in the Nation's Wars.'' The writer deems it befitting to quote the above, especially when speaking of the Negro soldiers of California during the pioneer days and the present-day Negro soldiers of California now serving in the World War.

The spirit of the times has directed our thoughts, writings and daily living to the study of war and Military Morale. It is impossible to eliminate the subject, try as we will. Since such is the case, it is befitting that we study the different types of soldiers now engaged in the present world war, beginning with the Negro.

The Negro soldier has been employed in the wars of the United States since Colonial times. It was during the early Colonial wars that so many free Negroes and slaves fought in the Continental Army. Slavery, at that period in the colonies, was different from what it was after the Declaration of Independence, when it developed into a commercial industry. During Colonial days the Negro slaves were brought into closer contact with their masters, and given some educational advantages and permitted to bear arms. This resulted in the Negro slaves often fighting in the Continental Army by the side of their masters.

There were no organized regiments of Negroes until the British raised two Negro regiments and placed them in service. Notwithstanding the fact that Negro soldiers, fighting in the Continental Army, had proven their courage and fighting qualities, the Colonies debated the advisability of arming the Negroes and making full soldiers of them, whether slave or free. While they debated the question, the British continued to enlist and organize Negro regiments and train Negroes as soldiers.

Historians never tire in speaking of the heroic death of the Negro Crispus Attucks, who was the first person to lose his life in defense of the Colonies. They have almost forgotten to mention the heroism of the Negro on Bunker Hill, by the name of Peter Salem. The heroism of Negro soldiers in the Revolutionary War is one of the most romantic in the history of that great struggle, both with the British forces and the Continental Army.

The -Continental Army did not decide to enlist Negro soldiers until after the wonderful praise bestowed upon Negro troops by the French General La Fayette and other French officers. Their praise of the courage, heroism and valor of the Negro troops fighting within the ranks of the Continental Army led to a deeper consideration of their worth and eventually to the New England States adopting a system whereby they offered as compensation to the slave his freedom if he enlisted and fought the common enemy. The records of the Continental Army, together with the writings of General George Washington, will endorse this statement and also numerous words of praise for the Negro soldiers by white officers serving over them. Thus we can truly say with the poet who wrote of Crispus Attucks:

> ''Black, and a man of might,
> He struck and fell for the right;
> Tho' he himself was 'neath Freedom's ban,
> He struck and died for his fellow man,
> Not the Black man, but the White.
> *   *   *   *   *   *
> The blood of the Black and the blood of the White
> Fomented a baptismal font for Freedom.''

It was Toussaint L'Ouverture, the great Negro General of San Domingo, who, in 1800, after freeing the island from slavery and declaring its independence, issued a proclamation which, among other things, said: ''Sons of San Domingo, come home. We never meant to take your homes or lands. The Negro only asks that liberty which God gave him. Your houses await you, your lands are ready come and cultivate them.'' And from Madrid and Paris, from Baltimore and New Orleans, the emigrant planters crowded home to enjoy their estates under a pledged word that was never broken. "No retaliation" was the motto and rule of his life. It has been the rule and motto of every Negro soldier ever since. Did not the Negro soldier pledge to himself "No retaliation?" How could he, having fought in the Revolutionary War and after the war was successfully won for the colonies, silently march away to again return to the shackles of a slave? If the Negro soldier did not carry in his heart the motto of that greatest of Negro generals, Toussaint L'Ouverture, "No retaliation," how could he have fought in the Civil War of the United States for one year without pay? It was that great Negro diplomat and statesman, the late Hon. Frederick Douglass, who, President Lincoln says, repeatedly urged him to employ Negro soldiers to fight for the Union. But, alas! after the Government decided to employ Negro soldiers, they also told Mr. Douglass they would not pay them the same as the white soldiers. Mr. Douglass, having confidence in the Negro, urged them to accept the opportunity to fight and prove their courage and manhood and not to accept any pay if by so doing they had to lower their standard as the equal of any other man on the battlefields. The Negroes, taking his advice, fought like none other. They set their standard not only for their own emancipation, but for unborn generations of Negroes, proving to the world by their valor, heroism and courage that they were not cowards. Although they had suffered for centuries as slaves, nevertheless they were men in the fullest sense of the word.

The average reader is familiar with the story of the Negro Color-Bearer in the famous 54th Massachusetts Regiment, who, when mortally wounded, exclaimed, while dying: "Colonel Shaw, the Old Flag never touched the ground!" This Negro soldier lost his life, but he dignified and held as sacred his position as color-bearer of the regiment. The martyred President Lincoln upon several occasions spoke of the Negro soldiers. This was especially noted when he spoke at the Sanitary Fair, in Baltimore, April 18, 1864. His address was on the meaning of the word "Liberty," but in the midst of his remarks he took occasion to speak on the painful rumor concerning the massacre of Negro troops at Fort Pillow, and said: "At the beginning of the war, and for some time, the use of colored troops was not contemplated, and how the change of purpose was wrought I will not now take time to explain. Upon a clear conviction of duty, I resolved to turn that element of strength to account, and I am responsible for it to the American people, to the Christian world, to history and in my final account to God. Having determined to use the Negro as a soldier, there is no way but to give him the protection given to other soldiers. * * * It is a mistake to suppose that the Government is indifferent to this matter, or that it is not doing the best it can in regard to it." At another time he made his words very clear when he said: "I was, in my best judgment, driven to the alternative of either surrendering the Union and with it the Constitution or of laying strong hands upon the colored element." The United States Government did not surrender its Constitution and the records of the Negro soldiers at Petersburg, Chapin's Farm, Hatcher's Run and at Appomattox are records of history and prove that the Negro soldier was worthy of the confidence entrusted in him.

What was the attitude of the Negroes in California? Were they willing to go, if called to the colors? They were not called, but enthusiasm ran high among the Negro people then living in California, many of whom went east as body servants to white army officers that they might be near the center of activities. There was a number in the City of San Francisco who held meetings and opened an office and registered their names in enlistment, forming a company and preparing themselves to serve the Government if called. The following is an account of a few of their meetings. Realizing the pleasure to an old pioneer of reading such, the writer has deemed it correct to quote them from a paper now in her possession, the only one in existence, in which it said: "Pursuant to notice, a public meeting was held in Scott Street Hall on Monday evening. Mr. Henry C. Cornish was appointed chairman and Louis N. Bell, secretary. The call for the meeting was read by the secretary together with spirited extracts from the *Anglo-African* relating to the Massachusetts 54th Regiment and the Fremont Legions. The proceedings of the previous meetings were read and the resolutions passed at that meeting were unanimously adopted as the platform for future operations.

"Mr. A. Furguson addressed the meeting and expressed his willingness to assist in raising a company of colored soldiers in California and offer their services to the United States Government for the purpose of aiding to subdue this unholy slave-holding rebellion. He stated that a commencement had been made and a few names enrolled. Mr. P. A. Bell read the names of those who would make the nucleus of a California regiment.

"Spirited and patriotic addresses were then made by Messrs. R. A. Hall, Meschaw and W. A. Hall. It was moved that a committee of three be appointed to correspond with the leading colored men of California and others who may be friendly to the project. The chairman reappointed the committee formed at the last meeting. Mrs. Priscilla Stewart made a few remarks on the importance of united action in the present crisis." The names of the men who signed to form the first Negro regiment in California will head the list of Negro Army Officers who have served in the wars of the United States Government and also those from California who won commissions in the National Army and are now serving in France in this World War for Democracy and the Liberty of the World.

After the Civil War had ended the enthusiasm of the colored men then living in California was just as great to be prepared to serve the Government in the case of another war. Their enthusiasm finally led to the forming of military companies all over the State. The first to organize and receive instructions was one which was formed in Sacramento, in Mr. William Quinn's barber shop. After organizing, they decided to employ an ex-army officer to teach them military tactics. They secured the services of Captain Crowell, who had seen service in the United States Army and after the Civil War was made postmaster of Sacramento, California. He instrusted this company of colored recruits for a period of one year, at which time they decided that they were competent to make a public appearance. They called themselves the "Sacramento Zouaves." The names of the officers of this company will be found also in the list of Negro Army Officers.

Their first public appearance was at the emancipation celebration held in Sacramento, January 1, 1868. The parade was headed by a white band and, just before it started, the company was presented with a silk flag by the daughter of Lieut. Gault. The Sacramento Zouaves made their first out-of-town appearance in San Francisco, where they were the guests of the "Branan Guards," another colored military company. This company was financed by the Hon. Sam Branan of San Francisco, after which the colored people named it in his honor. There were other military companies in San Francisco, namely, the "Lincoln Invincibles" and the "Richmond Blues," but the writer has not been able to procure any data concerning their organizations. These different Negro military organizations were rivals in everything except the celebration of the Emancipation Proclamation. The first celebration of the kind was held in the City of San Francisco, when the preliminary proclamation was issued. This celebration was held in Platt's Hall, and Rev. Thomas Starr King addressed the Negro people, notwithstanding he was ill and his physician had forbidden his leaving his bed. He made the address, went home and rapidly developed diphtheretic sore throat and died. His death was a great loss to everyone in California and especially to the Negro race. He is often spoken of as the one man who did more than any other to keep California in the Union. He traveled up and down the State, delivering lectures and encouraging patriotism. The State honored him with a Military funeral and also named one of their giant Redwood trees after him in memory of his lasting services to the State in her trying hour. After the Emancipation Proclamation was an actual law, the colored people held many great celebrations in the different churches. These different affairs were addressed by such orators as Bishop T. M. D. Ward and Rev. J. B. Sanderson. The orations of these men are a rich legacy to give to the Present-Day Negro of California.

The Civil War having passed into history, the next war of importance in which the United States Government took a part was the Spanish-American War. The American soldier of the African race served all during this war in the Cuban intervention. There were many who served as officers with Negro regiments. These men won honorable medals for bravery and heroism during battles, especially the one on San Juan Hill and at El Caney. Many of these men, since retirement, have located in California and their sketches will be found in this chapter.

The United States Army employed in this campaign the Regular troops of Negro soldiers known as the 24th and 25th Infantry and the Ninth and Tenth Cavalry, together with the 9th Immunes, 8th Illinois and the 23rd Kansas Regiments. The last two were officered throughout by negroes, the other regiments only having non-commissioned officers of the Negro race, notwithstanding these regiments had years of service in fighting the Indians on the frontiers. The regiments officered by Negroes gave a good account of themselves to the extent that it is a part of the history of that mighty struggle.

Recently there appeared in the *Army and Navy Journal* an article in defense of the Negro soldier. Among other things it said: "The class of colored men that join the army is vastly different from the class of colored men that cause all the racial disturbances throughout the South. The colored soldiers are men of high intellect and aspirations. They have to be to be allowed to enlist. They constitute, in the opinion of the writer, the pick of the colored men of this country who have been for financial reasons unable to attend any of the colored schools and colleges in their home States." This white writer who, as an army officer of the United States Army had personally come in contact with the Negro soldiers, formed a true estimate of the caliber of the average Negro soldier.

Spanish is the language of the Cubans, which necessitated the United States Government employing interpreters. Among the number was a member of the Tenth Cavalry by the name of Oscar Hudson. At the end of his enlistment he studied law and, coming to California, finally located in San Francisco where he now represents the Liberian Government at that port. He enjoys a large-paying practice, principally of Spanish people. He is an usher and a member of the Publicity Committee for Northern California Christian Science Church and, at this writing, is the treasurer of the Sixth Christian Science (white) Church of San Francisco. The writer is citing this from the sketch of Mr. Hudson to prove the statement of the white army officer when he said that the Negro soldier is a superior Negro to be allowed to enlist, and to also show the kind of Negro soldiers the United States Government honors with commissions. Mr. Hudson is a self-made man, his parents having left him an orphan when quite young. The United States Government, under the leadership of the then Commander-in-Chief of the Army, President McKinley, decided to reward the Negro soldiers, both non-commissioned and commissioned officers, together with the enlisted men who had won meritorious records in the Spanish-American War. The method used to reward these men was to organize two regiments of Negro Volunteers and officer them with these men. Acting upon the recommendation of the President, the War Department organized these two Negro regiments. The number of officers were selected by quota from each State. The men, when appointed, were and are still proud of their commissions because they were signed by the immortal President McKinley.

It has often been stated that Negroes would not make good officers and that Negroes would not obey their own men. In an effort to secure the exact truth of the services rendered by these men in the Philippine Insurrection, the writer addressed a letter to one of the officers serving with one of these volunteer Negro regiments in this campaign. The following is quoted from the reply of Captain Crumbly: "It has been said throughout the press and from the platform throughout the Nation * * * that our race would not be respectful and obedient to one another. The experience of the commissioned officers of the race who served during the war with Spain and in the Philippine Insurrection in the Volunteer Army of the United States, shows that this is not the truth of the matter. The soldiers of the Immune Regiments and the famous 48th and 49th Infantry were colored men and the record of those regiments compared, show that these troops under colored officers made as high mark in efficiency as any body of troops in any part of the army, whether regular or volunteers. Commanding generals serving with our troops across the Atlantic and Pacific all testify to their excellency; Brigadier General Bell is credited with having said that the army never had a more efficient organization than the 49th Infantry and deplored its having to leave his district to return to the United States for muster out. * * * Every officer of those regiments is proud of the records made and stands ready at all times to assure the people who think otherwise that our men can obey, and that we can command; that our people are capable of the highest development and to prove this an opportunity is all that is needed." Capt. Floyd Crumbly kindly furnished the writer with the names of all the officers who were commissioned in these two volunteer regiments. It remained for this, the present World War, to give to the Negro race the opportunity to prove to the world that they could command. Their first opportunity was when General Pershing was ordered into Mexico with a punitive expedition of United States soldiers. This expedition was composed of all the Negro regiments connected with the regular army, namely, the 25th and 24 Infantry, and the 9th and 10th Cavalry. It also contained many white regiments of both lines of the service. The white regiments remained to guard the border while the Negroes proceeded into Mexico with General Pershing.

The 10th Cavalry was in command of that splendid West Point graduate Negro officer, Lieut.-Colonel Charles Young (now Colonel). This officer had been called by the War Department back to the United States from Liberia, Africa, where he was representing this Government as Military Attache. Upon his arrival in the United States he was given orders to command troops with the expedition then going into Mexico. The reader will readily recall the splendid record made by the 10th Cavalry while in Mexico. The first mention of any actual fighting with the Mexicans was when the Mexican army fired on a detachment of Negro soldiers in command of Captain Morey. In this engagement ten Negro cavalrymen lost their lives and Captain Morey was severely wounded. Soon after this the *Army and Navy Journal* contained an article bespeaking the praise and loyalty of the Negro soldier. Among other things it said: "There are thousands of instances that could be mentioned showing the absolute loyalty of the colored troops in peace and war. Colored soldiers have given their lives for their officers and other white men. One instance was in the fight of the 10th Cavalry in Mexico during the last Pershing expedition, when three enlisted men refused to leave Captain Morey after he had been wounded, and they did not go until he had ordered them to do so. That is merely one instance out of many." And yet there was another instance occurring almost at the same date with another detachment of Negro soldiers under command of Lieut.-Colonel Young, who arrived in time to save General Dodd and his men from annihilation by a force of Mexican bandits who were attacking them at Parrall, Mexico.

The patriotism of the 10th Cavalry was commented upon in the *Army and Navy Journal,* under date of December 8, 1917, in which it said: " ' 'Of all organizations of the army as large as a regiment, the 10th Cavalry stands pre-eminent in its per capita subscription to the Second Liberty Loan,' writes Col. De R. C. Cabell of that regiment. With an aggregation of 1,329, officers and men, the 10th Cavalry subscribed for over two million dollars' worth of the bonds, more than $150 per man. It is a fact that this amount would have been materially increased had I not ordered that no man be allowed to pledge his pay to that extent that he would not have ten dollars on pay day.' Such patriotism from this regiment of colored men is worthy of publication."

During the Philippine Insurrection the hardest fighting was done by the 24th Infantry of Negro soldiers with General Lawton's command, and yet it remained just twenty years afterward before these loyal and heroic Negro soldiers were rewarded by the United States Government. The opportunity came when the War Department granted the request of the National Association for the Advancement of Colored People through their representative spokesman, Major Spingar, for a separate training camp for the training of officers to serve in the National Army to fight in the present World War. A separate training camp was opposed by many persons of both races. The argument used against it was that a man should first be a gentleman before he is made an officer in the United States Army. Then, if they were gentlemen and were to fight against a common enemy and make the world safe for Democracy, there should be no distinction made in their training, since the same requirements would be demanded in the execution of orders from the Commander-in-Chief from all the officers serving to win the war. After being convinced that if the Negro was to receive officers who would be in command as commissioned officers in the war, they would have to accept of a separate training camp.

After being brought to the realization of this fact, Negro men throughout the United States readily enlisted to train in a separate training camp. The War Department located this camp at Fort Des Moines, Iowa. There were graduated from this camp nearly seven hundred Negro Army officers. Of that number one hundred and ninety-eight were enlisted men from the Twenty-fourth Infantry and other units from the Regular United States Army. Many of these Negro soldiers were already non-commissioned officers. There were many in the list who were from the present day Negroes of California.

When the United States Government declared war upon the German Imperial Government, immediately there began rumors in the United States that this government did not intend to employ Negro soldiers in the war for oversea duty except as stevedores. Such rumors, in the face of such splendid war records of Negro soldiers who had fought in all the previous wars of this country did not make the Negro race in America very happy. To add to their unhappiness there were more lynchings of Negroes and the victims burned while alive, in the Southern States, together with the atrocities of the East St. Louis massacre of Negro residents, all tending to make Negro citizens of these United States wish that they had never lived to see this day. But "There is a Divinity that shapes our ends, rough-hew them as we may." In time the Congress of the United States passed in both branches a bill called "Conscription," or the "Selective Draft Act." It was approved and immediately signed by the President of the United States, Woodrow Wilson, in May, 1917. This was a little over a month after the declaration of war. This bill called for the registration of all men in the United States on June 1st who were of twenty-one to thirty-one years of age. It made no distinction as to race, color, position or wealth. All must register for service overseas or wherever the War Department might need them. "It then became clear to the Negro that in this the Negro boys saw plainly that they were to take their part and 'Tote half of the log.' " Thus, by signing this bill known as the "Selective Draft Act," the commander-in-chief of all the armies of the United States broke the first ground for a New Democracy in the United States of America.

In the great conflict of 1861 many wealthy persons hired substitutes to serve on the firing line. The instructions given to the Exemption Boards by the Secretary of War, and enforced throughout the United States, prevented any possible chance of any substitute filling anybody's place in the ranks of the National Army. They further started out in true Democratic fashion by being sent to the same training camps. In regard to the stevedore Negro regiments, the National Association for the Advancement of Colored People made a vigorous protest against all Negro regiments being made such. This resulted in the War Department announcing the number of such regiments alloted to the Negro people according to their quota, and that as many as possible would be officered by Negroes. After this statement but very few Negro men asked for exemption. They were all ready to make the supreme sacrifice for the good of their country. In the language of the late Booker T. Washington, who has been quoted as saying: ''I ask if a people who are thus so willing to die for their country ought not to be given the highest opportunity to live for their country?'' And thus, like a voice from the beyond, when there was mistreatment to Negro soldiers in Southern camps the successor to Dr. Washington, Major Motin, made a special visit to the commander-in-chief of all the armies of the United States, President Woodrow Wilson, to talk over the situation.

After this conference the President recommended to the War Department the appointment of Mr. Emmett J. Scott to act as advisor and assistant secretary to the Secretary of War, Newton Baker. Mr. Scott acted as secretary for the late Booker T. Washington for over eighteen years. Mr. Scott's duties are to look after the interest of the Negro soldiers. It was after this appointment that the Negro men rushed to enter the ''separate Training Camp for Negro Officers.'' This resulted in, after the successful graduating of the officers from the Training Camp at Fort Des Moines, the United States War Department opening smaller camps in different sections of the United States, where Negro men were trained in every branch of the army. It has gone even further, and those showing special aptness have been sent to the different Negro colleges to receive training in electrical engineering and other trades of use in the United States Army.

A little colored boy by the name of McKinley Anderson, who attended a rural school supported by the American Missionary Association somewhere in South Carolina, upon being requested by his teacher to write an article on the war, among other things said, in referring to the first draft Negro boys he had seen sent off to camp: ''Some how we've a feeling that those boys, if properly trained and given a square deal, are going to make a record not only for themselves but a record for the race; which will go down into history as the records of their grandfathers who fought with George Washington, and their fathers who fought with Grant and Roosevelt. Those boys and their families have a record for producing two-thirds of the food-stuff produced in 'X' County heretofore, and we will continue to grow and conserve food for them; and when they return, for we expect them back, we will welcome them as heroes of 'X' County, citizens of South Carolina and American boys who have helped make the world safe for Democracy.''

This Negro boy in his essay was right in his prophecy, because the National Army of the United States, now fighting in France for Democracy and the liberty of the world against autocracy, contains thousands of Negro soldiers and over a thousand Negro commissioned army officers, and many privates who have already won the French cross given for bravery under fire and at other encounters with the enemy. There are Negro expert marksmen as riflemen and, best of all, they have a hospital unit consisting of over a thousand trained orderlies, doctors, dentists, and recently the War Department has ordered Negro trained nurses. Negro soldiers thus far have behaved so gallantly and heroically in the face of fierce encounters that the American Associated Press has seen fit to give them first-page mention in the daily press throughout the Nation. It will not surprise the world if the final battle is fought by Negro soldiers commanded by Negro trained United States Army officers who will command their forces directly into Berlin and will bring back, to be placed in the Smithsonian Museum at Washington, D. C., the royal crowns of the Kaiser of Germany and the Emperor of Austria, together with any others necessary for the peace of the world.

The following will give the reader some account of the first Negroes in California who, during pioneer days, registered their names and formed a company and were willing and anxious for an opportunity to serve the United States Government in the Civil War. This data has been obtained from the *Pacific Appeal* of 1863, which said: ''A meeting was held on Wednesday evening, June 10, 1863, in the Athenaeum Hall on Washington street, San Francisco, California, of those who were willing to form a military company of colored men and, if accepted by the Government, engage in the war. It being necessary that a civil organization should be effected before a military company could be formed, Mr. Furguson was appointed as chairman and P. A. Bell secretary. On motion A. Furguson, S. J. Gromes and R. A. Hall were appointed a committee to draft rules for the temporary government. Messrs. W. H. Hall, L. H. Brooks, John Jones, P. Anderson and others addressed the meeting.

"Moved, we open a recruiting office in this place and that Mr. R. A. Hall be appointed recruiting officer. Carried. Moved that a vote of thanks be tendered Mr. George Smith for the gratuitous use of this hall. The following persons enrolled their names: A. Furguson, Nathaniel Wellington, F. G. Barbadoes, H. C. Cornish, S. J. Gromes, P. A. Bell, R. A. Hall, William H. Murry, George Smith, William Hall, C. H. Dutton, Jacob Yates, N. E. Speiths, J. Riker, Louis A. Bell, Allen Garvey, John Jones, Z. F. Bell, Owen Brown, William Freeman, William Walters, Charles Epps, James O. Smith; drummer boy, James Merritt. The names just quoted can be truly called the muster roll of the names of the first company of California Negroes who were willing to serve in the United States Army if called for service in the Civil War. There were other colored men of prominence connected with the white California militia or the Vigilante Committee of San Francisco. Mr. Charles Delvicho was a member of that committee. Captain John Jones, another colored gentleman, had charge of all the ammunition, and rifles of the Vigilante Committee which were stored in a warehouse used as their armory in San Francisco, California.

After the close of the Civil War enthusiasm ran high among the Negro people of this State to obtain military training, which eventually led to the forming of military companies of colored men all over the State. The Branan Guards, or the Lincoln Invincibles, were organized in San Francisco. Mr. Samuel Branan, a white gentleman of that city, paid for their equipment. The names prominently mentioned in connection with this organization were Captain John Jones, James Riker and Alexander G. Dennison. The Sacramento Zouaves was another Negro military organization. The names of their officers were Captain Pierson, First Lieutenant William Gault, Second Lieutenant William Quinn, Drummer Boy Albert Grubbs. Among the names prominently mentioned with this organization were Barney Fletcher, Bill Goff and Albert Grubbs (senior).

During the Philippine Insurrection the United States War Department had two volunteer Negro regiments officered by Negroes who, after their retirement, have located in California. Since it has been impossible to secure sketches from all now living in the State, the writer has deemed it fitting to quote the entire list of officers of these two regiments. They are as follows:

Forty-eighth U. S. Volunteer Infantry, William P. Duvall, colonel commanding regiment. Company "A": Captain, James E. Hamlin; first lieutenant, F. W. Cheek; second lieutenant, L. Washington. Company "B": Captain, A. Richardson; first lieutenant, W. H. Allen; second lieutenant, G. F. Marion. Company "C": Captain, S. Starr; first lieutenant, J. F. Powell; second lieutenant, J. C. Anders. Company "D": Captain, Jas. W. Smith; first lieutenant, J. H. Anderson; second lieutenant, G. W. Taylor. Company "E": Captain L. W. Dennison; first lieutenant, Jas. B. Coleman; second lieutenant, George Payne. Company "F": Captain, W. A. Hankins; first lieutenant, C. C. Caldwell; second lieutenant, J. Moore. Company "G": Captain, Wm. H. Brown; first lieutenant, J. W. Brown; second lieutenant, J. K. Rice. Company "H": Captain, W. H. Jackson; first lieutenant, H. J. Parker; second lieutenant, W. Green.. Company "I": Captain, R. R. Rudd; first lieutenant, L. M. Smith; second lieutenant, C. B. Turner. Company "K"; Captain, J. J. Oliver; first lieutenant, J. C. Smith; second lieutenant, F. R. Chisholm. Company "L": Captain, Thos. Grant; first lieutenant, P. McCowen; second lieutenant, W. Ballard; Dr. William A. Purnell, first lieutenant and assistant surgeon. Total officers, 57; enlisted men, 1,371.

Officers Forty-ninth U. S. Volunteer Infantry, Colonel William H. Beck, commanding regiment. Organized September 15, 1899. Mustered out of the service June 30, 1901. Dr. William C. Warmsley, captain and assistant surgeon; John H. Carroll, first lieutenant and assistant surgeon. Company "A": Captain, C. W. Jefferson; first lieutenant, L. H. Jordan; second lieutenant, A. H. Walls. Company "B": Captain, W. R. Staff; first lieutenant, Wm. R. Blaney; second lieutenant, Robert L. Goff. Company "C": Captain, Thos. Campbell; first lieutenant, W. H. Butler; second lieutenant, Beverly Perea. Company "D": Captain, F. H. Crumbly; first lieutenant, Jas. Thomas; second lieutenant, Geo. Payne.

First Lieutenants Thomas McAdoo, of San Diego, California; J. W. Clark, J. M. White, Thomas E. Moodey, W. H. Bettis, Levi Holt, Allen Lattimore, A. K. Barnett, served with Twenty-third Kansas Volunteer Negro regiment. Second Lieutenants Henry Taylor, A. M. Booker, William Green, J. D. Harkless, N. Singletary, George E. Payne, Oscar Overr, now of Allensworth, California. The First Battalion, Companies A, B, C and D, commanded by Major John M. Brown; Second Battalion, Companies E, F, G and H, commanded by Major George F. Ford, of Twenty-third Kansas Volunteer regiment.

William Beck, son of Lieutenant-Colonel Beck, served during the Spanish-American War as gunner's mate of the flag ship of the American fleet. Second Gunner's Mate Mr. Fred Overr, now of Pasadena, served on the Iowa of the American fleet.

The following are the names of the non-commissioned officers of the Twenty-fourth United States Infantry of Negro soldiers. These men all won high commissions when they graduated from the Separate Training Camp at Fort Des Moines, Iowa. The names are here recorded as they were in the Twenty-fourth Infantry: Regimental non-commissioned staff officers, Walter B. Williams, regimental sergeant major; Thomas E. Green, band leader; George A. Holland, Charles Ecton and George W. Winston, regimental supply sergeants; Elijah H. Goodwin, battalion sergeant major; Thomas A. Firmes, battalion sergeant major; Genoa S. Washington, battalion sergeant major; Roscoe Ellis, color sergeant; John W. DeHaven, color sergeant. Many of these men now live in California.

There have been several names given the writer since this chapter was completed with the officer's list. They are names first of a company of pioneer days namely L'Overture Guards, Captain R. J. Fletcher; First Lieut. Jos. Harris; Second Lieut. C. W. Whitfield; Secretary, W. J. Sims; Treasurer, T. M. Waters; Financial Secretary, J. T. Abrams.

The following names are of men who won commissions in the First Separate Training Camp for Negro Officers and are now serving with the National Army in France: Captain W. Bruce Williams, of Pasadena; he was the ranking Non-Commissioned Officer of the whole United States Army, Sergeant-Major of the 24th Infantry when he entered the Separate Training Camp, at Fort Des Moines, Iowa; he graduated with the rank of Captain; Dennis G. Mathews, First Lieutenant 350th Machine Gun Company; Jesse Kimbrough, First Lieutenant 365th Infantry; Dr. Leonard Stovall, First Lieutenant Medical Reserve Corps; Journer White, First Lieutenant 367th Infantry; Dr. Claudin Ballard, First Lieutenant Medical Reserve Corps. These men are all from Los Angeles. There are a number from San Francisco who made commissions. First Lieutenant Alberger, First Lieutenant Leonard Richardson, Captain Grasty, Captain Spar Dickey, First Lieutenant Leon Marsh and Chaplain Robson and Sergeant Gray of Los Angeles.

"Captain John Jones was born in the City of Lexington, Kentucky, on the 23rd day of October, 1829. When he was six years of age, his parents moved to Palmyra, Missouri, where he passed his youth until he was sixteen years old. Although all of his ancestors were free people, he lived in a slave State, where opportunities for an education were meagre, but, with it all, he obtained such education as his parents were able to give him, and which his unfavorable surroundings would permit. Even as a lad he evinced a disposition to obtain all the information that he could that dealt with the leading topics of the time. It was his delight to sit and listen to the discourses and arguments of the prominent men of his city.

"In 1846 he left his home to follow the United States Army into Mexico, and thereby saw some service in the Mexican War. Being too young to enlist as a regular soldier, he went as an officer's boy to one of the colonels in that army. He returned, however, in 1847 and took up his abode in St. Louis, where he obtained employment on one of the river steamers plying between that city and Natchez. It was on one of these steamers that he acquired the information and qualities which fitted him for the many positions of trust that he held in after years.

"In the spring of 1849, the stories of the great wealth that existed in the Golden State of California reached his ears and he determined to cast his lot in the Far West. At this time a fleet of prairie schooners was fitted out in St. Louis for the trip across the plains, and he decided to join it. After many hardships and several narrow escapes from the attacks of Indians, he arrived in the city of Sacramento in the fall of 1849.

"Of the trip across the plains Captain Jones used to relate a very amusing incident that occurred on the trip, which dealt with the perplexity of the Indian in some things. One day while crossing the Plains of Wyoming the caravan had halted under the shade of some large trees beside a running stream, when it was visited by a band of friendly Indians. Captain Jones was the only colored man in the party, and from later developments it appears that he was the first man of a dark skin that the Indians had ever seen other than those of their own people. During the wait he noticed that the Indians watched him closely and from time to time pointed toward him. He became so nervous over their actions that he seriously considered 'taking to the tall timber' at the first opportunity. Finally one of the chiefs came over to him and began addressing him in their Indian dialect. Of course, being unable to understand a word that the Indian said, he could only shake his head. At first the chief was inclined to get angry, as ho undoubtedly thought that Jones was a renegade Indian, trying to forsake his people. With this doubt in his mind, the chief began comparing things. He took Jones' hand

and placed it alongside of his and grunted 'All samee.' He then placed his cheek alongside that of Jones' and grunted 'All samee.' He touched Jones' mouth, ears, nose and eyes and then his own and grunted 'All samee.' He then rubbed his hand over his own hair and then over that of Jones and grunted loudly, 'No all samee.' When the Indians left the chief was murmuring 'All samee, all same; no all samee.'

"From Sacramento Captain Jones went to the 'Diggins' in Placer County, but things did not 'pan out' to his liking there, and after developing a good dose of rheumatism he went to San Francisco, where he remained practically the rest of his life. In San Francisco he gained the friendship of W. T. Coleman, of Vigilante fame, and through him became acquainted with the leading men of the early fifties in the State. In those days of good living and much money, the knowledge gained on the Mississippi river stood him in good stead and he easily secured employment as steward in one of the finest clubs of San Francisco, besides doing much private catering work.

"During the active period of the Vigilante Committee he was put in charge of the warehouse which served as an armory and as the council room of the committee. He was present when a bargeload of rifles was seized by the committee. These rifles were coming from Sacramento and had been sent by the governor to the Terry faction, who were opposing the Vigilance Committee. He was also present when Casey and Cora were hanged by the Vigilance Committee. He saw San Francisco destroyed by fire three times, and each time lost all of his possessions.

"Senator Broderick had taken a great fancy to Jones, and when he left for the National capital to represent California in the Halls of Congress, he took Jones along with him as his valet and confidential servant. Jones was in the immediate vicinity of the dueling ground when Senator Broderick, who had fired his gun into the air, was shot by Judge Terry.

"Captain Jones was prominently identified with all the activities of early California, especially those in which the interests of the people were concerned. Associated with such sterling colored pioneers as Anthony Osborne, Lige Hare, P. A. Bell, Peter Anderson, R. H. Wilcox, John A. Barber, Sully Cox, William Hall, Nat Godfrey, Dave Ruggles, Barney Fletcher, R. A. Hall, Fiddletown Smith, George W. Dennis, Sr., George Goodman and dozens of others. He gave his time, labor and money to any enterprise which tended to keep from the State those prejudices and hardships to which the colored people in the Southern States were being subjected. Many of the early Californians being persons from the South, they were endeavoring to shape the policies of California in such a way that it would be admitted into the Union as a slave State, and with this end that slavery might be planted in the State where free labor could have been very profitably used. This was actually tried when "Archy," a slave boy, was brought into the State by his master. Jones and his associates, * * * after considerable difficulty in preventing the master from getting Archy out of the State, succeeded in kidnapping him and hid him for a considerable period in the house of Mammy Pleasants. * * *

"In 1855, a fleet of palatial steamers was placed on the run from San Francisco to Sacramento, and Jones was given the stewardship of one of them. At this time the position was an enviable one, as the wages for a steward was $150 per month, and the perquisites were twice as much more. He afterwards became port steward of the fleet and was thereby able to make money. Like most old pioneers at this time, he imagined it would last forever, and money therefore slipped through his fingers about as fast as he made it. The great faults of the times were gambling and speculation, and he was not immune from either.

"One of Captain Jones' greatest efforts was the abolition of the colored schools of the State. Although he had a sister who was teaching in one of the colored schools, he accompanied a delegation to Sacramento to work for the passage of a law that would declare for mixed schools only in this State. Owing to the efforts of this delegation this law was passed. When he was asked why he would work for this law when its passage would put his sister out of employment, he replied that the advancement of the whole of his people was of more importance than the position of one, and that his sister would be benefited by the change by reason of her great pedagogic ability, and he foresaw aright, for immediately after the schools were mixed his sister was made principal of one of the finest grammar schools in Sacramento.

"One of the proudest moments in the life of Captain Jones was when he was elected captain of the Brannan Guards, a soldier company composed of colored men named after and financed by Sam Brannan, a man who had always shown the greatest concern for the welfare of the colored people of San Francisco. It was while he was captain of this company that the first celebration of the emancipation was held in San Francisco. With John A. Morgan he helped to organize the Morgan Cadets, and he had the pleasure of seeing his eldest son rise to the captaincy of that company of boys.

LIEUT. JOURNEE WHITE
367th Infantry (the Buffalos), 92nd Division, National Army, World's War.

SERGT. MIDDLETON SADDLER (Retired)
Spanish-American War.

"Captain Jones was noted for his oratory. His only peer at that time was William Hall, known as the colored silver-tongued orator. This oratorical gift made Captain Jones a very prominent figure in all of the activities of the time, political as well as otherwise.

"The lack of a superior education in himself and his observations of the value of education, made education his hobby, and he was ever doing something to further the educational advancement of the colored youth of the State. He valiantly struggled and many times denied himself many comforts during the latter years of his life in order that his offspring should not be handicapped in that regard, and with the result that his children were given every opportunity to provide themselves with that necessary adjunct to success in life. He had the pleasure of seeing his eldest son, the first colored youth to be graduated from the grammar school, from the high schools and the first to matriculate in the University of California, and he looked forward with keen anticipation to the day when he could see that son receive his degree and his other children follow in this son's footsteps, but death robbed him of that pleasure, as he died before that event occurred.

"In 1859 he married Sarah Rebecca Burke, a daughter of the prominent Hiner family, of Baltimore. The result of that marriage was two sons and four daughters, several of whom have become prominent in the political, social, fraternal and club life of the State. In 1873 Captain Jones accepted a position as steward of the Idaho Club, which he retained until his death, which occurred on the 31st day of August, 1881.''

It is with a great degree of pleasure, mingled with pain, that the writer is giving to the reader the following sketch of the late Colonel Allensworth, with whom she was personally acquainted from her early school days, in Cincinnati, Ohio, and the memory of his kindness and advice and his pure Christian character she holds as one of the sacred memories of her recollection. The lesson derived from a lecture given by him to children in Cincinnati, on "Mastering the Situation," has been as a guiding star through life. Colonel Allen Allensworth was intensely interested in the production of this book and gave the writer many valuable suggestions concerning its completion.

The late Colonel Allensworth was born a slave, and yet there are few, if any, who have made more out of life and done more for their fellow man. He was educated in the Roger Williams University, at Nashville, Tennessee, a Baptist institution. He added to his knowledge thus obtained by carefully making use of his spare time in obtaining information of value to his race and to mankind in general. He was appointed by the American Baptist Association to travel in the interest of the Baptist denomination and lecture to children.

Colonel Allensworth served in the Civil War, the Spanish-American War and the Philippine Insurrection. He was chaplain of the Twenty-fourth Infantry of Negro United States soldiers. He had charge of the school for enlisted men, and, aside from teaching them the English branches, saw to their moral education and entertainments. He was persevering, orderly, faithful and earnest in everything he undertook. He was a deep thinker and very careful of what he said. Mrs. Allensworth and daughters did not accompany him to the Philippine Islands, but remained at the Presidio of San Francisco, California.

Upon his retirement from the United States Army, he and his family located in Los Angeles, California. The War Department of the United States, upon his retirement with an excellent record, having served through three wars, honored him with the rank of Lieutenant-colonel (retired) of the United States Army. He immediately began to plan how he could further serve his race. Finding the climate of California so delightful, he soon decided that it would be just the place for thousands of poor Negro families struggling in the East against the cold and other disadvantages. After a careful consideration, he decided that California colored settlers could be of assistance to the members of the race in the East who would have the courage to come here to live. Whereupon he spoke to several public-spirited colored citizens, who readily joined and approved his plans. This resulted in their organizing a company for colonizing the Negro race in this the State of California. They subscribed a sum of money and decided to purchase a plot of land. In time they purchased land in Tulare County.

The men who formed the organization and worked for the success in having this land surveyed for a town site, immediately recognized the value of the advice, activities and influence of Colonel Allensworth, and they decided to petition the proper authorities and have the town site named after Colonel Allensworth. After considerable delay they secured the right to call it "Allensworth." It is governed, and with success, by Negroes.

Colonel Allensworth owed a great deal of his success in life to the true and faithful companionship of his wife, Mrs. Josephine Leavell Allensworth, who is equally as public-spirited and race-loving. She has gone hand in hand with him in every movement for the betterment of the race. (See ''Distinguished Women.'')

The death of Colonel Allensworth was most tragic, because, after passing through three wars, he was finally killed by a careless motorcyclist on the streets of Monrovia, California, a few miles out from Los Angeles, the accident occurring on a Sunday morning in September, 1914. The aged Colonel was on his way to preach in a small church of the village and had just stepped from a Pacific Electric street car when these men knocked him down and ran over him, killing him through their careless driving, his death, occurring within twenty-four hours afterwards without his regaining consciousness, was like a thunderbolt from a clear sky to the people of the State. He had spent the two years previous in dictating and assisting Professor Charles Alexander to write his autobiography. The book had been sent to the publishers and was ready to come off the press when he was killed.

Colonel Allen Allensworth was loved and respected by all who knew him. He was accorded a military funeral by the Grand Army Veterans of Los Angeles. Few people are privileged to live and die leaving so sweet a memory. There were memorial services held for him throughout the State and Nation. The race papers for weeks were making honorable mention of him. Many societies passed resolutions of respect and honor for his work for the betterment of the race. His death was felt keenly by all who were so fortunate as to have enjoyed his friendship, or even to have known him.

Captain Floyd Henry Crumbly was born in the City of Rome in the State of Georgia, May 10, 1859, son of Robert and Mariah Crumbly, his father a slave and his mother a free woman, a half-breed Indian. He received primary instruction from Rev. George Standing, one of the early missionaries of the Methodist Episcopal Church at La Grange, Georgia, obtaining the balance of his education in the United States Army and in the school of experience. He enlisted in the U. S. Army as a private, November 16, 1876, and was assigned to Troop ''I,'' Tenth Cavalry, Captain T. A. Baldwin commanding; promoted to corporal June, 1877; promoted to sergeant January, 1878; served at Forts Stockton, Richardson and Sill in the Indian Territory; served in all the Indian campaigns, operating in Texas and the Indian Territory, from 1877 to 1881, as sergeant-major and quartermaster sergeant during the Victoria campaign on the border of Texas and Old Mexico in 1880, under Lieutenant Henry O. Flipper, who was one of the best educated and best drill masters ever produced by West Point Military Academy, and who was, in every way, an officer and a gentleman. Mr. Crumbly was discharged from the army November 16, 1881, by reason of expiration of his term of service, with an excellent character.

He returned to his Southern home at Atlanta, Georgia, and engaged in mercantile business, building up an excellent trade and accumulating property. After the great financial panic during the Cleveland administration, young Crumbly found himself at the same place he had occupied when he first started. He was not discouraged, but again set out to rebuild on a clean record, with all accounts fully satisfied and with many strong friends in the wholesale trade. He was a one-third owner in the first drug store operated and owned by colored men in the State of Georgia. It was known as the Butler-Slater Drug Company, located on Auburn avenue, which business was succeeded by the Gate City Drug Company, now operating in that city and owned by Dr. Moses Amos and others, and which business is a creditable representation of the medical profession in any city. Dr. Amos, who was with the business at its early inception, is the oldest pharmacist in the State among colored people.

At the creation of the Orphan Home by Mrs. Carrie Steel, Captain Crumbly was chosen secretary of the trustee board of that home, which proved to be useful and sheltered and fed hundreds of orphans and dependent children. He is a member of the Masonic fraternity and was grand secretary and chairman of the committee on foreign correspondence of the Georgia jurisdiction for a number of years, lending his personal influence to the unification of Free Masonry in that State, from 1882 to 1898.

President McKinley appointed him a first lieutenant of the Tenth U. S. Volunteer Infantry July 5, 1898, during the war with Spain. He was mustered out of the service March, 1899, and again commissioned by the President to be captain in the Philippines. During this service, as well as during the Indian wars, Captain Crumbly was in many engagements on the field of battle, and on all the campaigns in all seasons of the year, enduring all privations of a soldier on the theater of military operations against hostile forces. He was appointed judge of the Court of First Instance at Paranaqua, in the Philippine Islands, and was charged with the duty to measure out civil justice to all native criminals. Special record is made of his command engaging insurrection forces at Santa Catalina, in the La Guna province, where, as was usually the case, our forces were out-numbered. He had fifty men with one hundred cartridges, fighting two hundred well armed insurgents, who were well-protected for the fight. The horse which the Captain rode was killed at the first volley from the enemy and several men were wounded after a desperate fight. The American forces under the captain charged the enemy's earthworks and routed them from their security, driving the main body into the bamboo thicket, killing a score or more and capturing a number of armed men, destroying the barracks, supplies, equipment and foodstuff and the entire town of Santa Catalina, consisting of approximately one hundred houses. The enemy was pursued, but eluded the Americans because of their knowledge of the trails leading through the bamboo forest. General Bell, commanding the district, issued orders of commendation for the splendid work done by the troops under Captain Crumbly's command.

In 1903 this contented citizen in time of peace, who was ever ready to answer "Here" when the call of the Nation was manifest, located in the City of Los Angeles, arriving there with broken health from campaign service and climatic conditions in the islands of the Pacific Ocean. He found here a climate that assisted in his full restoration and decided to make this State and section his future home, notwithstanding many inducements offered to him by some of the largest wholesale merchants of his Southern home to return to that city, one of whom stated that the business people of California would never appreciate his worth as a citizen as did the men of the South. However, this was not sufficient to cause him to return, believing that the men of the race should no longer confine themselves to the South, but should find a place, or make one, in every section of this great nation and the world at large wherever civilization was found.

Captain Crumbly assisted in the organization of the Department of the Columbia United States Spanish War Veterans, including all the States west of the Mississippi River, and was its first Commander. It is deemed proper to add here that he was one of the colored commissioners associated with Professor Crogman, Bishop Gains, H. A. Rucker, Rev. I. Garland Penn, John C. Dancy, Booker T. Washington and others for the great Negro building at the Cotton States and International Exposition in 1885. It was this body of men who after months of agitation secured a place on the opening day program of that exposition for Booker T. Washington as one of the speakers. Every race man of that time and every Southern white man admitted that this address was Booker T. Washington's master effort. * * * What he said to the ten thousand people there assembled was read with deep interest throughout the world wherever Associated Press news was sent.

Captain Crumbly is now at the head of a local movement in Los Angeles having for its purpose the establishment of a sanitarium for persons in the early stages of consumption, to prevent the spread of the disease as much as possible. He is engaged in the real estate business and is one of the commissioned notary publics of Los Angeles County, California.

It affords the writer great pleasure to give the sketch of Captain Crumbly to the reader because of the fact that he is thoroughly a race man and takes pride in doing whatever he can in promoting the interest of the race. Since coming to Los Angeles he has been one of the prime movers in the organization of the Y. M. C. A. and the "Forum," a club which meets every Sunday afternoon in the auditorium of the Y. M. C. A. and discusses questions of importance to the race.

Alfred D. Benston, the subject of this sketch, has a most interesting career. He has a mixture of Cherokee Indian blood, together with traces of Negro, and is six feet tall. He has seen service in the Civil War, as his record shows. Previous to coming to California he was a lumber merchant and inspector, holding the position as clerk and foreman of the yard of H. R. Deacon & Co., lumber merchants, of Philadelphia, Pennsylvania, serving the firm for over thirteen years at a salary of $22 a week and allowed $7 a day for expenses, holding the inspectorship of western, eastern and northern parts of the United States or the lumber district of Albany, Pennsylvania and the West.

After a time he left this firm and placed an advertisement in the New York papers for a position. His advertisement was answered by George M. Grant & Brothers, of New York, who were lumber merchants. Mr. Benston stood an examination before the firm in New York City and passed over six white competitors. He was employed by the firm and sent to Clarksville, Tennessee, where he measured and inspected a quantity of walnut lumber, subject to shipping to Philadelphia, Pennasylvania.

His knowledge of lumber and the different sections of the United States caused Mr. George North to engage him to sell twenty carloads of lumber. Mr. Benston's commission on the deal amounted to $15,000. After collecting this he decided to come to California and see what his prospects in the Golden West would bring him. He soon fell in love with Miss Minnie Dennis and they were married in San Francisco, California.

He then accepted a position with Mr. Parrott as butler, holding the same for seven months, when Mr. Timothy Hopkins, cashier of the Southern Pacific railroad, offered Mr. Benston a position on his poultry ranch at Menlo Park. He worked at poultry raising for four years, keeping seven incubators continuously busy, using between twelve and thirteen hundred eggs and losing less than five per cent. This poultry farm covered six acres. After the first year the daily output was five hundred eggs a day.

When Hon. William McKinley was elected as the President of the United States, he appointed General Dimond as superintendent of the United States mint, located in San Francisco. Since General Dimond was a G. A. R. man and a friend to Mr. Benston, who also held a war record, at the suggestion of Mr. T. B. Morton, the subject of this sketch made application for a position in the mint. His application was signed by Governor Stanford, General Dimond and Mr. Timothy A. Hopkins, after which it was forwarded to Washington, D. C. In twenty-eight days afterwards Mr. Benston received the appointment in the mint and retained the same until there was a change in the administration.

He then accepted a position with the Southern Pacific Railroad until there was another change in the administration, when he was again appointed to the assayer's department in the mint, serving in that capacity for eighteen years, when he was suddenly stricken at his work. He was ill for two years, after which he recovered and returned to his position. During his long service in the mint he has a record that was clear, having never been tardy or had to be called-down for insubordination by the superintendent. He made all the cupels used getting out all the leads used in the department. His cupels tooks the red ribbon at Philadelphia at the annual meeting of the assayers' departments of all the United States mints in 1911. This position was filled by Mr. Benston for years. The following is his military record:

"Certificate of Record. To all whom it may concern: Bequeathed to every American is a priceless legacy preserved to us by the valor of the boys in blue.

"This certifies that Alfred Benston enlisted from Lancaster County, Pennsylvania, to serve one year or more during the war, and was mustered into the United States service at Philadelphia, Pennsylvania, August 24, 1864, as corporal of Captain John T. Barnard's company "E," One Hundred and Twenty-seventh Regiment, United States colored Infantry, Colonel Benjamin F. Tracey, commanding. This regiment, composed of men enlisted and drafted in the State of Pennsylvania, to serve one, two and three years, was organized at Camp William Penn, Philadelphia, from August 23rd to September 10th, 1864. He was ordered to City Point, Virginia, in September, 1864, and attached to the First Brigade, Third Division, Tenth Corps Army of the James; later transferred to the Second Brigade, Second Division, Twenty-fifth Corps and Department of Texas. It participated in the siege operations against Petersburg and Richmond, Virginia, including engagements at Chapin's Farm, New Market Heights, Fort Harrison, Darbytown Road and Fair Oaks. It was on duty in trenches north of James River before Richmond until March, 1865; moved to Hatcher's Run, March 27, and the next day started on the Appomattox campaign, taking part in engagements at Hatcher's Run, Fall of Petersburg, pursuit of Lee, and Appomattox, or Lee's Surrender, Virginia, April 9, 1865. It was on duty at Petersburg and City Point until June, 1865, then ordered to Brazos, Santiago, Texas, and assigned to duty at various points on the Rio Grande until October. It was consigned into a battalion of three companies September 11th, and was mustered out of service October 20th, 1865.

The said Alfred Benston was taken sick in November, 1864, of chronic diarrhoea and was confined in a tent hospital at Point of Rocks, Maryland. While there his limbs were frozen and he was transferred to the general hospital at Fortress Monroe, Virginia, where he remained for seven months, and received an honorable discharge there on the 11th day of September, 1865, by reason of surgeon's certificate of disability and close of the war.

"He was with his command during its services as outlined until after the battle of Fair Oaks, Virginia, and rendered faithful and meritorious service to his country. He was born in Chester County, Virginia, on the 25th day of November, 1847. He was united in marriage to Minnie L. Dennis at San Francisco, California, July 14th, 1885, from which union were born four children, Alfred C., Marguerite L., Charlotte G. and Harold.

"He is a member of Lincoln Post, No. 1, Department of California and Nevada, Grand Army of the Republic; I. O. O. F. and F. and A. M. He was formerly a member of Robert Bryan Post, No. 80, at Philadelphia, Pennsylvania.

"He is employed in the United States mint, at San Francisco, California. These facts are thus recorded and preserved for the benefit of all those who may be interested. Compiled from official and authentic sources by the Sailors and Soldiers' Historical and Benevolent Society. In testimony whereof I hereunto set my hand and cause to be affixed the seal of the Society. Done at Washington, D. C., this 16th day of December, A. D. 1912.

"M. WALLINGSFORD, *Historian*, No. 6775."

Mr. Benston was transferred to the Lincoln Post at the request of General Dimond in 1889. He was a member of the post for a number of years when he was appointed sergeant major, in 1902, and continued for twelve years at fifty cents per post, occasionally filling the chair as adjutant and, during the illness of the regular appointee, Mr. Benston filled the chair for three months, and at the time of the adjutant's death he was appointed adjutant of the post, performing every duty of the office accurately and satisfactorily to other comrades up to the time of his last illness, during which he has been complimented by the commander of the post, who constantly visited him until he recovered and returned to his position in the post.

Middleton W. Sadler, the subject of this sketch, was born in 1873 in Marrietta, Georgia, which is located twelve miles from Atlanta, spending his youth in Alabama and Kentucky, attending the public school of Sheffield, Alabama. He entered the Kentucky University, at Louisville, in 1891, leaving before graduating to volunteer in the United States Army or military service in 1892.

Military career: His first duties took him to the frontier of Dakota and Montana, where he remained on duty until the outbreak of the Spanish-American War, of 1898. His regiment, the Twenty-fifth Infantry, was the first ordered to the front and they were first established at Camp Chickamauga Park, Georgia, where they remained only a few weeks before the regiment was ordered to take up advance position at Tampa, Florida, where it was put into condition for service on the Island of Cuba.

Cuban campaign began June 14, 1898. The regiment, with the Fifth Army Corps, embarked for service in Cuba, the expedition landing at Santiago, Cuba, June 22, 1898. Campaign on the island: The regiment disembarked under fire from the enemy June 25th, but the enemy being driven away, the troops halted for reconnoiter and observation on June 30. The Twenty-fifth regiment was called to the relief of the Rough Riders, which had been suddenly pounced upon by the enemy; a skirmish ensued and the enemy was driven off. The regiment was ordered into battle on July 1 against the enemy in fortification at El Caney. After a day's hard fighting the position was carried, and in the meantime the subject of this sketch had been slightly wounded in the left arm while leading his company in the terrific assault, he being first sergeant and all the officers having fallen in battle. For this service he was complimented in orders by his regimental commander and recommended for a commission in the volunteer forces.

After the fall of El Caney, the regiment turned on the City of Santiago, when it took part in storming San Juan. The regiment remained in action until the final surrender of the city, July 17, 1898. At the close of the Cuban campaign the regiment was ordered to the State of New York, where it remained until ordered to a permanent station in Colorado and Arizona. While in camp in New York, upon the recommendation of his regimental commander, the subject of this sketch was decorated by a medal given by Miss Helen Gould.

Sergeant Saddler's next active service took him with the Twenty-fifth Infantry to the Philippine Islands, July 1, 1899, while in an active campaign which was carried on against the natives for three years that followed. During this campaign he was engaged in twenty-two battles and skirmishes and remained with his regiment in the islands until peace was declared July 4, 1902.

Returning with his regiment from the islands, he took station in Nebraska, remaining with his regiment until promoted to the post non-commission staff by the Secretary of War, May, 1905. Upon his promotion he was again ordered to the Philippine Islands, where he served as post commissary sergeant until 1908. Upon his return from the island via Suez canal, having circumnavigated the globe, he was given a station in New York, remaining on that duty until he was again ordered to the Philippine Islands, January, 1912, remaining until 1915. His new station took him to the State of Kansas, where he remained until ordered for duty along the Mexican border. In the month of April, 1917, he was ordered home for retirement, having served the thirty years to entitle him to this privilege; twenty-five years of active service and foreign service. He was subsequently retired from active service, September 20, 1917.

Promotion, Recommendations: Although entering the service as a private, his attentiveness to duty soon won him promotion, first as corporal, sergeant, first sergeant, sergeant major, and post commissary sergeant. His military career is considered second to none, having served twenty-five years without a court martial or a single reprimand by his superiors.

The following recommendations were given to him when he was about to retire, and will give the reader a fair estimate of the high regard in which Sergeant Saddler was held by his superior officers:

"A soldier of proven courage and bravery."—General J. P. O'Neal.

"A gallant soldier, a man for whom I have great personal respect."—General A. S. Burt.

"A credit to the Army, a leader of his race."—Major General J. F. Bell.

"I have personally observed Sergeant Saddler for many years and find him to be courteous, painstaking, reliable and efficient."—Colonel A. R. Paxton.

"His character is without reproach."—Captain M. A. Maloy.

"I know of no man better qualified for a commission than Sergeant Saddler. I heartily endorse him for any honor a government may see fit to bestow upon him."— General E. F. Taggart.

"His excellent character, his habits of sobriety, his pure motives are matters of record wherever he has served."—General M. J. Lenahan.

"I have known Sergeant Saddler sixteen years. He has been one of the best men I ever commanded; painstaking, trustworthy, a soldier in every sense of the word."— Colonel R. L. Bush.

"I invite special attention to Sergeant Saddler for any commission and position of trust that may be bestowed upón him."—Colonel M. D. Crowin.

"I know of no man better qualified through long experience and faithfulness to duty for a commission of high grade than Sergeant Saddler."

"Order of Retirement. It is a pleasant duty of the post commander to announce to this command the retirement from active service of Middleton W. Saddler. Sergeant Saddler entered the service many years ago and served faithfully until its honorable close. Sergeant Saddler has seven discharge certificates, all signed by different commanding officers, showing character excellent. He also is the honorable wearer of five service medals and an active campaign badge. The closing of Sergeant Saddler's active career takes from the army a valuable soldier, a man that younger soldiers would well emulate. While his commanding officer is proud to know he has reached his goal, he regrets very much to lose his service. He carries into civil life a record second to none. He is known throughout the army as a model soldier. I congratulate him upon his valuable record and can only say, 'Well done, thou good and faithful servant.'

"L. R. Brown, *Colonel of the Coast Artillery Corps.*"

Since his retirement Sergeant Saddler and wife have purchased a beautiful home in Oakland, California. They are both active members of the Fifteenth Street A. M. E. Church, and are deeply interested in the uplift of the race in all movements, taking an active hand wherever needed. They both have delightful personalities, and the writer considers it a great privilege to give to the reader the military career of one who has won honors for the race.

Rev. George W. Prioleau, chaplain in the United States Army, born of slave parents, L. S. and Susan Prioleau, of Charleston, South Carolina, attended the public schools of that city and Avery Institute. In 1875, he attended Claflin University, Orangeburg, S. C. During the winter months from 1875 to 1879, he taught the primary public school of Lyons Township, Orangeburg County, S. C. He was converted and joined the A. M. E. Church, St. Mathews, S. C., his father being pastor. He served his church as leader of the choir, Sunday school teacher, superintendent, class leader, and local preacher; joined the Columbia, South Carolina, Conference December 1879, under Bishop Brown; was assigned as pastor to the Double Springs Mission, Lawrence County, S. C.

December, 1880, was sent to Wilberforce University by the Columbia, S. C., Conference, but, the Conference having failed to support him, he supported himself by working at his trade during hours of recreation in the harvest fields of Green and Clark Counties in Ohio, and was assisted by his father; was assigned to the Selma, Ohio, Mission by Bishop Shorter in the year 1881, held this charge three years; graduated from the Theological Department, Wilberforce University, June, 1884, with the degree of B. D.; taught in the public schools of Selma, Ohio, September, 1884, to September, 1885, and, in connection, was pastor of A. M. E. Mission, Yellow Springs, Ohio, North Ohio Conference.

Was appointed pastor of A. M. E. Church, Hamilton, Ohio, September, 1885; Wilberforce University, December 23, 1885; appointed pastor A. M. E. Church, Troy, Ohio, by Bishop Campbell, 1887; was elected to fill the chair of Ecclesiastical History and Homeletics, September, 1889; and, in this connection, was pastor of Trinity, A. M. E. Church, Wilberforce University; appointed Presiding Elder, Springfield District, North Ohio Conference, A. M. E. Church, September, 1890, in connection with duties as instructor at Wilberforce University. This dual position was held until September, 1892; elected delegate to the General Conference held in Philadelphia, 1892; was elected secretary for four consecutive times of the North Ohio Conference, North Ohio; President, Conference Sunday School Institute for three years; was appointed Pastor of St. John's Church, Xenia, Ohio, in connection with Professorship at Payne Theological Seminary; associate editor A. M. E. Sunday School Lesson Leaf for three years; was appointed

Chaplain of the 9th Cavalry, United States Army, by President Cleveland, April 25, 1895, with rank of Captain and served with the regiment until November 15, 1915, twenty years, six months and twenty days.

Transferred to the 10th Cavalry, November 15, 1915; was married after the loss of first wife February 27, 1902, to Miss Ethel C. Stafford, Kansas City, Kansas, February 20, 1905; two girls, Mary S. and Ethel S., and one boy are the fruits of this marriage. The Chaplain has crossed the Pacific Ocean six times; four with his regiment, and twice on detached service. He is a Thirty-third degree Mason, an Odd Fellow and was initiated as a K. P.; appointed D. D. G. M. by G. M. N. C. Crews, Jurisdiction of Missouri, over Arizona and New Mexico; organized William, H. Carney Lodge No. 89 G. U. O. of O. F.; reorganized Joppa Military Lodge No. 150, A. F. and A. M. He paid off a long standing debt of nearly $1,100 on the church at Troy, Ohio, and built the present structure; paid off a large debt on St. John's Church, Xenia, Ohio, and Payne A. M. E. Church, Hamilton, Ohio. His reports have always been satisfactory to the Bishop. Many souls were converted through his preaching at Hamilton, Selma, Xenia and in the army.

Chaplain Prioleau is the oldest ranking Chaplain in the United States Army. During the past year he was examined and was promoted to the rank of Major for exceptional efficiency. He has seen service during the Philippine Insurrection and was with the regiment in the Philippine Islands during the great cholera scourge and did all he could to give consolation to the dying, when it was not considered safe for him to do so, but he never forsook anyone whom he might comfort in their last hours of suffering. He holds a letter of commendation from Brigadier-General Strong for efficient services. He is now Chaplain of the 25th Infantry. He served twenty years and six months with one regiment, a longer term of service than any Chaplain has served in the United States Army. He will retire May 15, 1920.

Chaplain Prioleau has purchased an elegant, modern home for his family at Raymond and West Thirty-fifth Place, Los Angeles, and owns other valuable properties in California. He will make his home in Los Angeles, California.

Captain William Reynolds was born in Williams County, Tennessee. His father emigrated to Topeka, Kansas, when the subject of this sketch was four years old. He was reared and educated in the public schools of that city. He entered the volunteer service during the Spanish-American War, 1898. He organized the first company of the 23rd Kansas volunteer Infantry, and commanded as a Captain of Company ''A.''

After the regiment was mustered into United States service it was sent to Cuba, making a splendid record on guard duty in the Province of Santiago de Cuba. The command was under Major General Leonard Wood; during the engagement on San Juan Hill the 23rd Kansas was sent up into the mountains to head off Spanish reinforcements. This Spanish force surrendered, were disarmed, sent to Santiago de Cuba, and the 23rd Kansas occupied their barracks.

The 23rd Kansas, in connection with the 8th Illinois and 9th Louisiana Immunes, were assigned to six months' guard-duty in that province, in rounding up the Cuban Insurgents, and bringing them in, disarming them and sending them back to their farms; tearing down all Spanish block-houses and bringing peace to the Cubans. Company ''A'' was commanded to destroy the block-houses on San Juan Hill and to assist restoring to sanitary condition the entire island of Cuba. The ''Reconcentrado'' orders issued by Weyler (the butcher) caused the unsanitary conditions.

After the regiment was in Cuba three months, Major Ford, who had secured leave of absence from the government position he held in Washington, D. C., was compelled to return to the United States. In view of Captain Reynold's being senior officer, he was put in command of the 2nd, Battalion during the absence of Major G. W. Ford. This position was held by Captain Reynolds until the regiment returned to the United States in March, 1899.

After his return to the United States en route home, he stopped at Quindaro University, in Kansas, whereupon his brother, Prof. A. L. Reynolds, who was a member of the faculty, extended Captain Reynolds an invitation to deliver a lecture before the students, which he did on the subject ''The Spanish-American War.''

Captain Reynolds stood an examination for a position as Captain and his application was returned from the war department, with recommendations for Major, instead. He was recommended by Brigadier-General Ewers to Major-General Leonard Wood, Commander of the Division, as a tactician and disciplinarian, on account of first certificate of examination, When the War Department was fearful that this Government would be drawn into the World-War, it sent many letters to Captain Reynolds. Among these letters was one which the writer was permitted to read, in which it spoke of Captain Reynolds being registered with the War Department as qualified for an appointment as a Commanding Officer if volunteer forces should be needed, and suggestions as to preparedness.***Acting upon such, he immediately began to organize home guards in Pasadena and Los Angeles, and organized and officered, with former Spanish-American War Veterans (all colored), three companies of Negro soldiers. Mr. Oscar Hudson, of San Francisco, worked in the northern part of the State with the hopes of securing enough to complete a full regiment. Captain Reynolds is an expert marksman.

Captain Reynolds is a member of Friendship Baptist Church, and chorister of the same. He is a vocal teacher at his home in Pasadena. Captain Reynolds has one son, who is now somewhere in France with the National Army, Corporal Raoul Reynolds, Company "I," 365th Infantry, Expeditionary Forces, under General Pershing.

Captain Reynolds has given some attention to Fraternal organizations. He is Past Grand Captain-General of Knights Templar, of the State of California, also Past Master of the State of Kansas and Past Eminent Commander of the State of Kansas. During the past eleven years he has lived in this State, he has identified himself with Euclid Lodge No. 2; Past Master of the Blue Lodge; Past High Priest of the Red Cross; Past Eminent Commander of the Knights Templar.

Captain Reynolds has been happily married for over twenty-five years, to Miss Maggie E. Russel, of Topeka, Kansas. She, like her husband, is interested in everything for the uplift of the race; is a member of the Federated Women's Clubs and is Past Matron of the Eastern Star Lodge and Community Auxiliary Red Cross.

Chaplain Washington E. Gladden retired with the rank of Captain of the Twenty-fourth Infantry, United States Army. He was born in the State of South Carolina, in 1866. At the age of fourteen years he went to Great Bend, Kansas, where he found work in the Hulme & Kelly flouring mills. He worked there for twelve years, during which time he filled various positions from roustabout to that of chief engineer of the establishment. He also won a contest for champion sack-sewer of the mill, having sewed and packed six hundred and sixteen sacks in ten hours. While working at the mill he mastered, through correspondence, a course in electrical engineering.

Chaplain Gladden was always of a religious and missionary spirit. When he was only fourteen years of age, he organized a Sunday school, and would drive twenty miles into the country on Saturday night after his week's work was finished, and hold a religious meeting on Sunday in some desolate place in Kansas, returning to his work on Monday morning.

In 1889, the Chaplain made a trip to Africa in the interest of missions and to inform himself of the wisdom of an emigration scheme by many who were at that time preparing to emigrate to Africa. He made an extensive report that mission work in Africa was a failure due to the fact that those who were sent to the field lacked medical knowledge and sanitary information that would render them immune in the great epidemics that often broke out in South-Central Africa.

On his return to the United States, in 1890, he immediately entered the ministry, and was ordained and took charge of the First Baptist Church at Great Bend, Kansas. While pastoring at this place he took a special course of training at the Western College, Macon, Mo. In 1895 the Chaplain received a call to organize a work at Colorado Springs, Colorado, under the direction of the American Baptist Home Missionary Society of New York. This he accepted, and began work there in February, 1896. To learn that he succeeded in this enterprise one only has to visit the St. John's Baptist Church at Colorado Springs. Here he will find a modern church structure costing ten thousand dollars and entirely out of debt. This work was accomplished during the trying period of the great strikes in Colorado. One has but to know the history of this church to know something of the characteristics of this man. Discarding many of the generally-accepted principles of the Baptist Church and meeting often the criticism of his brethren in the Baptist ministry, he organized and administered his church on a strictly business plan, claiming that a church organization was a business, as well as a spiritual institution. Thus running his church on a cash basis and "pay as you go plan." This met the popular approval of the populace and he had no trouble in obtaining money at all times for the needs of the church. In civil life he was identified with all that made for the progress and welfare of the city and people. He is a fearless advocate of all the rights of American citizens alike.

His appointment to the position of Army Chaplain was like that of the call of John the Baptist, unsought and without public announcement, without the assistance of the newspapers or other political influences. No one seemed to know anything about it, or that the Chaplain was a candidate for the position until the President sent his name to the Senate for confirmation on May 21, 1906. The Chaplain accepted the position and was assigned to duty with the 24th Infantry, United States Army in the Philippine Islands, leaving San Francisco on July 25, 1906. He served with this regiment during the Pulahan Insurrection in 1906-7. He returned with the regiment to the

United States in 1908, and, for three years, was stationed at Madison Barracks, New York.

In 1909 the United States Government appointed a Board of Chaplains who were to make recommendations for more officers among the Chaplains. The subject of this sketch, Chaplin Gladden, was elected Recorder of the Board, and was the only man of the race who was a member of the board when it met at Fort Leavenworth, Kansas. He asked that chaplains be placed on the board for examining men for the position as chaplains.

Chaplin Gladden returned with the 24th Infantry to the Philippine Islands in 1911, completing a four-year foreign service in that country. He had the distinction of performing the first baptism by immersion in the Philippine Islands. During the time he was in the army, he made all grades in marksmanship, up to expert rifleman.

Chaplin Gladden was an engineer as well as a minister, and his skill in this made him adept at the wheel of a motion-picture machine. He operated the first machine of this kind ever shown in the islands. He used it for the entertainment of his men as well as all other creditable methods of entertainments. He encouraged the men in all manly athletic sports. He has been appointed on several army boards, and is an aggressive advocate of making the Army Post so attractive for the enlisted men that they will not seek pleasure in the dives that often surround a military reservation.

In the Philippine Islands his efforts reached the climax at Camp Stotsenburg, Pampanga, P. I. Here he established and installed a modern motion-picture plant that entertained from three to eight hundred men each evening. His Sunday evening religious services reached the number of 558 men at one service and averaged attendance of more than four hundred each Sunday evening during a period of three months.

Chaplain Gladden says: "The 24th Infantry U. S. Army has, like all other regiments, some few men who make trouble, but they are in the minority. We have a number of men who have spent their entire time with the regiment. They have honorable records for being true, brave men. It is probable that this regiment has the largest number of men with it who engaged in the Spanish-American War. They have two Spanish War Veterans Camps. Many of the men climbed San Juan Hill, engaged in the operations at El Caney, and did volunteer nurse duty at the fever-stricken camps in Cuba. In view of the fact that they would take a chance of being stricken by that dreaded disease yellow fever, when the call came for volunteer nurses the entire line went forward as one man, and many of them did die from the dreadful malady.

"In the ranks of the 24th Infantry we have many examples of thrift and ability. A number of the men have beautiful homes somewhere in the United States, as well as improved properties. These homes are all paid for. Many of the men have accounts in the savings banks. It is not an unusual thing to have one of them retire with a neat sum provided for his comfort. I have but to refer to the many beautiful homes owned by them in Oakland, Berkeley and many other cities in California. I know of men in this regiment who have retired and some of them in active duty today that have bank accounts from $5,000 to $25,000. This demonstrates the ability and possibilities of the men who can conform to army life and stay with it for years. Then if a young man does not desire to remain with the army he can return, at the end of his first enlistment, to civil life with a discharge as to character excellent, which is of great help to him in securing employment in the civil service branches of the government. There is also a post school provided for the men by the Government. The Chaplain is the superintendent of these schools. They run for five months of each year, and any young man can volunteer to attend these schools. Here the man made of the right kind of stuff can improve his opportunities and often prepare himself for some useful occupation in civil life."

Chaplain Gladden, on March 26, 1915, went with the 24th Infantry from Fort D. A. Russell, Wyoming, to the border where they joined the American Expeditionary forces into Mexico under General Pershing. He was placed in full charge of all the mail of the expedition. It was while handling a large sack of mail that he injured himself, which caused a very serious condition of the heart, and resulted in his having to be brought out of Mexico on a litter and he was taken to Fort Bliss, and from thence to the Letterman General Hospital of the Presidio of San Francisco, California, where he was confined to his bed for nine months. This unfitted him for further services and he was honorably discharged and retired from the army on May 23, 1917. He has decided to make Los Angeles his home and he and his family are comfortably located on Dana Street in that city, in a modern beautiful home.

William Nauns Ricks, the subject of this sketch, was born in Wytheville, Va., of mixed Indian parentage. On the Indian side, his mother's, he is a direct descendant of Powhattan, and on his father's side of Royal English and Indian blood. His maternal great grandfather was of Indian and Royal African blood. When quite a boy he realized that the few drops of African blood in his veins would make his life a difficult one. After seeing a lynching of a black youth he made a vow to himself that he would honor these drops of African blood by rendering service to the Negro race. He realized that he would have to struggle above the tide of prejudice. As a step in his preparation for his life's work, he worked his way on steamers, and, at the age of sixteen years, began his pilgrimage which took him several times to England. At the age of eighteen he went to Roanoke, Va., where he joined and was elected in due course Noble Grand of Kibar Lodge, of Odd Fellows, in that city, before he was twenty-one years of age. He was a member of the True Reformers; a brass band; sang in the Presbyterian Church choir; a member of dramatic clubs and several helpful organizations beside a military company.

In 1898 he enlisted in Company "A" 24th U. S. Infantry (regular service), and served ten months when he was discharged on G. O. No. 40. He re-enlisted and served twenty-seven months in the Philippine Islands and held the United States Medal for Service. Returned to the United States an invalid; went to Southern California where he became contracting plasterer. Afterward his right arm becoming impaired so as to make it impossible for him to follow the work, he sought other fields of endeavor. While living in Los Angeles he instituted and was one of the founders of the Men's Forum Club.

Mr. Ricks moved to San Francisco in 1904 and was married. He lost his wife, through an accident, in 1908. Shortly after locating in San Francisco he secured employment with the California Packing Corporation. Realizing the opportunities for advancement, he began attending business college at nights. This resulted in not only making him proficient and valuable to his employers but it secured for him an increase of salary annually during the eleven years' service. They recently made him head of a department over a force of men.

Mr. Ricks, like many others, moved to Oakland after the fire of 1906. He has been elected in that city to Past Chief Ranger of Foresters; Past National Aide de Camp, U. S. War Veterans, also past all the camp and department offices except Department Commander, which he refused three times. He is a member of the Fifteenth Street Church choir and many social uplift clubs, among which are the National Association for the Advancement of Colored People, having served on the executive board of the Northern California branch of this Association. He is teacher and founder of the Sunday School Improvement Club; Past President of the Limited Club; the Assembly Bay Cities Club, and recently was among the first to volunteer in an organization which was called "The Home Defense Club," out of which it was hoped to merge the "First Colored California Volunteer Regiment" for service during the present war. He was designated Provisional Captain of Company "C" of this proposed regiment.

Mr. Ricks has found time to take some part in politics, having at one time been a member of the State Republican Committee, and Judge of Elections in San Francisco. Mr. Ricks thinks that the greatest honor came to him when he was elected as a delegate to the Labor Union State Convention in 1907.

Mr. Ricks, as a recreation, writes poems and has done so since a boy. His first poem to be published in California was during his residence in Southern California, making its appearance in the *Daily News-Star*, of Pasadena, California, in 1902. Since then some of his poems have been published in the *New York Journal* and several magazines including *Sunset* and *Overland Monthly*. He has published some four or five hundred poems, his poem on "Lincoln" having appeared several hundred times on this Coast alone. He has published one book of poems called "The Whistle Maker." His writings show clearly that they are the product of a well-developed mind. Many of his poems will be found in the literary chapter.

Mr. Archie H. Wall, the subject of this sketch, was born in Franklin, Tennessee, Williams County, in 1857. He was educated in the school of experience, enlisted in the United States Army, February 18, 1876, at Nashville, Tenn., with the Twenty-fifth Infantry; served with the regiment until the Victorian campaign of 1880. All the troops in the campaign were from Fort Davis, Texas; thence to the Indian Territory, Fort Supply, serving six years and six months; thence to Fort Bayard, New Mexico, serving there six years; thence to Fort Douglass, Utah, at which time the declaration of war with Spain, or the Spanish-American War, began.

This regiment was ordered to Santiago de Cuba, disembarked June 25, 1898, and marched into battle July 1, serving on the firing line until July 14, 1898. Mr. Wall returned to Sibony de Cuba to the yellow fever camps and served in nursing yellow fever patients until August 26, at which time he embarked for New York. There were many personal friends among the soldiers who were immune to yellow fever and served as nurses from tent to tent. Among this number were Willis S. Bouncler, Abraham Benston, Jack Jones and R. E. Lee.

Mr. Wall related an unusual experience at San Juan Hill: ''The entire battalion of Seventy-first New York began firing on the Twenty-fourth Infantry of United States Negro Soldiers. Sergant Wall called the white commander's attention to the mistake he was making, as they were not the enemy. This instance occurred July 1, 1898. Sergeant Wall was caring for a number of soldiers who had been wounded in battle when he discovered this mistake of the commander of the Seventy-first New York. The Twenty-fourth Infantry of United States Negro soldiers was ascending San Juan Hill. The firing against them did not cease until Sergeant Wall threatened to report the white officer to Major General Shafter.''

After the Cuban campaign the Twenty-fourth Infantry returned to Fort Douglass, Utah. The regiment was ordered from there to the Presidio of San Francisco, and on July 19 embarked for Manila, arriving August 10, 1899. The regiment and the subject of this sketch, as a member of the Twenty-fourth Infantry, took part in General Lawton's advance, serving in Manila, Philippine Islands, until March 1, 1902.

Archie Henry Wall enlisted in the United States Army February 18, 1876, and was assigned to Company ''H,'' Twenty-fourth Infantry, August 13, 1876. He was made principal musician March 15, 1885, serving as such for eighteen years and having a company of never less than twenty-six musicians whom he trained. The following letters will give an estimate of the high regard in which Principal Musician Wall was held by his superior officers:

''Fort Ethan Allen, Vermont, February 11, 1903.

''To Whom It May Concern: Principal Musician A. H. Wall, band master of Twenty-fourth Infantry, United States Army, was on duty with his regiment in the campaign before Santiago de Cuba July 8 to August, 1898. On the 2nd day of July, 1898, Principal Musician Wall was of great assistance to me in caring for the wounded under fire of the enemy and, after dark, worked with others in digging a trench for burial of the remains of eight men who had died of wounds during the day. The location was on the ridge of the bank of the San Juan river. While digging the trench the Spaniards opened a terrific fire on our lines; Wall and his comrades were in a dangerous and much-exposed position, but, instead of abandoning their work, dropped into the trench. When the firing ceased they finished the trench and covered the remains after I held the services about midnight. I repeatedly saw Principal Musician A. H. Wall, band master of Twenty-fourth Infantry, U. S. A., while on duty. He was always neat and soldierly in appearance, respectful, well-behaved and attentive to duty.

''I take pleasure, from my personal knowledge of his genial conduct, in commending him to any one he may engage with for services he may be competent to perform.

''CHARLES S. WALKLEY,
''Chaplain, Artillery Corps, U. S. Army.''

The following is from the late Colonel Allensworth, a colored chaplain of the Twenty-fourth Infantry, U. S. Army:

''Fort Harrison, July 16, 1903.

''To Whom It May Concern: This letter of commendation is given to Archie H. Wall, principal Musician, U. S. Army, retired, late of the Twenty-fourth Infantry band, to certify that I have known him since 1866. He is prompt, faithful, and true to the interest of those who may place their confidence in him. He was one of the best musicians in the Twenty-fourth Infantry band and one of its reliable non-commissioned officers.

''ALLEN ALLENSWORTH,
''Chaplain, Twenty-fourth Infantry.''

''Fort Harrison, Montana, July 15, 1903.

''To Whom It May Concern: This is to certify I have known Principal Musician Archie H. Wall, band master, Twenty-fourth Infantry, since 1899. I consider him an excellent soldier and most manly, being honest, reliable, faithful and willing. In his retirement from active service the Twenty-fourth Infantry band loses one of its best and finest musicians and non-commissioned officers.

''JAMES A. MOSS,
''Captain and Adjutant, Twenty-fourth Infantry.''

''To Whom Is May Concern: I have known Principal Musician A. H. Wall, Twenty-fourth Infantry, for the past fifteen years, during which time for several periods he served directly under me, notably in the Santiago campaign, and I take pleasure in saying that I have always found him to be a brave, loyal and well-disciplined soldier and a sober, faithful and hard-working man.

''CHARLES E. TAYMAN,
''April 22, 1903.''   ''Captain, First Infantry.

The above-named officer presented Principal Musician and Mrs. Wall with a handsome and immense silver nut-bowl while at Fort Douglass, Utah. Principal Musician Wall told the writer that thirteen was his lucky number and recited the following to prove his statement: Signed to Company "H" August 13, 1876; sick in hospital thirteen days during his enlistment of thirty years. His oldest daughter was born June 13, 1888. He sailed from San Francisco to Manila July 13, 1903. He is a member of U. B. F. and charter member Spanish-American War Veterans, Guy V. Henry No. 3; also charter member Noah Ark, 3207.

Principal Musician Wall was married June 1, 1885, to Miss Fanny McKay, of Louisville, Kentucky. The union has been blessed by the birth of three children, Clifton, Florence Wall-Murry and Lillian Wall-Williams. The children are all musical. They were educated in the public school of Oakland and given every advantage. The girls are attractive and leaders in society of the Bay cities, marrying befitting their station. Their mother has a sketch in "Distinguished Women."

Mr. John W. Brown, the subject of this sketch, is the son of Mr. John B. and Julia Miner, of Falmouth, Virginia. When a boy of eighteen years he enlisted in the Ninth Cavalry and was considered a first-class rifle marksman; passed the examination and was made regimental clerk of the regiment (Ninth Cavalry); afterward took the examination for commissary sergeant.

During the Spanish-American War he was given a commission as second-lieutenant in the Ninth Immunes and served until that regiment was brought back from Cuba. When the insurrection begain in the Philippine Island he was given a commission as first lieutenant in the Forty-eight Infantry Volunteers regiment of Negro soldiers. After this campaign he returned to his former regiment, the Ninth Cavalry, the Forty-eighth having been mustered out of service. After twenty-seven years of service he was honorably retired with the rank of commissary sergeant.

Mr. Horace F. Wheaton, the subject of this sketch, aside from having a splendid musical education, has a military record worthy of historical prominence. The record is as follows: Horace F. Wheaton served in Company "L" of the Sixth Massachusetts State Militia, which regiment responded to the call in 1898, in the war with Spain. This regiment formed part of the army of occupation of Porto Rico, under General Miles, with whom they first went to Cuba, but did not land. While stationed at Utmado, Porto Rico, Mr. Wheaton was detailed as nurse in one of the field hospitals, where his experience gained from service and study at Tuft's College Medical School, Boston, Massachusetts, soon caused him to be promoted to acting hospital steward of Hospital No. 3, for officers, with full charge of the same. That his services were satisfactory is shown by his receiving a commission as second lieutenant in the Forty-ninth Infantry, U. S. Army of Volunters.

The requirements were to have served in the Spanish-American campaign with a meritorious record. When such eligibles were called from Massachusetts, as colored men, by the War Department at Washington, D. C., Mr. Horace F. Wheaton was one of the four chosen from the list submitted. The Forty-ninth Regiment, like the Forty-eighth, was organized for service in the Philippine Islands by act of Congress, March, 1899, to serve not later than June 30, 1901.

The subject of this sketch accepted his commission September 9, 1899. The regiment was organized at Jefferson barracks, Missouri; sailed for Manila December 2, 1899, arriving there January 2, 1900. On the Island of Luzon, in the northern part of Cagayan Province, skirting the shores of the China Sea, is where Mr. Wheaton saw the most service during the eighteen months on the island. He was on special duty of some kind, such as detached service from the company to which he belonged, with a detail of men doing guard or scout duty which was varied and arduous. He acted for some time as acting commissary and quartermaster of the military district where a battalion of the regiment was stretched over a long line of country. These and many other duties that devolved upon an officer he performed.

He participated in important captures which, with the satisfactory performance of his other duties, prompted Major Hinds, commander of the battalion above mentioned, to recommend him for an appointment as officer in the Native Scouts, Philippines. But the subject, being interested in medicine when he was mustered out, June 30, 1901, returned to Boston and took up the study of medicine in one of the colleges of that city. He did not finish, but decided to move to California, locating in Los Angeles, where he stood the civil service examination and was appointed as clerk in the postoffice of that city.

In regard to his commission, Mr. Wheaton says: "My commission I value very highly, not only for the office and honor it represents and the many experiences that it recalls, but because it is signed in the original handwriting of the martyred President, William McKinley, also his secretary of war, Elihu Root." Mr. Horace F. Wheaton is quite a musical factor in Los Angeles and was the leader of the largest concert orchestra of colored musicians that had ever been assembled in Los Angeles and which served during the colored Chautauqua of August, 1915.

Captain Henry Batie, the subject of this sketch, came to Los Angeles, California, from Grayson County, Texas, living in the State about seventeen years at the time of his passing, October 29, 1916. He was in the United States Army, as a member of the Twenty-fourth Infantry, during the Spanish-American War, serving first as a musician, then as corporal, then sergeant, of Companies "K," "G," "F," the band, and "L" company, quartermaster sergeant of the last named company while in Cuba.

Captain Batie, after the Cuban campaign, returned with his regiment to the United States and then to his home in California, where he re-enlisted. He afterwards went with Company "L" of Twenty-fourth Infantry, U. S. Army, to Skagway, Alaska, and when his last enlistment expired he remained in Alaska from May to December, 1899, after which he returned to Los Angeles and married Miss Roberta, daughter of Mrs. Sara Johnson, of San Diego, California. The union was blessed by the birth of one daughter, Katherine, who grew to be very patriotic and was a Red Cross worker to the time of her death, which occurred May 30, 1918, at the age of fifteen years.

Captain Batie, after locating in Los Angeles, took an active part in every movement of a benefit to the Negro race. He was an active member of the Afro-American Council and was on a committee of citizens who presented ex-President Taft with a gold card. He was also an officer of the General Harrison Gray Otis Marching Club, of Los Angeles. He spent several years attending lectures at the International Bible Institute, located in Los Angeles. He had about completed his course and was making preparations to launch out in such work when, after a few weeks of illness, he was called to his reward.

Captain Batie was highly respected, a beautiful, Christian gentleman. He was most happily married, and the grief of his passing led to the death of his only daughter in less than a year from the date of his passing.

Mr. Arthur Wilson, the subject of this sketch, was born in Charleston, South Carolina; joined the Twenty-fifth Infantry at Charleston, South Carolina, in 1866, and was honorably discharged at Jackson Barracks, Louisiana, in 1868. After being discharged from the army Mr. Wilson went to New York City. He left that city with a crew of eighty colored waiters and forty-two colored chambermaids, coming direct to San Francisco, California, where they opened the Palace Hotel. Mr. John Randolph was the head waiter of the crew. Mr. Wilson worked in the hotel for three years.

Afterward he accepted a position with the wholesale house of Fletchheimer & Goodekine, serving them for five years, after which time he went to work for the Pullman Car Company as porter, filling the position for five years, when he was given the appointment as private car porter on the Southern Pacific Railroad. He served in this capacity for twenty-five years when, on account of heart trouble, he was retired on a pension. He lived three years afterwards.

Mr. Wilson had several brothers living in the East, John, in Boston; William, in Akin, South Carolina; Edward and Chester, in Lynchburg, Virginia, and one sister, Maria. Mr. Arthur Wilson was married twice. His last wife was the youngest daughter of the late Rev. Sanderson. He was a trustee of the Fifteenth Street A. M. E. Church, of Oakland, a sincere and practical Christian gentleman and a devoted husband. His death occurred shortly after his wife's. They were a devoted couple and it is believed her sudden passing hastened his demise.

"Another private who won an honorable discharge, a Mr. Arthur Ellis, a private of Company "I," Eighth Regiment of Infantry of Illinois, volunteered on the 28th day of June, 1898, to serve two years, or during the war, is hereby discharged from service of the United States by reason of muster-out of the regiment at Chicago, 3rd day of April, 1899.

"FREDERICK BALLOU,
"Captain, Eighth Illinois Volunteer Infantry.

"Service, honest and faithful; character, good. Served in Spanish-American War in Cuba."

"Army of United States. To All Whom It May Concern: Know ye that Arthur Ellis, private of Troop "A" of the Ninth Regiment of Cavalry, who enlisted at Jefferson Barracks, Missouri, on the 28th day of March, 1908, to serve three years, is hereby honorably discharged from the Army of the United States by reason of expiration term of service.

"Said Arthur E. Ellis was born in St. Louis in the State of Missouri and, when enlisted, was thirty and nine-twelfths of a year old; by occupation a laborer No. 1; eyes, black; hair, light brown.

"Given under my hand at Fort Sam Houston, Texas, this 24th day of March, 1911.

"J. S. GULFOYR,
"*Lieutenant-Colonel of Cavalry, Commanding.*"

"Character, excellent. H. A. Sievert, Captain of Ninth Cavalry, Commanding Troop 'A.' Remarks: Service, honest and faithful; served in Philippine Islands, May 3, 1908, to May 15, 1909."

This record is especially interesting because the subject is a grandson of the pioneer barber of Oakland, a Mr. George Ellis.

It is with great pleasure that the writer is giving this sketch of a former officer in the United States Army, now practicing the profession as a doctor in the City of Oakland, a portion of which has been copied from the Howard University records, in which it said:

"William Whipple Purnell, Phar. D. M. D., Ophthalmia and Otology, 1895-8. Born January 25, 1869, Philadelphia, Pennsylvania, son of James W. and Julia A. Purnell; attended Howard University Normal and Preparatory Departments, 1880-5, afterward the Pharmaceutical College sessions, 21, 22, 1888-90, and Medical College, sessions, 23, 24, 25, and graduated Phar. D. in 1890, and M. D. in 1893. After which practiced medicine in Washington, D. C. Was appointed first lieutenant and assistant surgeon Forty-eighth United States Volunteers in 1899, Philippine Isles, during the insurrection."

Dr. Purnell served as assistant instructor in the Eye, Ear, Throat and Nose at Howard University from 1893 to 1898. He was appointed first lieutenant, assistant surgeon of the Eighth Immunes, United States Regulars, soldiers who were sent to Chickamauga Park, Georgia, to prove that it was not unhealthy. This regiment was afterward sent to Cuba and served during the Spanish-American War. At the close of the war it was returned to the United States and mustered out of service.

Dr. Purnell was appointed as first lieutenant and later captain-surgeon with the Forty-eighth Volunteer Infantry, serving with the regiment in the Philippine Islands during the insurrection. The regiment returned to the United States and was mustered out of service June 30, 1901. Mrs. Julia Brown, of Washington, D. C., mother of the doctor, crossed the continent to welcome her son's return to the United States. She advised him to locate in Oakland. Because of that advice today her son is the leading Negro physician of the Bay cities and enjoys a rapidly growing practice among Italians, Spanish and members of his own race. In 1895 he was married to Miss Theodora Lee, of Chicago, a granddaughter of the late John Jones.

The union has been blessed by the birth of one son, Lee Julian Purnell, to whom has been given the best education possible. He is very popular in all the schools he has attended. While at the Berkeley high he played basket ball and took part in football and other activities. After entering the University of California he was almost immediately made a member of the Big "C." He will graduate with the class of 1919 as an electrical engineer. The first semester after the United States entered the war, Lee Purnell was made a student officer and acted as such, drilling the lower classmen in military tactics twice a week. After the Government decided to establish an officers' training school at the University, Lee Julian Purnell entered the same with the hopes of winning a commission.

Dr. Purnell is a member of the Chamber of Commerce of Oakland, organizer of the Elks Lodge; director of the K. of P.; member of the Railroad Men's Association, Forresters and the Masons. Mrs. Purnell is one of the organizers of the Florence Nightingale Auxiliary to the Oakland Chapter of the Red Cross, a devoted member of the St. Augustin Mission of the Episcopalian Church and the Old Folks' home Executive Board.

The auxiliary of the Red Cross, under the leadership of Mrs. Purnell, did more active work and raised more money during a Red Cross drive than any other colored auxiliary in the United States. The California race women were enthusiastic in their effort to render service in the Red Cross during the recent World's War for Democracy. The State Federation of Colored Women's Clubs suspended all literary activities save the teaching of the different communities the value to the race of united war work in helping to win the war. The reports read at the annual meeting at Los Angeles and the appearance of the different auxiliaries, with their chairmen all in uniform, was an encouraging and inspiring sight. They aided in strengthening the Negro soldiers in the fight for a better place for the Negro people, after the war is won and peace has been declared and signed.

CHAPTER XXII

HISTORY OF THE NEGRO AT THE PANAMA-PACIFIC INTERNATIONAL EXPOSITION, SAN FRANCISCO, CAL.

This exposition was held to commemorate the greatest achievement of engineering skill ever accomplished by man—the completion of the Panama Canal. The exposition lasted from February 20 to December 4, 1915. The City of San Francisco was selected after a bitter fight between San Diego, California, and New Orleans, Louisiana, who tried, but in vain, to secure the honor of holding the exhibition or World's Greatest Exposition in their respective cities. The spirit and self-reliance of San Francisco finally won for her the honor. The committee representing the city, in addressing the Congress of the United States, among other things said that if given permission to hold the exposition in that city they would build the greatest of all expositions free of cost to the United States Government. This statement was remarkable because of the memory that less than five years previously the entire city was a mass of ruins from the earthquake and fire of 1906.

To build such a great exposition required money. The committee in charge who were entrusted to see that this pledge was kept, sold stock to obtain money for the project. The par value of the stock was one hundred dollars. Among the heaviest purchasers in the colored race was Mr. Walter A. Butler, of Oakland, and Mrs. Frazier, of San Francisco. This was a tremendous opening wedge for the Negro people in the building of this great exposition.

The exposition was nearly completed when one of the daily papers of San Francisco, the *Call-Post*, in an editorial asked its readers to suggest a pet name for this beautiful exposition, their suggestions to be sent in sealed envelopes to the editorial rooms of the paper. A committee, consisting of Mayor Rolph, of San Francisco; Mr. Henry Payote; Charles R. Fields, editor of the *Sunset* magazine; Supervisor Andrew J. Gallager, Paul Elder, publisher, and Haig Patigian, sculptor, was to pass on the names. There were thirteen thousand persons who submitted names, but the honor came to a colored school girl, little Miss Virginia Stephens, for being the first to suggest the name "Jewel City," a name that was voted the most correct. The papers in announcing the selection devoted almost an entire page telling of the decision of the committee. Among other things it said: "Jewel City, Fair's Pet Name. Committee makes selection christening great exposition. 'Jewel City' will be popular name for Panama-Pacific International Exposition. By unanimous agreement the committee of citizens appointed by Mayor Rolph and President Moore, which met yesterday afternoon to consider the suggestions of thirteen thousand Californians, decided 'Jewel City' was the phrase which best expressed the impression conveyed by the exposition. The name which most picturesquely described the architectural achievement of the fair. The decision of the judges will be popular with San Franciscans.''

A week later the paper had the following to say editorially: "People like the name 'Jewel City' for their fair. Popular title selected by the 'Call-Post' symposium passes into general usage. When the committee meets to select a name for an institution of such infinite variety as the Panama-Pacific International Exposition, there is always uncertainty about the result of the conference. Will the people accept the name so chosen? Will the name really be popular? When Mayor Rolph's citizen committee surveyed the hundreds of suggested popular titles for the exposition and unanimously chose 'Jewel City' as the most appropriate, they knew some thirty readers of this newspaper had offered that as their opinion. But they had no means of knowing that it would be the popular name with the people, that other publications and other people would adopt it as the most picturesque and striking name for the wonderland, within the green walls of the fair. The name was selected for cogent reasons. It sparkled with the gems of the 'Tower of Jewels' and it gave the dominating idea of beauty and preciousness which is inherent in the exposition. But the committee knew the public is whimsical and might not accept the idea. But it has. The name 'Jewel City' has caught the popular fancy and has been incorporated into the literature of the exposition. In the description of the exposition published in a booklet by a large local firm, 'Jewel City' is the synonym for the exposition. Futhermore, in the current number of the well-edited *Journal of Electricity* we find a handsomely illustrated article entitled, 'Illumination of Jewel City.'

"The young school girl of Oakland, Miss Virginia Stephens, who first suggested 'Jewel City' as the pet name for the fair has great reason to be proud of her faculty for striking a popular note and for first seizing on the word which to the world becomes obviously the right one.''

The writer considers this editorial just quoted of historical value; first, because it appeared one week after the selection of the name 'Jewel City,' and also because, in a few hours after the committee made their selection, they were told that the girl was a Negro child.

This little colored girl seems to have been blessed with unusual events from her birth, which occurred while her father, Mr. William Stephens, was private car man for the well-known family, the Crockers, of San Francisco and Burlingame. The family was very fond of Mr. Stephens and welcomed the birth of his daughter. When Miss Virginia Stephens was christened ''Virginia'' she was given a gift of a solid silver cup to commemorate the occasion by Hon. Francis Burton Harrison, the present Governor of the Philippine Islands. The reader will readily recall that the father of Mr. Harrison was the private secretary to, and was captured and imprisoned with Jefferson Davis, while he was President of the Confederacy.

Mr. William Stephens made no attempt to announce the identity of his daughter, lest she be denied the honor of naming the fair ''Jewel City,'' and notwithstanding the selection was made in January, there was no attempt to give her public recognition by the race until ''Alameda Day,'' which occurred late in June of that year. The colored citizens were asked to participate in the parade, whereupon the writer insisted that Miss Virginia Stephens be given a prominent place. Miss Mira Simmons, who at the time was president of the Colored Civic Center, and had the task of marshaling the colored people together, readily consented, which resulted in little Miss Virginia Stephens, together with seventy-five colored children, riding through the streets of San Francisco on a float in the parade, with a huge banner proclaiming the fact that Miss Virginia Stephens named the fair ''Jewel City.'' The writer at the time was a special feature writer for the daily *Tribune* (Oakland) and saw that proper mention was made through the press that the pet name of the fair, ''Jewel City,'' was given by a colored girl who rode in state in the parade on Alameda Day to and over the great exposition grounds.

The reader has traced the building and naming of the greatest exposition. We will now trace the Negro throughout the fair, showing the great progressive spirit of the West in his place in this the greatest of all expositions. The reader will now take an imaginary stroll with the writer through the predominating court of the exposition, which was called ''The Court of the Universe,'' and it has been said it was patterned after the square before St. Peter's at the Vatican, in Rome. The main entrance to this court was through the ''Tower of Jewels,'' a magnificent structure and thoroughly original in its every appointment, towering fully four hundred and twenty feet, hung with myriads of semi-jewels which were made of hand-cut glass by Austrian workmen and were just finished and on their way to the United States when the World's War was announced. These jewels were of the five soft pastel colors selected by Mr. J. Guerine, who had charge of the color scheme of the exposition. They sparkled in the noon-day sun and at night as real jewels, and were a wonderful sight.

There were two other gateways to this the greatest of exposition courts. These gateways were built after the pattern of the ''Triumphant Arch of Constantine,'' with the exception that they had placed on top groups of allegorical figures made of travitine. They had their own significance in carrying out the idea of the ''Court of the Universe.'' The first gateway after leaving the central gate, ''The Tower of Jewels,'' was that of the ''Nations of the East.'' On top of the ''Triumphal Arch of the Rising Sun'' were grouped, in imitation of sculpture, figures representing: The Arab Shiek on his steed; the Negro servitor, with fruit on his head; the Egyptian on his camel, carrying a Mohammedan standard; the Arab falconer, with bird on wrist; the splendid Indian Prince, on the back of the elephant, inside the howdah; the Spirit of the East; the Lama from Thibet, with his rod of authority; the Mohammedan, with his crescent, stands against a Negro servitor; the Mongolian on his horse.

Across the sunken gardens and on the opposite side of the Court of the Universe was the ''Gateway to the West.'' On the ''Triumphal Arch of the Setting Sun'' were figures of the ''Nations of the Occident.'' From left to right you see the figures of the French-Canadian, the trapper, the Alaskan, with her Totem-poles on her back; the Latin-American on horseback, the German, the Italian, the Anglo-American; the squaw, with her papoose basket; the American Indian on his horse; in the center the old prairie schooner drawn by the great oxen, and on the tongue of this schooner the figure of a hale and hearty young woman, representing the ''Mother of Tomorrow.'' Atop of the prairie schooner was ''Enterprise,'' represented by a kneeling figure with arms raised, pushing out, and on either side of this figure was a white boy and colored boy, representing the "Heroes of Tomorrow." In front marches that stalwart "Mother of Tomorrow." It has taken all these figures of the Occident to produce the work that is coming in the future, in the achievements due to the completion of the Panama Canal. Therefore they co-jointly express the "Mother of Tomorrow," a typical representation of the progressive spirit of the West, and especially California. In the "Nations of the East," the Negro is represented as a servitor; in the "Nations of the West" sitting on a level and facing each other a white boy and a colored boy with Enterprise or Energy pushing back of them, representing the "Heroes of Tomorrow." To prove the statement that this spirit of an equal chance with others at the P. P. I. E. the reader will now visit the last entrance to this "Court of the Universe." Unlike the other entrances, this had a bandstand in the center and overlooking the Bay of San Francisco. During the entire period of the exposition every afternoon the Philippine band, with their Negro leader, Major Walter Loving, gave a concert, and at the same hour there were concerts given by different famous bands with their great white leaders in the other courts of the exposition. There are numerous instances of this kind the writer might cite. Take, for instance, Alameda Day; they had a street parade in San Francisco in which Virginia Stephens rode in state. They also had in this parade two floats of Colored people, one of which contained colored ladies ,members of the Oakland Civic Center and clubs, and a float of seventy-five colored school children waving American Flags and the Bear Flag. After the parade had traversed the exposition grounds, the school children had a special program, and, among other things, a drill consisting in forming a human American Flag. The Negro children were included in this Flag-drill, together with all other races of children of Alameda County schools.

When the American Athletic University Track meet was held on the athletic grounds there were a number of colored boys. Aside from Howard Drew, there were Sol. Butler, R. Morse, Irving Howard and Binga Dismond. Such events often occur where colored college boys appear with white college or university boys. But this special event was given much publicity and especially the colored entries in the meet.

Another event that deserves more than a passing notice was the celebration of Lincoln Day. The parade that preceded the exercises, which were held in Festival Hall, was composed of regiments of Coast Artillery, a battalion of Marines, Naval detachments from warships in the San Francisco Harbor, Cavalry troops, Ambulance companies, and Field Hospital troops. This splendid parade was led by one thousand Negro troops, or practically all of the Twenty-fourth Regiment of U. S. Negro soldiers, then stationed at the Presidio of San Francisco. Three days previous this same regiment of Negro troops were selected to escort the Liberty Bell over the exposition grounds and through the streets of San Francisco to the Southern Pacific depot, where it started on its way back to Philadelphia.

In regard to Negro exihibits at the Exposition, there were not a great many because of the exposition that was being held in the City, of Chicago by the colored citizens throughout the Nation, in commemoration of the Fifty Years of Freedom. There were some colored exhibits at the exposition in San Francisco of a nature to reflect credit upon the race. In the Educational Palace, the Department of Education of the United States Government had a wonderfully arranged set of charts and pictures of historical value in that they showed the progress of the Negro race from the cotton fields of antebellum days to the holding of a post mortem and clinics in a colored hospital, surrounded by Negro doctors and nurses. Another set of charts portrayed the Negro in the industries and the sciences. They also had pictures of some of the leading schools for higher education, showing their grounds and buildings, and, in many instances, classes at graduation. This was especially noticeable in the picture of Meharry Medical College. The most interesting of all these charts, which had the effect of cheering those who thought that the United States Government was not interested in their progress, were the charts showing the race's greatest need for more doctors, dentists and men and women in the other professions. In another part of this exhibit was a well-filled bookcase of Negro books. The desks, chairs and the bookcase were the work of Negro students of Hampton Institute, located in Virginia. Adjoining this exhibit were several exhibits of work from the public schools for the race in Washington, D. C. The M Street high school, Normal No. Two, and also the Armstrong Manual Training School, all of Washington, D. C., had wonderful exhibits in water color paintings, domestic science, and architectural plans for a residence. The needle work, charcoal sketches, machinery, wood-turning and rugs were especially fine. Would that space permitted giving details of each exhibit from the Washington, D. C., colored schools. The Summer High School for colored in St. Louis had a collection of essays, and also two very creditable charcoal sketches, work of students, one by Miss Agnes Fort, and another by Miss Kate Smith. They were "Winged Victory" and a colored Episcopalian church of St. Louis.

In the Food Exhibit Palace, there was exhibited all during the fair an automatic citrus press, the invention of two colored people of Oakland, California. In the Idaho State Building there were two pieces of water-color paintings, work of colored public school children. In the Virginia State Building were hung pictures of the Colored Institute of West Virginia, showing the different buildings, grounds and pictures of a few students.

In the Mississippi State Building there was an entire room set aside for the exhibiting of the handiwork of colored students from the Tougaloo University, of Mississippi, these exhibits consisting of furniture for a dining room, andirons and hardware, together with the entire plans for a six-room house. They showed needlework which represented the progress of a student, from the making of a kitchen-apron to a reception gown, fancy French embroidery and many other dainty pieces of handiwork. This exhibit was the only exihibit,with the exception of a few products, in the Mississippi State Building. The exhibit by colored students from this State was noticeable, because of the bitter fight made by it to keep California out of the Union. It was the Hon. Jefferson Davis of Mississippi who led the Southern States to rebellion, and, after fifty years, this State was the only one in the Union with a creditable Negro exhibit. It was especially encouraging to the writer because it portrayed a better understanding between the races.

In the Palace of Fine Arts there was a magnificent painting by Henry O. Tanner, "Christ in the House of Lazarus." This painting received the gold medal. Mr. Tanner is one of five of the world's celebrated spiritual painters. He has many pictures that the Government of France has purchased from him, and they are now in the great art galleries of that country. There was also exhibited a finely executed hand-painted portrait of Mr. Tanner by a celebrated white painter from Philadelphia, a former teacher.

In the French Pavilion, the librarian and interpreter was a gentleman of French and Negro extraction, a Mr. Jean J. Adams, a cultured gentleman who was a graduate of the University of France. He was very much grieved over the manner in which the Germans were devastating the beautiful country of France. He was, as he said, glad that the war had at least begun, for France had for years lived on edge with the taunting of the Zeppelins. Often when there was a great fete day, a Zeppelin would suddenly land in their midst, or, at the still hour in the night, one would be aroused by cannonading. Upon inquiry you learned that the Kaiser had decided to call his men to practice a battle in the mountains just for exercise. He then sighed and said: "After all, it is better to be in actual war than to live in this constant dread; but ah! the sacrifice of human lives, for France will never surrender as long as a French man or woman can fight." Like all true Frenchmen, he loved dear Paris. He was the author of "The Chronology of History."

The Panama-Pacific International Exposition held many special days, at which times many colored people exhibited creditable stock or other things. It was impossible for the writer to visit all these different exhibits, but she has the pleasure of giving an account of one who exhibited and won several prizes. That lady is the daughter of a pioneer by the name of Mrs. Abigal Nugent of San Francisco. Her daughter, a Mrs. Margret Hatton, is interested in fine Persian cats. She was presented by a friend several years ago with a fine Persian cat, and immediately began the study of the care of such cats, which has resulted in the breeding of the celebrated "Prince You Know," which took the first prize in the Panama-Pacific International Exposition, and a special prize from an admirer.

The first prize given was a handsome silver cup, fully ten inches high and the blue ribbon, by the P. P. I. Exposition. Mrs. Hatton's "Prince You-Know" won first prize at the Cat show in Oakland, in 1914. Afterward Mrs. Hatton decided to join the Cat Club of that city. She has the distinction of being the only colored lady cat fancier on the Pacific Coast and a member of the Pacific Cat Club. The following account of this celebrated cat is quoted from *The Cat Courier*, June 15, 1915, in which it said. " 'Prince You-Know,' orange-eyed, white neuter, owned by Mrs. M. E. Hatton, of San Rafael, California, was judged best 'golden-eyed' white male kitten at the California Club cat show in Oakland, 1914. He also won two silver cups, among other specials. He won the same awards in the Pacific Coast cat show in San Francisco in 1914. He won two cups at the show when he was only six months old—quite a killing for a cat of that tender age." The following is from *The Western Cat Fancier*, published in San Francisco January, 1915: "Mrs. Hatton's 'Prince You-Know' won first prize in his class, 'Golden-eyed' white male kitten, and second prize as a novice of the same class, receiving a blue and red ribbon for the best white kitten under seven months descendant of 'Toodles.' He received a special prize, a silver cup. He won while as novice in the same class, and two special, a silver cup and a string of rose beads, and only six and a half months old." Mrs. Hatton has five Persian cats, "Lady Rowena," in open class, which in the novice class won yellow and pink ribbons at the Panama-Pacific International Exposition.

CHAPTER XXIII

THE END OF THE TRAIL

The beginning of the blazing of a new trail for the Present Day Negro in California is evinced by the doings of the following prominent Negro citizens:

Dr. Wilbur Clarence Gordon, of Los Angeles, who during the first month of the Spanish influenza epidemic, had one hundred and ninety-six new cases, besides his regular practice. Many of the new cases were families of well-to-do white persons, who employed this Negro physician and Negro trained nurses.

Mr. Errol Marshall, a successful Negro furniture dealer in Oakland, who was the first Negro in the State to receive the nomination as candidate for County Clerk of Alameda County. He lost the election by a small margin.

Mr. James Bishop, of Modesta, California, who has opened a first class carpet and house furnishing store in a town where he will have to depend almost entirely on white trade.

Rev. J. Stout, of the C. M. E. Church, who has succeeded in opening the doors of the public schools of the State to many Negro teachers.

Mr. C. E. Brunson, of Santa Monica, who had an objectionable sign removed from the pleasure pier of that beach town.

Rev. Shaw, of Los Angeles, whose partiotic sermons have greatly aided in the three million dollars subscribed by California Negroes to the Fourth Liberty Loan.

Frederick Madison Roberts, the first Negro ever elected to the California legislature. He represents the Seventy-fourth District. He was very ill during the first weeks of the first session, but recovered in time to be sworn in, and to cast his vote for National prohibition, and introduced sixteen bills of vital interest to the Negro race before the first recess of the first session of 1919.

Miss Gladys Reo Harris, the first Negro girl to graduate in sociology and stood the civil service examination in a class of sixty-seven, out of which seventeen passed. This colored girl passed and received an appointment as supervisor of charities among the colored people in Los Angeles County. Her work was so satisfactory that in less than a year she was given work among all races.

Hugh Mcbeth, a young negro attorney of Los Angeles, recently had the distinguished honor of addressing the Southwestern District Convention supporting the League of Nations at their executive sessions held at the St. Francis Hotel, San Francisco. The subject of Mr. Mcbeth's address was "The League of Nations as a Guarantee to Weaker People." Other speakers addressing that body were ex-President William Howard Taft, and Hon. Benjamin Ide Wheeler, President of the University of California at Berkeley.

Mr. William Shores (Daddy), who for thirty years has served as special officer of the Security Bank of Los Angeles, was recently honored by having his sketch and picture appear in the publication of the history of the Bank.

Captain T. Nimrod McKinney arrived in San Francisco, California, November 15, 1917, and immediately reported to the representatives of the Federal State Department, that Passport Frauds were being perpetrated by so-called American citizens in Japan and China, who had taken out citizenship papers, but who, upon the declaration of war against Germany by the United States, went to Siberia for the purpose of obtaining fraudulent passports and documents of former citizenship. The Princess Juliana, the Dutch steamer on which Captain McKinney and many of the above class of persons travelled from China and Japan, was detained in San Francisco, and all passengers of Russian and other descent were taken to Angel Island for a rigid investigation.

Captain McKinney soon discovered that it was not the policy of the War Department to assign colored Americans to staff positions such as a Captain Quartermaster administrative section in accordance with his qualification, and he accepted an invitation from the Women's Department Educational Propaganda Council of National Defense, and in this capacity gave one year of successful and effective service to his country without pay, and at the sacrifice of his own personal fortune. This was truly an act of heroism and sacrifice.

The *Manila Times* of the Philippine Islands under date of October 6, 1917, spoke of Captain T. Nimrod McKinney as a well-known local merchant who had received a Commission as Captain Quartermaster in the United States Army. The "Crisis," under date of April, 1918, made honorable mention of Captain McKinney and his standing in the Philippine Islands as a soldier, an organizer, author, and merchant. The Honolulu

Star-Bulletin, under date of November 16, 1917, said: ''T. Nimrod McKinney, manager of the Manila Commission Co. and the Manila Transportation Co., and Mrs. McKinney, are in Honolulu today en route to San Francisco. In their party are also Dr. Ramon Abril and wife and Ara Pueo, well known in commercial and Spanish social circles of Manila, who are on their way to Spain. McKinney reports that business conditions in Manila are booming and that the business men of the Philippine capital are mastering every situation brought about by America's declaration of war against Germany. He says: 'We can sell everything we can raise, but now have no bottoms with which to make delivery' * * * McKinney intends to enter the war service of the United States. * * * He passed through here eighteen years ago with the American army of occupation when it was bound for the Philippines. He is an officer on the quartermaster reserve corps.''

Lieut. Osceolo E. McKaine, in an article ''With the Buffaloes in France,'' in the Independent magazine, under date of January 11, 1919, said: ''* * * Perhaps the most significant and important phase of the war's reaction is the enthusiastic and unconditional acknowledgment by the colored soldier of intelligent, efficient and successful black leadership. He has acquired an inordinate and passionate love and respect for the colored officers. The black man, in the ranks demands black superiors. This acknowledgment, this love and respect, forever refutes the contention that black men could not successfully lead black men, for these black officers led their 'Buffaloes' successfully and sometimes brilliantly, in the carnage of Chateau Thierry, the bloody and bitter Argonne and in the eleventh hour drive on Metz. When the peace bells tolled their first stroke its echo found the old 15th New York (colored) the nearest American troops to the Rhine, and the 367th Infantry (the Buffaloes), the nearest Allied troops to Metz.'' Many of these officers were Californians. Among the number who won distinctive honors was Dr. Claudine-Ballard of Los Angeles, who won the Croix de Guerre, at Mont des Singes (monkey-mountain) on the banks of Ailette River, the key to the Hindenburg line. His citation follows:

''59-Division
''Infanterie
''Etat-major   ''Extract de l'Ordre decitations No. 62.

''Le General Rondeau, commandant L'Infanterie de la 59th Division, cite a l'Ordre de la Brigade. Le Lieutenant, Docteur Ballard, Claudius, der 37th, B. I. U. S. Pendant les operations du 30 Septembre and 13 Octobre, 1918, est reste a son poste quoque blessé et a soigne ses camarades avee un devotement extraordinaire jusqu'a ce que son Battaillon soit relevé.

''Le General Rondeau, Commandant.
..''L'F. D. 59.
''(Signed) RONDEAU.''

The English translation of the above is as follows:
''59th Division   November 24, 1918.
''Infantry
''Major General's Office.
''Extracts of Orders of Citation No. 62.

''General Rondeau, commanding the Infantry of the 59th Division, cites this Brigade order. Lieut. Dr. Claudius Ballard of the 370th Regimental Infantry, U. S. During the operations of September 30 to October 13, 1918, he remained at his post, although wounded, and administered aid to his comrades with an extraordinary devotion until his Battalion was relieved.

''General Rondeau, Commandant of the 59th Infantry Division.
''(Signed) RONDEAU.''

S. P. Johnson, eighteen years in Los Angeles, came from Emporia, Kansas. He entered the labor movement in 1903, was soon elected local representative, and has for the past fifteen years served as its business manager. In 1905 he was elected General Secretary of the International Union at a convention held in Kansas City, Mo., and has held the position ever since, the only colored man holding such a position over whites and colored in this country. Served seven years as Grand Master of the Odd Fellows of California, now serving his eighth year as Grand Secretary of the Grand Lodge; also Grand Patron of the Order of the Eastern Star Chapter of California; General Secretary Western Baptist Association; President of Kansas Club, and holds many other positions of trust: now in the undertaking business.

There has been a great number of the ''Black Boys of Uncle Sam'' from California who have won distinction in the recent World's War. Among this number is Sergeant

Edward Carlisle, a member of the 1st Battalion 367th Infantry, who won the Croix de Guerre for courageous conduct under shell fire and evacuation of French prisoners just before the signing of the armistice.

Sergeant Leonelle Fortier, member of Machine Gun Company, 365th Infantry, 92nd Division U. S. A. On guard duty with mounted guns in life boats for submarines while crossing the Atlantic ocean; operated a machine gun in the drive on Metz.

William Ragsdale, a first class private in the Medical Corps, 92nd Division, 365th Infantry, served eighteen months, during which time was on the field of action during the hardest fighting and administered to the wounded especially in the Marbarche Sector and in the drive on Metz.

THE BLACK BOYS IN KHAKI

By MRS. A. C. H. BILBREW

Black Boys in khaki,
  We're mighty proud of you;
You started in to make the Allies win,
  And you've seen the whole thing thru.

With your Anglo comrade by your side,
  Fighting for liberty,
Like him you shed your blood and died
  For a World Democracy.

No shot or shell nor swift shrapnel
  Could make you quake or quail,
But always steady at your post,
  You knew you dare not fail.

The monster cannon's mighty roar
  Was music to your ear,
The sickening deadly poisonous gas,
  You didn't dread nor fear.

You were a puzzle to the Hun,
  He could not understand
How you fought with rifle, bayonet or gun,
  And never missed your man.

The old 15th Infantry and 8th Illinois,
  Are in a class all their own;
Needham Roberts, and Johnson who won
  the Croix de Guerre
For holding off twenty-four Boches alone.

Black Boys in khaki,
  Your mothers are proud of you,
And they prayed to God to give you strength
  To prove you were soldiers true.

Your sweethearts, wives and children
  At home were staunch and true;
While you were out in No Man's Land,
  Their thoughts were all for you.

Black Boys in khaki,
  France is mighty proud of you,
For you fought like demons to save Paris,
  From the hands of the Fritzies, too.

When Alsace sighed and Lorraine cried,
  Till her streets with tears were wet;
With your Anglo comrade by your side,
  You helped America pay her debt.

Black Boys in khaki,
   America is proud of you,
For you have proven once for all,
   You're Americans thru and thru.

And if she could establish Democracy
   Away across the sea,
There is no doubt she'll bring it about
   In her own land of the free.

Then when she lifts her voice to sing
   "My Country, 'tis of thee,"
Twelve million strong we'll catch the strain,
   "Sweet Land of Liberty."

Black Boys in khaki,
   We're mighty proud of you,
You started in to make the Allies win,
   And you've seen the whole thing thru.

Dennis McG. Mathews, of Los Angeles, received his commission as First Lieutenant of Infantry in U. S. Army October 15, 1917, upon his graduation from the 17th Provisional Training Camp (colored) at Fort Des Moines, Iowa. He afterward entered the Divisional Infantry School of Arms, 86th Division, National Army, Camp Grant, Illinois, completing a special course of instruction in Machine Gunnery, Mechanism and Tactics section; later he qualified at the same school to instruct in Field Fortification. After reaching France he took a special course in Machine Gunnery at Gondrecourt, France, First Corporal School. He was second in command of Company C, 350th Machine Gun Battalion, 92nd Division, in the Metz sector the day the Armistice was signed, and when the Battalion ceased firing they found out that the Armistice had been signed fifteen minutes before. After the signing of the Armistice he was made Town Mayor of Lassay, Department of Mayenne, France, where there were two thousand soldiers and seventy-six officers billetted of the 349th, 350th and 351st Machine Gun Battalion. First Lieutenant Mathews had seen previous service with the 23rd Kansas in the Spanish-American War, and also in the Navy.

William Lee Bryson, of Los Angeles, was First Sergeant of Company D, 25th Infantry, U. S. A., and attended the Training School for Officers at Fort Des Moines, Iowa, and won a commission as Captain. He afterward served in France with the National Army with Company E, 367th Infantry.

Lieutenant Journee White, Los Angeles real estate operator, gave up his business to do his bit overseas. He was commissioned at Fort Des Moines, Iowa, October 15, 1917, and went to France with the 367th Infantry, or the "Buffaloes" as the regiment was afterwards called. For his gallantry and heroism in battle before Metz he was decorated with the Croix de Guerre along with the First Battalion of his regiment. After his return to Los Angeles the *Daily Express* honored Lieutenant White by publishing his picture and the following article which was headed "Officer Praises Colored Yanks' Courage in War:"

"That the American Negro displayed high courage in the world war is attested by Lieut. Journee White (colored), formerly Los Angeles real estate man, who has just returned wearing the Croix de Guerre. 'The Negro has done his part in this war,' said Lieutenant White today. 'He does not claim to have done any more than any one else, but he does want the world to know and give him credit for what he actually achieved. If he gets that it will be much.

" 'In front of the men with the 367th Infantry, 92nd Division (Buffaloes) the dark Americans were assailed with every possible German propaganda. The Germans tried to get us to give up, to play the part of traitors. To spy on the government, some of us were offered high commissions in the German Army. Others were offered high prices, and all were promised real liberty and democracy in Germany. Yet I do not know of a single American Negro having been shot for treason. His loyalty could not be shaken.' According to Lieutenant White his regiment saw its hottest fighting before Metz, one of the final and decisive battles of the war."

Lieut. White was the assistant regimental supply officer, having been promoted to the staff by Colonel James A. Moss, the organizer of the 367th Infantry (Buffaloes). There were one hundred colored California men in this regiment, all of whom made good. Special mention must be made of the splendid record made by some of these men who were drafted and as privates won commissions, namely: Sergeant Raoul Reynolds, Platoon Sergeant; J. H. Gray, to Sergeant, and Mr. Lucas to Second Lieutenant; also Josiah Banks for heroism, Windell Baker who was wounded at La Chapelle, St. Dil sector, and William Johnson who was killed while speeding to his Colonel with an important message, one of the most efficient of all messengers and a most loyal and obedient soldier. He died a hero. He was the first Los Angeles colored drafted man to be killed and was a member of the Supply Company, 367th Infantry, 92nd Division.

Aurelious P. Alberga, of San Francisco, won his commission as First Lieutenant at the Training School at Fort Des Moines, Iowa. He served as First Lieutenant, 365th Infantry R.C. He also served as Regimental Athletic Officer from November 4, 1917, for six months of training in the United States. During this time he conducted many boxing contests, cross country runs, baseball games and many other athletic events, and shows exceptional aptness for this kind of work.

F. C. Swertzer,
Captain and Adjutant, 365th Infantry.

On the evening of October 21, 1918, this officer with Colonel N. B. Marshall, Company A, 365th Infantry, conducted a raid on the German lines at Bois-Freharte, returning through a two-hour artillery box barrage without the loss of a man, and gaining valuable information.

John H. Sheffield,
Major, 365th Infantry.

Lieut. Alberga trained and instructed Company A from November 3, 1917, until this company went into Vorges sector.

Walter Lowe,
First Lieutenant Commanding Company A, 365th Infantry.

Last, but not least, little Charles Ragland, age twelve, member of Troop 102, L. A. Boy Scouts of America, won a medal from the U. S. Government for selling more Liberty Bonds than any other Colored Boy Scout in this State. He sold in the Fourth Liberty Bond drive ten Bonds, and one Cash Bond.

Sergeant Charles Raymond Isum, of Los Angeles, a native son of a native son (Thomas Isum, of San Jose). Sergeant Isum was drafted and from the ranks of a private was promoted for efficiency to Sergeant of the Medical Department and served with the 365th Infantry, First Battalion (the Buffaloes), serving in the front line trenches administering first aid in the Voges, St. Die Sector, Argonne Forest, and the Marbache Sector. Sergeant Isum saw eighteen months of service in France, during which time he administered to wounded soldiers. During the German raids of October 14-15, 1918, he administered to one hundred and twenty-seven men who had been gassed. After this he entered the ruined town of Pont-A-Mousson in the Marbache Sector. In this Sector he rendered first aid to and evacuated patients under constant shell fire from November 5 to November 10, 1918.

On the morning of November 10 he was ordered to move his station to Lesmenil which the day before had been in the heart of ''No Man's Land'' but had been captured by the 365th Infantry during the night of the 10th in the drive on Metz. He moved his station under a terrific barrage of German 75's and 155's. So terrific was the barrage that it was impossible to set up a station and he took refuge for the night in the ruins of an old farm house at Lesmenil. The Germans began a barrage of gas around the ruins of the farm house during the night, gassing all the occupants. The majority of those gassed were sent to the hospital on the morning of the eleventh of November, but Sergeant Isum refused to be evacuated, having a desire to be on the field of action when the war closed. He was afterward awarded the Wound Chevron by orders of Lieut.-Colonel Deitsch, Commanding Officer.

Personnel Intelligence Sergeant Henry Mahammitt Brooks, born in Williston, North Dakota, 1895. Educated in public schools of Orange County, California; graduated from the Huntington Beach High School, the only Negro boy to graduate in that county. He qualified for athletic work and was indorsed by the Athletic Association of Southern California and his private instructors for a position in the Kansas City public schools at Kansas City, Missouri. He was called into the service of his country from that city in October, 1917. He was made Corporal at Camp Lewis and Sergeant at Camp Grant, and later Personnel Intelligence Sergeant, and while serving in France was engaged in map making. He also taught physical culture during his eighteen months' service in the National Army. He was attached to the 350th Machine Gun Battalion, 92nd Division (the Buffaloes). He has prepared a book on ''The Trail of the Buffaloes in France'' and will publish it soon.

Lieut. Eugene Lucas, Company A, 368th Infantry, National Army, has resided in Los Angeles for over ten years, during which time was an emissary of the County Jail of Los Angeles County during Sheriff Hammell's administration, serving three years and seven months. He was later certified by the Civil Service Commission for a position as Water Front Guard at San Pedro, California, the present Mayor, W. T. Woodman, being president of the Harbor Commissioners at that time. Mr. Lucas filled this position until the call of his country through the draft of October 27th, 1917. He was sent to Camp Lewis, American Lake, Washington. He was sent to the officers' training school at Camp Funston, Kansas, January 5th, 1918. He graduated from the officers' training school April 19, 1918, and was assigned to headquarters troop, 92nd Division, in France July 22, 1918. He left the United States June 12, 1917, and arrived in France June 19, 1917. He saw service in the following Sectors: Vosges from August to September, and in the Muse-Argonne from September 25th to 30th, and in the Marbache Sector from November 1 until the signing of the Armistice. Received honorable discharge from military service at Camp Mead, Md., March 18, 1919, by order of Colonel Crnoyes, Commanding 17th Infantry U. S. A.

Lieut. Jessie Kimbrough saw service with the ''Buffaloes'' as a Machine Gun operator during the entire war and took part in some of the heaviest fighting with his command during their engagement at Verdun, and especially the Argonne Forest and Marbache Sector. Mr. Kimbrough is one of Los Angeles' favorite sons, where he has filled with honor many responsible positions.

There are many more men who have served with great honor and credit to the race in the recent World War. It was impossible to give each a sketch because this volume was completed and on the press when they returned. The author is proud of the ''Black Boys of Uncle Sam'' from California and elsewhere throughout the Nation, and some day will write their entire history, for there is no braver soldier in war than the Negro. He not only fights for the glory of his country, but for the betterment of the condition of the Negro race. He will gladly give up his life if it becomes necessary, because he knows by his sacrifice there will be one more hero who will force the issue and thereby blaze a better trail for untold Negroes, proving to the world they are worthy of every right and privilege granted to other citizens of this United States of America. God bless Negro soldiers for their valor and sacrifices.

CHAPTER XXIV

NOTES ON THE TEXT

"The Broderick-Terry Memorial real historical lesson; not the death of dueling, but the end of local slavery agitation. In erecting two shafts to mark the site of the historic encounter between Broderick and Terry, the Native Sons' Landmark Society has performed a patriotic service, but it would be unfortunate if those monuments serve only as reminders of the end of dueling in California. There is a broader meaning and a deeper significance in that tragic contest which was not only the last chapter in the history of the duel, in this State, but also the final page of the story of the attempt to carry California out of the Union. Of two such lessons why forget the nobler and manlier one? Broderick, despite defects so characteristic of the times, was a sincere and stalwart champion of the principles of Liberty. His mind admitted of no compromise upon the question of human freedom. Neither color, nor creed, could vary his application of the doctrine that men are born free and that no man comes into the world either with spurs on his heels or a saddle on his back.

"He was a Democrat until the democracy of the South became permeated with the determination to fight for the perpetuation of slavery. Broderick was for free labor, and to his efforts was very largely due the fact that this State was even temporarily carried out of the Union in 1850, when he offered a bill against the immigration of free Negroes; in 1852 he fought the fugitive slave law; in 1857, in the United States Senate, he delivered a sensational speech attacking the pro-slavery party, and a few months later, in another address, said: 'How foolish for the South to hope for success in such an encounter. Slavery is old and decrepit and consumptive; Freedom is young, strong and vigorous. The one is naturally stationary and loves ease; the other is migratory and enterprising.' It was for sentiments such as these that Broderick suffered the series of attacks which culminated in the insults which a vicious and radical code of honor demanded he should avenge by a duel These shafts are not to honor the men nor their duel, but to mark an historical incident, and for that reason the incident should be read in the light of its deeper significance."—(*San Francisco Chronicle*.)

California—the name; Dante's Divina Comedia, when he represented the mountain of Purgatory at the antipodes of Jerusalem crowned by the terrestrial Paradise.—Longfellow's note to the Purgatories; first note, to the Purgatories, Vol. II, Div. Com., p. 159. Herrara, dec. VIII, libro VI. Hale's "His Level Best." California, Dispute of the Origin of the Name. "Known twice as long as formerly supposed," says *Porto Rican Educator*. Long accepted beliefs as to the origin of the name California have been vehemently disputed by a new theory propounded by P. I. Miller, commissioner of education at Porto Rico, in a letter to Professor Charles Edward Chapman of the Department of History in the University of California. The earliest known use of the name California has been supposed to be its appearance in the novel, "Las Sergas de Espladian," published by Montalvo, in 1510, in which he told of the black Amazons ruling the Island of California. However, the same was really known twice as long ago as that, points out Commissioner Miller, for he calls attention to the presence of the name in the famous old French epic poem, "The Song of Roland," written about the close of the eleventh century, in which appears the line, "And those of Africa and those of California."—(Quoted from the *Daily Californian*, March 16, 1916.)

California, admission of the State of, to the Union. Senator Benton's speech as reported in the *Congressional Globe* of the Thirty-first Congress, 446; first session, Senate speech of Mr. Benton of Missouri, April 8, 1850. Senator Seward's speech on "Admission of California," *Congressional Globe*, March 11, 1850, p. 269, Thirty-first Congress, first session, under heading "California, Union and Freedom."

Colored Settlers—First on the Pacific Coast.—"California Miscellany," Vol. I, p. 9. Address on the history of California from the discovery of the country to the year 1849, delivered before the Society of California Pioneers at their celebration of the tenth anniversary of the admission of the State into the Union, by Edward Randolph, September 10, 1860, San Francisco. First colored settlers on Pacific Coast (p. 62), History of Santa Clara County, California, by J. P. Monroe Frazer, historian; also Bancroft's History of California, Vol. IV, p. 713; Vol. III, p. 413, 755; Vol. III, p. 230-248; Vol. IV, p. 400, 565; Vol. I, p. 175; Palou's Notices, I, 401-451. Settlement of Los Angeles, Padron de 1781, MS., Ortega, in St. Pap. MS. and Colon, I, 104-5.

Ceruti, Burton Edward, attorney at law. Crim. No. 1848. In bank, December 18, 1914. The People—Respondent vs. Burr Harris, appellant. The victim was a Mrs. Rebecca P. Gay, Christian Science practitioner, having her office in the H. W. Hellman

Building, in the City of Los Angeles, September 26, 1913. Arrested in San Diego, October 5, 1913; admitted killing victim with a blow on the head with a piece of iron pipe. Appeal from a judgment of the Supreme Court of Los Angeles County and from an order refusing a new trial; Frank R. Willis, judge. E. Burton Ceruti for appellant; U. S. Webb, attorney general, and George Beebe, deputy attorney general, for respondant. The judgment and order appealed from and affirmed. Melvin, J.; Henshaw, J. Angellote, J., and Sloss, J., concurred. California Report, 169, p. 53, 1914-15. C. P. Pomeroy.

The claim on behalf of the appellant was that he was subject to intermittant attacks of a particular phase of epileptic insanity, defined by the medical experts called in behalf as psychic epileptic equivalent, a condition where, instead of the usual convulsions, phenomena ordinarily known as epeileptic fits * * * are substituted from time to time certain disturbances of mentality, during which consciousness of the individual affected is so altered that he is deprived of his full possession of his usual faculties. He acts in a manner wholly foreign to his usual conduct, habits and mode of thought and thinks things are true that are not, and acts upon them because he believes they are true; that a characteristic of this phase of insanity is that while suffering under it the individual may become dominated with an idea, entirely imaginary, that he is being persecuted or threatened with injury from some source and will make a sudden and violent attack on some person his diseased mind suggests is the one persecuting or intending to injure him. These medical experts gave it as their opinion, from the evidence in the case and personal examination of the defendant, that he was suffering from a spell of this phase of insanity when he killed deceased and was insane when he did it, so that by reason thereof he was incapable of having a malicious intent to kill and incapable of deliberating upon the act of killing which he committed. The court permitted these experts to testify that, from the nature of his insanity, when the defendant killed the deceased he was incapable of resisting an impulse to do it. But the court at the same time stated that nevertheless it would instruct the jury that in this State the doctrine of irresistible impulse, as an excuse for crime, did not exist, and did so instruct the jury.

The alienists in the "People vs. Burr L. Harris" case were Dr. Charles L. Allen, physician in charge of the psychopathic department, Los Angeles County Hospital; Dr. Ross Moore, for the defendant; and Drs. James D. Fisher and Thomas J. Orbinson for the People. Dr. Thomas Nelson (colored) was called as witness in his capacity as family physician.

Crim. No. 1972, in bank, January 3, 1916. The People vs. Thomas Miller, appellant; p. 649, California Report, 171, Pomeroy, 1915-16. Richards, Carrier & Heany, J. W. & W. G. Gammill, for appellant; U. S. Webb, attorney general, and Charles Jones, deputy attorney general, for respondent. Appeal from a judgment of the Supreme Court of Santa Barbara County, S. E. Crow, Judge. The appeal was taken and a new trial granted and E. Burton Ceruti was employed to conduct the second trial. The alienists called at this trial were Dr. Charles Allen, of Los Angeles (referred to in the Harris case); Dr. L. L. Stanley, resident physician of the State Prison at San Quentin, for the defendant; and Drs. J. C. Bainbridge and Julius H. Hurst, for the People. The record of the Miller second trial can be found in the files of the Superior Court of Santa Barbara County, California.

Darden, Charles, attorney at law.—The following is an exact quotation of Judge John W. Shenk's decision in the land litigation case cited in Attorney Darden's sketch: "John W. Shenk's decision in the Superior Court of the State of California, in and for the County of Los Angeles. Benjamin Jones and Fanny Guatier, plaintiffs, vs. Berlin Realty Company, a corporation, and L. E. Dimit, defendants. 89-346. Findings of facts and conclusions of law. This case came on regularly to be tried before the courts on the 21st day of October, 1913. A jury trial having been waived by the respective parties and Charles Darden, Esq., appeared as attorney for the plaintiffs herein, and Ingall W. Bull, Esq., appearing as attorney for the defendants, and the Court having heard the proofs of the respective parties and considered the same, and the records and papers in the case and the arguments submitted both orally and by briefs filed to the Court of respective counsels for its consideration and decision, the Court now finds the following:

"That the facts alleged in the amended complaint one and each thereof is true. That the facts alleged in the answer, except so far as they are a reiteration of the facts alleged in the amended complaint, are not, nor is any thereof true. Conclusion of law: As conclusion of the law from the foregoing, it follows that the plaintiffs are entitled to a decree against the defendants; that the defendants, Berlin Realty Company, a corporation, should be required to sell and convey the real property described in the amended complaint to the plaintiff herein; upon the payment by the plaintiffs to said defendant corporation of balance of the purchase price, title or interest in said property against plaintiff; that plaintiffs are entitled to their cost. Let judgment be entered accordingly. Dated, February 24, 1915. John W. Shenk, Judge.''

Education.—The seventh proviso of Section 22, p. 235, in regard to organizing public schools. School Laws of 1855, of California Staute, said: ''Provided that the Common Council, on the petition of fifty heads of white families, citizens of the district, shall establish a school or schools in said district and shall award said school or schools a pro rata of the school funds.'' California Reports No. 2, 51, 9. California Stautes of 1861, ch. 467, p. 521. Senate and Assembly, Section 422, 394. California Reports, 1872-3, Tuttle 3372. People vs. McGuire, California Statute, 1860. Mary Frances Ward vs. A. J. Ward, California Report, 48, 1874, p. 36. First School.—Bancroft's History of California, Vol. 7, p. 716. Jacob Wright Harlan, California from 1840, 1888, in regard to Leidsdorff. School Laws.—1855, p. 235; Section 20, seventh proviso. California Stautes, School Laws, 1866, p. 397.

Fremont's Famous Ride, published in the *National Intelligencer* November 22, 1847. Jacob Dodson, servant of Captain Fremont, ''Bancroft's California,'' Vo. II, p. 782, with Captain Fremont in his famous ride from Los Angeles to Monterey, Vol. 4, p. 437; Vol. 5, p. 443. He was also with Fremont when he discovered Klamath Lake. Fremont's Famous Ride is quoted from Mr. McGroarty's ''California: Its History and Romance,'' in which it said: ''The following narrative, vouched for by John Bigelow, Fremont's eminent biographer, was published in the *National Intelligencer* of Washington, D. C., November 22, 1847. The journey was undertaken by Colonel Fremont to inform General Kearney of the outbreak of an insurrection at Los Angeles. It ranks among the most remarkable recorded in history.

''This extraordinary ride of eight hundred miles in eight days, including all stoppages and nearly two days' detention, a whole day and night at Monterey and nearly two days and a half at San Luis Obispo. Having been brought into evidence before the Army court martial now in session in this city, and a great desire being expressed by some friends to know how this ride was made, I herewith send you the particulars that you may publish them, if you please, in the *National Intelligencer* as an incident connected with the times and affairs under review in the trial of which you give so full a report. The circumstances we first got from Jacob, afterward revised by Colonel Fremont, and I drew them up from his statement The purpose will show, beside the horsemanship of the riders, the power of the California horse, especially as one of the horses was subject in the course of the ride to an extraordinary trial in order to exhibit the capacity of his race. Of course, this statement will make no allusion to the object of the journey, being confined strictly to its performance.

''It was at daybreak on the morning of the 22nd of November, 1846, that the party set out from La Ciudad de Los Angeles (the city in the southern part of Upper California) to proceed in the shortest time to Monterey on the Pacific Coast, distant fully four hundred miles. The way over a mountainous country, much of it unhabited, with no other road than traces, and many defiles to pass, particularly the maritime defiles of El Rincon or Punto Gordo, fifty miles in extent, made by jutting off a precipitous mountain into the sea, which can only be passed when the tide is out and the sea is calm, and then, and many places, through waves. The town of Santa Barbara and San Luis Obispo and an occasional ranch are the principal inhabited places en route. Each of the party had three horses, nine in all, to take their turn under the saddle. The six loose horses ran ahead without bridle or halter and required some attention to keep to their track. When wanted for a change, say a distance of twenty miles, they were caught by the lasso, thrown either by Don Jesus or the servant Jacob, who, though born in Washington, D. C., in his long experience with Colonel Fremont had become as expert as a Mexican with the lasso, as sure as the mountaineer with the rifle, equal to either on horse or foot, and always a lad of courage and fidelity.''

Fund Sanitary.—''Through the influence of Rev. Thomas Starr King, California organized the Sanitary Fund of the United States Army during the Civil War, and sent, in 1862, $480,000, and afterward $25,000 a month. California sent through its committee, during the war, to this Sanitary Fund, the sum of $1,200,000, and to the Christian Fund $34,000. These societies corresponded to the Red Cross of today.''

Homestead Law.—Califoria Statute, 1860, p. 87. An act extending the privileges of the homestead laws to certain persons and to regulate the creation of the same. Approved March 13, 1860.

Right of Testimony.—Article on ''Contact of Races,'' by John Archibald, a distinguished newspaper writer during pioneer times, and who afterward published his writings in a book called ''Contact of Races,'' in which the article quoted on the ''Right of Testimony'' appeared on page 36.

Mines and Mining.—History of Tuolumne County (Dick). This account is quoted from ''Hittell's History of California,'' Vol. III, p. 118. Rare, Ripe Gold and Silver Mining Company, San Francisco, April 10, 1868.

Rev. Thomas Starr King.—Unitarian minister, coming from New York to California in 1860. He was a great orator and a friend to the Negro in the fight for Freedom. He located in San Francisco, but soon became well-known all over the State and throughout the Nation. About this time the States were seceding from the Union and the Civil War was just beginning. This little minister, with poor health, forgetting his own welfare, fired with the importance of California remaining in the Union as a free State, traveled all over the State, giving lectures on ''Christianity and Humanity,'' until he startled and then electrified the people with his lectures. He only lived four years in California, during which time he won his place in the hearts of the people so thoroughly that at his death he was given a military funeral, and one of the giant redwood trees has been named in his memory and in honor of his services to the State.

Vigilance Committee.—John Jones had charge of the armory and council room of the committee. He was also body-servant to Senator Broderick.

San Francisco Bay.—Mrs. Zelia Nuttall has recently published a book through the Hackluyt Society of London, England. This book covers years of research work in the archives of Mexico and gives valuable information hitherto unknown. It is called ''A New Light on Drake'' (p. 317).

End of the Spanish Rule in California.—Fr. Zephrin Engelhardt, O. F. M., in ''Missions and Missionaries of California,'' Vol. I, p. 133, says that ''King Phillip V had given orders that the Missions of California should, at his expense, be provided with everything necessary for Divine worship, such as bells, images, vestments, lamps, olive oil and altar wine, and that some missions should be established and maintained from the royal treasury, but neither of these commands was carried out owing to the indifference or ill will of those that held office in Mexico. All these articles, besides clothing, tools, provisions, medicines, furniture, and implements, which they ordered for themselves or the Indians, were charged to the Upper Missions and paid for from the meager allowance, at the expense of the Missions.''

The Pious Fund.—The following brief history of the Pious Fund, and the right of the Roman Catholic church to its principal and income, is quoted from Hon. John F. Doyle's paper concerning the litigation of the same, in which he said: ''From the time of the discovery of California, in 1534, by the expedition fitted out by Cortez, the colonization of that country and the conversion of its inhabitants to the Catholic faith was a cherished object with the Spanish monarch. Many expeditions for that purpose were set on foot at the expense of the crown, during the century and a half succeeding the discovery. But though attended with enormous expense, none of them were productive of the slightest good results. Down to the year 1697, the Spanish monarchs had failed to acquire any permanent foothold in the vast territory which they claimed under the name of California.

The success of the Jesuit fathers in the Missions on the northwest frontier of Mexico and elsewhere induced the Spanish government as early as 1643, on the occasion of fitting out an expedition for California, under admiral Pedro Portal de Casant, to invite that religious order to take charge of the spiritual ministrations of it and the country for which it was destined. They accepted the charge, but the expedition failed, like all its predecessors failed (p. 6). It is a hundred years since the Jesuits were expelled from Lower California, yet to this day most that we know of its geography, climate, physical peculiarities and natural history is derived from the relics of the early missionaries.''

The following account is quoted from the same paper and will give the reader a clear idea as to the meaning and origin of the Pious Fund of California:

''Some Account of the Pious Fund of California and the Litigation to Recover It,'' by John F. Doyle. ''In the year 1857 I was retained and authorized by the Most Rev. Archbishop Alemany, of San Francisco, and the Rt. Rev. Bishop Amato, of Monterey, to take steps to recover for them, as official trustees of the Catholic Church and Catholic people of this State, the sum due by the government of Mexico to the church, on account of the Pious Fund of California, the properties belonging to which had been appropriated by Santa Ana, in 1842, to the use of the public treasury. Neither of the reverend prelates had any specific information on the subject of the Pious Fund, but its existence and confiscation were matters of public notoriety in the country, derived by tradition from the old missionaries. The archbishop had in his possession a few old papers, found among the archives of the diocese, which embraced copies of correspondence between the administrator appointed by the Mexican Government and the agent of the former bishop of Monterey, about the time of the seizure, wherein the latter had protested against the proceedings, but under duress had given a inventory of the properties.

From these papers I learned the circumstances of the seizure and something of the character and value of the property taken.

Under the authority of the archbishop and bishop I addressed a letter in July, 1859, to Hon. Lewis Cass, Secretary of State, requesting the interposition of the United States Government with that of Mexico in this favor, and I subsequently presented the claim to the mixed committee appointed under the convention between the United States and Mexico, July 4, 1868. The rule of the commission called for a Memorial of the Claim, as the pleading on the part of the claimant and prescribed its formal requests. With my memorial I filed a brief history of the Pious Fund, compiled and condensed from the results of many years' reading and study of Mexican history and Mexican books, in which I was fortunate enough to state the facts with such accuracy that none of its allegations were controverted.''

Pious Fund.—As given by Fr. Engelhardt in ''Missions and Missionaries of California,'' in which he said, ''Purchase of Upper California by the United States, in 1848, Mexico failed to pay any part of the income to the proper recipients in Upper California and as a consequence upon the information of the mixed committee under the Treaty of 1868, to adjust claims of citizens of the United States or of Mexico against the other governments. The Archbishop of San Francisco and the Bishop of Monterey and Grass Valley, through the American agent, presented the claim against the Republic of Mexico for the proper portion of the income of said fund. Bringing it to the attention of the mixed commission on March 30, 1870. Mexico in January 20, 1890, Wm. F. Horton, James G. Blaine, Secretary of State; John W. Forster, Walter Q. Gresham, John Sherman, W. R. Day and John Hay. The case was placed before the Tribunal of Arbitration at The Hague, which on October 14, 1902, unanimously decided and pronounced as follows: (P. 598) ''That the said claim of the United States of America for the benefit of the Archbishop of San Francisco and of the Bishop of Monterey is governed by the principle of resjudicata by virtue of the arbitral sentence of Sir Edward Thornton on November 2, 1875, amended by him October 24, 1876. That conformity to this arbitral sentence the Government of the Republic of Mexico must pay to the Government of the United States the sum of $1,420,682.67 Mexican, in money having legal currency in Mexico, within the period fixed by article ten, of the protocol of Mexico, of May 22, 1902. This sum of $1,420,682.67 will totally extinguish the annuities accumulated and not paid by the Government of the Mexican Republic. That is to say, this annunty of $43,050.99 Mexican, from February 2, 1869, to February 2, 1902. The Government of the Republic of Mexico shall pay to the Government of the United States of America on February 2, 1903, and each following year on the same date of February perpetually, the annuity of $43,505.99 Mexican, in money having legal currency in Mexico.'' Hence Mexico must forever each year pay to the Catholic authorities of Upper California on one-half of the Pious Fund property, which the Mexican Government confiscated and diverted into its treasury despite the intentions of the donors, and which sum annually amounts to the other half of the property of the Pious Fund property, and its income belongs to the Catholic Church of Lower California.''

Pious Fund.—As quoted from Hon. John McGroarty's ''California, Its History and Romance,'' in which it said: ''Archbishop Riordan, of San Francisco, Protocol of May 22, 1902, signed by John Hay, United States Secretary of State, and Senor de Aspiros, Mexican Ambassador, at Washington, D. C., by which the entire matter was settled with the permanent Court of Arbitration, under The Hague Convention of 1899. Report of Jackson H. Ralston, Agent of the United States, and Counsel in the matter of the Pious Fund case. The report was made to Hon. John Hay, Secretary of State, of the United States, on November 10, 1902 (see p. 915, Appendix II), Foreign Relation, U. S. vs. Mexico.''

Cabeza de Vaca.—''It is well known that Cabeza de Vaca wrote two principal works, both of which were published at Valladolid in 1555 by Frances Fernandez de Cordova. The first one of these two books is a second issue of the one translated here. The other gives an account of his vicissitudes in Paraguay, and what is now the Argentine Republic, and bears the title of 'Commentarios de Alva Nuez Cabeza de la Plata.' The print from 1555 is the earliest known of the 'Commentarios of Nanfragios' here translated. No earlier issue has been found; only two copies of it are known, one of which is perfect and is at the Lennox branch of the Public Library of New York, the other somewhat damaged at the British Museum. The oldest print of the 'Nanfragios' is from 1542 and was published at Zamora. Its text has been followed exclusively in this translation.''

The writer has deemed it of value to quote this preface from F. Bandeile's book, quoted elsewhere, and which has given valuable material concerning ''Estevancio,'' who was with ''Cabeza de Vaca'' while on the nine years' journey across the continent.

Estevancio.—The following is quoted from Fr. Zephyrin Engelhardt, O. F. M., who, in his "Missions and Missionaries of California," said in volume I, p. 24: "Lower California.—The poor returns which Cortez had obtained from his various costly enterprises did not deter Viceroy Mendoza from making other attempts to acquire more territory that would yield the wealth which all desired. At his request Friar Marco of Nizza, a Franciscan Friar of the Province of the 'Holy Gospel Mexico,' set out to explore the region to the north of Sonora, entirely unarmed and accompanied by Estevancio, the colored survivor of 'Narvaz's expedition.''

Slavery in California.—The following laws concerning slavery in the Spanish Colonies is given that the reader may fully understand the laws concerning slavery while California was Spanish territory, and is quoted from Help's 'Slavery in the Spanish Colonies,' in which it is said (Vol. I, p. 121): "Sept. 15, 1528. The same year was signalized by a Royal order in favor of the Negro. * * * in order to animate the Negroes to work, and to induce them to marry, the Emperor is informed that it would be well that they should be enabled to purchase their freedom, fixing the rate at twenty marks of gold, at the least, and he desired the authority to fix the rate. * * * Vol. 4, pp. 338-9-40. The foregoing laws and the privileges of the Indians must have rendered labor scarce in the Spanish Indies. The fatal consequence naturally ensued of an increased demand for Negro labor and accordingly licenses for importing seventeen thousand Negro slaves were offered for sale in the year 1551. In the following year Phillip the Second concluded a bargain for the grant of a monopoly to import twenty-three thousand Negroes into the Indies, and so the traffic went on until the great Assienti of 1713 between the English and the Spanish Governments was concluded respecting the importation of Negroes into Spanish America.

The number of Negroes imported to America between the year 1517 when the trade was first permitted by Charles the Fifth, to 1807, the year in which the British Parliament passed the act abolishing the slave trade, cannot be estimated at less than five or six million. * * * The Court of Spain was not inattentive to the treatment of the Negroes any more than that of the Indians. As early as 1537 there is a letter from Cuba, addressed by some official person to the Empress informing her majesty that the Negroes are stronger than the Indians, and that they were well fed, and that in accordance with the Royal order they have a holiday of four months duration * * * There is one law, however, of high importance in favor of the Negroes. * * * We command our Royal Audiences, that if any Negro or Negress, or any other person reputed slave should publicly demand their liberty, they should be heard, and justice be done them, and care be taken that they should not on that account of their demanding their liberty be maltreated by the masters (p. 340). The earliest law that declared the ground on which the Negroes could demand their liberty dates from the year 1528, in which it is provided that a Negro, having served a certain time should be entitled to his liberty upon the payment of a certain sum not to be less than twenty marks of gold, the exact amount to be settled by Royal Authority. That many Negroes did obtain their liberty may be inferred from the fact of there being several laws having reference to free Negroes enacted, for instance, what tribute they should pay, and with whom they should live and commanding that free Negresses, unless married to Spaniards, should not wear gold ornaments, pearls or silk.''

Slavery in California.—English Treaties is quoted from "The History of Slavery and the Slave Trade," by W. O. Blake, p. 250-302-553.

Auction of Slaves.—Quoted from George Tinkham's "Men and Events," pp. 157-8; Freedom Papers, from the California Archives, at the University of California, through the courtesy of Dr. Owen C. Coy; other papers from individuals, through the courtesy of Hon. Monroe Works, of Tuskegee Institute, of Tuskegee, Alabama, who published one paper of the writer's article on "Slavery in California," and which appeared in the Journal of Negro History for January, 1918, a slavery paper which he had secured concerning slavery in Los Angeles, California.

Returned to Slavery.—California Reports, No. 9, Expartra Archey and Report No. 2, pp. 424-6. Slaves emancipated through the courts of California, and friends, is quoted from the diaries of the late Rev. J. B. Sanderson, Bancroft's "History of California," George Tinkham's book "Men and Events," old newspaper files in the Bancroft Library, between the dates of 1848 and 1885. The account of Mammy Pleasants is quoted from the San Francisco Call, January 4, 1904, the Oakland Tribune, September 3, 1916, the last named being a reprint from the San Francisco News Letter. The marriage of a Manumitted slave—California Report No. 51, p. 120. Slavery in California—a paper by Prof. C. A. Duneway, read before the American Historical Society, 1910, a paper published in the Boston Transcript by Marion Reynolds, on "Slavery in California," "Memories of Slavery in California," by Cornelius Cole (Senator).

Soldier, Negro.—The Toussaint L'Ouverture proclamation is quoted from Wendel Phillips' estimate of "Toussaint L'Ouverture," and appeared in the book "Toussaint L'Ouverture and Hayti's Struggle for Independence," by C. W. Mossell, published in Lockport, N. Y., 1890.

Panama Pacific International Exposition.—This chapter, in a great measure, has been quoted as to the description of the different courts from the charming little book by Mrs. Juliet James, on "The Palaces and Courts of the P. P. I. E." This book was published in San Francisco during 1915.

Negro Press.—The pioneer history and the sketch concerning Phillip A. Bell has been quoted from the "Afro-American Press and Its Editors," by I. Garland Penn, and published in 1890.